Music in Latin America
and
the Caribbean

~

An Encyclopedic History

*Joe R. and Teresa Lozano Long Series in
Latin American and Latino Art and Culture*

Music in Latin America and the Caribbean

~

An Encyclopedic History

VOLUME 1

Performing Beliefs:
Indigenous Peoples of South America,
Central America, and Mexico

Edited by Malena Kuss

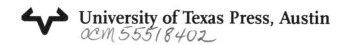 University of Texas Press, Austin

Music in Latin America and the Caribbean: An Encyclopedic History

A project of The Universe of Music: A History,
initiated by and developed in cooperation with

The International Music Council

First edition, 2004

Requests for permission to reproduce material from this work
should be sent to Permissions, University of Texas Press,
P.O. Box 7819, Austin, TX 78713–7819

⊗The paper used in this book meets
the minimum requirements of ANSI / NISO Z39.48–1992 (R1997)
(Permanence of Paper)

Library of Congress Cataloging-in-Publication Data

Music in Latin America and the Caribbean : an encyclopedic history / edited by
Malena Kuss.
      p. cm. — (Joe R. and Teresa Lozano Long series in Latin American and
Latino art and culture)
  Includes bibliographical references and index.
  ISBN 0-292-70298-1 (cloth : alk. paper)
    1. Music—Latin America—History and criticism. 2. Music—Caribbean
Area—History and criticism. I. Kuss, Malena. II. Series.

ML199.M858 2004
780´.98—dc22   2004012481

This work is dedicated to all the musicians whose creativity shaped vigorous cultures across the Americas; and to the memory of Barry S. Brook, Samuel Claro Valdés, and Guy Huot, whose vision nurtured my journey.

Malena Kuss

CONTENTS

Prologue...ix

Acknowledgments...xxvii

Native Peoples: Introductory Panorama 1
    Carol E. Robertson

Myth, Cosmology, and Performance 7
    Carol E. Robertson

Metamorphosis: Mythic and Musical Modes of Ceremonial Exchange among the
    Wakuénai of Venezuela...25
    Jonathan D. Hill

Brazil's Indigenous Universe (to ca. 1990): The Xavante, Kamayurá, and Suyá...........49
    Elizabeth Travassos

The Yawari Ritual of the Kamayurá: A Xinguano Epic 77
    Rafael José de Menezes Bastos

Music and Worldview of Indian Societies in the Bolivian Andes 101
    Max Peter Baumann

Local Practices among the Aymara and Kechua in Conima and Canas, Southern Peru 123
    Thomas Turino

Amerindian Music of Chile...145
  María Ester Grebe

Musical Culture of Indigenous Societies in Argentina.........................163
  Irma Ruiz

Fertility Ritual...181
  Carol E. Robertson

Music and Healing...187
  Carol E. Robertson

The Fundamental Role of Music in the Life of Two Central American Ethnic Nations:
  The Mískito in Honduras and Nicaragua, and the Kuna in Panama...............193
  Ronny Velásquez

Mexico's Indigenous Universe...231
  Marina Alonso Bolaños

Musical Traditions of the P'urhépecha (Tarascos) of Michoacán, Mexico.........247
  E. Fernando Nava López

Aerophones of Traditional Use in South America, with References to Central America
  and Mexico..261
  Dale A. Olsen

Epilogue...327
  Carol E. Robertson

Index..329

Contributors...401

Recorded Examples..403

PROLOGUE

MALENA KUSS

This unprecedented work covers in considerable depth the musical legacies of indigenous peoples, African descendants, Iberian colonizers and creoles, and other immigrant groups that met and mixed in the New World. Within a history marked by cultural encounters and dis-encounters, music emerges as the powerful tool that negotiates identities, enacts resistance, performs beliefs, and challenges received aesthetics. Approached from a number of perspectives, music mirrors an inner history that writers of contemporary fiction can penetrate and historians often fail to capture, providing a point of entry into spiritualized conceptions of the world that take shape in multiple and different ways of being musical. Collectively and individually, the peoples in this region welded powerfully expressive forms by resignifying ancient practices and breeding new life into fragments of traditions brought by colonists, slaves, and settlers. The infinite variety of musical responses to the New World's complex history, however, maps a wealth of vibrant and dynamic forms that set the region apart from any of its tributaries. This work was conceived to empower Latin Americans and Caribbeans to shape their own musical history, privileging their modes of representation and traditions of scholarship. It also was conceived to emphasize the role that music plays in human life. As such, it highlights the meanings that traditions carry among practitioners, as seen mostly through the lens of cultural insiders.

As the Polish/German scholar Walter Wiora predicted in an unassuming but prophetic book he called *The Four Ages of Music* (1961 in 1965), the twenty-first century was to be "the age of technology and global industrial culture" that eradicates the predominance of Western ["art"] music. A pioneer among Europeans in realizing the need to approach music history from a global perspective and break artificial barriers between folk and art musics, he relativized the perceived centrality of European culture by projecting it onto the larger canvas of past and future "ages"—such as prehistory, the age of high cultures of Antiquity and the Orient, and the age of globalization and diversity. He was bound, however, to assumptions of linear evolutionism in his conception of a historical sequence of hegemonic cultures, and to a perspective that ultimately remains "ethnocentric . . . [because] the configuration of *all* the world's music is formed about the Third [European] Age as a zenith; the rest is preparation and decline" (Treitler 1989b: 130–31). The age of globalization eradicates more than the centrality of any one culture, as it presupposes the simultaneity or interactive coexistence of many musics shaping a shifting quilt best represented in Foucault's image of the Archive as the site that accumulates and collapses [musical] discourses from the past and the present into a de-historicized metaphorical place. What the twenty-first century foreshadows is nothing less than the replacement of hegemonies by the concept of equivalence of cultures, each understood according to the terms of its own rationality.

We have divided the world into convenient geographic lumps we call "regions" that more often than not assume the connotations of "cultures," a concept that implies at least a metalevel of commonalities (among them Europe, Asia, and Africa, the original trinity contained within the *orbis terrarum* and prioritized in that order by the geographers of Antiquity). America erupted as a geographic entity only after it was "discovered" by Europeans, prompting Edmundo O'Gorman's famous epigraph: "At long last, someone has arrived to discover me!" (Entry for October 12, 1492, in an imaginary Private Diary of America) (1961: 9). Few such "virtual or implicit cultures"—which as totalities only can exist in our imagination—could be more complex or resilient to implicit organicism than the region that came to be called "Latin America." Extraverted branding (Agawu 2003: xii) is embedded in the colonialist act of taking possession, and the politics of naming for external consumption can turn upside down the logic that names have to correspond to that which they name. The story of how this externally-generated label was affixed to our "region" turned "culture" is but one strand in a web of foundational mythologies that writers of fiction, composers, and scholars often sublimate through pervasive irony.

AT LONG LAST, SOMEONE HAS
GIVEN US A NAME

Is "Latin America" a cultural or a geographic concept? This question, which neophytes frequently ask, was explored with unlimited imagination and no small dose of irony when, in the context of the Quincentenary of 1492 that catalyzed reappraisals, the Chilean writer Sergio Marras interviewed sixteen titans of Latin American literature and published these conversations under the title *América Latina: Marca registrada* (1992). To each of them he posed the same question: "Does Latin America exist"? After the cast of Spanish and Portuguese conquerors, colonizers, missionaries, and settlers had shaped the foundational *imaginaire* in a daunting corpus of chronicles spanning well over three centuries (1493–1819), recording events and customs while naming in the process fauna, flora, and some musical practices and instruments for which the foreign observers had no names, a new image of the vast territorial expanse between Patagonia and Mexico erupted upon the stage of history, this time credited to France. "Did you know that this business of 'latina' in América latina was not of our making?" says Mexican novelist Carlos Fuentes to Marras in one of the most provocative interviews. "No, it is nothing less than a French invention, like so many others: la Bardot, the *négligé*, cognac, the corset, and the *ménage à trois*. *L'Amérique latine* [a monolithic abstraction] is, in fact, the invention of Michel Chevalier (1806–79), the French ideologue of a panlatinism conceived to justify France's ambitions in the *Territoires d'Outre-Mer*." Specifically, this image was forged to further the political expansionism of Napoleon III (1808–73), which materialized in the short-lived imposition of an Austrian emperor on Mexico (1864–67) when President Benito Juárez defaulted on Mexico's foreign debt. Needless to say, "Maximilian was promptly shot down by a few soldiers who dispatched him in less time than the fastest rooster in Querétaro could crow, leaving poor María Carlota of Belgium a widow at the age of twenty-six" (Fuentes in Marras 1992: 15).

Michel Chevalier was a "communicator," continues Fuentes, not unlike those "brainstorming around a table at transnational corporations," where imaging is both reactive to existing preconceptions and active in carving a place for a new registered label (a *marca registrada* or *marque déposée*). The process of naming was seldom arbitrary in the New World. Columbus appears to have followed a hierarchical order in his baptisms, which corresponded successively to the Christian Savior, the Virgin Mary, the King and Queen of Spain, and the Royal Princess, when he called the first island he sighted San Salvador "in honor of His Heavenly Majesty who wondrously has given us all this," although he was aware that the Indians called it Guanahani; then Santa María de Concepción, Fernandina, Isabella, and Juana ("Letter to Santángel," February–March 1493). Because "things must have the names that correspond to them . . . , this obligation plunged Columbus into a veritable naming frenzy" wherein he appropriated the right to name as a form of taking possession of the "virgin world" unfolding before his eyes. Thus he named mountains, rivers, and capes by direct resemblance to elements in nature (like Islas de Arena, or islands of sand; and Cabo de Palmas, or cape of palm trees), and settlements after symbols of "his" world. These "acts of extended nomination" did not spare the Indians, as "the first men brought back to Spain were rebaptized Don Juan de Castilla and Don Fernando de Aragón" (Todorov 1984: 27–28). On occasion, the process of naming took the form of mistranslation, as in the case of the Yucatan Peninsula, according to a story that Tzvetan Todorov relishes, but does not substantiate. It appears that, to the shouts of the first Spaniards landing on the peninsula, Mayans responded with "Ma c'ubah than" (We do not understand your words), which the Spaniards heard as "Yucatan" and assumed it to be the name of the place (1984: 99). Todorov himself, so "sensitized to the misdeeds of European colonialism" by his own account (1984: 58) and relentless in his representation of Columbus as impervious to human alterity, seems to have accepted uncritically the French "invention" of an *Amérique latine* (1984: 49–50):

> The entire history of the discovery of America, the first episode of the conquest, is marked by this ambiguity: human alterity is at once revealed and rejected. The year 1492 already symbolizes, in the history of Spain, this double movement: in this same year [Spain] repudiated its interior Other by triumphing over the Moors in the final battle of Granada and by forcing the Jews to leave its territory; and it discovered the exterior Other, that whole America that would become *Latin* [my emphasis].

Amused by the concept that Chevalier tossed into the ideological market of the Western hemisphere's fledgling nations, Carlos Fuentes embellishes on the success of the French enterprise:

> The title suited us, *criollos* and mestizos, because we needed to distance ourselves from such traditional hispanophilic labels as Hispanoamérica or Iberoamérica, not only because our Motherland had fallen into global disrepute, but also because we had rebelled against her and were obstinate in our resolve to assert our differences and walk our own path. Moreover, we already suspected that the simple geographic term "América del Sur" would not protect us, because the United States already was seriously claiming "America" for itself, as it took possession of parts of Mexico and Caribbean islands in a voracious rush to plunder the remaining spoils. We could not but smile at this ingenious turn . . . toward a "latinidad" that turned us overnight into honorary French citizens. I am not going to criticize monsieur Chevalier because he did his thing rather well, so well, in fact, that we still believe in this tale (Fuentes in Marras 1992: 17).

Of course, the story would have been different if the reversal of history in *Mare nostrum: Discovery, Pacification, and Conversion of the Mediterranean Region by a Tribe from the Amazon* (Berlin, 1975) by Mauricio Kagel (b. 1931) had been more than a flight of fancy for his brand of experimental music theater or an expression of subliminal Desire (Kuss 1991: 10).

As for the much-berated colossus of the North, it appears that it narrowly escaped the fate of being called "Freedonia," or "Land of the Free," when this name was discarded after the communicators wrestling to find the right image received a letter alerting them that "donia" or "Doña" meant "woman" in Spanish, and thus Freedonia could be interpreted as "The Land of Free Women." ("Freedonia" survives in a map by R. H. Laurie published in London in 1830 and updated in 1832, 1833, 1834, 1836, and 1849.) Columbia or Colombia also was considered, but by then it had been snatched by the legendary Simón Bolívar (1783–1830) for the newly independent Viceroyalty of New Granada which, comprising Venezuela, New Granada (present-day Colombia and Panama), and Ecuador, was renamed Republic of Colombia in 1819 and is known as Gran Colombia to distinguish it from the smaller modern Colombia after the short-lived confederation disintegrated in 1830. Writing in 1962 about unity and diversity in "The Four Americas"—namely Indo-Spanish America, Portuguese America (Brazil), English America (the United States), and Anglo-French America (Canada)— the distinguished and controversial Colombian historian and statesman Germán Arciniegas (1900–99) argues that the United States is the only country in the world which does not have a name. "There are other confederations in the Americas, like the United States of Mexico, the United States of Venezuela, and the United States of Brazil. The philosophers gathered in Philadelphia to draw up the constitution . . . did not think of giving the new state a name of its own. To say 'United States' is like saying federation, republic, or monarchy" (Arciniegas 1962 in Hanke 1964: 237–38). By default and abbreviation, then, the nameless United States of America, not unlike Mexico, Venezuela, and Brazil, became just simply "America."

The question of whether "Latin America exists" addresses not the fact that the French invention is a misnomer, because neither Native Americans nor Africans and their descendants are "Latin," but when and at what levels cultural insiders identify with this act of utopian reductionism. When confronted with the question of why his literature did not contain a "Latin American or Latin Americanist coloration," the Argentinian Juan José Saer (b. 1937), who has been called one of the greatest living writers in the Spanish language, responded: "Of course not, because I am not a Latin American, I am Argentinian. To be 'Latin American' is an abstraction; it is like saying 'I am

European.' If I wrote like [the Mexican] Juan Rulfo, everybody would laugh at me. The language of a writer is 'maternal' in the broadest sense of the term, it is a language etched in many emotional elements. For a writer, language is essentially polysemic and connotative, namely the opposite of a metalanguage" (1987). Scores of cosmopolitan composers, who barely tolerate this form of extraversion, would identify with this statement. The tropification of stereotypes, or discourse centered on whether a "Latin Americanness" shines through (as in the question posed to Juan José Saer), also is replicated at the national level. When Aaron Copland visited seven South American countries on behalf of the Coordinator of Inter-American Affairs in 1941 and reported his impressions in an often-quoted article published a year later in *Modern Music*, he found it necessary to explain to an apparently uninformed U.S. audience that "lumping" was not such a good thing:

> To see the field of composition as it actually is down there we should of course stop thinking in terms of The South American Composer. No such person exists. South America, as we are often told but never seem fully to comprehend, is a collection of separate countries, each with independent traditions. Their musical developments are various and there is little or no musical contact between them. Brazilian, Colombian, Peruvian composers are just as different from each other as are Dutch, Hungarian, or Yugoslav composers. European music covers a lot of territory, and so also does South American (Copland 1942: 75).

Copland did not go far enough in his well-intentioned attempt to eradicate stereotypes, and he himself would have objected if his compositional poetics had been lumped together with Milton Babbitt's or Charles Ives' in the service of constructing the national myth or politico-cultural masterstory. If "The Latin American Composer" is a monolithic abstraction that obliterates national differences, "The National Composer" submerges and obliterates individual poetics. The former is a product of the discourse of difference stemming mostly from cultural outsiders; the latter feeds the tropification or construction of discourses on the politico-cultural national myth; and both contribute to the construction of stereotypes. Lodged in conceptual frameworks developed by German music historiography to marginalize and subordinate compositional aesthetics deemed antithetical to the

canonized metaphysics of purely instrumental music in the nineteenth century (Dahlhaus 1974; Fischer 1979), the tropification of "nationalism" is one of the most glaring examples of self-colonized and colonialist discourse (Kuss 1998). Composer Marlos Nobre (b. 1939) settled this core issue—whose complex nuances are treated at length in Volume 3 of this series—in response to one of those banal questions based on expectations of exoticism at a festival and conference held at Fort Worth's Texas Christian University in 2000: "I am Brazilian; I write music; I do not write Brazilian music." The same can be applied to scores of composers and particularly to the poetics of Alberto Ginastera (1916–83). In "El escritor argentino y la tradición" (1932 in 1974: 270), Jorge Luis Borges (1899–1986), whose cosmopolitan literature was not immune to the same expectations of "explicit Latin Americanness" as Saer's, once wrote that "The Argentinian cult of local color is a recent European cult that nationalists should reject for its foreignness" (El culto argentino del color local es un reciente culto europeo que los nacionalistas deberían rechazar for foráneo).

The implications of a concept frivolously conceived and often stereotypically applied, however, merged with the idea of a community of nations and established an interplay between frequently insurmountable national differences and utopian commonalities. Long before our "Latinidad" was fabricated in France, the Venezuelan Simón Bolívar had envisioned "the most immense, or most extraordinary, or most invincible league of nations the world had ever seen" after solidifying Peru's independence in 1826 (García Márquez 1989 in 1991: 74). His thwarted dream of integrating the fledgling American nations into a free and powerful single republic spanning from Mexico to Patagonia is the overriding theme in *The General in His Labyrinth* by the Colombian recipient of the 1982 Nobel Prize in Literature. "He had wrested from Spanish domination an empire five times more vast than all of Europe, he had led twenty years of wars to keep it free and united, and he had governed it with a firm hand ..." until 1830, the year of the General's last journey chosen by Gabriel García Márquez to weave his masterful web of historical fiction (1989 in 1991: 37). The foundational interplay between commonalities and differences in the early nineteenth century took the shape of an attempted redemption in the utopian dream of continental unity, which, conceived as a strategy to fence off the European Holy Alliance of the 1820s and face the increasingly powerful Anglo-America in the North, also could defeat internal anarchy, the new enemy of the fledgling republics. While the Bolivarian dream survives in the present-day Organization of American States, the figure of the Liberator remains firmly entrenched in the domain of myth. As historian David Bushnell put it, Bolívar "has been claimed as a precursor by every ideological current from the revolutionary Left to the extreme Right . . . . There is something about Bolívar to appeal to every taste and every age" (Hanke and Rausch 1999: 3; Bierck, Jr. 1999: 11).

Historically, an identification with the idea of a community of nations forged from within has been in constant flux and gains strength and substance at specific junctures. In the words of the revered U.S. historian Lewis Hanke, "There are moments of universal agony, of crisis, in which histories of continents [or countries] join hands to survive in the great tests with which are measured the characters of men and the vigour of their faith" (1964: 235). Few historical intersections validated the existence of a bond between Latin American nations as did, for instance, the sociopolitical movement that soared throughout the 1960s and 1970s giving tangible shape to rebellion against tyranny, dictatorships, and social injustice in the *Nueva canción latinoamericana* (addressed by Cuban scholar Clara Díaz Pérez in Volume 4 of this series). Prefigured in folklore revivals of the 1950s, the voices of *cantautores* (singers-authors)—such as the Chileans Violeta Parra (1917–67) and Víctor Jara (b. 1938–assassinated in Santiago de Chile, September 15, 1973), Argentinians Atahualpa Yupanki (1908–92) and Mercedes Sosa (b. 1935), Brazilians Geraldo Vandré (b. 1935) and Chico Buarque (Francisco Buarque de Holanda, b. 1944), Nicaraguans Carlos Mejía Godoy (b. 1943) and his brother Luis Enrique Mejía Godoy (b. 1945), Uruguayans Alfredo Zitarrosa (1936–89) and Daniel Viglietti (b. 1939), Mexicans Judith Reyes and Oscar Chávez (b. 1935), Peruvians Tania Libertad and Nicomedes Santa Cruz (b. 1925), and Venezuelans Lilia Vera (b. 1951) and Soledad Bravo (b. 1942), among so many others—carried the plight of voices suppressed by repressive regimes throughout the continent, spreading it at home and abroad well into the 1980s. The idea of a community of nations singing with one voice validated in this instance the substance of Latin America's existence.

HISTORICAL FICTIONS AND FICTIONAL HISTORIES

In "Questions of Conquest: What Columbus wrought and what he did not," the Peruvian novelist Mario Vargas Llosa calls the early chroniclers "the first Magical Realists . . . . The chronicles of Conquest form an astonishingly rich literature—a literature at once fantastical and true. Through these books we can rediscover a period and a place, much as the readers of contemporary Latin American fiction discover the contemporary life of a continent" (1990: 46). The fables constructed by the chroniclers, at once fantastical yet not confined to the domain of fiction, are the foundational writings that set the course of America's being in history. They are foundational because, by naming for the first time realities for which the namers had no names—and wherein naming becomes an art of approximation or translation—they mark a historical chasm, a rupture with the familiar that casts the past into an ontological void (González Echevarría 2006). In turn, this void obsesses history with questions of origins and concomitant fixations with identity. The "invented" historical being of America (forged by the European imagination after its own image) (O'Gorman 1961) took place in the domain of discourse and, initially, in the discourse of the chronicles. This corpus of letters, reports, diaries, and historical narratives spans from Columbus' letter to Luis de Santángel of February 1493 (González Echevarría 1990 in 1998: 43) to the early 19th-century writings of the Spaniard Diego de Alvear (1749–1830), respectively the first and last entries in Francisco Esteve Barba's monumental *Historiografía Indiana* (1964), the most comprehensive roadmap to chronicles from "discovery" (1492) to the birth of nations.

The fact that some writers of fiction would turn to the discourse of chronicles verging on myth in canonic works of contemporary literature (such as Gabriel García Márquez's *One Hundred Years of Solitude* [1967]) to define a poetics of history that defies verification, paradoxically validates them beyond the empirical level summoned by most scholars searching for historical certitudes of the verifiable variety. Most of all, the observations and events recorded in the chronicles, their multiple lines of transmission, and the utopias they catalyzed in the course of their European reception (as in the case of Garcilaso de la Vega's *Comentarios reales de los Incas* [1609] [Montiel 1992 and 2000]), constructed an *imaginaire* whose domain is neither temporal history nor atemporal myth—two domains that Europeans have kept safely apart (Kuss 1996 and 2005). Built on the discourse of difference, this *imaginaire* became as much a scaffolding for America's being in history as cathedrals superimposed on submerged Aztec temples—as is the case in Mexico City—became a part of the skyline of colonial cities.

Western epistemological orders traveled with conquerors, colonizers, and settlers, and later on with explorers and scientists in the nineteenth century, building and superimposing layers of discursive modalities through which Americans themselves would represent their own being in history. This led Tzvetan Todorov, who made the most of linguistic disencounters in his influential *The Conquest of America: The Question of The Other* (1984), to imply that America was not conquered by swords but by a mastery of language, or control of signs. The entrenched European belief in the superiority of written expression (verbal and musical) surfaces already in the foundational *Relación* of the Ur-cronista Fray Ramón Pané (1498 in 1991), a Catalan entrusted by Columbus to record in Spanish information on myths told to him by the Indians of Hispaniola in a branch of Arawakan, who, according to Todorov, repeats that, "Since the Indians have neither alphabet nor writing, they do not speak their myths clearly, and it is impossible for me to transcribe them correctly" (1984: 41). As a storehouse of images and versions of events seen from the start through the lens of the foreign observer, the foundational *imaginaire* mirrored epistemological orders in "perfected histories" written to fit a variety of objectives, while submerging ways of knowing that did not conform with the linear logic of European thought under layers of superimposed Western modes of representation (in an imaginary archaeology of discourses). The chroniclers themselves were not of one mind and often projected contradictory perspectives. Among them are the historically untrained conqueror/soldier who recorded firsthand observations; the friar committed to redeeming the oppressed Indian; the serene, apparently non-biased pioneer ethnographer who relied on our first "informants"; the classically trained humanist; the colonized Indian; the erudite mestizo; and the armchair historian filtering primary and secondary sources to fulfill the tasks of Crown-appointed official Cronista Mayor de Indias (1572–ca. 1793) (Esteve Barba 1964: 8–10, 112–36). Discourse, not praxis, forced a historical experience and representations of the

exuberant creativity it spawned into a procrustean bed whose implications for musicology (broadly defined) remain to be exorcised.

Five centuries later, self-awareness and the assimilation of texts that blazed a liberating trail (especially Edmundo O'Gorman's *The Invention of America: An inquiry into the historical nature of the New World and the meaning of its history* [1961] [Kuss 1993]) have catalyzed a flurry of creative scholarship in a number of disciplines that submit the received conceptual frameworks and their concomitant discursive modalities to critical scrutiny. Confining ourselves only to Peru as an instance, it is important to note that some of the paradigmatic texts generated within a more generalized movement of postcolonial revisionism have been driven by a need to heal fractured national identities and finally assimilate the trauma of Conquest, which is still an open wound in Andean countries and emblematic of current social struggles. Written by Peruvians to understand and sublimate their own historical experience, these texts are not addressed to the foreign consumer (extraversion) but directed inwards (intraversion). For instance, in *Entre el mito y la historia* (Hernández, Lemlij, Millones, Péndola, and Rostworowski 1987), ethnohistorians and psychologists engage in "archaeological" efforts to rescue patterns of Andean thought (see also Luis Millones, "Popular Dramas and Commemorations: The Incas of Carhuamayo," in Volume 3 of this series); in *Memoria del bien perdido: Conflicto, identidad y nostalgia en el Inca Garcilaso de la Vega* (1993), Max Hernández probes the subtending integrity of a universalist project while painting an intimate psychoanalytical portrait of the mestizo who wrote the vastly read *Comentarios reales de los Incas* (1609) to recover and reconstruct his conflictual identity (see also González Echevarría 1990 in 1998: 43–92); and in *Del paganismo a la santidad: La incorporación de los indios del Perú al catolicismo, 1532–1750* (2003), historian Juan Carlos Estenssoro Fuchs rescues the quest of Indians to be recognized as Christians, exposing the strategies of colonial power to perpetuate the myth of resistance in order to maintain a marginalized class that itself defined and ensured the perpetuity of the colonial structure, and challenging the entrenched essentialist view of generalized resistance to conversion by a static indigenous society incapable of change. Critical editions and rereadings of canonic texts also have proliferated. Among them, few are as paradigmatic as

Rolena Adorno's reading of native-born Felipe Guamán Poma de Ayala's *Nueva corónica y buen gobierno* (1615) as a comprehensive critique of colonialist discourse on religion, political theory, and history (1986 in 2000), as well as her critical co-edition of this text with John V. Murra (Guamán Poma de Ayala 1615 in 1980).

To the vibrancy and integrity that this research communicates and the potentially inexhaustible lines of inquiry it suggests, we must add literary criticism and, specifically, the work of Roberto González Echevarría, whose essay on "Latin American fiction and the poetics of history" sets the tone for our inquiry into the paradoxical encounters and disencounters we map in Volume 3 of this musical history. The vigor of postcolonial studies in a number of disciplines, however, has yet to emerge with the same generalized conviction from musicological quarters (Kuss 1993; 1998; 2005). Only a relatively small number of scholars—whose work is included in these volumes—are shaking the belief in the supremacy assigned to the entrenched masterstory defined by European- and, more recently, U.S.-centric frames of reference.

Musicology's relative isolation from contemporary criticism in the field of Latin American Studies begs one of the most important questions in postcolonial thought, best formulated by V.Y. Mudimbe in *The Invention of Africa: Gnosis, Philosophy, and the Order of Knowledge* (1988). Published by the same press that brought out O'Gorman's *The Invention of America* seventeen years earlier, Mudimbe's work scrutinizes "processes of transformation of types of knowledge" and "interrogates images of Africa":

> Western interpreters as well as African analysts have been using categories and conceptual systems which depend on a Western epistemological order. Even in the most explicitly "Afrocentric" descriptions, models of analysis explicitly or implicitly, knowingly or unknowingly, refer to the same order. Does this mean that . . . African traditional systems of thought are unthinkable and cannot be made explicit within the framework of their own rationality? My own claim is that, thus far, the ways in which they have been evaluated and the means used to explain them relate to theories and methods whose constraints, rules, and systems of operation suppose a non-African epistemological order (1988: x).

The questions this text raises and the foundations it jolts are echoed in Kofi Agawu's "The Invention of

'African Rhythm'" (1995) and in his polemical book, *Representing African Music: Postcolonial notes, queries, positions* (2003), whose "Introduction"—with a substitution of terms and names—easily could argue our case. At a metalevel, these "virtual cultures" share a similar predicament: no matter how culture-specific and profoundly different the processes by which these *imaginaires* were constructed, each has affected how members of these cultures represent themselves. As the Indiano says to Filomeno in Alejo Carpentier's *Concierto barroco* (1974: 76) when they part in a Venice train station after their adventure in "time" (defined as the substance of rhythm and history): "Sometimes it is necessary to see things from afar, even with an ocean in between, to see them up close" (*A veces es necesario alejarse de las cosas*, poner un mar de por medio, *para ver las cosas de cerca*).

HISTORY AS AESTHETIC CONSTRUCT

The mythological dimensions of Latin America's history, prefigured in the chronicles but not limited to their timespan, compel writers to turn to history for the themes of their fiction and seize larger-than-life heroes or villains (as in the portrayals of Bolívar by García Márquez in *The General in His Labyrinth* [1989 in 1991], and of the Dominican Republic's dictator Rafael Leónidas Trujillo Molina (1891–1961) by Mario Vargas Llosa in *The Feast of the Goat* [2000 in 2001]), or to mythological cycles of colossal proportions (as in García Márquez's *One Hundred Years of Solitude* [1967 in 1970], and Carlos Fuentes' *Terra nostra* [1975 in 1976]). The fact that reality can be more surreal than fiction also feeds an innate proclivity to mythologize it. In the speech he delivered when he received the Nobel Prize in 1982, García Márquez observed that "Independence from Spanish dominion did not spare us from insanity. General Antonio López de Santa Anna, three-time dictator of Mexico, staged magnificent funerals *for the left leg* he had lost in the so-called Guerra de los Pasteles (1983: 1).

From the perspective of a canonic corpus of contemporary literature as interpreted by González Echevarría in "Latin American fiction and the poetics of history," the opening essay in Volume 3 of this series, history then becomes fulfilled poetic prophecy. He writes:

> Modern Latin American novelists obsessively turn to Latin American history as source because they find there

the prolegomena of their narrative art—what comes first, how events determine each other, how causality works, who are the heroes and villains. History becomes in the works of Latin American novelists an *artistic construct* whose truth is *aesthetic* rather than documentary or factual, and more often than not runs counter to official histories found in textbooks and government pronouncements.

With different words, García Márquez expressed a similar thought in a famous dictum: "If historians have written fiction, it befalls us, the writers of fiction, to write the history" (Si los historiadores han hecho ficción, me parece natural que los escritores de ficción hagamos la historia). Aesthetic constructs override "official histories" because the latter served to construct powerfully political fictions whose colonizing purpose defined a conquest by mastery of [written] language, or control of signs. Always more precocious than musicology, literary criticism offered us twenty-five years ago a perfect formulation of this historical predicament:

> The New World occupies a doubly fictive place: the one furnished by the European tradition, and the one reelaborated by Latin American writers [and composers]. Writing within a Western tradition and in a European language, Latin American writers [and composers] feel they write from within a fiction of which they are a part, and in order to escape from this literary [or musical] encirclement they must constantly strive to invent themselves and Latin America anew (González Echevarría 1977 in 1990: 28).

Mastering the code becomes then a way out of "the imperialism of context" (*Ibid.*: 29).

Few have mastered the code or captured the dialogue between versions of history and the interplay of forces driving the structure of constraint, imitation, and subversion that shaped musical creativity in Latin America with more command of history as an aesthetic construct than Alejo Carpentier (1904–80) in *Concierto barroco* (1974), his most musical of fictions. In this novella, the towering figure of Cuban letters—who also wore the hats of music critic (1980), amateur ethnographer (1933 in 1979), music historiographer (1946), opera librettist (1931), and cultural critic (1977)—celebrates the coexistence of musical traditions that shape an incongruent whole through the metaphor of a Haendelian/Vivaldian baroque concerto grosso

disrupted by an African drumming that "does not fit," defying any received model of historical organicism or any attempt at cultural definition. In his masterful critical study of Carpentier's *oeuvre* (1977 in 1990), González Echevarría summons "the most tremendous concerto grosso the centuries have ever heard" as metaphor for an impossible harmony, a "cacophonous, indiscriminate fusion" of European, American, African, traditional, art, and popular musics and instruments of the most varied origins, "of which there need be no synthesis," and where the acceptance of heterogeneity is also an abandonment of an obsession with origins. Rather than "the autonomy of Latin American culture that Carpentier pursued in earlier writings," wherein identity assumes the character of a fusion (as in the magical realism of his only libretto [1931] and its paradigmatic musical setting by Alejandro García Caturla [1934]) (Kuss 1992), in *Concierto barroco* he "demonstrates the dialectics of dependence and independence that subtend any effort at cultural definition" (1977 in 1990: 266, 274). Latin America was postmodern before the age of postmodernism.

The wealth of mythologies that conditioned our "being in history" also conditions the search for the poetics of history in aesthetic constructs, both literary and musical. Transmutations of the foundational *imaginaire* are summoned not only in contemporary fiction but also define the very essence of a brand of creativity capable of transmuting the 18th-century French *contredanse* into tango and Anton Webern's *Symphony*, Op. 21 (1928) into Ginastera's *Cantata para América mágica* (1960) (Kuss 2000). Interpreting the poetics of history as an aesthetic construct demands challenging the basic tenets of the holy writ, namely the value-laden concepts of history shaped by Europeans and those within their gravitational field (see, for instance, Hans Heinrich Eggebrecht's masterful summary of approaches to European history [1980: VIII, 592–600]). It also demands abrogating the political imperative of assigning truth to the process of verification through the written document and claiming oral histories as a part of its domain (as Luis Millones does in "The 'Other' History: Provincial Reflections on the Discovery of America," a recovery of what he calls "parallel histories" in Peru [1985]). Moreover, it demands thinking of cultures as interdependent and fluid wholes, instead of—as anthropologist Eric R. Wolf put it brilliantly—"turning names into things by endowing nations and cultures with the qualities of internally homogeneous and externally bounded objects, thus creating a model of the world as a global pool hall in which the entities spin off each other like so many hard and round billiard balls, leading to the conception of a monolithic West counterposed to a monolithic East, both reified categories that interfere with our ability to understand their mutual encounter and confrontation" (1982: 6). In *Europe and the People Without History*, Wolf argues that we have created intellectual instruments (names that turn concepts into "things" = culture, society, nation) leading to the construction of static models that isolate phenomena, but have not yet devised instruments to name the changing interrelatedness that involves all agents of history, not only the predilect victors or carriers of torches of liberty (1982: 5–7; Kuss 1991: 3). A history that assigns the same value to all traditions and is defined by a heterogeneity "of which there need be no synthesis" and by an infinite number of intersections of time, place, and peoples, only can be served by a neutral model of history, such as Wolf formulated in his aforementioned work: "A web of temporally and spatially changing and changeable set of relationships, or relationships among sets of relationships" (1982: 6). We adopt this non-value-laden grid for our history of this region's musics.

Analyzing modalities of discourse (*d'après* Foucault) in paradigmatic narratives inclusive of writings that "literature proper" would exclude, González Echevarría tells us that the history of the Latin American novel has been told in various ways. The following statement captures a predicament that easily can be applied to the music historiography of Latin America:

> No matter what method the historian employs, the blueprint of evolution and change continues to be that of European literary or artistic historiography . . . . Ordinary categories like romanticism, naturalism, the avant-garde, surface sooner or later. If it is questionable that this historiographic grid is applicable to European literature, it is even more so regarding the literature of Latin America . . . . It is a hopeless task to force texts such as these into a conventional history of the Latin American novel (1990 in 1998: 38–39).

Likewise, when musicologists apply regulative concepts devised by Europeans for the European experience to compositions by Latin Americans—the simplest example of which is the indiscriminate transfer of style-period labels and/or aesthetic movements—they are dooming one historical experience and concomitant aesthetics to representation through the discursive modalities of another. If European-affiliated compositional techniques and procedures created analogies, links, and transformations of the European legacy, these intersections are not homological: the primordial condition of being in history through the discourse of difference subverted aesthetic results (Kuss 2005).

In *Myth and Archive: A theory of Latin American narrative* (1990 in 1998), González Echevarría accomplishes a monumental task: by analyzing modalities of discourse—rather than patterns of evolution and change supported by the scaffolding of facts of conventional historiography—he arrives at a reformulation of historical categories that are culture-specific. Working retrospectively from the modalities of discourse recovered in modern fictions, he identifies three epochs, each characterized by the pervasiveness of a different discursive modality—or period rhetorics—and by the structure of constraint, imitation, and subversion. These modalities, however, are relieved of their historicity when they reappear accumulated or stored in the modern Latin American narrative he calls the "archival fiction" (*d'après* Foucault) of the fourth epoch. Assigning the role of founder of archival fiction to Carpentier in *The Lost Steps* (1953 in 1956), whose narrator/protagonist is a composer, García Márquez's *One Hundred Years of Solitude* (1967 in 1970) stands as its archetype and Jorge Luis Borges as its guardian (1990 in 1998: 1–42).

The synchronic presence of de-historicized discourses defines history retrospectively, as a reconstruction of the past in the present (Treitler 1989a and 1989b), and reaches beyond Latin America's archival fiction. The year 1967 suggests a broader "confluence of historical coordinates"— Carpentier's metaphor for the elusive predicament of the region's musics (1977). In this particular intersection converge not only the publication of *One Hundred Years of Solitude*, the advent of archival compositions such as Alberto Ginastera's *Bomarzo* and Luciano Berio's *Sinfonia* (1968–69 [*O King*, 1967]), and an expanded revision of Umberto Eco's *Opera aperta: Forma e indeterminazione nelle poetiche contemporanee*, but also Foucault's dialogue with Raymond Bellour wherein he lends a shape to the figure of the "Archive," published under the title "On the Ways of Writing History" (1967 in 1999: 289–90):

xviii | PERFORMING BELIEFS: INDIGENOUS PEOPLES

Bellour: How do you situate yourself personally in this mutation that draws the most rigorous works of knowledge into a kind of literary adventure (an *aventure romanesque*)?

Foucault: Unlike those who are labeled "structuralists," I am not really interested in the formal possibilities afforded by a system such as language. Personally, I am more intrigued by the existence of discourses, by the fact that words were spoken. Those events functioned in relation to their original situation, they left traces behind them, they continue to exist, and they exercise, in their submerged subsistence in history, a certain number of manifest or secret functions.

Bellour: In that way, you surrender to the characteristic passion of the historian, who wants to respond to the endless murmur of the archives.

Foucault: Yes, because my object is not language but the archive, which is to say, the accumulated existence of discourses. Archaeology, as I understand it, is not akin either to geology (as the analysis of substrata) or to genealogy (as the description of beginnings and successions); it is the analysis of discourse in its *archival* modality.

Mastering the hegemonic code—divested of its hierarchies, values, and contextual meanings—to invert its signs and turn the received discourses into a fiction is then the way out of "the imperialism of context." Moreover, this strategy reverses the terms of the foundational *imaginaire* and balances the asymmetry of the initial historical predicament. Antithetical to the masterstory, the Archive, or de-historicized accumulation of discourses, is neither hegemonic nor does it canonize:

> Mythification is a version of the masterstory of escape from the strictures of the dominant discourse through fusion with one of the main objects of that discourse: myth. Heterogeneity of cultures, languages, sources, beginnings, is at the core of the Archive's founding negativity, a pluralism that is a subversion or sub-version of the masterstory. The Archive culls and looses, it cannot brand or determine. The Archive cannot coalesce as a national or cultural myth, though its make-up still reveals a longing for the creation of such a grandiose politico-cultural metastory (González Echevarría 1990 in 1998: 175).

If a center of gravity of modern culture in Latin America exists at all, it belongs as much to the visions projected by Carpentier as it does to Borges because, for the latter, it was never a question of rejecting the legacy of the West but rather embracing it in its totality to reorder its signs and turn it into a fiction. When Borges turns his encyclopedia of Western knowledge on its head, divesting it of its culture-specific contexts of interpretation, he cancels out its meanings to map out infinite possibilities of different associations, presenting "a vision of a place where all other places intersect" (Parks 2001: 42). Such reorderings of the legacy of the West require an *a priori* act of possession, a "mastery of the code" (González Echevarría 1977 in 1990: 29), without which there is no possibility of escaping the epigonic fate of the original predetermination (the "invention" of America as a replica of Europe). Mastery of the code to then decode and elicit multiple new readings that turn *the received culture into a fiction* by inversion of signs demands a critical attitude toward its legacy and its systems of explanation. Borges challenges the limits of this idea in "Pierre Menard, autor del *Quijote*" (1938 in 1974: 444–50) when its fictive author—an *absence*—reproduces his source *verbatim* to elicit the reading of a totally different work, not by "copying" the original but by "coming to the story *through the experience of Pierre Menard*" (Parks 2001: 41). In 20th-century music theater, the Borgean idea of appropriation and reordering surfaces in *Bomarzo* (1967), the second opera by Alberto Ginastera (1916–83) based on the homonymous novel (1962) and libretto by Manuel Mujica Láinez (1910–84) (Kuss 1987b and 2002). If the figure of the Archive, as defined by González Echevarría in his theory of Latin American narrative, is at once Library, Encyclopedia, History, and Sediment, the fiction that the *grotteschi* in Bomarzo's gardens suggested to Mujica Láinez subsumes all of these and takes possession of the Renaissance to invert its signs and reterritorialize it from a 20th-century perspective, as Borges reterritorializes Cervantes in "Pierre Menard." In *Bomarzo*, Ginastera aligns himself with the fiction that Borges inaugurates in 1938 with "Pierre Menard," wherein mastery of the code becomes the tool to strip the embraced culture of its hierarchies, values, and meanings and thus turn the legacy of the West into a fiction that reverses the terms of the foundational *imaginaire*. (The composer was well aware of this strategy: when I started working on *Bomarzo* a quarter of a century ago, he said to me with a big smile, "Don't forget to read 'Pierre Menard'.")

Each point of intersection in our relational web *d'après* Wolf defines different sets of relationships among the traditions involved. This value-free, cybernetic metaphor for history as a web of multileveled intersections of time, place, and peoples is not only inclusive of all traditions, but also accommodates hegemonic modalities of musical discourse or "period rhetorics," each with its respective strategies of subversion, as well as "archival" composition, namely the synchronic accumulation of discourses that defines modernity, which, as stated above, is not hegemonic (González Echevarría 1990 in 1998: 175). Within this neutral metaframework, however, each intersection or nodal point represents an interplay of culturally value-laden factors. Viewed as an Archive of intrahistories, each unfolding at its own pace, what Columbus wrought for Europe was the fulfillment of *another set of cultural possibilities*, "defined within and yet against a powerful totality" (González Echevarría). Rather than the West and the rest, the rearticulation of values in the acts of adoption, assimilation, and subversion relativizes certainties and challenges borders of a once sacrosanct space, implicitly de-centering it and irreverently breeding criteria for its critique (i.e., Latin American "culture" as mirror and critique of its tributaries). The regulative concepts of the hegemonic grid have been critically scrutinized by some enlightened Europeans (Fischer 1979; Finscher 1986–1987) and challenged, more or less irreverently, by scholars in the United States (Treitler 1989a and 1989b; Tomlinson 1995), to mention but a few. Musicologists specializing in Latin America are beginning to dismantle the tenacious hold of colonialist and self-colonized discourse. However, a culture-specific theory of "musical discourses" mediated by analysis and engendered by the terms of its own rationality, comparable to González Echevarría's theory of Latin American narrative, still lies dormant, waiting to be "discovered" by musicologists.

The four volumes that comprise our collaborative "encyclopedic history" are, by necessity, eclectic. We have not imposed theories of culture or history on the work of our authors, but intentionally embrace the multiplicity of approaches and perspectives that mirrors a broad range of differences in traditions of scholarship and training. There is, however, a subtending agenda, beyond the hope of stimulating research on a vast array of gaps. We believe that the unprecedented coverage of musical traditions in Latin America and the Caribbean in these volumes, which adheres to the principle that these have to be studied at the local level, can contribute in some measure to the eradication of essentialisms and to critical reassessments of the infinite ways in which cultural representation still relies on criteria and conceptual frameworks developed within the Eurocentric sphere of influence, including some models of cultural criticism stemming from vastly different historical experiences.

OUR "CULTURAL ADVENTURE"

... Son tantos los hilos ausentes
en toda urdimbre o toda trama,
que con ellos alcanza

en algún otro espacio
para un tejido completamente diferente ...

Toda historia, toda explicación, todo discurso,
son figuras trazadas por un momento en el aire,
formas a la deriva
que se enrollan a veces transitoriamente
en el perfil un poco más discreto
de una rama seca.

... So many are the absent strands
in every scheme or every web,
that with them we would have enough,

in some other space,
to weave another utterly different net ...

Each history, explanation, or discourse,
is a transient figure traced in the air,
forms adrift
that sometimes curl for a while
around the less ambitious shape
of a seared branch.

—Fragments from "Poesía vertical" by Roberto Juárroz, cited in Lelia Madrid's *La fundación mitológica de América Latina* (1989: 19) (my translation).

THE FOUR VOLUMES in this series are structured as parts of a single conception and gather 150 contributions by well over 100 distinguished scholars from 36 countries. In addition, the work includes approximately 30 hours of recorded sound and bibliographies that amount to a nearly comprehensive history of writings in the fields of Latin American and Caribbean music studies.

VOLUME 1, *Performing Beliefs: Indigenous Peoples of South America, Central America, and Mexico*, focuses on the inextricable relationships between worldviews and musical behavior in current and relatively recent practices of indigenous groups. Worldviews are built into how music is organized and performed, how musical instruments are constructed and when they are played, choreographic formations, the structure of songs, the assignment of gender to instruments, ritual patterns, and so on. Every essay in this volume addresses different levels at which this principle is manifested. Within this context, music is mostly an essential form of energy, a kinetic and transformative vessel that communicates with ancestors and the supernatural, heals, manipulates the forces of nature, bonds communities, or reenacts social tensions. The bridges cannot be crossed without the transformative power of music (or sound). Essays on fundamental concepts underpinning secular and religious practices of indigenous groups ("Native Peoples: Introductory Panorama"; "Myth, Cosmology, and Performance"; "Music and Healing"; and "Epilogue," all by Carol E. Robertson) articulate a framework for surveys mapping traditional practices of Native Americans in Argentina, Brazil, and Chile. In the case of Mexico, an overview of linguistically differentiated groups by Marina Alonso Bolaños captures merely the scope of the indigenous presence in that country and was commissioned expressly to question whether the rather vast anthropological literature on these groups has been matched by research on their musical practices. These surveys are complemented by case studies of rituals, performance traditions, and shamanic practices of specific groups (the Wakuénai in Venezuela; the Kamayurá in Brazil; the Aymara and Kechua in Bolivia and Peru; the Mapuche in Argentina; the Mískito in Nicaragua and Honduras; the Kuna in Panama; and the P'urhépecha in Mexico). Balancing this rich and still largely unexplored universe of meanings embodied in musical practices, Dale A. Olsen's substantive chapter on aerophones of traditional use probes the instruments that carry maximum cultural density among Native Americans. Two CDs with 44 examples illustrate the contributions to this volume, most of which were recorded in the field by the authors themselves.

In all cases, we sought the most widely recognized authorities to address these topics. The work of Irma Ruiz on Argentina, María Ester Grebe on Chile, Elizabeth Travassos on Brazil, Jonathan Hill on the Wakuénai, Ronny Velásquez on the Mískito and Kuna, Rafael José de Menezes Bastos on the Kamayurá, Max Peter Baumann on Bolivia, Thomas Turino on Peru, E. Fernando Nava López on the P'urhépecha, Carol E. Robertson on the Mapuche, and Dale A. Olsen on aerophones, represents a cross-section of classic research conducted between the 1970s and 1990s by two generations of scholars whose contributions to their respective areas of specialization remain largely unsurpassed. Within our "web of temporally and spatially changing and changeable set of relationships, or relationships among sets of relationships," each of these authors captured a specific intersection of time, place, and peoples susceptible to flux and interpretive challenge.

The index provides both concordances and definitions of the fluid local terminology we retained in order to fulfill one of the overriding principles that animates this project, which is to draw the Anglophone reader into culture-specific terms of explanation, instead of "translating culture" by representing it through the conceptual framework of the receiver. This is an important editorial issue because it redresses the general tendency, at least in the United States, to homogenize terminology in order to render it more accessible to cultural outsiders. Such simplification would have obliterated the linguistic creativity that peoples across the continent display to assert their local identities. This principle applies to instruments, genres, and "ways of naming" in general that often do not meet the Anglophone reader's expectations of concision.

VOLUME 2 addresses the reconfiguration of the Caribbean's complex sonic map after the Conquest and the strategies through which diverse groups assigned new meanings to their partially reconstructed traditions. The Caribbean was the stage on which the initial drama of Conquest was played out. As Sidney W. Mintz and Sally Price state in their introduction to *Caribbean Contours* (1985: 10), "to characterize Caribbean peoples as sharing some kind of special personality or philosophy would be to vulgarize the complexity of their pasts and the much differentiated societies in which they live today." Within different colonial histories, however, peoples in the Caribbean islands and in culturally related mainland areas (such as Guyana) shared the experience of slavery and the presence of Africans of varied origins whose musical legacy left an indelible mark on their creative strategies. Few authors can tell the compelling story of these strategies as does Olive Lewin, who, as the Great Lady of Jamaica and a scholar/participant in the musical life of her country, carries within herself the heart of the nation. If the creolization process spawned a broad range of new musical forms catalyzed by the

European and African legacies, the fluid process of self-representation has privileged an identification with a resignified African heritage. As Martha Ellen Davis states in her superb survey of oral traditions in the Dominican Republic, "each nation has its own discourse regarding its identity, based on a collective concept of its sociocultural composition and mythologized interpretation of historical events."

Prefaced by Argeliers León's masterful essay on the contribution of Africans and their descendants to concepts of timbric and rhythmic organization in traditional music, this volume includes studies of a representative cross-section of oral traditions in the Spanish-, French-, English-, and Dutch-speaking Caribbean. Among the latter is the moving "life story" of an 85 year-old man of African descent from Curaçao who, interviewed by Rose Mary Allen in 1984, recalls the traditional songs taught to him by his father and the struggle to subsist under the "pay for land" system that required those continuing to live on a plantation after Emancipation in 1863 to work for the owner a few days per week without pay. To underscore the significance of membranophones and idiophones in traditions of African provenance, the volume includes an organological study of *batá* drums and *güiros* in the context of Cuban *santería* by Victoria Eli Rodríguez, and an essay on African-Venezuelan percussion ensembles by Max Brandt.

Surveys of music archives offer basic information and summary descriptions of holdings that can facilitate access and kindle the interest of researchers. The 19 country profiles of islands and circum-Caribbean countries aligned primarily with Caribbean "culture" provide a context for the reader to situate topical essays within historical overviews of each geopolitical entity. Each country profile includes information on demographic composition, political status and history, religions, and languages spoken; the national anthem (with musical example); an overview of oral and written musical traditions; organization of musical life; a chronology of the nation's history; a brief section on communication media; a list of archives; and a selected bibliography.

VOLUME 3, which we would like to call "Latin America: Islands of History" *d'après* Marshall Sahlins, traces intersections ranging from pre-Columbian civilizations to late 20th-century composition, within which we chart the continuities and discontinuities that surface in this mosaic of expressions. In "Latin American fiction and the poetics of history," the opening essay, Roberto González Echevarría captures the fundamental characteristics of the "marvelous real" quality of a history that began as fiction (the historical being of America conjured up by the European imagination), feeding a capacity to mythologize reality and invert the terms of the foundational *imaginaire* in modern archival fictions. This special brand of creativity surfaces in the infinite ways in which the popular imagination reinvented received instruments, dances, traditions of performance, and concepts of music from its cultural tributaries, and this process continues.

The interplay of cultural identities that has characterized the New World experience for the past 500 years precludes any rigid separation between the domains of "folk," "urban popular," and "art" musical traditions. These reified categories curiously seem to have taken hold in Latin America only after the emergence of ethnomusicology in the United States, especially if we consider that distinguished music historiographers, such as the Uruguayan Lauro Ayestarán (1953), covered popular expressions as integral to the musical fabric of their respective nations (Kuss 1987a). Even the language discourages such separatism, since *música popular* denotes both "folk" and "urban popular" music. Argeliers León (1918–91), the towering figure of the previous generation of Cuban musicologists, addressed this issue, proposing a continuum of levels of ancestry and degrees of elaboration within three sociogeographic contexts as the basis for inductive categories that also bridge the gap between oral and written *música popular*: (1) primordial elements (factores antecedentes o primigenios), those closest to their sources, which are found mostly in rural oral traditions and rituals; (2) infra-urban musics (factor urbano primario), which, although already disengaged from rural and ritual contexts, rely on any object capable of producing sonority, and within which León situates the semantic field of traditional *rumba* (*yambú*, *columbia*, and *guaguancó*); and (3) the "elaborated" urban expressions (factor urbano elaborado), comprising the well-known genres associated with both old and new Cuban popular music (such as the *contradanza*, *habanera*, *bolero*, *guaracha*, *danzón*, mambo, cha-cha-chá, and others more recent) (León 1982). His disciple Olavo Alén Rodríguez proposed another definition of *música popular* based on information theory that differentiates this domain by the proportion and balance between familiar and unfamiliar quantity of aesthetic information (Alén Rodríguez 1984: 393–94; Kuss 1994: 935–36). Whether León's model is too evolutionary or even transferable to other cultural situations, and Alén Rodríguez's model is too exclusionary of contextual variables, remains arguable. The merit of these alternatives, however, rests on rejecting artificial separations between fluid domains. The same permeability applies to "art" music, whose also artificially constructed domain so often interacts with popular expression.

The disposition of contributions in this volume often subverts chronology to suggest precisely the seamless transitions between oral and written traditions and the complex mixes at these boundaries. For instance, Luis Millones' "Popular Dramas and Commemorations: The Incas of Carhuamayo," in which he recovers constructions of an "idealized oral history" in 20th-century representations of the death of Atahualpa, is followed by my essay on the same theme in its version for the lyric stage by the Lima resident Carlo Enrico Pasta (1817–98) on an original Italian libretto by Antonio Ghislanzoni (1824–93), which stands as the first opera on an Inca subject premiered in the Peruvian capital (Lima, 1877). Likewise, Beatriz Seibel's "The *Payadores* of the Río de la Plata," which traces the history of the old and idiosyncratic oral tradition of folk bards singing improvised verses to the accompaniment of guitar, is followed by an essay on *El matrero* (1929) by Argentinian composer Felipe Boero (1884–1958), an iconic work in the construction of the national masterstory whose protagonist is an emblematic *payador*. Essays on 20th-century composition in Volume 3 also establish links with oral traditions covered in previous tomes. For instance, the Andean panpipe called *siku* in Aymara, *antara* in Kechua, and *zampoña* in Spanish, which carries maximum cultural density in the organology of the region and plays an emblematic role in traditional music (see pp. 274–78 in this volume), is the theme deconstructed by two of Peru's most distinguished composers, Celso Garrido-Lecca (b. 1926) and Edgar Valcárcel (b. 1932). Entitled *Antaras* and *Zampoña sónica* respectively, both works were composed in 1968.

For Latin Americanists, who need both, the artificial separation between ethnomusicology and so-called historical musicology, as institutionalized in the United States, was only a necessary strategy of the former initially conceived to confront the institutionalized supremacy of the latter. Charles Seeger (1886–1979), who catalyzed the institutionalization of both disciplines in the United States, regretted the rift and often said that the study of all musics perhaps should be under the umbrella of ethnomusicology, "because we are all ethnic," or, conversely, under "musicology." We adopt this broadly defined concept of musicology throughout this work. Although we cannot claim interdisciplinarity as defined by James Clifford *d'après* Barthes in *Writing Culture* (1986: 1), namely "the creation of a new object that belongs to no one," this volume is enriched by the multi-disciplinarity converging in the sum total of individual perspectives from the fields of anthropology, ethnohistory, cultural theory, ethnomusicology, historical musicology, sociology, theater history, and literary criticism.

Organological studies published within the Anglophone sphere of influence often disregard the wealth of information that the vast instrumentarium indigenous to the Americas and adapted from its African and European tributaries can contribute to new approaches to taxonomy on a global scale, and to what Margaret Kartomi calls "an increased focus... on orally transmitted, culture-emerging concepts and classifications of instruments and ensembles" (2001: 308). The literature on instruments is vast (see pp. 262 and 320–24 in this volume for only a sample of published research). A chapter on string instruments of traditional use, placed in the context of colonial music in Volume 3 because chordophones—with the exception of the musical bow—were not known in the Americas before the arrival of Europeans, complements comparable studies of aerophones and membranophones/idiophones in the corresponding contexts of volumes 1 and 2.

Only exceptionally are tunings of instruments represented in conventional music notation. For pitch notation we have adopted a slightly modified version of the system used in *The New Grove Dictionary of Music and Musicians* (Sadie 1980: 1, xii), whereby middle C is c′, with octaves above as c″, c‴, etc., and octaves below as c, C, C′, C″, etc. Pitch-classes, defined as all possible octave transpositions of the same pitch (all Ds, regardless of octave register, constitute pitch-class D), are given in capital letters.

Seventeen country profiles of continental nations—from Argentina to Mexico—provide a historical overview of each geopolitical unit. As in Volume 2, country profiles include information on demographic composition, political status and history, religions, and languages spoken; the national anthem (with musical example); an overview of oral and written musical traditions; organization of musical life; a chronology of the nation's history; a brief section on communication media; a list of archives; and a selected bibliography. The CDs illustrating the contributions to this volume, whose length requires publication in two parts, include mostly examples not readily available in commercial recordings.

Beginning with Volume 3, indexes are cumulative. All four indexes are conceived as extensions of their corresponding volumes, insofar as they provide short definitions and concordances. The indexes in volumes 3 and 4, however, fulfill the additional function of linking entries throughout the already published tomes in the series.

VOLUME 4, *Urban Popular Musics of the New World*, focuses on transnational musics that feed from the vast canvas of traditional and academic practices mapped in the previous tomes. The introduction by Peter Manuel unfolds a panorama of musics that have transcended original boundaries and, conversely, musics created by "Latins" abroad, projected in turn throughout Latin America and the Caribbean. This essay includes sections on definitions (terminological paradoxes); the mass media; urbanization; transnational perspectives; class, race, and ethnicity; gender; music, imperialism, and empowerment; and a typology of a broad spectrum of expressions (from genres, such as the bolero, and semantic fields, such as Brazilian samba, to the sociopolitical *nueva canción* and rap). The contributions address some of the most dynamic and significant expressions configuring the sonic map of musics worldwide. Brazilian scholar Elizabeth Travassos, for instance, reminds us that samba—like Cuban *rumba*—is neither a genre nor a style, but a semantic field whose meanings have accumulated over the course of centuries: the exported image of samba as the urban music of an exotic Rio feeding the political economy of culture is only a recent face of this polysemic expression. Following a whimsical reading of the vast literature on the history of tango by Marta Savigliano, Ramón Pelinski provides a masterful essay on deterritorialized tango and Omar Corrado situates the idiosyncratic art of Astor Piazzolla in the context of signifying a city. A critical essay by Pablo Vila probing theory of interpellation and the construction of narrative identities balances, at the end of the volume, the theoretical and transnational perspectives in

Manuel's opening panorama. Especially because this repertoire has attracted the attention of cultural theorists worldwide, who often rely only on studies published in English, these invaluable readings by cultural insiders carry the potential of bridging a significant gap between traditions of scholarship. CDs with a generous dose of examples extracted from recordings produced mostly by local industries and a cumulative index of the 4-volume series complete the work.

When Garcilaso de la Vega named his influential memoir *Comentarios reales de los Incas* (1609), a chronicle whose wide European reception eventually would contribute to the egalitarian ideals that inspired the French Revolution and played a central role in the history of utopism (Montiel 1992 and 2000), by *reales* he meant that he was writing "the *real* history" of his people, certainly not the "royal" commentaries that mistranslators made it out to be (as in Alain Gheerbrant's edition [Garcilaso de la Vega 1609 in 1961]). We would not claim any such "truth" for any history, and especially not ours, because, as David Lodge (2004) states in his review of Terry Eagleton's *After Theory* (2003), "we cannot return to such an age of innocence." We do attempt, however, to displace the center of gravity of the reader and relativize his/her ways of knowing. Any work of a comprehensive nature only can capture fragments of history, partly because so much remains unrecovered, and mostly because it would take hundreds of volumes to cover the vast quantity of available research on all possible themes and historical intersections. In this respect, the 10-volume *Diccionario de la música española e hispanoamericana* directed by Emilio Casares Rodicio, with Victoria Eli Rodríguez and Benjamín Yépez Chamorro (1999–2002), a reference work that gathers contributions by hundreds of scholars, signals a new era in a field of study that my dear Nicolas Slonimsky called *terra incognita* (only for him, of course) when he, like Copland, visited a few Latin American countries in 1941 (Slonimsky 1945 in 1972: 1).

Above all, this work celebrates the creativity of countless musicians and the research they have inspired. It also celebrates the tenacity of the human spirit, because obstacles did not derail an enterprise that Samuel Claro Valdés lovingly called "our cultural adventure." We did not know where it would take us when we started it, energized by a commitment to the idea of providing a venue for peoples of the world to tell the story of their musics in their own terms and within their own frames of reference, values, and experiences. Thus, the mosaic of cultural practices captured in these pages is as rich as the diversity of perspectives on ways of knowing and "interpreting cultures." In the age of an interdependence that has been called "globalization" and its concomitant reaffirmation of local identities, we need to seize the possibility of making that elusive Other a part of our own narrative plot, not because it is politically correct or trendy to do so, or only through the often distant academic discourse of difference, but because an emotional rather than intellectual point of entry into a plurality of belief systems, and the *imaginaires* they sustain in a multiplicity of expressive forms, makes it possible for us to view our own not as "the true and right one," but as one more *imaginaire* among many. The certainty that it is theoretically impossible to translate the "feeling" of identification that practitioners and cultural insiders summon when they perform or listen to their musics should not deter us from trying.

In 1925, the Kuna chief Nele Kantule (1868–1944) started a successful political movement that, by 1938, had established the Kuna ethnic nation as one of the strongest on the American continent. The vigor of his commitment ensured the autonomy of his people, the preservation of his millenarian culture, and, so far against all odds, continues to guide their destiny. As an epigraph for the first volume that follows, I chose Nele Kantule's words, so wisely chosen by Ronny Velásquez (p. 212), which transcend their context and can define the purpose of my own journey:

I would like the culture of my race to survive within the universal framework of world cultures because only through the cultural expression of a people can we define the lasting legacy of the essence of their liberty, dignity, and respect as a nation.

Denton, Texas
August 11, 2004

REFERENCES

Adorno, Rolena 1986 in 2000. *Guamán Poma: Writing and resistance in colonial Peru*, 2nd edition. Austin: University of Texas Press.

Agawu, Kofi 1995. "The invention of 'African rhythm'," *Journal of the American Musicological Society* 48/3: 380–95.

2003. *Representing African music: Postcolonial notes, queries, positions*. New York and London: Routledge.

Alén Rodríguez, Olavo 1984. "La tradición popular y su significación social y política" in *Musicología en Latinoamérica*, ed. by Zoila Gómez García. La Habana: Editorial Arte y Literatura, 390–405.

Arciniegas, Germán 1962 in 1964. "The four Americas" in *Do the Americas have a common history? A critique of the Bolton theory*, ed. by Lewis Hanke. New York: Alfred A. Knopf, 235–49.

Arrom, José Juan 1971. *Certidumbre de América: Estudios de letras, folklore y cultura*, 2nd enlarged edition. Madrid: Editorial Gredos.

Ayestarán, Lauro 1953. *La música en el Uruguay*. Montevideo: Servicio Oficial de Difusión Radio Eléctrica.

Bierck Jr., Harold A. 1999. "Simón Bolívar: The life" in *People and issues in Latin American history: From independence to the present; sources and interpretations*, 2nd edition, ed. by Lewis Hanke and Jane M. Rausch. Princeton: Markus Wiener Publishers, 4–12.

Borges, Jorge Luis 1974. *Obras completas 1923–1972*. Buenos Aires: Emecé Editores.

Carpentier, Alejo 1931. *Manita en el Suelo*, opera bufa in one act and five scenes for narrator and puppets. Typewritten libretto, 16 pp.

1933 in 1979. *Ecué-Yamba-O*. Barcelona: Editorial Bruguera.

1946. *La música en Cuba*. México: Fondo de Cultura Económica.

1953 in 1956. *The lost steps*. New York: Knopf. English translation by Harriet de Onís of *Los pasos perdidos* (Madrid: Edición y Distribución de Publicaciones, 1953). Critical edition of *Los pasos perdidos* by Roberto González Echevarría (Madrid: Cátedra, 1985).

1974. *Concierto barroco*. México: Siglo Veintiuno Editores.

1977. "América Latina en la confluencia de coordenadas históricas y su repercusión en la música" in *América Latina en su música*, ed. by Isabel Aretz. México: Siglo Veintiuno Editores; Paris: UNESCO, 7–19.

1980. *Ese músico que llevo adentro*, ed. by Zoila Gómez. La Habana: Editorial Letras Cubanas, 3 vols.

Casares Rodicio, Emilio, with Victoria Eli Rodríguez and Benjamín Yépez Chamorro, editors 1999–2002. *Diccionario de la música española e hispanoamericana*. Madrid: Sociedad General de Autores y Editores, 10 vols.

Clifford, James 1986. "Introduction: Partial truths" in *Writing culture: The poetics and politics of ethnography*, ed. by James Clifford and George E. Marcus. Berkeley and Los Angeles: University of California Press.

Copland, Aaron 1942. "The composers of South America," *Modern music* 19/2: 75–82.

Dahlhaus, Carl 1974. "Die Idee des Nationalismus in der Musik" in *Zwischen Romantik und Moderne: Vier Studien zur Musikgeschichte des späteren 19. Jahrhunderts*. München: Musikverlag Emil Katzbichler. English translation by Mary Whittall, "Nationalism and music" in *Between romanticism and modernism: Four studies in the music of the later nineteenth century* (Berkeley and Los Angeles: University of California Press, 1980), 79–101.

Eagleton, Terry 2003. *After theory*. New York: Basic Books.

Eco, Umberto 1967. *Opera aperta: Forma e indeterminazione nelle poetiche contemporanee*, revised and expanded edition. Milano: Bompiani.

Eggebrecht, Hans Heinrich 1980. "Historiography" in *The new Grove dictionary of music and musicians*, 20 vols., ed. by Stanley Sadie. London: Macmillan, vol. 8, 592–600.

Estenssoro Fuchs, Juan Carlos 2003. *Del paganismo a la santidad: La incorporación de los indios del Perú al catolicismo, 1532–1750*. Lima: Instituto Francés de Estudios Andinos (IFEA).

Esteve Barba, Francisco 1964. *Historiografía indiana*. Madrid: Editorial Gredos.

Finscher, Ludwig 1986–1987. "Weber's *Freischütz*: Conceptions and misconceptions," *Proceedings of the Royal Musical Association*, vol. 110: 79–90.

Fischer, Kurt von 1979. "Zum Begriff NATIONAL in Musikgeschichte und deutscher Musikhistoriographie" in *Zwischen den Grenzen: Zum Aspekt des Nationalen in der neuen Musik*, ed. by Dieter Rexroth. Mainz: B. Schott's Söhne, 11–16.

Foucault, Michel 1967 in 1999. "On the ways of writing history" (conversation with Raymond Bellour) in *Aesthetics, method, and epistemology*, ed. by James D. Faubion. New York: The New Press, 279–95. English translation by Robert Hurley of "Sur les façons d'écrire l'histoire" (entretien avec R. Bellour), *Les Lettres françaises*, No. 1187 (15–21 juin 1967), 6–9; reprinted in *Dits et écrits, I: 1954–1975*, 2nd edition, ed. by Daniel Defert and François Ewald, with Jacques Lagrange (Paris: Gallimard, 2001), 613–28.

Fuentes, Carlos 1975 in 1976. *Terra nostra*. New York: Farrar, Straus, & Giroux. English translation by Margaret Sayers Peden of *Terra nostra* (México: J. Mortiz, 1975).

García Márquez, Gabriel 1967 in 1970. *One hundred years of solitude*. New York: Harper & Row. English translation by Gregory Rabassa of *Cien años de soledad* (Buenos Aires: Editorial Sudamericana, 1967).

1983. "La soledad de América," *Boletín* (La Habana, Círculo de Cultura Cubana) 7 (February): 1–2.

1989 in 1991. *The general in His labyrinth*. New York: Penguin Books. English translation by Edith Grossman of *El general en su laberinto* (Madrid: Mondadori España, 1989).

Garcilaso de la Vega 1609 in 1961. *The royal commentaries of the Inca*, ed. by Alain Gheerbrant. New York: Orion Press.

1609 in 1982. *Comentarios reales*. México: SEP—Universidad Nacional Autónoma de México (UNAM).

González Echevarría, Roberto 1977 in 1990. *Alejo Carpentier: The pilgrim at home*. Austin: University of Texas Press. Spanish edition, *Alejo Carpentier: El peregrino en su patria* (México: Universidad Nacional Autónoma de México, 1993).

1990 in 1998. *Myth and archive: A theory of Latin American narrative*. Durham: Duke University Press. Spanish translation by Virginia Aguirre Muñoz, *Mito y archivo: Una teoría de la narrativa latinoamericana* (México: Fondo de Cultura Económica, 2000).

2006. "Latin American fiction and the poetics of history" in *Music in Latin America and the Caribbean: An encyclopedic history*, 4 vols., ed. by Malena Kuss. Austin: University of Texas Press, vol. 3 (in press).

Guamán Poma de Ayala, Felipe 1615 in 1980. *El primer nueva corónica y buen gobierno*, ed. by John V. Murra and Rolena Adorno, with translation and textual analysis of Quechua by Jorge L. Urioste. México: Siglo Veintiuno Editores, 3 vols.

Hanke, Lewis, editor 1964. *Do the Americas have a common history? A critique of the Bolton theory*. New York: Alfred A. Knopf.

Hanke, Lewis, and Jane M. Rausch, editors 1999. *People and issues in Latin American history: From independence to the present; sources and interpretations*, 2nd edition. Princeton: Markus Wiener Publishers.

Hernández, Max 1993. *Memoria del bien perdido: Conflicto, identidad y nostalgia en el Inca Garcilaso de la Vega*. Lima: Instituto de Estudios Peruanos (IEP)—Biblioteca Peruana de Psicoanálisis (BPP).

Hernández, Max, Moisés Lemlij, Luis Millones, Alberto Péndola, and María Rostworowski 1987. *Entre el mito y la historia: Psicoanálisis y pasado andino*. Lima: Ediciones Psicoanalíticas Imago.

Kartomi, Margaret 2001. "The classification of musical instruments: Changing trends in research from the late nineteenth century, with special reference to the 1990s," *Ethnomusicology* 45/2: 283–314.

Kuss, Malena 1987a. "Toward a comprehensive approach to Latin American music bibliography: Theoretical foundations for reference sources and research materials" in *Latin American masses and minorities: Their images and realities*, 2 vols., ed. by Dan Hazen. Madison, Wisconsin: SALALM Secretariat—Memorial Library, University of Wisconsin, vol. 2, 615–78.

1987b. "Bomarzo" (1967) by Alberto Ginastera in *Pipers Enzyklopädie des Musiktheaters*, 7 vols., ed. by Carl Dahlhaus and the Forschungsinstitut für Musiktheater der Universität Bayreuth directed by Sieghart Döhring. Munich and Zürich: Piper Verlag, vol. 2, 382–86.

1991. "Round Table II: Contributions of the New World to the music of the Old World," *Acta musicologica* 63/1: 3–11.

1992. "The confluence of historical coordinates in Carpentier/Caturla's *Manita en el Suelo*" in *Musical repercussions of 1492: Encounters in text and performance*, ed. by Carol E. Robertson. Washington, D.C.: The Smithsonian Institution Press, 355–80.

1993. "The 'Invention' of America: Encounter settings on the Latin American lyric stage," *Revista de musicología* (Madrid, Sociedad Española de Musicología) 16/1: 185–204.

1994. Review of *Essays on Cuban music: North American and Cuban perspectives*, ed. by Peter Manuel (Lanham, Maryland: University Press of America, 1991) in *Notes, Quarterly journal of the Music Library Association* 50/3: 934–41.

1996. "Ficción e historiografía: Las crónicas españolas como fuentes para la etnohistoria musical americana," *Oralidad: Lenguas, identidad y memoria de América* (La Habana, journal of the Oficina Regional de Cultura de la UNESCO para América Latina y el Caribe [ORCALC]) 8: 13–22.

1998. "Nacionalismo, identidad y Latinoamérica," *Cuadernos de música iberoamericana* (Madrid, Instituto Complutense de Ciencias Musicales) 6: 133–49.

2000. "La certidumbre de la utopía: Estrategias interpretativas para una historia musical americana," *Música* (La Habana, Boletín de Casa de las Américas, Nueva Época) 4: 4–24.

2002. "'Si quieres saber de mí, te lo dirán unas piedras': Alberto Ginastera, autor de *Bomarzo*" in *Ópera en España e Hispanoamérica*, 2 vols., ed. by Emilio Casares Rodicio and Álvaro Torrente. Madrid: ICCMU (Instituto Complutense de Ciencias Musicales), vol. 2, 393–411.

2005. "Western thought from a transcultural perspective: Decolonizing Latin America" in *Enciclopedia della musica Einaudi*, 5 vols., ed. by Jean-Jacques Nattiez. Torino: Giulio Einaudi Editore, vol. 5 (in Italian translation, projected 2005).

León, Argeliers 1982. "Notas para un panorama de la música popular" in *Ensayos de música latinoamericana: Selección del Boletín de música de la Casa de las Américas*. La Habana: Casa de las Américas, 235–45. English translation by Peter Manuel, "Notes toward a panorama of popular and folk musics" in *Essays on Cuban music: North American and Cuban perspectives*, ed. by Peter Manuel (Lanham, Maryland: University Press of America, 1991), 3–23.

León-Portilla, Miguel 1988. *Time and reality in the thought of the Maya*, 2nd enlarged edition. Norman: University of Oklahoma Press.

Lodge, David 2004. "Goodbye to all that," review of *After theory* by Terry Eagleton (New York: Basic Books, 2003), *The New York Review of Books* 51/9 (May 27): 39–43.

Madrid, Lelia 1989. *La fundación mitológica de América Latina*. Madrid: Editorial Fundamentos.

Marras, Sergio 1992. *América Latina: Marca registrada*. Buenos Aires: Grupo Editorial Zeta.

Millones, Luis 1985. "The 'Other' history: Provincial reflections on the discovery of America" in "Preliminary report on the Quincentenary planning conferences," unpublished document gathering presentations delivered on November 21-22, 1985, prepared by Magali M. Carrera. Washington, D.C.: The Smithsonian Institution—Directorate of International Activities, 1986.

Mintz, Sidney W., and Sally Price, editors 1985. *Caribbean contours.* Baltimore and London: The Johns Hopkins University Press.

Montiel, Edgar 1992. "America — Europe: In the mirror of Otherness," *Diogenes* (Paris, journal of the International Council of Philosophy and Humanistic Studies sponsored by UNESCO) 159: 25–35.

    2000. *El humanismo americano: Filosofía de una comunidad de naciones.* Perú: Fondo de Cultura Económica; Paris: UNESCO.

Mudimbe, V.Y. 1988. *The invention of Africa: Gnosis, philosophy, and the order of knowledge.* Bloomington: Indiana University Press.

Mujica Láinez, Manuel 1962 in 1964. *Bomarzo,* 2nd edition. Buenos Aires: Editorial Sudamericana. English translation by Gregory Rabassa (New York: Simon and Schuster, 1969).

O'Gorman, Edmundo 1961. *The invention of America: An inquiry into the historical nature of the New World and the meaning of its history.* Bloomington: Indiana University Press.

Pané, Ramón 1498 in 1991. *Relación acerca de las antigüedades de los indios: El primer tratado escrito en América,* 9th edition, with a preliminary study, notes, and appendix by José Juan Arrom. México: Siglo Veintiuno Editores (first edition, 1974).

Parks, Tim 2001. "Borges and his ghosts," *The New York Review of Books* 48/7 (April 26): 41–45.

Sadie, Stanley, editor 1980. *The new Grove dictionary of music and musicians.* London: Macmillan, 20 vols.

Saer, Juan José 1987. "Soy argentino, no latinoamericano," interview by Leonardo Moledo in *Clarín* (Buenos Aires daily, Supplement "Cultura y Nación," January 15), 2.

Slonimsky, Nicolas 1945 in 1972. *Music of Latin America.* New York: Da Capo Press.

Todorov, Tzvetan 1984. *The conquest of America: The question of The Other,* trans. by Richard Howard. New York: Harper & Row. English translation of *La Conquête de l'Amérique* (Paris: Éditions du Seuil, 1982).

Tomlinson, Gary 1995. "Ideologies of Aztec song," *Journal of the American Musicological Society* 48/3: 343–79.

Treitler, Leo 1989a. "History, criticism, and Beethoven's ninth symphony" in *Music and the historical imagination.* Cambridge, Massachusetts: Harvard University Press, 19–45.

    1989b. "The present as history" in *Music and the historical imagination.* Cambridge, Massachusetts: Harvard University Press, 95–156.

Vargas Llosa, Mario 1990. "Questions of Conquest: What Columbus wrought and what he did not," *Harpers* 281/1687 (December): 45–53.

    2001. *The feast of the goat.* New York: Farrar, Straus & Giroux. English translation by Edith Grossman of *La fiesta del chivo* (Madrid: Alfaguara, 2000).

Wiora, Walter 1961 in 1965. *The four ages of music,* trans. by M. D. Herter. New York: W. W. Norton. English translation of *Die vier Weltalter der Musik* (Stuttgart: W. Kohlhammer, 1961).

Wolf, Eric R. 1982. *Europe and the people without history.* Berkeley and Los Angeles: University of California Press.

ACKNOWLEDGMENTS

This project owes its existence to the imagination of Barry S. Brook (1918–97), which knew no limits. A distinguished 18th-century scholar, he was a futurist who rekindled the spirit of French encyclopedism in vast international projects whose boundaries were set only by the size of the planet. Driven by an insatiable curiosity that defied confinement to "areas of specialization" (in one membership directory he appeared under "interests unlimited"), he wrote as much about his beloved classic period as he did about computer applications to musicology. If the idea was to create a graduate program in music at The City University of New York's Graduate Center (1967), he sought the best scholars and established a community of teachers and students ranked fourth in the country at last count; if he saw the need for bibliographic control of literature about music, he envisioned a tool that could serve the needs of scholars worldwide (RILM Abstracts of Music Literature, 1967–); if recovering 18th-century French symphonies in a 3-volume dissertation (1962) that earned him the Dent Medal of the Royal Musical Association (1965) was only a start, he set out to capture *The Symphony 1720–1840* in a 60-volume set (1979–1986) that made available in modern editions a repertoire we now can hear on the radio; and if music iconography was still a largely unexplored field, he proceeded to centralize it in the Répertoire International d'Iconographie Musical (RIdIM), a project he founded in 1971. This he did while working on the critical edition of Pergolesi's complete works, contributing to Haydn's critical edition, pursuing a facsimile edition of 17th- and 18th-century French operas, enriching the field of thematic catalogues, venturing into Stravinsky's *Pulcinella*, and much more.

After these projects were well under way, the challenge had to be upgraded. The idea of creating a world history of musics, which the Polish musicologist Zofia Lissa had advanced in the 1970s, found fertile soil in Barry Brook's imagination, and he proposed it to the International Music Council (IMC) during his term as president of this organization (1982–83). A Non-Governmental Organization formally established in 1949 at UNESCO's request, whose founders include Charles Seeger and Luiz Heitor Corrêa de Azevedo, the International Music Council is committed to furthering cultural understanding among peoples worldwide by spearheading cooperation between its member organizations, supporting the work of its regional and national committees, and promoting scholarship and performance within a unified conception of the field of music. I would like to acknowledge the extraordinary and uninterrupted support received from the International Music Council over the years, and the very generous funding received from UNESCO through the IMC during the planning stages of this project. Special thanks are due to former Directors General of UNESCO Amadou-Mahtar M'Bow and Federico Mayor; to four IMC presidents, Lupwishi Mbuyamba, Jordi Roch, Frans de Ruiter, and Kifah Fakhouri; to former Secretaries General Nils Wallin and Guy Huot, and current Secretary General Damien Pwono; and to Silja Fischer, for the countless ways in which she sustained cooperation between this project and the IMC. Guy Huot, who served as IMC Secretary General between 1987 and 2002, shared with me much of the history of our partnership, which he not infrequently turned into fodder for banter in several languages, preferably Latin.

A generous grant from the Rockefeller Foundation singlehandedly made it possible for us to continue developing the volumes on Latin America and the Caribbean in the early 1990s. I also wish to acknowledge the symbolic but no less significant contribution of the Inter-American Music Council (CIDEM) which, through its indefatigable Secretary General Efraín Paesky, helped us with a small grant.

The authors and/or the editor of this work, however, are responsible for the choice and the representation of facts contained in these volumes, and for the opinions expressed therein, which are not necessarily those of institutions to which they are affiliated, funders, and other partners, and do not commit these organizations. The designations employed and the presentation of the material throughout this publication do not imply the expression of any opinion whatsoever on the part of funders and partners concerning the legal status of any country, territory, city, or area of its authorities, or the delimitation of their frontiers or boundaries.

I am deeply indebted to the distinguished scholars who serve on our Board of Directors, which was chaired by Barry S. Brook until 1996, for the wisdom, experience, and wide-ranging perspectives they brought to our discussions, and for their unfailing support at decisive junctures in the history of this project. Individually and collectively, Israel Adler, Simha Arom, Hans Åstrand, Dorothea Baumann, Kifah Fakhouri, Ludwig Finscher, J. H. Kwabena Nketia, Jordi Roch, Frans de Ruiter, and Trân Van Khê, provided invaluable and indispensable advice over the course of many years (see also p. 399 in this volume).

The International Association of Music Libraries, Archives, and Documentation Centers (IAML), represented on our Board of Directors by former IAML president Barry S. Brook until 1996, provided a forum for discussion of our aims and played a significant role in the early development of our project. I would like to thank Maria Calderisi and Catherine Massip in particular, both former IAML presidents, for the countless ways in which they provided support and encouragement.

When the first conversations about shaping a world history of music took place at a meeting co-sponsored by the International Music Council and the Brazilian National Committee in São Paulo (1980), J. H. Kwabena Nketia proposed that I take charge of the coverage of Latin America and the Caribbean. At my request, and following my proposal that the distinguished Chilean musicologist Samuel Claro Valdés (1934–94) share with me the coordinatorship of this coverage, he was invited to join "our cultural adventure" as coordinator for Latin America. Likewise, Olive Lewin, assisted by Maurice Gordon, accepted the responsibility of coordinating the coverage of the Caribbean. We divided our tasks, and Samuel Claro Valdés worked tirelessly on commissioning articles until his failing health made it impossible for him to continue. Revered by Latin Americans, Samuel Claro Valdés left us a legacy of scholarly distinction and unwavering integrity. I shall always treasure the memory of working with a man whose generosity of spirit was legend.

Many institutions lent us their support during the planning stages of this project. I would like to acknowledge first and foremost the generous contribution of The City University of New York's Graduate Center and its Graduate Program in Music for sustaining our efforts between 1987 and 1996. The Swedish Royal Academy of Music, through its Secrétaire Perpétuel Hans Åstrand, a renowned scholar who made countless contributions to this project, organized a meeting in 1984; CENIDIM, the Centro Nacional de Investigación, Documentación e Información Musical of Mexico's Instituto Nacional de Bellas Artes, hosted a planning meeting in Mexico City in 1985; the Brazilian Musicological Society, through the kind efforts of musicologist Antonio Alexandre Bispo, invited us to São Paulo in 1987; the Smithsonian Institution welcomed us in 1988; and CIDMUC, the Centro de Investigación y Desarrollo de la Música Cubana directed by Olavo Alén Rodríguez, arranged an extraordinary display of talent when we traveled to Havana to discuss contributions by Cuban authors in 1992.

While institutional support was vital, we could not have materialized our goals without the talent and knowledge of our authors, who made this work possible. Confining myself only to Volume 1, I would like to thank Carol E. Robertson for contributing a record number of stimulating essays and for our nurturing friendship of many years. I also am grateful for the generosity with which Jonathan D. Hill, Elizabeth Travassos, Rafael José de Menezes Bastos, María Ester Grebe, Irma Ruiz, E. Fernando Nava López, and Ronny Velásquez responded to my relentless questioning during the editorial process.

Words cannot convey my gratitude for the professionalism and personal commitment shown by my production family. David Seham, the head of KP Company whose experience in the art of bookmaking proved invaluable, designed and oversaw the typesetting by the brilliant Gregory Orpilla, and both spared no efforts to decipher my intentions; Linda Strube proofread every page (several times), caught typographical errors in indigenous languages beyond the scope of her mastery of style, and taught me to love the English language; Kenneth Yarmey, a superb music calligrapher, copied all the musical examples included in this volume and stood by me steadfastly during difficult years; sound engineer Seth B. Winner made magic with field tapes to produce the CD masters; Philip Baczewski and Ben Bigby solved technical puzzles and responded instantly to my Angst of malfunctioning equipment; Gregory Straughn and Rebecca Ringer, two former students, facilitated many inquiries and warmed my heart with their intelligent and reliable research assistance; and Fred Leise, the first truly professional indexer I encountered after a long and expensive search, taught me the principles of his art by remote control from Chicago and made it possible for me to produce an index that also benefitted from conversations with anthropologist Erica Hill. Last but not least, I could not have enriched or revised the bibliographies appended to each contribution without the help of the entire staff of the University of North Texas Music Library. Music Librarian Morris Martin not only heads one of the best music libraries in the country, but also sets the tone for the high quality of service provided by his dedicated staff. Jean Harden, Susanna Cleveland, and Mark McKnight (who also contributed a survey of Latin American and Caribbean music collections in the United States for Volume 3), answered endless inquiries, and multilingual Arturo Ortega solved bibliographic puzzles in three languages. Donna Arnold, Music Reference Librarian, however, bore the brunt of my reluctance to search databases and rely instead on her expertise. Her patience and humor made each query a blast.

Most of the professional translations we commissioned at exorbitant cost to this project had to be rewritten. This is why I remain forever indebted to those whose flair for linguistic transfer of thought made my work on final versions less daunting. I want to thank Robert W. Showman for his extraordinary translations, John P. Murphy for shouldering difficult tasks with characteristic integrity, Victoria Cox and Paula Durbin for their mastery of metaphors, and Martha Ellen Davis for helping me arrive at a final

version of Argeliers León's polysemic and highly connotative prose.

Robert Stevenson, my mentor at UCLA whose contribution to our knowledge of music in Latin America is unmeasurable, generously accepted to grace our volumes with an article on compositions of the colonial period for which he refused to accept an honorarium, and helped me shape the coverage of national anthems with his uncanny control of the literature. Most of all, I am indebted to him for shaping my own early career, for teaching me so much through the example of his own writings, and for our long friendship.

Many colleagues and friends helped in tangible and intangible ways. Steven Friedson, Bernardo Illari, and John P. Murphy, all of them presently teaching at the University of North Texas, generously came to my rescue in countless ways. Dorothea Baumann applied her brilliant mind to unravel puzzles, especially on acoustics, and Anthony Seeger enriched our sound component by allowing us to reproduce a fragment from one of his extraordinary recordings of Suyá songs. I shared epiphanies and frustrations with Victoria Eli Rodríguez and Benjamín Yépez Chamorro, who, as a natural *repentista*, often was inclined to reply in verse. Anne Gurvin displayed her diplomatic skills on numerous occasions to ensure the survival of this project, and Electra Yourke never failed to sustain me with her contagious and unflappable belief in practical solutions. My lawyers Norman Solovay and Alan Bomser kept perilous situations at bay, and Chalón Rodríguez Salinas, a physician by profession and an expert in all things pre-Columbian by choice, kept me healthy and put at my disposal any photos I might want from his now famous collection.

In many ways, each new work is an homage to those who came before us. This applies not only to the prolific Robert Stevenson, still young at 88, but also to many pioneers, among them Carlos Vega, Isabel Aretz, Francisco Curt Lange, Domingo Santa Cruz, Juan Orrego-Salas, Lauro Ayestarán, Luiz Heitor Corrêa de Azevedo, Carlos Alberto G. Coba Andrade, José Ignacio Perdomo Escobar, and, for me, the everlasting memory of my close friendship with Charles Seeger. Their legacies live on in our volumes in explicit and implicit ways.

If Barry Brook set the wheels in motion, I owe the gift of completion to my mother, Elenita Kuss-Hieble, and to my son, Peter Sanders, the steady guardians of my dreams who made it possible for me to devote six undisturbed years to reshaping the entire original conception, editing, rewriting, retranslating, indexing, and overseeing the entire production of a tetralogy that grew from one act to four (or five, considering that Volume 3 requires two parts lest we render it unwieldy or carry it in a wheelbarrow). To them, and to all those who directly or indirectly became a part of this experience, whether I have included their names here or not, I offer my thanks.

A chance encounter with Theresa J. May, Editor-in-Chief and Assistant Director of University of Texas Press, brought this project home. I am deeply grateful to her for renewing my faith in the existence of that knowledgeable and committed editor/publisher who steers the ship home with a human and firm hand. I also would like to thank Joanna Hitchcock, Director of University of Texas Press, for her support of this project, and Allison Faust, Lynne Chapman, David Cavazos, Ellen McKie, David Hamrick, Nancy Bryan, Amy Tharp Nylund, Heather Crist, Lauren Zachry-Reynolds, and Sharon Casteel, for sustaining so efficiently the long tradition of professionalism of this prestigious press.

M.K.

VOLUME 1

Performing Beliefs:
Indigenous Peoples of South America, Central America, and Mexico

Native Peoples: Introductory Panorama

Carol E. Robertson

Wait! On this blessed day,
thou Hurricane, thou Heart of the Sky-Earth,
thou giver of ripeness and freshness,
and thou giver of daughters and sons,
spread thy stain, spill thy drops
of green and yellow;
give life and beginning
to those I bear and beget,
that they might multiply and grow,
nurturing and providing for thee,
calling to thee along the roads and paths,
on rivers, in canyons,
beneath the trees and bushes;
give them their daughters and sons.

May there be no blame, obstacle, want or misery;
let no deceiver come behind or before them,
may they neither be snared nor wounded,
nor seduced, nor burned,
nor diverted below the road nor above it;
may they neither fall over backward nor stumble;
keep them on the Green Road, the Green Path.

May there be no blame or barrier for them
through any secrets or sorcery of thine;
may thy nurturers and providers be good
before thy mouth and thy face,
thou, Heart of Sky; thou, Heart of Earth;
thou, Bundle of Flames;
and thou, Tohil, Auilix, Hacauitz,
under the sky, on the earth,
the four sides, the four corners;
may there be only light, only continuity within,
before thy mouth and thy face, thou god.
(*Popol Vuh*, trans. by Dennis Tedlock
1985: 221–22)

THE MAYA SAGES who created the *Popol Vuh*, the sacred book of the dawn of life, tell us that the first great lords fasted, cried their hearts out, and intoned this prayer so that their human progeny might prosper. And prosper they did. The first Americans began to cross the Bering Strait around 30,000 B.C.E. and within 20,000 years this hemisphere was populated from Alaska to Tierra del Fuego. By the third century of the Common Era, the peoples of what is now southern Mexico, Guatemala, and Honduras had carved ornate stone ceremonial centers out of dense jungles and had committed their songs and histories to an enigmatic system of writing.

Their neighbors to the north and south also had emerged as builders of cities and states. Between 600 B.C.E. and 800 C.E. Cuicuilco and Teotihuacan (central Mexico), Monte Albán (Oaxaca), Kaminaljuyú and Tikal (Guatemala), Tiwanaku (Bolivia), and Nazca (Peru), and many other nascent theocratic states explored approaches to governance, technology, and artistic excellence.

By the fifth century C.E., the city of Teotihuacan had become a jewel of urban planning and, according to some archaeologists, accommodated over two hundred thousand inhabitants. From this axis, the trade of agricultural and manufactured goods extended north into what is now New Mexico and south into what is now Guatemala. Although Teotihuacan was abandoned by the eighth century, its splendor influenced Tenochtitlan and Tlatelolco, the cities that dazzled the Spanish *conquistadores*.

The Incas of the central Andes also amassed wealth and influence through both trade and conquest. By the fifteenth century their voice could be heard as far north as Panama and as far south as northern Patagonia. Textiles, gold, silver, salt, musical instruments, and many other manufactured items scattered throughout Andean archaeological sites attest to the economic and military impact of their expansion. They engineered vast irrigation projects that facilitated specialized agriculture 12,000 feet above sea level. Potatoes, oca, quinoa, ullucus, guanaco meat, and fish provided a high protein, high fiber diet for a population of at least five million people in Peru, Bolivia, and Ecuador.

However, not all indigenous peoples before the coming of the Europeans built vast cities and farms. During 30,000 years on this continent native peoples developed many forms of subsistence and social organization, adapting always to the exigencies of habitat and ecology. The sparse settlement of some areas juxtaposed to the human ferment of cities and empires makes the population of the Americas at the time of Columbus' arrival extremely hard to estimate, for communities could range from less than 100 to over two hundred thousand people.

In 1924, Rivet and Sapper assessed the indigenous population of the entire hemisphere at 50,000, while in 1934 Means estimated that there were up to 32,000 people in the Andes alone (Dobyns 1966: 396). Stannard, influenced by the findings of Dobyns (1966), summarizes drastic changes in demographic estimates occasioned by accelerated archaeological discoveries and new methods of calculation:

Less than twenty-five years ago conventional scholarly opinion held—as it had for generations—that the pre-Columbian population of the Americas was somewhere between 8 and 14 million persons, with no more than a million in North America. Today's historians and anthropologists commonly accept figures up to ten times as high—as many as ten million in North America, twenty-five million in central Mexico alone, and 90 to 112 million for the entire hemisphere. If correct, such estimates mean that the population of the Americas in the 15th century was equal to that of Europe, including Russia, at the time (Stannard 1989: xv).

The calculation of both pre-Columbian and contemporary indigenous populations has profound political implications. Because the death knell of European contact pierced the very heart of America, estimates have tended towards conservatism: the horror of genocide is too great to fathom. The long-term physical, spiritual, and psychological devastation of the *conquista* is augured in *The Fall of Tenochtitlan*,

a lament by an anonymous 16th-century Mexica composer/poet:

Our cries of grief rise up
and our tears rain down,
for Tlatelolco is lost.
The Aztecs are fleeing across the lake;
they are running away like women.

How can we save our homes, my people?
The Aztecs are deserting the city:
the city is all flames, and all
is darkness and destruction.

Motelchiuhtzin the Huiznacahuatl,
Tlacotzin the Tlaicotlacatl,
Oquitzin the Tlacatecuhtli
are greeted with tears.

Weep, my people:
know that with these disasters
we have lost the Mexican nation.
The water has turned bitter,
our food is bitter!
These are the acts of the Giver of Life . . .
(from *Cantares mexicanos*, in León-Portilla 1962: 146).

The voyages of Columbus, the sacking of Mexico and Peru, and the traffic in human bodies and souls unleashed by the *conquista* ignited a war that persists to this day in Guatemala, El Salvador, Peru, Brazil, and in pockets of resistance throughout the Americas. The five-hundred year crusade to stamp out all opposition to the Cross and its political machinery has bequeathed a ragged indigenous cultural profile: while the native population of Argentina constitutes less than 0.6% of the nation, the population of Peru and Bolivia is 60% Kechua and Aymara. The people of Guatemala are overwhelmingly Maya-Quiché, while the peoples of the Antilles and Uruguay hold but a trace of Indian blood (Steward and Faron 1959: 457).

An accurate count of indigenous peoples today is hindered by dynamics that are both internal and external to the communities under consideration. In the mid-twentieth century, estimates of native populations in South and Central America and Mexico ranged from 14 to 20 million members of some 300 indigenous groups, but demographers rarely specified the criteria by which they reached these numbers (Stannard 1992).

How might one count "Indianness"? In the United States, standards for inclusion in a tribal configuration vary greatly from group to group. Indeed, the rules for inclusion may change significantly from generation to generation. Twenty years ago, tribal affiliation among Eastern Cherokee required members to prove that they were at least one thirty-second Cherokee. Gradually, this fraction changed to one sixteenth and currently efforts are being made to change the ratio to one eighth (Herndon, personal communication). Manipulating these fractions reflects, in part, a system in which government services are allotted according to a provable percentage of Indian blood. These formulations are particularly ironic in the face of the failure of the federal government to address central issues of Indian sovereignty and economic viability.

The problem in Latin America is equally complex, and has been fueled by linguists, anthropologists, and ethnomusicologists who have taken it upon themselves to decide when a community is "Indian enough" or when it has become too "acculturated" for statistical inclusion. Neither model takes into account the multiple models of identity that might coexist within a community. Moreover, in some situations, lineage, moiety, village, or village subsection may do more to define an individual's self-perception than language or tribal designation.

The designation of Indian "cultures" is directly tied to language classification. Europeans have attempted to classify "Indios" according to the languages they speak since the early stages of the *conquista*. The first grammars of indigenous American languages followed the style of the Arabic grammars used by the Catholic clergy of 15th-century Spain in their efforts to convert the Moors. A more systematic approach was heralded in 1708 by Adrianus Reeland, who compared the features of languages he referred to as Brazilian, Peruvian, Chilian, Pocoman, Carib, Mexican, Virginian, Algonkin, and Huron. Long before the Bering Strait was first charted (1730) and after its discovery by Russians in 1648, Reeland suggested that, if a common origin was to be found among the tongues of the Americas, it would have to be traced through the languages of Asia (Haven 1856: 56, cited in Key 1991: 4).

To this day, the comparative study of indigenous languages rests on the compilation and comparison of word lists, a method pioneered by Catherine the Great, who set in motion an effort to compare the languages of the known world, grouping them according to similarities discerned through word lists. She personally prepared word lists that were sent around the globe through diplomatic channels. Her requests for special attention to newly-discovered Indian languages even reached George Washington and his fledgling nation. Catherine commissioned Peter Pallas to edit her work, which he published under his name in 1786–1787 (Key 1980). Mary Ritchie Key, who has addressed linguistic change in South American Indian languages, characterizes the grouping of language families that arise from the word list method as being the result of rather arbitrary decisions made by scholars who are either "lumpers" or "splitters" (1991: 9). Thus, conclusions about linguistic kinship are heavily influenced by the personality and experiential reality of the observer. Word lists have varied over time from twenty-six items (Balbi 1826 in Key 1991: 5) to the two hundred items listed by Morris Swadesh (1955, 1959). Ultimately, the problem of classification of languages into families rests on decisions made on the basis of similarities perceived by individual linguists juxtaposed with locational contiguity and the migration of groups in and out of geographic regions. "Families" consist of languages that hold enough similarity to afford a certain degree of mutual intelligibility. Of course, language change forces us to juxtapose similarities in time and space with the methods and knowledge of the linguist. Consequently, the number of language families identified among indigenous peoples of South America has varied tremendously in the last century: the 73 language groups proposed by Daniel Brinton in 1892 were increased by Cestmír Loukotka to 94 in 1935 and 117 in 1968. In his "Ethno-Linguistic Index," Loukotka lists more than 3,000 individual South American dialects (1968: 405–38).

The determination of language families in Mesoamerica has been influenced by characteristics assumed to have been common among cultural groups in pre-Conquest times. Summarizing work begun in Mexico and Guatemala four centuries ago, Jorge Suárez offers an inventory of calculations ranging from 14 to 88 language families, and estimates that 100 to 190 Indian languages are spoken to this day in Mesoamerica, including Garífuna (Black Carib), a language imported from South America in the late eighteenth century (Suárez 1983: 11).

The pitfalls of language classification and of "lumping" or "splitting" traits derived from word lists illustrates some of the difficulties involved in any discussion of indigenous musics of the Americas. Ethnomusicological field research and the laboratory classification of musical instruments and performance styles has produced inventories of peoples, rituals, tuning systems, and traits that render similarities and differences. But the complexities of linguistic and/or musical competence lead us to ponder whether language, notions of "race," or ritual participation can dictate inclusion. For example, among the Argentine Mapuche, a grandmother may speak "deep" (rich in metaphoric layerings) Mapuche; yet her daughter may speak only Spanish and her grandaughter, having learned Mapuche in a Salesian mission school, may speak fluent, but "surface" Mapuche. Digging deeper, we might find that the Mapuche-speaking grandmother may really consider herself Ranquel, but has taken on the label Mapuche to satisfy the "lumping" tendencies of the federal government. To further confuse matters, the Spanish-speaking daughter may have married a *winká* (non-Mapuche) who has learned the tribal language and even participates actively in annual rites of increase (see Carol Robertson, "Fertility Ritual," in this volume). Here our notions of "Indianness" are reduced to dust, and we are left with an articulation of inclusion based on ritual/social participation and the complexity of individual and community identities adapted to specific circumstances.

The linear construction of scholarship usually negates the processes through which we and others arrive at a sense of "belonging" within a particular group. Instead, we have invented terms that cause us to distance ourselves from our subject matter as it was experienced during our research. These terms are the foundations of a discourse in which "we" talk about "them"; we translate who "they" are to others who are more or less like us. But if "they," the Indios, seem too much like us—if they dress, speak, worship, or sing in ways that seem familiar to us—they have become "acculturated." These labels stigmatize those societies that no longer fit our ideas of what and who Indians should be. Often, regardless of whether communities identify themselves as indigenous, we marginalize them through our imposed classification systems. Our tendencies toward reductionism ignore subtle differences in worldview within indigenous communities. This same reductionism ignores that the terms *indio*, or *paisano*, or *caboclo* (in Brazil) signal a reality of the Other constructed by non-Indians—a reality that lumps peoples who have co-existed with European worldviews for five centuries with peoples who have "discovered" Europeans within our lifetime.

Perhaps an even greater void in our discussion concerns the myriad ways in which native peoples respond to incursions by Europeans, mestizos, and other outside groups. For example, the Makiritare of the Upper Orinoco (Venezuela) have incorporated two contrasting images of the Spanish invader in the Watunna, their creation narrative: the White Man, Iaranavi, is associated with the white egret, an emissary of beauty, wisdom, generosity, and light. It is Iaranavi who is remembered as the powerful master of iron, a precious metal that, when embodied in the thunderous arcabuz, invokes the power of the heavens. But Iaranavi's shadow, Fañuru (from "español"), is a dark, treacherous figure—a rapist, cannibal, and despoiler of the land who dragged his own god into the center of the village and crucified him (Civrieux 1980: 6–7). Although the Makiritare have had little contact with the *español* since the late eighteenth century, the indelible mark on their psyche left by the European presence has been absorbed into the very heart of their cosmology.

Highland Peruvian and Mexican dance-dramas also represent the conqueror in more than one way. In the dramatizations known as *Moros y cristianos* (see Béhague's "Music and Dance in Ritual and Ceremony" in these volumes), the Spaniard is aligned with the triumph of good over evil, of Christianity over what the Catholic Church labeled as "paganism." But in contemporary re-enactments of the death of the Inca Atahualpa, the Spaniard or, more specifically, Pizarro, becomes the enigmatic betrayer of the Kechua of old. In the town of Carhuamayo, a community that many would consider highly "acculturated," Pizarro enters the dance arena in his best finery, making gestures that honor the stately Coya women surrounding him. In an unexpected moment, he stealthily draws a dagger from his cloak and slits the throat of the Coya. From her throat chicha (corn liquor) flows to the ground, for the *wira* or life force of the People is being sucked dry. The Death of Atahualpa (Millones 1992), whether performed in an *Indio* or mestizo community, is a potent act of resistance to conquest. So, in defining the parameters of "native" cultures we must emphasize that peoples constantly "reinvent" themselves. Every ritual, every performance event, every story told about the past is part of that process of continuous creation and re-creation of aboriginal identity.

Ethnographies and cultural classifications often seem to imply that acculturation or *mestizaje* involves some pivotal moment when the Indian becomes less and less Indian, until she or he falls off the scale of Indianness. But is there really some invisible line that an individual or community crosses over to cease being Indian and to become mestizo? Is there a particular moment when a Tarahumara fiddle player tunes his instrument in such a way that he trades in his Tarahumara aesthetic for a foreign one? Musical, relational, linguistic, and ritual changes have been unfolding in the indigenous cultures of the Americas since the first crossing of the Bering Strait. In the Nahuatl world, sages continue to count years and cycles, predicting the emergence of a Fifth World in the year 2012. As they mark the passage of time, they continue to reinvent themselves and their world. They have done this many times before. But now, because they often draw on a European aesthetic or play on instruments introduced by Spanish conquerors, they are judged less Indian. Perhaps we give the slaughter of conquest too little importance and the culture of the conqueror too much importance, thus creating a double standard of acculturation. Would an Aztec (Mexica) composer seeking to recreate Toltec aesthetics cease being Aztec and "become" Toltec by virtue of his involvement in a culture that was ultimately foreign to him?

Native cultures have been borrowing from each other for thousands of years: the Mexica took many of their artistic and spiritual cues from the Toltecs; the Atacameños of northern Chile emulated the instrumental traditions of the northern Kechua; peoples along the Xingú River borrow repertoires and rituals from one another at this very moment. In similar ways, native cultures took ideas, names, even religious pantheons from the Spaniards, Portuguese, French, and British, as they do today from North American protestant missionaries.

The analytic categories spawned by ethnographic research should remain no more than convenient, temporary tools for grasping complex bodies of information. Furthermore, we must always remember that cultures move back and forth in many directions as they struggle to reinvent their identities in times of great change. Anthony Seeger has documented a striking example of the ebb and flow among the Kiriri of Bahia, Brazil, who have been in contact with Brazilian institutions and ideas for centuries. They even were recognized throughout Brazil for being specialists in certain genres of Brazilian music. And yet, in the early 1990s the Kiriri underwent a conceptual, cultural, and musical

transformation that allowed them to "reinvent" their identity. Resisting the appropriation of their land by entrepreneurs, they cleared a collective garden atop one of the hills they had reclaimed and began performing a ritual known as the *toré*, learned a decade earlier from another Indian community. This music started as a cult activity on the reservation and mushroomed into a central social ritual of resistance: "The collective performance of this clearly indigenous ceremony on top of the hill in full view of their non-indigenous neighbors was an important symbolic affirmation of Kiriri 'Indianness' and a musical argument for their rights to the land they were occupying" (Seeger 1992: 454).

The methodological issues raised above affect the ways we read and write about native cultures of the Americas. The essays that follow illustrate many different approaches to documentation, interpretation, and representation. On the whole, they attempt to explicate the interrelationships between music and other ways of knowing the universe, for lists of traits and classifications of musical styles are sterile notions unless they appear woven into the fabric of social discourse and ritual action. The ways in which people "perform" their particular universe remain just beyond our reach unless we can embrace these richly textured myths, rituals, and performance practices as embodiments of the paradox, conflict, beauty, pain, and loss that mark all human experience. Whether from the deserts, mountains, or rainforests, all of these cultures have found intricate ways of explaining the relationships between sound, social organization, time, and the sacred. Strategies for survival vary greatly from one indigenous group to another, yet in every society the relationship of individuals and groups must be negotiated in time and space. Musical performance is always a key ingredient in our formulations of the universe, for it creates an arena in which the known and the unknown, the revered and the feared, the past and the present can co-mingle, where the deepest recesses of the subconscious can be jarred or reaffirmed, and where the core images of being human can be evoked.

REFERENCES

Brinton, Daniel G. 1892. "Studies in South American native languages," reprinted from *Proceedings of the American Philosophical Society* 30/137: 45–105. Philadelphia: Printed for the Society by Mac Calla & Co.

Civrieux, Marc de 1980. *Watunna: An Orinoco creation cycle*, trans. by David M. Guss. San Francisco: North Point Press.

Dobyns, Henry F. 1966. "Estimating Aboriginal American population: An appraisal of techniques with a new hemispheric estimate," *Current anthropology* 7/4: 395–416.

Haven, Samuel F. 1856. *Archaeology of the United States; or, sketches, historical and bibliographical, of the progress of information and opinion respecting vestiges of antiquity in the United States.* Washington, D.C.: Smithsonian Institution (Smithsonian contributions to knowledge 8). Reprinted with an introduction by Gordon R. Willey (New York: AMS Press for the Peabody Museum of Archaeology and Ethnology, Harvard University, 1973).

Herndon, Marcia 1994. Personal communication, June 13.

Key, Mary Ritchie 1980. *Catherine the Great's linguistic contribution.* Carbondale, Illinois: Linguistic Research.

Key, Mary Ritchie, ed. 1991. *Language change in South American Indian languages.* Philadelphia: University of Pennsylvania Press.

León-Portilla, Miguel 1962. *The broken spears: The Aztec account of the Conquest of Mexico*, with translations from Nahuatl into Spanish by Ángel María Garibay K., English trans. by Lysander Kemp. Boston: Beacon Press.

Loukotka, Cestmír 1968. *Classification of South American Indian languages.* Los Angeles: Latin American Center, University of California, Los Angeles (Reference Series, ed. by Johannes Wilbert, vol. 7).

Millones, Luis 1992. "The death of Atahualpa" in *Musical repercussions of 1492: Encounters in text and performance*, ed. by Carol E. Robertson. Washington, D.C.: Smithsonian Institution Press, 237–56.

Pallas, Peter Simon 1786–87. *Linguarum totius orbis vocabularia comparativa.* St. Petersburg: I. C. Schnoor, reprinted with a preface by Harald Haarman. Hamburg: Buske, 1977.

Popol Vuh, The Mayan Book of the Dawn of Life 1985, trans. by Dennis Tedlock. New York: Touchstone—Simon and Schuster.

Pottier, Bernard ed. 1983. *América Latina en sus lenguas indígenas.* Caracas: UNESCO—Monte Ávila Editores (UNESCO series "América Latina en su cultura").

Reeland, Adrianus 1708. "De linguis americanis," *Hadriani Relandi dissertationum miscellanearum*, 3 vols. Trajecti ad Rhenum: G. Broedelet, 1706–1708, vol. 3.

Seeger, Anthony 1992. "Performance and identity: Problems and perspectives" in *Musical repercussions of 1492: Encounters in text and performance*, ed. by Carol E. Robertson. Washington, D.C.: Smithsonian Institution Press, 451–61.

Stannard, David E. 1989. *Before the horror. The population of Hawai'i on the eve of Western contact.* Honolulu: Social Science Research Institute, University of Hawai'i.

1992. *American holocaust: Columbus and the conquest of the New World.* New York: Oxford University Press.

Steward, Julian H., and Louis C. Faron 1959. *Native peoples of South America.* New York: McGraw-Hill.

Suárez, Jorge A. 1983. *The Mesoamerican Indian languages.* Cambridge and New York: Cambridge University Press.

Swadesh, Morris 1955. "Towards greater accuracy in lexicostatistic dating," *International journal of American linguistics* 21/2: 121–37.

1959. *Mapas de clasificación lingüística de México y las Américas.* México: Universidad Nacional Autónoma de México (Cuadernos del Instituto de Historia, Serie Antropológica 8).

MYTH, COSMOLOGY, AND PERFORMANCE

CAROL E. ROBERTSON

Myth as explanation—Myth as performance—Myth, performance, and the unfolding of time—Songs of life and death: A Mesoamerican story—Songs of the animal powers: The jaguar in South America—Myth, performance, and human organization—Conclusions

MYTH AS EXPLANATION

MYTHS LIE AT the core of all human understanding. They permeate our dreams, our value systems, our social transactions, our formulations of history, and our pursuit of answers through ritual enactment and scientific exploration. Myths allow us to acknowledge pattern and chaos and to place ourselves within histories that attempt to make sense of the paroxysms of life and death. The underbelly of all belief systems—from rational science to ancestor veneration—is riddled with assumptions about the nature of the universe and the pathways that lead to transcendence.

When regarded as symbolic configurations rather than literal statements, myths can have broad applications that surpass time and place. All humans grapple with their own individuation and survival, and with the ways in which they fit (or do not fit) into a social world. Myths often outline stages of maturation and rites of passage through which individuals can grow into whole beings. Because each of us must develop a sense of self within the social settings that we come to protect and perpetuate (as our "culture"), we also extract from myths basic clues to group survival. In this sense, the images of myths have been used for millennia to justify and replicate the status quo. On the other hand, some myths suggest that the vessel of culture must sometimes be shattered and transgressed to ensure regeneration:

some crises demand that the hero break the most basic rules of society to engender new solutions. Thus, notions regarding the maintenance and implosion of paradigms are deeply embedded in myth.

Because myths reflect the deepest recesses of the human psyche they can withstand long distances, undergoing alterations and reinterpretations that accommodate particular social structures and ecological niches. For example, many myths reference the rebirthing of individuals into new social and spiritual dimensions during a single lifetime; but the ritual practice of symbolic rebirthing may take strikingly different forms in a matrifocal, equatorial society versus a patrifocal, sub-arctic society. According to Campbell, the symbolic references of mythical explanation are concerned with relationships rather than causes and are determined by historical as well as geographical variables:

> The first and most important historical distinction to be recognized is that between literate and nonliterate orders, and among the latter, that between primary and regressed mythologies, that is, those of isolated tribes whose myths and customs have been derived in large measure from the Bronze or Iron Age or even later high-culture systems. Geographically, an important distinction is to be seen, furthermore,

between the mythologies of Old Stone Age tribes inhabiting the great animal plains of postglacial Europe, Siberia, and North America, and those of the jungles of the tropical equatorial belt, where plants, not animals, have been the chief source of sustenance, and women, not men, the dominant providers (1983: 9).

These variables are important to our discussion, which covers a vast area ranging from the northern Mexican desert to the rocky icelands of Tierra del Fuego. The performance traditions of this continent include instances in which the sacred beings of myths may be invoked by men and women equally, by women only, or by men only. In some cases the protagonists of myths and of sacred time may materialize into different life forms: jaguars, deer, rock formations, musical instruments, or vines and mushrooms that open a hallucinogenic pathway into the sacred. Moreover, many of the peoples discussed have had extensive and prolonged contact with distant cultures, whereas other groups have remained in relative isolation until the twentieth century.

MYTH AS PERFORMANCE

Mythological structures and teachings are rendered accessible to communities through ritual enactment. Indeed, stories of ancestors and deities often describe sacred performances through which worlds are created and human and ecological features are set in place. Performances within myths (by extraordinary beings) establish the ordering of primordial worlds, the dynamics of life and death, the creation of extraordinary beings and their relations, tests of heroic prowess, processes through which spiritual power is accumulated, predictions about recurring patterns of time, and boundaries of appropriate behavior for the human descendants of deities. Performances of or about myths (by ordinary beings) constitute an enactment of belief wherein humans can impersonate and/or mediate the sacred and rehearse the formulas that generate order in the cosmos and in everyday social life. Through music, dance, vocalization, and dramatization, ritual performances bring about an "embodiment" of the myth in the celebrants. In other words, for the myth to take on its full potency, the word must become flesh.

In many of the ancient myths of the Americas, Creation is put into action through sound, either

spoken or sung. The *Popol Vuh*, a central mythological account of the Quiché of Guatemala, was assembled and written down by a 16th-century princely priest who had come into contact with Christianity. The destruction in 1524 of Utatlán by Alvarado resulted in a mass migration of survivors to Chichicastenango. It was here that the manuscript was translated into Spanish by Father Francisco Ximénez at the beginning of the eighteenth century. The original preamble in Quiché assures us that *re u xe uber izih varal quiche ubi*, "this is the beginning of the ancient traditions here in Quiché":

Here we reveal all that was previously secret, the great revelations of Tzacol [the Creator] and Bitol [the Shaper], Alom [Mother-Goddess] and Qoholom [Father-God], father-god and mother-god, and of Hunahpú Vuch [Goddess of Dawn], Hunahpú Utiú [God of Night], Zaquo-Nima Tziís [Grandmother-Goddess], Nim-Ac [consort of the Grandmother-Goddess], Tepeu [king or sovereign], Gucumatz [green-feathered serpent, i.e., the Quiché counterpart of the Maya Kukulcan and the Aztec Quetzalcoatl], U Qux Ho [Water Spirit], U Quz Paló [Sea Spirit], Ah Raxa Lac [Lord of the Earth] and Ah Raxa Tzel [Lord of the Sky] (Ximénez ms. ca. 1701–1703, fol. 1; Arias-Larreta 1968: 188, 240; translation by C. Robertson).

Among these original protagonists, Gucumatz and Tepeu, called the "Creator and Maker," become the agents of the deep feelings and thoughts of "Heart of Heaven, the divine mind, which is the first and supreme God, Huracán..." (Arias-Larreta 1968: 189). Gucumatz and Tepeu put the thoughts and feelings of the Divine Mind into creation through the utterance of the Divine Word, which engenders immediate power and action. The quality of sacred language was so different from human speech that, in the final stages of creation, a priesthood was established to interpret and mediate sacred sound.

In contrast, the creation myth of the Keres of Laguna Pueblo (southwestern United States) describes the unformed cosmos as the domain of Tse che nako (Thought Woman/Spider Woman) (Allen 1986: 13), who chants life into two sacred bundles that become the sisters Uretsete and Naotsete (She Who Matters and She Who Remembers). These twins "give human form to the spirit which was the people" (Allen 1983: 1) and chant into being all the languages of the earth. Chant contains the seed or active principle that weaves the thoughts of the Creator, Tse che nako, into coherent patterns. This complex creation myth remains in Keres oral tradition to this day:

> In the center of the universe she sang. In the midst of the waters she sang. In the midst of the heavens she sang. In the center she sang. Her singing made all the worlds. The worlds of the spirits. The worlds of the people. The worlds of the creatures. The worlds of the gods. In this way she separated the quarters. Singing, she separated. Upon the face of the heavens she placed her song. Thus she placed her song. Thus she placed her will. Thus she wove her design. Thus sang the Spider. Thus she thought (Allen 1983: 1).

In ritual performances, the ability to put thought into action through sacred utterance provides a link between humans and their life source. Contemporary Mapuche peoples of Andean Argentina (not to be confused with the Chilean Mapuche) acknowledge the sonic nature of the cosmos and the sacred nature of sound through the use of a ritual language essential to supplications (*lukutún*) and through the performance of lineage songs (*tayil*) and sacred chants (*öl*) that link the living to creator beings and to original ancestral families (Robertson 1979; Robertson-DeCarbo 1977). Many Mapuche state that sacred beings are deaf to ordinary speech and can be reached only when women birth sound into sacred chant. When asked about the origin of these songs, Mapuche ritual specialists, known as *witakultruntufe* ("the woman who carries the drum") explain that the language and chants of ritual are remnants of the sounds used to put the cosmos in motion. Thus, as in the Quiché and Keres accounts, myth "must" be embodied through performance, for the very nature of the universe is sonic and the transmutation of thought and spirit into matter is achieved through the act of "sounding."

MYTH, PERFORMANCE, AND THE UNFOLDING OF TIME

Myths evoke dimensions of sacred time and space that both parallel and intersect human experience. Because we have devised a literal, linear tradition of communication and translation in the Euro-American intellectual tradition, we tend to regard myths as stories that are not "true." However, in the indigenous traditions of the Americas nothing is truer than myth, for symbols are not confused with that which they reference. The reference is seen as part of a pattern of recurring relationships that shift somewhat according to where cyclical and linear time intersect. Thus, a myth can be interpreted through ritual performance in ways that speak to the specific crises and needs of a temporal community. As we shall see later on, myths also can be recast, distorted, or manipulated to legitimize specific power structures and dogmas.

In linear thought myth is relegated to a distant, dormant past, but in cyclical thought myth is experienced as an integral part of the unfolding of current events. Maya astronomers of southern Mexico saw the movement of the planets as an affirmation of the cyclical nature of time and the multi-dimensionality of space. Inscriptions and stone carvings dating to the fourth century C.E. document the unfolding of events that repeat themselves and must be kept in motion through complex ritual performances (León-Portilla 1973). This pattern of recurrences gives rise to what we call "prophecies," a misleading term for what are not so much predictions as they are descriptions of the events of the past or present in their future permutations.

These descriptions of things that are happening simultaneously in the past, present, and future often use similar symbolic forms to reference unfolding events. Thus, in myths found among many peoples, including the Caribbean Taínos (Puerto Rico, Cuba, Hispaniola), the Incas (Peru) and the Aztecs, Mayas, and Purépecha of Mexico, the coming of the Spaniards is anticipated through symbols, omens, and predictions of outcome that hold remarkable similarities. The historian Tzvetan Todorov suggests that this uniformity is the result of "retrospective reformulations" of history (1984: 74), i.e., that these prophecies were made "after" the event itself had taken place. But if we accept the possibility of a multi-dimensional concept of time in which past, present, and future intermingle, we might be able to accept that ancient indigenous sages knew of the coming of the Spaniards because they had experienced the *conquista* long before it ever occurred in linear time.

Thus, for many peoples of the Americas myth was and is a description of events happening in complementary time strata. Like the boundaries of time, the boundaries that separate spirit from matter are fluid and susceptible to sound frequencies. For the ancient Mayas the cultivation of the arts and sciences culminated in a core insight: matter is created by a concentration of energy (Arias-Larreta 1968; Robertson 1992). This is where sound again becomes crucial to our understanding of a worldview, for the time and space in which myth takes place can be accessed through the use of sound, and the transmutation from spirit to matter or matter to spirit can be accomplished through sonic technologies.

In Peru, Mochica potters of the third and fourth centuries C.E. portrayed priests in ecstatic flight. Some of these vessels and figurines indicate that flight was induced or accompanied by sound: an apprentice aids the priest in his journey by playing a raftpipe or beating a drum (Benson 1975; and Olsen 1992). These depictions refer to mystical teachings that also were represented in Nazca pottery (beginning some 1800 years ago) wherein hawks and other birds receive the strength to fly up to the sun from the San Pedro cactus (*Trichocereus pachanoi*).[1] Here the "symbol" is the bird, a possible "referent" is the human soul (or the shaman's soul), and the "vehicle" of flight is a potent hallucinogen that transmutes matter into spirit. To this day, traditional healers of the Americas use sound and/or psychotropic substances to induce a physical/psychological/spiritual state that breaks down the thin membranes separating spirit and matter (see Dobkin de Ríos 1972; Reichel-Dolmatoff 1975; Wilbert 1975; La Barre 1976; Grebe 1979–1980).

Given these tenets of transmutation, sound also could be used to bridge life and death, particularly if death is a journey that takes the deceased into yet another stratum of time and space. Describing depictions of death and the afterlife painted on Mochica pottery, Benson concludes: "Musical instruments appear in almost every afterlife scene and on many modeled skeletal pots; they are frequently held or played by priest figures. The evidence is strong that they are death-associated and that at least some of them indicate the otherworld, or the preparation for it" (1975: 116). These remarkable vessels link ancient mythology to the present, for they depict drums, raftpipes, notched flutes, conch shells, rattlepoles, and other instruments that continue to play an important role in Andean death rituals.

Songs emphasizing the deeds and genealogies of great leaders, documenting battles and defeats, and listing events of social significance indicate that notions of cyclical time coexisted with a tacit awareness of linear time. Simmons has discussed several examples of epic performances involving poetry, song, and dance noted in early chronicles: the *areíto* traditions of Hispaniola, where the lives of chiefs were retold through song and dance; the *teocuicatl* epics of the Aztecs, wherein myths were used to justify imperial expansion; and various types of historically-based performances among indigenous peoples of Nicaragua, Honduras, Colombia, and Paraguay (1960: 103).

Among the Incas, epic poetry could be sung, recited, or dramatized. Many epics described events in the beginning of time, or *purumpacha* (uninhabited or empty time), relating these to the legendary appearance of founding heroes and dynasties (Arias-Larreta 1968: 120). Ancient songs that revived ancestral memory and lamented the death of an Inca with elaborate accounts of his deeds and his character have become known in Peru as *cantares históricos* (Lara 1967: 317–18; Schechter 1979: 191).

Epics were used even in the most remote corners of the Andean empire to recall uprisings against the Incas. Some of these incidents are documented in the *Crónicas de Indias*: the uprising of the *collas* led by Xipana; the mutiny of Tocay Capay and his *huallacanes*; the struggle of the Chimú against serfdom. The play *Ollantay* depicts a late 14th-century uprising against the hegemonic rule and class structures imposed by the Incas. The warrior after whom the drama is named defies the laws that separate nobles from commoners to pursue a dangerous liaison with the fair Cusi-Coyllur, daughter of the Inca Pachacutec (Arias-Larreta 1968: 126–27; see also Betanzos 1551 in 1924; Farfán Ayerbe 1952). Through song, dance, and poetry (inseparable ingredients of Andean performance) both the strength and fragility of an empire and the complex relationships between order and chaos were re-enacted. The tradition of collapsing time and representing resistance through dramatization persists in this region to this day. Contemporary Kechua-speaking peoples continue to rehearse their resistance to domination through the dramatic event known as "La muerte de Atahualpa," which depicts the Inca Atahualpa's 16th-century struggle against Spanish colonization (Millones 1992; see also Millones,

---

1 Mochica civilization flourished on the northern coast of Peru from 200 B.C.E. to 700 C.E., when it was assimilated into the Huari empire. Nazca culture, on the southern coast, was contemporaneous with the Mochica State. The plain of Socos, centered in the Nazca area, is the site of the large land-drawings that have thus far defied Western scientific explanations.

"Popular Dramas and Commemorations: The Incas of Carhuamayo" in these volumes).

Thus, the actual "practice" or performance of myth and history stands as a place where line and circle intersect. It is important to remember that among the Incas, as well as for the Mayas and Aztecs (and their descendants), different belief systems coexisted long before the arrival of Christianity. Moreover, no matter how deeply we analyze the multiple references of a symbol, there is a level of understanding that is only accessible to those who practice the belief system—those who embody it through performance.

SONGS OF LIFE AND DEATH: A MESOAMERICAN STORY

Death appears as a central theme in the Aztec and Yucatec-Maya song texts that survived the Spanish invasions and book-burnings of the sixteenth century. Indeed, many composers seem deeply preoccupied with and ambivalent about the nature of life, death, and the hereafter. Their focus on death can be understood in part through the reinterpretations of cosmology that characterized their epoch and the manipulations of dogma that were used to justify Aztec imperialism.

The *teotlatolli* (divine words) and *teocuicatl* (divine songs) of the Nahuatl-speaking Mexicas (Aztecs, ca. 1300–1521 C.E.) told of five cosmic ages or "suns" representing different stages of creation. Each sun referenced a consecutively perfected and evolved world characterized by the introduction of a particular element or primordial force—earth, wind, water, and fire. These forces ruled earlier worlds until the beginning of the present epoch, known as the "Sun of Movement" (León-Portilla 1980: 27–29).

The god Ometeotl stood at the center of these consecutive stages of creation. Ometeotl was one of the many names of a dual being comprising the all-begetting Father and universal Mother, or Tonacatecuhtli and Tonacacihuatl. The Toltecs (ca. 750–1150 C.E.) also invoked him/her as Quetzalcoatl (Precious Feathered Serpent or Precious-Feathered-Twins), whom they sometimes paired with Coatlicue, the Mother goddess of the "skirt of serpents" (León-Portilla 1980: 19, 220). The duality of the sacred is also reflected in the Nahuatl names Ometecuhtli-Omecihuatl (Lord/Lady of Duality, also known as Xolotl-Cuaxolotl), Tlaltecuhtli (Lord/Lady of the Earth), Centeotl (He/She God of Maize), and Xochipilli/

Macuilxochitl, two of the names of the deity of music and all other arts (León-Portilla 1988: 13).

The worship of the benevolent Dual God, Ometeotl, was introduced to the people of Mesoamerica by the historic Quetzalcoatl. Named after the Feathered Serpent, this 12th-century mystic made a pilgrimage to Huapalcalco, where he devoted himself to meditation. Awed by his wisdom and extraordinary powers, the Toltecs chose him as their ruler. Under his leadership the city of Tula became a gathering place for composers, scientists, artisans, and tradesmen; many towns, palaces and temples were built and the arts flourished. The exile and death of Quetzalcoatl (ca. 1150 C.E.) brought about the collapse of Tula and the eventual ruin of the Toltecs. Many defeated Toltecs migrated south, spreading belief systems that extolled the god Quetzalcoatl, known in Quiché and Cakchiquel as Gucumatz, and in Yucatec Maya as Kukulcán (León-Portilla 1980: 19–21).

The accounts collected by Bernardino de Sahagún from indigenous informants some years after his arrival in Mexico in 1529 and during the sixty years he lived in New Spain (see *Códice Matritense, Códice Florentino*, and León-Portilla 1969: 15–16) state that the fall of Quetzalcoatl and the city of Tula was precipitated by the appearance of a god named Tezcatlipoca. Just as the mystic Quetzalcoatl mirrored the name of an important deity, Tezcatlipoca—whether god or man—carried the name given to the four sons of the creator Ometeotl. The four Tezcatlipocas (Smoking Mirrors) had appeared during the manifestation of Ometeotl that formed the first epoch. These brothers, born of an androgynous father/mother, were the white, black, red and blue primordial forces that set the sun in motion. After working together to bring order and bounty to the world, one of the Tezcatlipocas sought to aggrandize himself, angering his brothers and the other gods. Quetzalcoatl intervened in this cosmic struggle, destroying the earth and the first sun. Each consecutive stage of creation was again destroyed by attempts by one of the Tezcatlipocas to surpass his brothers.

The fifth era augured the appearance of human beings and the age of the "Sun of Movement." By this time a truce had been made between the four warring gods and each one had been given power over a different cosmic quadrant and cardinal direction.

The Fifth Sun had materialized through a massive and voluntary sacrifice of all the gods, who shed their blood so that the new creation could come to fruition.

These patterns of destruction and creation led the Aztecs to mark the end of certain calendrical cycles with rites in which all fires were put out and then rekindled to represent the terrifying passage from one sun into another (Fig 1). According to the *Tonalamatl*, the sacred astrological books of the Aztecs, the Fifth Sun was destined to end in a cataclysm that would leave the world in chaos (León-Portilla 1980: 28–29).

This apocalypse also had been foreseen in the *chilames*, the oral histories and prophecies of the Mayas of Yucatan. The twenty-year period called *4-Ahau Katun* (4-Lord-Twenty-Years), corresponding to 1477–1497 C.E., was awaited with foreboding:

The *Katun* [the twenty-year period of time] is established at Chichen Itza. . . . The quetzal bird shall come. Kukulkan [Quetzalcoatl] shall come, the green bird shall come. Blood vomit shall come. Kukulcan shall come with them for the second time. It is the word of God. The Itza shall come (Roys 1967: 161; León-Portilla 1988: 3).

Fig. 1: New Fire Ceremony performed every 52 years at the end/beginning of each calendar cycle. Seven priests impersonating deities surround the fire that will rekindle hearths throughout the Aztec empire (*Códice Borbónico*, 1938 edition: 34). Courtesy of the DeGolyer Library, Southern Methodist University, Dallas, Texas.

Fig. 2: Schematic rendering of the cosmos, where four cardinal directions emanate from the center (*Códice Fejérvary-Mayer*, 1945 edition: 1). Courtesy of the DeGolyer Library, Southern Methodist University, Dallas, Texas.

The *Annals of Cuauhtitlan* and other extant codices of the people of Central Mexico tell us that in the year 13-Flint (1492 C.E.) "the Sun was devoured" (folio 58). The *Third Relation* of the chronicler Chimalpain Cuauhtlehuanitzin, based on the ancient texts of Mexico, describes additional calamities that occurred in 13-Tecpatl/1492:

Here, there was disease, the sun was devoured, there was hunger. . . . A mountain, between the volcanoes Iztaccihuatl and Popocatepetl, split. Water sprang from the interior of it, and many ferocious beasts devoured the children . . . (León-Portilla 1988: 4).

The appearance of Hernán Cortés also was accompanied by portents that spelled disaster. In the *Códice Florentino*, Sahagún's informants assert that in the year 12-House (1517) the temple of sun/war god Huitzilopochtli burst into flames, the temple of the fire god Xiutecuhtli was struck by lightning, fire streamed through the sky, the wind heated the water until it boiled, the earth goddess Cihuacoatl would wail night after night for her children, a strange, mirror-topped bird appeared, and monsters roamed the streets of Tenochtitlan. These and additional omens appearing in 1519 led the counselors of Motecuhzoma II (Moctezuma) to speculate that Cortés might be the returning Lord Quetzalcoatl.

The Aztecs, who saw themselves as the chosen race and as the "Children of the Sun," sought to avert these prophecies and their own final destruction through a reinterpretation of cosmology: if the gods of previous epochs had been able to restore life and engender humans by sacrificing their own blood, humans could perpetuate the Fifth Sun and prolong their existence by sacrificing their own blood.

The Aztecs of the fourteenth century destroyed their own records and the sacred books of the peoples they had conquered, rewriting history so that they could inherit the mantle of the much-admired Toltecs. Ironically, they replaced the Lord/Lady of Duality with a god who might protect them from annihilation: Huitzilopochtli, the Divine Warrior. The priests of this deity taught that warriors who perished in the shadow of Huitzilopochtli would survive death to become companions of the Sun. According to the eminent Mexican scholar, Miguel León-Portilla,

> Huitzilopochtli is the Mexican interpretation of Tezcatlipoca, "The Smoking Mirror," a double, and later on a fourfold manifestation (present in the four quadrants of the world [Fig. 2]), of the supreme Ometeotl, the Dual God. Huitzilopochtli was, in sum, the warriors' own conception of [the] Toltec Tezcatlipoca, and, ultimately, of the primeval Ometeotl (1988: 12).

The terror of Tezcatlipoca's destructive powers led Aztec warriors to offer the blood not only of prisoners of war but also of their most beloved family members in sacrifice to the thirsty Huitzilopochtli, thus seeking to perpetuate life as the gods of the four earlier epochs had done through mysterious self sacrifices. In the sixteenth century, Diego Durán (1579–81) collected oral histories documenting a ceremony in which Ahuitzotl, Lord of Tenochtitlan from 1469 to 1481, sacrificed 80,400 people to his god. By the time Cortés imprisoned Motecuhzoma II, death had become an obsession and warfare had taken on an aura of mysticism for the Aztecs, much as it had for the invading Spaniards.

Because the myths that sustain warfare and carnage are ultimately fragile, their retelling and interpretations must be closely regulated. The Aztecs sought to control the *teocuicatl* or divine songs and the epic poems recalling the birth of Huitzilopochtli, subjecting new compositions to censorship and manipulating performances to justify the expansion of their empire. The *Códice Matritense* describes the process of church/state approval that ensured the purity of the dogma:

> The tonsured priest of "The Mother of Pearl Serpent" was concerned with the songs. If someone composed a song, he consulted with him, so that he could . . . dispatch the singers to his house. When someone composed a song, he had to pass judgment upon it (folio 260 r.).

Based on the descriptions in Diego Durán's *Historia de las Indias de Nueva España*, León-Portilla adds that

> The obtention of approval meant, among other things, that the submitted composition could be intoned in public, as nothing in it contradicted the prevalent dogma. Evidence exists that not only the sacred "official" hymns, which were chanted in the religious ceremonies throughout the year, but also many of the poems were conceived to be sung in one way or another. Thus for the native Mesoamericans, as has been the case in other ancient cultures, the universe of poetry existed closely related to music and also to dancing, with the participants often dressed in a variety of costumes, in a sort of performance anticipating the appearance of drama. Some of the extant poetic texts in Nahuatl [see *Cantares mexicanos*] are in fact accompanied by musical notation and imply the active participation of various persons. Their singing takes the form of a dialogue through which human and divine beings communicate (1980: 45).

The florid glorification of warfare through ritual song and dance is evident in the first and fourth verses of the one surviving text by Macuilxochitl (b. 1435), daughter of the state counselor, Tlacalel. Macuilxochitl (Five-Flower) is one of the names of Xochipilli, deity of song, dance, poetry and all other aspects of performance and artistic endeavor (see Fig. 3). Although the codices frequently show women engaged in performance, this is the only song composed by a woman that survived the *conquista* (see Fig. 4).

Fig. 3: Stone sculpture of Xochipilli, deity of song, poetry, and dance. Photo by Manuel Álvarez Bravo (León-Portilla 1967). Courtesy of Dr. Miguel León-Portilla.

I.
I raise my songs,
I, Macuilxochitl,
with these I gladden the Giver of Life,
may the dance begin!

IV.
Slowly he [Axayacatl] makes offerings
of flowers and feathers
to the Giver of Life.
He puts the eagle shields
on the arms of the men,

there where the war rages,
in the midst of the plain.
Like our songs, like our flowers,
thus you, warrior of the tonsured head,
give pleasure to the Giver of Life.

(León-Portilla 1967: 165)

Many songs in Nahuatl show evidence of strong dissent against the warring ways of the Aztecs. The numerous surviving works of Nezahualcoyotl (1402–1472), sage, composer, architect and Lord of

Texcoco, show the confluence of the Aztec focus on Huitzilopochtli and the earlier mythology of the Toltecs, attributed to the wise Quetzalcoatl. Nezahualcoyotl built vast palaces and halls dedicated to musical performance and artistic excellence. As a warrior, he had to engage in battle and participate in rituals with which he frequently expressed disagreement. He attempted on several occasions to dissuade his peers from human sacrifice and ultimately ceased to participate in the state religion (León-Portilla 1969: 45).

Nezahualcoyotl was a composer/sage, or *tlamatinime* ("he who understands things") in the deepest sense of the word. The themes of his songs address the fragility and temporality of life, the inevitable paradox of death, the enigma of humankind in relation to the Giver of Life, the mysteries of the land of the dead (Mictlan), the reality of disembodied spiritual beings, the doubts engendered by experience, the difficulties of grasping the creative force that animates all life (represented by "He Who is Continually Inventing Himself"), the importance of trying to find and speak "true words" and the meaning of "flower and song" (León-Portilla 1969: 48). The latter expression, "flower and song," was the Nahuatl metaphor for art and symbols, and was at the heart of Central Mexican semiotic discourse. Like the historical Buddha, Netzahualcoyotl taught that the path to enlightenment required the act of fully embracing one's humanity. Understanding could be entered and cultivated through the arts, which presented the possibility of immortality:

> My flowers will not come to an end,
> my songs will not come to an end,
> I, the singer, raise them up;
> they are scattered, they are bestowed.
> Even though flowers on earth
> may wither and yellow,
> they will be carried there,
> to the interior of the house
> of the bird with golden feathers.
>
> (Ms., *Collection of Mexican Songs*, fol. 16 v.;
> translated by León-Portilla 1980: 243–44)

In the cosmology of Nezahualcoyotl and many of his peers, the mysteries of life rest in the hands of the Lord of Near and Close, Tloque Nahuaque, who through his own flowers and songs paints all life on earth in his *amate*-bark book:

> With flowers You write,
> O Giver of Life;

> with songs You give color,
> with songs You shade
> those who must live on the earth.
>
> Later you will destroy eagles and ocelots;
> we live only in Your book of paintings,
> here, on the earth.
>
> (Ms., *Romances de los señores de la Nueva España*,
> fol. 35r.; translated by León-Portilla 1980: 244)

The temporality of life, which wilts like a flower, pervades the Nahuatl song texts that survived the *conquista*. Indeed, this theme persists in Nahuatl songs to this day, as shown by Mexican anthropologist and linguist Fernando Horcasitas: "The wistful laments over the withering of flower and song are not dead. In the mountains of northern Puebla, during a curing ceremony at the entrance of a cave, I heard a Nahua woman in her cups, half tears, half laughter, sing":

> Let there be violin playing,
> Let there be guitar playing.
> May I enjoy myself, may I laugh before the world!
> I am only here for a while, I am only passing;
> Tomorrow or the day after I will be under the earth,
> I will become dust.
> Let us drink our liquor, let us enjoy it!
> Today, this afternoon, we will rejoice,
> We will laugh here.
> Let those who are sour forget their sourness,
> Let those who are angry forget their anger.
> Not every day, not every afternoon,
> Will we be here to enjoy life on earth
> (1980: xvi).

Mesoamerican conceptualizations of the sacred have transcended both time and culture, surviving the cataclysmic changes of the last five hundred years. The paradoxical concepts of the duality of the sacred and the motherhood/fatherhood of God, the significance of sacrifice and the inevitability of death are central to the ways in which the peoples of Mesoamerica have "converted" Christianity to fit their own cosmologies and ceremonial needs. With few exceptions, indigenous peoples throughout the Americas have chosen to build shrines to the Mother of God rather than to the Son of God. The Son of God becomes the symbol of sacrifice—the god who must die so that humans may populate the earth and, at the same time, the human whose blood must be shed so that the gods may live. Beginning in the late seventeenth century, hundreds of converts to Catholicism joined orders of *penitentes*, flagellating and mortifying (killing) their flesh to achieve salvation

Fig. 4: Drawing of women composers from the *Códice Florentino*, p. x (León-Portilla 1992: 176). Courtesy of Dr. Miguel León-Portilla.

and composing *alabanzas* (or *alabados*) to praise the Mother and Son of the Creator. Thus, notions of life and death were again reshaped to blend the mythologies of the conqueror and the conquered.

SONGS OF THE ANIMAL POWERS: THE JAGUAR IN SOUTH AMERICA

The periodic destruction of the universe by fire, flood, or darkness is described in the myths of people throughout the Americas. The jaguar often stands at the center of these explanations of cosmic regeneration as a symbol of transformation and knowledge. Among the Makiritare of Brazil and Venezuela, the beginning of European colonization marks the period of mythic time characterized by the appearance of the *fañuru* (Carib *pañoro*, or *español*), beings whose greed and madness leads them on an up-river pilgrimage of pillage, murder, rape, and cannibalism. Eventually, the *fañuru* kill the creator god, Wanadi, on a cross. The 1775 Makiritare uprising against the Spanish is recalled in oral tradition as a mythic stage in which the great shaman Mahaiwadi and his jaguar *demodede* (spirit double) put in motion yet another cycle of destruction and regeneration:

Mahaiwadi lived on the banks of the Arahame. He was very wise. He was *huhai* [a medicine man who defends the village against evil powers]. He took his *demodede* out of his body. No one saw him. He hid in the jungle, playing maraca, singing, smoking. He went to the mouths of the Arahame, the Kuntinama, the Tamatama. He threw tobacco leaves and *wiriki* [small quartz crystals] all around there. He called the *mawadi* [giant spirit anacondas]. Then he went to Kashishare (Casiquiare). He threw his maraca in and hid in the forest. He just stayed there singing and smoking.

The *Fañuru's* canoes turned over and the *mawadi* ate them. Some of them left their canoes and ran into the jungle. Mahaiwadi lay down in his hammock. He left his body there as a trick. He went out in a new body, like a jaguar. He sent the jaguar into the forest to eat the *Fañuru*.

When his task was finished, the jaguar summoned the people:

He screamed: "The *Fañuru* are in my stomach. You can come out of your caves now."

Mahaiwadi woke up. He turned into a bird and took off singing: "Free, free, I'm free." That's how he sang.

When Mahaiwadi died, a star crossed the sky. They say his *demodede* was returning to Heaven. They keep Mahaiwadi's skull and bones in the Arahame as proof, as a reminder. They have power. They cure the sick (Civrieux 1980: 158).

Throughout the continent, the jaguar is a crucial symbol of the creation/destruction cycles of the cosmos. Beginning ca. 1300 B.C.E., the Olmecs carved enormous representations of their Jaguar God in stone. Jaguar masks made of green mosaics have been found in many ancient Olmec sites. Elements of this deity became associated with the Mesoamerican Rain God (known in Nahuatl as Tlaloc) and are invoked to this day in ritual performances held by the descendants of the Maya and Quiché (Fig. 5).

In the Hohódeni-Baniwa myths of the upper Río Negro (northwestern Amazon), it was the jaguar, Yaperikuli (=Iñapirrikuli, literally "made out of bone"), who engendered the primordial hero, Kuai (=Kuwái), with his thought. Kuai excreted the pebble which became the present world. The voice of the jaguar, which in current rituals is embodied in the resonant bass tone of wooden trumpets, made the earth open and increase with each note of the song. Robin Wright states that "*whenever* the jaguar-song occurs in myth or shaman-song, it indicates [that] a transformation—*Ipadámawa*—is being made" (1981: 382). When the hero Kuai, son of the jaguar, is eventually burned by the cosmic fire at the center of the earth, he is reborn in immortal forms, "including the multiple forms of musical flutes and trumpets and the sounds that generate the distinctions between species of animals and people (linguistic groups)" (Sullivan 1988: 70). Thus, "Kuai's spirit lives an immortal existence in the Other World, while Kuai's body is represented in the sacred flute, *Kuai*, which men play today" (Wright 1981: 532). (See the Dzáwinai, literally "keepers of the jaguar" version of this creation myth by Jonathan D. Hill, "Metamorphosis: Mythic and Musical Modes of Ceremonial Exchange Among the Wakuénai of Venezuela," in this volume.)[2]

Throughout the Americas the jaguar may appear as male, female or a male/female pair. It is often the female manifestation of the jaguar that is the most fearsome, for the very life force of women emanates from the great felines. The Canelos Quichua (Ecuador) account for the soul-substance of women through a myth in which Apayaya, the black jaguar grandfather, captures a pregnant woman and extracts the twins from her womb, raising one of them as a jaguar son. The son eventually slays his father and reigns over the animal kingdom. His mother is later instructed by the female spirit of garden soil and pottery clay, Nunghuí, to differentiate the domain of cultivated land from the forests. Jaguars and cougars protest this demarcation and are killed by caymans (alligators). This intricate mosaic of stories-within-stories informs female spirituality, lineage structures and origins, and long-

standing patterns of social organization (Whitten 1976: 55–56).

The initiation rites of Barasana (Colombia) males involve elaborate performances focusing on the *He* house. The flutes and trumpets used in the second phase of the ceremony are fed tobacco snuff by the shaman, who blows the substance into the instruments through the air holes. The initiates, whose food intake and behavior have been restricted for the two months preceding these rites, have been kept away from the sacred *he* flutes. At sundown of the second day of this stage of the ritual, the initiates, whose hair has been cut and whose bodies have been covered with black paint, are instructed to sit in a fetal position and to remain motionless. They must accept the cigars, coca and *yagé* (a psychotropic drink made from the *Banisteriopsis caapi* vine) in this womb-like position. Only after ingesting these offerings are the initiates allowed to see the instruments as each *he* flute is slowly paraded in front of them. As they are played, the instruments breathe and come alive, emitting the roar of the ancestral jaguar: "The *he* instruments, brought from the forest, breathe life into the house. At Fruit House [the earlier stage of the rite], this same life-giving ancestral breath is blown from the trumpets over the piles of fruit so that its soul is changed and becomes ripe and abundant, and at *he* house, it is blown over the initiates themselves to change their souls and turn them into strong adults" (Hugh-Jones 1979: 151).

Wherever the jaguar appears, it walks the fine line between chaos and order. Many jaguar myths speak of destruction and dismemberment, not in the sense of sacrifice but in the sense of transformation. Human beings are meant to learn from these acts that the dismantling of the self is often necessary for growth and healing. *Nahôre* dances among the Toba (Bolivian

---

2 The term Wakuénai can be glossed as "people with whom we speak" and includes the Dzáwinai, Waríperídakéna, Ádzanéni, Kumadámnainai, and Hohódeni peoples of the Isana and Guainía river basins. These groups speak mutually intelligible dialects of the language Waku, all trace their cultural origins to mythical emergence from the ground at a place near Hípana on the Aiarí River ("The Center of the World") and all intermarry. "Wakuénai" is used by Jonathan D. Hill in his contribution to this volume (see "Metamorphosis: Mythic and Musical Modes of Ceremonial Exchange Among the Wakuénai of Venezuela") in lieu of "Baniwa," a term designating all Arawakan speakers along the Isana river and its tributaries in Brazil; "Curripaco" is a name used in Colombia and Venezuela to refer to all Wakuénai groups. Baniwa and Curripaco are both local terms. Baniwa is the name of a distinct northern Arawakan group living in Venezuela whose language is not mutually intelligible with Waku. Curripaco denotes a dialect of Waku that is associated with the Ádzanéni phratry of the Guainía River (= Río Negro) and is therefore not an ethnologically precise term for the Wakuénai as a whole. The use of different ethnonyms reflects the geographical position of Wakuénai lands, some of which are in Brazil and the rest in Venezuela and Colombia.

Fig. 5: The Jaguar as Lord of the Animals (Aztec) (*Códice Telleriano-Remensis*, 1963 edition: 9 verso). Courtesy of the DeGolyer Library, Southern Methodist University, Dallas, Texas.

Chaco) focus on the healing powers of the jaguar and provide a context within which young women are initiated into the animal powers that they will receive at death. In the dance, young men circle around the initiates, lashing their loins with strands of cloth. Thus having been killed, the girls lie "dead" in the center of the dance circle, where they are "attacked" by a healer impersonating a jaguar. He revitalizes each girl not by harming her, but by performing a series of healing actions: "He puts his mouth to the girl's breast, sucks it on two spots and blows on it, after which he spits out what he pretends to extract. Then he treats the head in the same way, sucking it and blowing on it" (Karsten 1923: 73). Toba men undergo no major initiations, and it is women who are more frequently transformed into jaguars after death. The ritual encounter of women with the jaguar, who in appearing to attack and destroy actually heals, brings them into contact with a cosmic force that pulsates between life and death.

The identification of shamanic healers with jaguars can be found from the earliest chronicles of the *conquista* to the ethnographies of the twentieth century. Among the Desana (Tukano) of Colombia

> . . . it is thought that a shaman can turn into a jaguar at will and that he can use the form of this animal as a disguise under which he can act as a helper, a protector, or an aggressor. After death, the shaman may turn permanently into a jaguar and then manifest himself in that form to the living, both friend and foe, again in a benevolent or malefic way, as the case may be. . . . The connection is so close that shamans and jaguars are thought to be almost identical, or at least equivalent, in their power, each in his own sphere of action, but occasionally able to exchange their roles (Reichel-Dolmatoff 1975: 43–44).

The mythical domain is populated by many other animals, all of whom have special powers and attributes. Many kin groups trace their ancestry, special characteristics, or protective spirits to these animals. We have focused on the jaguar because of its association with creative and destructive cycles and because of its special link with transformation, especially through the introduction of fire, which marks the emergence of civilization. In *The Raw and the Cooked* (1969), Claude Lévi-Strauss links the emergence of fire and the technology of cooking food to the emergence of culture and social organization. In the myths of Native American peoples it is often the cosmic jaguar that brings fire, the transformative element that moves humans into a social world.

MYTH, PERFORMANCE, AND HUMAN ORGANIZATION

Participation in a social world requires a grasp of the myths that illuminate common assumptions among members of a population. Such esoteric knowledge is usually gained through performance, for it is in the act of recreating the myth that the performers and their audience (both human and extra-human) collapse time and become one with the ancestors and spirits. The performance of myth also serves to legitimize the power structures that bind and define a society.

Among the now extinct Selk'nam of Tierra del Fuego in southernmost Argentina and Chile, the songs, dances, and costumes of the Hain initiation ceremony were used to reinforce the power of men over women:

> The [male initiation] rite has come to an end. The *kloketen* now knows that [the god] Shoort is only a man and he may have guessed already that all the spirits are the same. . . . He will be repeatedly admonished never to tell the women "the secret" nor ever to mention to them what transpires in the Hain [ceremony]. He will be warned time and again that he will be spied upon when he returns to normal life, that if he lets out the slightest hint of the forbidden knowledge to the women or to the children, he will be immediately killed as well as the woman in whom he confides (Chapman 1977: 6).

The protected secret of the Hain was that men and their gods are one and the same. Beneath the secret was yet another: these secrets originally had been given to women who held sway over the behavior of men. Led by Kra, the Moon Woman, the women sought to deceive the men into submission. Led by Kran, the Sun Man, the men killed the women and stole their secrets, thus cementing the primordial antagonism between Sun and Moon, mirrored in the social antagonism between men and women (Gusinde 1931 in 1975: 859–69). Ironically, the songs of the Hain ceremony of induction into manhood, which the *kloketen* initiates were instructed to keep secret, were recorded for Anne Chapman by Lola Kiepja, a woman who was the last representative of her people. The fact that Lola Kiepja was able to record many hours of secret male ceremonial material from memory suggests that the division of ritual repertoires by gender was as permeable as the division between gods and men (Robertson 1987: 227–28).

The Kalapálo of the Upper Xingu Basin (Brazil) also focus their central rituals on mythic as well as social gender antagonisms. The women's *Yamarikumalu* and the men's *Kagutus* ceremonies exclude members of the opposite sex. According to Ellen Basso, "the *Yamarikumalu* features collective performances by the women of a variety of songs, whereas during the *Kagutu*, men (normally in groups of three) play on large flutelike instruments of the same name. . . . Women must not see the flutes or the men playing them; men can observe the women singing during the *Yamarikumalu*, but they are supposed to keep a respectful distance" (Basso 1985: 261).

Again, the flutes are kept from women but are female in origin. These are the kinds of instruments anthropologists frequently have referred to as "phallic." However, "the language used by the Kalapálo to talk about the *kagutu* is characterized by metaphors of female sexuality. The shape and appearance of these large, tubular instruments, rather than seeming phallic to them, are likened to the female sexual organ: the mouth of the flute is called its "vagina" (*igïgï*), and when the set of *kagutu* is stored in the rafters of the sponsor's house during periods when it is not played, the instruments are said to be 'menstruating'" (Basso 1985: 304).

The menstrual power of women is one of the elements that men seek to control ritually. Among Guayakí peoples of Paraguay, female behavior directly affects the endeavor of hunters. A hunter becomes attractive to the forest beings and to game when his wife is giving birth or menstruating, when his daughter reaches menarche, or when his wife aborts a child (Clastres 1968: 23–24). Hunting is the one activity that puts men on a par with women as shedders of blood. The ability of women to shed their own blood associates them with the cataclysms and transformations of past worlds.

Myths that explain successions and inversions of gender-based power are ubiquitous in rites of initiation. Sullivan suggests that,

> by following the mythic history of initiatory processes and by noting the degree to which male and female initiatory processes overlap, one can see how male

initiation seems to have stolen, borrowed, or shared the regenerative strategies of females. . . . Whereas women's initiation displays the hiddenness and constancy of the powers of dissolution and metamorphosis, male initiation more often highlights the violence of change inherent in all symbolic display (1988: 344).

Further research may reveal the extent to which ritual repertoires reflect these tendencies throughout the continent.

The performance of myth also exists in permutations that emphasize the need for cooperation and reciprocity that crosses gender, moiety, or kinship boundaries. The processes of life described in myths often require male/female pairings, and the effectiveness of collaboration has entered the imagination of many storytellers, including the composers of the Inca empire. Garcilaso de la Vega translated a song in his *Comentarios reales* (1609) in which a heavenly *ñusta* (a woman or maiden of royal lineage) works with her brother to produce rain. The female aspects of precipitation are hail, rain, and snow. The male dimension requires the action of "fierce men and not tender women," and results in thunder and lightning, produced when brother rain breaks his sister's water vessel (Garcilaso 1609 in 1953: 149–51, reproduced below).

The people of ancient Peru reflected this tension between male and female in ceremonies performed to bring rain and fertility and in rites honoring the Sun God and his descendants, the Incas. The gender play between Sun and Moon remains part of Andean oral tradition to this day. Many aspects of ritual performance mediate such cosmological and social appositions. (See Max Peter Baumann, "Music and Worldview of Indian Societies in the Bolivian Andes," in this volume.)

Sometimes performance reenacts the introduction of a particular technology, such as the cultivation of corn, manioc, potatoes, or other staples. In some cases, ritual enactment of the arrival of such knowledge is accompanied by assertions of ownership or transmission of information that transforms the lifeways and worldviews of a community. The telling of stories and the enactment of myths that involve transformation or metamorphosis always seem to involve song. Because the knowledge referenced by song, dance, and gesture is often linked to the survival of a people, it continues to be as important to indigenous cultures today as it was five centuries ago. In his study of the Suyá (Brazil) Mouse Ceremony, wherein men sing for their sisters and boys sing for their mothers, Anthony Seeger says:

> It should be clear that Suyá song meant much more than what we call music today. It was far from being simply entertainment. Songs were obtained from dangerous beings through an intermediary who had lost his or her spirit through the actions of a witch, or who had confronted foreigners and learned from them. They had to be performed carefully and seriously. Ceremonies and their associated songs transformed members of the society and also each individual's experience of self and social relationships. Song was associated with euphoria and with personal and society-wide transformations. Songs, and the Mouse Ceremony among them, were not something at the periphery of essential experience, but at its very center (1987: 61).

CONCLUSIONS

Although he later denied the integral relationship between ritual performance and myth, Lévi-Strauss was keenly aware of the link between the mythical and the musical experience: "Mythology and music have in common the fact that they summon the listener to a concrete form of union, with the difference, however, that myth offers him a pattern coded in images instead of sounds. In both cases, however, it is the listener who puts one or several potential meanings into the pattern, with the result that the real unity of the myth or the musical work is achieved by two participants, in and through a kind of celebration" (1981: 654).

Every society develops ideas about the nature of the universe that influence its development and technological goals. The difference between ideology and mythology is that the latter always embraces a mystical component—a means of communing with the sacred and transcending the common boundaries of temporal existence. Out of the generalized notions of time, space, and performance summarized above, peoples of the Americas devised "technologies" that helped them expand their experience. Rather than emphasizing a material technology that would produce mechanical flight, they embraced a technology that led to pneumatic flight. Rather than compartmentalizing experience only into linear segments, they searched for the interconnectedness of forms of energy and the recurring patterns of events, thus validating a simultaneously linear and spiral experience of time.

The cosmologies of the Americas are many. We sometimes encounter a culture in which two or more systems of explanation have coexisted for centuries. What appears to the outsider as a contradictory panoply of beliefs is experienced by the participant as part of the paradox of life. In most cases, that paradox is constantly mirrored in each culture's complex

Cúmac ñusta	Hermosa doncella	Beautiful *ñusta*,
Torrelláaiquim	Aquese tu hermano	your brother there
Puiñuy quita	El tu cantarillo	your vessel
Páaquir cayan	Lo está quebrantando	is breaking
Hina mantara	Y de aquesta causa	and for this reason
Cunuñunun	Truena y relampaguea	come thunder and lightning;
Illapántac	También caen rayos	lightning also falls.
Camri ñusta	Tú, real doncella	You, *ñusta*
Unuiquita	Tus muy lindas aguas	your lovely waters
Para munqui	Nos darás lloviendo;	you will rain down;
Mai ñimpiri	También a las veces	at the same time
Chichi munqui	Granizar nos has	you will hail;
Riti munqui	Nevarás asimesmo	you will snow.
Pacha rúrac	El Hacedor del mundo	The Maker of the world,
Pacha cámac	El Dios que le anima	the God who breathes life into it,
Vira cocha	El gran Viracocha,	the great Viracocha,
Cai hinápac	Para aqueste oficio	for this task
Churasunqui	Ya te colocaron	they chose you
Camasunqui.	Y te dieron alma.	and gave you a soul.

(Garcilaso de la Vega 1609 in 1953: 151; Spanish trans. by Garcilaso of a song collected by Father Blas Valera; English trans. by C. Robertson.)

relationship with the land and the cosmos. The ways in which these systems of relationships came to be were told throughout the continent in myths that circumscribed and explained the nature of life. Over time, systems of spiritual relationships became the model for social relationships. In these myths, as they have been bequeathed to the people of our century, sound appears time and again as an important tool for creation and regeneration. The Aztec composer Nezahualcoyotl alluded to this process in his hymns to Tloque Nahuaque, "He Who is Continually Inventing Himself." The unfolding of creativity through constant reinvention offers an apt metaphor for the way the "sounding" of myth works in our lives, for performance allows us to collapse temporality and bring mythical and present time into one and the same experience.

REFERENCES

Allen, Paula Gunn 1983. *The woman who owned the shadows.* San Francisco: Spinsters—Aunt Lute.
1986. *The sacred hoop: Recovering the feminine in American Indian traditions.* Boston: Beacon Press.
"Anales de Cuauhtitlan" in *Códice Chimalpopoca* (16th-century manuscript in Nahuatl at Mexico's National Museum of Anthropology), facsimile edition, study, and Spanish translation by Primo Feliciano Velázquez, 2nd edition. México: Universidad Nacional Autónoma de México—Instituto de Investigaciones Históricas, 1975.
Arias-Larreta, Abraham 1968. *Literaturas aborígenes de América.* Buenos Aires: Editorial Indoamericana.
Basso, Ellen 1985. *A musical view of the universe: Kalapalo myth and ritual performances.* Philadelphia: University of Pennsylvania Press.
Bastien, Joseph W. 1978. *Mountain of the condor: Metaphor and ritual in an Andean ayllu.* St. Paul, Minnesota: West Publishing Co.
Benson, Elizabeth 1975. "Death-associated figures on Mochica pottery" in *Death and the afterlife in Pre-Columbian America*, ed. by Elizabeth Benson. Washington, D.C.: Dumbarton Oaks Research Library and Collections, 105–44.
Betanzos, Juan de 1551 in 1924. *Historia de los Incas y Conquista del Perú. I: Suma y narración de los Incas* por Juan Díez de Betanzos. *II: Relación de la Conquista del Perú* por Miguel de Estete, ed. by Horacio Villanueva Urteaga. Lima: Imprenta y Librería SANMARTI.
Campbell, Joseph 1983. *The way of the animal powers*, vol. 1, *Historical atlas of world mythology*. London: Summerfield Press.
Cantares mexicanos (15th/16th-century manuscript in the National Library of Mexico), facsimile edition by Antonio Peñafiel as *Cantares en idioma mexicano*. México: Oficina Tipográfica de la Secretaría de Fomento, 1904.
Chapman, Anne 1977. *Selk'nam chants of Tierra del Fuego, Argentina.* Liner notes, Folkways Records, No. FE 4179.
Chimalpahin Quauhtlehuanitzin, Domingo Francisco de San Antón Muñón ca. 1606–1631. *Diferentes Historias originales de los reynos de Culhuacan y México, y de otras provincias* (Nahuatl manuscript in the Colegio de San Pedro y San Pablo, Boturini and Aubin collections), ed. by Ernst Mengin (Hamburg, 1950); facsimile edition by Ernst Mengin in *Corpus codicum americanorum medii aevi*, 3 (Copenhagen, 1949–1952).
Cieza de León, Pedro de [after 1553] in 1880. *Segunda parte de la Crónica del Perú, que trata del Señorío de los Incas Yupanquis y de sus grandes hechos y gobernación.* Madrid: Marcos Jiménez de la Espada.
Civrieux, Marc de 1980. *Watunna: An Orinoco creation cycle*, trans. by David M. Guss. San Francisco: North Point Press.
Clastres, Pierre 1968. "Ethnographie des indiens Guayakí," *Journal de la Société des Américanistes* 57:8–61.
Codex Borbonicus (Mexican manuscript in the Library of the Palais Bourbon), facsimile edition with commentary by Karl Anton Nowotny. Graz: Akademische Druck- und Verlagsanstalt, 1974.
Codex Fejérvary-Mayer (Pre-Columbian manuscript in the Free Public Museum of Liverpool, M 12014), facsimile edition with commentary by C. A. Burland. Graz: Akademische Druck- und Verlagsanstalt, 1971.
Códice Borbónico. Manuscrito pictórico antiguo mexicano que se conserva en la biblioteca de la Cámara de Diputados de París (Palais Bourbon). México: Librería Anticuaria G. M. Echaniz, 1938.
Códice Fejérvary-Mayer. Manuscrito pictórico antiguo mexicano que se conserva en el Museo de Liverpool. Mexico: Librería Anticuaria G. M. Echaniz, 1945.
Códice Florentino (Laurentian Library, Florence), facsimile edition. Mexico City: Archivo General de la Nación, 1979, 3 vols. In Bernardino de Sahagún's *Historia General de las Cosas de Nueva España*, trans. and ed. by Arthur J. O. Anderson and Charles E. Dibble (Santa Fe, New Mexico and Salt Lake City: School of American Research and University of Utah, 1950–1982), 12 vols.
Códice Matritense de la Real Academia de la Historia (Nahuatl texts of the Indian informants of Sahagún in the Real Academia de la Historia, Madrid), facsimile of vol. 8, edited by Francisco del Paso y Troncoso. Madrid: Hauser y Menet, 1907.
Códice Matritense del Real Palacio (Nahuatl texts of the Indian informants of Sahagún), facsimile edition of vol. 6 (part 2) and vol. 7 by Francisco del Paso y Troncoso. Madrid: Hauser y Menet, 1906.
Códice Telleriano-Remensis. Pictografías mexicanas del siglo XVI, con interpretación en lengua española de la época. Actualmente en la Biblioteca Real de Bruselas / Con un estudio y paleografía en francés por Mr. E. T. Hamy y ahora vierte al español actual la Dra. Carmen Cook de Leonard. México: Librería Anticuaria, G. M. Echaniz, 1963 [facsimile of Paris: Duque de Loubat, 1899, with a study by E. T. Hamy].
Dobkin de Ríos, Marlene 1972. *Visionary vine. Hallucinogenic healing in the Peruvian Amazon.* Prospect Heights, Illinois: Waveland Press.
Durán, Fray Diego 1579–1581 in 1971. *Book of the gods and rites of the ancient calendar*, translated and edited by Fernando Horcasitas and Doris Heyden. Norman: University of Oklahoma Press.
Farfán-Ayerbe, José María B. 1952. *El drama quechua Apu-Ollantay.* Lima: Editorial Politec—José Pardo [Publicaciones Runa-Simi, No. 1].
Garcilaso de la Vega, Inca 1609 in 1953. *Comentarios reales de los Incas.* Puebla, Mexico: Publicaciones de la Universidad de Puebla, 2 vols.
Grebe Vicuña, María Ester 1979–1980. "Relaciones entre música y cultura: El kultrún y su simbolismo," *Revista INIDEF* (Caracas) 4: 7–25.
Gusinde, Martín 1931 in 1975. *Die Feuerland Indianer*, vol. 1, *Die Selk'Nam*, translated and with commentary by Johannes Wilbert as *Folk literature of the Selknam Indians.* Los Angeles: UCLA Latin American Center (Latin American Studies Series, vol. 32).

Harrison, Regina 1989. *Signs, songs, and memory in the Andes: Translating Quechua language and culture.* Austin: University of Texas Press.

Horcasitas, Fernando 1980. "Preface" to Miguel León-Portilla's *Native Mesoamerican spirituality.* New York: Paulist Press.

Hugh-Jones, Stephen 1979. *The palm and the pleiades: Initiation and cosmology in northwest Amazonia.* Cambridge: Cambridge University Press.

Karsten, Rafael 1923. *The Toba Indians of the Bolivian Gran Chaco.* Abo (= Turku), Finland: Acta Academiae Aboensis (Humaniora 4), reprint edition (Oosterhout, The Netherlands: Anthropological Publications, 1970).

La Barre, Weston 1976. "I narcotici del Nuovo Mondo: Riti sciamanistici e sostanze psicotrope," *Terra Ameriga* (Genoa) 12/37–40: 31–40.

Lara, Jesús 1967. *La cultura de los Inkas,* vol. 2 of *La religión, los conocimientos, las artes.* La Paz (Bolivia): "Los Amigos del Libro."

León-Portilla, Miguel 1967. *Trece poetas del mundo azteca.* México: Universidad Nacional Autónoma de México—Instituto de Investigaciones Históricas.

1969. *Pre-Columbian literatures of Mexico,* trans. by Grace Lobanov and the author. Norman: University of Oklahoma Press.

1973. *Time and reality in the thought of the Maya,* trans. by Charles L. Boilès, Fernando Horcasitas, and the author. Boston: Beacon Press.

1980. *Native Mesoamerican spirituality.* New York: Paulist Press.

1988. "Mesoamerica 1492, and on the eve of 1992," Working papers No. 1. College Park, Maryland: Department of Spanish and Portuguese, University of Maryland.

1992. *Fifteen poets of the Aztec world.* Norman and London: University of Oklahoma Press. Revised and enlarged translation of *Trece poetas del mundo azteca* (México: Universidad Nacional Autónoma de México—Instituto de Investigaciones Históricas, 1967). Revised and enlarged Spanish edition, *Quince poetas del mundo náhuatl* (México: Editorial Diana, 1994).

Lévi-Strauss, Claude 1969. *The raw and the cooked,* vol. 1 of *Mythologiques,* trans. by John and Doreen Weightman. New York: Harper and Row.

1981. *The naked man,* vol. 4 of *Mythologiques,* trans. by John and Doreen Weightman. New York: Harper and Row.

Means, Philip Ainsworth 1928 in 1973. *Biblioteca andina: Essays on the lives and works of the chroniclers, or, the writers of the sixteenth and seventeenth centuries who treated of the pre-Hispanic history and culture of the Andean countries* (New Haven: Connecticut Academy of Arts and Sciences), reprint edition. Detroit: Blaine Ethridge Books.

Millones, Luis 1992. "The death of Atahualpa" in *Musical repercussions of 1492. Encounters in text and performance,* ed. by Carol E. Robertson. Washington, D.C.: Smithsonian Institution Press, 237–56.

Olsen, Dale A. 1992. "Implications of music technologies in the pre-Columbian Andes" in *Musical repercussions of 1492. Encounters in text and performance,* ed. by Carol E. Robertson. Washington, D.C.: Smithsonian Institution Press, 65–88.

Poma de Ayala, Felipe Guamán 1615 in 1980. *El primer nueva corónica y buen gobierno,* ed. by John Murra and Rolena Adorno, with translations from Kechua by Jorge L. Urioste. México: Siglo Veintiuno Editores, 3 vols.

Popol Vuh, The Mayan Book of the Dawn of Life 1985. (Manuscript of the Quiché text and 1701–1703 Spanish translation by Fr. Francisco Ximénez in the Edward E. Ayer Collection, Newberry Library, Chicago), edition and translation by Dennis Tedlock. New York: A Touchstone Book—Simon and Schuster.

Reichel-Dolmatoff, Gerardo 1975. *The shaman and the jaguar: A study of narcotic drugs among the Indians of Colombia.* Philadelphia: Temple University Press.

Robertson, Carol E. 1979. "'Pulling the ancestors': Performance practice and praxis in Mapuche ordering," *Ethnomusicology* 23/3: 395–416.

1987. "Power and gender in the musical experiences of women" in *Women and music in cross-cultural perspective,* ed. by Ellen Koskoff. Westport, Connecticut: Greenwood Press, 225–44.

1992. "The dance of Conquest" in *Musical repercussions of 1492: Encounters in text and performance,* ed. by Carol E. Robertson. Washington, D.C.: Smithsonian Institution Press, 9–30.

Robertson-DeCarbo, Carol E. 1977. "Lukutún: Text and context in Mapuche rogations," *Latin American Indian literatures* 1/2: 67–78.

Romances de los Señores de la Nueva España (manuscript in the National Library of Mexico) in Ángel María Garibay K.'s *Poesía Náhuatl,* vol. 1. México: Universidad Nacional Autónoma de México—Instituto de Investigaciones Históricas, 1963.

Roys, Ralph L. 1967. *The book of Chilam Balam of Chumayel.* Norman: University of Oklahoma Press.

Sahagún, Fray Bernardino de (16th century). *Florentine Codex: General history of the things of New Spain,* Books 1–5, 7–12, trans. by Arthur J. O. Anderson and Charles E. Dibble. Santa Fe, New Mexico: School of American Research, 1950–1963 (see *Códice Florentino, Códice Matritense de la Real Academia de la Historia,* and *Códice Matritense del Real Palacio* above).

Santa Cruz Pachacuti Yamqui Salcamayhua, Don Juan de 1613? in 1879. "Relación de antigüedades deste reyno del Pirú" in *Tres relaciones de antigüedades peruanas.* Madrid: Ministerio de Fomento de España.

Schechter, John M. 1979. "The Inca *cantar histórico:* A lexico-historical elaboration on two cultural themes," *Ethnomusicology* 23/2: 191–204.

Seeger, Anthony 1987. *Why Suyá sing: A musical anthropology of an Amazonian people.* Cambridge: Cambridge University Press.

Simmons, Merle L. 1960. "Pre-Conquest narrative songs in Spanish America," *Journal of American folklore* 73/287: 102–11.

Sullivan, Lawrence E. 1986. "Sound and senses: Towards a hermeneutics of performance," *History of religions* 26/1: 1–33.

1988. *Icanchu's drum: An orientation to meaning in South American religions.* New York: Macmillan.

Todorov, Tzvetan 1984. *The conquest of America. The question of the Other,* trans. by Richard Howard. New York: Harper and Row.

Whitten, Norman E. Jr. 1976. *Sacha Runa: Ethnicity and adaptation of Ecuadorian jungle Quichua.* Urbana: University of Illinois Press.

Wilbert, Johannes 1975. "Eschatology in a participatory universe: Destinies of the soul among the Warao Indians of Venezuela" in *Death and the afterlife in Pre-Columbian America,* ed. by Elizabeth Benson. Washington, D.C.: Dumbarton Oaks Research Library and Collections, 163–90.

Wright, Robin Michael 1981. *History and religion of the Baniwa peoples of the Upper Río Negro Valley,* 2 vols. (PhD diss., Anthropology: Stanford University).

METAMORPHOSIS

Mythic and Musical Modes of Ceremonial Exchange among the Wakuénai of Venezuela

JONATHAN D. HILL

Social organization in the northwest Amazon region—Kwépani, *the dance of Kuwái:*
The mythic origins of kwépani; Kwépani, *social gestures and performance;*
Interpreting kwépani—Pudáli: *ceremonial exchanges between affines: Overview of ceremonial*
activities; The internal structure of pudáli; Déetu, *the collective evocation of shamanistic power;*
The metamorphosis of the coconut palm grub (mútsi)—*Glossary*

THIS ESSAY EXAMINES musical performances, dances, and other activities that make up two distinct, yet interrelated, genres of ceremonial event among the Wakuénai, an Arawak-speaking people of the Venezuelan Amazon. The term Wakuénai can be glossed as "people with whom we speak" and includes the Dzáwinai, Waríperídakéna, Adzanéni, Kumadámnainai, and Hohódeni peoples of the Isana and Guainía (Río Negro) river basins in Venezuela, Colombia, and Brazil. These groups speak mutually intelligible dialects of the language Waku, all trace their cultural origins to mythical emergence from the ground at a place near Hípana on the Aiarí River ("The Center of the World"), and all intermarry.

Throughout the Upper Río Negro region and the adjacent Vaupés region to the south and west, indigenous peoples have elaborated upon the symbolic importance of the jaguar in their ceremonial and ritual activities. For the Wakuénai of Venezuela, the jaguar embodies powers of mythic creation and transformation that socialize individual persons and mediate in social relations among intermarrying groups. In mythic narratives, the jaguar's voice is said to have brought the creation of animal species to completion, and the Wakuénai evoke these creative powers in their initiation rituals by playing enormous "jaguar bone" trumpets over the sacred food of male initiants. In these sacred ritual contexts, Wakuénai elders become the jaguar-ancestors of myth by collectively creating the musical sounds of the jaguar's voice and thereby assume the power to define fully socialized humanness in terms of the asymmetrical power relations between mythic ancestors and living descendants. In less sacred ceremonial contexts, the hierarchical relations of power between mythic jaguar-ancestors and living human descendants are opened up into more egalitarian, socially inclusive performances. Through a genre of collective singing known as "wheel-dance," lines of male and female dancers come to embody the opening and closing of the jaguar's mouth, symbolizing the local kin groups' power to control relations of trade and intermarriage with other kin groups. For the Wakuénai, the jaguar is not merely a symbol representing the creative powers of mythic ancestors but also the source of ritual and ceremonial performances through which human beings take on the ancestral powers of defining individual humanness and mediate in collective relations of exchange.

By interpreting performances in broader contexts of myth, history, and social relations, we begin to understand how the Wakuénai musically construct two fundamentally different dimensions of bodily, social, and cosmic space-time. The vertical dimension of space-time is a metaphor for generational time, or the relations between mythic ancestors and their descendants, and also for developmental time, or the individual's passage from stage to stage in the life cycle. The horizontal dimension of space-time is a metaphor for the "opening up" of closed, hierarchically ordered patrilineal families into accepting "others" through trade relations and intermarriage, that is, the dispersal at any one point in time of hierarchically defined closed units to create new social "others" and expand relations among distinct groups. Following a brief overview of Wakuénai social organization, this study proceeds to a more detailed exploration of the cycle of myths about the two creations of the world in the time of Amáru and Kuwái, the primordial mother and son.[1]

In this myth cycle, the Wakuénai explain the coming-into-being of a human social order in which adult men are differentiated from adult women, animal nature is distinguished from socialized human being, and all categories of social and natural being are defined in relation to the life-giving powers of mythic ancestors. In the first part of the myth cycle, the voice of Kuwái musically names-into-being the species and objects of nature "from above" as he flies through the sky. The vertical dimension of space-time is subsequently created and mediated through a series of mythic movements between sky and earth that reaches completion when Kuwái descends for the last time into the village of mythic proto-humans and imparts the creative forces of musical naming power to Dzúli, the first owner of sacred chants (málikái). After doing so, Kuwái is pushed into a bonfire, causing the world to shrink back to its original miniature size. In the second part of mythic creation, an enormous palm tree erupts from the ashes of Kuwái, and this tree is made into a set of sacred flutes and trumpets that become the principal embodiments of ancestral power in human society. Amáru and the women then steal these sacred instruments from the men, setting off a battle between the sexes in which the flutes and trumpets are played in various locations. The horizontal dimension of space-time opens up as the sounds of Kuwái's sacred flutes and trumpets are produced in new places away from the center of mythic space.[2]

The two types of ceremonial event to be considered here are collective processes of symbolically constructing vertical and horizontal dimensions of mythic space-time in the contexts of human society and history. *Kwépani*, or the "dance of Kuwái," is a ceremonial gathering in which adult, initiated men from a number of villages amass a large quantity of wild fruits and play the sacred flutes and trumpets of Kuwái while lashing each other with ritual whips (*kapéti*). Women and children remain in seclusion during *kwépani*, and interaction between men and women is restricted to occasional dance-songs (*kápetiápani* or "whip-dance") that take place inside the house where women are secluded. The musical dances of *kwépani*, together with the symbolism of wild fruits and ritual whips, outline male-controlled processes of constructing vertical relations of power between mythic ancestors and human descendants. *Kwépani* is a process of social continuity and regeneration that unfolds through symbolically mediated movements of ancestral power "downwards" from one generation of adult men to the next and the complementary movements "upwards" of individual men as they progress through developmental stages of the life cycle.

Pudáli is a two-part cycle of male- and female-owned ceremonies in which a guest group brings a gift of smoked meat to a village of people who are classified as affines ("marriageable others" or in-laws). In the opening stage of *pudáli* ceremonies, guests and hosts remain clearly separated as the former play large ensembles of flutes and trumpets in circular dances around the gift of food. At later stages in *pudáli* ceremonies, the boundaries between guests and hosts are progressively relaxed and transcended. Musical performances are central to the process of establishing and, later, transcending boundaries between different local groups. In *pudáli* ceremonies, men and women participate together in constructing the horizontal dimension of Kuwái's mythic creation by musically opening up relations of trade and intermarriage between the descendants of different mythic ancestors. The transition from relatively fixed musical performances in large collective ensembles to more improvisatory, individualized performances constructs an expanding, horizontal dimension of mythic power along which persons, foods, and artifacts flow back and forth between groups of people living in different places.

The two types of ceremonial event, *kwépani* and *pudáli*, form two contrasting parts of a more general

---

[1] A "Glossary of indigenous terms" used here may be found at the end of this article, preceding the "References."

[2] This analysis of Wakuénai myth has been greatly influenced by Terence Turner's interpretation (1985) of the Northern Kayapó myth of the origin of cooking fire.

poetics of exchange in Wakuénai society. In *kwépani* ceremonies, the nuances of mythic meaning constrain the explosive creativity of musical sounds, resulting in relatively stable, cyclical (or reversible) patterns of musical and bodily movements that embody social processes of continuous, predictable change and renewal. In *pudáli* ceremonies, mythic meanings are transferred to increasingly dynamic musical and choreographic movements through variations of pitch, timbres, rhythms, and tempos, that directly embody processes of social expansion and transformative exchange. At a deeper level of analysis, the vertical and horizontal dimensions of space-time are linked, "the one ensuring the continued production of a people and food, and the other ensuring the proper exchange of these between groups of people" (Jackson 1983: 202). As this indigenous poetics of ceremonial exchange is based upon images of metamorphosis, or the transformation of a natural form into its opposite within the context of a single species of being, musical and other symbolic expressions underlie connections between the vertical and horizontal dimensions of space-time.

SOCIAL ORGANIZATION IN THE NORTHWEST AMAZON REGION

The Arawakan peoples of the Isana and Guainía rivers area refer to themselves as Wakuénai, or "people with whom we speak" (see Map) and they have maintained deeply rooted relationships of warfare, trade, and intermarriage with their eastern Tukanoan neighbors to the south and west. Like the Cubeo of the Cuduyarí River (Goldman 1979), the Wakuénai organize themselves into internally ranked patrilineal families that are localized in riverine territories and can act together as a defensive unit to repel outsiders. There is clear evidence of a historical connection between the Wakuénai and the Cubeo: "one of the Cubeo phratries

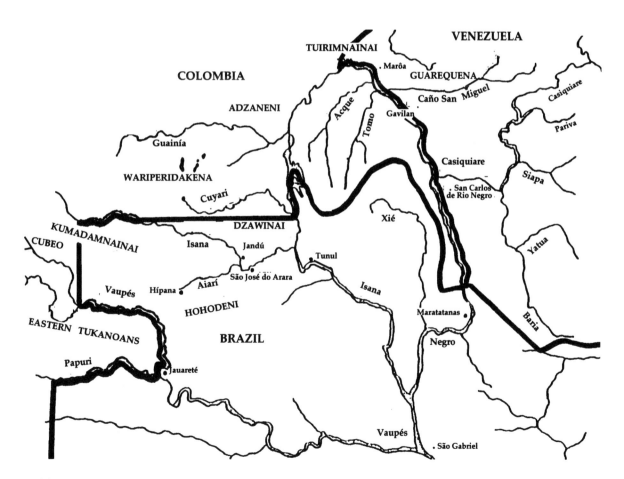

Map of the northwest Amazon region centered around Wakuénai lands in the Isana-Guainía drainage area of Venezuela, Brazil, and Colombia.

was, in fact, once Arawakan" (Goldman 1979: 26). In-depth studies of Wakuénai language and social organization are just beginning to appear, still lagging behind the study of eastern Tukanoan societies. Comparison of northern Arawakan and eastern Tukanoan social organization and of the intermediate Cubeo system promises to reveal cultural relations of great complexity.

Throughout the northwest Amazon region, local patrilineal groups integrate into larger, hierarchically ranked confederations, called phratries. Among the Wakuénai, each phratry consists of four or five named patrilineal families ranked in a serial order according to the mythic order of emergence of totemic ancestors from beneath the waterfalls at Hípana, a village on the Aiarí River in Brazil. In everyday social contexts, the names of the highest ranked sibs (or non-marriageable persons within the same phratry) serve as terms of social reference and conveniently mark the social boundary between blood related kin (*nukítsiñápe*) and "marriageable others" (*apána náiki*, "other people," or affines). Relations among phratries are not ranked but characterized by competition and shifting alliances among parties of equal status.

In spite of historical dislocations during the Rubber Boom (ca. 1860–1920) and more recent migrations of local patrilineal groups into new areas, Wakuénai phratries remain strongly associated with specific riverine territories. The continuous occupation of riverine areas by patrilineal phratries is supported by a rule that requires newly married couples to take up residence in the community of the husband's father's kin group after a brief, one-to-two year period of bride service. In recent years however, residence patterns have begun to change, and in some villages a large proportion of families resides in the community of the wife's kin group.

Young men are expected to live in their wives' villages and work for their prospective fathers-in-law. This period of labor for the wife's family, called bride service, is a way of socially legitimating relations of intermarriage between different patrilineal families. The young men are required to cut new manioc gardens for their fathers-in-law and provide their households with fish and game meat. Personal accounts of bride service depict it as a critical transition in young men's lives, when they undergo intense scrutiny and obey strict rules of respect for their future in-laws. Young men who are judged to be lazy or incompetent in their fulfillment of bride service duties

can be sent away without their brides. This veto power of fathers-in-law is greatly feared, and young men who fail the test of bride service suffer a sort of social death.

Tensions between fathers-in-law and sons-in-law are elaborately expressed in Wakuénai myths about the primordial world of mythic beginnings. In a cycle of narratives about this distant past, the trickster-creator (Iñápirríkuli) evades a series of lethal traps set for him by his father-in-law, a cannibalistic animal-human named Kunáhwerrim. Competition and rivalry between in-laws is a continuous theme in the entire cycle of myths about Iñápirríkuli and the unfinished world of mythic beginnings.

KWÉPANI: *THE DANCE OF KUWÁI*

The mythic origins of *kwépani*

In the cycle of narratives about Amáru and Kuwái, Wakuénai storytellers describe the coming-into-being of a differentiated world of male and female human beings, mythic ancestors, and animal nature from an earlier space-time of animal-humans living at the Center of the World in Hípana. The central characters of the narrative cycle are Iñápirríkuli, the trickster-creator; Amáru, the first woman; and Kuwái, the son of Iñápirríkuli and Amáru. The cycle consists of two distinct parts, a first creation in which Kuwái's humming and singing names-into-being the species and objects of nature, and a second creation in which Iñápirríkuli and Amáru compete for control over sacred flutes and trumpets.

Part I

Amáru became pregnant after having incestuous sexual relations with Iñápirríkuli but was unable to give birth because she had no birth canal. Iñápirríkuli called upon animal-intermediaries to open up a passageway that allowed Kuwái to escape. Together with his younger brother, Dzúli, Iñápirríkuli took Kuwái away from Amáru and placed him in a house in the corner of the sky (*líwanápu éenu*). Kuwái grew very rapidly and broke out of his place of confinement. As he flew about the sky, his humming and singing was a powerful sound that opened up the world (*kémakáni hliméetaka hekwápi*) and created all the species of animals, birds, and fish. Four boys (Hérri, the youngest brother of Iñápirríkuli, and three of his nephews) were out in the forest and saw the monstrous, world-opening body of Kuwái. From then on the boys had to fast on drinks made from wild forest fruits and stay in a special hut in the forest.

One day Kuwái flew down to the forest canopy above the boys' roofless shelter and tempted them by dropping *guaco* fruits to the ground. Hérri refused to eat the fruits, but each of the other three boys ate some. Kuwái caused a great rainstorm and transformed himself into a huge rock cave. The three boys who had eaten the forbidden fruits entered the cave, which was really the mouth of Kuwái, and were eaten alive. Only Hérri survived by refusing to enter the cave. Kuwái flew over to the Isana River, where he vomited up the remains of the three boys before returning to his corner of the sky. Iñápirríkuli sent a wasp-person up to lure Kuwái back to the village at Hípana with some coconut palm grubs (*mútsi*). Intoxicated with the smell and taste of these grubs, Kuwái revealed the secret of his life-giving powers in a mythic dialogue with Kálimátu, the messenger. When Iñápirríkuli learned this secret, he prepared a large bonfire on the village plaza and ordered his brothers to harvest wild fruits to make palm liquors.

Kuwái appeared in the sky above the village in the form of the jaguar-ancestors and came down to the village at Hípana. He led the men inside and began to sing and chant so that Hérri, the first initiate, could end his ritual fast. Iñápirríkuli failed to learn the songs and chants because he was too busy doling out liquor to other men in the village. Only Dzúli, the first chant-owner (*málikái limínali*), had the patience to sit through the entire night and memorize all of Kuwái's songs and chants. Between chants, Kuwái and Iñápirríkuli led the other men in singing *kápetiápani* ("whip-dance") around the bonfire. After concluding the last song of initiation, Kuwái went outside to dance *kápetiápani*, and Iñápirríkuli pushed him into the bonfire. As Kuwái's body burned, the newly created world contracted back to its original, miniature size. Dzúli whipped Hérri across the back and ordered him to eat the sacred food (*káridzámai*).

Part I of the Kuwái myth cycle is about the creation of a uniquely human social order in which people define their humanness through ritual fasting and seclusion, immortalizing the life-giving principle of Kuwái's powers by learning to perform sacred chants and songs, and eating the sacred food of the ancestors. The first creation of the world unfolds primarily along the vertical dimension. Initially, Kuwái is removed to a place that is "above" and outside the social space of the village at Hípana, and he creates the species of animal nature by musically naming them from the skies "above" the forests and rivers. The remaining myths of Part I are concerned with reversing Kuwái's initial

movement up and outside into a final movement down and inside the social space at Hípana. The return of Kuwái down to the ground at Hípana is not a simple, direct movement from up in the sky to down on the ground but a more complex series of movements. Kuwái's first return to the ground is only half-finished, since he returns to the forest outside the village and remains in the intermediate vertical zone of the forest canopy.

The mythic process of reversing Kuwái's initial movement is paralleled by the reversal of physiological processes. Initially, Kuwái is stuck inside Amáru's womb and escapes to life in the external world through the intervention of his father and father's brothers. This initial motion from inside to outside the body is gradually transformed into the reverse process, or the passage of food from outside to inside the body. Again, the halfway point comes when Kuwái eats and vomits the three boys who prematurely end their fast by eating the *guaco* fruits. The processes of movement of bodies and foods across the boundaries of the human body are juxtaposed in a single mythic episode. In the next section of the myth, Kuwái's eating of *mútsi* grubs foreshadows the eventual movement of Kuwái's musical naming power into the social space of human beings on the ground in Hípana and the movement of sacred food into the body of the first initiate.

As previously pointed out, the vertical dimension of space-time is a metaphor for generational time, or the relations between mythic ancestors and their descendants, and also for developmental time, or the individual's passage from stage to stage in the life cycle. At the same time, the vertical relations between elders, adult men, and children are transformed into a ritual hierarchy of specialists, or chant-owners, who control the life-giving powers of Kuwái and mediate the relations between jaguar-ancestors and children undergoing the passage to adulthood.

Part II

Iñápirríkuli returned to the site of Kuwái's fiery death and found that an enormous *macanilla* palm had grown from Kuwái's ashes. He knocked the palm tree down with a long stick, and the wood fell into a pile of short, hollow logs. Iñápirríkuli blew through them and found that they made the sounds of all the different species of forest animals, birds, and fish. He also made the enormous jaguar-bone *(dzáwinápa)* trumpets of male initiation by lashing bark from the *yébaro* tree around a small trumpet called *molítu* (a species of small frog). Amáru and the women stole the flutes and trumpets of Kuwái from Iñápirríkuli and the world opened up for a second time as Amáru and the women ran away from Iñápirríkuli and played Kuwái's instruments in various places along the Isana, Vaupés, and Guainía rivers. Whenever Iñápirríkuli caught up with Amáru, she escaped with Kuwái's flutes and trumpets through an underground passage that led back to her home at Mútsipáni ("Coconut palm grub-dance") on the Aiarí River.

To put a stop to this, Iñápirríkuli organized all the men at Hípana into a group, disguised as *molítu* frogs, and confronted Amáru at Mútsipáni. Iñápirríkuli knocked Amáru and the women unconscious with a bolt of lightning, and the *molítu*-men rushed in to take Kuwái's flutes and trumpets back to Hípana. Iñápirríkuli woke up Amáru and the women by blowing tobacco smoke over them, and he told them that Kuwái's instruments had turned into animals, birds, and fish. Amáru did not believe Iñápirríkuli's explanation, so he invited her to attend a *kwépani* ceremony at Hípana. At the ceremony, Amáru and the women remained inside a special house while the men danced and played Kuwái's flutes outside. The men fastened small patches of fur, feathers, and fish-skin onto the ends of a stick and pushed them inside the house to convince Amáru that Kuwái's instruments had indeed turned into animals. Finally, Iñápirríkuli showed the men how to make the jaguar-bone trumpets for male initiation before going to live in the celestial paradise of the ancestors. Amáru left this world to live in the eastern sky, and Kuwái returned to his corner of the sky.

In the second part of the myth cycle, the world created in Part I is turned upside-down and inside-out. The initial movement of Kuwái, who now takes the form of a palm tree, is a falling down to the ground, a downward movement which is reversed by Kuwái's movement back up into the sky. Also, the focus in Part I on bodily processes of eating, fasting, and vomiting gives way in Part II to a concern for social processes of inclusion and exclusion among groups of people. The ambivalent status of women in a patrilineal, patrilocal social world generates the second, horizontal creation of the world. Amáru and the women can take control of Kuwái's life-giving powers only if they go across the world from the center at Hípana to other places far downstream. In essence, the second creation is a metaphor for the

opening up, or dispersal, of a single, hierarchically ordered patrilineal family, into a collective order consisting of "we people here" and a plurality of "those other peoples there" with whom "we" have relations of trade and intermarriage. Whereas Part I of the myth cycle describes the transformations leading to a vertically differentiated cosmos of generations and developmental stages, Part II is about the creation of social others through the opening up of a horizontally differentiated world of historically developing political relations among a number of distinct peoples. In doing so, Part II of the narrative cycle also resolves the problem of incestuous sexual relations that set the entire cycle in motion at the beginning of Part I.

In the final stage of the myth cycle, Iñápirríkuli invents the first *kwépani* ceremony as a way of convincing Amáru and the women that Kuwái's flutes and trumpets have turned into animals, birds, and fish. Although the myth portrays this event as a simple confrontation or polarity between men and women, the underlying social process is actually more complex. At one level, *kwépani* is a process of socializing the biological procreativity of individual women into the collective reproduction of society through exchanges of blood female kin for wives between groups of men. Like Amáru, the primordial human female of myth, each individual woman is guaranteed a significant role in reproducing society by virtue of her ability to give birth to new life. As individuals, however, men have no such capacity, yet they can take symbolic control over social reproduction through forming groups which agree upon principles of mythic descent and exogamous marital relations. At this level, *kwépani* is a process of socializing female procreativity into collective exchanges between groups of men. At another level, *kwépani* embodies an opposing process in which groups of men can only obtain control over reproduction through assuming non-human, animal identities. The simultaneous gaining of wives through the loss of female blood-relations is symbolically expressed in *kwépani* by a paradox: the power to control Kuwái's flutes and trumpets that men gain through forming into groups is offset by their loss of human identities. This simultaneous gain/loss of blood-kin in marriage is symbolically expressed in the first *kwépani* as a loss of men's identities as individual human beings. Through collectively desocializing themselves vis-à-vis their wives and female kin, male flute players in *kwépani* dance out their alienated selves and become other peoples' "others." Only after this collective act of negation can their identities as full human beings—or descendants of the mythic ancestors—be restored through Iñápirríkuli's gift of the jaguar-bone trumpets for male initiation.

Kwépani: social gestures and performance

Kwépani ceremonies are social gatherings at which two local groups play the sacred flutes and trumpets of Kuwái over an offering of wild fruits. The owner of *kwépani (kwépanímnali)* is the male leader of the guest group bringing a ceremonial offering of wild fruits. Members of affinal groups are also invited to participate in *kwépani* but are not required to bring an offering of wild fruits.

The polarity between men and women is a constant feature of *kwépani*, beginning with the exclusively adult male activity of harvesting wild fruits. The owner of *kwépani* organizes the collection of wild fruits and the making of sacred flutes and trumpets from *macanilla* palms. Upon returning to the village, the men cover the instruments with palm leaves so that women and children cannot see them. The women and children depart for the hosts' village in separate canoes, ahead of the adult men, whose canoes bear the offering of wild fruits and the sacred flutes and trumpets. Women and children arrive in the hosts' village around four in the afternoon, and they quickly go inside a special house set aside for all women and children. The owner of *kwépani* and his male kin play the sacred *wáliáduwa* flutes of Kuwái as they approach the hosts' village. As they enter the village, the guest men dance in a procession with the leaders playing *wáliáduwa* flutes. Younger men carry the offering of fruits up onto the village plaza and pile it in front of the host men. The three *wáliáduwa* flute players are followed by men bearing the two *máariawa* flutes, the *molítu* flute, and a variety of other flutes and trumpets named after animal and bird species. From time to time, the *molítu* flute is sounded during the opening dance of *kwépani*.

As the guest men play *wáliáduwa* flutes and dance around the pile of wild fruits, the host men stand in a line, shoulder to shoulder. The principal costume of the men is a crown of palm leaves with a bundle of wild fruits tied on and hanging down their backs. In addition, long strands of sweet-smelling *tsipátsi* grass are tucked into the headdresses of palm leaves and hang down over the men's shoulders. The host

headman (*pantímnali*, or "house-owner") and the owner of *kwépani* distinguish themselves by wearing special capes made from small pieces of animal fur patched together.

The music of *wáliáduwa* flutes, a set piece that is invariably played at the beginning of the *kwépani*, provides the main theme of opening dances. *Wáliáduwa* is the only type of wind instrument in *kwépani* that is not named after a forest animal or bird species. *Wáli-* is a prefix meaning "new" or "newly," and *-áduwa* is an adjectival suffix widely used in sacred *málikái* chants and songs to make up spirit-names of natural species and objects. The prefix *wáli-* is used in the terms for individuals who have undergone a change in social status: *wálikáni-rú*, the newborn infant; *wálimerú*, the newly initiated girl; or *wáli'táki*, the newly fasted (initiate). When asked about the meaning of the term *wáliáduwa*, informants explained that the three flutes are the outer three fingers of the hand of Kuwái. They also associate the term *wáliáduwa* with old women. This paradoxical juxtaposition of opposing meanings is a key to understanding ceremonial activities in *kwépani*. *Wáliáduwa* literally means "new-like" and yet carries implicit meanings that associate it with elderly women and the hand of Kuwái because *wáliáduwa* performances in *kwépani* are a process of renewing the social order in which all adult men, past the age of initiation, collectively give and receive lashings with dance-whips (*kapéti*) and form the body of Kuwái.

While the host men watch, the guest men dancing immediately behind the *wáliáduwa* flute players lash them with *kapéti* whips. The loud sounds of whips striking the backs of *wáliáduwa* flute players punctuate the mournful sounding melody that the men play (Recorded Ex. 1). Immediately following this opening dance, the host men play the same *wáliáduwa* melody as the guest men watch. The whips are temporarily put aside and men play duets on flutes and trumpets named after various animal and bird species, such as *dápa* (paca, a large rodent) and *dzáate* (toucan).

Shortly before sunset, the men pick up *kapéti* whips and begin to sing *kápetiápani*, or whip-dance. The dancers pound the handles of their whips on the ground in unison with each other and with the stomping of the right foot on the ground. After circling a few times around the pile of wild fruits, the column of male singer-dancers circles around the women's house and gradually penetrates to the inside. At this early stage of the ceremony, the women remain respectfully silent as they join the men as dance partners in *kápetiápani*.

During this performance, two men remove the sacred flutes and trumpets of Kuwái from the dancing ground to a port at the river's edge designated as off limits to women and children. The sets of instruments belonging to hosts and guests are deliberately mixed up in a single heap so that in later dances there is no distinction between instruments made by the host and guest men. As the *kápetiápani* performance comes to an end, the owner of *kwépani* leads the column of male and female dancers out of the women's house, and the hosts' headman announces that women can go to bathe and fetch water from the river. The two leaders stand facing one another across the displayed pile of wild fruits and make formal speeches of offering and acceptance. The fruits are then taken inside the hosts' house, and a period of drinking fermented manioc beverages and juices made from the wild fruits lasts until shortly before midnight. Women and children are sent back into seclusion, and the men go down to the river to bring out the sacred flutes and trumpets of Kuwái for a second time. Standing near the door of the house, *molítu* flute players carry on playful dialogues with the women inside. The women ask the *molítu* player who its "owner" is, and the man playing the flute must not answer with his own name but with another man's name. The *molítu* flute is a short, thick piece of *macanilla* palmwood that produces only a single tone. By holding one hand over the opening of the flute opposite the mouthpiece, a man can produce semi-distinct "words," or stress patterns that resemble words. Once the *molítu* player has passed the test of disguising his identity from the women, he transforms into a sort of musical oracle to which pregnant women can address the question of whether their unborn children will turn out to be male or female.

At midnight, the men perform a second *wáliáduwa* dance and whipping ceremony. The melody of this late-night performance is somewhat more cheerful than the solemn music of the opening *wáliáduwa* dances. The period from midnight until shortly before dawn is a joyous celebration filled with dancing, singing, and drinking. Using their special form of speech, the *molítu* flute players "ask" women for fermented drinks until all the men have become inebriated. Inside the house, women consume large quantities of beer and add to the general atmosphere of euphoria by singing and joking.

The night of festivities reaches a climax when the men begin to sing *kápetiápani* for a second time and enter the house to dance with the women (Recorded Ex. 2). When the men's voices are first heard, the women pause briefly from their boisterous talking and singing. Once the line of male singer-dancers has entered the house, however, the women accompany the *kápetiápani* song with their own personal songs (*pákamarántakan*). One of the senior women stands in the middle of the dance-circle and makes long, high-pitched shrieks that can be heard above the din of male and female singers, ecstatic conversations, laughter, and the low thumping of whip handles and feet against the ground. In the background, some men begin to play a low, throbbing bass ostinato on *dápa* trumpets outside the house, and a *molítu* player lets out an occasional shrill blast on his flute. This moment is the musical, social climax of *kwépani*.

In the very early morning, just as the eastern horizon starts to grow light, the joyous atmosphere of the night of drinking and musical performances is brought to an abrupt halt. Men, women, and children fall silent as two *máariawa* flute players perform *tsépani*, the final dances of Kuwái (Recorded Ex. 3). *Tsépani* commemorates the mythic episode in which Kuwái ate the three nephews of Iñápirríkuli who had broken their fast by eating *guaco* fruits. In a second performance, the two *máariawa* flute players are joined by three *wáliáduwa* flute players, who perform the same melody that they had played in the opening dances of *kwépani* (Recorded Ex. 4). Finally, the men send Kuwái back to the forests and rivers away from the village by playing the *wáliáduwa* and *molítu* flutes as they embark in a canoe. The *kwépani* ceremony ends with the sounds of Kuwái's flutes fading into the distance and the voices of birds and people beginning a new day (Recorded Ex. 5).

Interpreting *kwépani*

The *kwépani* ceremony contains a wealth of symbolism that reenacts basic metaphors and patterns of relations established in narratives about Kuwái's transformations of human society and the cosmos through music. The entire ceremonial process builds up to *tsépani*, a solemn evocation of the fate of Máarináriéni and the other two boys who were eaten alive by the mythic Kuwái. *Tsépani* places *kwépani* firmly into the vertical dimension of mythic creation by evoking the moment when Kuwái's singing-into-being of upper and lower worlds was exactly halfway finished. *Kwépani* is thus an episodic construction of the vertical axis of generational relations between ancestor spirits and their human descendants through collectively negating the horizontal relations of exchange between different peoples. Not so much an exchange of wild fruits between groups of men, *kwépani* is a vertical exchange of wild fruits, male pain, and male loss of individual identity to mythic jaguar-ancestors in return for a rejuvenation of the social order. It does assert that adult males are ultimately able to bring about and control the collective renewal of society through loss of identity and symbolic death.

The specific symbolism of instruments, dances, and other activities embodies a basic underlying ambiguity or paradox between the life-giving and life-taking powers of Kuwái and the mythic ancestors. The ambiguous association of *wáliáduwa* flutes with both newness and old age hints at this larger ambiguity between life and death, or gain and loss. By playing flutes and trumpets that simultaneously represent parts of Kuwái's mythic body and natural animal species, male dancers paradoxically bring Kuwái and his musical creation of the cosmos to life through acting out the collective loss of male life in *tsépani*. The *molítu* flute performances are perhaps the clearest expression of this gaining and losing of power in the vertical dimension of space-time. In both myth and ceremony, the *molítu* frog symbolizes the adult men's collective acquisition of Kuwái's powers from women. This power is openly exhibited in *molítu* flute performances when women ask male flute players to tell them the sex of their unborn children, an expression of collective male control over women's fertility and reproductive powers. However, in taking control over Kuwái from the women, the men must undergo a process of loss of their identities as individual human beings (i.e., transformation into animals). *Wáliáduwa* flutes, *molítu* flutes, and the enactment of collective male death in *tsépani* are ways of transforming the ambiguous gain and loss of female lives in horizontal relations of exchange into the simultaneous gain and loss of male lives in vertical relations between ancestors and their descendants.

The symbolic significance of wild fruits as a form of sacred food is supported by various details of mythic discourse and ceremonial activity. Wild palm fruits are literally the highest species of edible food, the ones most vertically removed from the social world of fully adult, human beings on the ground. In *kwépani*, the falling of palm trees and the downward motion of fruits is a metaphor for the passage of generational time, or the collective replacement of a generation of elders by a younger generation of adult men. The palm trees themselves form mediating links that connect the celestial region of Kuwái and the ancestors to the terrestrial world of human beings. The importance of palm trees as a symbol of vertical, generational relations in *kwépani* is also evident in the basic rule that pairs or larger sets of flutes and trumpets must be constructed from continuous pieces of a single felled trunk of *macanilla* palm. By implication, ensembles of male flute players in *kwépani* reunite the cut pieces of palmwood into a single entity, or an image of the body of Kuwái, prior to being cut down and made into musical instruments.

The costumes of male musician-dancers in *kwépani* add another layer of meaning to the symbolism of palm trees. Aside from the two ceremonial leaders, the men wear crowns of palm leaves and hang bunches of wild palm fruits down their backs. In a sense, the men become palm trees in *kwépani*, since by donning palm leaves and fruits they transform their bodies into "trunks" that connect upper and lower regions of body, society, and cosmos. By ceremonially whipping each other's bodies, the men evoke the mythic act of chopping down the tree of Kuwái. At the same time, they complete the circle of symbolic connections between musical instruments and the mythic body of Kuwái by making their bodies into living drums, the striking of which forms a percussive sound that evokes the downward motion of felled palm trees. Later, the same whips are used to make a percussive, rhythmic accompaniment to *kápetiápani* songs by banging the whips' handles against the ground. In short, *kápetiápani* completes the palm trees' downward motion, and the ground itself becomes a percussive instrument.

The musical performances making up *kwépani* provide further clues to its interpretation. First, *kwépani* begins and ends with the same solemn trio of *wáliáduwa* flutes. The identity of opening and closing melodies provides a strong sense of continuity to the ceremonial events. In addition, the specific performances of *wáliáduwa*, *molítu*, *dzáate*, and other music are highly repetitive and stable. Like the opening and closing melodies played on *wáliáduwa* flutes, all the intervening performances consist of a simple theme played over and over with only the slightest amount of variation. This lack of change is highly significant, since the underlying purpose of the ceremony is to effect a controlled transition of sacred power from one generation of men to the next.

The musical performances of *kwépani* also have a dynamic, progressive character, insofar as they change from an original emphasis on the exchange of pain (whips) between male musician-dancers, to a concern for the dynamic interplay of male and female singer-dancers, and finally to the evocation of collective male death in *tsépani*. The contrast between highly formalized, unchanging male singing in *kápetiápani* and the spontaneous, emotional outbursts of women's *pákamarántakan* is very important.[3] Women's singing embodies the ambiguity of horizontal exchange relations within a patrilineal society, with the women's spontaneity energizing the men's concern for controlling the vertical descent of power from mythic ancestors to human descendants via the elders. In the more purely male sphere of instrumental music, the performances evince a progressive change from individual to collective evocations of Kuwái's powers. The superimposition of three *wáliáduwa* and two *máariawa* flutes in *tsépani* integrates the five fingers of Kuwái's mythic hand and connects the five segments of Kuwái's complete body, thereby closing the circuit between jaguar-ancestors and human descendants.

Viewed as an isolated entity, the *kwépani* ceremony is a socio-religious process of constructing the vertical, generational dimension of social and cosmic relations. However, the musical performances of *kwépani* become more fully intelligible when compared with musical and other activities of *pudáli*, or ceremonial exchanges of meat for vegetable products between kin groups related by marriage.

PUDÁLI: *CEREMONIAL EXCHANGES BETWEEN AFFINES*

Overview of ceremonial activities

Pudáli is the social mechanism for creating and renewing relations of exchange between "marriageable others" or groups outside the blood-related patrilineal family. It thus represents the horizontal opening up of the family (*náiki*) to include a broader universe of "we people here" and a plurality of "those other

peoples there." In most respects, *pudáli* is a secular ceremonial process in which both men and women play active roles and musical performances are not directly linked to the powerful beings of sacred myth. However, the symbolism of musical instruments and performances in *pudáli* does include a number of allusions to sacred ritual powers, such as the shaman's power to journey back and forth between the world of living peoples (*hekwápiríko*) and *íyarudáti*, the dark netherworld where the souls of recently deceased persons linger for a time before transmigrating to ancestor spirits in the celestial paradise. The symbolic connections between *pudáli*, intermarriage, and shamanistic curing rituals are important for understanding how *pudáli* ceremonial cycles contribute to the broader, musico-poetic view of body, society, and cosmos that is described in the Kuwái myth cycle. The following analysis of *pudáli* explores this higher-level symbolism of shamanistic power as it emerges in the context of a more general process of transforming the initial social opposition between hosts and guests, or kin and affines, into a mythic space-time that overrides categorical differences between blood kin and in-laws, human and non-human beings, and male and female humans.

The performances in *pudáli* encompass an elaborate array of instrumental music, songs, and dances. None of these performances are considered to be sacred, or highly powerful, like the songs and chants known to ritual specialists, or the flute and trumpet music performed in *kwépani*. Perhaps because of its secular, unrestricted character, the *pudáli* genre of *mádzeru* embodies a kind of moral, social power which is equally shared by all adult men and women in Wakuénai society. The dance-music of *pudáli* forms the egalitarian sub-stratum of Wakuénai musical culture, the infrastructural framework of ideas, sounds, and movements within which more restricted genres of instrumental dance-music and the highly restricted genres of *málikái* chants and songs are located and defined from the bottom up. *Pudáli* is a socio-musical process of food exchange that orients Wakuénai society to root paradigms, or " . . . emotionally loaded, ethically impelled metaphors that give form to action in publicly critical circumstances" (Victor Turner 1977: 74). More specifically, the dance-music of *pudáli* outlines a process of collectively constructing the space-time of mythic beginnings. For the Wakuénai, this mythic space-time is described in narratives about the origins

---

3   See Goldman (1979) on the Cubeo mourning ceremony *(oyné)*.

of Iñápirríkuli, the trickster-transformer, and Káali, the originator of bitter manioc and other cultivated plants. Mythic beginnings are outside of the present human social order and prior to the cultural separateness of humans and animals and of male and female humans. The precultural, presexual past of mythical origins is also described in narratives as a period of unceasing, violent acts of treachery between kinsmen (Iñápirríkuli and his brothers) and affines (Kunáhwerrim, the leader of cannibalistic animal-people). The significance of musically evoking the precultural, presexual space-time of myth in *pudáli* ceremonies is rooted in beliefs and attitudes about the potential problems created by social "others," or affines. Indeed, the metaphors employed can be interpreted as an indigenous strategy for coping with dangerous social "otherness" and converting it into social alliance and reciprocal exchange.

The *pudáli* cycle is a perfect example of the horizontal extension of generalized and balanced reciprocal exchange (Sahlins 1972; Laughlin 1974), from their normal ranges within the patrilineal family and phratry outwards to more distant members of the same ethnolinguistic group. Viewed internally, each ceremony provides an arena for the generalized sharing of food and female dance-partners with "other people" (*apána náiki*) who are usually regarded as potentially dangerous competitors for the same resources. Viewed as a whole, the two-part male and female cycle of *pudáli* ceremonies gives active expression to balanced reciprocity through exchange of equivalently valued food surpluses, smoked meat and processed manioc pulp. Balanced exchanges of the products of male and female labor are a symbolic preproduction, in miniature, of the exchanges of male labor for female labor in the institution of bride service. Performances of dance-music are crucial to the success of the symbolic substitution of food for humans in the exchange process, since they provide the symbolic channel for transcending the cultural boundaries between humans and non-humans and between maleness and femaleness. In short, musical evocations of the presexual, precultural space-time of mythic beginnings construct a set of emotionally charged, ethically impelled expressive metaphors for coping with the publicly critical situation of social interaction and intermarriage with potentially dangerous "others."

Pudáli ceremonial cycles celebrate the simultaneous climax of horticultural and fishing activities at the beginning of the long wet season. The male-owned ceremonies open when a local group visits a host group of actual or potential in-laws and formally offers them a gift of smoked fish or game meat. The male owner of *pudáli* leads his kin group and their wives into the hosts' village in a procession of flute-players, trumpet-players, singers, dancers, and food-bearers. Large ceremonial trumpets, named after a species of large, striped catfish (*kulírri* in Wáku, a species of *Brachyplatystoma*), create a deep, rumbling drone that represents, or imitates, the sound of a river full to the brim with spawning, migrating fish. Male trumpet-players and female dancers circle around the heap of smoked fish in dances named after the white, spotted, and red-tailed *Leporinus* fish (*táari, dúme,* and *dúpari,* respectively). In front of the trumpet-players, a pair of *máwi* flute-players and their female dance partners lead the counterclockwise procession, which varies slightly in each of the three *leporinus* dances (Fig. 1). The music of these opening dances consists of a highly standardized *máwi* flute duet, which is the most commonly heard musical performance in the *pudáli*. This *máwi* flute duet can be heard on the accompanying sound component (Recorded Ex. 6).

Other musicians often join in the *leporinus* dances to make the procession larger and more impressive. *Tsikóta* flute-players, *déetu* flute-players, and *píti* whistle-players, attach themselves to the tail end of the *kúlirrína* trumpet-players and play as loudly as possible to be heard over the other, larger instruments. The sound of different instruments, such as the *máwi* and the *déetu* flutes played together (Recorded Ex. 7) is not like a carefully orchestrated ensemble of wind instruments but a heterophonic collage of sounds ranging from the lower melody of the *máwi* flutes to the ear-piercing high notes of the *déetu* flutes. To a Western-trained musician, the overall sound of these opening dances appears cacophonous, yet it is precisely this image of unrestrained, chaotically superimposed voices which creates the auditory point of entry for collectively evoking the space-time of mythical beginnings. The opening dances of *pudáli* transfer to a nonverbal musical level the social meaning of the event: a gathering of male and female voices without the imposition of hierarchical, centralized control. Higher and lower musical voices, female and male dancers, are fully and simultaneously given public expression.

The hosts listen to their guests' music and watch their dances "from a distance" until sunset. Then the owner of *pudáli* and the male house-owner or host headman make formal speeches of offering and

Fig. 1: Men and women playing *máwi* flutes and *kúlirrína* trumpets (Hill 1981). Courtesy of the author.

accepting the gift of smoked fish and game meat, which is taken inside the host's house until the next morning. At night, the hosts offer their guests drinks of manioc beer (*padzáoru*) inside their house and come outside to participate in special *kúlirrína* trumpet-dances around a bonfire. In the morning, the heap of smoked fish and game meat is redistributed to host and guest families alike, setting off a day of feasting and individual dancing in which men of the host village dance with women of the guest village and vice versa. Depending on the supply of food and the sentiments of male and female dancers, male-owned *pudáli* ceremonies can last up to four days and nights in a row. At the end of the opening, male-owned ceremony, the guests offer their *kúlirrína* trumpets, emblazened with designs representing their phratry, to the hosts as reminders of the closing ceremony which is owed to balance their guests' generosity.

In a closing *pudáli* ceremony held several weeks later, a female owner of *pudáli* (*púdalímnaru*) organizes the production of a large quantity of grated, processed manioc pulp as an offering to the guests of the first ceremony. The internal structure of ceremonial events follows the same basic sequence of dancing around the food in large, collective ensembles, drinking and dancing around the fire at night, and individual dancing on the day after food redistribution. However, the formal speeches of offering and accepting the food are made by women, the *púdalímnaru* and *pantímnaru* (female house-owner, or host), respectively, rather than male leaders. Also, the *kúlirrína* trumpet-dances are replaced in female-owned, closing ceremonies by dance stomping tubes (*wáana*) and a series of songs specific to these instruments.

In terms of Wakuénai social organization and the local ecology of the Upper Río Negro region, *pudáli* ceremonial cycles provide an arena for the playing out of respectful give-and-take between intermarried groups at times of an abundance of fish. Through a gradual process of asserting the collective boundary between kin and in-laws ("others"), transforming the boundary through food exchange and drinking, and transcending it through individualized musical dances, *pudáli* ceremonies serve as a cultural means for converting potentially dangerous social otherness into relatively safe social oneness through bride service and intermarriage between patrilineal descent groups. At the same time, *pudáli* ceremonial cycles place these social processes into a naturalized interpretive framework by metaphorically comparing human social reproduction with the reproduction of natural species. One key to this dominant metaphor of *pudáli* is the native term for the activity of dancing in ceremonies. *Lirrapaka*, or "he dances," is the same verb used to refer to the spawning behavior of *leporinus* and other fish species. Thus, *pudáli* ceremonies are in one sense an elaborate, playful courtship activity between potential marriage partners which evokes the natural spawning behavior of fish species as a dominant metaphor.

The internal structure of *pudáli*

Each *pudáli* ceremony, whether male- or female-owned, consists of three distinct stages articulated by the exchange and later redistribution of a large quantity of food. In the first stage, men and women of the guest group enter their hosts' village and perform collective dance-music around an offering of food which is conspicuously displayed on the plaza outside the hosts' houses. During this initial stage, the hosts are strictly forbidden to dance, play music, speak, or directly interact in any other manner with their guests (and vice versa). The formal speeches of offering and accepting the gift of food are the first step in transforming the collective boundary line between hosts and guests (or kin and affines). These speeches include an assurance by the owner of *pudáli* (the guests' ceremonial leader) and the hosts' leaders (*pantímnali* and *pantímnaru*, or male and female house-owners) that no one in their respective groups has brought poison (*mahnéti*) or other harmful substances. Stylistically, a good speech begins with a slow, deliberate rhythm and accelerates gradually until the flow of speech is quite rapid.

After the formal speech of accepting the gift of food from the sponsors of *pudáli*, the hosts' ceremonial leaders take the food inside their house and store it on platforms suspended between the horizontal cross beams. A large bonfire is lit on the dancing plaza outside, and the guests are invited to come inside the house to drink manioc beer and a variety of other mildly alcoholic beverages. Throughout this transitional late-night period men and women sing personal drinking songs, called *pákamarántakan*, in which they ask one another for drinks. These personal songs all make use of the same descending melodic structure, but the song verses are created in a completely spontaneous manner depending on the social situation of the performers and audience. The

emotional tone of *pákamarántakan* songs can range from deepest sorrow over the death of a spouse to the most ribald humor aimed at friends or relatives present in the *pudáli* ceremony. In one *pákamarántakan* song, a woman of the *Waríperídakéna* phratry grieves over the death of her husband and her subsequently marginal status as a widow with two young children to feed. In another song, two elders, a woman and a man of different phratries, make ironic comments about the laziness and poor behavior of young people who are present in the audience and can be heard laughing in the background.

The *pákamarántakan* drinking songs provide a musical channel for individuals to communicate across the social boundary between hosts and guests, or kin and in-laws. The songs are also an occasion for making social commentaries which are generally kept at the level of private gossip rather than public performance. Every adult participant in *pudáli* knows how to perform *pákamarántakan* songs, making them the most generalized and unrestricted genre of vocal music in Wakuénai culture.

At the same time as men and women drink together and sing *pákamarántakan* inside the hosts' house, the guest men surround the outside perimeter of the house in performances on *déetu* flutes, which are named after the coconut palm weevil, a shiny black insect which feeds on sweet sap by sucking with its long proboscis. In performances on *déetu* flutes, the guest men imitate the natural feeding behavior of *déetu* insects by surrounding the hosts' house and playing their flutes up into the space between the thatched roof and the walls of the house (Recorded Ex. 8). In this way the *déetu* flute-players are said to "suck" fermented drinks out of their hosts, who come outside with large quantities of manioc beer. One by one, the flute-players lower their raised instruments and drink until they vomit.

These flute performances mark the beginning of an important transition, a modulation in the social meaning of *pudáli* ceremonies, since for the first time a single type of instrument is played without the accompaniment of *máwi* flutes and other instruments. The collective activities of sucking and regurgitating evoke the transformational powers of shamanistic curing, which revolve around the shamans' attempts to suck disease-causing agents out of their patients' bodies and release these substances after linking them with external, supernatural causes of disease. The *déetu* flute performances of *pudáli* transpose the shamanistic techniques of sucking and vomiting, seen as reversals of basic physiological processes, to a collective level and, in doing so, define *pudáli* as a cultural event which is concerned not only with the social relations between kin and in-laws but also with the symbolic relations between human beings living in this world (*hekwápiríko*) and the spirits of recently deceased persons in the dark netherworld (*íyarudáti*). By implicitly evoking the reversible space-time of shamanistic transformation, the *déetu* flute performances signal the beginning of a collective transition from a secular, social process of food exchange to a mythical process of disintegrating the symbolic boundaries between humans and animals, and between men and women.

In the very early morning (*déepitwawátsa*), just when the first gray light of dawn becomes visible in the eastern sky, the hosts come outside and participate with the guests in special dances around the bonfire. In male-owned, opening ceremonies, the hosts and guests play *kúlirrína* trumpets around the fire without the accompaniment of *máwi* flutes. This dance is named after the resin (*máini*) used to cover the woven resonators of *kúlirrína* trumpets, and the stated purpose of the dance is to cook the *máini* resin. The sound of the *kúlirrína* trumpets played without *máwi* flutes serves as a cadence which brings the transitional late-night period of *pudáli* to a close. At the end of these dances, the guest men give their *kúlirrína* trumpets to the hosts as reminders of their duty to hold a closing, female-owned ceremony several weeks later. The *kúlirrína* trumpets are the only musical instruments exchanged in this manner. The guests and hosts do not exchange *máwi*, *tsikóta*, or *déetu* flutes but keep them stored underwater for use in future ceremonies.

The third stage of *pudáli* begins after the redistribution of food in equal portions to guest and host families alike in the early morning. The social boundary between host and guest, or kin and affine, is now totally dissolved in this daytime period of feasting and dancing. Individual men of the host group dance with individual women of the guest group and vice versa in *máwi* and *tsikóta* flute duets named after various species of fish, forest animals, and birds. Unlike the highly standardized *máwi* and *tsikóta* flute pieces performed in the first stage of *pudáli*, the flute duets of the third stage of *pudáli* allow pairs of male flute-players and female dancers to display their talents as musicians and dancers through improvisation.

In general, female-owned *pudáli* ceremonies have the same three-part structure as the opening, male-owned ceremonies: 1) large, standardized ensembles of *máwi* flute-players and other instruments prior to the offering of a food-gift; 2) drinking songs, *déetu* flute-dances, and performances around a bonfire in the transitional late-night period; and 3) improvisatory, individualized flute duets during the daytime period of feasting after the food-gift has been redistributed. The principal difference between female-owned and male-owned *pudáli* ceremonies is that in the former a series of dance-songs, called *wáanapáni*, takes the place of *kúlirrína* trumpet dances. The rhythmical, percussive sound of dance stomping tubes (*wáana*) which accompanies these song-dances is the source of the sub-genre's name, *wáanapáni* ("stomping tube dances"). These songs all have a single melody, but there are significant variations in the song texts and dance formations during the course of ceremonial events. In the opening song, the guests sing as a large group in unison as they circle around the food-gift of processed manioc pulp on the village plaza. Their voices are heard together with *máwi* flutes and other instruments. In the transitional late-night period of *pudáli*, the guests and hosts form separate lines of dancers and perform *dzúdzuápani* ("wheel dance"), in which a miniature, circular fish-net (*dzúdzumáka*) is suspended over the bonfire between two poles carried by the lead singers of the hosts and guests. After the opening lines of the song, the lead singers and their female dance-partners split off from the two columns of response singers and begin to circle the fire. They move rapidly and change their direction frequently, so that the fish-net in the middle often dips down into the upper flames of the bonfire. The two pairs of singer-dancers have to whirl around at exactly the same moment to prevent letting too much slack into the lines holding the fish net, which could fall into the fire and burn. During these maneuvers, the response singers remain stationary in two opposing lines (hosts and guests), marking time with their *wáana* stomping tubes. When the lead singers reach the verse "we open the jaguar's mouth" (*níni námaru liákanínu yáwinúma*), the two lines of response-singers dance backwards, away from one another, until they are several steps apart. A few verses later, the lead singers call for the reverse of this movement: "I want to close the jaguar's mouth" (*nínika númaka tárumi liákani yáwinúma*). Then the two columns of response singers and female dancers move back together until they have closed up the space that separated them (Recorded Ex. 9).

The *dzúdzuápani* song-dances bring an end to the transitional, late-night period of female-owned *pudáli* ceremonies just as the playing of *kúlirrína* trumpets "to cook the *máini* resin" brings an end to the late-night period of male-owned *pudáli* ceremonies. Beyond this analogy between the timing of *dzúdzuápani* and *kúlirrína* trumpet dances of the late-night period, there are important symbolic connections between the material construction of the miniature fish-net used in *dzúdzuápani* and that of *kúlirrína* trumpets. The small, wheel-shaped fish-nets of *dzúdzuápani* are made from *dzámakuápi*, a species of vine that also is used to make a wheel that connects the mouthpieces of *kúlirrína* trumpets to their large, woven, and resin-covered resonators. *Kúlirrína* trumpets are generally not considered to be sacred instruments and women are allowed to watch men making them, except for the moment when the wheel of *dzámakuápi* vine is inserted into the trumpets' resonators to connect the short tubes of *máwi* palm which serve as mouthpieces. At this moment in the trumpets' construction, when they are being closed up, women of childbearing age are told to leave the vicinity so that they will not die when giving birth in the future. The men claim that a woman's unborn child would become stuck inside the womb if she were to observe the closing up of the *kúlirrína* trumpets. Thus, the wheel of *dzámakuápi* which remains hidden inside the *kúlirrína* trumpets during male-owned ceremonies becomes the center of open, public display in the *dzúdzuápani* "wheel-dances" of female-owned ceremonies.

Viewed as a whole, the three stages of *pudáli* outline a process of establishing, transforming, and dissolving the social boundary between hosts and guests, or kin and affines. This three-stage process is expressed through a number of symbolic mediums. First, in terms of musical dancers, both male- and female-owned ceremonies begin by asserting the boundary between groups of kin and affines by prohibiting members of the two groups to dance together while the food-offering is still displayed outside on the village plaza. The boundary between male and female dancers is transformed during the *kúlirrína* and *dzúdzuápani* dances of the late-night period by allowing groups of hosts and guests to dance, sing, and play music together. Finally, the individualized, improvisatory flute duets of the period of daytime feasting express a complete transcendence of the boundary between hosts and guests. Individual men of the host group are allowed to dance with individual women of the guest group and vice versa.

A similar process is expressed through food symbolism. During the first stage, the food offering is heaped up and displayed outside during the first part of the ceremony. After the food-gift has been accepted and taken inside by the hosts, the guest men and women are likewise invited to enter their hosts' house for drinking and singing. Finally, the food is redistributed in a manner that parallels the breaking down of clearly defined host and guest groups in the individualized performances of the third stage of *pudáli*.

In terms of distribution of instruments, *pudáli* begins as a series of dances in which different types of instruments are played together and later, in the late-night period, transforms into dances in which only one type of instrument is played (e.g., *kúlirrína* trumpets or *wáana* stomping tubes). Sounds outline a parallel process in which a standard, relatively fixed *máwi* flute piece with no changes in phrase length and only minor tonal variations is eventually transformed into highly improvisatory flute duets named after animal species. On the day of feasting after the redistribution of the *pudáli* food-offering, guest men take host women as their dance partners (and vice versa) in *máwi* and *tsikóta* flute duets named after animal, fish, and bird species. Unlike the highly standardized flute duets of the opening stage of *pudáli*, the duets played during the day of feasting are improvisatory and make use of the principle of theme and variation. Each piece begins with a simple melodic theme made up of six notes played in an interlocking manner, alternating the longer, "male," and shorter, "female" flutes. The accompanying CDs include an example of these duets, the *dzawírra* (a fish), played on *máwi* flutes (Recorded Ex. 10). The improvisatory variations on themes are carried out in two ways: 1) expanding and shortening the length of phrases; and 2) changing the pitches used within each phrase. Because of this flexible approach, no two performances of a flute duet are exactly the same. Thus, the third stage of *pudáli* serves as a social context for allowing individual men to display their individuality as musician-dancers.

Déetu: the collective evocation of shamanistic power

Pudáli ceremonies evoke the mythic space-time of the closed, precultural world of the trickster-creator and his animal enemies. The origins of *pudáli* are explained in a narrative about this remote mythic past of Iñápirríkuli. Káali, a younger brother of Iñápirríkuli and the originator of manioc and all other cultivated plant species, taught his children (Káaliéni) how to sing *pákamarántakan* and play the dance-music of *pudáli* so that they would know how to properly ask other people for food and drink. At the same time, the symbolism of musical and verbal performances in *pudáli* also alludes to the transformational space-time of Kuwái's second, horizontal creation of the world (the opening up of the world as Amáru and the women played the flutes and trumpets of Kuwái in various places). An allusion to the process of sacred mythic creation comes in the *dzúdzuápani* or "wheel-dance" songs performed at the end of the transitional late-night period in female-owned *pudáli* ceremonies. "We open the jaguar's mouth" subtly refers to the collective process of opening the social boundaries between kin groups that define themselves internally as descendants of the jaguar-ancestors. The *dzúdzuápani* performance also embodies the principle of mutual interdependence between kin and in-law, since guests and hosts form two separate lines of dancers, each forming a "jaw" of the jaguar-ancestor. The two columns of dancers move back together in order "to close the jaguar's mouth," implying that there must be coordination and unity between guests and hosts in order for the "jaguar" to eat, and thus to survive. Immediately after *dzúdzuápani*, the offering of food is redistributed, and guests and hosts join in a day of feasting, drinking, playing music, and dancing together without the restrictions on guest-host interactions that characterized earlier stages of *pudáli*.

In a more general sense, the musical performances of *pudáli* implicitly evoke the two sacred creations of the Kuwái myth cycle through a concern for food and eating as metaphors for the processes of internalization and externalization. The mythic, life-threatening situation of Kuwái at birth, who was stuck inside the womb of Amáru, is evoked during the men's construction of *kúlirrína* trumpets by the requirement that adult women must not be present at the time of the instrument's closing out of fear that their unborn children will become stuck inside their wombs. At the same time, *kúlirrína* trumpets connect this implicit, sacred meaning to the secular social process of exchange between kin and affine, since the guests present the instruments to their hosts at the end of the late-night period of singing and drinking. Both the implicit, sacred meaning of the trumpets and their value as tokens of exchange are engulfed in the symbolism of the natural process of fish-spawning runs. Through such multivocality, dances and

instruments in *pudáli* collapse metaphorical comparisons between self and other, male and female, and human and non-human into part-to-whole relations between people and food, or eating and reproducing, all elements of the ambiguous totality of sacred, mythic processes of creation.

Pudáli is also connected to sacred, ritual powers through the belief that *lidánam* spirits of the dead spend their time in *íyarudáti* drinking and performing the musical dances of *pudáli*. Shamans enter into hallucinogenic trances in order to travel to the houses of the dead in *íyarudáti* so that they can bring back the lost souls of sick individuals. The mythic prototype of shamanistic journeying is Amáru's undergound escape from Iñápirríkuli from places far downstream back to her home at Mútsipáni near the center of the world at Hípana. Amáru's mythic reversal of the transformation of "we people here" into "those other peoples there" established the reversibility of the horizontal dimension of Kuwái's mythic creation. In like manner, shamanistic curing rituals aim at reversing the process of soul-loss in patients whose human body-shaped souls (*likáriwa*) have traveled to *íyarudáti*, the place where the sun falls on the western horizon.

The imagery of shamanistic power does not erupt all at once in *pudáli* but emerges in subtle, musical and verbal styles of expression in the first stage of ceremonial activity. First, the heterophonic collage of instrumental melodies and sounds in large collective dances around the food offering is similar to the superimposition of melodic voices that are not rhythmically synchronized with one another in shaman's songs (*málirríkairi*). For shamans, these sounds are a musical bridge for crossing over into the space-time of the spirits of the dead in *íyarudáti*. In *pudáli*, the use of heterophony serves as a collective point of entry into the space-time of mythic beginnings. A second example of allusions to shamanistic power is the use of acceleration, gradual rising of pitch, and increasing volume in the formal speeches of offering the food gift. These stylistic devices are consistently employed in shamanistic singing and give a musical shape to the idea of movements through space-time (Hill 1983).

Heterophony and the musical cadence of ceremonial speech in the early stages of *pudáli* lead up to the more overtly shamanistic symbolism of *déetu* flute performances that evoke shamanistic power through the guests' activities of "sucking" and regurgitating gifts of fermented drinks from their hosts. When we follow this metaphorical relation between shamanistic curing and ceremonial flute performances to its implicit conclusion, it leads to an interpretation of the ceremonial house, filled with drinking, singing men and women, as a sort of collective body which must be collectively shamanized (sucked) by the guest men. In this sense the *déetu* flute performances are collective evocations of shamanistic power that transform *pudáli* from a potentially dangerous encounter with "others" into a relatively secure environment for the exchange of foods, instruments, and musician-dancers between affinal groups.

The organization of pitches in *déetu* flute performances adds to the sense of reversible space-time embodied in the activities of sucking and vomiting. As can be seen in Example 1, the music of *déetu* flutes remains stable, lacking change in melodic shape and phrasing. Unlike the *máwi* flute duets, which consist of melodic units with clearly defined phrasing, the *déetu* flute music consists entirely of a simple, rhythmical alternation between higher notes of short duration and lower notes of longer duration. The musical effect of these sustained, lower notes coming at very regular intervals creates a feeling of circular, repetitive movement.

Like the *kúlirrína* trumpets, the *déetu* flutes refer multivocally to both human gender attributes and the reproductive behavior of non-human species. The *kúlirrína* trumpets do so through the sounds which they produce, said to represent the sound of a stream full of spawning *leporinus* fish, and through the sexual meanings attributed to their material construction. The *déetu* flutes establish the same metaphorical comparison between human sexuality and the reproductive behavior of non-human species but in a very different manner. Because the flutes are all the same length, they refer to neither male nor female gender. At the same time, performances on *déetu* flutes in the late-night period of *pudáli* represent the natural eating, or sucking, behavior of *déetu* insects. These shiny black weevils are attracted to the smell of sap oozing from palm trees. As they feed on the sap, they deposit tiny larvae into the pith of the felled tree. After a few weeks, these larvae turn into large, oily white grubs (*mútsi*) which the Wakuénai harvest, roast in a fire, and savor as a delicacy. In *pudáli*, the imitation of the feeding, or sucking, behavior of adult *déetu* insects is a powerful expression of the idea of a non-sexual form of reproduction. Indeed, the life

cycle of *déetu* weevils as a cyclical process of metamorphosis constitutes an image of spontaneous self-reproduction. The *déetu* insect metonymically collapses the metaphorical relation between eating and reproducing, for it deposits its larvae, or reproduces itself, in the same place and at the same time as it feeds itself through sucking the sap of damaged or felled palm trees. Thus, the *déetu* performances are highly condensed symbolic activities which simultaneously frame a natural process of non-sexual, self-reproduction and a mythical process of collectively constructing a reversible, shamanistic space-time.

The metamorphosis of the coconut palm grub (*mútsi*)

Kwépani and *pudáli* are in many respects opposite processes of ceremonial exchange. *Kwépani*, or the dance of Kuwái, is a collective construction of the vertical, generational dimension of time between mythic jaguar-ancestors and their human descendants, enabling one generation of adult men to replace another in the hierarchy of ritual power within the local patrilineal kin group. *Pudáli*, on the other hand, is the opening and closing of horizontal relations of exchange between distinct, mythically defined kin groups, allowing potentially dangerous affinal "others" to become "one of us" (and vice versa) through acts of giving, eating, drinking, singing, dancing, and playing music together.

This contrast between *kwépani* and *pudáli* is concretely expressed in different ways of constructing musical instruments in the two ceremonies. In *kwépani*, each pair or set of instruments must be constructed out of a single, continuous section of hollowed-out *macanilla* wood. The three *wáliáduwa* flutes, associated with the three outer fingers of Kuwái, for example, are always made from the trunk of a single felled palm tree, and the men must avoid cutting away any of the wood between each of the three logs. A clean cut must be made in between each log so that the mouthpiece of the longer and thicker, female flute is identical in circumference to the lower end of the shorter and thinner, male flute. In opposition to this practice, each individual *máwi*, *tsikóta*, *déetu*, or other flute used in *pudáli* is cut from the trunk of a separate *máwi* palm tree. Thus, the manner of constructing flutes in *kwépani* calls attention to the vertical, continuous growth of palm trees, whereas the cutting of separate palms for each flute used in *pudáli* expresses the importance of discontinuous, horizontally separate plant growth.

The basic principles for attributing gender or sexual meaning to the musical instruments of *kwépani* and *pudáli* are diametrically opposed. The *wáliáduwa* and *máariawa* flutes used in *kwépani* ceremonies are classified as either "male" or "female" depending on their relative length and thickness (Fig. 2). Longer, thicker flutes (those made from the base of a felled palm) are called "female" (*ínarruátsa*), whereas shorter, thinner flutes are called "male" (*átsiátsa*). This application of gender to musical instruments makes perfect sense in the context of the more general associations in *kwépani* that link maleness to vertical height above the ground and contact with celestial mythic ancestors. The only exception to this principle is the *molítu* flute, a short, thick instrument made in only one size and strongly linked to concepts of male sexuality. In *pudáli* ceremonies, flutes are classified according to exactly the opposite rule: longer, thicker flutes are called "male," whereas the shorter, thinner flutes of each pair are called "female." This opposition between rules for attributing gender to musical instruments in *kwépani* and *pudáli* reflects the broader opposition between gender relations in the two ceremonial contexts. *Kwépani* presupposes the polarity of male and female genders from beginning to end, whereas *pudáli* starts from the principle of gender reciprocity and works steadily toward representations of presexuality, or a mythic state of unity between maleness and femaleness that preceded the eruption of gender differences in the mythic space-times of Kuwái and Amáru.

The only exceptions to the rule of gender attribution in *pudáli* are instruments that are made in only one size and played in sets of three or more, such as the *kúlirrína* trumpets and *déetu* flutes. The *kúlirrína* trumpets, as we have seen, have their own unique gender meanings that associate them with the birth of Kuwái and the concept of ambisexuality, or maleness and femaleness

in one being (Fig. 3). *Déetu* flutes are regarded as nonsexual entities, since they come in only one size and refer to an asexual process of natural reproduction through egg laying and metamorphosis.

Kwépani and *pudáli* also embody opposing processes of loss of individual identity and individualization, respectively. In *kwépani*, the individual musician's identity is either disguised (as in *molítu* flute performances) or submerged into an ensemble of men who collectively bring together the parts of Kuwái's mythic body. *Kwépani* culminates in the superimposition of three *wáliáduwa* and two *máariawa* flute players in *tsépani*, a symbolic uniting of the five fingers of Kuwái. *Pudáli*, on the other hand, proceeds in the opposite direction, from large, collective ensembles of musician-dancers playing a variety of different instruments to small, individualized performances with only one kind of instrument.

In terms of pitch variation, *kwépani* ceremonies allow for little or no improvisation of melodies and rhythms by individual musicians. In addition, the changes produced at different stages of *kwépani* are stabilized by the playing of identical *wáliáduwa* flute melodies at the beginning and end of the ceremony. *Pudáli* outlines the opposite process of moving from relatively unchanging melodies in the beginning to improvised, dynamic melodic and rhythmical variations at the end.

The symbolic oppositions between *kwépani* and *pudáli* include other dimensions of the two ceremonial contexts. However, the examples given above are sufficient to demonstrate that *kwépani* and *pudáli* are collective constructions of the vertical and horizontal dimensions of body, society, and cosmos. These oppositions are evidence that the Wakuénai perceive of and express the interrelations between vertical and horizontal dimensions as a fundamental opposition between two ways of ordering experiential reality, most specifically the problematic experiences of collectively

Ex. 1: Transcription of *déetu* flutes played without accompaniment; melodic intervals found in *máwi* flute duets and songs are absent.

reproducing a male-controlled hierarchy of ritual power, and of initiating male-female exchange relations between local kin groups.

The specific symbolic oppositions between *kwépani* and *pudáli* underlie a more profound contrast between two modes of exchange that place different weightings on the relationship between myth and music. *Kwépani* embodies a mythic mode of exchange insofar as its richness of meaning arises less from variations in the organization of musical sounds than from the multiplicity and complexity of ways in which

instruments, performers, and performances are choreographed to explore the nuances of meanings that originate in the Kuwái myth cycle. In *kwépani*, mythic meanings act upon and constrain musical sounds to produce a minimum of musical change. The quasi-speech of *molítu* flute players, for example, is a "mythification" of sound in which the acoustic organization of human speech is superimposed upon the sound of *molítu* flutes. *Pudáli*, on the other hand, is a musical mode of exchange in which sounds act upon mythic meanings to produce a maximum of

Fig. 2: A pair of "male" (longer) and "female" (shorter) *máwi* flutes (Hill 1981). Courtesy of the author.

Fig. 3: After being painted with white, uncooked resin, *kúlirrína* trumpets are dried in the sun (Hill 1981). Courtesy of the author.

musical change. The richness of meanings in *pudáli* is only secondarily based upon the subtleties of mythic meaning and emerges most directly from the variety of ways in which materials, sound structures, and choreography are employed in creatively transforming social boundaries between humans and non-humans, kin and affines, and men and women. *Kúlirrína* trumpet dances, *déetu* flute performances, and *dzúdzuápani* dances all give active expression to the musicality of the presexual, precultural space-time of mythic beginnings. The *déetu* flute players make this transference to non-verbal, musical expression of myth explicit, since they transform both the social process of "asking" the hosts for drinks and the *déetu* insects' natural feeding behavior into a purely musico-choreographic event (only musical sounds and drinks are exchanged, no words).

The opposition between mythic and musical modes of exchange is perhaps most evident in the contrast between the *molítu* flute performances in *kwépani*—where myth acts upon, or constrains, music—and the *déetu* flute performances in *pudáli*—where music transforms myth. At the same time, it is

precisely in the multivocality of *molítu* and *déetu* as animal symbols that the Wakuénai construct a higher level of meaning and poetically mediate between the mythic meanings of sound and the musicality of mythic speech and behavior. Despite the multiplicity of contradictions between mythic and musical modes of exchange in Wakuénai social and religious life, the two modes come together at a higher level to form a poetics of social exchange that centers around the nexus of symbolic meanings attributed to *molítu* frogs and the metamorphosis of *mútsi* grubs into mature *déetu* weevils. More generally, this indigenous poetics of exchange is based upon the desocialization of human social processes towards the domain of nature. Both the prevalence of myth in *kwépani* and the prevalence of performance in *pudáli* depend upon symbolic processes of removing activities of exchanging power, foods, artifacts, and people from the realm of human society to the non-human domain of animal nature. At this higher level of meaning, mythic and musical modes of exchange form complementary parts of a poetic process of symbolically predetermining the value of exchange activities in Wakuénai social life. In *kwépani* and *pudáli*, the *molítu* frog and the *déetu* weevil serve as condensed symbols for constructing a higher level of meaning that mediates the fundamental dialectic between vertical and horizontal dimensions.

The *molítu* frog is a quintessential symbol of male control over the life-giving powers of Kuwái. In the second part of the Kuwái myth cycle, men transformed themselves into an army of *molítu* frogs when they accompanied Iñápirríkuli to take the sacred flutes and trumpets away from Amáru and the women at Mútsipáni. In this sense, the *molítu* frog is a metaphor for the power to transform Mútsipáni, or female control over Kuwái, into *Kwépani,* or male control over Kuwái and the vertically defined relations of power within the group. Outside of sacred myths and ceremonies, *molítu* frogs are an important symbol of cooperative relations between male and female laborers in the annual cycle of shifting horticulture. In this more secular context, *molítu* frogs are considered to be children of Káali, the mythic originator of cultivated plant species and *pudáli* ceremonies. The singing of *molítu* frogs at the beginning of the short, September-to-November dry season is interpreted as a sign of Káali telling men when to select and cut areas of forest for new gardens (Hill 1983, 1984). Likewise, the *molítu* frogs' singing at the end of the long dry season in late March is a signal for men and women to begin planting manioc and other crops in their newly cut and burned swiddens. In general, people feel that their labor is easier, more productive, and less dangerous if they work in synchrony with the mythical calendar of the frogs' singing. Thus, in addition to their ceremonial and mythic significance as sacred symbols of collective male control over the vertical relations between mythic ancestors and their human descendants, the *molítu* frogs are just as firmly associated with the mythic character of Káali and the annual cycle of horticultural activities. In other words, *molítu* is a doubly significant animal symbol for the Wakuénai insofar as it

simultaneously evokes the mythic, world opening powers of Kuwái and, like the *déetu* flutes of *pudáli*, the transformation of mythic, natural and social processes into performance.

The double significance of *déetu* weevils arises from the duality of the species' natural means of reproducing by laying eggs in palm trees and the subsequent metamorphosis of white *mútsi* grubs into black *déetu* weevils. In *pudáli*, the *déetu* flute performances embody a transformation, through shamanistic transference to sound, of the horizontal social boundary between hosts and guests, or kin and affines. In addition, the men's act of imitating the natural feeding behavior of *déetu* weevils implicitly evokes the insects' manner of reproducing through laying eggs in the soft inner pith of felled palm trees, which in turn serve as both "womb" and food source for the eggs as they develop into *mútsi* grubs. The life cycle of *mútsi-déetu* insects is a natural metaphor that connects the horizontal opening up of social relations in *pudáli* to the vertical dimension of sacred, mythic power in *kwépani*. The palm trees that serve as wombs and food for developing *mútsi* grubs are also symbols of the vertical connection between mythic ancestors and living descendants, and male musician-dancers in *kwépani* symbolically transform their bodies into palm trees by wearing crowns of palm leaves and bundles of wild palm fruits. More importantly, however, is the direct role of *mútsi* grubs in sacred myth as the food that intoxicates Kuwái and persuades him to reveal the secrets of his powers. *Mútsi* was the source of the mythic transformation of Kuwái's musical naming power, or the "powerful sound that opened up the world," from a monological, purely musical force of nature into a dialogical, verbal, socialized form of communication. *Mútsi* grubs brought about this all-important transformation of sound into mythic discourse, enabling the life-giving powers of Kuwái to be transferred to Dzúli, the first chant-owner.

Figure 4 summarizes the poetics of Wakuénai ceremonial exchange. The opposition between mythic

Molítu flute in *kwépani*
mythification of musical sound
(music converted into mythic speech)

Déetu flutes in *pudáli*
musicalization of mythic speech
(mythic speech converted into musical sound)

Molítu frog as Káaliéni
musicalization of mythic speech
(mythic speech converted into musical sound
of frogs' singing)

Mútsi grub in Kuwái's myth
mythification of musical sound
(conversion of musical naming power into mythic
speech, or dialogue)

Fig. 4: The poetics of ceremonial exchange.

and musical modes of exchange is mediated through using the multivocality of animal symbols to express the inextricable connections between the conversion of sound into mythic discourse and the transformation of mythic speech into musical sound. Like the metamorphosis of white *mútsi* grubs into black *déetu* weevils and back again, the poetics of ceremonial exchange transforms musical sound into mythic meaning and vice versa. Through metamorphosis and autoreproduction, the vertical and horizontal dimensions of bodily, social, and cosmic creation transform into one another.

GLOSSARY OF INDIGENOUS TERMS AND CHARACTERS

Amáru: The primordial human female of myth and mother of Kuwái.

dápa: Sacred trumpets named after the *paca*, played during *kwépani* ceremonies and in male and female initiation rituals.

déetu: A large, shiny, black, species of coconut palm weevil; also, the name of flutes played by guests to "suck" fermented drinks out of their hosts during the late night period of *pudáli* exchange ceremonies.

dzáate: Toucan; also the name of pairs of sacred flutes played in *kwépani* ceremonies.

dzáwinápa: Jaguar-bone, or large conical trumpets played in male initiation rituals to represent the jaguar-ancestors.

dzúdzuápani: Wheel-dance performed with *wáana* dancing tubes and singing at the end of the late night period in female-owned *pudáli* ceremonies.

Dzúli: A younger brother of the trickster-creator, Iñápirríkuli, and the first owner of the sacred songs and chants, called *málikái*.

hekwápiríko: The world of living human beings.

Hérri: Youngest brother of Iñápirríkuli.

Hípana: A village along the Aiarí River in Brazil, the place regarded as the center, or "navel," of the world where the mythic ancestors emerged from the ground and where Kuwái is brought down to the ground in myth and initiation rituals.

Iñápirríkuli: The trickster-creator of myth and father of Kuwái.

íyarudáti: The dark netherworld of recently deceased persons and the place where shamans travel in song.

Káali: A younger brother of the trickster-creator, Iñápirríkuli, and mythic originator of cultivated plant species and all things associated with horticulture, including *pudáli* exchange ceremonies.

kadápu: Sacred ritual whips made of a vine, called *dzámakuápi*, used only for striking male and female initiates.

kapéti: Ritual whips used for marking time in collective dance-songs called *kápetiápani* performed in *kwépani* ceremonies and in male and female initiation rituals.

káridzámai: Sacred food of the mythic ancestors consisting of hot-peppered, boiled meat over which *málikái* songs and chants have been performed.

kúlirrína: Large trumpets made by lashing woven resonators to short tubes of *máwi* palm; named after a species of large catfish (*kulírri*) and played in ensembles during the opening dances of male-owned *pudáli* ceremonies.

Kuwái: The monstrous, primordial human being whose musical voice and instruments powerfully opened up the world.

kwépani: Kuwái-dance, or ceremonial exchanges of wild fruits over which the sacred flutes and trumpets of Kuwái are played.

likáremi: The celestial paradise of Iñápirríkuli where the mythic ancestor spirits live, a place of eternal light and total purity.

máariawa: Sacred flutes named after the white heron (*máari*) played in *kwépani* ceremonies and in male and female initiation rituals; said to represent the thumb and index finger of Kuwái.

málikái: A complex genre of mythically powerful speech, including spoken, chanted, and sung performances in various sacred ritual contexts.

málikái limínali: Chant-owner, or ritual specialists who know how to perform and interpret *málikái* prayers, chants, and songs.

malírri: Shaman, or ritual curer.

máwi: A species of palm used to make flutes and trumpets played in *pudáli* exchange ceremonies and the name of the longest kind of flutes.

molítu: A species of small frog (unidentified) and namesake of short flutes played in sacred ceremonies and rituals; symbol of Iñápirríkuli's recapturing of Kuwái's sacred flutes and trumpets from Amáru and the women in myth and also a child of Káali used to schedule horticultural activities.

mútsi: White palm grubs that mature into *déetu* insects; in myth, the food used to lure Kuwái down to his fiery death at Hípana.

Mútsipáni: *Mútsi*-dance, or the mythic home of Amáru on the Aiarí River.

pákamarántakan: Personal drinking songs sung by men and women during the late night period of *pudáli* ceremonies and by women during the late night period of *kwépani* ceremonies.

pudáli: Ceremonial exchanges of meat and manioc products between affines.

tsépani: Final dance-music of *kwépani* ceremonies, evoking the mythic episode in which Kuwái ate and vomited three boys who had prematurely ended their ritual fast and uniting the five fingers of Kuwái's mythic hand.

tsikóta: Smaller flutes made of *máwi* and played in *pudáli* ceremonies.

wáana: Stomping tubes, or hollowed out logs, rhythmically pushed against the ground in female-owned *pudáli* ceremonies.

wáanapáni: Dance-songs performed with *wáana* stomping tubes in *pudáli*.

wakaítaka yénpiti: "We speak to our child," or female initiation rituals.

wakapétaka yénpitipé: "We show our children," or male initiation rituals.

wáliáduwa: Sacred flutes played in sets of three during *kwépani* ceremonies to represent the outer three fingers of the mythic hand of Kuwái; the term means "new-like" and refers to the implicit theme of social renewal in *kwépani* ceremonies.

REFERENCES

Chernela, Janet 1983. *Hierarchy and economy of the Uanano-(Kotiria) speaking peoples of the middle Vaupés basin* (PhD diss., Anthropology: Columbia University).

Goldman, Irving 1979. *The Cubeo: Indians of the northwest Amazon*, 2nd rev. ed. Urbana: University of Illinois Press.

Hill, Jonathan D. 1983. *Wakuénai society* (PhD diss., Anthropology: Indiana University).

1984. "Social equality and ritual hierarchy: The Arawakan Wakuénai of Venezuela," *American ethnologist* 11: 528–44.

1985. "Agnatic sibling relations and rank in northern Arawakan myth and social life" in *The sibling relationship in lowland South America*, ed. by Judith Shapiro and Kenneth Kensinger, 25–33 (Working papers on South American Indians, no. 7. Bennington College, Bennington, Vermont).

Hugh-Jones, Christine 1979. *From the Milk River*. Cambridge: Cambridge University Press.

Hugh-Jones, Stephen 1979. *The palm and the pleiades*. Cambridge: Cambridge University Press.

Jackson, Jean 1983. *The Fish people: Linguistic exogamy and Tukanoan identity in northwest Amazonia*. New York: Cambridge University Press.

Journet, Nicolás 1981. "Los Curripaco del Río Isana: Economía y sociedad," *Revista colombiana de antropología* 23: 127–82.

Laughlin, C. D. 1974. "Deprivation and reciprocity," *Man, Journal of the Royal Anthropological Institute* 9: 380–96.

Matos Arvelo, Martín 1912. *Vida indiana*. Barcelona: Editorial Mauci.

Nimuendajú, Kurt 1950. "Reconhecimento dos Ríos Içana, Ayarí, e Vaupés. Relatorio [1927] apresentado ao Serviço de Proteção aos Indios do Amazonas e Acre, 1927," *Journal de la Société des Américanistes* 39: 128–70.

Reichel-Dolmatoff, Gerardo 1971. *Amazonian cosmos: The sexual and religious symbolism of the Tukano Indians*. Chicago: University of Chicago Press.

1976. "Cosmology as ecological analysis: A view from the rain forest," *Man* 11: 307–18.

1985. "Tapir avoidance in the Colombian northwest Amazon" in *Animal myths and metaphors in South America*, ed. by Gary Urton. Salt Lake City: University of Utah Press, 107–44.

Sahlins, Marshall 1972. *Stone Age economics*. Chicago: Aldine Press.

Sorensen, Arthur 1967. "Multilingualism in the northwest Amazon," *American anthropologist* 69: 670–84.

Turner, Terence 1985. "Animal symbolism, totemism, and the structure of myth" in *Animal myths and metaphors in South America*, ed. by Gary Urton. Salt Lake City: University of Utah Press, 49–106.

1988. "Ethno-Ethnohistory: Myth and history in native South American representations of contact with Western society" in *Rethinking history and myth*, ed. by Jonathan D. Hill. Urbana: University of Illinois Press, 235–81.

Turner, Victor 1977. "Process, system, and symbol: A new anthropological synthesis," *Daedalus* 106/3: 61–80.

Wright, Robin 1981. *History and religion of the Baniwa peoples of the Upper Río Negro valley* (PhD diss., Anthropology: Stanford University).

Wright, Robin, and Jonathan D. Hill 1986. "History, ritual, and myth: Nineteenth-century millenarian movements in the northwest Amazon," *Ethnohistory* 33: 31–54.

RECORDED EXAMPLES

1. *Wáliáduwa* flute duet played in a circle around display of wild fruits in hosts' village; men give each other whippings.

2. *Kápetiápani* song-dance performed between midnight and dawn; women singing *pákamarántakan* songs, laughing, and drinking manioc liquor; *molítu* flute and *dápa* trumpets heard in the background.

3. *Máariawa* flute duet played shortly before dawn, announcing the beginning of *tsépani*.

4. Two *máariawa* and three *wáliáduwa* flutes played together in *tsépani*.

5. *Wáliáduwa* flute duet played in the canoe, leaving village at the end of *kwépani*.

6. *Máwi* flute duet, opening dances of male-owned *pudáli* ceremonies.

7. *Máwi* flute duet and *déetu* flutes played together, opening dances of *pudáli*.

8. *Déetu* flute performance during the late night period of *pudáli*.

9. *Dzúdzuápani*, or "wheel-dance," a *wáanapáni* song-dance performed around fire just before dawn.

10. *Dzawírra* (fish), *máwi* flute duet.

BRAZIL'S INDIGENOUS UNIVERSE (to ca. 1990)

The Xavante, Kamayurá, and Suyá

ELIZABETH TRAVASSOS

Demographic, linguistic, and cultural considerations—Landmark studies in the twentieth century: Helza Camêu's great effort at systematization—Music among the Xavante Indians of the State of Mato Grosso—The Kamayurá of the Xingu Indian Park—Vocal music of the Suyá Indians—Toward the possibility of comparative studies

WHEN JEAN DE LÉRY visited Brazil in 1557–1558, as part of a colonizing and missionary expedition sent by Calvin to "Antarctic France" (the short-lived, mid-16th-century French colony in present-day Rio de Janeiro), he recorded in his travel diary the first transcription of a native Brazilian melody (Fig. 1). Known since then as *canidé ioune* ("yellow macaw" in the Tupi language), a title taken from the texts also recorded by Léry, this song was heard among the now extinct Tupinambás in Rio de Janeiro and became one of the most cited documents in Brazilian musicological literature. The best known music histories of Brazil, especially those that dedicate several chapters to oral traditions, invariably mention Léry's transcription of this Tupinambá song in their introductions, or in the first chapter dealing with the origins—or "pre-history"—of Brazilian music. Most of these histories, however, neglected to discuss the reliability of this document (Almeida 1942; Melo 1908 in 1947).

One of the factors that determined the curious destiny of this Tupinambá song was the lack of documentation on indigenous music in Brazil until recent times. The Jesuits, who since their arrival in 1549 had instituted the need and the structure for teaching European music to the indigenous population (Leite 1949), did not record any native musical expressions, although they allowed it and even stimulated it. In their writings, they made references to indigenous musical instruments, musical practices, and to occasions when there was playing, singing, and dancing. Their documentary legacy, however, excludes musical transcriptions.

From the time of contact with the Europeans and until the beginning of the twentieth century, very little was known about indigenous music. This situation changed in the 1970s and thereafter, when several studies were published whose focus was the musics of aboriginal populations. Some include sound documentation recorded in the field. Most of these studies were carried out by anthropologists and thus reflect a preoccupation with comprehending music within its cultural context. Present-day knowledge of indigenous groups precludes any generic treatment of native musical cultures in Brazil, or any delineation of "musical areas" based on uniformity of features. Jean-Michel Beaudet, however, observed certain relationships between the musics of several groups from lowland South America, based on his critical listening of available recordings:

Ces parentés restent encore à prouver solidement par les études ethnomusicologiques à venir, lesquelles commenceront certainement par mettre en valeur la variété et la multiplicité culturelle de cette région (1982: 151).

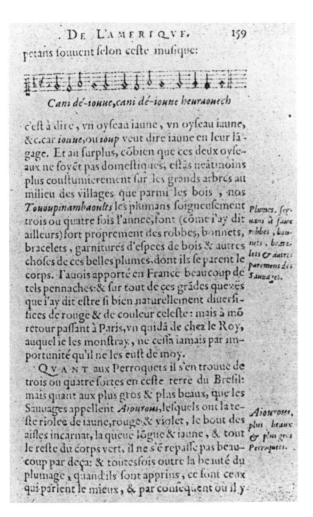

Fig. 1: *Canidé ioune*, reproduced in Camêu 1977: 87, from Jean de Léry's *Histoire d'un voyage faict en la terre du Brésil*, third edition, 1585.

These relationships remain to be solidly proven by future ethnomusicological studies, which will certainly begin by stressing the diversity and cultural pluralism characteristic of this region.

Contemporary researchers have chosen to focus on the music of a single indigenous group, or on small areas of intense cultural exchange between several groups. This recent tendency to study individualized ethnic groups has resulted in valuable contributions to knowledge, albeit at the expense of comparative analyses. For this reason, we have chosen the musics of three ethnic groups studied in the 1970s for the present essay. Several landmark studies carried out before 1970 should be noted: the production of the first sound documents by a Brazilian researcher; a brief moment of interest in indigenous music in the official music schools, which did not continue; and archival research

based on phonograph and museum collections. Each of these initiatives reflects different concerns, from the preservation of documents for research and teaching, to the transformation of these documents into objects of analysis, or the emphasis on music as a focus of study. The latter characterizes most of the recent research, although there are considerable differences among the authors' perspectives. To speak about indigenous music in Brazil is, essentially, to speak about the knowledge gained so far about the subject, since only through this knowledge is it possible to come into direct contact with these geographically remote musics. Direct observation of such a vast universe is impossible, even for the most avid and active group of field researchers. The idea of uniformity of phenomena implied by the expression "indigenous music," which had been assumed a priori in earlier times, has now been abandoned. "Indigenous music" is no longer a system that owes its existence to the polarization between "Indians" (as "primitive") and "civilized" peoples, but rather a group of distinct traditions that must be studied within their own cultural idiosyncracies, and about which the limited knowledge gained so far precludes generalizations. Before addressing some of the significant pre-1970s studies and focusing on our survey of three ethnic groups, we shall provide some general background on demography, linguistic groups, and efforts to categorize indigenous groups according to cultural and inter-ethnic criteria.

DEMOGRAPHIC, LINGUISTIC, AND CULTURAL CONSIDERATIONS

In 1957, Darcy Ribeiro estimated the number of indigenous groups in Brazilian territory at approximately 143. These were differentiated by language, culture, and by their situation of contact with national society, amounting to a total of roughly 100,000 individuals (Ribeiro 1957). In 1986, the Indigenous Missionary Council (CIMI) estimated the number of identified indigenous groups at 220, with a total population of 220,000 persons. In addition, there were probably 30,000 Indians not settled in villages and belonging to tribes that had not yet established contact with national society (Porantim 1986; Ecumenical Center for Documentation and Information [CEDI] 1987). In 1996, the total population was estimated at 300,000 persons, of which 280,000 live in indigenous territories (Ricardo 1996). The higher figures for the 1990s can be attributed to several factors, including the increased knowledge about several groups, which until the 1950s were isolated or simply excluded from official documents, and to the demographic growth of the indigenous population as a whole. It is important to remember, however, that many groups were decimated or suffered violent depopulation due to illness, loss of territory, and precarious living conditions.

Many imprecise and incorrect facts about Brazil's indigenous peoples and their situation were the object of verification, updating, and systematization by a research project of the Ecumenical Center for Documentation and Information (CEDI). This collaborative project published three volumes (*Povos indígenas do Brasil*), each dedicated to one geographic area. Precise and updated information about each group is difficult to obtain because the sources are dispersed or outdated, and because Brazil shelters indigenous peoples throughout its enormous territory.

These groups have been classified according to linguistic and cultural criteria, as well as by their degree of inter-ethnic contact. Regarding linguistic criteria, large stocks of genetically-related languages have been identified. These are the Tupi and Macro-Gê stocks, the Arawak, and Carib groups, which make up several families. There are also smaller groups whose incorporation into these main stocks is still uncertain, as well as isolated languages that have not yet been related to any as yet constituted linguistic family:

1. Tupi stock: it includes the Tupi-Guarani, Munduruku, Juruna, Arikêm, Tupari, Ramarâma and Mondé families;
2. Macro-Gê stock: it includes the Gê, Bororo, Maxakali, Karajá, and Botocudo families;
3. Arawak;
4. Carib;
5. Families that do not belong to the large groupings include the Tukano, Pano, Katukina, Mura, Txapakúra, Makú, Nambikwára, Guaikurú, and Yanomami (Rodrigues 1986).

Eduardo Galvão (1960 in 1979: 193–228) undertook a classification according to cultural criteria valid only for Brazil. He based his criteria on contiguous spatial distribution of cultural elements, geographic area, and contact situation. His classification rendered eleven cultural areas. It is, however, too early to determine whether these cultural areas are congruent with the musical data collected so far (Map 1).

In 1957, Darcy Ribeiro distinguished four categories, defined according to contact situation criteria: isolated;

in intermittent contact with national society; in permanent contact; and integrated. Isolated groups live in zones that have not yet been reached by the advancing frontiers of Brazilian society and maintain cultural autonomy. Those that are in intermittent contact with national society maintain cultural autonomy but have acquired needs that require economic relations with the non-indigenous population. The groups in permanent contact, according to Ribeiro, have lost their socio-cultural autonomy and are dependent on the regional economy while maintaining their traditional customs. Integrated groups are those that do not differ in any way from the Brazilian population with which they live, except for ethnic identity: they consider themselves Indians and are perceived as such by other ethnic groups. Assimilation itself or the "fusion of indigenous groups into national society as an indistinguishable part of it" would be exceptional (Ribeiro 1957 in 1977: 434). From these categories, it would be impossible to infer the degree to which each group has retained the integrity of its musical traditions. Remnants of indigenous groups, for instance, such as the Tremembé population living on the coast of Ceará and "integrated," according to Ribeiro's meaning of the term, maintain the ritual practice of the *torém*, in which one dances to the sound of traditional songs, in spite of all the transformations that have given rise to their present lifestyle. The Tremembé, who today speak Portuguese, sing their chants in a dead native language during the performance of the *torém*. These chants are both linguistically and musically different from the musical expressions of the region they inhabit, and this is a sign of their desire to identify instead with their own tradition (Torém/CE, 1979, see Discography). The retention of a musical tradition, as in this case, may occur even when a group is categorized as "integrated," according to Ribeiro's criteria. As more documentation is collected and greater knowledge gained, these linguistic and cultural classifications may serve as reference for comparative musical studies. At the present time, we cannot even hypothetically formulate a delineation of indigenous musical areas since we lack the documentation to justify such hypotheses.

LANDMARK STUDIES IN THE TWENTIETH CENTURY

A summary and evaluation of the contribution of chroniclers, missionaries, travelers, ethnographers, and musicologists to knowledge about the music of

Map 1: Indigenous cultural areas, 1900–1959 (Galvão 1960 in 1979: 207).

LEGEND:
  I. Norte-amazônica
  II. Juruá-Purús
  III. Guaporé
  IV. Tapajós-Madeira
  V. Alto Xingu
  VI. Tocantins-Xingu
  VII. Pindaré-Gurupi
  VIII. Paraguai
  IX. Paraná
  X. Tietê-Uruguai
  XI. Nordeste

Brazil's indigenous peoples from 1500 to 1964 was carried out by Helza Camêu (1977: 20–67). In this survey, the author attempted to show that the music of the Indians, as differentiated from other musical traditions in Brazil, retained its integrity in spite of indoctrination, colonization, and the transformations imposed on the indigenous peoples' way of life in the course of almost five centuries. For Camêu, it was important to evaluate the extent to which one can reliably speak of "authentic" indigenous music in the twentieth century without "distortions" resulting from contact with other traditions because—among other reasons—some observers may have exaggerated the effects of acculturation on the musical lives of the natives. In a chapter devoted to the role of catechism (1977: 68–81), Camêu concludes that, in spite of its efficacy as an instrument of conversion, the teaching of European music carried out by the missionaries did not succeed in eliminating the character of indigenous traditions. At best, indoctrination reached isolated individuals or small groups and did not have considerable effect on ethnic identities. This preoccupation with authenticity is absent in the texts of other contemporary authors, both because they do not use such categories as "authenticity" and "integrity" in reference to musical traditions, and because they proceed from the assumption that indigenous musics did not enter into significant processes of "fusion" with those of European or African origin in Brazilian territory. According to Anthony Seeger (1986), the low level of interaction between European and indigenous traditions could be attributed to the physical distance that separates the native peoples from Brazil's densely populated centers, as well as to the structure and timbre of indigenous musics and their reliance on religious and power structures that make removal from original contexts difficult.

Concerned with identifying "authentic" features in the second half of the twentieth century, Camêu considers the Tupinambá chants recorded by Léry as a point of reference from the distant past. If, however, we can assume minimal interaction and maximum retention of traditional features in the sixteenth century, these European transcriptions of indigenous music are suspect at best. This is the case of the chants recorded by Léry, even more so when it is known that the transcriptions appeared only in the third edition of his *Histoire d'un voyage faict en la terre du Bresil, autrement dite Amérique* (1585). (See John P. Murphy, "The Ethnohistory of Amerindian Peoples: Brazil," in these volumes.) Subsequent alterations would make these examples even less credible: while the words and melodic lines of the Tumpinambá chant would appear in Rousseau's *Dictionnaire de musique* (Paris, 1768), Rousseau thanks Marin Mersenne for that "Canadian" musical example (Harrison 1973: 7). The question of authenticity in Léry's transcriptions and changes made thereafter also was examined by Luiz Heitor Corrêa de Azevedo (1941). Cautiously, Camêu avoids drawing too many conclusions from such controversial documents.

Throughout the seventeenth, eighteenth, and nineteenth centuries, superficial transcriptions of music and dance were omnipresent in the works of travelers, missionaries, and scientists. This was due, possibly, to the ubiquity of music and dance in ceremonies, perhaps the most public and visible aspect of social life and the most attractive to the outside observer (we are not taking into account the secret ceremonies that are carried out privately). From this period, there are many descriptions of musical instruments, some simply mentioned, others described more carefully. (See Dale A. Olsen, "Aerophones of Traditional Use in South America," and John P. Murphy, "The Ethnohistory of Amerindian Peoples: Brazil," in these volumes.)

In the nineteenth century, the work of naturalists and ethnologists gained importance. Naturalists did not exclude the indigenous population from their field of observation. Their contributions with regard to music are very heterogenous, and are partially determined by their personal backgrounds and specific areas of interest, which may or may not have

included specialized musical knowledge. Oliveira Filho stressed that the authors who were generically characterized as "travelers" in Brazil constituted "a well differentiated universe of intellectual producers" (1987: 92). It also should be remembered that iconographical records of dances, rituals, and musical instruments were very often documented by artists or scientists who used drawings to record animal and vegetable species, landscapes, and human types. The Music Division of Rio de Janeiro's National Library carried out a wide-ranging survey of Brazil's musical iconography from the sixteenth to nineteenth centuries that focused especially on documents on paper or canvas in its own collection (photographs were not included in the survey). The results were presented in an exhibition catalogue (Biblioteca Nacional 1974).

The first works whose central concern was the music of indigenous peoples appeared in the early decades of the twentieth century, although few were the product of field work and direct observation by the authors. Manizer's (1934) study, in this sense, is an exception. Roquette-Pinto (1917 in 1976) documented the music of the Paresí and Nambikwára Indians in the field, but he was essentially a collector, in this case delegating the study of the musical material to another person.

Manizer was in Brazil between 1914 and 1915 on a study mission from the Museum of Anthropology and Ethnography of the Russian Academy of Sciences. He stayed in several indigenous areas (Kadiwéu, Xavante, Terena, Kaingang, Botocudos, and Krenak) for varied periods of time, the longest being among the Botocudos in the State of Espírito Santo. Based on these short visits, Manizer described the musical occasions he witnessed or heard about from informants. He recorded observations on dance, body position of the musicians, speech, shouts, and other manifestations associated with musical performances. He collected and examined musical instruments, which he described in detail. He transcribed some songs with the help of a violin on which he played the melodies until he, with the aid of informants, could be sure of the accuracy of what he had transcribed. Except for the documentation produced on the Botocudos, the information remains brief and superficial.

What impressed Manizer most about the Botocudos was the special intonation of a certain type of speech that approaches song, and the fluid passage from lament to song. He concluded that song was intimately linked to the word, lending itself to the expression of very intense emotions. He described the circular dance of the Botocudos, which was performed at all important events, and recorded eleven melodic excerpts that were sung as refrains, following a kind of "recitative" (a European term) by a soloist. Within this group of melodies, Manizer recognized a "scale of well established tones" (1934: 320), because the intervals of major and minor triads were frequently found, although he did not formulate such a scale. Unlike other authors, Manizer avoided generalizations about indigenous music. His annotations about actual performances based on first-hand observations are not found in other works of the time, most of which were carried out from recordings in archival collections.

Although Helza Camêu recognized the importance of the work of Roquette-Pinto and his pioneering efforts with regard to sound documentation in Brazil, she looked skeptically upon the results published in *Rondônia* and states that "[the songs recorded there] cannot be considered as valid ethnological documents in view of confessed distortions and misinterpretations thereof" (1977: 51). Roquette-Pinto was a physician and Professor of Anthropology at the National Museum who, in 1912, accompanied Lieutenant Colonel Antônio Pireneus de Sousa, of the Strategic Telegraph Lines Commission led by Rondon, on a mission to create communication between the capital (Rio de Janeiro), Cuiabá, and Amazonas. Roquette-Pinto was the first researcher in Brazil to record sound on a research trip and, curiously, he did so among the Indians.

Roquette-Pinto recorded by phonograph "the music of the principal Paresí songs." Among the Nambikwára, he filmed two dances and recorded other musical excerpts. The transcriptions and comments on Paresí music and the description of the musical instruments are credited to Professor Astolfo Tavares. The existence of the group's own musical system was not considered: the series of sounds produced by the Paresí flutes is compared with the seven-tone diatonic scale and the differences betweeen them explained as "gaps" or "anomalous intervals" in Paresí music. These technical misconceptions were pointed out by Camêu (1977: 52). Nonetheless, the information about musical instruments supplied by Roquette-Pinto is precious: some, like the nose ocarina and the trumpet with a resonating chamber, were documented by him for the first time in Brazil. His recordings and the information later published in *Rondônia* (1917 in 1976) were continually consulted by different scholars interested

in indigenous music (Corrêa de Azevedo 1938, for example), or in indigenous music as an example of so-called "primitive" music (Mário de Andrade 1942 in 1980). Some of the Paresí songs he documented became as well known as the old *canidé ioune* of the Tupinambá that Jean de Léry published in the 1585 edition of his 1578 *Histoire*.

Erich M. von Hornbostel (1923 in 1979–1982) contributed a seminal study of the collections of phonograms and musical instruments of the Makuxí, Taulipáng and Yekuâna groups who inhabit the border between Brazil and Venezuela, in volume III of Theodor Koch-Grünberg's 5-volume *Vom Roroima zum Orinoco* (1917–1924). The three groups are Carib-speaking peoples and, according to Hornbostel's conclusions, their musics can be approached together because they possess a considerable number of common characteristics. Only the Yekuâna depart from this common character, as they also present physical and cultural differences. These studies also make references to the Wapixána, Arawak-speaking neighbors who sang together with the Makuxí.

Hornbostel described musical instruments in technical detail and, in all cases, compared them with similar instruments stemming from other parts of the world. He approached their place of origin and routes of diffusion according to the Kulturkreislehre, typical of European scholarship of that time. The most common types of instruments found among these Carib-speaking groups were idiophones (rattles with stringed fruits and animal claws, some tied to a stamping tube; globular rattles used by shamans; and tubular rattles *de trançado*, that is, with external nets of interwoven vegetal strands), as well as aerophones (shell and wooden trumpets, whistles, vertical and transverse bone flutes, bamboo clarinets, etc.).

The songs from the phonogram collection were analyzed from the viewpoint of intonation, tonal structure, melodic contour, and rhythm (no instrumental music was transcribed). According to Hornbostel, highly variable intonation is characteristic of these songs, which exhibit great flexibility in the size of intervals, a phenomenon he attributes to a natural tendency of solo song without melodic or harmonic accompaniment. This type of intonation makes the task of transcription more difficult because conventional notation presupposes stability of intervals. For this reason, and although the intervals had been measured in cents, the musical transcriptions only can approximate a schematic profile of the melodies. The tonal structure, according to Hornbostel, is based on relations of perfect fourths and fifths, and on conjunct motion in intervals of seconds, filling in the fourths and fifths. Thus, in the midst of variable intervallic ranges, Hornbostel could discern some general tendencies, which he synthesized in "formulas of tonal structure" (1923 in 1979–1982: 356), though falling short of formulating a system of scales. These formulas were divided into three groups: (a) those in which minor thirds and tritones predominate; (b) those referable to the hemitonic pentatonic scale (five degrees with semitones); and (c) those referable to the anhemitonic pentatonic scale (five degrees without semitones).

The songs do not follow any rigid metric scheme, although attempts to metrify them reveal a preference for groups of three, as exemplified in triplets contained in binary measures. They even reveal a stable tempo, which Hornbostel considers fundamental in danced songs. Significant differences were found between the average tempo of the slower Makuxí and Taulipáng songs, and the faster Yekuâna songs, which the author relates to ethnic characteristics.

The tempo also is surely influenced by the physiology of the tribes: among the Yekuâna it is more lively, faster, on the average (MM 57) than among the Taulipáng (MM 47) and Makuxí (MM 49). According to this, the "tempo of an ethnic group" seems to offer an anthropological trait that is not properly taken advantage of (1923 in 1979–1982: 359).

The Yekuâna further distinguish themselves by presenting simpler musical forms and therefore, according to Hornbostel, more "primitive" ones, which he takes as an indication to characterize their culture in general, projecting an evolutionary bias typical of European scholarship of his generation. Hornbostel concludes that the Indian songs present common characteristics: melody is formed by the juxtaposition of descending intervals of approximately a minor third; the rhythm is made up of the juxtaposition of short beats, or by the dissolution of a longer value into small sequences of short sounds. In essence, he concludes that small units are always juxtaposed, like "pearls on a string."

These pioneering works here summarized "inaugurated" the documentation and analysis of indigenous music in Brazil. Although at the time indigenous music was treated as a whole, as "primitive" music, the need to study ethnic musics individually was being shaped by some of these initial observations.

In her overview of the contributions to knowledge about Indian music, Helza Camêu included the works of Luciano Gallet (1934) and Luiz Heitor Corrêa de Azevedo (1938 and 1941), both scholars with a principal background in music who were interested in the analysis of indigenous traditions. They opened a field of study in the official music schools that remained practically unexplored, even after the publication of Corrêa de Azevedo's thesis (1938), which was presented in the competition for the Chair of Folklore at the old National Music School of the University of Brazil. Both Gallet and Corrêa de Azevedo, and especially the latter, dedicated their more systematic efforts to studies of popular (non-indigenous) musical traditions. The study of indigenous music at the National Music School was developed from Roquette-Pinto's recordings and from transcriptions, such as the Tupinambá chants in Léry's *Histoire*. The attempt to institutionalize the study of indigenous traditions was indicative of a general concern with the ethnic roots of Brazilian music, which dominated the national musicological scene, rather than with a need to understand aboriginal musics as a contemporary reality. It is in this context that Corrêa de Azevedo's thesis (1938) must be understood. In it, the musical expressions of the Indians are referred to as a group of uniform musical traditions that lent themselves to generic discussion of characteristics, implying that principles valid for a single group also were applicable to all groups.

Corrêa de Azevedo discusses Gallet's statement that Brazilian Indian musics exhibit intervals smaller than the semitone. Based on the phonograms of the Rondon Commission (Roquette-Pinto) and on the Paresí flutes in the National Museum, he states that the melodies could be organized on the basis of diatonic/ heptatonic scales, unfolding the "feeling of chords emanating from the harmonic series . . . and generally from tonality itself" (1938: 26). To explain this assertion he does not discard European influence through the musical tools of indoctrination. Neither does the rhythm stray from European conceptions, according to Corrêa de Azevedo. His attention was drawn to repetitions, which he understood as a universal constructive principle evident to him in the simple form of textual reiterations. He also observed procedures for elaborate repetitions that rely on "resources analogous to those used in our music" (1938: 41). Motivated by an evident sympathy towards indigenous peoples, Corrêa de Azevedo tended to look for approximations and similarities between native music and Western European traditions. Mitigating the opposite view—that of radical differences—he outlined a bridge between musical worlds that he perceived as very diverse and led the reader to understand that, beyond the singularities of each case, there were universal principles at work, and that "primitive" music (the category used in his text) is, above all, music.

HELZA CAMÊU'S GREAT EFFORT AT SYSTEMATIZATION

Camêu's contribution is not limited to a broad-ranging survey of the literature on musical practices in the course of over four centuries, since she also proceeded to analyze a substantial body of musical documents. Her work differs from that of her predecessors in the breadth of sources consulted, the themes dealt with, and the concern with defining analytical procedures, pointing out at every step the difficulties encountered and dangers implied in the application of methods of European musicology to such a heterogenous body of materials and often fragile data.

The unpublished documents used by Camêu are the recordings made by Darcy Ribeiro (Mbayá, Ofayé, Urubu-Kaapor and Kadiwéu groups), Max Boudin (Urubu and Maxakali groups), and Egon Schaden (Guarani group) during the 1940s, which brought cooperation between anthropologists and musicologists in Brazil. These were transcribed and analyzed while she worked in the Studies Division of the old Indian Protection Service. The transcriptions are found in the Musical Supplement at the end of her book (1977: Supplement 1–67). The titles of her chapters reflect that her concerns were predominantly musical: intervals and tuning, articulation, development, unity, durations and rhythm, series of pitches and chromaticism, tendency tones, polyphony and harmony, sound qualities, vocal music, etc. She broadens her perspective in the last two chapters by considering the social function of music and the symbolism of musical instruments, suggesting the importance of understanding music in relation to other aspects of culture. Her approach, an innovative one for Brazil, proposed the need to understand the musical reality of each ethnic group, and only then proceed with comparisons. While generically placing indigenous music at the highest level of priority, she admitted that these priorities would differ from group to group. Camêu insisted on the need to deal scientifically with musical phenomena and avoid interpretations based on the observer's own aesthetics. She also believed that it was necessary to seek in each group a standard for conceiving and practicing music, and then place these standards on a scale of musical development.

Working from bibliographic sources and museum collections, Camêu also relates and describes—for the first time in the Portuguese language—a considerable number of indigenous instruments. These are grouped into three large categories (percussion, wind, and strings), each subdivided according to the peculiarities of sound production and materials used. This brief reference to Camêu's work cannot possibly do justice to the monumental contribution she made in her unprecedented effort at synthesis.

The 1970s and 1980s witnessed a growing interest in indigenous music that is reflected principally in the publication of studies and sound recordings by several anthropologists who have carried out field work. Their concerns include the documentation, study, and even learning of the music of peoples among whom they worked. Prominent concerns include the contextualization of musical phenomena and the belief that they must be approached from questions such as "who," "when," "where," "how," and "why," in Anthony Seeger's (1977) terms. Music is not only a group of sounds for musicological analysis but rather a cultural and social fact whose comprehension requires anthropological knowledge of the human groups that produce it; its understanding, in turn, must emerge from the system of ideas within which music carries significance. As will be seen below, researchers concentrated on the role and social functions of music and on native musicology and aesthetics. Seeger's "journalistic" questions synthetically announce the importance that field research would assume in contemporary investigations, since only in situ can the answers to these questions be sought. Essentially, late twentieth-century studies incorporate methodologies from the field of ethnomusicology, which was not part of Brazilian curricula until very recently.

MUSIC AMONG THE XAVANTE INDIANS OF THE STATE OF MATO GROSSO

The Xavante, a Gê-speaking group, were pacified during the 1960s after a long history of conflict with national society. Pacification, according to practice in Brazil (undertaken both by the State and by missionaries), consists of establishing non-hostile relations with indigenous groups that are in open conflict with the populations they maintain contact with, or with groups that refuse to maintain regular contact with non-indigenous populations (Ribeiro 1977: 151). In the 1990s, the Xavante live in seven areas of which five are reservations, and are assisted, in some cases, by the Salesian missionaries (Map 2). They total about five thousand Indians (CEDI 1987). Their music was studied by Desidério Aytai, a Hungarian living in Brazil. The product of field research he began in 1960, *O mundo sonoro Xavante* was presented as an academic thesis to the Catholic University of Campinas in 1976, and was published in 1985. Aytai contributed the most extensive repertoire of musical transcriptions presently available on any indigenous group.

Among the Xavante, songs and dances abound for rituals, daily activities such as hunting and home construction, and those that articulate the cycle of daily life: morning songs (*dapraba*), noon songs (*dadzarono*), evening songs (*dahipopo*) and midnight songs (*mara'wawa*). The generic Xavante term that designates collective song and dance is *daño're*. *Dapraba*, *dadzarono*, and *dahipopo* are types of *daño're* differentiated by dance gestures and the appropriate hour of their performance (Graham 1984).

As Aytai points out, the musical life of the Xavante is eminently communal because collective performance is by far the most frequent and, in it, adult men are—in a certain way—the protagonists of musical practices. The Xavante woman rarely sings and her role in the renovation and expansion of the repertoire is less prominent than that of men.

Xavante songs are "received" in dreams, when the spirit wanders through distant places. The "dreaming" of songs and their incorporation into the repertoire are the domain of the adult male who has fulfilled the initiation rites, has pierced his ear, and uses appropriate ornaments. After the "musical" dream, the individual repeats and perfects the piece in a low voice or with his companions. The song is presented publicly in the village square on a formal occasion, where it is judged by the elder men, who accept or reject it. The criteria for evaluation are not known, but the quality of interpretation upon first singing seems to carry significance (Aytai 1985: 25). The women rarely "receive" music in dreams, and the same is true

for children and young people up to the age of the *wapté*, the group of young, uninitiated men.

A basic principle underlying the system of beliefs and social organization of the Xavante, which they share with other Gê-speaking groups, is a dichotomy or polarization between the "natural" and "cultural" domains that takes on different forms of representation. For instance, this principle rules the organization of space. The village square and the men's house (more specifically the single men's house, at the stage of seclusion in preparation for the initiation rites), are conceived as masculine places and appropriate for public life. In contrast, the group of houses distributed in a semi-circle around the plaza is the domestic space, associated with the feminine and children's realms. Laura Graham (1984) observes that the laments (*choros*), an expression of individual emotion related to loss and separation performed in the domestic space, constitute a genre associated with the private sphere and with the feminine domain. Supporting this statement is the fact that women may "dream" *choros* but would never "dream" *daño're*, the songs associated with public life. These, in turn, are collective songs danced in the plaza and manifestations of an age group. Even though *daño're* are acquired in a dream by an individual, the transmission process makes the *daño're* collective, "no longer belonging exclusively to the individual who dreamed it" (Graham 1984: 170). This author attempts to show a significant correlation between the principle that opposes the cosmological orders of culture and nature and the male and female (or social and intimate) organization of space, and musical practices—more specifically *choros* or laments (*dawawa*), collective songs (*daño're*), and masculine oratory.

The central village square is the space conceived as the nucleus of social life, the site where men meet and political leaders speak. Oratory, which is different from daily speech, both because of its content and its systematic use of special intonations, repetitions, and parallelisms, is the domain of adults who carry high social prestige and exercise political leadership. It is in the square that groups of men dance the *daño're*, whose linguistic content is quite simple: there are no syntactic connections forming sentences but only words. In the case of laments, as sung by men and women in their houses, language is reduced to syllables and vowels practically stripped of semantic content, suggesting an association of this genre with the less social and more natural forms of

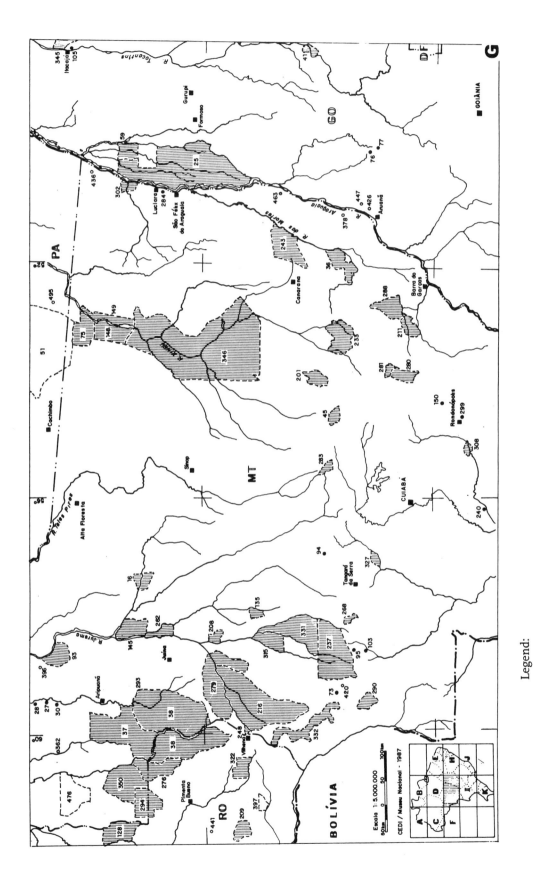

Legend:

346: Xingu Indian Park
36, 201, 233, 243, 280, 281, 288: Xavante areas

75: Capoto area
148, 149: Jarina area

Map 2: Areas inhabited by indigenous groups in Mato Grosso (CEDI 1987: 133).

communication. Consequently, the more distant the musical genre is from individual feelings and the spaces of domestic or intimate life, the more complex its linguistic content. The degree of melodic elaboration, however, seems to be inversely proportional to linguistic complexity, since the linguistically simpler laments (*choros*) unfold longer sequences of sounds and more ornamented melodic lines than the *daño're* (or male-owned, collective songs). Among the Xavante, whose ways of conceiving and organizing space are linked to cosmology, it seems clear that the place "where one sings" and "where one delivers a speech" (or formalized verbal expression, such as the chiefs' oratory) differentiates the verbal and musical genres.

Aytai's classification (1985: 106) reflects the breadth of the Xavante repertoire. It is based on function (for the generic groups) and native nomenclature (for the specific types), in the absence of a native classificatory system for music. We reproduce here only the generic categories, although the criteria based on function is flexible and often transcends specific uses because, as the author indicates, a song meant for a celebration can also be performed to articulate the cycle of daily life, or for another occasion:

> According to information from several Xavante singers, a chant for a festive day can occasionally be transformed—after the holiday—into another type of chant, generally the types that articulate the day (*dapraba, dadzarono,* or *dahipopo*). This suggests that the songs—or part of the songs—lack immanent properties (melodic, rhythmic, temporal, structural, textual, or other properties) that make them specific to one type of song or to one kind of function (Aytai 1985: 194, 199).

The following generic categories were identified by Aytai:

A. Songs that divide the cycle of daily life;

B. Songs related to subsistence (for hunting, construction of huts, request for food, songs for the preparation of corn, and preparation of the *jabuti* turtle);

C. War songs (calls to war, commemoration of victories);

D. Songs for festivals (*festas*) and sporting events (races, fights, festival of the *Way'ā*, the naming of women, the piercing of boys' ears, the *wamñorõ* festival, the *bate-água* festival);

E. Songs related to the social organization of specific groups;

F. Healing songs;

G. Rain songs (to make the rain stop);

H. Songs related to emotions, life, death (laments or *choros,* lullabies);

I. Songs to illustrate legends;

J. Acculturation songs (praises and songs related to Western ideas);

K. Special cases (which include songs that Aytai could not classify, miscellaneous types);

L. Instrumental and mixed music.

Within these categories, the *dawawa* type of *choro* or lament constitutes a special genre which the Xavante themselves do not consider as "song": they are individually performed and express nostalgia or longing (*saudade*) for a dead parent or a distant friend. The laments belong to the singer, accompany him throughout his life, only can be transmitted to wives, and cannot be sung by any other musicians. There are laments sung by a couple, each member performing his or her individual lament simultaneously, or by several men, as in Example 1.

When many Xavantes sing their individual laments at the same time, the result can be similar to heterophony, in the style of certain Suyá songs, as we shall see below. There is no polyphony in either instrumental music or music for voice and instruments. In the latter, the voice is always accompanied by instruments of indefinite pitch.

The *louvores* or songs of praise constitute a category that merits explanation. Aytai classifies them as "acculturation songs" because they pay homage to saints of the Catholic Church. In contrast to other

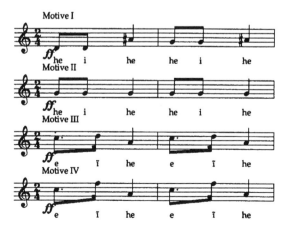

Ex. 1: Motives from *choros* (laments) sung by four Xavante men (Aytai 1985: 68).

songs, they have extensive texts, exclude meaningless syllables, and always deal with ideas introduced by the missionaries. Although their melodies possess clearly outlined contours and contain fewer repetitions, they are not simple assimilations of Western influences: they are Xavante songs that present a perceptible change in relation to the traditional style.

Although vocal expression is demonstrably more important than instrumental music, several types of rattles and a stamping tube often accompany song. There are also melodic instruments, such as the *umreñiduruture* flute, a relatively rare instrument, made of a small gourd with two holes; it produces three basic sounds with which melodies are built, but the instrument at times serves as a rattle, because the gourd contains the hooves of *queixada* (a type of pig). The majority of these flutes produce intervals of a minor third and perfect fifth, starting from the lowest sound. The *upawã*, a transverse bamboo flute without finger holes, produces three sounds (the variation of frequencies is obtained by closing the open end of the tube with the hand or by blowing more intensely), and it is used before the youths' ritual fight. The double *tsidupo* flute, made of two bamboo tubes, is always played in an interlocking manner with another identical flute.

Besides the eminently collective and vocal nature of Xavante music, other notable characteristics include a firmly regular rhythm that allowed Aytai to use meters in his transcriptions (Recorded Ex. 1). In several songs, however, mixed meters were noted. The strong tempi are marked by rattles and, during dance, by the strong stamping of the feet on the ground. Instrumental music and some laments depart from metric regularity. With few exceptions, however, most phonograms include strong beating of time. One example of the less frequent, irregular metric style is illustrated in Example 2.

As the songs are "received" in dreams, the Xavante do not always understand the meaning of the dreamed

words. Consequently, song texts might consist of only two or more words whose meaning is not always clear even to the Xavante, or only of meaningless syllables. According to Aytai, some syllables communicate ideas, as, for instance, *wé*, which means "beautiful, agreeable, good."

The high incidence of repetition, whether of one sound or of inner sections in a performance, is a phenomenon to which Aytai dedicates detailed statistical analyses. Example 3 (a *dadzarono* or noon song) illustrates the characteristics described above.

Based on his 131 transcriptions, Aytai examined several analytical questions, particularly those that refer to pitch organization. Eliminating songs that consisted of one and two pitches, that by definition could not be said to rely on a scale, he concluded that Xavante music lacks reference to a fully developed system of scales. The idea seems to be congruent with the fact that melodic instrumental music carries little significance within the tradition. However, a scale formed by a minor third, major second, and perfect fifth carries statistical significance, and for this reason Aytai considers it a "potential scale" (1976a: 78). The *dapraba* below is partially referable to this scale (Ex. 4).

Variation in pitch and progressive distancing from the original tuning also were observed during the singing of the songs, including those sung in unison. These, as well as pitch gliding and tempo variations, are explained as ornamental effects. Examples of Xavante music available on a commercial recording are found in *Música Indígena* (see Discography).

THE KAMAYURÁ OF THE XINGU INDIAN PARK

The Xingu Indian Park, an area reserved in 1961 by the Brazilian government, originally included 22,000 square kilometers, extending from the tributaries of the Xingu River to its mid-course.

Ex. 2: Xavante song of preparation for battle (Aytai 1985: 181).

Ex. 3: *Dadzarono* or noon song (Aytai 1985: 85).

Subsequent demarcations of the park reduced an area in which fourteen indigenous groups of diverse languages and cultures presently live. From time immemorial, the Alto Xingu region has been occupied by the Awetí and Kamayurá (Tupi linguistic stock), Kalapálo, Nahukwá-Matipú and Kuikúro (Carib), Mehináku, Yawalapiti and Waurá (Arawak), and Trumai (isolated language). Thanks to the natural isolation provided by waterfalls and virgin forests, they sought refuge there from external aggression while consolidating a relative measure of cultural uniformity. Besides these groups, the Txikão (Carib), Suyá, Metuktire, and Panará (Gê), Kayabi, and Juruna (Tupi), who previously inhabited other territories that were progressively occupied by national society, were brought to the park and they do not participate in the

Ex. 4: *Dapraba* or morning song (Aytai 1985: 119).

Alto Xingu culture (Map 3). The Metuktire group is presently settled in the areas of Capoto and Jarina, to the north of the park. The population of the park, together with the two areas just mentioned, totals 2,345 individuals (CEDI 1987). Practically all the groups in the Xingu Indian Park were or are the focus of anthropological and linguistic research, but their musics have not been thoroughly studied. Rafael José

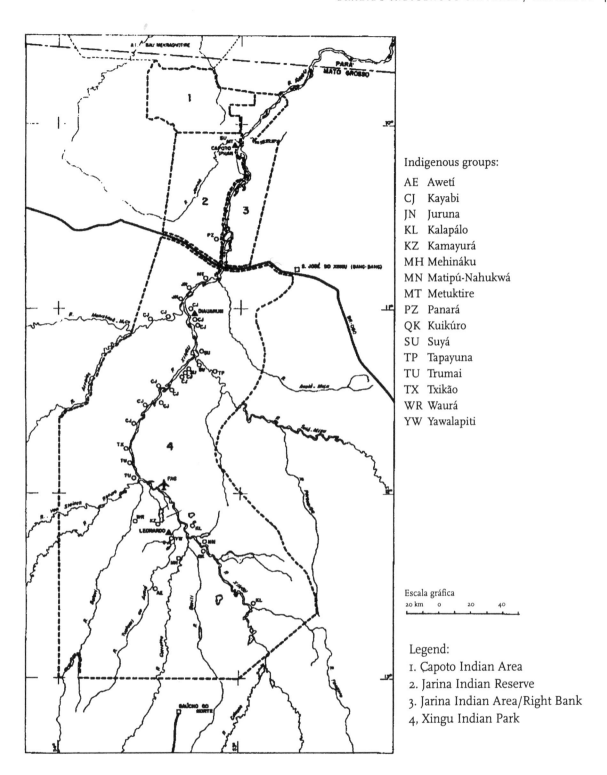

Indigenous groups:

AE   Awetí
CJ   Kayabi
JN   Juruna
KL   Kalapálo
KZ   Kamayurá
MH   Mehináku
MN   Matipú-Nahukwá
MT   Metuktire
PZ   Panará
QK   Kuikúro
SU   Suyá
TP   Tapayuna
TU   Trumai
TX   Txikão
WR   Waurá
YW   Yawalapiti

Escala gráfica

20 km   0   20   40

Legend:
1. Çapoto Indian Area
2. Jarina Indian Reserve
3. Jarina Indian Area/Right Bank
4. Xingu Indian Park

Map 3: The Xingu region (São Paulo: CEDI, 1985–1986 [Aconteceu especial, 17]).

de Menezes Bastos has studied the music of intertribal rituals of the Alto Xingu region which, together with matrimonial and commercial exchanges, represent a significant manifestation of the relations between different indigenous groups in that area (see Menezes Bastos, "The Yawari Ritual of the Kamayurá: A Xinguano Epic," in this volume). An earlier publication by the same author on the "musicology" of the Kamayurá deals principally with the native categories identified for their own music by this Alto Xingu group (1978 reissued 1999). In the 1978 study, Menezes Bastos constructs taxonomies that result from a two-tiered set of correlations: from the Kamayurá musical level to the Kamayurá verbal level, and from the latter to the scientific language used by the non-native researcher. The most inclusive category covers an area that refers to "any sound stream" (ihu). Then "any sounds" (also ihu) are distinguished from "language" (ñe'eng), the latter in turn including speech (also ñe'eng) and music (maraka). The Kamayurá criteria for contrasting these categories are as much acoustical (since they rest on "analysis of the distinctive physical manifestation of each subtype of 'sound stream'" [1978: 99]) as they are semiological (since only language transmits thought, as differentiated from other types of "sound streams"). The type of sound source (human beings, supernaturals, animals, inanimate beings) is implicitly considered as well, with ñe'eng being typical of human beings. In practical terms, only humans are capable of speech and music-making: the latter is a privileged domain they share with some birds. The acoustic criteria for defining classes of sound are: range ("small" or "big," that is, high or low); intensity (weak or strong); timbre (spoken = falado, struck = batido, rattled = chocalhado, kneaded or "massaged" = amassado, broken = partido, slightly touched = roçado, dragged = arrastrado, etc.); consistency (soft or hard); and density (diffuse or concentrated). The hitting together of two stones is a "hard" sound, while the wind lightly touching tree leaves is "soft." The sound of a rattle, made up of multiple sounds, is diffuse, while striking is a directed and concentrated sound.

The domain of music (maraka) includes the categories of kewere (prayer) and several subcategories,

with each musical style corresponding to a ritual or ritual phase (Menezes Bastos 1978: 107; see Fig. 2). According to the author, "the Kamayurá conceptualize the maraka category in terms that are no longer merely acoustical or semiological, but specifically musicological" (1978: 107).

Kewere is a therapy applied to organic illnesses, used by healers who work with traditional medicine, but different from the process of shamanism, which operates on the patient's soul. On the strictly musical level the two healing practices also differ. Other groups of the Tupi-Guarani linguistic family assign a similarly crucial role to music in shamanistic rituals, imbuing it with the power to restore relations between humans and the supernatural world, which is populated by potentially evil spirits.

In the identification of sound phenomena conceived as music (maraka), other criteria also come into play: duration (long or short), speed (slow or fast), and the syntactical process. With regard to the latter, the Kamayurá distinguish, for instance, such concepts as theme (ipỳ, literally foot) and its elaboration process through repetition, variation, and transformation in the course of a musical performance.

Musical instruments are treated according to their hierarchy in the taxonomy of the maraka category. The marakatap (or musical instruments) constitute one means of music-making, a broad category divided into "music proper" and "musical accompaniment." The first encompasses singing or playing wind instruments —that is, preferentially melodic music—while "musical accompaniment" implies the use of instruments incapable of melody, that is, mostly idiophones of indefinite pitch. The sounds that "sing," that is, that can vary in duration and amplitude, constitute "music proper."

The names of many instruments derive from the principal material from which they are made and refer to the occasion for which they are used. They are further distinguished by the degree of expertise of the performer who plays them, as for apprenticeship or actual performance. (In general, the small sizes are for training, as in the case of instruments of the same type with varying dimensions.) They also can be

Maraka (music)
1. kewere (prayer) 2. maraka (music)
kwarỳramaraka   yaku'iamaraka   tawurawãnãamaraka
music for Kwarỳ'p music for Yaku'i music for Tawurawãnã

Fig. 2: Native taxonomy of the domain of music (maraka)

classified according to context (singing, dancing, recreation), number of modules required for their construction, and number of players necessary for performance.

In the Alto Xingu there are sacred flutes (*yaku'i*) rigorously forbidden to women, such as those among the Tukano Indians of the Vaupés River in northwest Amazonia. The Kamayurá explain the taboo in light of a myth that narrates how, in the remote past, a culture hero imprisoned the fish of the rivers, which he then reproduced in wood. The hero gave them voices [flutes] and reserved them for men. After the women appropriated them, thus reversing the social roles, the flutes were again returned to the masculine realm, a restoration of the order that still prevails: no woman should dare approach the *yaku'i*. During the ritual of the same name in which these flutes are played, the women are confined to their homes.

The musical instruments in the Alto Xingu are played in groups of two, three, or four, often with interlocking technique. When this technique is not used, instrumental groups create multi-part relationships. Songs can be performed by one singer, or in groups of two, three, or more performers. Instrumental music is exclusively masculine, while the women sing and dance. The relationships between instruments symbolically correlate with social kinships: a pair of instruments is a couple—man and wife; groups of three or four instruments are fathers and sons. In some rituals, groups of two (such as in the *kwarỹ'p*), and three performers (such as in the *yaku'i*) predominate.

On the basis of recordings, the soundscape produced by these instrumental groups was examined by Jonathan Hill (1979), who called attention to the different procedures for elaboration of a phrase-theme in the course of a performance: addition of sounds and augmentation of the phrase played by the "music master," who holds the central role in the typical trio of *yaku'i* flutes for the ritual of the same name; diminution of the number of sounds and contraction of the phrase-theme in the music most likely played on *takwara* "clarinets" for the bamboo (*takwara*) dance; and lack of syntactical changes in the phrase-theme played in alternation by paired *uru'a* flutes for the *kwarỹ'p* ritual. Thus, symbolically distinct musical styles can be inferred from different rituals.

In addition to instrumental music, song and dance also are part of these occasions. The *kwarỹ'p* ritual was researched by Pedro Agostinho (1974).

Characterized as a cycle in several stages, *kwarỹ'p* is an intertribal event that celebrates and remembers deceased chiefs. During *kwarỹ'p*, the girls come out of seclusion and the relatives of the dead, who are remembered on the occasion, end their period of mourning. The cycle contains sequences of specific songs performed by "music masters" accompanied by two apprentices, in addition to the *uru'a* flute pairs.

Kamayurá music has a mythic and supernatural origin: it was from the body of a supernatural *mãma'ẽ* jaguar (*onça*) that a culture hero extracted the musical instruments. In the present as well, music is acquired from the *mãma'ẽ* by the "music masters," in dreams or solitary walks through the forest. Once received, it is first transmitted to the apprentice and learned on the instruments assigned to training, and only later presented to the community.

Unlike other indigenous groups, the Kamayurá formalize the transmission of musical knowledge through "masters" who excel in specific styles and possess the craft of building and playing the musical instruments, thus attracting prestige and wealth for themselves. When an individual who is stricken by some spiritual illness sponsors a specific ritual linked to the spirit causing it, he must contract a specialist in the music of that ritual. This fact provides a measure of the power and social status that music masters carry, particularly among the Kamayurá and other groups in the Alto Xingu.

The intertribal rituals in the Alto Xingu only can be considered in the context of cultural exchange and factional politics (Menezes Bastos 1984–1985). The complexity of the intertribal relations at play becomes clear in shamanic practices: the song texts of the *payemeramaraka* ritual (or music of the shamans) are in Arawakan languages (Mehináku or Yawalapiti); the great shamans—who officiate at the rites—are Kamayurá; the principal "music masters" belong to other groups; and so on. All this makes it difficult to talk about Kamayurá shamanistic music without considering the contributions of other groups. A comparative approach to the music and shamanistic beliefs of several Tupi groups would be welcomed.

The *payemeramaraka* ritual is distinguished from other shamanic practices by its divinatory "seeing and hearing" sessions, whose purpose is to identify the root of evil to which an illness may be attributed. It is carried out in the Alto Xingu by both the Kamayurá and other neighboring tribes. Healing sessions (using the smoke of tobacco), in which malignant objects are extracted from the body of the ailing person, can occur separately or as part of the *payemeramaraka*. The musics for this ritual were examined in their Kuikúro and Kamayurá versions, which are structurally identical (but containing the variations in texts that always occur, from one session to another, no matter what ethnic group the officiator belongs to). Accompanied by rattles, three shamans perform a song whose central part is the responsibility of the "music master," heterophonically imitated by his assistants. This central part is the "music proper," including text, melody, and rhythm. Around it there develops, simultaneously, another type of expression peripheral to the song (in Menezes Bastos's terminology) that includes speaking to the spirits and to the sick person's lost soul, performed by other shamans. The song of the community of shamans is accompanied by a series of other ritual activities: journeys in search of the ailing person's soul, healing with tobacco smoke, exhortations to the spirits, etc. Example 5 is a transcription by Menezes Bastos of the song of the chief shaman (1984–1985: 161), with the author's free translation of the text.

Musical features include repetition of a rhythmic pattern, with frequent variations of tempo; melodic motives that always are associated with the corresponding text; and considerable repetition of motives. The song precludes regular metrification and its tempo is very variable. Typical of Alto Xingu shamanistic rituals, it shares with the rest of the Kamayurá repertoire the structure that Menezes Bastos calls the "nucleus-periphery": a nuclear musical center to which peripheral elements—be they musical or not—are added. A recorded shamanic chant of the Kamayurá is available in *Música Popular do Norte-4*, side A, band 4 (see Discography).

háhue– blowing, healing with smoke
kaminū– the mythical twins Sun and Moon

nátuhutaakalá– I said
halỳ yó– the name of a *mãma'ẽ*

Ex. 5: Kamayurá shaman's chant (Menezes Bastos 1984–1985: 161).

VOCAL MUSIC OF THE
SUYÁ INDIANS

The Suyá are a group of about 150 individuals who live on the Suyá-Miçu River, a tributary of the Xingu River (Map 3). Their village, typical of Gê-speaking Indians, has houses arranged in a circle surrounding the square, where most of the ceremonies take place. Besides the residences, which house several nuclear families, there is a men's house for meetings that can include singing. The Suyá already had settled in the Xingu region when the Xingu Indian Park was established and maintain contact with Alto Xingu groups as well as with those who resettled there more recently. They share basic sociocultural traits with other family groups of the Gê linguistic stock, but are closer to the so-called northern Gê (Apinayé, Kayapó, and Timbira) than to the central Xavante or the southern Kaingang and Xokleng.

Practically all Suyá music is vocal, as it is among the Xavante. As far as we know, this appears to be characteristic of Gê linguistic groups. They use rattles for musical accompaniment and play Alto Xingu flutes that make their way into the village without incorporating them into their traditional performances. The word *ngére*, which designates music among the Suyá, also designates "ceremony," as well as a specific genre of songs.

The emphasis on vocal music is part of a larger system that assigns high value to oral expression, particularly masculine oratory. One of its forms, the formal "plaza language," is the domain of political leaders and serves to exhort fulfillment of collective duties. Suyá vocal genres were studied from a comparative perspective (Anthony Seeger 1987: 25–51) and constitute a continuum ranging from speech to song, rather than a roster of contrasting forms. All genres organize timbre, pitch, and duration of sound, but in diverse ways, with different emphases and varying degrees of structuralization. Thus, speech or *kapérni*, in all its forms and including informal speech, instruction (*sarén*), song (*ngére*), and invocations (*sangére*, occasionally used to cure illness), can be compared with regard to fixity of texts, use of language, length of phrases, and authority inherent in them. In general, the most structured expressions and those that take place on the most formal occasions are restricted to adult and older men:

All Suyá spoke everyday speech; most people would tell narratives; adult men and women would perform

invocations. But other forms were quite restricted. Only adult men and women orated, and some forms were supposed to be performed only by political and ceremonial leaders. Songs were originally learned by a few, specially endowed men and women and might only be performed by certain sex-, age-, and name-based groups (Seeger 1987: 49–50).

Speech and hearing are complementary faculties whose meaning also carries ethical values for the Suyá. The ability to hear and speak well is desirable and considered "social" behavior, in opposition, for example, to the special vision of male or female witches, which is dangerous and malevolent. Thus, the use of "plaza language" and the singing of a song genre *(akia)* are not only forms of expression but ways of achieving culturally established ideals for adult men, while the "bad speech" of the witches does not have a place in the public arena because it is condemned by the code of behavior.

The symbolism of the ear and lip disks, which constitute the Suyá's principal body ornaments, was interpreted by Seeger (1980) on the basis of the group's concepts of speech, hearing, vision, and smell. By decorating the lower lip and the earlobes with heavy disks, the group emphasizes orality and listening as principal means of perception, transmission, comprehension, and expression of their fundamental values. According to Seeger, the absence of instrumental music has something to do with the enormous importance attributed to oral forms of expression.

Suyá music is ceremonial. In their ceremonies, the two pairs of moieties of the tribe, constituted on the basis of names of individuals, play an important role; these groups cross between themselves and those formed on the basis of kinship and political loyalties, weaving a web of relations of diverse types that make the village a unit and not merely a group of houses. The initiation ceremonies for young men are quite elaborate. They live for some time in the men's house, leaving it upon the birth of their first child, when they join the wife's family. The passage to adulthood is marked by the piercing of the ears and lips, and by the use of disks, which up until a short while ago indicated the status of adult man; these ornaments are being abandoned.

It was from an ethnography of an initiation ritual (the Mouse Ceremony, in which a boy receives his name from his mother's classificatory brother, a name that determines the moiety to which he will belong, body painting he will use, with whom he will sing, etc.) that Anthony Seeger approached the principal vocal forms of the Suyá, including songs (1987). It is precisely song and the use of some types of speech that clearly characterize ceremonial periods, making them stand out from the flow of daily life. There are no work songs, love songs, or lullabies among the Suyá: all their music is confined to rituals.

The comparison between two important genres of Suyá songs (*akia* and *ngére*), as well as the analysis of each and the examination of the context in which they appear, permitted Seeger (1977, 1979) to discern some characteristics of Suyá music. The ceremonies include these two song genres, structurally identical and constituted as well by a dual division, which is related to the dualism in the group's social organization and cosmology. In his essay about the *akia*, Seeger (1977) deals not only with a musical genre but also with the relations between music and society: the shouted song called *akia* is seen "in light of the cosmological and social organization of the Suyá, and in search of the principles that are common to them."

The Suyá conceptualize the structure of their songs by separating, in each strophe, the part sung with text (*sinti iarén*, or "telling the name") and those in which only song syllables are sung (such as the *kuré*, or "coda," sung to the syllables te-te-te-te in Example 6). The songs as a whole are divided into two parts: *kradi* (first half) and *sindaw* (second half). The first and second halves are structurally equivalent and contain the same sections. Figure 3 (Seeger 1987: 43) schematizes the structure of Suyá songs.

There are examples of *akia* and *ngére* in the sections dedicated to songs in *A arte vocal dos Suyá* (1982, see Discography) and on the cassette that accompanies *Why Suyá Sing* (Seeger 1987). The internal divisions of the songs are not made on the basis of the text alone, as it may seem: they correspond to distinct musical sections. Example 6 shows the "telling the name" section, which evolves on a melodic level, and the "coda" section, in which

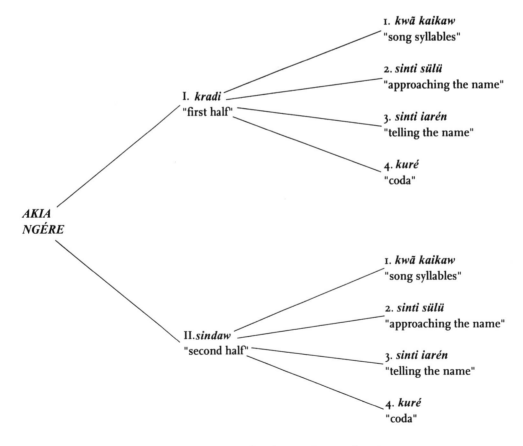

Fig. 3: The structure of Suyá songs (Seeger 1987: 43).

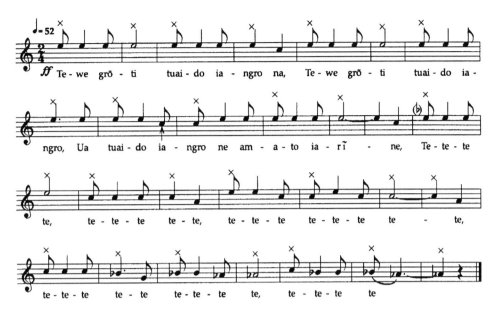

Ex. 6: *Akia* of the Suyá transcribed by Eero Tarasti (Seeger 1977: 47; Recorded Ex. 2). (X indicates rattle; upward arrow indicates micro-interval above pitch.)

the profile of the melody changes and becomes descending (Recorded Ex. 2). This pattern of melodic construction also is found in other *akia*. In the genre of songs called *ngére*, the stylistic characteristics are different: there appears to be no marked contrast in melodic approach between the sections "telling the name" and "coda."

The *akia* are a source of pride for the Suyá, who consider them a distinctive trait of their ethnic group. They are individual, masculine songs performed in a high register and in "shouted" style, which is expressed by the term *akia* itself that can mean "to shout" in other contexts. Several men singing their *akia* simultaneously, as is the custom in Suyá ceremonies, create heterophony, since the individual songs are performed all at once without concern for adjustments of tempo, "combination" of melodic lines, or coordination among the singers at the beginning or end of the song. The *akia* repertoire is constantly renewed by the appearance of new songs which, in a certain sense, belong to their singers. The *ngére*, conversely, are collective songs, sung in unison in a low register, and identified not with individuals but with ceremonial groups. Participation in ceremonies and, consequently, in collective singing is determined by a man's name, which defines the ceremonial moiety to which he belongs.

According to the Suyá, men sing *akia* for their sisters, a fact Seeger interprets as the way men have of communicating with their sisters without violating the rules of behavior that restrict their relations with

female blood relatives once they have left the house where they were born. The Suyá observe the uxorilocal rule of residence: boys leave their homes to live in the men's house at a certain time in their lives; when they marry, they go to live with their wife's family, distancing themselves spatially and socially from their mothers and sisters. The *akia*, which are shouted to be heard at a distance so that the individual singer can be identified, are the vehicle that overcomes the spatial, social, and psychological separation between a Suyá man and his sisters (Seeger 1977).

The "women's laments" (*choros femininos*) are the only example on the record *A arte vocal dos Suyá* (1982) of an exclusively feminine manifestation. Suyá women sing generally in accompaniment to men, which shows that their participation in traditional Suyá music is smaller. They narrate myths, they intone invocations (*sangére*) as often as men do, but their full participation in performance as singers takes place only during rituals acquired from Alto Xingu neighbors. This is explained, in part, by the fact that many women were kidnapped from these neighboring groups at the beginning of the century (this being a part of Suyá behavior rooted in myth), and at a time when depopulation threatened the existence of the Suyá group.

The songs the Suyá sing stem from three different sources. Their ceremonial repertoire includes very old songs whose origins are described in myths; songs they have learned and appropriated from outsiders; and songs transmitted to the community by "men without spirits." These are persons whose spirits have been snatched from their bodies by a male or female witch for malevolent reasons and dwell in a specific domain of the natural world, where they can hear these songs from animals, plants, and insects. They are the "composers" who then transmit these new songs to the community. Ceremonial specialists are recruited from among these individuals: they lead collective singing, and their role is complementary to that of the chiefs, although political leaders never are "men without spirits." Because these songs stem from a process of metamorphosis, they are believed to possess transformative power and for that reason are performed in initiation ceremonies, where the change in an individual's social status is effected. In all three cases, the realms from which songs are acquired are seen as external to Suyá society. According to Seeger, the principle that governs the creative and innovative process in music is always to bring into Suyá society songs that "belonged" to domains other than their own, thereby incorporating the knowledge (which is power) as well as the "material resources of strangers into social reproduction of their own society" (1987: 52–64).

TOWARD THE POSSIBILITY OF COMPARATIVE STUDIES

The number of existing studies about the musics of Brazilian Indians, added to those that are in progress, is not very substantial compared to the number of groups whose music is entirely unknown. Perhaps for this reason, what stands out most of all is diversity, rather than unity. At the heart of a plethora of styles, however, is the integral role of music and dance in ritual and ceremony, its potential as a means of communication with the supernatural world, and its role in the construction of identities (of sex, age group, ceremonial group, ethnic group). Future research will be able to build on these observations and consider them in all their dimensions and implications.

Some authors object to the joint treatment of indigenous musics (as, for example, Menezes Bastos 1974: 52). They argue that it would be inevitable to select a few musical characteristics that are comparable from group to group, and this would result in the elimination of others and in the omission of their particular meaning for the culture from which they stem. The difficulty may be temporary, however, and accumulated knowledge should permit, at the appropriate time, a team approach to comparative

studies. Some commonalities between the musics of linguistically and culturally related groups, or issues that have been persistently raised in the specialized literature, already can be identified. Although premature at the present time, it would be important to verify if there are common principles at work in the musics of these groups, if there are similar ideas and concepts, and if the aesthetic values that govern musical life are to some extent shared by them.

The Gê-speaking groups, it appears, prefer vocal music and their songs are collective, without giving special attention to individual performance. The individuality of the singers is suppressed, because what is important is "with whom one sings," as Seeger observed in reference to the Suyá (1979: 385). In societies where dual divisions create strictly ceremonial groups whose existence is principally manifested through song, it is reasonable to expect collective songs to be a constant, despite the stylistic differences between them. Even when individual performance is significant and when the singer is especially linked to his song (in the role of "author," if this term can be used, or "owner" of the song), it occurs on occasions of collective performance: the individual performance is subsumed into its simultaneity with others, as happens when many Suyá sing their *akia* at the same time, or when several Xavante perform their *choros* (laments). It should be remembered that collective song is not always in unison: the collective songs of the Krahó Indians (of the same linguistic family)—of which there are examples on the record *Música Indígena*—display what could be called a simultaneous multiplicity of individual performances. The music of the Krahó is also essentially vocal (Melatti 1982: 31).

Examples of "polyphony" or multi-part texture are found generally among the Tupi-speaking groups: the case of Kamayurá instrumental multi-part performance cited above; the war songs of the *yawaci* ritual of the Kayabi Indians (Ex. 7), in which a soloist alternates with a female group; and the songs of the Kayowá transcribed by Helza Camêu (Ex. 8), also in responsorial style, are instances of multi-part performances. The alternation between soloist and chorus "collectivizes" musical practice without leveling the roles of each part. In some cases, the role of the chorus is to make the solo part more evident, as we believe occurs in the songs of the *yawaci* ritual among the Kayabi. These groups also have collective songs, but there appears to be greater individuation of musical activity among them.

The Kamayurá and other Upper-Xingu Indians have "music masters" whose musical knowledge and experience are greater than that of the rest of the group. Their knowledge is transmitted to the apprentices, and when they sing and play, the rest dance or listen. The ceremonial leaders found among the Suyá are also individuals who carry specialized knowledge. However, while they lead the collective singing and create an ideal performance of a ceremony, it is assumed that all members of the community participate in musical activities according to their sex, age, and affiliation to the ceremonial groups.

The Tupi-speaking peoples place special significance on shamanism. As a rule, the shamans are specialists in ritual music on the strength of their power to communicate with the supernatural world, which is the source of some musical genres, rather than on their musical ability. In this case, collective participation is clearly under the musical direction of the shaman, or else the latter carries out by himself the musical activities required of his position. The condition of "specialist," however, is not always adequate for shamans. Among the Arawété, for instance, practically all the men are shamans, and all regularly sing according to "visions" or "dreams" that connect them with the dead and the gods (Viveiros de Castro 1986). It is common to find two types of shamanistic rituals among these groups: one that makes use of blowing, healing with smoke, and suction; and another, properly musical, in which there

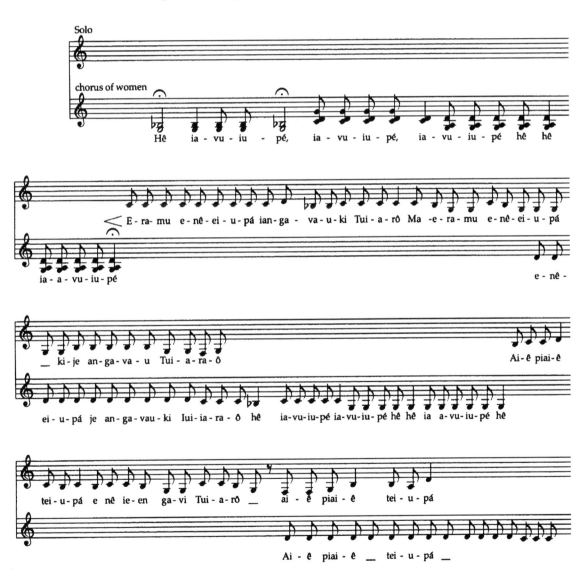

Ex. 7: Excerpt from a song for the *yawaci* ritual of the Kayabi Indians.

In performance, the chorus proceeds in two parts, as follows, always accompanied
by *maracá* and *tamborim*. The fifths 'glide', precluding precise intonation.

Ex. 8: Kayowá song in responsorial style, transcribed by Camêu (1977: Supplement, 44).

is collective dancing, singing, and playing under the leadership of one or more shamans. This is the case of the *kewere* and the *payemeramaraka* of the Kamayurá, and the *reza* and *maraká* of the Kayabi (Travassos 1984).

As far as we know, the Tupi groups distinguish themselves by the practice of more purely instrumental music, sometimes multi-part, as in the case of the Kamayurá. These Indians possess a greater variety of wind instruments, which is even more striking in areas of cultural exchange between several groups (the Kamayurá, for instance, have thirteen types of aerophones). This statement, however, cannot be taken as a general rule because exceptions soon appear: the Kayabi possess only two types of flutes (Grünberg 1967) whose construction and use recently have become extinct. Of their musical instruments, only a small bone flute remains for the shamans to summon

spirits during rituals. The loss of the flutes, coinciding with a series of contemporaneous events triggered by intensified contact with national society, can perhaps be explained by their expendable role in the group's musical life: men played them as a form of entertainment, rather than for reenactment of beliefs, as in ritual.

Although the existing documentation is scant and always oriented toward specific concerns, some musical aspects have been repeatedly addressed with regard to different groups. Pitch organization is one such aspect. Some researchers have observed variable intonation of pitch in vocal music, a fact that interferes with attempts to map intervals within a specific style and with identification of scales. Even those who do not specifically discuss problems of variable intonation admit difficulties in transcription and stress the schematic nature of traditional music notation. Hornbostel (1923) noted the variable intonation of pitches in songs of three Roraima groups, without determining their scales. Pioneers such as Gallet (1934) and Corrêa de Azevedo (1938) discussed how to treat intervals that defied codification according to the tempered diatonic and chromatic scales: was there a different intervallic system at work (Gallet), or did the intervallic "deviations" assume a diatonic base (Corrêa de Azevedo)?

Camêu and Aytai attempted to apply objective criteria in determining scales, assuming the principle that intervals could be graphically identified as seconds, thirds, etc. They based their findings on their listening experience with musics of the Urubu-Kaapor, Kadiwéu, Mbayá, and Xavante. Camêu did not consider the intervallic deviations frequently found in indigenous musics as elements of a system, regarding them instead as the result of "inflections of the languages, deficiencies of the interpreter, or dispositions peculiar to groups or tribes" (1977: 102). From examples chosen at random, Camêu argued for the existence of a natural concatenation of intervals in sequences that outline triads and seventh chords. For her, "the musical line is always clearly shaped, allowing the possibility of oral and graphic reproduction" (1977: 107). Corrêa de Azevedo (1938) advanced this observation with regard to other groups. To identify nuclear pitches, Camêu placed in ascending order all the pitches found in the music of a given group, and then identified the most frequently repeated tones and those functioning cadentially within a melody. Hornbostel and Aytai adopted different procedures. Hornbostel established "structural formulas," not from the totality of pitches in the sample (as did Camêu), but from the totality of intervals. Aytai, similarly, searched for a system of scales in the high percentage of recurring intervals among the totality of pitches found in a sample, but concluded that the samples were not referable to a system of scales. From this evidence, it appears that this approach to pitch organization produced disappointing results and only proved a reality of disconcerting heterogeneity. Beaudet (1982: 153) corroborated this perception: "Chez aucune ethnie n'apparaît clairement d'échelle dominante lors d'une simple écoute; et il apparaît encore moins d'échelle privilégiée par l'ensemble des ethnies des basses terres d'Amérique du Sud." This is due to the different methodologies used by the researchers and the limited scope of their research (relatively few ethnic groups), and also to the very nature of the musical materials with which they worked. The traditional,

European-derived parameters of analysis, such as pitch structure and rhythm, have been abandoned for other aspects whose analysis seems more fruitful for the study of these musics.

Anthony Seeger (1987), for instance, examined a very specific issue—the recurrent rise in pitch in *agachi ngére* (a genre of collective songs for the rainy season)—which had been observed in other repertoires but rarely considered as a significant aspect. Among the Suyá, not only is the occurrence of this "deviation" in tuning noteworthy, but also the fact that the singers periodically return to the initial level of intonation. Isolating this characteristic made possible some revelations about the musical aesthetics of the Suyá. They distinguish the high and low registers (characteristic of the *akia* and *ngére*, respectively), indicating the location of the sounds in the singer's throat: high up in the throat or with "small throat" for higher pitches, and in the lower part of the throat, or "big throat" for lower pitches. Singing the *ngére* with a "big throat" is an ideal pursued by the men, and in particular older men, from whom a better musical performance is expected. Thus, although they do not purposely elevate the tuning, the group formed by a leader who is a ritual specialist and whose voice is appreciated, and by young men, seeks to return to the low pitches that define a good performance of the *ngére* genre. While the Suyá did not discuss absolute pitch, "they were very interested in relative pitch (higher or lower than the mid-range), which was associated with age, genre, and the authenticity of the singers" (Seeger 1987: 101–102).

Some researchers have shown that ordered bodies of ideas and values concerning music exist among indigenous groups. The Kamayurá classify sounds found in nature and those produced by the human voice and by musical instruments. The Suyá speak about their pieces in terms of their proper form and about aspects they consider relevant about their styles:

> This structure [of songs] is clear to the Suyá (although it took me some time to discover it) and should put an end to statements to the effect that Indian music has little structure and no closure. There is in fact considerable structure, only the grossest of which I have treated here (Seeger 1979: 390).

More is also being learned about the processes of transmission of musical knowledge. Among the Xavante and the Suyá, musical training is central during periods of seclusion for preparation to enter adult life. The ceremonies are also occasions of musical instruction for young men. In an anthropological sense, an initiation ritual could be seen as a social "institution," but "schools" in the Western European sense do not exist. Seeger (1987: 17–18) relates that boys, during the Mouse Ceremony, "rehearsed" the songs under the leadership of an adult in a camp outside the village, and performed during their assigned night for presentation before all the adult men. Among the Xavante, the non-initiated boys undergo musical training directed by members of other age groups. This training (which, as in the Suyá case, consists basically of repetition) occurs in the single men's house, and the period of residence in this house is largely that of preparation for full participation in collective singing.

As stated above, our comparative criteria only can remain tentative at this stage in our knowledge of individual indigenous groups. One recent study, by Jonathan D. Hill (1994), explored the intrinsic connections between musical practices and the social construction of history in three cultural areas of Lowland South America: 1) the northern Arawakan peoples of the Upper Rio Negro in northwestern Amazonia; 2) the Tupi-Guarani peoples of coastal Brazil and Paraguay; and 3) the Gê-speaking peoples of central Brazil. In this paradigmatic study, Hill attempts to demonstrate that musically dynamic genres of ritual "speech" are directly employed in all three regions in constructing symbolic space-time of movements away from the center of the mythic and social worlds. According to Hill, musically dynamic genres of ritual speech provide the basic means for opening up the predominantly verbal, semantically constructed worlds of myth and society, into more open-ended, expansive processes of social reproduction, or history. He also observes that, although the musicality of ritual speech is central to the construction of history in all three regions chosen for comparison, the resulting patterns of social reproduction outline three radically diverse historical trajectories (1994: 1).

The emphasis on musical diversity that prevails in recent studies reflects far-reaching theoretical changes in both anthropology and ethnomusicology. It parallels an emphasis on cultural diversity and attention to ethnic self-identifications and cognitive structures, which should replace generic and external labels, such as "Indian." These new avenues have proved fruitful, as in the case of Anthony Seeger's "musical anthropology" of the Suyá (1987), and other contributions mentioned

in these pages. In spite of the tendency of some authors to concentrate on a single ethnic group, new comparative levels between particular musics and cultures are being devised, as, for instance, in the study by Jonathan Hill quoted above (1994). Finally, it should be remembered that studies of particular ethnic musics can raise our awareness of other conceptions of music, while cautioning us not to impose our own subconscious categories on other peoples' expressions and ways of life.

—Translated by John P. Murphy

REFERENCES

Agostinho, Pedro 1974. *Kwarìp: Mito e ritual no Alto Xingu.* São Paulo: Editora Pedagógica e Universitária [EPU]—Editora da Universidade de São Paulo.

Almeida, Renato 1942. *História da música brasileira.* Rio de Janeiro: Briguiet e Cia.

Andrade, Mário de 1942 in 1980. *Pequena história da música,* 8th ed. São Paulo: Livraria Martins Editora.

Aytai, Desidério 1976a. "O sistema tonal do canto xavante," *Revista do Museu Paulista* 23: 65–83.

1976b. *O mundo sonoro Xavante* (PhD diss., Anthropology: Pontifícia Universidade Católica de Campinas).

1985. *O mundo sonoro Xavante.* São Paulo: Universidade de São Paulo (Coleção Museu Paulista, Etnologia, vol. 5).

Azevedo, Luiz Heitor Corrêa de 1938. *Escala, ritmo e melodia na música dos índios brasileiros.* Rio de Janeiro: Rodrigues e Cia.

1941. "Tupinambá melodies in Jean de Léry's *Histoire d'un voyage faict en la terre du Brésil,*" *Papers of the American Musicological Society, annual meeting 1941.* Richmond: William Byrd Press, 1946, 85–96.

Beaudet, Jean-Michel 1982. "Musiques d'Amérique tropicale: Discographie analytique et critique des amérindiens des basses terres," *Journal de la Société des Américanistes* (Paris) 68: 149–203.

Biblioteca Nacional 1974. *Três séculos de iconografia da música no Brasil.* Rio de Janeiro: Divisão de Publicações e Divulgação (Catalogue of the exhibition, containing 18 postcards).

Camêu, Helza 1977. *Introdução ao estudo da música indígena brasileira.* Rio de Janeiro: Conselho Federal de Cultura, Departamento de Assuntos Culturais.

CEDI (Ecumenical Center for Documentation and Information)—Museu Nacional 1987. *Terras indígenas no Brasil.* São Paulo.

Gallet, Luciano 1934. *Estudos de folclore.* Rio de Janeiro: Carlos Wehrs.

Galvão, Eduardo 1960 in 1979. "Áreas culturais indígenas do Brasil, 1900–1959" in *Encontro de sociedades: Índios e brancos no Brasil,* ed. by Eduardo Galvão. Rio de Janeiro: Paz e Terra 193–228.

Graham, Laura 1984. "Semanticity and melody: Parameters of contrast in Shavante vocal expression," *Latin American music review* 5/2: 161–85.

Grünberg, Georg and Friedl 1967. "Die materielle Kultur der Kaybí-Indianer: Bearbeitung einer ethnographischen Sammlung," *Archiv für Völkerkunde* (Vienna) 21: 27–89.

Harrison, Frank 1973. *Time, place, and music: An anthology of ethnomusicological observation, c.1550 to 1800.* Amsterdam: Frits Knuf.

Hill, Jonathan D. 1979. "Kamayurá flute music: A study of music as meta-communication," *Ethnomusicology* 23/3: 417–32.

1994. "Musicality and the construction of indigenous histories in Lowland South America," communication presented at the 48th International Congress of Americanists, Stockholm.

Hill, Jonathan D., editor 1988. *Rethinking history and myth: Indigenous South American perspectives on the past.* Urbana: University of Illinois Press.

Hill, Jonathan D., and Fernando Santos-Granero, editors 2002. *Comparative Arawakan histories: Rethinking language family and culture area in Amazonia.* Urbana and Chicago: University of Illinois Press.

Hornbostel, Erich M. von 1923 in 1979–1982. "La música de los Makuschí, Taulipang y Yekuana" in *Del Roraima al Orinoco* by Theodor Koch-Grünberg. Caracas: Ediciones del Banco Central de Venezuela (Colección Histórico-Económica), vol. III. (Spanish translation of *Vom Roroima zum Orinoco*. Stuttgart: Strecker und Schröder Verlag, vol. III.)

Leite, Serafim 1949. "A música nas escolas jesuíticas do Brasil no século XVI," *Cultura* (Rio de Janeiro, Ministério da Educação e Saúde, Serviço de Documentação) 2: 27–39.

Manizer, H. H. 1934. "Música e instrumentos de música de algumas tribus do Brasil," *Revista brasileira de música* (Instituto Nacional de Música da Universidade do Rio de Janeiro).

Melatti, Julio Cezar 1982. "Nota sobre a música Krahô," *Revista goiana de artes* (Goiânia) 3/1: 29–40.

Melo, Guilherme de 1908 in 1947. *A música no Brasil: Desde os tempos coloniais até o primeiro decênio da República.* Rio de Janeiro: Imprensa Nacional.

Menezes Bastos, Rafael José de 1974. "Las músicas tradicionales del Brasil," *Revista musical chilena*, 125: 21–77.

1978. *A musicológica Kamayurá: Para uma antropologia de comunicação no Alto Xingu.* Brasília: Fundação Nacional do Indio. Second edition (Florianópolis: Universidade Federal de Santa Catarina, 1999).

1984–1985. "O 'Payemeramaraka' Kamayurá: Uma contribuição à etnografia do xamanismo no Alto-Xingu," *Revista de antropologia* (São Paulo) 27/28: 139–77.

Oliveira Filho, João Pacheco de 1987. "Elementos para uma sociologia dos viajantes" in *Sociedades indígenas e indigenismo no Brasil*, ed. by João Pacheco de Oliveira Filho. Rio de Janeiro: UFRJ (Federal University of Rio de Janeiro)—Marco Zero, 84–148.

Porantim (Brasília) (Suplemento) 1986, vol. 13, nos. 83–84 (janeiro–fevereiro).

Ribeiro, Darcy 1957. *Culturas e línguas indígenas do Brasil.* Rio de Janeiro: Centro Brasileiro de Pesquisas Educacionais.

1977. *Os índios e a civilização.* Petrópolis: Editora Vozes.

Ricardo, Carlos Alberto, editor 1996. *Povos indígenas no Brasil, 1991–1995.* São Paulo: Instituto Socioambiental.

Rodrigues, Aryon Dall'Igna 1986. *Línguas brasileiras: Para o conhecimento das línguas indígenas.* São Paulo: Loyola.

Roquette-Pinto, Edgardo 1917 in 1976. *Rondônia.* São Paulo: Cia. Editora Nacional.

Seeger, Anthony 1977. "Por que os índios Suyá cantam para as suas irmãs?" in *Arte e sociedade: Ensaios de sociologia da arte*, ed. by Gilberto Velho. Rio de Janeiro: Zahar Editores, 39–63. (See also "Sing for your sister: The structure and performance of Suyá *akia*" in *The ethnography of musical performance*, ed. by Marcia Herndon and Norma McLeod [Norwood: Norwood Editions, 1980], 7–43.)

1979. "What can we learn when they sing? Vocal genres of the Suyá Indians of central Brazil," *Ethnomusicology* 23/3: 373–94.

1980. *Os Índios e Nós: Estudos sobre sociedades tribais brasileiras.* Rio de Janeiro: Editora Campus Ltda.

1986. "Cantando as canções dos estrangeiros: Brasileiros e música de origem portuguesa no século XV," communication presented at the Colloquium of the International Council for Traditional Music, Lisbon (unpublished manuscript).

1987. *Why Suyá Sing: A musical anthropology of an Amazonian people.* Cambridge: Cambridge University Press.

Travassos, Elizabeth 1984. *Xamanismo e música entre os Kayabi do Parque do Xingu.* Rio de Janeiro: Museu Nacional—Universidade Federal do Rio de Janeiro.

Viveiros de Castro, Eduardo B. 1986. *Araweté: Os deuses canibais.* Rio de Janeiro: Jorge Zahar Editora—ANPOCS.

DISCOGRAPHY

A arte vocal dos Suyá. Compiled by Judith Seeger, Anthony Seeger, and the Suyá community. São João del Rei, 1 LP record and notes, Tacape 007 (1982) (Série etnomusicológica).

Música indígena. Universidade Federal de Goiás-SESU-MEC, Pró-Reitoria de Pesquisa e Pós-Graduação, Tacape 009 (Série etnomusicológica, Coleção Fontes Culturais da Música em Goiás, 1).

Música popular do Norte-4. Marcos Pereira recordings, MPA 9355 (1976).

Torém/CE. *Documentário sonoro do folclore brasileiro*, No. 30. MEC-Fundação Nacional de Arte, Campanha de Defesa do Folclore Brasileiro, CDFB 030 (1979).

RECORDED EXAMPLES

1. *Dapraba* (morning song) of the Xavante sung by Tsipre. Recorded by Desidério Aytai in the Sangradouro area in 1969 or 1974. Used by permission, courtesy of the author.
2. *Akia* of the Suyá ("Akia de adultos," or "shouted" song of adults, see Ex. 6) in *A arte vocal dos Suyá*, side B, band 4. Compiled by Judith Seeger, Anthony Seeger, and the Suyá community. São João del Rei, 1 LP record and notes, Tacape 007 (1982) (Série etnomusicológica). Used by permission from Anthony Seeger.

THE YAWARI RITUAL OF THE KAMAYURÁ

A Xinguano Epic

RAFAEL JOSÉ DE MENEZES BASTOS

The Kamayurá: history and social structure—Alto Xingu intertribal ritual—The Yawari ritual: The Yawari of June, 1981; The Dusk "instance"; Analysis of the Dusk "instance"; The Afternoon "instance"; Texts of the Afternoon "instance"; Description of the rest of the Yawari—Interpretation of Yawari

THE KAMAYURÁ INDIANS total about two hundred people and live in the Xingu Indian Park. The park is located in the northern part of the Brazilian State of Mato Grosso, on lands extending from the headwaters of the Xingu River to its mid-course. The Xingu is a large tributary of the Amazon River. The Kamayurá live there as members of a unique system of social articulation. The so-called Xinguano tribes are located in the southern part of the Xingu Indian Park and include the Kamayurá themselves (who are Tupi-Guarani speakers); the Awetí (Tupi, an isolated family); the Kalapálo, Kuikúro, and Nahukwá-Matipúhy (Carib); the Yawalapiti, Waurá, and Mehináku (Arawak); and the Trumai (who speak an allophylian language). In the northern part are the tribal groups that can be called "Xinguese": the Kayabi (Tupi-Guarani); Juruna (Tupi, an isolated family); the Metuktire, Suyá, and Panará (Gê); and the Txikão (Carib).

At the present time, the Xinguano are located around the Leonardo Villas Bôas Post, while the Xinguese are under the sphere of influence of the Diauarum Post. The Trumai, Panará, and Metuktire are exceptions to these rules: the Trumai live halfway between the two posts, and the other two peoples around the Kretire and Jarina posts. The present-day Xingu Indian Park, founded in 1961, formerly named Xingu National Park, is now administered by the Fundação Nacional do Índio, or FUNAI, a Brazilian government body linked to the Ministry of Justice, which is responsible for assistance to the indigenous peoples in the country (see Map for the distribution of these indigenous groups in 1992).

The Xinguano tribes are the oldest inhabitants of the Alto Xingu (Upper Xingu), within a historical sequence that appears to grant the Carib- and Arawak-speaking groups greater historical precedence, followed by the Kamayurá, Awetí (Tupi), and Trumai. Among the Xinguese, the Juruna and Suyá are apparently the oldest tribes in the area. The rest of the tribes arrived there only recently, including the Tapayuna (Gê), who entered the Xingu Indian Park in the 1970s, residing there with their Suyá hosts (Seeger 1981: 49) until the early 1990s.

What appears to be unique in the system of social articulation in effect in the region is that all these indigenous groups make up an intertribal, polyethnic society with several layers, dating back to at least the sixteenth century, which underwent profound demographic rearrangements after the arrival of the Europeans. Because it is difficult to gain access to the region, the Alto Xingu has been, throughout history, an indigenous refuge area. In this way, repeated waves of fugitives from "civilization"—invaders of the indigenous sanctuary—were added to a proto-Xinguano, Carib-Arawak formation in a process that caused extinctions and massacres, rearrangements and changes, and which paradoxically found relative repose—though always on the move—with the

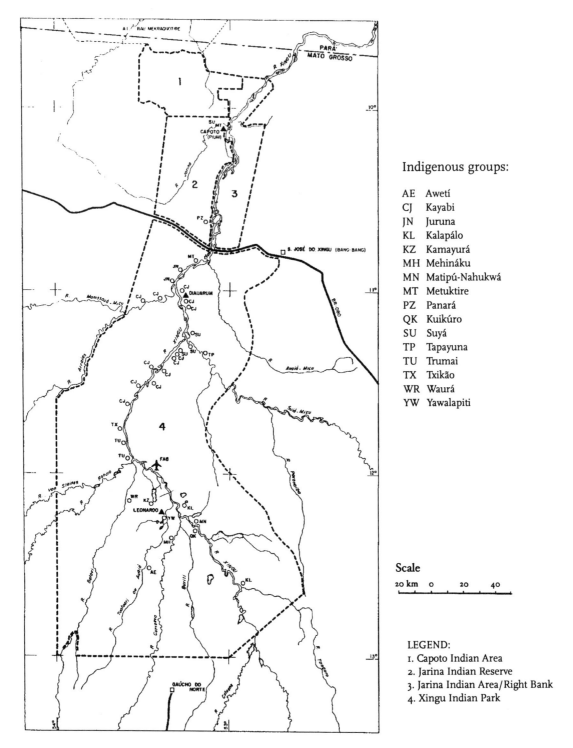

Indigenous groups:

AE   Awetí
CJ   Kayabi
JN   Juruna
KL   Kalapálo
KZ   Kamayurá
MH   Mehináku
MN   Matipú-Nahukwá
MT   Metuktire
PZ   Panará
QK   Kuikúro
SU   Suyá
TP   Tapayuna
TU   Trumai
TX   Txikão
WR   Waurá
YW   Yawalapiti

Scale

20 km   0   20   40

LEGEND:
1. Capoto Indian Area
2. Jarina Indian Reserve
3. Jarina Indian Area/Right Bank
4. Xingu Indian Park

Map: The Xingu region (São Paulo: CEDI, 1985–1986 [Aconteceu especial, 17]).

consolidation of the Brazilian state in the region. This happened only in the 1960s, with the creation of the Xingu National Park, an initiative of the Villas Bôas brothers.

The first layer in this system, as it appears today, is the so-called Xinguano Society. Here, polylingualism is incipient, there is no *lingua franca* (Portuguese has not reached that status), and intertribal rituals play an extremely important role. In these rituals, music appears as a language of special significance that mediates between myth-cosmology and the kinetic and visual arts (dance, painting, and ornamentation). This Xinguano society, formed by the Xinguano groups with the marginal inclusion of the Juruna and Suyá, constitutes, so to speak, the essence of the Alto Xingu as well as its popular image, both nationally and internationally. The second layer in this system can be understood in terms of the totality of Indians in the Park, or Xinguese society. Here, the Portuguese language appears as a pidgin, commercial exchanges carry great importance, and political language has a significant impact on the construction of a generic indigenous identity. The final layer in the system is what can be called Xinguara society, the arena of contradictory relations between the indigenous world and national Brazilian society.

The land question has acquired decisive significance, and a pan-indigenous diplomacy is actively maintained in tribal territories, which are always threatened by pressures from agribusiness, mining companies, and large infrastructural projects such as dams and highways. Aside from its posts, the Park has an additional "civilized" enclave that belongs to the Brazilian Air Force near the Diauarum post. Since the 1970s, a federal road (BR-080) has been cut through the land, and large, export-oriented farming and ranching enterprises (fazendas) virtually have surrounded the park. In the 1980s, an energy threat loomed: the projected construction of several large dams in the course of the Xingu River. If materialized, this would totally change the ecology of the region. These three layers should be perceived as interdependent, thus influencing each other, rather than as isolated levels in a system that, in this case, has been constructed by the observer for the purpose of penetrating an indigenous reality.

THE KAMAYURÁ: HISTORY AND SOCIAL STRUCTURE

The name "Kamayurá" is derived from kãma-yúla, a term of Arawakan origin that seems to refer to cannibalism. Originally, and currently in a residual way, the term refers to the Tupi invaders of the area. Kamayurá tradition reveals that their arrival there in the eighteenth century took place in several waves from the North, supposedly from the Tapajós-Xingu and Xingu-Araguaia river junctions. This same oral tradition

discloses the crucial fact that the present-day Kamayurá did not constitute a uni-ethnic group at the time of their entry into the Alto Xingu but included several predominantly Tupi-speaking peoples. Sometimes together, sometimes separately, these invaders fought to obtain refuge in the Carib-Arawak sanctuary under pressure from the European colonizing presence. Especially the Apyap ("those who hear?"), perhaps the principal formative group of the future Kamayurá, possessed an efficient war machine and a culture characterized by witchcraft and shamanism, structurally linked to war and cannibalism. All this was associated with the institution of the flute house (or men's house), the sacred space of male initiation where the great yaku'i flutes are kept (Menezes Bastos 1978 and 1986). The yaku'i flutes must not be seen by women, but women may hear them. Symbolically, they represent male menstruation, a sign of creativity that the men envy.

In this process of invading the Carib-Arawak sanctuary, the proto-Kamayurá (that is, those groups that eventually constituted their present-day, single-village formation) maintained highly differentiated relations with the host tribes. According to native tradition, the proto-Kamayurá perceived the Arawak as the Other par excellence, and Arawak lands—especially those of the Waurá—were the object of dispute here. Relations with the Carib, on the other hand, were marked by matrimonial exchange, though permeated by aloofness or "respect." Other invaders—the Juruna, the Suyá, and the Trumai—were competitors of the Kamayurá. Their competition was made explicit by a rich history of warfare, summarized, for instance, in the captivity of the Trumai by the Kamayurá. Finally, the foreign European presence is immanently felt here. In native Kamayurá oral tradition, the invasion of the region by foreigners in search of young male and female slaves is indelibly registered. Thus, when the German naturalist Karl von den Steinen headed his expeditions to the Alto Xingu in 1884 and 1887—the first official incursions into the area—his visits did not cause great surprise among the Indians, even less so the objects he carried with him and, in particular, metallic instruments (Steinen 1894 in 1940, and 1942).

Based on Kamayurá oral history and on ethnographic studies, the structure and history of their system of social articulation may be defined as a process of organization of differences, rather than as a system characterized by sociocultural uniformity, the essence of prior models of explanation. Thinking of the Alto Xingu as an always open and moving system in its organization of differences allows us to interpret the music of the Kamayurá, not as a generic "Xinguano music," but as a cultural subtradition of the area. Contrary to the theses of Pierre Clastres (1978, 1982), according to which the indigenous societies of the region would constitute autonomous and isolated worlds, the lowlands reveal an eminently relational universe in which systems of communication play an absolutely vital role that antedates the European invasion.

ALTO XINGU INTERTRIBAL RITUAL

Xinguano intertribal ritual, to which the (Xinguese) Juruna and Suyá have marginal access, comprises a highly varied group of festivals that participants explain in terms of a ternary, sequential structure. According to this explanation, myth-cosmology is the system's "entrance"; the dance, feathers, and body painting its "exit"; and the music mediates between them, as a "pivot." Thus, if myth-cosmology establishes the archetypal characters and their relationships—active in mythic time (mawe)—and the bodily arts actualize these models in historical time (ang), the music transforms word into flesh, translating cognition into motility and performance.

The organization of a Xinguano intertribal ritual includes cooperation between at least two tribes, hosts and guests. The ritual is generated by the sponsor (–yat) who, at the nucleus of the ceremony, takes responsibility for food and gifts for the guests. Also, from the hosts, three people in most cases are in charge of regimenting the host-participants, exhorting them to ideal behavior. These are the questioners (ye'engyaret). The music masters (maraka'yp) will carry out the liturgy of the festival with their apprentices (–namĩpy) and assistants (hawat). Depending on each case, the liturgical expression takes place in vocal or instrumental terms, or both; there are masculine, feminine, and mixed rituals. The signal for carrying out a ritual is almost always given by the death of a villager.

The Kamayurá are convinced, like other Tupi peoples (according to Viveiros de Castro 1986), that the firmament is sustained—and thus separated from the earth—by immense and powerful vultures that feed on human souls. Were these vultures to starve, they could no longer hold up the heavens. Their starvation thus augurs apocalyptic doom. The souls of common mortals attempt to travel to the celestial village when they leave the body and are then pursued

by hawks employed by the soul-devouring vultures. In this journey, the souls are aided by the living, who shout from the earth to scare off the hawks. The souls of the powerful, that is, of the politico-diplomatic and ritual chiefs, have a greater chance of reaching the celestial village through the mediation of Kwaryp, a ritual studied by Pedro Agostinho (1974). The terror of the Kamayurá at the death of their souls is not related to being devoured by the gods but to their fear of being transformed into the gods' feces. The organization of the rite among the guests includes the same roles, but in an ad hoc manner, especially in relation to the sponsor and questioners.

THE YAWARI RITUAL

The Yawari ("Jaguatirica"), an intertribal Xinguano ritual, probably had its origin in a vector that joins the Trumai with the Tupi Kamayurá and Awetí. In Kamayurá, the term yawari means ocelot (jaguatirica, the Leopardus pardalis). The word also signifies the spine of the tucum palm tree. Eduardo Galvão (1960 in 1979), the first ethnologist to study this ritual, noted that the historical connection between the Trumai and the Kamayurá and Awetí had been registered since von den Steinen's (1894 in 1940: 140, 148–50) and Schmidt's visits (1942: 365–66), as well as confirmed by Kamayurá tradition. From these sources, one can postulate an origin of the Yawari in the confluence of the Xingu-Araguaia rivers. The diffusion of the Yawari in the Alto Xingu was simply overwhelming: at the time of von den Steinen's and Schmidt's expeditions, it was almost limited to its original boundaries (Trumai, Kamayurá, Awetí); at the time of Galvão's first visits in the 1940s, only the Mehináku, among the Xinguano, did not practice it, but it was known by the Suyá, among the Xinguese. The Mehináku, however, adopted it about twenty years later (Gregor 1977: 281). The Yawari may be referred to, then, as a Xinguano rite, without detracting from its original Tupi-Trumai character, which is always marked in the native consciousness.

The Yawari of June, 1981

The following Yawari, studied in 1981, involved the Kamayurá as hosts and the Matipúhy as guests. The Yawalapiti were associated with the Kamayurá and also described themselves as hosts. No data exist to compare the Yawari reported here to those of other Xinguano tribes. Keeping in mind that in the Alto Xingu there is no sociocultural uniformity, but always the organization of differences, we will refer to this Yawari as one version within the Kamayurá subtradition of the ritual. There may be as many subtraditions as there are Xinguano tribes, and one Xinguese subtradition, that of the Suyá, according to Seeger (1980, 1981). In the description that follows, fictitious names are used to protect the personal identities of the participants.

In 1977, a young Kamayurá adult by the name of Storm died of malaria in Brasília, where he had been taken in an attempt to save his life once the native medical resources and those of the Xingu Indian Park had failed. His body was returned to the village of Yawaracingtỳp for burial. Yawaracingtỳp is the name of the present-day Kamayurá village, meaning "place full of *yawaracing* spines" (*yawaracing* also means a type of feline).

With Storm's mortal remains resting in a hammock at the house of his father (Plato), three of his cross-cousins (Uno, Duplo, and Triplo) exhort Plato to authorize Storm's burial. Plato, furious and overcome by grief, cannot accept the death of his son and accuses Gorgias, the great Kamayurá ritual chief, of having caused the death through witchcraft, thus making the soul of Storm into the food and future feces of the divine vultures. Only after much insistence by Storm's three cross-cousins would Plato accept the betrayal that his son's death represents. For the Kamayurá, death is a metaphorical betrayal: the dead person abandons the living as if to become the betrothed of the gods (and, paradoxically, to be devoured by them). Storm was then buried by his cross-cousins, who are now called his gravediggers (or planters).

With the dry season at its height and after many mutual consultations involving the other inhabitants of Yawaracingtỳp, Gorgias and Aristotle (the Kamayurá's great politico-diplomatic chief), decide to carry out a Yawari dedicated to Storm. For this, however, they must ask Plato's permission, and only after many conversations with his co-residents does Plato accept. Sponsoring a Yawari is extremely expensive because the sponsor must provide food for the participants from his village during the entire festival and, afterwards, for the guests from another village. On the positive side, this is perhaps the greatest opportunity to acquire prestige and power. Plato accepted this duty only to the extent that he

guaranteed the support of his domestic group and of Aristotle, his parallel nephew.

Soon after Plato's resigned acceptance, the group of sponsors, centered on Plato himself and on Aristotle, went to ask for authorization from Isolda (Aristotle's wife) for the festival to take place. Isolda is the person among the Kamayurá who has hereditary rights over the Yawari and nothing can be done without her permission. She agreed, and the group then went to the house of Sebastian, the music master of Yawari. They asked Sebastian if he would be willing to direct the festival's musical liturgy. He said that he would think about it and requested information about the presents and offerings that he would earn from the sponsors for carrying out the ritual, which the sponsors guaranteed. He said that he would respond later and that they should wait for him in the village's central yard.

For the purpose of the present Yawari, the Kamayurá village can be schematically represented as in Figure 1. Ỳpawu is a large lake about one kilometer from the village. The residences are large circular spaces made of wood and straw that shelter extended families. These typically consist of a group of mature brothers with their conjugal families, along with their daughters' husbands and children. Only prestigious males can capture coresident wives of their sons.

Shortly afterwards, Sebastian appeared at twilight in front of the flute house, where the rest of the participants in the ceremony were awaiting him. His arrival signified his acceptance of leading the ritual, and the formal opening of the Yawari took place as evening fell on June 7, 1981.

One of the basic musico-choreographic structures of the Kamayurá's world assumes a relationship between nucleus and periphery. In the nucleus are the music master, his apprentices and assistants, and the other mature people. On the periphery are the young adults, adolescents, and children. This structure applies to both the instrumental and vocal music, or a combination of both, and to both men's and women's music, or to their mixture. The nucleus performs what the Kamayurá's system classifies as "music itself"—typically songs in the case of vocal music, of which Yawari is one example. These songs always are performed in sequence, with the repertoire of a ritual being constructed by blocks of songs. The role of the music master is to lead the nucleus in singing, providing to the other members the model for the

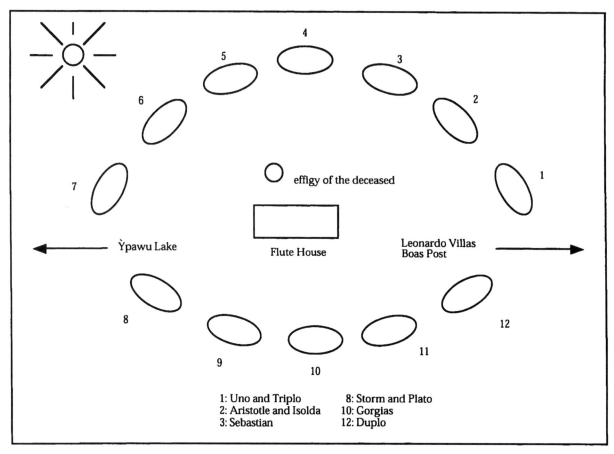

Fig. 1: Schematic representation of a Kamayurá village.

sometimes heterophonic repetition of songs. In general, the texts of these songs have a mythic, narrative character and report events from mythic time (*mawe*). The periphery is characterized by the performance of musico-linguistic onomatopoeias that imitate the voices of animals. In the case of the Yawari these are characteristically those of felines and hawks, which respectively represent terrestrial and celestial man-eating characters. In Kamayurá and Alto Xingu mythology in general, the felines are seen as representing the transformation of a cross-relative into an affine. The hawks point to the divine universe and are seen as "employees" of the soul-eating vultures, their soul hunters. Thus the hawks represent the Other par excellence, cross-relatives who only can be defined as affinal to the extent that one considers the dead person—and humans in general, as destined to die—to be the betrothed of the gods. In the Kamayurá kinship system, the regimentation of affines is effected among the cross-cousins.

In the Yawari, music with dance characterizes the day repertoire, music without dance the noctural one.

Yawari dance music uses four choreographic formations: procession, group, line, and wedge. In the procession, the participants form a row with the nucleus in the middle. In the group, the dancers position themselves to form a giant circle, with the nucleus at the center and the periphery surrounding it. The line has the nucleus at its center and the periphery at its extremes. Finally, the wedge is an arch with the nucleus in the middle and the periphery at its points. The procession and the line always move frontwards, and the group moves toward the front and back, although avoiding movements made with the back turned. In the wedge formation, the participants jump while remaining in the same place. The nocturnal Yawari music characteristically is performed with the participants seated in front of the flute house, facing East.

From another perspective, the Yawari repertoire is classified by the Kamayurá according to emblematic animals: forest cat (*yawaracing*), elongated ocelot (*yawaripep*), curassow (*mỹtũ*), and chicken (*karakarakõ*). These emblematic animals refer to divisions of the

Kamayurá day, which begins at dusk and ends the following afternoon. Thus, in Kamayurá culture, the day is always six hours ahead (or eighteen hours behind) in comparison with the reckoning of time that places point zero at midnight.

The universe of music and words in the Yawari song system is subdivided into seven large *cantos* (or sequentially arranged groups of songs) and "vignettes" (the groups of songs performed by the periphery that are characteristically musico-linguistic onomatopoeias). These *cantos* signal parts of the Kamayurá day: Dusk (*noitinha*), Night (*noite*), Late Night (*noite funda*), Dawn (*madrugada*), Curassow (*mutum*), Close of Dawn (*clausura da madrugada*), and Afternoon (*tarde*). The present text deals with the *cantos* for Dusk and Afternoon, exactly those that occur at the beginning and end of a Kamayurá day, the first being music to be sung while seated, the second being music to be danced. In addition, this essay concentrates only on what occurs on the first day of the Yawari, the rest being treated tangentially.

The Kamayurá Yawari described here took place in June of 1981, during a period of eleven days, that is, from dusk on June 7th to the morning of the 18th. Music is here both essence and nucleus, and the analytical model takes this fact into account.

According to what can be seen in the musico-poetic corpus presented below, the Yawari involves a narrative (a set of texts) set to music (a group of songs) whose characters are essentially heroes, that is, they are archetypes and therefore larger than common mortals, bordering on the divine. For this reason, the characters fulfill at each moment the designs of Fate, Rule, Chance, and God. It is in this sense that the Yawari is an epic. Its heroes are epic rather than tragic, to use this classical distinction borrowed from the tradition of studies of Mediterranean epics (Rocha Pereira 1986).

The Dusk "instance"

The formal opening of the Yawari took place, then, at Dusk on the 7th of June 1981, with the participants seated on a tree trunk in front of the flute house. Then the following was sung without interruption (Ex. 1; Recorded Ex. 1).

The musical transcriptions shown below constitute an "instance" of the Dusk sequence, according to definitions that follow shortly, from the repertoire of the Forest Cat. It consists of four "vignettes" (numbers 1, 8, 9, and 10) and six songs (2, 3, 4, 5, 6,

and 7). The vignettes function as pillars or markers of "instances"; vignette M of the excerpt under analysis points to the start of an "instance," and generally indicates the beginning of songs. Vignettes 9 and 10 display an interlocking technique: vignette 9 begins with two soloists called *tawato* (a type of hawk), followed by the chorus in dialogue with the jaguar (*yawat*, *Pantera onca*); vignette 10 involves two singers called *tawato'i* (another type of hawk). The "texts" of the vignettes are onomatopoeias of the voices of various animals. Shortly after the solo entry of Sebastian (the music master), Gorgias (his assistant and Kamayurá ritual chief) sings M, in which he is soon accompanied by the chorus. Once M is completed, Gorgias and the chorus begin to repeat what is sung by Sebastian, who continues with the song until its end.

By "instance" we mean a concrete realization of a sequence, approximately in the sense in which de Saussure (1967) distinguishes between *parole* and *langue*. The "sequence" is a deduction created by the analyst, displayed at the level of rules, which does not operate at a conscious level in the minds of the natives. This differentiation also can be approximated to that which Chomsky (1971, 1975) constructs between performance and competence, respectively. It is the analysis of concrete musical performances (instances) that permits the conceptual generation of a "sequence," namely the universe of rules governing the performance of "instances."

The following are approximate, condensed translations of the texts of the Dusk "instance."

1. **M**
(voice of the hawk: o, ho)
(voice of the ocelot: hoy, wo)

2. **Motekey**
I, the ocelot, will burn the *jacubim*
It makes me happy to shoot another fish, which I
    desire, with an arrow
It makes me happy to burn the *jacubim*
It makes me happy to shoot another fish, which I
    desire, with an arrow
I, the ocelot, am going to.

3. **He nu yawari**
You, another ocelot, which I desire,
Desire beeswax
You, yellow ocelot.

Ex. 1: Dusk "instance," transcription by Rafael José de Menezes Bastos. Abbreviations: Y solo = solo entry by Sebastian; W = Gorgias accompanied by chorus; M with slash = absence of M (which is vignette no. 1).

Ex. 1: *(continued)*

ka mi wa ye wa ry   ha ya ka tu wa ry hy   ka mi wa ye wa ry hy   hay hay hi ha i

hay hi hay hi   hi   hay hi hay hi   hi   hay hi   hi   hay hi   hi   hay hi ha i

6. Nuterihiyu

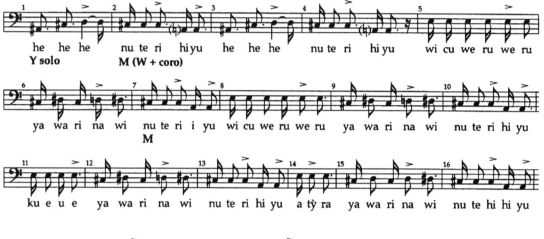

♪ = 176-184

he he he   nu te ri hiyu   he he he   nu te ri hiyu   wi cu we ru we ru

Y solo   **M (W + coro)**

ya wa ri na wi   nu te ri i yu   wi cu we ru we ru   ya wa ri na wi   nu te ri hi yu

M

ku e u e   ya wa ri na wi   nu te ri hi yu   a tỹ ra   ya wa ri na wi   nu te hi hi yu

he he he   nu te ri hi yu   he he he   nu te ri hi yu   hi cu e ru e ru   ya wa ri na wi

nu te ri hi yu   hi cu e ru e ru   ya wa ri na wi   nu te ri hi yu   a tỹ ra   ya wa ri na wi

nu te ri hi yu   he he he   nu te ri hi yu   he he he   nu te ri hi yu

7. Yahaha

♪ = 120-126

y a haha   ha   y hi a haha   hi a haha   ha   y hi a haha

Y solo   **M (W + coro)**

Ex. I: *(continued)*

ha   y   he ru a ta mi a ha ha heru wa ta mi a ha ha

ha   y   he ru wa ta mi a ha ha   ha   y   hi a   ha ha

ha   y   hi a   ha ha   ha   y   he ru wa ta mi a ha ha

he ru   wa ta   mi a   ha ha   ha   y   he ru wa ta mi a   ha ha

ha   y   hi a   ha ha   ha   y   hi a   ha ha   ha   y

8. M (same as 1)

9. T

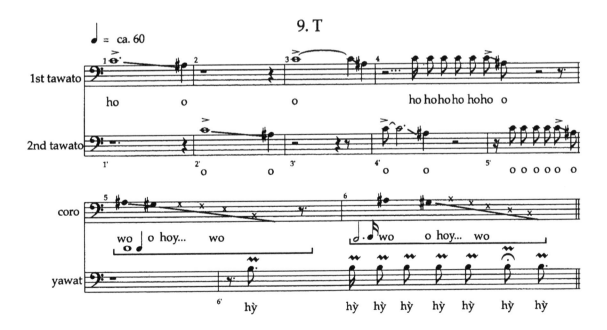

Ex. 1: *(continued)*

10. T'

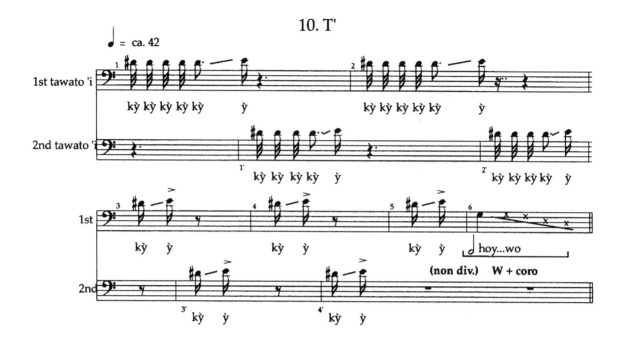

4. **Horowỳ**

    The ocelot is of our same blood,
    Oh cross-cousin
    She, your cross-cousin, the *camaíua* (a type of tree),
       kills me
    Oh ocelot.

5. **Kamiwaye**

    I am *kamiwa* (a type of tree)
    Ocelot
    I am *kamiwa* of the water
    I am the model sponsor of the water,
    Ocelot.

6. **Nuterihiyu**

    You, yellow *jacubim*, share his father
    Who comes from the ocelot
    You share his father, my affine (related by marriage).

7. **Yahaha**

    Let us go, we ourselves, ocelot
    Share yourself a bit with me
    Let us naturalize ourselves, we ourselves,
    Oh ocelot.

8. **M (same as 1)**

9. **T**

    (voice of the Hawk: o, ho)
    (voice of the ocelot: hoy, wo)
    (voice of the jaguar: hỳ).

10. **T'**

    (voice of the *tawato'i* [hawk]: kỳ)
    (voice of the ocelot: hoy, wo).

Analysis of the Dusk "instance"

Vignettes. In the texts of the vignettes (1, 8, 9, 10), there is an opposition between the celestial world—represented by the birds of prey, *tawato* and *tawato'i*—and the earthly, forest world—represented by the felines, ocelot and jaguar. This opposition points to the relationship between men and gods (birds) and men and nature (forest animals), the first of which is metaphorized by cross-relatives, the second by affinal relations. This is on the plane of the living; on that of the dead the picture is reversed, with cross-relatives becoming affinal and vice versa: the dead person abandons or divorces himself from the living and marries himself to the gods. It is important to point out that both the hawk and the ocelot are intermediaries "hired" by powerful beings of their same world: the divine vultures, who sustain the cosmos, and the jaguar. Moreover, this whole system of emblematic animals carries political implications for Kamayurá society: the jaguar represents the powerful, the eminent man, basically an older, conspicuous father-in-law / brother-in-law / brother, who holds socially fertile and effective power. At the opposite end of this overly human power stands the socially sterile yet extremely wise power of the pubescent recluse, represented by the small hawk *(tawato'i)*, with its absolutely accurate vision.

Songs. Something very similar happens with the texts of the songs. In song 2, the ocelot and the *jacubim* burn and shoot each other with arrows. "To burn" is the Kamayurá metaphor for "jealousy," or the fear of loss. For the Kamayurá, fear is desire itself, and what was a "burn" becomes a wound from an arrow of envy. In the Kamayurá system of relations, cross-cousins compete for the same women, that is, they "burn" each other (in the Kamayurá sense of the word). In another way, however, what this jealousy reveals is desire. This desire points to an intention to return to immortal life, when women and men constituted asexual beings, without desire, the cause of humankind's fall. In song 3 the same grammar reappears, an opposition that is really one side of the triangle: cross-relatives (the ocelot and the yellow ocelot), who compete for the same women, are jealous and yet desire one another. Beeswax, in the Yawari, covers the point of the dart, namely the instrument with which hosts and guests attack each other in the sporting game that they will play, as we will see below. In song 3, beeswax is as much fear as it is desire. Song 4 proposes, with glowing logic, the basic mathematical equation of the triangular Kamayurá kinship system: cross-relationship or irreciprocity is the abyss only cancelled by marriage (affinity) or consanguinity. The Kamayurá system of kinship terminology, in the form of terms of address, summarily prohibits the expression of cross-relationship, turning it into consanguinity. Still, in song 4, *camaíua* is a type of tree used by the Kamayurá to build houses, a fact that the song uses metaphorically to point to the cross-cousin of the cross-cousin. Song 5 will bring another pan-Xinguano ritual, the *Kwarỳp* (Agostinho 1974), into the setting of the Yawari. Here the primordial process of becoming human is dramatized, showing how humans originated in wood *(kamiwa)*, an archetypal wood that the demiurge Mawucini (he who rattles the stick) enchants, turning it into spouses for the jaguar. In *Kwarỳp*, the effigies of the humans commemorated—powerful men—serve in the end for the fertilization and thus continuity of the waters of Ỳpawu Lake. In Yawari, by contrast, these effigies are burned, that is, they suffer a process of radical transformation, from one domain to another: they leave the world of the living and enter that of the dead.

Song 5 is a poem about this. In song 6, what is said in song 4 is reiterated: cross-relatives share the same ancestry. Finally, song 7 is an exhortation to the cross-relatives to abandon the mortal world of contracts and trade, of marriage and human desire. There Curassow Head (Mỳtũakang), the great hero of the Yawari, the great traitor and the one who makes people jealous, invites the betrayed and the jealous ones to return to the primordial cosmos, the space-time whose essence is eternal.

Scale structure of the Dusk "instance." Songs 2 through 5 of the present "instance" are referable to scales that can be reduced to the following resultant scale, with their tonal center (a black note on the staff) transposed to C (Ex. 2). In this scale, the formation A–C–D is absolutely constant, G# and C# appearing optionally. This is represented on the staff by the placement of G# outside the brackets, and of C# with an Ø underneath.

Ex. 2: Resultant scale derived from songs 2 through 5.

Songs 6 and 7 are referable to the resultant scale shown in Example 3.

Ex. 3: Resultant scale derived from songs 6 and 7.

Here, C–E–F–F# constitute the constant segment of the resultant scale, C# and G being statistically optional. On a higher level of synthesis, we include below the general resultant scale to which the entire "instance" is referable, derived from the preceding two (Ex. 4).

Ex. 4: Composite scale for the entire "instance" (songs 2 through 7).

In Example 4, the "round" notes from Ex. 2 should exclude the "square" notes from Ex. 3 and vice versa. This points to something crucial about the general resultant scale (Ex. 4): the existence there of two paths, the first being a scalar design around the tonal center, the second moving upwards from it. These two paths oppose each other while maintaining a mediant relationship, anchored in the tonal center (C). Such an opposition takes place because of the minor and major thirds involved, the "mediant" tonal relationship becoming explicit by the fact that A and E are the most perfect "synonyms" of C in the scale under consideration, which is a model (Lévi-Strauss 1980). In the texts of songs 2 to 5 (the first set), disjunction—to burn, to desire (jealousy and envy)—becomes the basic sentiment, while in songs 6 and 7 (the second set), conjunction—to share—dominates the meaning of the texts.

The Afternoon "instance"

After the opening of the Yawari, all return to their houses. On the same Kamayurá day (7–8 June, or "our" 8th of June), around 5 P.M., the Yawari is resumed. Dances in the form of procession (7), group (20), line (3), and wedge (2) are performed in sequence with short interruptions. The choreographic formation leaves Plato's house, sponsor of the ritual, and moves in procession to the center of the village, in front of the flute house. After the procession, the participants form a group and move in this formation to the front of Plato's house, and then they return again to the center of the village. They stop once more and, a short time later, they form a line facing East and parallel to the front of the flute house. Finally, in a wedge, and around the effigy of the deceased, they perform the rest of the "instance" (Fig. 2).

The procession is headed by four pubescent recluses called *tenotat* (those who go in front). These recluses, identified with the small hawk *tawato'i*, are opposed in age and political status to the powerful individuals (ritual and politico-diplomatic chiefs). On the other hand, these recluses are recognized as the most pure and trustworthy experts on the essential world, and also display the best aim in the game of darts. Such purity and trustworthiness are encouraged by the kind of life that the *tenotat* are obliged to maintain: separated from the world in special rooms in their houses, they should learn almost everything from their elders; they should hardly speak, only hear and see; and they may not engage in sexual intercourse, eat soiled foods, or drink impure beverages.

The mature adults, in spite of constituting the nucleus in musical and choreographic terms, appear on the periphery as unique characters and present themselves as male-female couples. The boys and young adults, on the other hand, are integrated as collective characters and present themselves as a single group. Even Sebastian, Aristotle, and Gorgias participate in this sort of "tragicomic chorus."

During the entire "instance," the musical and interpretive disagreements between the music master (Sebastian) and Gorgias (his assistant) were very conspicuous: Gorgias sang "a" for "o", "u" for "ÿ", and "m" for "p," so as to confound the verbal clarity of the song. In terms of the music, the assistant played triplets instead of eighth notes; a sextuplet in place of a septuplet; he placed accents in the wrong places; produced microtonal deviations where he should not have, and so on. Therefore, Gorgias did not show himself to be a good assistant, who, in Sebastian's view, should simply repeat what the master performs and invents; he behaved, instead, like someone competing for political and aesthetic primacy. This was very clear when, at some point in the dances, Gorgias would sing the equivalent of "owner of the feces of we others" instead of "owner of the shaming of we others," as it should be. In Kamayurá, the two expressions are easily switched in a play on words. This provoked indecorous laughter from the participants but, at the same time, a profound resentment and hate in Sebastian (the music master).

At the end of another song, Sebastian, the master, probably wishing to begin the next song quickly, hummed the sound "m." The chorus, meanwhile,

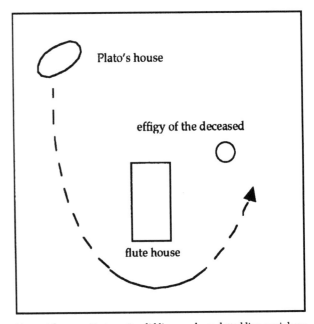

Fig. 2: Afternoon "instance"; solid line, nucleus; dotted line, periphery.

under the command of Gorgias, which in no way repeated the master's "m," took up again the beginning of the song, a decision that, again, provoked anger in Sebastian. The sound "m" is a fundamental point of articulation in Kamayurá music, particularly suited for the control of tuning.

During the entire performance in line formation, the participants were especially excited, erupting in exhortations for the heroic performance of the Kamayurá and severely criticizing the rest of the tribes in the area, especially the Carib. Soon, M was sung (see Ex. 1), after which the formation in a line advanced—representing a combat charge—toward the effigy of the deceased, around which they formed a wedge (Fig. 3).

From the advance until reorganization in the form of a wedge, the group progressed in a Dantesque tumult, striking feet and pieces of wood, cheering and offering encouragement, shouting ferociously. The only ones who did not behave in this manner were Sebastian and Plato, who remained in front of the flute house. This was followed by a chastisement of the effigy of the deceased. First, the four *tenotat*, costumed as *tawato'i*, attacked the effigy successively. The attack occurred in the spot marked by a cross in the diagram (Fig. 3). The attacks were verbal and literal, with darts: they criticized the "imitation" or effigy of the deceased, who left the world of the living and entered that of the dead as the bridegroom of the divine vultures who support the heavens. Next, it was the turn of the boys, characterized as *yerep* (birds).

Shortly after came the *tawato* and *tawato'i* couples. The remaining couples gradually attacked the effigy of the deceased, and the chastisement became generalized.

After the attacks, M (Ex. 1) was sung, the formation having dispersed to converge in front of the flute house. It was around 6:50 P.M. on June 8 or, in Kamayurá terms, the very end of June 7–8.

The following are approximate, condensed translations of the texts of the Afternoon "instance."

Procession

1. **M** (see 1, M, Dusk "instance")

2. **Wicíka**
   About the *socó* (a type of bird) you, and the wasp:
   My younger brother shot darts at you in the presence of the champions.

3. **Hipỳwa**
   That person in front of me is the owner of the hit (*acerto*) on the foot,
   The master (of) the wood (your younger brother)
   Your bow (it is the younger brother), it is generous, so it hits
   Your wood, oh my younger brother
   In your direction, in my direction, arrows are shot, which hit
   Your wood, your bow, is generous (and therefore accurate)
   In your direction, in my direction, arrows are shot, which hit,
   My younger brother is generous, accurate, in shooting arrows.

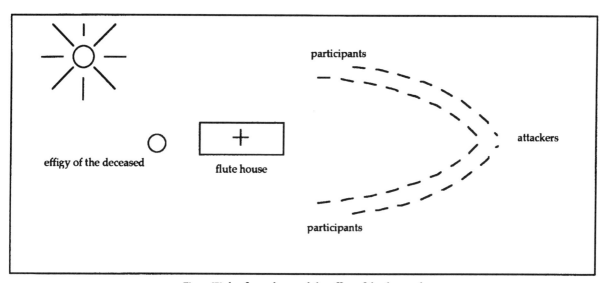

Fig. 3: Wedge formed around the effigy of the deceased.

4. **Yaw yauk**

Bathe yourself, you, gull

Bathe yourself, gull, *rei-congo* (name of a bird)

You become similar to the *guandu* (fruit of bean-like plant)

You become dry.

5. **He he he he**

Courage, you!

Courage, killer!

6. **Awíri he**

Courage, you Awetí

You, Awetí, yellow lightning bug

Ocelot, you.

7. **M**

Group formation

1. **M**

2. **Kakariye**

I, gull, said to the small one:

You, gull, ocelot,

Are the owner of the shaming of we others

(the owner of our feces).

3. **Kakaye he**

You and I are gulls,

We ourselves are gulls,

You are a gull, ocelot

The gull burns me

Gull, ocelot, you are the sheath of the divine-natural

The sheath of the heels of we ourselves

The ocelot is the food, the pleasure, of the divine-natural.

4. **Hahaye**

You and I are gull and ocelot,

Inajá (a type of palm tree) and wasp.

5. **Wakỳ he**

Awaken from fear, you and I, ocelot:

The yellow ocelot desires, but does not desire, you

You desire, but do not desire, the yellow ocelot.

6. **Wahỳ**

I shoot with arrows those from the village of the little gull

I shoot you with arrows, the father of the ocelot.

7. **Wakỳ**

Awaken from fear, you and I, for the hit (of a dart) your hit, ocelot,

The hit of we others, ocelot

Awaken from fear, you and I, ocelot, for the hit with the arrow

Your hit, with an arrow, ocelot

The hit of we others, ocelot, with an arrow,

Your reproduction, your genealogical blood

Is the same as we ourselves

The (right) hand of we ourselves is good.

8. **Wa'ỳ hỳ ye**

Awaken from fear, you and I, to shoot with arrows

Where are you, my younger brother, my wood, ocelot, ocelot?

That one there, that one there, whose mother is made of wood?

Where is my younger brother, owner of the *marimbondo* (wasp)?

Here is my younger brother, with the look of the *kari* (a type of fish)

Where will be the younger brother, the wood, of we ourselves?

9. **Heyu mãni**

You, yellow *mandi* (a type of fish)

You, small ocelot

You come from the awakened fear

The lightning bug, young adult, comes from you.

10. **Wỹra**

You are the loathing that the bird feels for the "pointed stick"

You are a killer, you, you, bird.

11. **Iwaya'i**

Iwaya'i (a type of palm tree),

Ocelot.

The daughter of your paternal aunt,
Your lover,

Witnessed your wounding by an arrow in the testicle.

12. **Hãya hayá**

I am the owner of the ocelot, oh ocelot

My younger brother (also) will be,

Those who hit correctly with arrows (also) will be.

13. **Himanĩ**

Mandi, he is *mandi* (a type of fish),

He is an ocelot.

You, younger brother, are the good right hand of the Yawari,

You are the owner of the *macaúba* (a type of palm tree), my younger brother, of the Yawari.

14. **Hiwaní duye**

He is *mandi*, I am a yellow *mandi*

You are the owner of the food, of the
pleasure
You are a champion.

15. **Wakute**

(translation unavailable to the author)

16. **Ha'á hahá'i**

Ocelot, ocelot.

17. **Há'i Há'i**

Ocelots,

You (plural) took revenge, with arrows, on my younger
brother.

You (singular) are not the owner of revenge, of
wounding

You are not (ethically and aesthetically) magnificent.

18. **Nukaya**

Killer, killer, ocelot, ocelot,

Our festival is about the causing of jealousy.

19. **Yawarinawi I**

Elongated ocelots, coming from ocelots

You and I are ocelots

you are the father of the ocelot.

20. **M**

Line formation

1. **M**

2. **He haha'i**

You, ocelot, yellow ocelot

Are exclusively other, owner of we ourselves

The other (which is you) in front of me, who was
seen.

3. **M**

Wedge formation

1. **Chastisement of the effigy of the deceased.**

2. **M**

Texts of the Afternoon "instance"

In Kamayurá thought, if the older brother is seen as an example of the exercise of power, the younger brother is seen as potentially preserving genealogical excellence. Song 2 from the procession defines the object of the entire "instance": the confrontation of the wasp *(marimbondo)*, an insect that is agile and accurate in its "arrow hits," with the *socó* (a type of bird), a disheveled, long-legged creature. Here, "you"

is the wasp, the younger brother of an older person who remains hidden in the text of the song, proud of the performance of his younger brother, who is so magnificent that he transforms the most eminent champions into weak-legged *socó* birds. Song 3 is an unlimited praise for the ability and generosity of the younger brother. The ankle, almost the heel, as in Homeric Greece, is a symbol of masculinity in Kamayurá martial arts. To have the ankle wounded by another person equals to supreme humiliation. In song 4, the singular form of "you" *(você)* soon turns into "you" plural *(vocês)*, which demonstrates that, in reality, it is not individuals who are confronting each other here but groups (brothers). Song 5 urges the killer to have courage, a theme taken up again in song 6, when the younger brother is identified with the lightning bug, a luminous insect. For the Kamayurá, before the birth of the Sun and the Moon, offsprings of the primordial jaguar and grandchildren of Mawucini, the world was lit only by insects like the lightning bug.

In song 2 of the group section, shame is equated with feces, a sign of death. The words of song 3 elucidate the game—triangular in the singular, biangular in the plural—that characterizes Kamayurá culture. In Kamayurá language, the pronoun structure establishes three basic types of personas: in the singular "I," "you" (the person being spoken to), and "him" (the person being spoken of); in the plural, the tripartite structure of the first person is binarized to "we ourselves" and "we others," the first form joining "I" and "you," the second, "I" and "him." In song 3 the adversaries, those who are burned and become jealous, are paradoxically joined together. What binds them? The poor humans are nothing but the food, the pleasure of the gods. Song 4 returns to the encounter between adversaries, an epic encounter emblematized by the precision of the wasp and the aggressive thorns of the *inajá* (a kind of palm tree). Song 5 exhorts "we ourselves," or "I" plus "you," to remain vigilantly awake at night, synonymous of courage, equating sleep with fear (and death). This accomplished, the poem does something stupendous: it establishes the equivalence of desire and lack of desire, bonding love and hate. The "ourselves" in song 6 are, again, taken apart. Song 7 is a type of "development" of song 5, as is song 8. Song 9 returns to the exhortation to remain awake, the state of the "wise" ones. The disjunction in the "ourselves" of song 10 is catalyzed by disgust (shame, feces, fear, and death). Song 11 states that the object of desire (the daughter of the paternal aunt, the loved one) is, at the same time, under the triangular geometry of jealousy, a testimony of the most humiliating and ridiculous absurdity. Desire is death itself in Kamayurá culture, so extraneous and at the same time so familiar. The texts of songs 12 to 16 reiterate previous texts. In song 17, the hidden older brother becomes angry: the *socó*, the *guandu*, the weak-legged [bird] finally take revenge on junior's ego in an ethically reprehensible way, since vengeance only can take place within the sphere of reciprocity. If there is no debt, if there is no credit, if there is no memory, ultimately, of "buying and selling," there can be no economy of vengeance. Song 18 subsumes Kamayurá poetics: the hero says that Yawari is a festival about the causing of jealousy. Perhaps the best definition of Yawari should not go beyond this simple statement. Song 2 of the section in the form of a line states something fundamental about Kamayurá cosmology: that a person who reveals himself to others loses power, thus making himself vulnerable.

Scalar structure of chants for the Afternoon "instance." The composite scale to which the chants of the Afternoon "instance" are referable can be divided into three large configurations, distinctively related to the choreographic schemes: procession (Ex. 5), group (Ex. 6), and line formation (Ex. 7). This refers to the absolutely crucial fact that, in Kamayurá culture, there is a meaningful correlation between the structure of music and dance in which dance appears to carry the highest level of irreducible abstraction. This reveals meaning as well: the Kamayurá discourse about the constitution of ritual, according to which myth / cosmology serves as the ritual's point of entry and the bodily arts as its point of exit, with music as the transformative pivot, is not merely an idea but also its concretization.

There are two resultant scales in the configuration illustrated in Example 5, involving songs 2, 4, and 6 on the one hand, and songs 3 and 5 on the other. There is a clear contrast between these two scales, the first of which is chromatic and the second diatonic. From both the native and the researcher's viewpoint, this contrasting relationship reveals that the music does not simply underscore what the song "says" but—much to the contrary—it reinterprets the texts. The Kamayurá say that "the words go into the music," wishing to point to the fact that the texts are "judged" by the music, a critical language.

The scales in Example 6 define three large areas (I, II, III). The configuration as a whole appears as a continuous mechanism of chromaticization, in the direction of the increasingly filled-in pitch series. Area III (which involves songs 5, 12, 13, 15, 17, 18, and 19) has its preferential region in the ascending major third, starting from the tonal center. Similarly, area II (songs 6 and 11) centers around the perfect fourth above the tonal center. Area I (song 3) has as its defining region the augmented fifth, ascending from the tonal center. Finally, in Example 7, which includes a single song (2), the scale appears to occupy a middle ground between the two previous configurations.

Comparison of referential scales, Dusk and Afternoon "instances." Dusk finds its basic compositional mechanism in diatonic dyads. The minor third interval is as generalized as to constitute a "tonal center." This minor third is sometimes ascending, sometimes descending, with predominance of the latter. On the other hand, in the Afternoon "instance," the basic mechanism of musical elaboration consists of chromatically "filling in" a diatonic space. From this point onwards, the phrase will be elaborated by manipulation of the original sequence of pitches. This manipulation is always chromatic, and the process of transposition, with more or less subtle variations, is basic to it.

The Kamayurá say: "Ye'eng imaraka apỳpe" (the texts go inside the music). What does "to go inside" signify in Kamayurá? Politics in the more elemental sense of principle, force, violence. Music, then, is the weak force that rules over the strong force of the word. In Kamayurá culture, only dance can go beyond the music—or come closer to it, depending on the direction of the arrow of time.

Description of the rest of the Yawari

Preludes, days 1 to 4 of the ritual. If during the first day of the Yawari only one Dusk "instance" and one Afternoon "instance" were performed, the ritual on the following days became increasingly complex. The eleven days of the Yawari can be understood schematically as unfolding in the following phases: preludes, outbreak, resumption, eve, and encounter. The preludes extend over the first four days of the ceremonies: the opening described above was repeated on the second day; it was replaced with a derived "instance" on the night of the third day; and nothing was heard during the same period on the fourth day.

With respect to the eve phase, the remaining days were filled with "instances" derived from those of Afternoon described above, all with chastisement of the effigy of the deceased, and followed—on the third and fourth days—by *brincadeiras* (jest), or musico-choreographic performances dominated by a jocular spirit. In this way, the preludes are defined, at night, by the presentation of an opening or something derived from it, or even by the absence of song, and, in the afternoon, by an "instance" derived from those for Afternoon, followed by chastisement or another type of derivation of Afternoon, also leading to chastisement, after which a *brincadeira* can take place.

Outbreak, days 5 and 6. This phase took place over the two following days. From an extra-musical point of view, this phase is defined by an especially rich morning period. In this way, on the fifth day (11–12 June), and shortly after a long chastisement, the cleansing ceremony was performed. This ceremony, which took place on the shore of Lake Ỳpawu, involved the ingestion of a beverage made with *kỳe*, followed by induced vomiting. *Kỳe* is a type of sharp grass (the name translates as "knife" in Portuguese), abundant in Xinguano shores. Very early in the morning, the young adults who were to participate in the Yawari games went to Lake Ỳpawu's shore, collected large quantities of *kỳe*, cooked them, then drank and regurgitated this kind of tea. This ceremony marks the beginning of sexual abstinence and fasting of the dart-throwers: they can no longer eat fish (daily food of the Kamayurá), only birds (extremely well broiled), cooked beans, and sweet cereals. Finally, they also must sleep only for a short time, and never at night.

On the sixth day, there was a rehearsal of the game of Yawari: the Kamayurá team divided itself into two groups, simulating the hosts and guests. For the game, each participant has long darts, their points covered with beeswax. These darts are launched manually with a wooden instrument in the shape of a fish (a launcher), which has an opening at one end where the dart fits. For defense, the participants use a bundle of sticks, placed vertically in relation to the body. The ideal point to wound an enemy is on his ankle. Once the darts are thrown, the defender tries to avoid them with the help of his bundle of sticks and through subtle body movements (without walking). The upper part of the body cannot be hit. The aim of the participants is to hit first, and

responding with a revenge hit never will be valued as highly as a first-time hit. There is no scoreboard for this game, since the hits cannot be added up, as they are essentially different. Finally, victory belongs to the person who succeeds in hitting first, and to his group, the contest always being performed in pairs, according to age. After this rehearsal, those who were gravediggers of the deceased person being commemorated, and afterwards those who held the role of questioners in the festival, were named, by the sponsors, as *pariat* (inviters). These inviters left on the morning of 12–13 June for the village of the Matipúhy Indians to invite them to the festival.

Resumption, days 7 and 8. On the morning of the seventh day, the inviters returned to the Kamayurá village with the notice of consent, on the part of the Matipúhy, to the honorable invitation. Then the inviters cleaned an area around two hundred meters from the village, in the direction of the Leonardo Villas Boas Post. This area was to be the future campsite of the guests, and had to be provided with firewood and other comforts. On the morning of the eighth day, in this phase of resumption that included the 13–14 and 14–15 of June, the darts of the Kamayurá participants were blessed by Gorgias, the great ritual chief of the Kamayurá. On the afternoon of this same day, the smoking (blessing with smoke) of the darts was repeated, followed by an "instance" derived from Afternoon, and chastisement.

Eve, days 9 and 10. The eve phase represents the maximum extension of the "fan" structure that describes Yawari so well. On this night of the ninth day there was a chastisement, followed by a derivation of Dusk, another chastisement, a Dawn, a Curassow, a Deep Night, an Opening of Dawn, all ending with another chastisement. In the morning, a Deep Night was sung, followed by a Night, another Deep Night, and still another. In the afternoon a mix between Dusk and Afternoon "instances" was performed, followed by a chastisement and another session of smoking the darts. On the night of the tenth day, only an opening was sung. In the morning, the *pariat* (inviters) went to fish for the hosts, except for one of them (Duplo), who had gone to meet the Matipúhy on their way to the village of their Kamayurá hosts. During twilight—always in this space—the Yawalapiti arrived in Yawaracingtỳp.

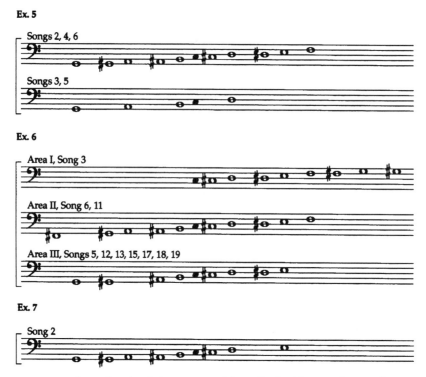

Exs. 5, 6, and 7: Scalar structure of chants for the Afternoon "instance."

Encounter, day 11. Finally, on the eleventh day, the encounter took place. There were several chastisements by the hosts, which were followed by a single one on the part of the guests. Afterwards, the guests returned to their camp. The Kamayurá sang all night. Very early in the morning, the Kamayurá did a chastisement. Next, the Matipúhy dignitaries entered the village patio. Soon, the Kamayurá sang a derivation of Dusk, followed by a chastisement. Next, the team of Matipúhy singers-dancers-players entered the village and chastised the effigy of the deceased. Then there was a game of Yawari that the hosts won. Once the game was over, Aristotle and Plato delivered the funeral eulogy for Storm, the beautiful adult who had been stolen from life so early. Afterwards, they wept copiously. At this moment, three people left the resting place of the Matipúhy dignitaries in the patio of Yawaracingtỳp, and moved toward Aristotle and Plato, who were still weeping. These three Matipúhy—who would be the ones to make Storm into the ultimate Other by validating his death and, thereby, his betrothal to the gods—received cereal from the sponsors, then wept intensely. Next, these three Matipúhy collected the effigy of Storm, as well as his bows, darts, and dart-launchers (which his father lovingly kept) and burned them all in a stupendous bonfire. This accomplished, the Matipúhy sang a derivation of Afternoon, repeated by the

Kamayurá. Then the inviters directed the visitors to Lake Ỳpawu to bathe, which was followed by visits by the Matipúhy to the houses of Kamayurá relatives or friends. Finally, the Matipúhy left for their village. Plato sadly collected the ashes of Storm's possessions and buried them.

INTERPRETATION OF YAWARI

How can the Yawari be understood, based on this ethnographic fragment, more a faction than a fiction in the Latin sense of these terms (Geertz 1978)? What follows is an extremely compressed version of the Yawari myth, as Gorgias presented it to this author, with the intention of making us understand what we had witnessed.

In the old days, in the Trumai village of Wawaniwani, the chief surprised his cross-cousin Curassow Head (Cabeça de Mutum) having sexual relations with his two wives. He already knew of these encounters and, that day, said to his wives that he was going fishing. He did not go fishing, however. His wives said to him, as always, that they would go to the garden. They made manioc cake. When the wives went to the garden, the chief followed them and hid there. He then witnessed the amorous encounter. At this moment, he left his hiding place and shot an arrow at Curassow Head, who was hit in the neck and, running, took cover in a thicket near the village. The chief set fire to the thicket, which stung the hair of Curassow Head. In the village, all could see Curassow Head's wound and burn. He became profoundly ashamed and decided to go to the extreme north, land of savage peoples. The chief, overtaken by jealousy of his cross-cousin and anger at his wives, returned to his house. He spent much time without going to the "circle of smokers." The Curassow Heads (the group of brothers whose older brother was Curassow Head) traveled to the land of the savages. They took manioc flour with them. The walked for many days, always stopping at night to eat and sleep by the waters' shores. They encountered many wild animals and suffered hardship. When the manioc flour was about to run out, they noticed signs of smoke in the distance. They walked much more and were completely out of manioc flour when they arrived at a garden. There, an old woman was roasting potatoes. They ate potatoes and asked the old woman: "Are the savages going to kill us?" The old woman responded, "They are very good. They are having a festival now. Do not be afraid. I will take you to the village." Then they went. The name of the people? Payeta, ancestors of the Trumai. Their language was similar to that of the Trumai, and similar, also, to the Kamayurá language. So, the Curassow Heads went to the village of the savage Payeta. There, they were doing Yawari. The Curassow Heads were received very well. They ate many roasted potatoes, plenty of beans, *mohet* (non-alcoholic beverage), and *kawĩkỳtã* (sweet *kawi*). The Payeta were doing Yawari. They sent *pariat* (inviters) to [invite] the Anumania. The Anumania are ancestors of the Awetí. They ate humans. The Curassow Heads witnessed the entire festival, trying to learn all of it, to hear, and keep it in their heads. They lived for many years with the Payeta, waiting for their shame to end, and for the jealousy of their cross-cousin to dissipate, far away. They returned, then, to Wawaniwani. The old woman gave them manioc flour. They traveled for many days. They endured hunger and confronted immense dangers. They arrived in their village of origin, where they were very well received: there was no more shame or jealousy. The respect had been restored. Curassow Head (no longer the group but the older brother) then became the music master or *maraka'ỳp* of the Yawari, teaching it to the Trumai, in the old days. Afterwards, all the others (Xinguano) came to learn it as well. The Awetí, in the old days, already knew it. They learned it with the Anumania. The Yawari narrates how Curassow Head resists many arrows from his cross-cousin. That is the way Yawari is.

When the chief surprises his cross-cousin Curassow Head making love to his wives in Wawaniwani, what actually is happening can be construed as an act of fulfillment of fate, namely the regulation of irreciprocal behavior between equidistant members of the system that includes them. The only surprise in the narrative is the act of witnessing: in Kamayurá culture, the first persons to become aware of a betrayal are the husbands themselves. What the Trumai chief is doing when he decides to witness the betrayal is an act of public acknowledgement. From that point onward, Curassow Head becomes publicly indebted to the chief, who, in turn, proceeds to legitimize vengeance or "credit." On the one hand, the traitor will have his neck wounded by an arrow and his hair burned, leading to shame and public humiliation of the great hero. On the other hand, the grieving and angry chief will remove himself from the village's public places. In this manner, to the jealous and envied chief corresponds the jealousy-provoking and envious Curassow Head.

What happens next in the narrative is quite extraordinary: the traitor travels to the extreme North, the Kamayurá symbol of savagery, in a true descent into an inferno. The humiliation of the first scene of the myth gives way to heroism in the second, mixing comedy and tragedy. However, something even more remarkable is to follow. The teleology of this descent is nothing less than the search for the Yawari festival itself, namely the machine that sets in motion and justifies everything that has taken place. What will be sought is something that almost was possessed—jealousy and envy—not as emotions in themselves but as ritual objects. Furthermore, these are taken from where an alliance is unthinkable, that is, from the North, the space of the savage peoples. In this manner, "events" in historical time (*ang*) create an intervention on mythical time (*mawe*). This is astounding for Kamayurá culture because its members think of the Yawari ritual—at least schematically—as the great force that organizes the world and creates the cosmos from chaos. Furthermore, this is remarkable because nothing less than a ritual is sought, one which is like a cyclotron pointing to the beginning of "beginnings," or human dissatisfaction with human-cosmic codes. We suggest that this second scene of the myth seeks to establish that the alliance or marriage between envy and jealousy, and the opposite pulsations of these two emotions, constitute interdependent voices of a single polyphonic fabric which, consequently, should not be viewed as reciprocal failures. Instead, if desire exists, everything should be validated by the existence of desire, either as original sin, or as the first price paid for the process of becoming human. Desire is the death of desire as well as its price.

If the foregoing interpretation addresses the codes of the myth, what might be the message of the ritual itself? We suggest that the Yawari, using the social world of humans as a metaphor, is a discourse on cosmic trade, wherein death is the great object of desire. But desired how, and by whom? Death is desired jealously by Plato, who represents the betrayed chief of myth, the great Jealous and Envied one, and it is desired enviously by the gods, symbolized in Curassow Head. In this polyphonic fabric, the world of mortals interfaces with the immortal realm of the vultures. This is because, in the worldview of the Kamayurá, socialization already implies renouncing both invulnerability and the impotent rejection of death, all under the threat of the fall of the heavens if the vultures do not have food (souls) to survive. Within this framework of beliefs, Storm is the great object of desire, a metaphorical wife of the living and beloved of the gods.

In the opening Dusk sequence of the Yawari, of which only one "instance" has been analyzed here, the song texts construct a discourse that targets the customary ethics of the tripartite universe of Kamayurá kinship. Within this context, what does music do? The texts establish the ethos of denial of death as currency of the cosmic trade (in songs from "instances" not discussed in this essay); rivalry, as well as jealousy and shame, in the face of struggle for the same desires (in songs 2 to 5); and sharing as renunciation of the sexual, and as a return to resigned, amorous idleness (in songs 6 and 7). Assigning itself an eminently axiological role, music will pronounce judgment on this discourse: it will refer to rivalry as the territory of Evil (in songs 2 to 5, see Ex. 2) and, distinguishing it from sharing, it will place the latter as a return to a natural order of things in the domain of the Good (in songs 6 and 7, see Ex. 3). Moreover, the scales derived from these "fields" (Exs. 2 and 3), with their composite (see Ex. 4), establish these ethical polarities as non-Manichaean, non-equivalent opposites.

In the Afternoon sequence, of which only one "instance" has been discussed here, jealousy will be established as negation of primordial joy, and desire as ludicrous, itself a negation of prototypical austerity. This part of the ritual rekindles the question of divinization of the human as human itself, with its music critically questioning any idea of "genesis."

Here, music proposes a paradoxically divine state of humanity, or the teleology of a desire beyond good and evil.

The questions posed by the substance of the Yawari ritual can be considered relevant to indigenous societies in Lowland South America in general (Albert 1982; Viveiros de Castro 1986). For instance, the discourse on cross-relationality is a fundamental index of this assertion. Cross-relationality places the domains of the social (human) and the cosmic (human-divine) on the same path of reflection. The universality of questions, however, should not be construed to mean that indigenous groups are socioculturally equal. On the contrary, this Lowland world is built upon the organization of differences. Here, small societies hold on stubbornly to their specificities, and, while loving the "exotic," never submit to homogenization.

In the Alto Xingu, the Yawari is inscribed in a Trumai-Tupi (Kamayurá-Awetí) historical nexus that, in turn, points to the Tapajós-Xingu and Xingu-Araguaia river junctions. This geography is the setting of an immense game of war and peace, wherein neither is construed as a failure, that at once builds and destroys societies. Moreover, what happens in a part of this territory becomes a model for the entire subregion. Consequently, the study of Yawari represents an important step toward an understanding of these societies as prominently relational worlds, open and moving. Without a doubt, these characteristics of the peoples who inhabit Lowland South America harbor the question of *artisticidade* (artistry) as fundamental and recurrent in the area. We refer to "artistry" rather than to "the arts." What we would like to suggest is radical: in this indigenous universe, everything is art, artifice, deception, enticement—a real and essentially true simulacrum.

REFERENCES

ABA (Associação Brasileira de Antropologia) 1955a. "Convenção para a grafia dos nomes tribais," *Revista de antropologia* 3/2: 150–52.
    1955b. "A grafia dos nomes tribais brasileiros (listagem dos etnônimos," *Revista de antropologia* 3/2: 125–32.
Agostinho, Pedro 1974. *Kwarýp: Mito e ritual no Alto-Xingu.* São Paulo: Editora Pedagógica e Universitária [EPU]—Editora da Universidade de São Paulo.
Albert, Bruce 1982. *Temps du sang, temps des cendres: Représentation de la maladie, système rituel et espace politique chez les Yanomami du sud-est (Amazonie brésilienne)* (PhD diss., Social Anthropology: University of Paris, X).
CEDI (Ecumenical Center for Documentation and Information—Museu Nacional 1987). *Terras indígenas no Brasil.* São Paulo.

Chomsky, Noam 1971. *Linguagem e pensamento.* Petrópolis: Vozes. English edition, *Language and thought* (Wakefield, Rhode Island: Moyer Bell, 1993).

1975. *Aspectos da teoria da sintaxe.* Coimbra: Armênio Amado Editor. Portuguese translation of *Aspects of the theory of syntax* (Cambridge: Massachusetts Institute of Technology [M.I.T.] Press, 1965).

Clastres, Pierre 1978. *A sociedade contra o estado.* Rio de Janeiro: Livraria Francisco Alves.

1982. *Arqueologia da violência: Ensaios de antropologia política.* São Paulo: Editora Brasiliense.

Galvão, Eduardo 1960 in 1979. "O uso do propulsor entre as tribos do Alto-Xingu" in *Encontro de sociedades: Índios e brancos no Brasil,* ed. by Eduardo Galvão. Rio de Janeiro: Editora Paz e Terra, 39–56.

Geertz, Clifford 1978. *A interpretação das culturas.* Rio de Janeiro: Jorge Zahar Editora—ANPOCS. Portuguese translation of *The interpretation of cultures: Selected essays* (New York: Basic Books, 1973).

Gregor, Thomas 1977. *Mehináku: The drama of daily life in a Brazilian Indian village.* Chicago: University of Chicago Press.

Lévi-Strauss, Claude 1980. "A noção de estrutura em etnologia" in *Os pensadores: Claude Lévi-Strauss,* ed. by Marilena Chauí. São Paulo: Abril Cultural, 1–43.

Menezes Bastos, Rafael José de 1978. *A musicológica Kamayurá: Para uma antropologia da comunicação no Alto Xingu.* Brasília: Fundação Nacional do Índio (FUNAI). Second edition (Florianópolis: Editora da Universidade Federal de Santa Catarina, 1999).

1986. "Música, cultura e sociedade no Alto-Xingu: A teoria musical dos Índios Kamayurá," *Latin American music review* 7/1: 51–80.

1989. *A festa da "Jaguatirica": Uma partitura crítico-interpretativa* (PhD diss., Social Anthropology: University of São Paulo).

Rocha Pereira, Maria Helena 1986. "O herói épico e o herói trágico," *Kriterion* (Universidade Federal de Minas Gerais) 27/76: 1–23.

Rodrigues, Aryon Dall'Igna 1984–85. "Relações internas na família lingüística Tupi-Guarani," *Revista de antropologia* 27–28: 33–53.

1986. *Línguas brasileiras: Para o conhecimento das línguas indígenas.* São Paulo: Edições Loyola.

Saussure, Ferdinand de 1967. *Curso de lingüística general.* Buenos Aires: Editorial Losada. Spanish translation of *Cours de linguistique generale,* ed. by Charles Bally and Albert Sechehaye (Paris: Payot, 1916).

Schmidt, M. 1942. *Estudos de etnologia brasileira.* São Paulo: Companhia Editora Nacional.

Seeger, Anthony 1980. "A identidade étnica como processo: Os Índios Suyá e as sociedades do Alto-Xingu," *Anuário antropológico* 78: 156–75.

1981. *Nature and society in central Brazil: The Suyá Indians of Mato Grosso.* Cambridge: Harvard University Press.

Steinen, Karl von den 1894 in 1940. "Entre os aborígenes do Brasil Central," separatum from Nos. 34–58, *Revista do Arquivo Municipal* (São Paulo).

1942. *O Brasil Central.* São Paulo: Companhia Editora Nacional.

Viveiros de Castro, Eduardo Batalha 1986. *Araweté: Os deuses canibais.* Rio de Janeiro: Jorge Zahar Editora—ANPOCS.

RECORDED EXAMPLES

Dusk "instance" (see transcriptions, Ex. 1).
1. M
2. Motekey
3. He nu yawari
4. Horowy
5. Kamiwaye
6. Nuterihiyu
7. Yahaha
8. M (same as 1)
9. T
10. T'

MUSIC AND WORLDVIEW OF INDIAN SOCIETIES IN THE BOLIVIAN ANDES

MAX PETER BAUMANN

Ritual, music, and dance—Symbolic dualism in panpipe ensembles:
The ira/arka *principle in its diverse manifestations; Julajulas; Lakitas; Sikuris—*
Panpipe representations in pre-Columbian times—Symbolic dualism as worldview:
cosmological approach—Appendix: Instrumentarium

MEMBERS OF INDIAN societies constitute more than half of the Bolivian population. Most of them live in small rural settlements in the Altiplano (mountain plateau) and in the *cordilleras* (mountain chains) at an altitude of 2,500 to 4,500 meters above sea level. The Spanish term "Indio" refers primarily to feelings of social and cultural solidarity among these groups. Indians live primarily off the land, growing various kinds of potatoes, corn, wheat, *quinoa* (a kind of barley), and beans. These vegetables and the stock of llama, sheep, some cows, and pigs make up their staple diet. They speak at least one of the Indian languages as their mother tongue and identify with the traditional Andean cultural heritage. Kechua- and Aymara-speaking farmers constitute the numerically largest linguistic groups. In the Andean highlands, and for the sake of simplicity, Indians who speak one of these languages are designated as Kechuas or Aymaras, using the Spanish plural. Kechua is spoken primarily in the departments of Cochabamba, Oruro, Potosí, and Chuquisaca, as well as in some provinces of the Department of La Paz. The language is the Runa Simi (language of the people) that evolved from the classical Kechua of the Inca Empire (1438–1537). The Aymara language survived in the vicinity of the pre-Inca ritual sites of Tiwanaku on Lake Titicaca. The Aymaras or Kollas live primarily in the highlands of La Paz, as well as in relatively large areas in the departments of Oruro

and Potosí. Many Aymara musical terms and concepts seem to have been transmitted to the Kechua-speaking peoples in this area.

The Chipayas, a smaller group, still survive near Lake Coipasa in linguistic and cultural isolation. Their language, Chipaya, is spoken today by fewer than 1,000 people. Presumably, the Chipayas were among the first settlers of the central Andes, along with the Urus of Lake Titicaca. The Callawayas (Kallawayas) hold a unique position within the Kechua-speaking provinces of Bautista Saavedra, Muñecas, and parts of the provinces of Tamayo and La Paz. Approximately 2,000 Callawayas use their own Machchj-juyai language (literally, "language of the compatriot or companion") but generally speak Kechua. The Callawayas differ culturally from the Kechuas and Aymaras, although many reciprocal influences are evident, especially in the realms of music and musical instruments.

RITUAL, MUSIC, AND DANCE

Music, dance, song, and ritual are closely intertwined in the Bolivian highlands. Dance is present in almost all group-oriented forms of music-making. The Kechua term *taki* (*taqui*, song) denotes language that is sung, rhythmicized melody, and dance. Each of the three key terms, *takiy* (to sing), *tukuy* or *tukay* (corruptions of the

Spanish *tocar* which means "to play"), and *tusuy* (to dance), emphasizes one aspect of a holistic musical behavior. These three aspects complement one another and signify the inherent unity of structured sound, movement, and symbolic expression.

Musical behavior always is embedded in a particular context within the annual cycle of religious rituals. The types of music-making and singing are determined by the agricultural cycle of the rainy season (when the seed is sown and the harvest is brought in) and the dry season (when the earth is tended and plowed). In general, the seasons also determine the kinds of musical instruments, melodies, and dances that should be performed. Numerous festivals are celebrated for the earth deities, and offerings of smoke, drink, and animal sacrifices are made when the ground is tilled and the seeds are sown, as the plants grow, and as people pray for a rich harvest. Each celebration has its own set of melodies (*wirsus* or *tonadas*) and its own musical instruments. Music and dance are expressions of joy and offerings to honor Father and Mother Earth (Pachatata and Pachamama).

Today the various festivals also must be considered in connection with the historical layers and traditional reinterpretations that have been superimposed on them through time. Often, for example, the old Inca calendar, the Christian or Gregorian calendar, and the annual agricultural cycle simultaneously influence such celebrations. All these different elements and fragments play their own roles and frequently interact with each other.

The cosmological-religious worldview of Indians in the Altiplano often seems to be partly syncretistic. Traditional central Andean beliefs still survive, blended to a limited extent with the Christian conception of faith and worship in a relationship of reciprocal influence. The Virgin Mary is associated with the timeless principle of mother earth or Pachamama. Throughout the centuries, Christian religious figures, such as the Virgin Mary, have become syncretized with elements of Pachamama as a fundamental principle, which manifests itself in individual, local virgins (*mamitas*), such as the Virgen de la Candelaria, Virgen de Copacabana, Virgen del Carmen, and Mamita Asunta (Virgen de la Asunción).

Pachamama is the mother of humans, the source of all fertility, and the symbol of growth and decline, within an overall concept of time and space. During the rainy season in the Department of Oruro, for

example, *charkas* or *pinkillos* are sounded in honor of Pachamama to express gratitude for the first good harvest of the season. *Charkas* are duct flutes of various sizes (built similarly to the recorder) that are played by men to accompany the dances, together with a cow horn, or *pututu*. Unmarried girls accompany these instruments in a high falsetto voice, saying "Takisun Pachamamaman mañarisun" (Let us sing and invoke Pachamama).

Various duct flutes such as *charkas*, *pinkillos / pinkollos*, *mohoceños / aymaras*, *ch'utus*, *tokurus*, and *tarkas / anatas* traditionally are played during the rainy season, that is, starting on All Saints' Day (November 1) until the carnival season in February or March. These instruments belong to the rainy season, which is the "female" time of the year. The distinction between "female" and "male" times of the year can be seen as a partial remnant of the old Inca calendar. According to this calendar, the sun festival of the "king" (Inti Raymi), which was the main festival of the dry season, was followed by the festival of the "queen" (Koya Raymi). The wooden duct flutes symbolize the female principle of irrigation, of becoming fertile after the quiet and dry time; they express joy over the sprouting seeds and the harvest. The connection of these instruments with the element of water is emphasized by the fact that they are sometimes filled with water before being played, saturating them with the liquid and therefore making them airtight. Because Christian religious concepts were superimposed on the festivals, the duct flutes also are closely related to the numerous festivals dedicated to the Virgin Mary that take place during the rainy season, such as the Fiesta de la Concepción (December 8) and the Fiesta de la Candelaria (February 2). The instruments proclaim delight over the Christmas season and the New Year. The Bolivian summer solstice (December 21) coincides with the high point of the rainy season (called *paray mit'a* in Kechua) and also with Christmas festivities. Varying somewhat in length according to latitude, this season lasts from around the beginning of November to the end of March or the beginning of April.

On the other hand, panpipes and notched flutes made of hard bamboo are associated with the male principle, represented also by the sun, the dry season, and the wind. Played predominantly during the dry season, these instruments are closely linked to the "male" festivals that take place during the other half of the year, such as Santa Cruz (May 3) and Corpus

Christi (end of May / beginning of June), as well as to the numerous festivals that honor particular male saints, such as Tata Santiago and Tata Agustín. These feasts are all linked to the concept of Pachatata or Tatapacha (*tata* = father). The dry season (called *ruphay mit'a* in Kechua), reaches its high point with Inti Raymi on June 21, the Bolivian winter solstice. Soon thereafter, the great festival of San Juan takes place on the coldest night (June 24). During this dry season, the instruments predominantly used are the notched flutes made of bamboo (*kenas, chokelas, kenakenas, lichiwayus, pusi-ppias*) and panpipes (*sikus, sikuras, antaras, julajulas, lakitas*).

Pachamama and Pachatata thus manifest the Andean concept of the earth, which is a dualistic principle of energy; each is a part of a pair and the completion of the other. In its internal symbolic dualism, a pair symbolizes the energizing poles of the inner bondage of the world.

The transcendent dimension of the sky above the earth is represented by Mama Killa (Mother Moon) and Tata Inti (Father Sun), a complementary pair of precontact deities. The temple gates dedicated to the moon and sun in the pre-Inca temple sites at Tiwanaku already were considered a pair of opposites. Later, under Christian influence, Tata Inti was renamed Tata Santísimo (Holy Father / Ghost) and Mama Killa was reinterpreted as Mama Santísima by the Indians. Both principles stand for the same symbolic dualism that, as an enduring pattern, flows through all forms of being and transcends space and time. The Kechua phrase "Tukuy ima qhariwarmi" (Everything is man and woman) expresses the concept that each member of a pair contains an element of the other member (Platt 1976: 21): the female half contains a male element, although it is predominantly female, and vice versa. The concept is thus one of double dualism or quadripartition. This basic principle regulates all existing structures on earth and in the sky, human beings, the world as creation, animals, and plants. Symbolic dualism also extends to the social order and to agricultural life: it is man who tills the soil, opening it so that woman can plant the seed. The united strength of the pair thus releases new energy. By analogy, the mountains contain the mainly male-oriented centers of power in their holy peaks, which are given such names as *tatas, apus, achachilas,* or *mallkus* (*mallku* is the condor, the master of the mountains). The mountains provide the water to fertilize the land. This contrasts with the feminine energies of the flatter lands and valleys, where female spirits dwell (*awacha, awila, mamita, t'alla*). All local centers of energy are assigned specific names of male or female deities or saints, who are invoked on particular occasions and are offered music, drink (*aqha* / Spanish, chicha), and incense (*q'oa*) during the ritual of *ch'alla* or during an animal sacrifice (*wilancha*).

The fundamental principle of symbolic dualism often surfaces in various local manifestations of "deities / saints" and "spirits" *(lugarniyoj)*. Among the Chipayas, the protective spirits Mallkus and Samiris play an important role in the fertility of land and cattle. Sajama, the holy mountain, is celebrated with offerings so that he will yield the life-giving water and thus fertilize the female-associated fields, the Mother Earth. The male spirits of the earth (*jurq'u*) have their female counterparts in water holes (*warmi jurq'u*). According to an old mythical narrative, the sun people were birthed from the love between the mountain Illampu and Lake Titicaca.

Within this system of beliefs, human beings live in a world (*kay pacha*) situated between heaven and earth. On the one hand, wise men, called *yachaj* by the Kechuas and *yatiri* by the Aymaras, function individually as knowing mediators. Through prayers and songs they establish a connection between deities and humans inhabiting this world. On the other hand, the collectively celebrated music rituals and festivals, through honoring and offering, create a common bridge between the sacred and the profane, between above and below, between growing and dying, and between Pachamama / Wirjin María and Pachatata / Tata Kruz (Father Cross). Such collective celebrations are known as *tinku* and *tinka* (in Spanish, *encuentro*) and include fertility rites, weddings, processions, and other festivities, some influenced by Christianity. The ritual *tinku*, a mock battle between two groups, is a powerful, aggressive event, while the *tinka*, a ritual meeting of contrasting groups, is a peaceful occasion. The *tinka* itself represents a union of complementary parts, "the important ritual action of bringing together separate and yet contrasting parts, such as highlands and lowlands, vertical and horizontal kin groups, and the living and dead" (Bastien 1978 121f.). It is a symbolic union "to express a bond of unity, distinctiveness, and reciprocity" that represents a third unit created by an "interlocking" principle. Power, energy, and reproduction emanate from this new, third unit.

SYMBOLIC DUALISM
IN PANPIPE ENSEMBLES

Panpipe ensembles can be viewed as a paradigm of the symbolic dualism and anthropomorphic cosmology described above. The traditional panpipe ensembles of the Bolivian highlands use the playing technique of "interlocking" pairs. Each ensemble consists of several pairs of instruments, and each pair combines a female instrument with a male counterpart. The pairs can be multiplied to create several registers within a range of two to five different octaves. Playing in pairs is encountered in specific panpipe ensembles, such as the *maizus, julajulas, julu-julus, chiriwanos, lakitas, antaras* or *sikus, sikuras,* and *phukunas,* namely in the most traditional ensembles of Aymara-, Chipaya-, and Kechua-speaking peoples.

With few exceptions, the rural music ensembles (*tropas*) consist of identical melody-playing panpipe types. All panpipes appear in a "choral" setting, as uniform panpipe pairs. In contrast to the urban folk groups (*conjuntos*) of mestizos, the Indians do not mix panpipes with other instruments such as the notched flute (*kena*), the duct flute (*pinkillo / tarka*), or with string instruments (*charango / guitarra*). Panpipe ensembles can be classified either as *tropas* of single-row panpipes without drum accompaniment, or as *tropas* of double-row panpipes with drum accompaniment. Most panpipe ensembles consist of several pairs of different-sized instruments, which is to say that more than one pair of panpipes is needed to cover several registers. Exceptions include the *maizu* ensemble of the Chipayas and a few others in which pairs of panpipes appear only in one register.

In most cases a pair is composed of one instrument with an odd number of pipes and another with an even number of pipes, although some ensembles have pairs of instruments with the same number of pipes. In either case, when the pair is expanded by addition of instruments of the same type, those instruments maintain the same numerical composition. The pipes of each instrument usually are bound together in raft form according to size. Each member of a pair is played by one musician.

Figures 1 and 2 show the specific pairs of panpipes as they are found in the most common ensembles. Underlined numbers indicate stopped pipes, plain numbers designate open pipes. (In addition to the panpipes discussed below, see the Appendix to this article, "Musical instruments and ensembles in the

Name of panpipe ensemble	Pair of stopped pipes	Distribution
maizus (or *chiriwanos*)	(3) and (2)	Chipayas
julajulas	(4) and (3)	Kechuas / Aymaras
julu-julus	(4) and (3)	Aymaras
chiriwanos	(4) and (3)	Kechuas / Aymaras

Fig. 1: Number of pipes in different ensembles of single-row panpipes (without drum accompaniment).

Name of panpipe ensemble	Pair of double-row panpipes	Distribution
lakitas / sikus	(6+6) and (5+5)	Aymaras / Kechuas
lakitas / sikus	(7+7) and (6+6)	Aymaras / Kechuas
lakitas / sikus	(8+8) and (7+7)	Aymaras / Kechuas
phukunas	(7+7) and (6+6)	Callawayas
ayarichis	(7+½7) and (7+½7)	Kechuas
sikuras / sikuris	(17+17) and (17+17)	Aymaras / Kechuas

Fig. 2: Number of pipes in different ensembles of double-row panpipes (with drum accompaniment).

Bolivian Andes," for illustrations of Figs. 1 and 2 and for other instruments used in the area.)

The *ira/arka* principle in its diverse manifestations

According to native terminology and explanations given by musicians, each member of a panpipe pair carries a male or female connotation. *Ira* is the dominant, male-oriented instrument that usually starts the melody and leads the panpipe playing, while *arka*, its complement, follows. *Ira* and *arka* are blown by two players in alternation: while *ira* begins playing one to four notes, *arka* rests and then continues the melody as *ira* rests, and so on. In this way, *arka* and *ira* combine their notes to create a particular melody that results from an interplay of interlocking parts.

The Aymara word *ira* or *irpa* denotes "leader" or "the one who leads" and represents a male principle. Other names used for the same concept are *sanja, pussak / pussaj* (from the Kechua *pussay,* to lead), and the Spanish *guía* (leader) or *primero* (the first). The Aymara word *arka* denotes the female counterpart, "the one who follows." Other names for *arka* are the Kechua *khatik / qhatij* (from the infinitive *qhatiy,* to follow) and the Spanish *trasguía* (after the leader) or *segundo* (the second). Although it is quite likely that *arka* and *ira* are Aymara words, they also are used by speakers of Kechua. In Aymara ensembles, the male *ira* panpipes are often the instruments with the smaller number of pipes, while the opposite is true in Kechua ensembles.

To illustrate the complexity of different panpipe ensembles, three of the most common types will be described in detail, focusing particularly on the tuning and distribution of the pipes and on individual pitch ranges. These are a *julajula* ensemble from Lagua Lagua (in the Department of Potosí); a *lakita* ensemble from Llauro Llokolloko (in the Department of La Paz); and a *sikuri* ensemble from Chilca Grande (in the Department of Cochabamba).

***Julajulas* (Department of Potosí).** The *julajula* panpipes (Fig. 3) are played in pairs whose male member (*ira*) has four stopped pipes and the female (*arka*) has three stopped pipes. The pipes of both instruments are tuned in sequential perfect fourths, with the exception of one major third.

The seven tones produced by the two instruments form a descending anhemitonic pentatonic scale (D–B–A–G–E). The pairs of the ensemble of the village of Lagua Lagua are tuned in five octave registers: *ch'ili* (meaning "small" in Kechua); *tijli* ("slender" in Aymara); *liku* ("the third" in Aymara); *mali* (probably from the Kechua *malta / mallta* that refers to objects of a middle range); and *machu* (see Figs. 4a and 4b). This ensemble is composed of 16 players or eight pairs (1 *ch'ili*; 3 *tijli*; 2 *liku*; 1 *mali*; and 1 *machu*).

The *machu* ("old" or "patriarchal") pair is played by the two oldest musicians. In principle, the larger the panpipes, the older the musicians playing them: the smallest panpipes are played by the youngest, the *tijli*

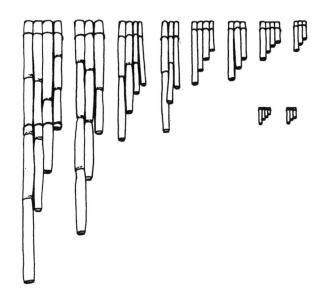

Fig. 4a: Set of *julajula* panpipes.

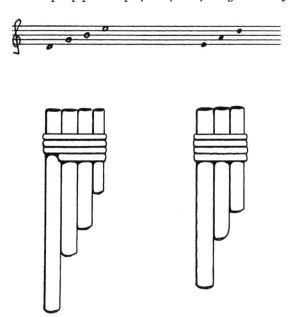

Fig. 3: Pair of *julajula* panpipes (*ira*: 4 and *arka* 3) in the *liku* register (29 cm).

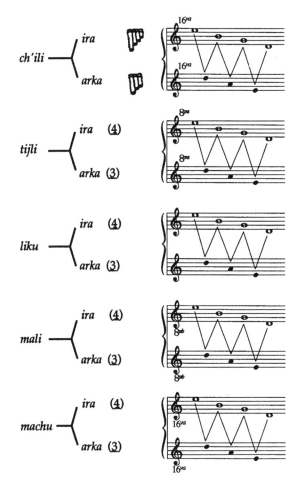

Fig. 4b: Tuning of *julajula* panpipes illustrated in Fig. 4a.

Fig. 4c: *Julajula, arka* instrument. Arampampa, north of Potosí, 1978.
Photo by Max Peter Baumann, courtesy of the author.

Ex. 1: *Julajula* panpipes: *baile chúkaro* (Lagua Lagua), transcription of the *liku* pair (Recorded Ex. 1).

by the next youngest, and so on. Individual *julajula* melodies sound "simultaneously," in parallel octaves over four or five registers (Fig. 4c). In the transcription of a *baile chúkaro* ("wild dance") from Lagua Lagua, the pitches of *ira* are represented by downward stems, and those of *arka* by upward stems (Ex. 1; Recorded Ex. 1).

The *baile chúkaro* of the *julajulas* is performed during the dry season, especially on the Fiesta de la Cruz (May 3). The central church plaza (Fig. 5) is divided into quadrants, each of which has its own *julajula* group. The complementarity of opposites is manifested also in the symbolic division of the quadrangular space into moieties, the higher *aransaya*

(or *hanansaya*) and the lower *urinsaya* (*hurinsaya*). The groups meet in the plaza for the *tinku* or ritual encounter, each with its *julajula* ensemble, and perform their *baile chúkaro*. First, the ensembles play separately on each half of the church plaza; later, after the ritual "battle" of the two moieties, they unite in a procession to visit the four altars (*eskinas* or corners).

Tinku symbolizes the encounter or union of two opposite groups, or *ayllus* (communities) of above (*aransaya*) and below (*urinsaya*), and their coming together from the four corners or directions. A few days before the actual *tinku*, the *julajula* players move forward to the plaza from their distant villages in a serpentine line-dance, one after another, according to

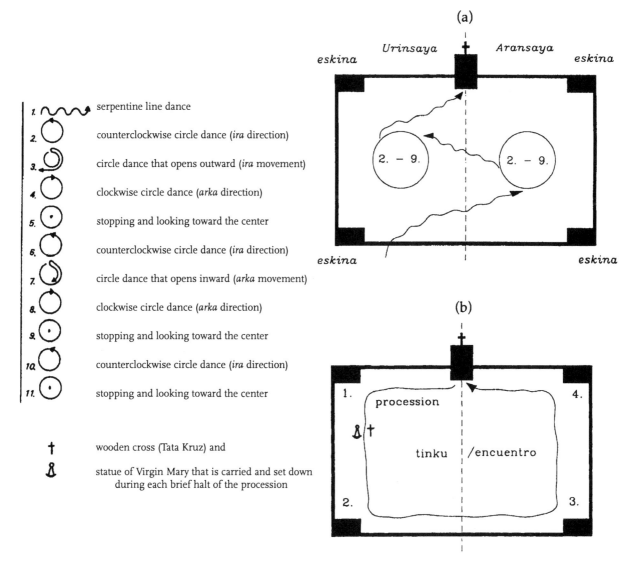

1. serpentine line dance
2. counterclockwise circle dance (*ira* direction)
3. circle dance that opens outward (*ira* movement)
4. clockwise circle dance (*arka* direction)
5. stopping and looking toward the center
6. counterclockwise circle dance (*ira* direction)
7. circle dance that opens inward (*arka* movement)
8. clockwise circle dance (*arka* direction)
9. stopping and looking toward the center
10. counterclockwise circle dance (*ira* direction)
11. stopping and looking toward the center

† wooden cross (Tata Kruz) and

𝄞 statue of Virgin Mary that is carried and set down during each brief halt of the procession

Fig. 5: Basic structure of *julajula* dance figures: (a) tower and plaza with the four directions (*eskinas* = corners, *altares* = altars), dancing at the beginning of the festival; (b) *tinku* and the subsequent procession at the end of the festival.

the hierarchy determined by the size of their instruments. The oldest and most experienced musicians, playing the largest panpipes, head the line. Once they arrive at the church plaza, they perform choreographic figures on the "*aransaya*" side of the square. The dance then moves diagonally across the square to the "*urinsaya*" side and the same sequence of figures is repeated. Following this, the musicians kneel at the entrance of the church, near the tower, and play a *plegaria* or prayer. From there they go to a village compound, near the church plaza, where they stay for the next ten days of festivities. The groups are lodged also in accordance with the hierarchical concepts of *aransaya* and *urinsaya*, and the four different directions. The square or *plaza t'alla* (*t'alla* meaning woman) is a local representation of Pachamama; the church tower or *torre mallku* is the male counterpart (Fig. 5).

In the symbolic center of the plaza / tower, the complementary elements of the male and female principle are united in the ritual meeting, the *tinku* or *encuentro*, and the playing also is described as *encuentro*, *contrapunto*, or *tinku*. Thus, all entities, male and female, unite at the center, as expressed by the saying "Everything is man and woman." The encounter reenacts the symbolic dualism of the female and male principle on several levels:

In space: the two moieties, *aransaya* / *urinsaya*; the four directions, two by two; the dance figures on both sides of the plaza;
In time: during the dry season, performing a melody proper to a particular fiesta;
In the transcendent world of Pachamama / Pachatata, Santísima / Santísimo, and Mama Asunta / Tata Kruz: one fertility ritual;
In the human world: men (*qhari*) are the musicians, and women (*warmi*) are the dancers with flags (*whipalas*); also panpipe players (*arka* / *ira*);
In nature: bamboo instruments, associated with wind and dryness;
In the social hierarchy: *ira* / *arka*; *machu*, *mali*, *liku*, *tijli*, *ch'ili*;
In the musical form: sections AA and BB, and the combination of A and B in section C, their *tinku* or *encuentro* (see Ex. 1).

Lakitas (Department of La Paz). The same *arka* / *ira* principle of the *julajulas* also applies to *lakita* ensembles. Although the *lakitas* are double-row panpipes and, in our illustration (Fig. 6), composed of a double row of eight or seven single pipes tuned differently than the *julajulas*, the second row of pipes serves basically for resonance. The pipes of the

second row are cut off at an angle at the bottom and thus sound softly as open pipes, at an octave higher than the stopped melodic pipes. The individual pitches shared by *arka* and *ira* are tuned at intervals of major and minor thirds (Fig. 6). The pairs *ch'ili*, *liku*, and *sanja* are tuned an octave apart, and melodies are performed according to the same interlocking principle that characterizes other panpipe ensembles. *Lakitas*, however, are accompanied by four *wankara* drums (Ex. 2; Recorded Ex. 2).

In Kechua, the names of the stopped pipes are *tokanan* (playing the melody), *tapasqa* (stopped), or

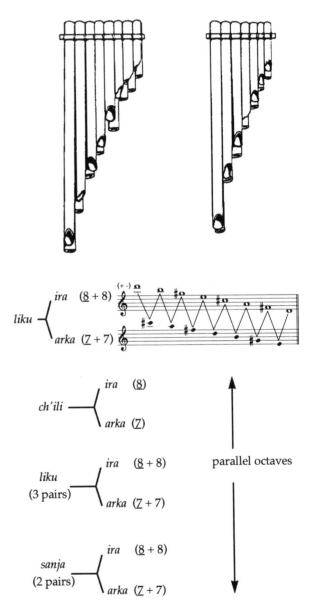

Fig. 6: Pair of double-row panpipes (*ira*: 8+8 and *arka* 7+7) in three octave registers (*ch'ili*, *liku*, *sanja*).

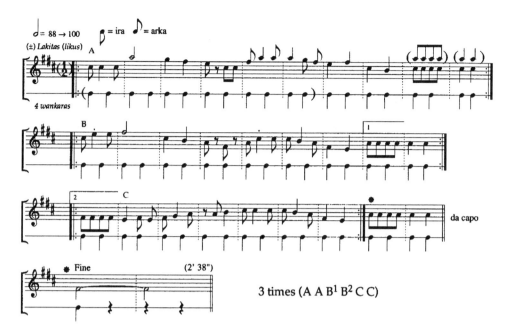

Ex. 2: *Lakitas* (Llauro Llokolloko), transcription illustrating the interlocking technique of the *liku* pair that plays in the middle register (Recorded Ex. 2).

qhari (man). The open pipes have different names in different languages: in Aymara, *phallkja* (fork) or *q'asa* (notch / nick); in Kechua, *kacharisqa*; and *compañía* in Spanish. Another name for them is *china* (little woman). Once more, the complementarity of opposites in a pair is expressed through these terms.

Lakitas ("the chosen ones") are played during the dry season, as is usually the case with panpipes. The *lakita* dancers express the ritual purification and preparation of the land before the sowing begins, in order to entreat Pachamama to grant a good harvest. The musicians dance around the *mallkus* and *t'allas* (male and female heads of communities). Two pairs of women dance around the musicians, spinning llama wool by hand into a ball of yarn with a small wheel (*k'apu / rueda*).

Sikuris (Department of Cochabamba). The dualistic *arka / ira* principle functions similarly in *sikuri* ensembles. Also called *sikuras* or sometimes simply *sikus*, the *sikuris* belong to the large type of double-row panpipes. As a rule, the individual instruments have 17 stopped melodic pipes, bound together in raft form (Fig. 7). A second row of open pipes of the same number and lengths is bound in front of the first row. Although the pipes are "tuned" in diatonic intervals, the tunes played are not diatonic but most often pentatonic. In *sikuris*, both components of the *arka / ira* pair share the same tuning and construction, in

sharp contrast to other panpipe ensembles. The equal pairs play their melody in three different registers (Fig. 7): the *ch'ili* pair and the *liku* pair sound in parallel octaves, while between them the *tarke* pair plays a parallel fourth below *ch'ili*, namely a parallel fifth above *liku*. Unlike the interlocking manner in which *ira* and *arka* play in *julajula* and *lakita* ensembles (illustrated in Exs. 1 and 2), the *ira* and *arka* of *sikuris* use an alternating technique whereby *arka* always echoes the pitch played by *ira* (Ex. 3; Recorded Ex. 3).

The panpipe players, accompanying themselves with four *cajas* (drums), dance in a circle around three dancers representing an old man (*achachi / abuelo*), his small child (*kulyaqa / wawa de los abuelos*, child of the ancestors), and the *umajala* ("naked head," perhaps symbolizing death), who rings a llama bell (*campanilla*) (Fig. 8). Outside the circle there is an old woman, called *awicha* or *abuela*, who is the child's mother and represents the spirit of the arable land. She is played by a man in woman's clothing, who spins yarn with a spindle and is pursued by an evil spirit (Supay) wearing a devil's mask and carrying a cow horn (*pututu*). The *awicha* is anxious to prevent any harm done to the child and thus leads the evil spirit away. Within the safe area of the *sikuri* circle there are also two female dancers (*warmiwaillis*).

The *achachi* adopts the symbolic role of the old man who plows the field, and the *awicha* is the

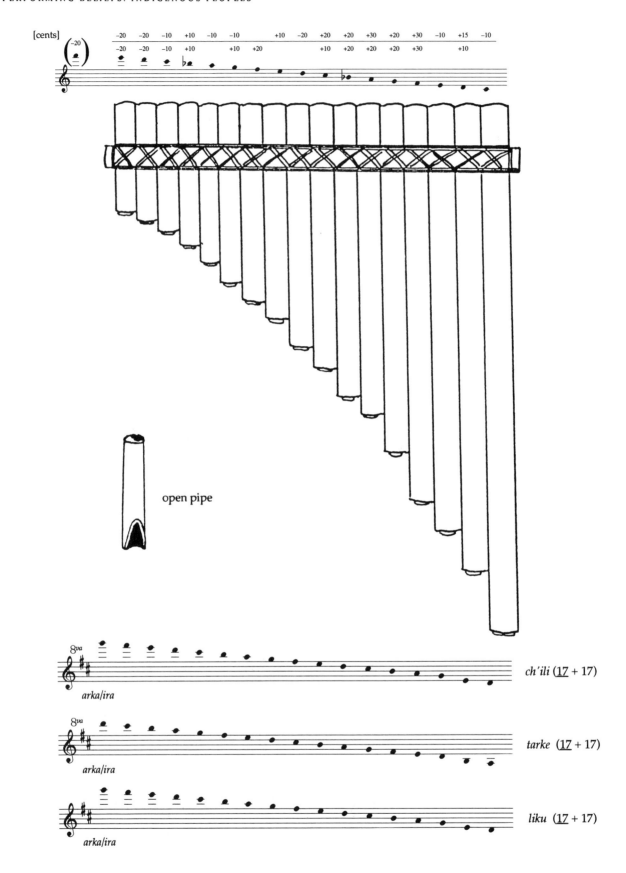

Fig. 7: *Sikura*, double-row panpipe (*ira* or *arka*), with tuning of each pipe above, and *ch'ili*, *tarke*, and *liku* registers below.

Ex. 3: *Sikuris* (Chilca Grande, Tapacarí). Transcription of only the *liku* pair, with *pututu* and accompaniment of drums, performing a *wayño* in alternating technique (Recorded Ex. 3).

Ex. 3: *(continued)*

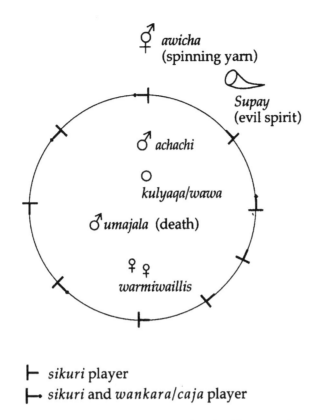

├─ *sikuri* player

├─• *sikuri* and *wankara/caja* player

Fig. 8: *Sikuris,* dance circle with *achachi* and *awicha* (Tapacarí).

woman who sows; both are constantly surrounded by danger. *Achachi* represents the male spirit of the mountain, *awicha* that of the female arable land. *Awicha* is also the mother of potatoes. In addition, dancers alongside the *umajala* wear a stuffed female vicuña on their hats and also a male *kuntur* (condor).

The circle dances of all these panpipe ensembles are associated with the dry season of the agricultural cycle and represent the giving of thanks for the past harvest as well as prayers for the next season. These are addressed to Pachamama (Wirjin) and Pachatata (Tata Kruz), respectively the female and male spirits of the ancestors (*awicha* and *achachi*).

PANPIPE REPRESENTATIONS IN PRE-COLUMBIAN TIMES

Ethnohistorical data, such as the observations recorded by early chroniclers, complement information from field research and vice versa. In this context, the writings of the Inca Garcilaso de la Vega (1539–1616) concerning panpipes may constitute one of the earliest descriptions of the interlocking techniques mentioned above:

[Each instrument consisted of] . . . four or five double pipes of cane. These were bound together so that the pitch of each pipe would successively rise a degree above its neighbor, after the manner of organs . . . . Their way of playing was this. One member of the quartet would start by blowing a note. Then another player would blow a pipe sounding at the distance of a fifth or any other desired consonance above or below the first note. Next, still another player would blow his note, again at any desired consonantal distance. Finally, the fourth played his note. By keeping up this sort of thing they ranged from lowest to highest notes at will, but always in strict time. They did not know how to vary their melodies with small note-values but always stuck with whole notes (Garcilaso 1609: fols. 52v–53 [recte 51v–52] translated in Stevenson 1968: 277).

In addition, we find early representations of playing in pairs in figurines or relief paintings on vessels, and in drawings on ceramic pieces from the Moche and Chimú cultures. Paired instruments from the Nazca culture also have been discovered by archaeologists. In fact, when panpipe representations show pairs of identically constructed counterparts, our knowledge of the traditions of playing in the panpipe ensembles

Fig. 9: Festival of the Spirits of the Dead. In the center, two musicians are shown playing a pair of panpipes (of seven and six pipes). Illustration from a Mochica ceramic vessel (Kutscher 1950: 31). Reprinted by permission.

Fig. 10: Ceramic vessel showing two musicians playing panpipes (of seven and six pipes). Moche culture, northern Peru. Staatliche Museen, Preussischer Kulturbesitz, Museum für Völkerkunde, Abtl. Altamerikanische Archaeologie, VA 17 625. Photo by Waltraut Schneider-Schütz. Reprinted by permission.

Fig. 11: Musicians with panpipes (5 + 5) and ceramic trumpets (*pututus*) (Kutscher 1950: 30). Reprinted by permission.

described above allows us to infer an intention to depict an interlocking technique (Figs. 9–13). Evidence of complementary counterparts in the *arka / ira* sense is reinforced by representations of panpipes tied together in pairs with string, as, for example, on a Mochica ceramic vessel (Fig. 9, Kutscher 1950: 31). The tradition of tying two instruments together with string seems to have continued up to the twentieth century (Vargas 1928: 8).

Based on this information, we can advance the following hypotheses concerning precontact panpipe ensembles:

(1) Panpipes of clay and bamboo have been known since pre-Inca times.

(2) They have played an important role in ritual life and often were buried with mummies or associated with skeletons and death.

(3) Double-row panpipes made of bamboo also date from precontact times.

(4) Early representations of panpipe players in pairs, as well as the discovery of early paired instruments, suggest the use of interlocking techniques.

(5) Individual panpipes had from two to twelve pipes. The paired instruments had an odd or even number of pipes, or combined an odd and even number of pipes in a pair.

(6) Playing in octaves and parallel fifths already was known in pre-Inca times.

SYMBOLIC DUALISM AS WORLDVIEW: COSMOLOGICAL APPROACH

The *arka/ira* principle stems from the anthropomorphic worldview of precontact Andean cultures, based on the concept of dualism and quadripartition. According to this view of the cosmos, everything consists of two complementary parts, with the human body used as a metaphor. The right and left sides are associated respectively with the male and female principles. These

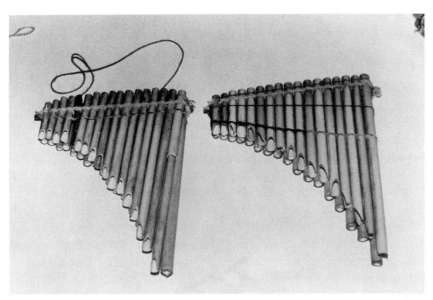

Fig. 12: *Sikuras. Ira* and *arka* pair of panpipes (17 + 17) of a Wilcalacaya ensemble, Province of Tapacarí, Department of Cochabamba, 1982. Photo by Max Peter Baumann, courtesy of the author.

are divided again into two different and opposite moieties: the head above is associated with birth, and the feet below are associated with death. Everything in existence has elements of life and death that interlock with one another, and the proportion of one element in relation to the other changes in the course of living. "In the Andes almost everything is understood in juxtaposition to its opposite" (Duviols 1974), or, as Bastien (1978: 104) states:

> Lineages, for example, are distinguished between the man's and the woman's kin group; siblings are classified into youngest and oldest; and communities have upper and lower sections. Ritualists always serve two plates to each earth shrine. For example, if a shrine is male, then a plate also is set for the female companion. Shrines usually are served in pairs, such as young and old, mountain and lake, and helper and owner. Ritual teaches Andeans the complementarity between contrasting parts of a pair.

Bastien's investigation further describes how the macrocosm of the Andean mountains is reflected symbolically in the microcosm of the human body and vice versa. Symbolic dualism also is expressed metaphorically in local society, the individual, and the life cycle: all forms of being are marked by the interacting powers of symbolic dualism. For instance, musicians from Huayñopasto in the Department of Oruro lay out their *sikuris* on the ground in the pattern of a human body, creating a symbolic representation of this shape (Fig. 13). We can see the importance of

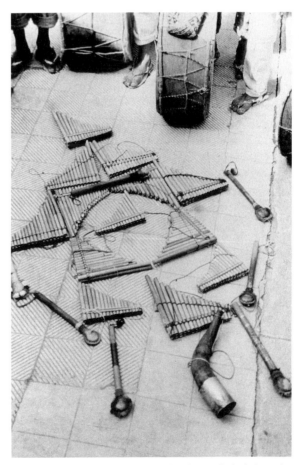

Fig. 13: *Sikuri* ensemble arranged in the shape of a body by Indians from Cantón Sepulturas, Province of Cercado de Huayñopasto Grande, Department of Oruro. Thirteen instruments (each 7 + 7), in addition to one cow horn (*pututu*) and seven drumsticks that belong to the seven *wankaras* (drums). Photo by Max Peter Baumann, courtesy of the author.

pairs in this composition, which reflects moieties with a heart in the center.

The *sikuris* represent the basic anthropomorphic idea that all things can be understood as a pair of opposites: each individual instrument contains a row of stopped pipes (male) and a row of open pipes (female). Each dualistic unit can be recreated in further complementary pairs. The interlocking technique of the *tinku* reflects the joining of opposites on several levels. *Ira* and *arka* assume added meaning in the body-like grouping of individual panpipes. The instrument that symbolizes the head (*uma*) is placed opposite the heart (*sonqo*). The latter is enclosed by a double *sikuri* pair, reflecting the four directions of the wind in vertical and horizontal directions. The number four symbolizes the completeness of the former Inca Empire or Tawantinsuyu, as well as the metaphorical unity within its plurality. The four parts enclose the heart, the seat of life and blood. The individual parts of the body represent at once the various territorial links (*ayllus*), as well as the merging of horizontal and vertical directions.

To summarize, the *ira* and *arka* principle can be characterized as an interpretive model for the following manifestations:

ira (the leader)	*arka* (the follower)
—right side, front	—left side, back
—sun (*inti*), dry season	—moon (*killa*), rainy season
—East, light, day	—West, darkness, night
—mountains, cold areas (*chirirana*)	—plains, valleys, temperate areas (*patarana*)
—above (*aransaya*)	—below (*urinsaya*)
—land of man (*jatun ayllu*)	—land of woman (*masi ayllu*)
—counterclockwise direction	—clockwise direction
—birth of the sun, upward direction, awakening	—death of the sun, downward direction, dying
—organization, cleansing	—production, planting
—plowing	—sowing
—to begin, dominant, leading	—to end, subordinate, following
—larger, male	—smaller, female
—*qhari*, Pachatata, Tata Kruz	—*warmi*, Pachamama, Wirjin
—Santísimo, Achachi	—Santísima, Awicha
—condor, Mallku, Torre Mallku	—puma, Plaza T'alla
—corn	—potatoes
—bamboo, panpipe (*siku*), notched flute (*kena*)	—wood, duct flute (*pinkillo, tarka*)
—circle dance that opens outward	—circle dance that opens inward

The dualistic principle is related to (1) men and women, as well as to society, nature, animals, and plants in the human world (*kay pacha*); (2) the transcendent dimension above (*janaq pacha*); and (3) the interior world below (*ukhu pacha* or *ura parti*) (Platt 1976: 23). In the middle dimension where humans dwell, music and musical instruments have their determined function, as parts and manifestations of this cosmological order. The symbolic duality of *arka* and *ira* subsumes an overall structure that expresses the unity of its opposite poles.

In addition, the principle of double dualism of time and space is related to the hierarchical order of the life cycle. The principle of complementarity and opposition, at once uniting and dividing its halves, offers a fourfold asymmetrical equilibrium. As in a year, with its dry and rainy seasons, each part has its growing and dying half. In general, male authority is occupied with organization, and female authority with production. Together, both elements provide the security for reproduction in time and space, in the natural and social orders, and in the music itself. During festivals, the bringing together of opposite elements is always the fundamental part of the ritual, which functions as the mediation between *ira* and *arka* opposites.

Ethnographic data are often incomplete and reflect more the fragmentary nature of the research material and the limited perspectives of a few informants than the ideal cosmological structure of a complex traditional system. This is especially true for the Andes, where acculturation processes have a long history, and where precontact concepts have been submerged by reinterpretation and syncretism due to the impact of colonization. The general dualistic concept of anthropomorphic *arka* and *ira* often was blended with the Christian male/female concept of Christ and the Virgin Mary. Vis-à-vis this dualism, the triadic social organization of the Inca empire (priests, warriors, and farmers, namely knowledge, power, and fertility) came to an end with the weakening of the sacerdotal and martial classes. However, agricultural life continued and still expresses in some ways the precontact worldview of Andean peoples. As a result of acculturation between precontact traditions and the Christian system of beliefs in specific areas, the views of most informants are often partial and fragmentary. In addition, it seems that—as in other dualistic societies—the individual, as well as a particular group, usually has knowledge of only one moiety. Thus a more complete cosmological view is the result of a process of reconstruction. The native cosmology emerges from an interpretation of the ethnographic data, complemented by ethnohistorical and archaeological facts. Furthermore, the ethnographic data highlight the past discrepancies and even misunderstandings with respect to the two competing sets of cultural concepts. A comparison of ethnographic and historical approaches leads to a holistic view that takes into account the native and hispanic cultural components. The symbolic and complementary dualism itself becomes a part of the process of understanding.

REFERENCES

Bastien, Joseph W. 1978. *Mountain of the condor: Metaphor and ritual in an Andean ayllu.* St. Paul, Minnesota: West Publishing Co.

Baumann, Max Peter 1979. "Der Charango—zur Problemskizze eines akkulturierten Musikinstruments," *Musik und Bildung* 11: 603–12.

1981a. "Julajulas—ein bolivianisches Panflötenspiel und seine Musiker," *Studia instrumentorum musicae popularis* 7: 158–63.

1981b. "Music, dance, and song of the Chipayas," *Latin American music review* 2/2: 171–222.

1982. "Music of the Indios in Bolivia's Andean highlands," *The world of music* 25/2: 80–98.

1983. *Sojta chunka Qheshwa takis Bolivia Llajtamanta/Sesenta canciones del Kechua boliviano.* Cochabamba: Centro Pedagógico y Cultural de Portales.

1985. "The Kantu ensemble of the Kallawaya at Charazani (Bolivia)," *Yearbook for traditional music* 17: 146–66.

1985a. "Saiteninstrumente in Lateinamerika," *Studia instrumentorum musicae popularis* 8: 157–76.

1990. "Musik. Verstehen und Struktur. Das ira-arka-Prinzip im symbolischen Dualismus andiner Musik," *Beiträge zur Musikwissenschaft* 32/4: 274–83.

Bolaños, César 1985. "La música en el antiguo Perú" in *La música en el Perú.* Lima: Patronato Popular y Porvenir Pro Música Clásica, 2–62.

Díaz Gainza, José 1977. *Historia musical de Bolivia,* 2nd. ed. La Paz: Ediciones Puerta del Sol.

Duviols, Pierre 1974. "Duality in the Andes," paper presented at the Andean Symposium II, American Anthropological Association, Mexico City, November 20.

1977. *La destrucción de las religiones andinas (conquista y colonia).* México: Universidad Nacional Autónoma de México— Instituto de Investigaciones Históricas (Serie de historia general, 9).

Garcilaso de la Vega 1609. *Primera parte de los comentarios reales.* Lisbon: Pedro Crasbeeck.

González Bravo, Antonio 1948. "Música y danza indígenas," *La Paz en su IV centenario, 1548–1948.* La Paz: Edición del Comité pro IV Centenario de la Fundación de La Paz, 3: 403–23.

d'Harcourt, Marguerite, and Raoul d'Harcourt 1959. *La musique des Aymaras sur les hauts plateaux boliviens d'après les enregistrements sonores de Louis Girault.* Paris: Société des Américanistes, Musée de l'Homme.

d'Harcourt, Raoul, and Marguerite d'Harcourt 1925. *La musique des Incas et ses survivances,* 2 vols. Paris: Paul Geuthner.

Kutscher, Gerdt 1950. *Eine altindianische Hochkultur.* Berlin: Verlag gebr. Mann.

Martí, Samuel 1970. *Alt-Amerika. Musik der Indianer in präkolumbischer Zeit.* Leipzig: VEB Deutscher Verlag für Musik (Musikgeschichte in Bildern, Bd. II Lieferung 7).

Platt, Tristan 1976. *Espejos y maíz: Temas de la estructura simbólica andina.* La Paz: Cuadernos de Investigación CIPCA 10.

Stevenson, Robert 1968. *Music in Aztec and Inca Territory.* Berkeley and Los Angeles: University of California Press.

Vargas, Teófilo 1928. *Aires nacionales de Bolivia,* vol. I. Santiago de Chile: Casa Amarilla.

DISCOGRAPHY

Bolivia: Panpipes. Recordings by Louis Girault (1950–73). Edited by the International Institute for Comparative Music Studies. Commentary by Xavier Bellenger. 1 LP stereo, EMI-Italiana 3C/064–18528 (1981) (Musical Atlas: UNESCO Collection); Reissued on CD, AUVIDIS/UNESCO (1987), D 8009.

Instruments and music of Bolivia. Recorded in Bolivia by Bernard Keiler. Commentary. 1 LP stereo, Ethnic Folkways Library FM 4012.

Música andina de Bolivia. Grabaciones y comentario: Max Peter Baumann. 1 LP stereo, Lauro LPLI/S-062 (1979).

Musik im Andenhochland, Bolivien / Music in the Andean highlands, Bolivia. Recordings and commentary, Max Peter Baumann. 2 LPs stereo, MC 14 (1982) (Museum Collection, Museum für Völkerkunde, Berlin).

Songs and dances of Bolivia. Compiled and edited by Ronnie and Stu Lipner. Commentary. 1 LP stereo, Ethnic Folkways FW 6871.

RECORDED EXAMPLES
(from the field work collection of Max Peter Baumann)

1. *Julajula* panpipes: *baile chúkaru* (see Ex. 1).
   Instruments: 16 *julajulas* (1 pair of *machus*, 1 pair of *malis*, 2 pairs of *likus*, 3 pairs of *tijlis*, 1 pair of *ch'ilis*).
   Group: 16 campesinos from Lagua Lagua, Cantón Santiago, General Bilbao Province, Department of Potosí (Q 706). June, 1980.

2. *Lakita* panpipes: *wayñu* (= huayno) (see Ex. 2).
   Instruments: 12 *lakitas* (2 pairs of *sanjas* or *jachas*, 3 pairs of *likus*, 1 pair of *ch'ilis*) and 4 *wankaras*.
   Group: Mallkus de Aransaya y sus Lakitas, Community of Lauro Llokolloko, Cantón Caquiaviri, Pacajes Province, Department of La Paz (Q 567). October, 1978.

3. *Sikura* panpipes: *wayño* (= huayno) (see Ex. 3).
   Instruments: 9 *sikuras* (5 *likus*, 1 pair of *tarkes*, 1 pair of *ch'ilis*), 4 *cajas* (large drums), 1 *pututu* (cow horn), 1 *campanilla* (small llama bell).
   Group: 15 campesinos (including eleven musicians and two women dancers) from Chilca Grande, Tapacarí Province, Department of Cochabamba (Q 689a). June, 1980.

APPENDIX
Musical instruments and ensembles in the Bolivian Andes

In addition to the panpipes discussed in detail above, the following instrumentarium is found in the Bolivian Andes (for further information on these instruments, see Baumann, *Musik im Andenhochland* 1982, under Discography).

1. PANPIPES
1.1. Single-row panpipes (without drum accompaniment)

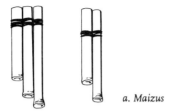

a. Maizus

a. MAIZUS (or *chiriwanos*, pl.) 20 cm: Panpipes of the Chipayas, played in pairs. One pair consists of one instrument with two stopped pipes and another with three stopped pipes, (2) and (3). The three-pipe panpipe is considered masculine (*lutaga* = man; informants also refer to this instrument as *ira*, or "the one who leads"). The two-pipe instrument is considered feminine (*mataqa* = woman; the instrument also is called *arka*, "the one who follows"). A *maizu* ensemble is composed, for instance, of three *arka* panpipes, one *ira* panpipe, and an additional vessel flute (*wauqu*).

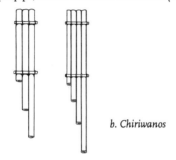

b. Chiriwanos

b. CHIRIWANOS / JULAJULAS / JULU-JULUS, 90 cm: Panpipes of the Kechuas and Aymaras, played in pairs, composed of one instrument with three stopped pipes (*arka*) and another with four (*ira*). The pipes are tuned on the basis of an anhemitonic pentatonic scale. Like most other panpipes, they usually are bound together in raft form, ordered according to size. An ensemble is composed of several pairs of panpipes of different sizes covering distinct octave registers.

1.2. Double-row panpipes (with drum accompaniment)

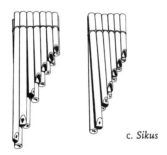

c. Sikus

c. SIKUS / LAKITAS / PHUKUNAS / ANTARAS (Span. *zampoñas)* 40 cm: These terms designate different kinds of double-row panpipes, played in pairs. Each individual instrument is composed of a row of stopped pipes tuned to different pitches, and a second identical row of open pipes. For example, the first member of the pair may have five stopped pipes of different lengths (5) and five open pipes of the same corresponding lengths (5). This instrument is designated in abbreviated form as (5+5). The other member of the pair may be an

instrument of (6+6). The members of the *siku* pair of (5+5) and (6+6) complement each other by playing in an interlocking manner. Players blow the stopped pipes and the open ones behind are heard in soft resonance an octave higher.

Other types of double-row panpipes have a larger number of stopped and open pipes, as, for example, the pair of *siku* instruments with (6+6) and (7+7), or even a *lakita* pair with as many as (7+7) and (8+8). Each pair is present in the ensembles always in different sizes covering different registers.

d. Ayarichis

d. AYARICHIS, 60 cm: Instruments with a double row of pipes in which the first row is composed of seven stopped pipes; the second row is also stopped, but with the pipes only half as long as the corresponding pipes in the first row, (7+1/2 7). These instruments always are played in pairs; the second instrument of the pair is constructed in the same way. In Chuquisaca the *ayarichi* ensemble is composed, for example, of a larger- and a smaller-sized pair of panpipes that are accompanied by two large drums and a *charango*.

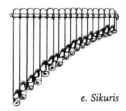

e. Sikuris

e. SIKURIS or SIKURAS (also *sikus*), 30 cm: Double-row panpipes, each of which has 17 stopped pipes of various lengths and 17 open pipes of corresponding length (17+17) and (17+17). They are joined in raft form, arranged according to size, and appear in pairs of identical construction. Each pair can be used with other pairs of different registers, for example, an octave or a fifth apart.

2. NOTCHED FLUTES (WITH DRUM ACCOMPANIMENT)

The notched flutes are half-stopped endblown flutes of various sizes, with an incised notch against which the breath is directed.

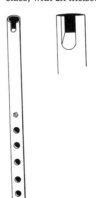

f. KENA (QENA, QUENA) / KENA-KENA / CHOKELA / LICHIWAYU, PACEÑO, 50 cm: These flutes usually have six front finger holes and a thumb hole. They are played in two to three different sizes and tuned in different registers. A *kena* ensemble often consists of 12 to 24 instruments accompanied by a small drum (*tambor*), infrequently with a *tambor* and a *bombo*.

f. Kena

3. DUCT FLUTES (USUALLY WITH DRUM ACCOMPANIMENT)

3.1. *Pinkillos* (simple duct flutes)

g. PINKILLO / PINCOLLO / PINCULLO / PINKAYLLO / WAKA-PINKILLO / TARKA / CHARKA / CH'UTU / PFLAWATA / FLAWATA / ROLLANO, 30 cm: Different flutes, each provided with a mouthpiece plugged with a woodblock (similar to the principle of the recorder). The plug can protrude, as a block, or can be beak-shaped, adapted to the mouthpiece. According to their construction the duct flutes are either whole tubular flutes or flutes made of a tree branch cut in half, hollowed out inside, then fitted together again, provided with a block and a duct, and finally tied together with llama or sheep nerve fibers.

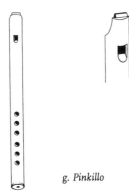

g. Pinkillo

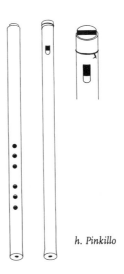

h. Pinkillo

The small *waka-pinkillo* has only two front finger holes; there are other *pinkillos* with four or five front finger holes. Most types of *pinkillos* have six front finger holes (*tarkas, charkas, ch'utus, rollanos*). The *tarka, charka, ch'utu* or *rollano* ensembles are often composed of two to four different sizes of the same type of flute, and each size also can be represented by several equal flutes. With the exception of the *charkas*, most duct flute ensembles are rhythmically reinforced by either a large or small drum, or by both simultaneously.

h. PINKILLO (inserted plug), 90 cm

i. TARKA, 47 cm

j. ROLLANO (*pinkillo*), 1 meter

i. Tarka

3.2. Multipart duct flutes

k. PINKILLO MOHOCEÑO / (JATUN) AYMARA / AYKHORI, 1.5 m: These types of duct flutes are very long, ranging in size from 1.2 up to 2.2 meters. Because of their length these instruments have a small or longer tube attached to them that doubles back and enables the player to blow into it as with a bassoon. These long duct flutes with five or six finger holes are known as *tokuru / mohoceño / aymara / aykhori / burdón* or *contrabajo*, and normally are played together with the smaller types of simple duct *pinkillos* (e.g., the *tokuru* together with 9 other simple duct *pinkillos* in the *pujllay* ensemble from Tarabuco, or the *mohoceños* together

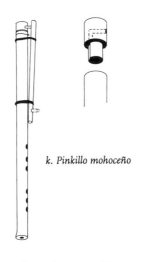

k. Pinkillo mohoceño

with several simple duct *pinkillos* in the *mohoceñada*). Most of the time, one, two, or even three small drums struck with two beaters complete these flute ensembles.

L. MUCH'A (PINKILLO), 1.2 m

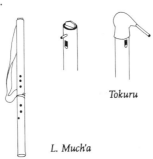

L. Much'a

Tokuru

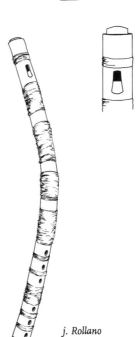

j. Rollano

3.3. Transverse flute

m. Phalawita

m. PHALAWITA / PFALA / CHARAZANI / CH'UNCHU / PÍFANO / PITO, 38 cm: These are different names for a similar type of *flauta traversa* that may have originated in post-Columbian times. If the instruments have more than six front finger holes they are additionally supplied with a thumb hole. The *ch'unchus* of the Callawayas at Charazani have, for example, six front finger holes. Two different sizes of flutes (4 *altos* and 2 *bajos*) are blown in parallel fifths and play together with a large *wankara* and a small *retuela* drum.

4. VESSEL FLUTES

n. Wauqu

n. WAUQU, 10 cm: Vessel flutes or ocarinas are made of clay or of the hull of a tropical fruit. The *pulu* of the Aymaras has no finger hole, while the *wauqu* of the Chipayas has one. The vessel flutes normally are played together with panpipe ensembles (e.g., 4 *pulus* together with the Aymara *julajula* panpipes; or a *wauqu* together with the Chipayan *maizus*).

5. NATURAL TRUMPETS AND REEDS

o. Pututu

o. PUTUTU / DOTI, 40 cm: These are animal horns that serve as signaling instruments and also are used in various panpipe or *pinkillo* ensembles. Among the Chipayas the instrument is called *doti*.

p. Waqra pututu

p. WAQRA PUTUTU, 60 cm: A *pututu* that is a combination of several animal horn pieces inserted into one another.

q. PHULULU / PHULU-PUTUTU / TIRA-TIRA / CAÑA, 4 m: A calabash, an animal horn, or a horn-shaped leather goblet, which functions as a resonator, is attached to the end of a bamboo tube between 15 cm and 3 to 4 meters in length. These names designate different kinds of trumpet-like instruments. Only the *caña* of Tarija is a transverse trumpet; the *tira-tira* from northern Potosí and the other instruments of this type are longitudinally blown. The trumpets are played in smaller as well as larger ensembles during carnival (Potosí) or during the Festival of San Roque in Tarija.

q. Caña

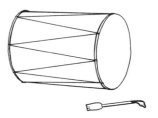

r. Erke

r. ERKE / ERKENCHO, 40 cm: A small bamboo tube with a beating reed is inserted into the cut-off end of an animal horn. It is a "clarinet" without finger holes, often played by women in *pinkillo* ensembles at carnival time or by men together with a little drum (*cajita*).

6. DRUMS (MEMBRANOPHONES)

6.1. Large drums

s. Pfutu wankara

s. PFUTU WANKARA, 45 cm / WANKARA, 60 cm / CAJA / BOMBO: These are large double-headed drums, which are struck with a padded beater (*wajta, tokana*). The bottom skin is often crossed by a snare (*charlera*). The *pfutu wankara* is a large double-skin tubular drum whose height is greater than its diameter. Large drums accompany particular panpipe ensembles, such as those of *sikus* or *sikuras*.

t. Wankara

t. WANKARA

6.2. Small drums

u. Wankarita

u. WANKARITA, 30 cm / TAMBORA / TAMBORIL / TAMBORCITO / CAJITA / RETUELA: These are small double-headed cylindrical drums, usually struck with two beaters, and provided with a snare. The small drum often accompanies *kena, chokela,* and *pinkillo* ensembles. The pair of *bombo* and *tambor* membranophones generally accompanies *lakita* or *tarka* ensembles.

7. IDIOPHONES

v. Campanilla

v. CAMPANILLA / CAMPANA, 6 cm: Llama bells of bronze, in various sizes and played in ensembles of flutes or *guitarrillas*, often accompany the dance of men and women.

w. Ch'ajch'as

w. CH'AJCH'AS, 25 cm / CH'ULLU-CH'ULLUS / SUILA JUT'AS (pl.): These terms indicate different types of jingles, or small rattling objects. In the *ch'ajch'as* or *chullu-chullu*, several pig or goat hooves are bound together to form a rattle. The rattle sounds to the movement of the dancer. In folk groups it indicates the rhythmic ground pattern.

x. Espuelas

x. ESPUELAS, 21 cm: Another type of rattle, large spurs of forged iron are attached to the wooden sandals of the musicians from Tarabuco. Small perforated plates of sheet metal are threaded on a rod that joints the forked ends of the spurs, in a manner resembling a sistrum. These plates strike against each other with each step of the carnival dancers.

y. Matraca

y. MATRACA, 31 cm: A simple wooden box cog rattle is sometimes used in panpipe performances. The *matraca* is of Spanish origin.

z. Triángulo

z. TRIÁNGULO, 35 cm: In the panpipe ensemble of the Callawayas in particular, a large forged iron triangle is played along with the drum rhythm.

Local Practices Among the Aymara and Kechua in Conima and Canas, Southern Peru

Thomas Turino

"Indian" identity, regionalism, and social dynamics—General musical and aesthetic features—Musical culture in Conima, Puno: Musical life in Conima; The instrumental traditions; Musical style and composition; Musical occasions in Conima—Musical culture in Canas, Cuzco: Mestizo and new musical traditions in Canas; Older musical traditions in rural Canas; Comparison of the Caneño and mestizo charango *traditions; Musical style and contexts—Conclusions*

"INDIAN" IDENTITY, REGIONALISM, AND SOCIAL DYNAMICS

IN HIGHLAND PERU, the instruments, practices, and meanings of music vary widely from one region to another and according to the identities of social groups within the same region. When left to themselves, rural Kechua- and Aymara-speaking peoples in the southern sierra, considered the most conservative indigenous area of the country, define their social identity and musical styles largely in terms of localized communities and regions, rather than using broad categories of ethnicity or class as the basis of social solidarity.

Because of centuries of domination, Kechua and Aymara speakers have become painfully aware of the three major social categories created within Peruvian colonial and national discourses: *Indio, mestizo* ("mixed Spanish and indigenous heritage and culture"), and *criollo* ("born in the Americas of Spanish descent"). People identified as Indians were forced to work in the mines during the colonial period, and as peons on *criollos'* and mestizos' land from the colonial period until 1969 (the year President Juan Velasco Alvarado initiated the agrarian reform). "Indian" identity was, in part, constructed and maintained by members of higher social groups as a means of retaining this labor pool. "Indio" became, and remains, a term of disparagement. To symbolically counter discrimination against rural highlanders and to create links with such groups, Velasco replaced the word with *campesino* (peasant) in state discourse. People and cultural practices identified as "Indian" have been systematically marginalized and oppressed by the state and local elites for much of Peru's history. Often denied access to opportunities and upward social mobility within the dominant society, indigenous Andeans bolstered their own social unity at the local level as a means of defense and distanced themselves both culturally and, when possible, geographically (Schaedel, Escobar, and Rodríguez 1959: 13). This bilateral process of separatism operates as a dialectic since self-view is influenced by how others, particularly people of greater power, view the social position of an individual or a group. In some Peruvian highland regions, social separatism partially accounts for the maintenance of strikingly distinctive Andean musical practices and sensibilities, when compared with mestizo and *criollo* musical practices. At the same time, efforts on the part of church and state to alter Andean ideology and culture by force (as, for instance, the "extirpation of idolatry" campaign of the late sixteenth and first half of the seventeenth centuries), and attempts to link Andeans to the colonial and republican states, resulted in syncretisms that also affected contemporary local practices and worldviews.

The most efficacious moves to link rural indigenous communities to the state during the republican era were generated by the government of Juan Velasco Alvarado (1968–1975) in an explicit attempt to integrate the economy and society (Velasco 1971: 48). Aided by improved mass media and transportation, Velasco's agrarian, educational, and media reforms disseminated a nationalist ideology among the youth of rural communities more profoundly than before. Crucial to Velasco's impact was the promise of social mobility that the agrarian and educational reforms convincingly communicated to rural southern Peruvians. An unfavorable shift in the person-land ratio around World War II spurred tremendous migrations to the cities, connecting urban centers with the countryside more directly than ever before. Migration and return migration, as well as Velasco's cultural politics, especially have affected rural people growing up since the 1950s. By now these generations are culturally distinct from their parents and grandparents in important ways.

In major cities such as Lima, rural highland identifications (with ethnic, class, and regional components) have been perceived by migrants as a liability, and hence some people have tried to deny or downplay this background. But simultaneously, since the 1960s, regional highland identities also have become an increasingly important basis for social and political unity and action among some migrants, leading to a strengthening of pride in local highland music and other selected practices. At present, musical styles from all over the highlands are performed in Lima by migrants, as are commercialized versions of regional country music, and new syncretic forms such as *cumbia andina* (a blending of the urban *cumbia* and the highland *wayno*, Turino 1990a). Local highland musical styles have

come to serve as central identity emblems for migrant groups that often are organized in formal regional associations. By the 1980s the performance of highland music and dance was as much a coastal-urban as a rural phenomenon, although the processes and meaning of musical production remain extremely distinct between rural villagers and the migrants in Lima, tempering common notions of the "continuity" of highland culture in the city. (See Millones, "Social Function of Music and Dance in Andean Territory" and "Urbanization and Popular Music in the Andes," in these volumes.)

Because of the regional nature of highland music and the fluid, relative character of social identities, all but a few generalizations about Andean musical practices and meaning are problematic. This chapter thus compares two specific musical cultures: among older Aymara speakers of the District of Conima in the Province of Huancané, Puno, and among Kechua speakers of the Province of Canas in the Department of Cuzco (see Map). An account of these cultures can illustrate the local nature of their music, the sustained distinctiveness and coherence of rural Andean musical aesthetics and practices, and the profound impact of migration and nationalizing trends on local musical cultures, a complex and significant topic (Romero 1990; Turino 1988, 1991, and 1993).

GENERAL MUSICAL AND AESTHETIC FEATURES

Several commonalities in the aesthetic values and musical characteristics of Conima and Canas apply to indigenous Andean musical production more widely. A preference for high tessitura and a dense quality of sound is evident in both locales, affecting the instruments used, specific performance practices, ensemble organization, and the overall musical sound (often a dense unison, sometimes approaching heterophony or parallel polyphony). The organization of music emphasizes repetition (of motives and entire pieces) and the use of subtle levels of contrast, both of which distinguish indigenous musical production from urban-Western and mestizo practices. A more general aspect of Andean sensibility stresses the synthetic joining or fusion of complementary or opposing entities: large / small, male / female, insider / outsider, sacred / non-sacred, comical / serious, plant / animal, human / divinity, *hanan* (high) / *hurin* (low), sometimes around a central point or

Map: Areas of musical ethnography in Peru.

entity. This multileveled synthetic conception of the world manifests itself continually in cultural practice, as, for instance, in the meaning of the *Achach K'umu* dance, the relationship between the roles of the *ira* and *arka* panpipes, and in the overall three-voice group structure of *sikuris, tarka,* and *pitu* ensembles in Conima. (See Baumann, "Music and Worldview of Indian Societies in the Bolivian Andes," in this volume.)

MUSICAL CULTURE IN CONIMA, PUNO

Conima, in the Aymara-speaking Province of Huancané, is a rural district on the Peruvian Altiplano (high plateau, about 12,500 ft.) on the northern shore of Lake Titicaca and the Bolivian border. The district is divided into six *ayllus* (a pre-Columbian term for politico-geographical-religious community units), and these are often further subdivided. The economy of the *ayllus* is based on subsistence agriculture and animal husbandry, each family's agricultural plots being distributed within a crop-rotational system of four geographical *suyos* (quarters) and located at different altitudes to maximize productivity and to guard against climatic catastrophes; this is a pre-Columbian pattern (Murra 1975; Bastien 1978; Wilson 1988). Most older rural Conimeños have a minimal involvement with the money economy, but family members' urban employment and cultivation of cash crops in the tropical forest region (Sandia) do supply some income for *ayllu* dwellers.

Mestizos live in the district capital town of Conima, which, although considered to be outside the *ayllus,* serves as a center for specific fiestas and political activities (the high school also is located in the town). With the exception of certain economic and ritualized relations (such as coparent relationships), *ayllu* dwellers tend to avoid social contact with mestizos whom they call *q'ara* (a negative term to denote outsiders). In the *ayllus,* a man simply refers to himself as *hak'e* (person) or as a member of his community. Self-identified mestizos attempt to maintain a social distinction between themselves and "Indios" by disparaging their cultural practices (such as coca chewing, although I have sometimes witnessed mestizos chewing coca).

Although most men and middle-aged/younger women are to some extent bilingual, Aymara is the primary language of the *ayllus.* Basically Christian concepts of *Dios creador* (God the creator), Jesus, and various Catholic saints have been incorporated into the local religion and are seen as additional sources of power, although in ritual life far greater emphasis is placed on maintaining relationships with local Andean divinities, especially the *achachilas* (divinities associated with specific mountains, also translated as "place") and Pachamama (the Earth mother). In almost all musical and social occasions, a ritual with coca and alcohol *(t'inka)* is performed as an act of reciprocity with the local divinities. Like people elsewhere in the Andes, Conimeños told me that "if we do not feed the Earth, the Earth will not feed us."

Reciprocity and egalitarianism are central to social relations in the *ayllus* of Conima. The unity, identity, and solidarity of the community are granted greater importance than individual identity (Albó 1974). Two facts in the musical realm are linked to these core values: any male is welcome to perform with his community ensemble regardless of his ability, and there is no room to highlight soloists in Conimeño ensembles. A further consequence of the strong identity of individual groups (for which music serves as a primary emblem) and of the marked factionalism between social units is a strong tendency toward inter-community musical competition.

Musical life in Conima

In keeping with the strong communal orientation in the *ayllus* of Conima, almost all musical activities involve relatively large ensembles in public fiesta contexts; ensembles are community based. Individual performance, even to practice music, is virtually nonexistent. Vocal music is much less important than the traditions involving large wind ensembles. Brass bands, which are extremely common throughout the Peruvian sierra, are found in several of the *ayllus* and perform mainly in the mestizo patronal fiesta held in the district capital (San Miguel, September 29), at other mestizo-oriented events (school anniversaries, national fiestas), and at occasional weddings in the *ayllus.* String instruments, found in most regions of the Peruvian highlands, are not currently used in Conima, not even among mestizos who live in the district capital.

Conimeño musical culture revolves around five Andean wind ensemble traditions: (1) *sikus* (double-row panpipes, accompanied by large double-headed drums, *bombos,* or with snare and bass drum during the Easter fiesta); (2) five-hole *pinkillus* (vertical cane duct flutes accompanied by *cajas,* which are large, deep-sounding snare drums); (3) six-hole *pinkillus* with *cajas;* (4) *tarkas* (wooden vertical duct flutes with snare and bass drum); and (5) the *pitu* or *falawatu* (side-blown cane flute with snare and bass drums). Each ensemble plays specific musical genres and is associated with particular occasions and times of year. *Pinkillus* are played during the rainy season, from Todos los Santos (November 1) through carnival, and for roof-raising fiestas any time of year. *Tarkas* only are played during carnival. *Sikus* are played at public fiestas during the dry season (Easter through October) and at weddings throughout the year. *Pitus* are played in May, August, and for the children's *pastores* dance at Christmas.

The ensembles range from twelve to, more rarely, fifty players and, as is generally true of Andean indigenous musical practice, melodic instrument types are not mixed in ensemble. Only men play musical instruments in Conima. To my knowledge, the only female instrumental tradition in Peruvian indigenous culture of the central and southern highlands is that of the small *tinya* drum, a pre-Columbian practice (Guamán Poma de Ayala 1615 in 1980).

Traditionally most men in the *ayllus* of Conima play all of the instruments with their specific community-based ensembles. Due to intense migration of individuals of working age since the 1960s and changes in interests and values, most young men have not taken up the practice of *tarkas, pinkillus,* and *pitus.* Young men do play *sikus,* largely because of the current popularity of this music in Peruvian urban centers among Puneño migrants; there is even a *sikuri* ensemble connected to the local high school in Conima. *Pitus, tarkas,* and *pinkillus,* however, have not become as well-known or popular in the cities (Turino 1988 and 1990b), and the young people of the *ayllus,* who are influenced by urban trends, have followed suit.

Until recently other instruments (the single-row *kallamachu* and *locopallapalla* panpipes, and the end-notched *chokela* flutes) were regularly played in Conima. When I asked Conimeños in one village why they no longer played the *chokelas,* a former specialty of theirs, I was told that all the men who knew this tradition had migrated away or were too old to play. The depopulation of the district also has reduced the number of potential fiesta sponsors for the less important events, thus leading to the decline of certain dance and instrumental traditions. Older people in the *ayllus,* for whom these fiesta traditions serve as joyous focal points of social life and community identity, are saddened by their disappearance. They express both disappointment and understanding in regard to the youth's lack of musical participation and their desire to move away.

The instrumental traditions

The *siku* used in Conima has interdependent *ira* ("the one who leads") and *arka* ("the one who follows") panpipes, played by paired musicians in interlocking fashion; the pitches of the scale alternate between the two panpipes. Many observers have interpreted this manner of performance as a manifestation of the communal nature of Andean musical performance and the core values of reciprocity and binary complementarity. Indeed, Conimeños say that it is not even possible to play the *siku* correctly as a solo instrument. On unisons and octaves, pitch variations of up to forty cents (about twenty cents sharp and flat) are common in the tuning of a given *siku* and between instruments of a tuned consort, which helps to create a dense sound quality. "Dense sound" refers to a consistent overlapping and blending of discrete fundamentals and overtones to produce a thick unified texture. In Conima, and more widely, the *ira* and *arka* panpipes each may have a second resonating row on which corresponding tubes sound roughly an octave higher, again in accord with the preference for a dense, breathy sound.

The manner of playing *tarkas, pinkillus,* and *pitus* results in a similar density of sound. All these flutes are played so that the same variance in intonation results. Unlike the *siku,* these flutes are consistently overblown, in keeping with the preference for high tessitura (that is, lower tessituras are possible, but not utilized), and the forceful blowing technique results in a dense, breathy sound, rich in overtones.

The *siku, tarka,* and *pitu* ensembles use instruments tuned to different registers to produce a sound approximating parallel harmony. *Sikuris* potentially can use nine parts organized into three groups within a range of three parallel octaves (Ex. 1, from high to low, with the pitches given being approximate for the lowest tube on each instrument). Conimeños consistently state that the middle *malta* part is the main melody-carrier and that the other parts sound in accompaniment to the *malta* part and *malta* group. The *malta* part may be played by as many as six pairs, while the other parts only have one to two pairs. The central parts thus produce the

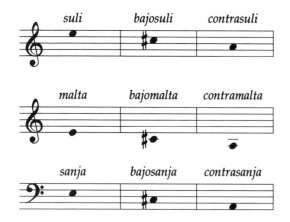

Ex. 1: Pitches for the lowest tube on each instrument.

primary energy and are the musical fulcrum of the ensemble, with the high and low parts ideally being balanced in volume around the *maltas*.

Pitu and *tarka* ensembles each use three parts (*suli*; *malta*, or *ankuta*; and *sanja*, or *tayka*), with the outer parts tuned an octave apart and the central part being a fifth (or fourth in some *pitu* ensembles) above *sanja*. As with the *sikus*, the *maltas* in *pitu* ensembles are denser in texture and are considered the main melody-carrying part. In *tarka* ensembles, Conimeños say that each of the parts should be equal in prominence, the central one thus being distinguished only by pitch. It is significant that the *tarka* tradition came into the region recently, allegedly in the 1930s, from Bolivia. *Sikuris* and *pitus* are older traditions in Conima and are organized around the more prominent central parts, as were the now-defunct, single-row *kallamachu* panpipe ensembles in Conima (Fig. 1).

The major aesthetic principle of *sikuri* ensemble performance and of the other Conimeño instrumental traditions discussed here is group blend: "playing as one," or "sounding as one instrument." Conimeños state that an individual player should not stand out; his pitches should not "escape" from the dense sonic fabric of the ensemble. Individual variations and improvisatory techniques are present, moving some performances from strict parallel polyphony toward a blended heterophony. According to Conimeños, however, these techniques should be used in ways that augment the density, overlap, and interlock without making the individual player stand out. Groups also are judged by their volume. Blowing on panpipes should be as forceful as possible, helping the group to create a powerful sound

and, at the same time, filling the entire tube (not just its mouth) with air to avoid "staccato" playing and harsh overblowing that would cause the *siku* of an individual player to "escape" (Recorded Ex. 1).

Musical style and composition

Almost all music in Conima is based on a standard AA BB CC form. A general feature of the music is the constant repetition of motivic material throughout the three sections. Sections B and C often are distinguished from A only by one or two short motives, a new juxtaposition of previously used motives, or slightly altered versions of the earlier motives. Most music in Conima is in binary meter with syncopated rhythms. Scale types vary from one genre and instrumental tradition to the next, but the two most common types are six- and seven-tone scales with a flatted seventh degree; the first third in the scale may be either major or minor. In Conima the *tarkeada* genre is unusual in its prominent use of various anhemitonic pentatonic scales, reminding us again that *tarkas* constitute a relatively new and distinct tradition in this area.

In many indigenous fiesta traditions, the same pieces are used every year for specific dances and occasions, and are shared by the various communities within the region. In Conima, however, the ensemble of each *ayllu* creates two or three new pieces for a given fiesta or dance every year, one of which serves as the ensemble's emblem for that year's fiesta and is played more often than other pieces. The music is created communally by the musicians who attend the rehearsal one or two evenings prior to a fiesta, in a kind of group brainstorming session, or individually, prior to the rehearsal (Turino 1989). It is extremely formulaic within a given genre, and the repetition of motives across sections also reduces the amount of new material necessary. The formulaic, repetitive nature of Conimeño music also facilitates rapid learning for community musicians who want to play during the fiesta but who do not necessarily attend the rehearsal.

In Conima a tremendous emphasis is placed on original composition as a sign of an ensemble's (and its community's) competence. This is particularly evident when various groups from different *ayllus* compete musically for the favor of the spectators in the plaza of the district capital. Conimeños will criticize an ensemble that enters the plaza without a new composition or with one that mainly plays other ensembles' material.

Fig. 1: *Sikuris* performance in the District of Conima (Turino 1985). Courtesy of the author.

Because the musical ensembles represent their communities in district-wide fiestas, maintaining a distinguishing playing style also is stressed.

Ensembles differentiate their performance styles by playing at consistently faster or slower tempos and by different types of ornamentation. Some *sikuri* groups change their consort size/pitch from one fiesta to the next (usually within a semitone) for variety and originality, and drumming patterns also distinguish panpipe ensembles. Although these mechanisms for differentiating ensemble styles may appear minor by Western standards, they generally are recognized as major differences by Conimeños. I have listened to discussions lasting over an hour in which consensus was reached about the size of the consort that should be used for an upcoming fiesta. On one occasion, after the decision had been reached, a member of the group commented: "We will kill them with this one," referring to a change of about a quarter tone and the effect that it would have on their musical competition. Small distinctions are recognized as making major differences in Conima. Within this scale of contrasts, the originality of an ensemble's style and compositions is extremely important for marking community identity and competence.

Musical occasions in Conima

Within the annual cycle of public fiestas there is approximately one festival per month somewhere in the district. Some are celebrated by a single *ayllu* or community, while larger events such as carnival and Todos los Santos involve all the communities. Life-cycle events, including the "first hair cutting" *(sikuri music)*, weddings *(sikuris* or brass bands), and roof-raising (five-hole *pinkillus),* are also occasions for musical performance. With the exception of the mestizo-controlled patronal fiesta of San Miguel (September 29, featuring brass bands, costumed mestizo dances, and a contracted *sikuri* ensemble from a local *ayllu*), and the mestizo festival for La Virgen de la Asunción (August 15), the other annual musical occasions are linked to the local agricultural, political, and indigenous religious cycle, even though the events often take Catholic names (Valcárcel 1946). It is typical of syncretism in the Andes for indigenous communities to invest European symbols and events with local meanings (Bastien 1978: 69).

Candelaria. In Conima, for example, the fiesta of the Virgen de la Candelaria (February 2) is the occasion for an important agricultural ceremony as well as for courting activities. The event is dedicated to the "first sacred products" of the harvest rather than to the Virgin, who is rarely mentioned in the religious rituals. Early on the morning of February 1, the *vísperas* (the day preceding the main fiesta), the elders and the religious specialist of the *ayllu* go into the fields and select the largest, most developed products of each species. After the performance of *ch'alla* (libations with alcohol) and of a *t'inka* for Pachamama, the produce is taken to the home of that year's fiesta sponsor to be ritually prepared.

Dressed in red ponchos, the community musicians (who will play both the five- and six-hole *pinkillus* for this event) gather outside the sponsor's house at mid-morning to warm up. The young people who will dance start to arrive, dressed in festive clothing. While the elders are preparing the sacred products inside the house, the musicians perform the *wifala* dance on five-hole *pinkillus*, walking in a circle outside (Fig. 2).

The *wifala* is a courting dance performed during the rainy season by young people who move with a simple shuffling step in a large single-file circle, loosely alternating males and females. After each repetition of the piece, the dancers turn 360 degrees with their hands in the air. Each piece is danced for as long as twenty minutes or more. At certain points in the afternoon, men and women sing alternate verses of an unaccompanied song comparing the girls to flowers and a garden; Candelaria is thus one of the few public performance contexts in Conima that include vocal music. In the texts, sexual imagery is cloaked in metaphors expressing playful themes as well as those of fertility and productivity. Competition between the sexes also is expressed in the text in ways similar to those described below for Canas.

At mid-afternoon the elders emerge from the sponsor's house carrying the prepared sacred products on their backs in woven shawls. After a meal is served and a *t'inka* performed, the community, led by the elders and the musicians, dances up the mountain to the earth shrine of the *achachila* (the place of power). The musicians perform the more "serious" six-hole *pinkillu* music during the part of the event that directly involves the sacred products.

Accompanied by the six-hole *pinkillus* and *cajas,* the community dances around the earth shrine. Rituals and special prayers are performed for the first products. The ritual specialist instructs the sacred first products to call others of their kind from the earth in abundance so that the houses will be filled with great quantities of food. Simultaneously, the younger dancers go to a site below the *achachila's* place and resume the *wifala*. Later in the evening, the community returns down the mountain dancing to the music previously played on six-hole *pinkillus*.

Carnival. In community events such as the fiesta of the Virgen de la Candelaria, competition between the musical ensembles of different *ayllus* is not an issue. Two or three days of the week-long fiesta of Carnavales involve festivities within each *ayllu* that also are related to agricultural ritual and the prosperity of the community. During the opening and closing days of Carnavales, however, the different community ensembles play *tarkas* or five-hole *pinkillus* in the town plaza, and the ensembles compete for spectators, dancers, and prestige. Ensembles are judged by several criteria: the overall quality and originality of their music; whether their sound is loud and powerful enough to attract and hold attention; and, perhaps most importantly, the length

Fig. 2: *Wifala* dance accompanied by five-hole *pinkillus* in the District of Conima (Turino 1985). Courtesy of the author.

of time they can endure remaining in the plaza to provide entertainment for the people.

Ensembles stand next to each other around the plaza and alternate performances. For the most part each ensemble maintains a social distance from the others, celebrating separately with dancers and onlookers from its own community. As the afternoon wears on, the ensembles begin to perform their best pieces. Neighboring ensembles now begin to perform simultaneously, each trying to play louder and longer than the others. Fiestas in the plaza invariably grow in

intensity as the afternoon progresses into evening and the alcohol takes hold. Spectators enter the dance; emotional conversations and even fist fights occur. Conimeños throw themselves heart and soul into these events, which are the joyous and cathartic focal points of the annual social cycle.

Satiri. Other major fiesta traditions in Conima involve costumed dance dramas. The dance known as *satiri* (planter of tubers) is performed during the Fiesta de San Isidro (May 15). Accompanied by *sikuri* ensembles, community dance groups compete in the town plaza for the favor of the spectators. The masked dancers dress clownishly as peasants and carry toy digging sticks. In a period of about two hours, they reenact the entire agricultural cycle, including the distribution of communal land (no longer actually practiced), the clearing and cleaning of fields, planting and hilling of rows, the agricultural rituals of the Virgen de la Candelaria, Carnavales, Easter, and finally the harvest.

Although the dance is considered a serious depiction of the agricultural cycle and of the people's own lives and rituals, the performances are characterized by humorous antics and entertaining horseplay for the pleasure of the spectators. From my perspective, the Conimeños seemed to be parodying themselves in even their most sacred acts, such as the *t'inka*, which was enacted in an outrageous manner. When I asked friends about this, they found no paradox between the comic performances and the seriousness of the dance's meaning. Held directly after the harvest, this fiesta celebrates the completion of another annual cycle.

Achach K'umu. A second dance drama, *Achach K'umu* (hunch-backed old man) or *Auki Auki* (mountain divinity), is performed for the Fiesta de Santa Cruz (May 3), accompanied by *pitu* ensembles (Fig. 3). The dancers have dual roles: through costuming and dramatic behavior they represent the Spanish in a comical and satirical way, while also portraying the local *achachilas* in a serious manner. Spanish hats and knee pants are juxtaposed with animal masks made of goat skins, and animal fur is worn on the hands and feet. The *achachila* is thought of as an old man, and the dancers carry large walking sticks. At the beginning of the fiesta, the dancers climb to the top of a mountain that is an *achachila*. They set fires and "mysteriously" emerge from the smoke as if coming out of the mountain.

When I questioned older Conimeños as to how the dancers could comically satirize the Spanish and seriously portray the mountain divinities at the same time, one man responded: "It has to be that way. A dance has to mean many things, it cannot have only one meaning." This response sheds light on the synthesizing aspect of Andean sensibility, the tendency to see things as necessarily including multileveled sets of opposites, and on the complex imagery in performance.

MUSICAL CULTURE IN CANAS, CUZCO

Located southeast in the Department of Cuzco, Canas is an isolated *puna* (high altitude) region of treeless, rolling hills dotted with stone outcrops and small lakes. The contemporary indigenous population speaks Kechua. Due to the altitude and cold temperatures, subsistence tuber agriculture and the raising of animals (llamas, alpacas, sheep, and cattle) are the main economic activities. The province contained a number of large haciendas until the beginning of the agrarian reform in 1969.

The following account describes the musical culture of the districts around Descanso, especially Langui, Layo, and Checca, located south of Yanaoca, the provincial capital (see Map above). Surrounded by sparse, widely dispersed Kechua-speaking communities, the small district capitals are inhabited by mestizos and people in social transition, as in Conima. Also as in Conima and most of the southern sierra, many people of working age have left the area to seek employment in cities and towns. Life in the barren *puna* region of Canas is unusually harsh.

The people of the region generally are referred to as *chunchos* (horsemen), since they often travel by horseback over the vast *puna*. The region is linked to the "horseman" cultures of other *puna* regions in the departments of Cuzco, Apurímac, Ayacucho, Arequipa, and Puno, labeled collectively as the "area Qorilazo" (lassos of gold) by the Montoyas (1987). The people of rural Canas maintain typically Andean patterns of communal labor exchange *(ayni)* and work projects, as well as community decision-making processes. However, according to a local stereotype that my own observations confirm, Caneños are more individualistic in spirit than the Kechua valley people or the Aymara of Conima. Due perhaps to the extremely difficult environment in which they live, Caneños also are known as a hard and sometimes dangerous people. As in Conima, Catholicism has been introduced among the indigenous population, although in their rituals they pay greater attention to Pachamama, the *apus* (mountain divinities), and local earth shrines.

Mestizo and new musical traditions in Canas

In the district capitals of Canas, the mestizos host fiestas for the patron saints as well as other Catholic festivals. Two different ensembles are used for these

Fig. 3: *Achach K'umu* dancer with *pitu* players in the District of Conima (Turino 1985). Courtesy of the author.

events, as in mestizo fiestas throughout Cuzco. Often hired from outside the region by mestizo sponsors, brass bands and *orquestas cuzqueñas* accompany costumed and social dancing, playing the repertoires for specific costumed dances (Verger 1945; Mishkin 1946: 465; Smith 1975; Turino 1982) or the standard Cuzqueño repertoire of *waynos* (Roel 1959) and *marineras* (Romero 1985). The *orquesta cuzqueña*, found throughout the department, has one or two *kenas* (end-notched flutes), one or two violins, diatonic harp, bass drum, and commonly accordion or mandolin. Violins and *kenas* play the melody in harmony, largely involving thirds and fifths, the harp has a bass function, and the accordion supplies harmonic accompaniment as well as melody. Combining different types of melodic instruments and timbres is typical of mestizo ensembles, contrasting fundamentally with traditional indigenous practices.

A string band style (with regional variations, e.g., Ancash, Ayacucho, Apurímac, southern Cuzco) has been popularized by radio since the 1960s and adopted by rural people in Canas, many of whom own transistor radios. This type of string band tradition for *wayno* performance was produced and distributed commercially in Lima for migrant consumption, especially during the 1950s and 1960s (Lloréns Amico 1983; Turino 1988). Its feedback to rural areas has been an important force for change in many highland regions of Peru, Conima being an exception. The melody is sung solo (by both men and women) or in duos using parallel thirds. One or two mandolins (considered a mestizo instrument by Caneños) serve as the primary melodic and solo instruments. Several guitars provide harmonic accompaniment; a bass runs between verses and a *kena* or harmonica might be added. Young indigenous musicians in Canas also have taken up the *bandurria*, an instrument shaped like a mandolin with 16–20 strings in four courses (INC 1978: 144–46), which is to be found in the neighboring Province of Canchis largely because of the broadcasts of *bandurria* music from Cuzco. The string band style and the *bandurria* are used in informal contexts (as at home among friends), but have not been incorporated into local fiesta and ritual traditions.

Older musical traditions in rural Canas

The older musical traditions practiced by indigenous people in Canas include Kechua songs (that is, agricultural and animal fertility songs, as well as courting and carnival songs), and such instruments as the *pinkullu, kena,* and *charango.* In contrast to Conima, music is sometimes performed solo in formal and informal contexts; vocal music is extremely important; and a string instrument, the *charango,* has been incorporated into local festivals and agricultural rituals, including the *papa tarpuy* (potato planting).

Kechua songs are sung in most musical contexts, with or without instrumental accompaniment. Both men and women sing, depending on the context, but women are by far the preferred singers, and the high, lilting voice quality of young girls is preferred to the deeper voices of older women. Along with the frequent use of falsetto, this reflects the traditional Andean preference for high tessitura. One time while walking with a friend during a fiesta, we passed a young girl singing particularly high. My companion turned to me beaming and, with real satisfaction,

said, "That is how a voice should sound!" The vocal quality consists of nasal head and throat singing without vibrato, in contrast to the singing style with vibrato (from the diaphragm) preferred by mestizos and standard for the commercialized *wayno* style in the cities.

In Canas, group or solo singing with instrumental accompaniment is basically in unison or octaves. Parallel polyphony as heard in Conima, elsewhere in Puno, and in Bolivia, is totally absent in Canas. The unison is lax, especially with instrumental accompaniment: singers often enter a phrase independently and treat the melodic relationship with the instrumental line in a free manner, sometimes creating a heterophonic effect. This freer relationship among performers contrasts with the Conimeño ideal of "playing as one."

The instruments. The *kena,* a vertical end-notched flute (made of plastic PVC tubing, cane, or metal), is one of the instruments commonly played in Canas. In indigenous performance practice, the first finger hole (farthest from the rounded or square mouth notch) is left open. A loose embouchure creates a breathier sound than that preferred by urban-mestizo *kena* players and European-trained flutists. Also in contrast with the mestizo *kena* style, vibrato is not used by rural Caneño performers. In keeping with the value of high tessitura, the overblown second octave and part of the third are used primarily. *Kenas* are played for informal musical occasions, such as at home or while walking to and from the fields before and after work. They are usually played solo for the musician's own enjoyment or with an informal string band. Presently, the *kena* is considered a casual, unimportant instrument, and is not currently used in any of the local fiestas or rituals.

The *pinkullu* in Canas is a flute that differs substantially from its Aymara namesake in Conima ("pinkillu" is another pronunciation of "pinkullu"). Unlike the shorter (53 cm) cane variety found in Conima, the *pinkullu* of Canas is a duct flute made out of wood, approximately 99 cm in length, and over 3.8 cm in diameter. The branch of wood is cut in half, hollowed out (half stopped at the bottom), then bound back together with llama gut. It has six top finger holes, only four of which are played. Due to the length of the instrument, the performer must often tilt his head back and stretch his arms to reach the top four holes. Various pitches for each stop (octaves and fifths) are obtained through non-sequential fingerings and overblowing. The *pinkullu* produces a particularly dense, breathy sound, and may be played solo to accompany unison singing, or in a loose unison with other *pinkullus*. Any number of players may come together to perform as the spirit and occasion move them, but it is not formally a large ensemble tradition as in Conima, and it is not accompanied by drums. (In fact, drums are not used in Kechua music of Canas.)

As in Conima, the *pinkullu* is played in Caneño fiestas and earth fertility rituals throughout the rainy season (November to March or April). The rainy season in the Andes is a particularly important time for rituals dedicated to Pachamama. According to a musician in Canas, the term *pinkullu* has a phallic significance *(ullu* means penis = *uyu;* see Hornberger 1977: 100), and its use in fertility rituals with the open female earth is thus symbolically consistent. In Conima, however, people did not attribute any sexual significance to the *pinkillu*. Hence, while the *pinkillu/pinkullu* is associated with the same season in both regions, the symbolic meaning of the seasonal association does not seem to be shared. (See Dale A. Olsen, "Aerophones of Traditional Use in South America," in this volume.)

It is generally accepted that pre-Hispanic cultures did not have string instruments (see Ercilia Moreno Chá, "Chordophones of Traditional Practice in South America, Central America, and Mexico," in these volumes). The Andean *charango,* a chordophone, developed during the colonial period (ca. 1700), based on the model of the guitar or vihuela but much smaller in size. Contemporary Caneños explain the size reduction in two ways: it made the instrument more portable than the guitar, and the shorter string length allowed for higher-pitched tunings. Both the practical and the aesthetic reasons may well have been involved in the innovation (Fig. 4).

Because the *charango* is, by its very nature, "mestizo" (namely, a hybrid innovation), writers have categorically considered it "non-Indian" (for instance, Céspedes 1984: 217). Oddly, similar arguments are not made in regard to duct flutes, although their pre-Columbian existence has yet to be demonstrated. In any event, such a position is based on a static view of culture that precludes innovation and the borrowing of ideas.

In Canas, Kechua-speaking peoples and mestizos alike associate the *charango* with the former group; with the exception of the *papa tarpuy* fiesta, it is usually played only by young indigenous musicians during courtship. In fact, because of social prejudices, mestizos in this region tend not to play it in order to remain distinct. Mestizos do play the *charango* elsewhere in southern Peru, however, and in a manner that differs fundamentally from indigenous performance. Such players frequently associated the *charango* with mestizo identity, an indication that ethnic associations with the instrument are fluid (Turino 1984). A summary comparison of the indigenous Caneño and urban-mestizo *charango* traditions will highlight some basic differences in aesthetics and performance practices between these two groups.

Comparison of the Caneño and mestizo *charango* traditions

In Canas and in most places in Peru, the *charango* has a flat wooden back and looks precisely like a miniature guitar (the size of a ukulele or smaller). The instrument has ten or twelve thin metal strings grouped into five courses.

The low octave string found in the center course on mestizo *charangos* is usually absent in Canas and is uncommon among indigenous players generally. Lately, however, some Caneños have added a lower octave string to the fifth course, in imitation of the *bandurria* of the neighboring Canchis province. The direct influence of the *bandurria* is indicated by the fact that these instruments use the standard Canchis *bandurria* tuning as well. Several different *charango* tunings are used in Canas, depending on the player, and they can be a step or more above the standard A minor tuning used by mestizos (Ex. 2). The higher-pitched tunings, the flat-backed sound box, and the numerous thin metal strings, characteristic of indigenous instruments, create a sound in keeping with Andean preferences for a high, strident, and dense sound.

While in Canas, I had with me a larger, round-backed *charango* with nylon strings and with a low octave string in the center course. Caneño players consistently voiced a dislike for this instrument, saying that it was too "hoarse" *(ronco)* and that it sounded like a guitar rather than a *charango*. They said that a *charango* should *chillar* (cry out, screech, referring to a high-pitched sound) and should "cry out like a cat." In contrast, the larger round-backed type has become increasingly popular with Peruvian mestizos in recent years precisely for the deeper quality that the Caneños rejected.

Fig. 4: Charango player in the market, Canas (Turino 1985). Courtesy of the author.

Although the indigenous *charango* in Canas, southern Peru, and Bolivia is only strummed, plucked and strummed sections are alternated in mestizo practice. Mestizos say that they use the plucking/strumming contrasts so that their listeners will not become bored (Turino 1984), and this is partly a result of performance context—the urban stage versus a rural participatory fiesta. In Caneño culture the deliberate use of such obvious contrasts is not an aesthetic concern. The more open approach to performance allows for repeating the strummed verse indefinitely, whereas mestizos tend toward more closed, structured forms—namely, introduction (strummed), verse (plucked), verse (plucked), verse (strummed), verse (plucked), postlude or *fuga* (strummed).

In traditional contexts, such as courting fiestas and the *papa tarpuy*, only *charangos* are played together to accompany singing and dancing whereas mestizo players frequently combine the *charango* with guitar and other instruments in ensemble. The *charango* was not typically included in the recently created string bands in Canas, which suggests a kind of conceptual

Ex. 2: A minor tuning of the *charango* used by mestizos.

compartmentalization between the older local tradition and this new one.

The approaches of mestizo and indigenous players to *charango* performance are distinct in other ways. In their plucked renditions of melodies, mestizos use parallel thirds and triadic harmonic progressions (for instance, V/III–III–V7–i). The indigenous approach to performance is conceived melodically rather than harmonically. In Canas and throughout southern Peru, indigenous players strum a repeated melodic ostinato or a song's melodic line. The melody is usually played on a single course and strummed along with the remaining open strings, producing a dense sound rather than the more punctuated, plucked melodic renditions that mestizos prefer (Recorded Ex. 2).

Although the Caneños and indigenous players of other regions whom I interviewed consistently numbered the strings of guitars and mandolins sequentially (from high to low: 1, 2, 3, etc.), approximately five of these same players conceived of the *charango* string order with the central course as 1, numbering and tuning the instrument out from there. It is possible that such conceptions of *charango* string order are idiosyncratic to certain players for other reasons (such as finding these tuning orders easier and numbering their strings accordingly). Nonetheless this finding is suggestive in light of the way that Conimeño panpipe and *pitu* harmony is conceived—from the center outward—and in relation to weaving in Cuzco, which also is conceptualized symmetrically in relation to the center of a piece or design.

Musical style and contexts

Musical genres often are named for specific functions and occasions. Although in Conima new pieces are created each year for major fiestas to distinguish individual community ensembles and each instrumental genre has a large repertoire, in Canas the same few pieces are used annually for given events and are shared by all communities in the region. Here it is the particular tunes that serve as indices for specific occasions whereas in Conima it is the genre-specific formulas.

Charango music. The *charango* is used primarily by young men during a sequence of courting activities that has a limited repertoire of *kashuas,* or circle dances. Chroniclers specifically define the *kashua* as a circle dance, indicating a long history for the term and its general meaning (Guamán Poma de Ayala 1615 in 1980: 288; Cobo de Peralta 1653 in 1895, iv: 231). The two main *kashua* pieces used for courting in Canas are the *punchay kashua* (day *kashua*) and the *tuta kashua* (night *kashua*). The former uses three pitches and the latter four. The metric-rhythmic scheme hovers ambiguously between duple and triple feeling with the phrases lasting six beats, in keeping with the *kashua* choreography (Turino 1983: 88).

Like all Conimeño music, these *kashuas* are typical examples of the way Andeans use intense repetition of musical material, and of the aesthetic principle that subtle changes mark major differences. In the *punchay kashua* (Ex. 3), the three-beat a and b are essentially identical in all but their first and final pitches. Sung syllabically, this song atypically has a kind of refrain (section B).

The *tuta kashua* (Ex. 4) follows these basic characteristics, but has only one section comprised of four three-beat phrases (a b a b). The first two beats of each phrase are identical.

In occasions of reciprocal labor exchange for the planting of potatoes, the workers sing and dance to a particular song known as *papa tarpuy* accompanied by *charango* during rest periods. The song text is humorous or satirical in nature, addressing the owner for whom they are working. This song also has a four-pitch scale, and the two repeated phrases (AA BB) are rhythmically identical (Ex. 5). Both men and women enter at will, singing in unison and accompanied by the *charango*.

Pinkullu music. Among the most dramatic occasions for vocal-*kashua* and *pinkullu* performance are the ritual battles that take place in various locations, notably Tocto and Chiaraje, between December and February. Caneño communities come against each other fighting with slings and rocks; often wounds and even deaths result. The pre-Columbian tradition of ritual battle in the Andes remains widespread today (Betanzos 1551 in 1924; Molina 1572 in 1947; Gutiérrez de Santa Clara 1603 in 1904–1929; Alencastre and Dumézil 1953; Gorbak, Lischetti, and Muñoz 1962; Brownrigg 1971–1972; Hopkins 1979). Referred to as *tinku (tinkuy,* "to come together," as well as "point of encounter"), the battles fit within a larger field of meaning that involves the meeting and joining of opposite forces (Isbell 1978: 113; Allen 1988: 206–7).

The battle of Chiaraje takes place on an isolated plain, surrounded by several small mountains. Men and women of the five *ayllus* of the district of Checca travel for hours to the site by foot, horseback, or truck to confront their ritual enemies from Langui and Quewe who unite on the opposing side. The men who take part in the battle call it a "game" and often explain their participation by saying that "the game is beautiful." The event's function as an earth fertility ritual is expressed in participants' statements that the winning side will gain a good harvest and prosperity for the year to come. From the pre-Hispanic period to the present, animals have been sacrificed and blood (a symbol of life) has been "fed" to Pachamama in earth fertility rituals as a reciprocal act (Guamán Poma de Ayala 1615 in 1980; Bastien 1978).

The two opposing groups occupy hills at opposite sides of the field of battle. Women stay on their respective hilltops as men enter the fray on horseback or on foot. With slings and rocks, each side tries to drive its enemies to the foot of their hill and hold them there, thus dominating the field and winning; this occurs in two sessions, from around 10:30–12:00 A.M. and 2:30–4:00 P.M.

At midday the men return from the battle to their hill camps for food, drink, and a fiesta with the women. In 1982, after most had finished eating on the Langui-Quewe hill, seven women of all ages (18–60) joined hands in a circle and began singing and dancing the *"kashua* of Chiaraje." At first the song and dance were unaccompanied, and more women gradually joined in. After about ten minutes, the women asked some *pinkullu* players to accompany them, and one man began to play. The *pinkullu* and voices used different pitches, since the women had already started singing and the pitch of the *pinkullu* is relatively invariable. Throughout the performance, the women changed the pitch level of their singing without regard for the flutes. Another *pinkullu* player soon joined the first, who was standing outside the women's circle. Before they began playing, they carefully checked the tuning of the two instruments and found them acceptable. Hence the tuning of the voices with the flutes remained random, while care was taken for the flutes to play in a well-tuned unison.

The performance, which lasted several hours, was organized around the singing of the women. They performed five different melodies in medley for varying lengths of time (between 3 and 20 minutes each), and the first melody sung was brought back several times during the performance. A pattern of microtonal rising was apparent during the performance of the first melody. Microtonal rising (in which the melody pitches maintain the same relationships while the melody as a whole rises gradually in pitch) is unusual in the Andean highlands and is more common among Amazonian groups (Seeger 1987). Four of the melodies were tritonic, while the fifth had four pitches. As is typical of Andean music, they used one, two, or three short repeated phrases (e.g., abac, abab, aaaa) with a high degree of motivic repetition between the phrases. Sometimes the singing exhibited a rather free, unmetered character. The singing was syllabic, and the exact rhythms varied with the text. The *pinkullu* players performed freely interpreted versions of the

Ex. 3: *Punchay kashua.*

Ex. 4: *Tuta kashua.*

Ex. 5: *Papa tarpuy.*

sung melodies and entered or rested independently of the singers. As the afternoon battle began, the *pinkullu* players and other men left the hilltop. The women kept singing and dancing, and continued on during their trip home (Fig. 5).

The other major context for *pinkullu* performance occurs during carnival week, when private and semi-private rituals take place at the earth shrines. A family, perhaps with neighbors and friends, gathers around the place of power to "feed the earth." The shrine is a hole in the ground that may be marked with stones. Fires are made, as coca, alcohol, and food are given to Pachamama in reciprocal exchange for the life she gives, as Caneños explicitly state. The burning of offerings is symbolic of the earth "eating" or consuming them (Bastien 1978). After the offerings, a male in the household often plays the *pinkullu* to accompany group singing and dancing.

In addition to these semi-private rituals, a major fiesta is held in the capital of each district on a specific day during carnival week. People begin streaming into town in the morning from the surrounding communities, dressed in festive clothing. The male dancers arrive on horseback with their *pinkullus* in hand. In outlying streets and in fields at the edge of town, the people dance, eat, drink, and celebrate.

The most elaborate male *chuku* ("helmet," the traditional hat of Canas) dancers wear the high boots typical of Qorilasso culture, black pants, a decorative jacket, and a hat decorated with colored ribbons. Around the waist they wear a spectacularly colored (red or pink) thick skirt of yarn. The male dancers are said to represent a male llama laden with wool. Women wear typical, festive clothing, and their hats are decorated with ribbons and flowers. The carnival dance is performed by individual couples or between groups of men and women, while spectators gather to join in the fun. The men play *pinkullus*, and both men and women sing to accompany the dance. The dancers do a hard stamping step to the music. The women hold their bodies erect, and the men bend over forward so that the movement, aided by their yarn skirts, gives them an animal-like appearance. The male pursues the female, who whips her partner with a leather thong as they circle around each other. At the climax of the dance, some men hold their long *pinkullus* in both hands and try to capture their partners between the *pinkullu* and their arms. The pair wrestles strenuously until the male forces his partner to the ground, explicitly suggesting human lovemaking.

This dance combines a wealth of meaning into a single performance, particularly in the context of Carnavales, a time of heightened sexual activity and earth and animal fertility rituals. The male dancer's role as a male llama combines the images of animal fertility and human sexuality. Men play the carnival melody solo, in pairs, or in groups in unison. They also may alternate performing the melody on *pinkullu* and singing verses. Often one or two women sing basically in unison with their partners' flute melody. Toward the end of a performance, men and women also alternate sung verses in a kind of duel between the sexes. The performance includes occasional *pinkullu* interludes.

The song texts usually include boasting, sexual challenges, and insults; as the performance warms up, men and women begin singing simultaneously without concern or reference to where the other is, melodically or in the text. These are gleefully aggressive shouting/singing competitions between men and women, rather than an "ensemble performance" as understood in Conima. People enter into the singing, *pinkullu* playing, and dancing at will; a loose unison as well as a musical free-for-all may result (Recorded Ex. 3).

The melody for this carnival music utilizes four pitches. Its phrase structure is generally aabc, but the musical form is flexible, depending on the text sung. Most texts are four-line stanzas, each line joined to one musical phrase. The stanzas can be extended to six or even eight lines, particularly when men and women are challenging each other for the last word. When this happens, the flute players and singers will merely repeat musical phrases b and c. In one such case the man sang four lines:

> On my horse
> I am going to carry you off
> My life, you will carry off
> you want my life.

In the heat of the song duel, the woman did not wait for the man to finish but entered about five beats behind with a six-line answer:

> How will you be able [to carry me off]
> Girls from Langui are quick
> If you are able, take me
> If you are not able, leave me
> Because this one [referring to herself] is single
> This one is an apple.

Fig. 5: *Pinkullu* player at noontime during the ritual battle of Chiaraje, Canas (Turino 1985). Courtesy of the author.

A large repertoire of formulaic verses is available to singers to suit the occasion or the message they wish to express. Formulaic text improvisation occurs when singers combine pre-existing and new lines. These texts are laden with sexual imagery, challenges, and invitations. For example, a woman sings:

> A single girl can fall
> A tree can fall
> You can mount [her] like a mule
> Another year you will mount [her].

CONCLUSIONS

These sketches of musical life in Canas and Conima reveal similarities as well as regional and cultural differences between Aymara and Kechua communities. The most obvious contrasts between the two involve musical instruments and genres, which are dependent on local custom throughout the Andes. In Conima and in general with the Aymara of Peru and Bolivia, vocal music is relatively rare and unimportant, while in Canas it is central.

The relative unimportance of vocal music seems to be a general characteristic of Aymara communities in Peru and Bolivia (Tschopik 1946; Buechler 1980). Common throughout the Peruvian sierra, songs for agricultural and animal fertility ceremonies, and work related events, are performed in Canas but not in Conima, with the exception of roof-raising.

In both Conima and Canas, vertical duct flutes (pinkillu/pinkullu, tarka) are associated with the rainy season, the earth, and agricultural rituals, but the sexual significance of this connection does not seem to be shared. In the Andes, musical meaning must be studied at the local level. The complete lack of string music among the Aymara in Conima is only local, because the Aymara of Chucuito have a tradition of charango performance. The importance of drums in Conima is typical of many Andean flute traditions; the absence of drums in Canas is not a Kechua trait per se.

The basic approach to musical performance in Canas and Conima offers another major contrast. In Conima, music is performed only in large ensembles, and solo playing or even practicing alone are practically non-existent, while in Canas, music is used in casual, private contexts, and there is more solo playing during fiestas. Although the most important musical occasions and traditions are linked with communal events in indigenous Andean society generally, Conima represents an extreme and unusual case where music only is performed in such contexts. Although group singing and instrumental performance are associated with fiestas in Canas, the individual performer's relationship to the group is conceived in a more loosely knit fashion, resulting in a heterophonic or free-for-all style. In both cases these distinct approaches to musical performance are consistent with the strong value of community solidarity in Conima and the more individualistic ethos in Canas.

In Conima, competition between communities is realized primarily through musical performance during fiestas, as the originality of new compositions and ensemble style serve as important markers of community identity and competence. In Canas, inter-community competition is realized primarily during the ritual battles (tinku), and musical competition takes place more prominently between the sexes in song duels during carnival and courting-kashuas (Turino 1983). The annual composition of new tunes is not a feature of Caneño musical culture, which emphasizes formulaic composition and improvisation of song texts.

Three- and four-tone scales are the mainstay in Canas while six- and seven-tone scales are heard most frequently in Conima. Neither case substantiates the oft-repeated generalization (following d'Harcourt 1925) that contemporary Andean music is predominantly pentatonic. The two isolated cases presented here suggest that further ethnographic analysis is needed to determine the ethnic/class, regional, and contextual associations with the admittedly widespread pentatonic scale. Various musical forms are heard in Canas but none approaches the strict AA BB CC structure of Conimeño music.

In addition to all the features that serve to distinguish these localized musical cultures, certain aspects that unite them have been underlined: the dense sound and high tessitura, the economic repetition of a limited number of motives, and the prolonged (open-ended) repetition of entire pieces, as well as the avoidance of stark contrasts. Genres are frequently identified by context of use and, likewise, instruments are tied to specific occasions and functions. Only the same type of melodic instruments are played together. In both locales, musical performance is a non-specialist activity.

Most of these characteristics were highlighted in the comparison of the urban-mestizo and indigenous-Caneño charango traditions and point to the distinct musical and cultural sensibilities of indigenous and mestizo musicians. Although this will come as no surprise to Andeanists, some scholars continue to question the validity of discussing indigenous Andean groups as culturally distinct from other segments of the larger society because of the long history of interaction. I have suggested that bilateral processes of separatism, strategic in nature, may account in part for the maintenance of distinct local identities and cultural practices—this, in fact, being one result of the harsh nature of the interaction.

At the same time, musical life in Conima and Canas is being affected by urban migration and migrant music in the cities, as well as by public education and the media. The advent of string bands and charangos tuned like bandurrias in Canas, and the decrease in the number of instruments, dance traditions, and fiestas in Conima, serve as examples. With the exception of sikus, young Conimeños show little interest in the local musical traditions, whereas in Canas, as of 1982, young men still performed the charango as part of local courting customs. Increased interaction with "national society" seems to be diminishing Conimeño traditions while it may be perceived as augmenting the number of resources in Canas (as, for instance, the addition of the string band). Hence, in Peru, even the relation to the "national" and its impact on regional musical practice is variable and must be assessed at the local level.

REFERENCES

Albó, Javier 1974. "La paradoja aymara: Solidaridad y faccionalismo," *Estudios andinos* (Lima) 4/2: 67–110.

Alencastre, Andrés, and Georges Dumézil 1953. "Fêtes et usages des indiens de Lagui," *Journal de la Société des Americanistes* 42: 1–118.

Allen, Catherine J. 1988. *The hold life has: Coca and cultural identity in an Andean community*. Washington, D.C.: Smithsonian Institution Press.

Bastien, Joseph W. 1978. *Mountain of the condor: Metaphor and ritual in an Andean ayllu*. St. Paul, Minnesota: West Publishing Co.

Betanzos, Juan de 1551 in 1924. *Historia de los Incas y Conquista del Perú. I: Suma y narración de los Incas por Juan Diez de Betanzos. II: Relación de la Conquista del Perú por Miguel de Estete*, ed. by Horacio H. Urteaga. Lima: Imprenta y Librería Sanmartí.

Brownrigg, Leslie Ann 1971–1972. "El papel de los ritos de pasaje en la integración social de los Cañaris quichuas del austral ecuatoriano," *Folklore americano* 19/20: 17, 92–99.

Buechler, Hans C. 1980. *The masked media: Aymara fiestas and social interaction in the Bolivian highlands*. The Hague: Mouton.

Céspedes, Gilka Wara 1984. "New currents in música folklórica in La Paz, Bolivia," *Latin American music review* 5: 217–42.

Cobo de Peralta, Bernabé 1653 in 1895. *Historia del Nuevo Mundo*, 4 vols., ed. by Marcos Jiménez de la Espada. Sevilla: Imprenta de E. Rasco, vol. 4.

Gorbak, Celina, Mirtha Lischetti, and Carmen P. Muñoz 1962. "Batallas rituales del Chiaraje y del Tocto de la provincia de Kanas, Cuzco-Perú," *Revista del Museo Nacional* (Museo Nacional de Historia, Lima) 31: 245–304.

Guamán Poma de Ayala, Felipe 1615 in 1980. *El primer nueva corónica y buen gobierno*, ed. by John Murra and Rolena Adorno, with trans. from Kechua by Jorge L. Urioste. México: Siglo Veintiuno Editores, 3 vols.

Gutiérrez de Santa Clara, Pedro 1603 in 1904–1929. *Historia de la guerras civiles del Perú (1544–1548) y de otros sucesos de las Indias*, 6 parts, ed. by Manuel Serrano y Sanz. Madrid: Librería General de Victoriano Suárez.

d'Harcourt, Raoul, and Marguerite d'Harcourt 1925. *La musique des Incas et ses survivances*. Paris: Paul Geuthner, 2 vols.

Hartmann, Roswith 1971–1972. "Otros datos sobre las llamadas 'batallas rituales'," *Folklore americano* 19/20: 17, 125–35.

Hopkins, Diane 1979. "Play of enemies: The interpretation of a 1772 ritual battle in southern Peru from historical and symbolic perspectives," paper presented at the 43rd International Congress of Americanists, Vancouver.

Hornberger, Esteban S., and Nancy H. Hornberger 1977. *Tri-lingual dictionary: Quechua of Cusco, English, Spanish / Diccionario tri-lingüe: Quechua de Cusco, inglés, español*. [s. l.]: LCA, 3 vols.

INC (Instituto Nacional de Cultura) 1978. *Mapa de los instrumentos musicales de uso popular en el Perú*. Lima: Instituto Nacional de Cultura, Oficina de Música y Danza.

Isbell, Billie Jean 1978. *To defend ourselves: Ecology and ritual in an Andean village*. Austin: Institute of Latin American Studies, University of Texas at Austin. Repr. ed. (Prospect Heights, Illinois: Waveland Press, 1985.)

Lloréns Amico, José Antonio 1983. *Música popular en Lima: Criollos y andinos*. Lima: Instituto de Estudios Peruanos.

Mishkin, Bernard 1946. "The contemporary Quechua" in *Handbook of South American Indians*, 7 vols., ed. by Julian H. Steward. Washington, D.C.: Smithsonian Institution, Bureau of American Ethnology, vol. 2, 411–70.

Molina, Cristóbal de 1572 in 1947. *Ritos y fábulas de los Incas*. Buenos Aires: Editorial Futuro.

Montoya, Rodrigo, Luis Montoya, and Edwin Montoya 1987. *La sangre de los cerros: Antología de la poesía quechua que se canta en el Perú*. Lima: CEPES, Mosca Azul Editores y UNMSM.

Murra, John 1975. "El control vertical de un máximo de pisos ecológicos en la economía de la sociedades andinas" in *Formaciones económico-políticas del mundo andino*. Lima: Instituto de Estudios Peruanos.

Roel, Josafat 1959. "El wayno del Cuzco," *Folklore americano* 6/7: 129–246.

Romero, Raúl 1985. "La música tradicional y popular" in *La música en el Perú*. Lima: Patronato Popular y Porvenir Pro Música Clásica, 214–86.

——— 1990. "Musical change and cultural resistance in the central Andes of Peru," *Latin American music review* 11: 1–35.

Schaedel, Richard P., Gabriel Escobar, and Antonio Rodríguez 1959. *Human resources in the Department of Puno*. Lima: Southern Peru Regional Development Project.

Seeger, Anthony 1987. *Why Suyá sing: A musical anthropology of an Amazonian people*. Cambridge: Cambridge University Press.

Smith, Robert J. 1975. *The art of festival, as exemplified by the fiesta to the patroness of Otuzco: La Virgen de la Puerta*. Lawrence, Kansas: Department of Anthropology, University of Kansas.

Tschopik, Harry Jr. 1946. "The Aymara" in *Handbook of South American Indians*, 7 vols., ed. by Julian H. Steward. Washington, D.C.: Smithsonian Institution, Bureau of American Ethnology, vol. 2, 501–73.

Turino, Thomas 1982. "Communication in performance: The fiesta of the Virgen del Carmen, Paucartambo, Peru" (Master's thesis, Ethnomusicology: University of Texas at Austin).

——— 1983. "The charango and the sirena: Music, magic, and the power of love," *Latin American music review* 4: 81–119.

——— 1984. "The urban-mestizo charango tradition in southern Peru: A statement of shifting identity," *Ethnomusicology* 28: 253–69.

——— 1988. "The music of Andean migrants in Lima, Peru: Demographics, social power, and style," *Latin American music review* 9: 127–49.

——— 1989. "The coherence of social style and musical creation among the Aymara in southern Peru," *Ethnomusicology* 33: 1–30.

——— 1990a. "Somos el Perú: 'Cumbia andina' and the children of Andean migrants in Lima," *Studies in Latin American popular culture* 9: 15–37.

——— 1990b. "The history of a Peruvian panpipe style and the politics of interpretation" in *Ethnomusicology and modern music history*, ed. by Stephen Blum, Philip Bohlman, and Daniel Neuman. Urbana: University of Illinois Press, 211–32.

——— 1991. "The state and Andean musical production in Peru" in *Nation-states and Indians in Latin America*, ed. by Greg Urban and Joel Sherzer. Austin: University of Texas Press.

——— 1993. *Moving away from silence: Music of the Peruvian Altiplano and the experience of urban migration*. Chicago: University of Chicago Press.

Valcárcel, Luis E. 1946. "The Andean calendar" in *Handbook of South American Indians*, 7 vols., ed. by Julian H. Steward. Washington, D.C.: Smithsonian Institution, Bureau of American Ethnology, vol. 2, 471–76.

Velasco Alvarado, Juan 1971. *La voz de la revolución: Discursos del Presidente de la República General de División Juan Velasco Alvarado 1970–1972*, vol. 2. Lima: Ediciones Participación.

Verger, Pierre 1945. *Fiestas y danzas en el Cuzco y en los Andes.* Buenos Aires: Editorial Sudamericana.

Wilson, David J. 1988. *Prehispanic settlement patterns in the lower Santa Valley, Peru.* Washington, D.C.: Smithsonian Institution Press.

RECORDED EXAMPLES

1. The *sikuri* ensemble Centro Social Conima performing an untitled piece in the *lento* genre typical of *sikuris*. This genre is performed typically at weddings and other public fiestas for social dancing. Twenty panpipe players and two *bombos* (drums) are heard in this example. The piece was recorded at the home of one of the musicians in August of 1986.

2. Solo *charango*-vocal rendition of a *tuta kashua* performed by Raúl Quispe. Quispe, a boy in his late teens, was recorded at the weekly market in Descanso, Canas, in March of 1981. The *charango* performance heard here is typical of the indigenous style. The *charango* had twelve metal strings.

3. Carnival dance, recorded in Layo, Canas, in February of 1982. An unidentified, informal group of people from the districts of Langui and Layo are performing during the carnival celebration; the singing is accompanied by *pinkullus*.

AMERINDIAN MUSIC OF CHILE

MARÍA ESTER GREBE

The Aymara of the northern Tarapacá highlands: Cattle-marking songs; Carnival; Patron saint fiestas; Potato-sowing ritual (Pachallampe)—*Atacameño music: Sowing ritual* (Fiesta de la semilla); *Cattle-marking and animal increase ritual* (Floramiento del ganado); *Ritual cleansing of irrigation ducts* (Limpia de canales)—*Mapuche music*—*Kawéskar music*

THIS ESSAY SURVEYS the living musical traditions of four indigenous societies: the Aymara of the northernmost Tarapacá highlands; the Atacameño of the northern Atacama desert highlands and plateaus; the Mapuche of southern Chile, from the Bio-Bio River to the Chiloé archipelago; and the Kawéskar of the southernmost channels and archipelagos. The Aymara, Atacameño, and Mapuche are agriculturalist and/or pastoralist peoples who belong to the Andean cultural area and share a heritage of traditional musics and instruments that can be considered as a set of distinctive variants of a common Andean legacy. By contrast, the Kawéskar are a small group of shellfish gatherers who belong to the domain of the Fuegian nomadic hunting and gathering paleo-Indian societies, which, up to several decades ago, also included the Yámana and the now-extinct Selk'nam. Although each of these four societies is affiliated with isolated linguistic stocks, most of them are bilingual (Aymara-Spanish, Mapu-dungu-Spanish, and Kawéskar-Spanish). The Atacameño's Kunza language, however, has been replaced by Spanish and survives only in ritual song. Aymara, Atacameño, and Mapuche peoples excel as weavers and pottery-makers, and also have been skilled silversmiths.

Research on these indigenous groups was carried out during the first half of the twentieth century by such distinguished scholars as C. Wellington Furlong (1907–1908, see Discography); Félix de Augusta (1910 in 1934, and 1911); Martin Gusinde (1931–1939); Erich M. von Hornbostel (1936 and 1948); Carlos Isamitt (1935, 1937, 1938); and Grete Mostny, Fidel Jeldes, Raúl González, and Fernando Oberhauser (1954), among others. Although the Aymara and Mapuche musical legacies remain in full force at the close of the twentieth century, traditional performances among the Atacameño and Kawéskar are less frequent. In spite of ongoing processes of acculturation, however, indigenous groups continue to perform their traditional musics. It is interesting to note that most indigenous musicians acknowledge the differences between past and present musics by dividing their repertoires into "old" and "new," assigning these terms to the fixed traditional and the free acculturated styles and structures, respectively. The domain of indigenous music in Chile should be perceived as Native American strongholds that coexist with the basic Hispanic foundation of national culture, itself characterized by regional and ethnic variants. Whenever the contact between Hispanic and indigenous cultures has been continuous and/or intense, it either has resulted in new hybrid forms or it has led to a gradual decline of the indigenous tradition.

Among Native American peoples, life is predestined by supernatural forces and powers that articulate the relationships between the natural, mythical, and human domains. Their world is both poetic and symbolic (Picón-Salas 1966: 12). Humans are not able to control nature. Their destiny is preordained by humanized gods and spirits, and by a spiritualized nature. Music is a part of the mythical, the natural, and the human realms. To characterize the whole cultural system and its underlying meanings (of which music is a specific means of communication), worldview, ritual, and core symbols should be considered (Grebe 1978: 85).

Worldview provides the broad framework of explanations that clarifies systemic, structural, and functional relationships of a cultural whole. In terms of its conceptual, cognitive, and affective meanings and formal expressions, music is inextricably linked to such an overall cosmological framework. As a kinetic reenactment of myth, ritual condenses a range of cultural patterns in a more concentrated fashion than ordinary, non-ritual experience. Music is frequently an integral part of ritual communication, with basic and meaningful roles in the various ceremonial actions. Symbolic behavior and cultural objects, such as specific kinds of performances and instruments, provide a point of entry into a holistic understanding of music in culture.

Furthermore, symbolism may reveal ways in which cultural and musical patterns are related at levels that are not evident to the immediacy of experience. Symbols are polysemic, even when the inter-relationships between heterogeneous realities that articulate a whole, a complex configuration, or a system, may not be apparent or explicit. Symbols can translate human experience into cosmological terms and explain the hidden relationships of a cultural event or fact. They project their inner meaning onto a deeper reality and communicate paradoxical contents that could not be expressed otherwise (Eliade 1967: 129–35).

Among the indigenous peoples of Chile, music belongs primarily to the sacred domain and secondarily to the secular, where it appears in the interactions of domestic groups as part of their social life, family gatherings, work, and leisure-time activities.

Although it is difficult to characterize the musical features of these groups as a whole, due to the scarcity of primary aural sources and reliable musical transcriptions, it is possible to present a synthesis based on working knowledge, many years of field work, and aural experience. Only those features that are persistent, widespread, and essential for an understanding of musical behavior are considered here.

Musical forms are based on sequences of repetition and variation of short, juxtaposed melodic cells, which generate sets of subtle, discrete, and meaningful transformations. Strophic forms are generated either by poetic texts, dance patterns, or symbolic representations.

Pitch systems tend to be foreign to Western European equal temperament, and approximation to the latter generally indicates musical acculturation. Tritonic, tetratonic, and pentatonic scales tend to show analogies with—or cultural borrowings from—Western European sources. Narrow melodic ranges prevail throughout, with extensions that cover the octave plus adjacent tonal segments. Wider ranges are to be found only in specific musical categories and styles. Heterophony, parallel intervals, and empirical harmony appear mainly in the repertoire of specific chordophones, and in choral and instrumental ensemble musics. The presence of typically Western European harmonic patterns, such as I–V and I–IV–V–I, as well as specific kinds of repeated pitch patterns and drones, frequently indicate assimilation of Western European sources.

Either free or regular strophic rhythms characterize different musical categories and styles. Isometric and polymetric sequences appear either in fixed or extemporized performances. Although natural pulse prevails, recurring regular accents are to be found in specific kinds of dances and songs. Variations of free tempo determined by expressive needs are a dominant feature. Fixed or stable tempo with sudden changes between slow and fast sections are to be found only in specific types (such as the well-known Aymara *huayño*).

Among the expressive features of vocal music that indigenous groups share are lack of vibrato, nasality, vocal tension, glissando, appoggiatura, and portamento. A rich variety of devices is employed: pulsation, glides, falsetto, extremely high or low and extremely loud or soft sounds, inhalation, cantillation, yells, sobbing or weeping, whispering or humming, aspiration, *bocca chiusa*, emphatic accents, tonal fluctuations, and oscillation and deflection. There is a predominance of extemporization, based on the principle of transforming shared melodic patterns or short melodic cells.

As a whole, these features are meaningless unless they are considered as structural and stylistic configurations that characterize specific musical categories and styles within each indigenous culture, and as part of a process of symbolic communication. These features also reinforce shared stylistic patterns and establish means by which listeners identify with their own cultural traditions.

THE AYMARA OF THE NORTHERN TARAPACÁ HIGHLANDS

The Aymara are the second largest indigenous group of the central Andean area after the Kechua. Their domain extends over part of the highland territories of four neighboring countries: Bolivia, southeastern Peru, northwestern Argentina, and the highlands of northern Chile. Before the domination of the Incas, the Aymara were divided into various independent warring states (Tschopik 1946: 507). Unity was achieved by means of the shared Aymara language.

The Aymara living in Chilean territory occupy the southwestern part of the Aymara area—the highlands of Tarapacá in the northernmost part of Chile—which exhibits idiosyncratic regional features. Although the Aymara lived in virtual isolation in the past due to insufficient means of communication and transportation, they more recently have increased their mobility. The frequency of travel and contacts with the lowlands increased during the 1980s, allowing market transactions and social interactions with kinsmen and close friends. This change also has exposed their traditions to greater exogenous influence. Although the Aymara are bilingual, Spanish is today the predominant language and loss of Aymara is particularly noticeable among young people. This is because Spanish is acquired early, displacing the Aymara mother-tongue and reducing it to a secondary role (Grebe 1986a: 47). Although adult women are more competent in Aymara than adult men, perhaps because they are more isolated than men in the rural areas and lack mobility, the opposite is true for their respective competence in Spanish.

The Aymara divide the cosmos into three worlds: *araj-pacha*, the upper world of the sacred celestial bodies; *taipi-pacha*, the middle world of the mountain spirits, agricultural spirits, and saints, which is also the world of humans; and *manqha-pacha*, the under-

world inhabited by Seren'-mallku and his wife, the spirits of music and water, and the sacred wild animals (Grebe 1980: 127–85; 1981: 61–79). In this tri-layered cosmology, music is a part of the underworld. It is conceived as a language generated in myth and embedded in cosmology, and as "melody-generated-in-nature." Seren'-mallku is said to create all music from the underground sources of water, and in the rustling sounds of nature's waterfalls, springs, brooks, and rivers. Seren'-mallku is thus invoked for melodic inspiration, for adequate tuning and tone quality of the musical instruments, and for the musicians' ability to synchronize during performance. The experience of the Aymara musicians who visit Sereno's springs on the eve of a ritual fiesta is of deep emotional significance, as if they were entering a mystical domain. They listen in silence to the music of water in nature and transfer the melodies to the instruments. Seren'-mallku is believed to be the source of all melodic inspiration and the progenitor of a cumulative musical repertoire for instrumental ensembles. This legacy is a powerful means of communication and the necessary condition for a good ritual performance.

According to the beliefs of the participants in ritual, Aymara music is inextricably linked to the cosmological and ritual realms. Musical categories and styles are included in the domain of broader cosmological categories, followed by ritual categories. General and specific music and dance categories belong to the domain of ritual. The following categories, in hierarchical order, represent the native taxonomy of the Aymara and include the musical traditions associated with them (Grebe 1980: 198).

The two main cosmological divisions are:

uywir-parte, the cults of the herding/mountain and agricultural/earth spirits; and

dios-parte, the worship of Catholic saints, including the syncretic cult of celestial bodies and the church's guardian spirits.

Of the four ritual categories (cattle-marking, carnival, patron saint fiesta, and potato-sowing), the cattle-marking and carnival rituals belong to the cosmological *uywir-parte*, and the patron saint fiesta and potato-sowing to the cosmological *dios-parte*.

Each music and dance genre is associated with one of the four rituals (Grebe 1980: 197–287). Cattle-marking songs are either unaccompanied (solo or collective performance) or accompanied by the *bandola* (a type of *bandurria*, a flat-bodied plucked chordophone), and categorized according to the specific animal or person to which each song is addressed (for instance, *tonos* for the llama, alpaca, sheep, sacred animals, or shepherds).

Carnival music and dance comprises *tonos* ("tunes," accompanied songs), *ruedas* (round dances), *tarkeadas* (ensemble of indigenous wooden flutes) and *orquesta* (ensemble music with two *kenas*, guitar, mandolin, fiddle, and an occasional accordion).

Patron saint fiesta music includes four kinds of ensembles: *sikuras* (ensemble of large panpipes), *lakitas* (ensemble of small panpipes), *lichiguayos* (large *kena* ensemble), and *banda* (brass band). (See Max Peter Baumann, "Music and Worldview of Indian Societies in the Bolivian Andes," and Thomas Turino, "Local Practices among the Aymara and Kechua in Conima and Canas, Southern Peru," in this volume.)

Potato-sowing music includes special *tonos* and *ruedas* (accompanied songs and round dances), whose texts refer to the events that take place in ritual contexts.

Music and dance sub-genres or species consist of further subdivisions of the four ritual categories and their specific music and dance genres into various specific pieces, which correspond to sets of individual songs and dances with salient stylistic features and identifiable choreographic and poetic characteristics.

Cattle-marking songs

These are performed during the *enfloramiento* or *floreo*, an animal increase rite dedicated to the cattle and their protective spirits. The rituals take place two or three weeks before carnival, and their central activity is the flowering and marking of the cattle with colored wool. The Aymara believe that domesticated animals belong to the cosmological domain of the *uywir-parte* and to the herding/mountain spirits to whom most ceremonial actions and invocations are addressed. There is a rich repertoire of cattle-marking songs that vary regionally in style and context. Their importance as a means of ritual communication is reflected in an elaborate folk taxonomy.

The songs are categorized first according to the specific animal to which each song is addressed, including those for sacred animals and shepherds. Second, the songs are categorized according to gender, with separate songs for female and male animals. And third, there are variants divided according to the specific functions and actions of the animal. Songs are dedicated to the two kinds of sacred, emblematic animals associated with herding, the *chullumpe* bird and the *tite* mountain-cat; others are dedicated to shepherds, such as love songs or songs in dialogue between shepherds, or between the shepherds and the animals in their keep.

Each cattle-marking song is based on a single melody, frequently divided into two phrases, with several slightly varied repetitions according to differences in text and mood of the performance. Male and female animal songs may be tonally identified by their respective major diatonic or pentatonic scales. For instance, songs for shepherds and sacred animals are usually pentatonic. Each male or female animal song may be recognized by characteristic isometric or bimetric patterns, repeated throughout. Melodies often fall within ranges smaller than the octave. Tempos are moderate and stable. Performances are generally accompanied by the *bandola*, a colonial chordophone similar to the *bandurria* with sixteen strings grouped into four courses of four. The strings are either strummed or plucked, using a V–I chord pattern. Songs also can be performed by two singers in duo, or collectively, by an unaccompanied group. These songs are valued for their strong expressive quality and display of musicianship, which is recognized in vocal and instrumental synchronicity, precision, and subtlety within the norms of the local style. The skill of the performer is a condition for success, as is the lively atmosphere of interaction that occurs during the early stages of the ritual.

Carnival

This major communal event closes the annual agricultural and herding cycle, coinciding with the harvest period and the seasonal migration of cattle. Its purpose is to re-enact a celebration of the earth and the fertility of animals. Carnival is an exuberant event, widely disseminated and popular, that promotes interaction, friendship, and love affairs. Its ritual activities imply rights, duties, and reciprocities of ritual leaders and kinsmen, who renew their network of interactions and reinforce communal and village identity and solidarity. Carnival symbolizes the end and beginning of annual cycles. Its symbols provide a tangible paradigm of pastoral and agricultural life, centered on cattle increase and abundant harvest.

Music and dance function as permanent means of ritual communication, linking activities and underlining symbolic meanings. This is the case with the animal-sacrifice melody performed at the opening of the highland Carnival of Isluga, when two male white llamas are sacrificed to the mountain-spirits. The ritual slaughtering, agony, and death of the animals are accompanied by *pinkillo* (a reed aerophone) solos or duets. Thereafter, a metonymic association is established. Because the *pinkillo* melodies and heterophonies are associated with ritual sacrifice itself, they will function as substitutes for this offering and its transcendent meaning throughout carnival. Consequently, transformations of *pinkillo* melodies constantly will be heard throughout performances at other musical events, as counter-melodies added to songs, dances, and their instrumental accompaniments. A similar case occurs in the middle-highland Aymara Carnival of Socoroma, rooted in Hispanic models. The carnival spirit, represented by a huge straw man decorated with flowers and agricultural produce, is the *carnavalón* or mythical protective spirit of the planted fields who symbolizes fertility and plentiful harvest. As a focal point of every carnival event, he parades jointly with the *alférez* (ritual leader), his wife, and the *tarkeada* (aerophone ensemble). The contiguity or intimate association between *tarkeada* music (with its sophisticated dances) and the *carnavalón*, *alférez*, musicians, and dancers, produces a metonymic association between this myth and *tarkeada* music, which then functions as background context and substitutes for the key concept of fertility of the earth and its polysemic transformations.

In the upper highlands Carnaval de Isluga, songs (*tonos*) and round dances (*ruedas*) are performed by a team or *pandilla* of male musicians and young female dancers who belong to the same village. Each *pandilla* emblematically represents its own *alférez* (leader) and includes *bandola* and *pinkillo* performers as well as a group of singers. The leader is an expert solo singer and *bandola* performer who alternates with the responsorial singing of the choral group. Their music accompanies the round dance performed by the young female dancers, which consists of counterclockwise and clockwise turns in small steps. Each girl holds in her right hand a colorful woolen snake (*culebrilla*) that symbolizes her sexual maturity and fertility. Young unmarried men observe the dancers to choose a partner and marriage alliances

usually start at this event. In the case of the middle-highlands Carnival of Socoroma, songs and dances are performed by the entire ritual community of the village, under the leadership of an expert solo singer and guitar player. He organizes the responsorial communal singing and the round dance, in which men's step-dancing (*zapateo*) is currently included and all villagers of both sexes may participate. Due to its Hispanicized mestizo features, we can speculate that some ancient symbolic elements have been replaced or transformed.

Carnival songs, song texts, and dances are the means through which Aymara peoples identify with their culture, with their natural and social environments, and with the ritual leaders and actors, who are also emblems of their ethnic group. Their melodies are either short and simple or extensive and elaborate, with repetitions and inserted refrains. Each melodic pattern represents a song and comprises two, three, or four strophic phrases referable to either major or minor heptatonic, hexatonic, or pentatonic scales. Melodies usually cover the range of an octave, in isometric or bimetric sequences, brisk and stable tempi, and intervallic structures that reveal either Aymara or Hispanic foundations. They are accompanied by either *bandola*, guitar, or ensembles.

The men's vocal style is characterized by a tense, emphatic, and self-assertive delivery with strong accents, high register and volume, some nasalization, and raspiness. In contrast, women's singing style exhibits a shy, non-emphatic vocal delivery with extra-high registers sung softly. The mood of the performance is joyful, reaching its climax during the last two days of carnival.

Two instrumental ensembles are employed in the middle-highland Carnaval de Socoroma: *tarkeada* and *orquesta*. The *tarkeada* is an aerophone ensemble comprised of four to eight players of *tarkas* (indigenous duct flutes with six finger holes, in three different sizes and registers). Their instrumental style is characterized by an idiosyncratic tone color with rich use of overtones and a typical raspiness. *Tarkas* are supported by two membranophones, a small frame drum (*caja*) and a large bass drum (*bombo*). The musical style is based on a multipart texture in parallel intervals at the fifth and octave, underlined by the time-line of the *bombo* and the rhythmic subdivisions and flourishes of the *caja*. This ensemble music accompanies sophisticated choreographic patterns performed by mixed-coupled dancers, who design interlocked, mirror-like shapes. The *orquesta* is a mestizo ensemble that comprises two *kenas* (vertical notched flutes), mandolin, guitar, and fiddle, the latter frequently omitted. The melodic framework is provided by the two *kenas* and underlined by a single plucked mandolin, while the strummed guitar and mandolin provide the harmonies (V–I) and time-line. While the first *kena* renders a highly ornamented version of the melody, the second *kena* plays a simplified version. Rhythmic clapping and vocalizations by a solo or chorus enliven the interludes. Song texts refer mainly to love or sentimental topics. The ensemble performs *takiraris* (a dance), and accompanies evening and night carnival communal dances.

Patron saint fiestas

These are celebrated in each Aymara village to honor the local patron saint. As a communal event, the fiesta gathers the local community and also kinspeople and friends who have migrated to the lowlands but return for the event as visitors. This celebration shares the common basic organization and content established by the centralized model of the Catholic church, with regional and local variants. This is a syncretic ritual into which the indigenous worldview has inserted Catholic elements, holistically conceptualized as a macro-representational folk model. Led by the *mayordomo* and/or the *alférez* (ritual leaders), this event is divided into three main parts: antevespers, vespers, and patron saint day. While the first emphasizes the indigenous components, the second and third reenact syncretized Christian patterns. The rich symbolism of the Aymara worldview underlies many formal Catholic events, particularly in the reenactment of the myth of Sereno, the water music spirit, and of the *achichis* (or *achachis*), the ancestral spirits. This symbolism surfaces in the music, because instrumental ensemble musics are believed to be controlled by Sereno, and because the male-female panpipes and their respective pitches behave anthropomorphically.

Four categories of ensemble music are to be found in the patron saint fiesta: *sikuras* (large reed panpipe ensemble), *lakitas* (small plastic or reed panpipe ensemble), *lichiguayos* (large *kena* ensemble), and *banda* (brass band). The *sikuras* and *lakitas* (panpipes) are the most important native instruments of the Aymara, differing from other aerophones in their

diffusion and use. Other aerophone ensemble instruments, such as the *lichiguayos*, *kenas*, and *tarkas*, have a restricted local use and, in some regions, are becoming less used or even extinct. By contrast, panpipes are widely disseminated throughout the whole Tarapacá area and used regularly by both old and young generations of indigenous peoples. Changes in the manufacture of *lakitas* can be seen in the new plastic instruments, which show acculturation due to the influence of urban lowlands.

Sikuras comprise a maximum of twenty mature male performers. Their reed panpipes of fourteen or eleven pipes are divided into three registers: *contra* (high), *likhu* (middle), and *sankha* (low). Within each register, the panpipes are grouped into male-female pairs to provide an interlocked performance of complementary strong-weak beats. Each musician simultaneously performs a panpipe and a drum. The musicians' circular layout implies the performance of counterclockwise and clockwise collective and individual turns. The typical musical texture is a pentatonic polyphony in parallel fifths and octaves, punctuated by the even beats of the drums. All the *sikura* pieces, marches, processions, and farewells have a solemn and ceremonial character. They consist of a short, free introduction, the presentation and repetitions of a basic melody in its multi-part setting, and a brief final section similar to the introduction. The *sikuras* are emblematic of the *mayordomo*'s ritual role and status, and escort him almost permanently. In the northernmost region of Chile, this ensemble is to be found only in some areas of the upper highlands.

Lakitas comprise a maximum of fourteen young male performers: twelve (six pairs) of panpipes, a large bass drum (the *bombo*) and a small frame drum (*caja*). Their plastic or reed panpipes of either six (male) or seven (female) pipes are divided into two registers, the higher *likhu* and the lower *sankha*, which provide an interlocked performance of complementary pitches. Their spatial layout is linear and excludes circular turns. Both dance and church music are included in their repertoire.

Dances include *huaynos*, *takiraris*, *cumbias*, *valses*, and *cuecas*; church music comprises *dianas*, *marchas*, *procesiones*, and *benditos*. The texture is based on a simple octave doubling of a basic pentatonic, hexatonic, or heptatonic melody, punctuated by the *bombo* and *caja* drums. Like the *sikuras*, *lakitas* are emblematic of the ritual leadership of the *alférez* and escort him wherever he goes. This ensemble is widely disseminated throughout the villages of the Aymara highlands and also is found in neighboring lowland urban areas as a consequence of Aymara migrations.

Lichiguayos is a specifically Aymara aerophone ensemble that comprises four to six players of *kenas* (large notched-reed vertical flutes) in two or three different registers, accompanied by *bombo* (bass drum). These instruments have a rectangular notch in the embouchure and six finger holes, plus a thumb hole that provides a diatonic tuning. Since the ensemble carries an association with the *alférez* or ritual leader (as do *sikuras* and *lakitas*), it leads processions and marches dedicated to the patron saint in a few highland villages. The mature and experienced players perform only solemn ritual marches, processions, and *takiraris* (dances) in slow tempo, underscored by the drumbeats. Their spatial layout is either linear or circular, the latter involving turns similar to those of the *sikuras*. Melodies consist of brief, repeated phrases, in either major or minor European modes, or in minor pentatonic or hexatonic in native style. Both styles are characterized by isometric patterns, as well as by slow or moderate tempo. They share with the *sikuras* and *tarkeada* the texture in parallel fifths and octaves. The musical style of the *lichiguayos* has a sweet and penetrating timbre and a dense ornamentation, strong accents, and short legato articulation.

The *banda* is a brass band ensemble of six standard instruments—trumpets and bass tuba—and two drums (a large bass drum, and a small military drum). This ensemble shares repertoire with the *lakita* panpipes' church and dance music. Consequently, alternate performances of *banda* and *lakitas* are frequent in patron saint fiestas. The brass band's increasing popularity began in Bolivia and Peru as well as in the Chilean lowlands. Today, the Aymara express a preference for this ensemble due to its brilliant sound and loudness, thus threatening the survival of the older, traditional reed and wood aerophone ensembles.

Potato-sowing ritual (*Pachallampe*)

This ritual and its music are addressed to Pachamama, the Earth mother. It is still performed in some areas of the middle Aymara highlands, where potato crops carry great significance. Although we may assume that this ritual is of pre-contact and pre-Christian origin, its domain is presently restricted to the communal lands of the church. Ritual activities are controlled by the *alféreces* (ritual leaders), who use potato crops as a source of economic support to defray the cost of the patron saint fiesta. Ploughing is the task of men and sowing is reserved for women, while songs and round dances are performed with accompaniment of guitar and *bombo*. The closing event of this ritual is a large communal meal and dance. The performance of *pachallampe* songs is responsorial: while expert musicians lead in extemporized solo singing, the dancers and other ritual actors perform responsorial refrains. Each song consists of a basic melodic pattern of short phrases, performed within a fixed metrical sequence and in slow tempo. The melodies are either major hexatonic or minor pentatonic within the range of an octave to an eleventh. Vocal style is expressive and emphatic, with strong accents and embellishments. The choreographic gestures follow the model of the carnival's *rueda* (round dance), with its usual turns and step-dancing.

Viewed as a whole, three pervasive principles of symbolic structures are present in Aymara ritual music: duality, symmetrical relationships, and sexual differentiation (Isbell 1978: 11–14, 207; Grebe 1980: 274–77). Duality is to be found in the recurrent binary divisions and repetitions of pieces, duets, complementary oppositions of melodies, and simultaneous renderings of musical events. Symmetrical relationships appear in spatial layouts and mirror-like dance movements of musicians and dancers, and in joint performances of various ensembles. Sexual differentiation is enacted in the contrasting singing styles of men and women, the exclusion of women from instrumental performance, and in the male and female native categories of cattle-marking songs, panpipes, and panpipe music. Through the enactment of these principles, the Aymara peoples project their belief in fertility and the regeneration of the social and cosmic orders, central to their worldview. Music and dance are then integral to the network of multivocal and polysemic symbolic structures that condense deep meanings and identify the Aymara universe as a whole.

ATACAMEÑO MUSIC

During the pre-Hispanic period, the Atacameño or Likan-Antai settled in the Atacama desert of northern Chile, extending from the Loa to the Salado River basins, including the Salar de Atacama. For a long time, this was an area of transit and interaction between different Andean cultures. The impact of Spanish colonization set in motion an ongoing process of cultural change, with gradual assimilation of European cultural patterns that included the adoption of the Catholic religion and the Spanish language. Until the nineteenth century, when Spanish gradually replaced the indigenous languages, Kunza, Aymara, Kechua, and Spanish were spoken. The indigenous Kunza language, still undeciphered, survives only in ritual song. Also declining are song texts and invocations in Kunza. In some of the highland villages, remnants of Kechua and Aymara coexist with Spanish, due to exchanges and reciprocities with the neighboring areas of Jujuy and Salta in Argentina, and with the Bolivian highlands. Archaeological findings have clarified these associations, uncovering a shared legacy from the ancient Tiwanaku (Tiahuanaco) high Andean culture. These cultural contacts have clarified several features of the Atacameños' musical past (Grebe 1974a: 20).

The main Atacameño rituals, in which indigenous songs in Kunza language were performed and still may be, are the *fiesta de la semilla* or *minga de maíz* (sowing ritual), *floramiento del ganado* (cattle-marking ritual), and the *limpia de canales* (cleaning of the pre-Hispanic irrigation ducts). The extant carnival song texts are, however, in Spanish.

Sowing ritual (*Fiesta de la semilla*)

This fertility ritual is dedicated to Pachamama, the Andean Earth mother, and takes place during the ploughing and sowing of the maize fields and patches. In the *ayllus* (smallest communal units) of San Pedro de Atacama, before the sowing takes place, *tinka* or *convido* offerings are made as payment to the earth, water, and ancestor spirits. These offerings include *ulpiada* (a mixture of ground corn or wheat and local *chicha de aloja* or carob-tree drink), wine, and coca leaves. One portion of the *ulpiada* and wine are poured into a small earth-pit, as symbolic "payment" to Pachamama, requesting the protection of the Earth-mother, water, and ancestor spirits for successful sowing and seed growth. The remainder of the *ulpiada* is sprinkled, together with the coca leaves, over the seeds. In Peine, *tinkas* or *convidos* are performed by men and women after sowing. On this occasion, they burn *koba* incense (*sahumerio*). At the end of the ritual, songs in Kunza and Spanish and the *túskalu* tap-dance used to be

performed in the past. This practice is now rare among the Atacameños (Mostny, Jeldes, González, and Oberhauser 1954: 89, 166). A transcribed fragment from an old recording documents these features (Álvarez and Grebe 1974: 31).

Cattle-marking and animal increase ritual (*Floramiento del ganado*)

The *floramiento del ganado* is a ritual of increase performed for the cattle and their protective spirits. It could take place seven or fifteen days before carnival, during carnival, on St. John's day (June 23–24), at Christmas, or New Year's. Inside the corral, the Atacameños burn *koba* incense and make *tinka* offerings, while invoking the earth and the mountain, and ancestor spirits on behalf of the cattle. Llamas, sheep, and goats are marked with ear-cuts, wool earrings, and flowers of various colors; the remaining, larger animals are marked with hot irons. Later on, in the closing phase of the ritual, and/or in the house of the cattle-owner, they perform the *chururito* dance-songs in either Kunza or Spanish for the llama or sheep (Mostny, Jeldes, González, and Oberhauser 1954: 92). The *chururito* are circular counterclockwise dance-songs performed by both men and women, with hand-clapping and guitar accompaniment. In some Atacameño villages, however, this ritual music is no longer practiced.

Ritual cleansing of irrigation ducts (*Limpia de canales*)

The *limpia de canales* is the most important Kunza ritual still performed in some highland villages (Grebe and Hidalgo 1988: 90–94). Its main activity, which consists of the ritual cleaning of pre-Hispanic irrigation ducts, is shared by the entire community. It proceeds from lower to higher ducts, ascending gradually until the birth of the waterfall is reached. In Socaire, there is a sacred site (*merendadero*) next to the sources of water, where the main secret ceremony takes place. There, the Atacameños burn aromatic plants (*koba* incense) and make symbolic offerings (*kajcher*) to the mountain, water, earth, and ancestor spirits, prepared in a bottle filled with *chicha de aloja*, with tied bags of ground cereals and llama fat (*tuftuka*), and with symbolic ornaments of flamingo feathers. Invoking first the mountain spirits, followed by the water, earth, and ancestors, the ritual leader (*cantal*) delineates a cross on the ground at the center of the shrine or *cobero*, where the *koba* incense is burning. While naming each of the mountains that provide irrigation water, the *kajcher* offerings of ground cereals, llama fat, and flamingo feathers are burnt over the cross, followed by the *chicha de aloja* with which a circle is made around the cross. These offerings are a payment to the mountain, water, and earth spirits for the irrigation received that promoted fertility, and to the pre-Hispanic ancestors who built the irrigation ducts.

The concluding phase of the ritual calls for the performance of the *talatur* dance-songs near the source of the waterfalls. The *talatur* includes circular counterclockwise dance-songs with tap-dancing, accompanied by three indigenous instruments. These are the *clarín,* a long side-blown natural trumpet similar to the *erke* of Argentina; the *putu,* a natural horn related to the Aymara *pututo;* and the *chorromón,* an ancient metal bell with three male and three female bells, or two male and four female bells, identical to pre-Hispanic archaeological specimens (Grebe 1974a: 19, fig. 12). The *talatur* song performed by the *cantal* "is believed to be the song of water." It can be heard near the waterfalls and it is learned from the water-spirit, Tata-Putarajni (Barthel 1959: 25–45; Grebe and Hidalgo 1988: 94). In fact, the natural sounds of the waterfalls produce harmonic overtones which, according to native beliefs, generate the song of the water-spirit and reappear in the human sounds of vocal and instrumental ritual melodies.

The archaic ritual music of the Atacameños, which survives mainly in these three rituals, is characterized by a solemn, epic, and pensive mode of performance. Its formal features are based on repetitions and transformations of a nuclear phrase, whereby the length of each piece depends on its poetic text, function, and context. Long renderings tend to prevail in ceremonial music. Some stylistic elements that recur include the use of tritonic melodies whose basic pitches correspond to a major triad, with a clear tonal center; collective performances in unison or heterophonic textures; simple and flexible rhythmic patterns based on additive meters regulated by prosodic accents; generally syllabic or slightly ornamented, "throaty," and—with some frequency—excessively high and loud vocal performances; and moderately slow, quiet, and stable tempo. Within this soundscape, the *clarín, chorromón,* and *putu* produce freely improvised accompaniments within the limits of their potential range. These indigenous instruments lend Acatameño music an archaic quality reinforced by the use of an extinct language (Kunza) in the *talatur* dance-songs of the ritual cleaning of irrigation ducts.

Due to the strong similarities between the archaic Atacameño style and that of other, less acculturated indigenous peoples, such as the Shuar of Ecuador and the Indians of the Argentinian Chaco, and taking into account practices of acculturated groups such as the Diaguita-Calchaquí of Argentina, it is generally assumed that the musical practices of the Atacameños reach back to pre-Hispanic times. There is little evidence to support the proposition that this style developed under the influence of the early military music of Spanish armies, as an imitation of trumpet fanfares (Álvarez and Grebe 1974: 42–45).

Borrowings from music of Hispanic origin surface in the use of strophic forms based on witty texts, rich in double meanings and wordplay; tonal or modal melodies of narrow range, and repetitive rhythms with refrains; solo songs with either guitar or ensemble accompaniments of guitars, harps, flutes, and *caja* (frame drum); faster tempos; and an extroverted, carefree mood. Performances of mestizo music among the Atacameño take place in rituals influenced by Hispanic traditions, such as carnival, patron saint celebrations, and other Catholic fiestas, whose music derives from genres brought by Spanish colonists or Catholic missionaries. On the other hand, the Atacameños have borrowed elements from the musical traditions of their Aymara neighbors. This resulted from frequent reciprocities and exchanges between the Atacameño and Aymara peoples, and from the frequent participation of Bolivian pilgrims and Chilean Aymara in major ceremonial events of the Atacameño—such as Ayquina—where their characteristic pentatonic melodies and syncopated rhythmic patterns are played on *cajas,* panpipes, *kenas,* and other Aymara aerophones.

The inextricable relationship between Atacameño music and its cultural context is represented in the coexistence or integration of bicultural components, in their indigenous instruments, and also in the symbolism of the myth of Tata-Putarajni, the spirit of water and water-music. During the ritual of *limpia de canales,* the *maestro* or master of the *talatur* teaches his disciple how to acquire knowledge of ritual music and dance reserved only for a few initiates. The master and his disciple perform the *convido* offerings dedicated to Tata-Putarajni. According to the testimony of an experienced *maestro,* master and disciple listen to "a water-melody which is not understood . . . . The master listens. And then he goes on singing the *talatur* melody. The water runs continuously. It is then heard how the water is singing the *talatur* (or *talando*). This occurs during the vespers of the ritual cleaning of irrigation ducts. Then, the water is noisy. It is not heard as a song but as a special noise. It is as if someone were singing *talatur* from afar" (Grebe and Hidalgo 1988: 94). The one who sings is Tata-Putarajni. Hence, the song of water, a triphonic melody born from and within nature, is musical discourse engendered by myth. This symbolic conception of the origin of music is closely related to the Aymara myth of Sereno, the water-music spirit of the Andean highlands (Grebe 1980: 158–89; 1981: 69–73).

Andean symbolism surfaces in Atacameño musical instruments. The *chorromón* is a pre-Hispanic bell (Grebe 1974a: 23–25), formerly composed of twelve or eight bells grouped in male-female pairs, but now more often composed of six. These consist of two low-pitched male bells, and four high-pitched female bells. Even numbers carry positive connotations in the Andean area, and the pairs of bells represent the human couple, the basic Andean social unit. In the *talatur*, symbolic dualism also is found in the male *clarín* trumpet (*tatai clarín-clarín*) and the female *putu* horn (*mamai putu-putu*), which lead the men's and women's performances, respectively. This musical dualism corresponds to the symbolism that pervades Andean cultures and is built into musical practices by the enactment of the principles of duality, symmetrical relationships, and sexual differentiation.

MAPUCHE MUSIC

The Mapuche, the largest indigenous society living in Chilean territory and the carriers of one of the most vigorous native cultures on the American continent, have maintained their traditions in spite of distinctive regional variants and interaction with non-Mapuche populations. Four-hundred years of war against the Spanish and, later, the Chileans—from the sixteenth to the end of the nineteenth century—have contributed to their sociocultural continuity and to the preservation of Mapuche ethnicity.

Mapuche means "people of the land" and the term is used—properly or improperly—as a synonym for *araucano* (Araucanian). At the present time, the Mapuche's extensive geographical domain covers segments of three Chilean regions, from the Bio-Bio River to the Chiloé archipelago. The Mapuche categorize themselves into four regional groups: Pewenches (people of the East), who live in the area of the *araucaria* pinetree, in the Andean mountain slopes; Williches (people of the South), who live south of the Toltén River from Valdivia to Chiloé; Lafkenches (people of the West), who live in the coastal areas; and Pikunches (people of the North) who, in the past, had settled north of the Bio-Bio River. All these groups share an ancestral culture and their own Mapu-dungu language. The Pikunches became extinct due to the impact of conquest and colonization, and the Williches have been absorbed by the southern mestizo population (Faron 1956: 435). In the 1990s, the Mapuche areas most densely populated are in Cautín and Malleco, followed by the Neuquén area of Argentina. In both countries, Mapuche peoples characteristically share a subsistence economy based on agriculture and herding, supplemented with handicrafts. They excel in weaving, pottery, and wood- and stone-carving. They are also skilled silversmiths. Extended family households are patrilineal/patrilocal residential units in dispersed hamlets—each usually consisting of a single lineage—located near the fields. Since 1867, changes in the reservation system have reshaped land tenure, but residential rules tend to be preserved.

The complex belief system and ritual practice of Mapuche religion have been kept partially hidden, well preserved, and integrated into a dualistic cosmology. The main carrier of these traditions is the shaman or *machi*, who performs several ritual roles: religious, healing, divinatory, and artistic (music, poetry, dance, and drama). The *machi* is the mediator between humans and the supernatural forces that regulate life, welfare, destiny, health, and the survival of human beings. Mapuche beliefs and worldview are enacted and communally shared in the powerful recitations and songs of the *machi*. The fact that ritual music communicates and enacts their system of beliefs has contributed effectively to cultural survival, and to the strong sense of ethnicity and social integration of the Mapuche peoples.

Mapuche worldview is enacted in specific ritual songs and mythical recitations. These describe how the cosmos was vertically conceived as an orderly and stratified whole divided into seven square worlds or platforms (of equal size) superposed in space, and how the latter represent either good or evil supernatural or natural domains, dwelling places of interacting gods, spirits, and humans. An ancient Mapuche cosmogonic myth tells us that these worlds were created in descending order, taking as a model the creator's highest platform. They are *wenu-mapu*, the highest four good supernatural worlds inhabited by gods, spirits, deceased shamans, caciques, and ancestors, where divine music is generated and performed. *Rangiñ-wenu* is the middle-high evil supernatural world inhabited by evil spirits (*weküfe*). *Mapu* (earth or land) is a natural world—good and evil—inhabited by humans, where human music is performed and shaman's songs and recitations connect the natural and supernatural domains. *Minche-mapu*, the lowest supernatural underworld, is inhabited by dwarf-like evil spirits (*laftrache*) (Grebe, Pacheco, and Segura 1972).

The *rewe* or symbolic sacred space of the shaman represents these superposed worlds or cosmic platforms in the shape of a ladder with either seven or four steps. Commonly, the *rewe* of seven steps is anthropomorphic, with the carved head of a god on its highest step. Hence the *rewe* is an icon, a concrete polysemic symbol of the cosmos: a shrine, a ladder, a cosmic tree, a god, a ritual center, and a micro-semantic space in which the shaman's music and dance are performed.

The horizontal shape assigned to each of these worlds or cosmic platforms is squared and oriented according to the four cardinal points, taking the East (the site of sunrise and of the Andes) as a focal point. The penultimate lower world or cosmic platform (*mapu*) represents the native land, "the land of the four corners," whose center is the Mapuche's own lineage and reservation. Good or evil connotations are assigned to each of the cardinal points: East is the best; South is good; North is less than good, or bad; and West is the worst. In ritual performances, these conceptions of space are symbolically enacted in the selection or rejection of spatial orientations and locations of musicians and dancers. Repeated circular counterclockwise movements starting from the East organize specific kinds of ritual music and dance performances that represent symbolically the traditional conception of time governed by the sun's counterclockwise circular movements starting from sunrise (Grebe 1987: 61–67).

If the *rewe* is an icon that symbolically represents the vertical conception of the Mapuche cosmos, the *kultrún* (shaman's drum) is a related icon that depicts the horizontal conception of cosmic space; indeed, the *kultrún* is a symbolic microcosmos (Grebe 1973: 24–28). Worldview is clearly projected in the *kultrún*'s morphology and decoration. The design on its skin represents the supernatural world and its diverse immaterial components; the wood vessel and the small objects introduced inside its hollow body represent the natural world and its various material components. Thus, the skin's design depicts the four divisions of the square earth or cosmic platforms according to the cardinal points. Its wood vessel, carved out of a sacred laurel tree, symbolizes the cosmic tree, whose icon is the *rewe*. This cosmic tree has the power to propel its owner into the high worlds during trance. The various small objects introduced into the drum's cavity represent not only the shaman's power, healing capacities, and good fortune, but also the abundance of food supplies, such as animals, domestic fowls, and cereals, stressing the strong meaning that fertility carries in Mapuche culture.

The *kultrún* represents not only a dynamic synthesis of the universe, which embodies both cosmic and earthly, immaterial and material components, but also her owner, the *machi*. This occurs during the ceremonial construction of the instrument, when the *machi*'s voice is symbolically introduced into the drum. From that moment onward there is a complete identification between the *machi* and her instrument. The *kultrún* becomes the vessel and symbol of her own voice and spiritual powers.

Embedded in the *kultrún* and its performance is the symbolic number four, which represents both the four beneficial platforms of the supernatural domain and the "land of the four corners" of Mapuche worldview, divided according to the cardinal points. As an ubiquitous positive symbol, the number four reappears in cosmological, mythical, ritual, medical, and musical structures as well as in their parts and fragments, groupings and divisions, number of participants, and objects. In the context of Mapuche numerical symbolism, even and odd numbers represent and embody positive and negative cosmic powers, whose meanings may be understood in the context of the dualism that pervades Mapuche culture.

In the dual conception of the Mapuche's complex cosmology, both nature and the supernatural—with their various phenomena and constituent elements—are symbolically related in terms of the opposition of good and evil: cosmic and earthly regions, temporal and spatial orders, cardinal points, numbers, colors, stars, planets, and so on (Grebe, Pacheco, and Segura 1972: 83). Ritual performances involving music and dance are inextricably bound to this cosmological order.

Worldview, myth, and beliefs provide a point of entry into the meaning of performances and into the cognitive framework of indigenous conceptions of time, space, movement, number, and color.

Within this framework, *tayil* is a special category related to the domain beyond the human and the earthly in which "spiritual" music is to be found. As such, *tayil* contrasts with the "human" music of the Mapuche and thus it is excluded from the native musicians' shared knowledge of traditions. The performance of *tayil* is a complex and unique sensory experience for both the performer and the listeners. It is a process of communication between entities from two different cosmic strata: *wenu-mapu*, the four highest beneficial platforms of the Mapuche gods, and *mapu*, the earth. Ritual actors believe that *tayil* is a song that attracts the divine auxiliary eagle-spirit (*ñamku*) to the earth. The performance of the song calls this eagle-spirit, which descends upon the center of the ritual field and returns to *wenu-mapu* when the performance is finished (Grebe 1989: 69–85).

Tayil is a powerful ritual song and means of communication generated by the gods and given only to a few chosen human beings. These include all shamans and some non-shamans, both men and women, who excel in musicality and/or have kinship ties with deceased shamans and *tayiltufes* (performers of *tayil*). The power of *tayil* rests in its capacity to attract the auxiliary eagle-spirit to the human domain by creating the necessary conditions to compel its descent. A communication cycle is developed between the divine and the human *tayil* performer, and between him/her and the ritual community. The *tayil* accompanies not only the shaman's trance but also the ostrich-dance (*choike-purrún*) in their respective ritual contexts. It reproduces and reenacts on earth the "divine music" performed by the gods, which belongs to the time of mythic origins. The Mapuche believe that these gods practice their own rituals in the *wenu-mapu*, singing their *tayil* in the supernatural domains. *Tayil* is an expression of sacred time that implies a concentrated and intense perception of ritual time and space, constituting a transcendent experience for the ritual actors and their respective congregations. (See also Carol E. Robertson, "Fertility Ritual," in this volume.)

Although there is no generic term for music in the Mapuche language (Mapu-dungu), the term *ül*, which means both song and poetry, replaces it (Augusta 1916 in 1966: 290): *ülkantún* is the act of singing, and *ülkantufe* the one who sings. Almost all kinds of

Mapuche music are sung, including dance music with instrumental accompaniment. In fact, Mapuche musicians use the term *ülkantún* as a general category that embraces all kinds of music. There are two broad kinds of *ülkantún*: "divine" and "human." The former is represented by *tayil*, the latter by sacred (ritual) and secular genres of earthly origin. Further distinctions are made between *kuifi-ülkantún* (ancient traditional music) and *we-ülkantún* (new or present-day music, including acculturated types), and between *wentru-ülkantún* (men's music) and *domo-ülkantún* (women's music).

The basic Mapuche taxonomy divides "human" music (*ülkantún*) into a basic dichotomy: *machi-ülkantún* (ritual music), which encompasses almost every kind of ritual music, including dance-music; and *mapuche-ülkantún* (secular music), which comprises unaccompanied solo songs performed at social events to communicate feelings and ideas. Ritual music is regarded as older, fixed, more important, and powerful. Secular music is said to be of more recent origin, less important, free, and for entertainment. Ritual music is categorized according to the specific ritual function and performed only for religious, medical, and/or communal purposes. Secular performances currently take place at semiformal, informal, or casual social events. Both categories continued to be retained vigorously as important means of communication and interaction in the lives of Mapuche peoples. Ritual and secular musics share an extemporized musical and poetic rendering, based on preexisting traditional patterns that are adapted, transformed, and recreated according to the performance mood, local style, and context of the specific musical event. The good singer is also a poet who must create in his/her song an intimate integration and correspondence between a melody (*ngëñum* or *wënën*) and its oral poetry (*dungun*) (Augusta 1910 in 1934: 269–70; 1916 in 1966: 33). In the same manner, the lexeme *purrún* denotes choreography and dance-music as an integrated whole.

It is difficult to draw a full taxonomy of present-day Mapuche music due to its complexity and regional diversity. Musicians and ritual actors agree, however, on the general division of "human" music into ritual and secular. The category of ritual music and dance (*machi-ülkantún*) is itself divided into four main groups, according to function: communal rituals, initiation, healing, and communication ceremonies. Communal rituals include the *ngillatún* or fertility ritual songs and dance-music, and the shaman's funeral songs and dance music (*machi-elwün*). Initiation rituals comprise the shaman's new (*machilwün*) and post-initiation songs and dance-music (*ngeikurrewén*). Healing includes simple therapeutic songs for curing mild or acute diseases (*ülutún*); complex ritual songs, dance, and trance-music for severe or chronic diseases (*datun*); and diagnostic songs and trance-music for recognition of the disease through a divination process (*pewutún*). In the fourth ritual category, the shaman communicates with her auxiliary spirits and with the deceased master-shaman's spirits through *pillantún* and *pichi-pillantún* ritual songs.

Under the general category of secular "human" music (*mapuche-ülkantún*) are unaccompanied songs performed at intimate social gatherings of family and friends, and only occasionally at communal events. These can be considered according to their function, namely narratives, lyrical songs, work songs, drinking songs, and lullabies. Narrative songs are among the favorites at social gatherings, as they recount travels (*amual-ülkantún*), recall lineage or family ancestors (*cheski-ülkantún*), and evoke historical times (*ayakán-ülkantún*). Lyrical songs create a means of social interaction and can express love (*ayüwün-ülkantún*), nostalgia (*uñotuam-ülkantún*), welcome (*ngen-ruka-ülkantún*), joy (*ayüwkli-piuke-ülkantún*), sadness (*weñankën-ülkantún*), and wedlock (*mafún-ülkantún*). Although work songs are less frequently performed, these can accompany work-searching (*këdau-ülkantún*), communal work (*minkako-ülkantún*), hut-building (*rukán-ülkantún*), sowing (*nganën-ülkantún*), wheat or maize grinding (*kudi-ülkantún*), spinning (*kulio-ülkantún*), and weaving (*ngërrewe-ülkantún*). Drinking songs are commonly performed by men and are sung while drinking wine or chicha (*pütún-ülkantún*), and while drinking in bars (*pütu-peyüm-ülkantún*). There are three native types of lullabies, and these are mainly sung by women: *pichiche-ülkantún*, *ngëmautungé-pichiche*, and *kupül-pëñeñém*.

Mapuche peoples assign positive powers to ritual music. Stemming from the supernatural domain of *wenu-mapu*, this power is embodied in the shaman, who mediates between the mythical and human realms. The shaman's powerful mediation through song is essential to restore health and to attract the gods' and spirits' attention toward humans' requests. Ritual music is both transcendent and a vehicle for social and cultural communication.

Secular music, on the other hand, is taken more lightly. It is a pastime that stimulates emotional responses expressed in laughter, smiles, and even tears. These songs also provide an important emotional outlet for the male or female singer and encourage social interaction. As a means of communication at public gatherings, assembly songs are performed by those "who take advantage of these occasions to release emotion or to call general attention to some matter of personal concern to the singer"; the moods of these assembly songs "may vary from naïve and joyful to slanderous, bitter, or ironic" (Titiev 1949: 2).

In both repertoires, song texts provide guidelines for musical form, style, and expression. These improvised texts create an elaborately figurative poetic discourse that employs metaphoric wordings based on the prosodic speech-rhythms and metric patterns of the Mapuche language (Grebe 1986b: 47–66). Dance patterns also regulate the musical features of their instrumental accompaniments.

Although Mapuche ritual and secular musics are clearly differentiated in style and structure, they have common features. Improvisation prevails, based on short melodic patterns repeated and developed in a chain of subtle variations. These patterns differ according to personal singing styles and regional features. Symbolic dualism is pervasive in the divisions and subdivisions into two or four units and their multiples that predominate in overall formal designs and structural details. Recurrent melodic contours tend to rest on low tonal centers. There are three main scale-types: a pentatonic scale with tritonic, tetratonic, and hexatonic derivations; a tritonic scale whose main pitches correspond to a major triad; and a scale based mainly on regular or irregular sequences of thirds (Augusta 1911: 687–98; Grebe 1974b: 66–73; González 1986: 247). Rhythmic and metric groupings are determined either by poetic texts or by dance patterns. Frequent portamentos and glissandos embellish the melodic line.

Ritual music is distinguished by its strong emphasis on twofold repetitions of musical phrases, text, and larger ritual units. Most rituals are performed at dusk and repeated at dawn, each time with four basic sections and/or songs. Fixed melodic and rhythmic patterns tend to predominate, although sometimes a fixed accompaniment serves as background to a free vocal melody. Regular tempo is punctuated by strong dynamic accents. A solemn, dignified expression characterizes ritual style, which has various features in common with other indigenous cultures of North and South America. Therapeutic ritual music is accompanied by the *kultrún*, to which a bell-rattle (*kaskawilla*) and a gourd-rattle (*wada*) may be added. Other shamanistic ensembles may include *kultrún*, *trutrukas* (long vertical natural trumpets), *pifülkas* (vertical flutes without finger holes), and *nolkiñ* (short vertical natural trumpets) among other instruments (Grebe 1973: 23–25; González 1986: 4–52). (For musical traditions of the Mapuche in Argentine territory, see Irma Ruiz, "Musical Culture of Indigenous Societies in Argentina"; and Carol E. Robertson, "Fertility Ritual," in this volume.)

As ritual art, music and poetry, dance, and drama are univocal expressions inextricably bound to cosmology, myth, and native medicine. Through their rich web of symbolic expressions, Mapuche peoples project a dualistic conception of the cosmos that operates throughout the field of music, both sacred and secular (Grebe 1974b: 53–75).

KAWÉSKAR MUSIC

The Kawéskar, with the Yámana and the now-extinct Selk'nam, are the main hunting and gathering societies of the southernmost regions of South America. On the basis of extant archaeological records, it is assumed that they arrived approximately 11,000 years B.C.E. (Massone 1987: 8–9; 1989: 129–30). Along with the Patagonian Tehuelche and Hausch of Argentina, they seem to belong to the most ancient indigenous groups that populated America.

The Kawéskar and Yámana were canoe nomads, mainly shellfish gatherers, fishermen, and sea-hunters who inhabited the rainy forests of the Pacific channels and archipelagos. The Selk'nam were pedestrian nomads, hunters and gatherers who wandered throughout the continental eastern steppes and forests of the southernmost regions, including the meridional Patagonian steppe as well as the northern and southern areas of Tierra del Fuego. There is evidence of a close cultural relationship between the Kawéskar and Yámana, found in their respective somatic features and in their material and immaterial cultures, and reinforced by cultural contacts between these groups. Differences are to be found in their respective languages.

The peoples of these three Fuegian societies lived in scattered and small family clusters, which joined larger congregations for specific communal rituals of their ethnic groups (Steward and Faron 1959: 383, 397, 405). Kinship ties and patrilineal-patrilocal groups connected by marriage alliances reinforced family integration. The exogamic band had imprecise boundaries, and the nuclear family was the most consistent primary group. Seasonal transhumance and nomadic behavioral patterns provided the essential resources for a family subsistence economy. Differences of age and gender were the main factors of labor division: men's hunting and fishing, and women's gathering were the basic, complementary activities. Low productive output resulted from their nomadic subsistence economy and a peculiar interaction with nature and the supernatural. A simple and rudimentary material culture was based on the need to carry only a few essential objects.

The coastal area of the Pacific that the Kawéskar and Yámana inhabited is one of the most inhospitable environments on earth. It is an irregular area covered with ice and snow, continually exposed to storms, winds, low temperatures, and insufficient sun. Despite their rudimentary technology, they had complex ideational and religious systems that provided a broad set of explanations about the natural and supernatural worlds.

The Kawéskar canoe nomads wandered throughout the Pacific channels and fjords in search of large shell-fish banks, sea mammals, wild birds, fish, and wild fruits for gathering, hunting, and fishing. Whenever a whale was stranded on a beach, nuclear families gathered and performed communal rituals, thereby renewing their social interaction. The same applies to their artistic expressions—song, dance, oral literature, and visual arts—which were to be found more frequently in the context of myth and ritual.

Since the 1930s, cultural contact with Chilean sea-wolf and otter hunters and sailors has generated various cultural borrowings that have modified some of the basic Kawéskar ideational and behavioral patterns. Various components of their material culture have been replaced, with overt changes in clothing and utensils. Critical changes in nutritional patterns and value system have contributed to the decay of both health and moral standards. According to José Aylwin, the Kawéskar global population consisted of 101 acculturated persons in 1995. Only 12 have remained in their original settlement in Puerto Edén; 64 have migrated to the southern city of Punta Arenas; and the remaining 25 are scattered throughout different locations in southern Chile.

Among the latter, two have settled in the capital city of Santiago. Kawéskar music has been seriously affected by this acculturation process reaching all aspects of Kawéskar society.

Fuegian music survives mostly in ethnological sound recordings. These include C. Wellington Furlong's cylinders on the Yámana and Selk'nam (1907–1908); Martin Gusinde's and Wilhelm Koppers' cylinders on the Yámana, Kawéskar, and Selk'nam (1923–1924); Carleton S. Coons and Alberto Medina's recordings of the Kawéskar (1959); Rodolfo Casamiquela's on the Selk'nam (ca. 1966); Grebe's field recordings of the Kawéskar (1971) (see Grebe 1974c: 81–82); and Anne Chapman's two recordings of the Selk'nam of Tierra del Fuego (1972 and 1977). Musical transcriptions are included in the work of Gusinde (1931–1939), Hornbostel (1936 and 1948), Emperaire (1963), and Grebe (1974c). These documents reveal close links between Kawéskar and Yámana musics, as well as points of convergence and divergence between them and the music of the Selk'nam. On the whole, Fuegian musics share overt affinities in various constituent elements of their musical discourse.

Early reports indicate the coexistence of two distinct Kawéskar musical repertoires: the now-extinct religious music, which included initiation and funeral ritual music, and the surviving secular music, mainly related to daily activities and the expression of emotional experiences. The types of songs related to work, leisure, and emotional expression include zoomorphic mimetism in songs on sea-wolfs and sea-ducks, characterized by onomatopoeic descriptions of animal movements and other distinctive features; expressive songs on love, and lullabies; and children's play-songs, which describe and/or represent ideas, movements, or activities relevant to the enculturation process. Other themes refer to the relationship between humans and nature, hunting and gathering activities, and other aspects of Kawéskar life.

Kawéskar songs are characterized by the use of nonsensical syllables, a relevant feature of Fuegian sung poetry, and by the absence of instrumental accompaniment. Although musical instruments seem to be extinct, reports indicate the past existence of idiophones and aerophones such as percussion sticks, shell-rattles, shaken fur-mantles, and bone flutes (Hornbostel 1936: 365–66; 1948: 88–89).

Musical structures are dependent on speech-forms. They are constructed on the principle of continuous metamorphosis of a melodic nuclear unit or cell whose juxtapositions generate a musical mosaic. Two ancient formal categories coexist: short song (canto corto) and long song (canto largo), both of which are either of minimal or brief length. Shared song-types provide musical frameworks that generate clusters of individual variants created by each performer.

What we may label as a monotonic recitation is categorized as canto or song by the Kawéskar: a recitation based on a single melodic axis surrounded by adjacent indeterminate pitches is considered a song. We may assume that the natives' aural experience allows the perception and discrimination of microtonal components that are neglected by Western aural training and its tempered system. Kawéskar tonal organization involves sequences based on oscillations and fluctuating intonation within the framework of a non-tempered musical system; melodies of one to five pitches with a clear tonal axis organized within a very narrow range; and conjunct microtonal intervals, seconds, and minor thirds. Melodic movement is organized in centripetal trajectories, with small ascending and descending movements around the axis, which occasionally may be transferred to an adjacent pitch. Variety is created by subtle changes in performance practice.

The free prosodic rhythm of Kawéskar song is generated by speech patterns. The text also generates metrical patterns, which are irregular and additive. Iambic and trochaic meters are employed in alternation, inversion, or in various combinations. Tempos are moderate and maintained throughout.

Kawéskar songs are characterized by a lack of gradual dynamics, with prevailingly soft or moderate loudness maintained throughout a performance. In spite of an overt contrast with the emphatic, accented, and intense style of the Selk'nam, the Kawéskar style preserves a few typical dynamic accents derived from linguistic prosody. These accents are focal points of the melodic patterns. The most remarkable feature of Kawéskar articulation is produced by the glottal-stop, a typical linguistic trait. It consists of a sudden stop within the articulation of certain words or syllables that produces a small silence interpolated within the corresponding melodic pattern. Vocal timbre is relaxed, with some nasality and a tone quality that could be qualified as guttural. Expressive devices include interpolations of speech, laughter, and expiration/aspiration.

The intense process of cultural change that has brought about a disintegration and near-extinction of Kawéskar society also is reflected in a parallel process of musical acculturation (Grebe 1974c: 96–107). Since the 1930s, the Kawéskar rituals declined, becoming extinct after 1950. As a consequence, a large and complex corpus of religious practices, including initiation, funeral, and shamanistic rites, have been lost. The hunting of wild animals gradually diminished due to the significant decrease of the original fauna and to the competitive activities of Chilean sea-wolf and otter hunters. As hunting and gathering have been replaced by household handicrafts among the Kawéskar, a variety of zoomorphic mimetic songs have lost their function and disappeared. Only three are still remembered and sung by a few elder members of the Kawéskar community: the songs of the fine sea-wolf, the bully sea-wolf, and the sea-duck. Although children's games and play-songs were favorite activities, today they are recalled only by a few adults as a remembrance of their childhood. Only three kinds of game-songs were performed: playing round, the swing, and making fire. The Kawéskar state that the main contributing factors have been the learning of new Chilean children's games and game-songs at the local school, and the lack of adequate playground space in the Kawéskar reservation of Puerto Edén. Other obvious causes are the loss of the native language and ethnic identification by younger generations due to efficient enculturation.

In the past, songs frequently were performed during men's activities while fully interacting with nature. These have been replaced by indoor cottage industries and the manufacture of handicrafts, where love-songs and lullabies currently are sung. Although in earlier times songs were performed at social gatherings, solo songs now are performed in solitude. This change may be explained by a lack of social integration, by adaptation to the new environmental conditions, and by fear of discrimination and criticism from those who neglect the Kawéskar's native traditions and language.

The chain of musical testimonies of oral tradition is practically broken. This coincides with a crisis of ethnic identity that affects the younger generations. Formal education in elementary schools stresses the patterns of national culture and neglects native traditions. Radio programs also disregard native culture. Singing in Kawéskar has become a rare and solitary activity of adults for whom tradition is a nostalgic meditation and a melancholic experience. The singers avoid facial expressions and bodily movements, projecting a visible lack of energy and vitality.

Temporal organization shows a shift toward metric regularity or symmetry, which appears to indicate musical acculturation. In those cases, a song becomes rather mechanical and static, weak in its power of expression. Absolute metric regularity, however, is absent from older songs. Another relevant feature is tempo. Metronomic measurements of the oldest musical samples recorded by Gusinde (1923–1924) and transcribed by Hornbostel (1948: 100–1) indicate that their average (MM = 71) was slower than the average (MM = 77) samples of Coons and Medina (1959), transcribed by Grebe (1974c); Grebe's own field recordings of 1971 and their corresponding transcriptions (Grebe 1974c) show a further increase in average tempo (MM = 90). This factor provides reliable evidence of musical change. From it we can infer that the Kawéskar's perception of time has speeded up, as a consequence of their gradual adaptation to the different conception of time that prevails in their present environments.

Dynamics and articulation show an abandonment of strong emphatic accents. If the repertoires recorded by Coons and Medina (1959) are compared with Grebe's (1971), one can appreciate the richer articulation of the former and the loss of articulation complexity and glottal-stop frequency in the latter. Timbre and special interpretative devices indicate that old Kawéskar vocal music was characterized by more vocal tension expressed in emphasis, pathetic feeling, imposing character, solemnity, dignity, and austere harshness. In later vocal music, these attributes are either absent or have been considerably weakened.

Earlier Kawéskar music was related to dance, pantomime, and mimicry, conveying a now-lost expressive vigor; later music retains only its relation to the Kawéskar language and its patterns of speech. Song style has changed, communicating a feeling of solitude, meditation, nostalgia, and melancholy. These musical performances are the sounds of a culture verging on extinction.

REFERENCES

Álvarez, Cristina, and María Ester Grebe 1974. "La trifonía atacameña y sus perspectivas interculturales," *Revista musical chilena* 28/126–127: 21–45.

Augusta, Félix José de 1910 in 1934. *Lecturas araucanas.* Padre Las Casas: Imprenta Editorial "San Francisco."

   1911. "Zehn Araukanerlieder," *Anthropos* 6: 684–98.

   1916 in 1966. *Diccionario araucano.* Padre Las Casas: Imprenta Editorial "San Francisco."

Barthel, Thomas S. 1959. "Ein Frühlingsfest der Atacameños," *Zeitschrift für ethnologie* 84: 24–45.

Eliade, Mircea 1967. "Observaciones metodológicas sobre el estudio del simbolismo religioso," *Metodología de la historia de la religiones* by Mircea Eliade and J. M. Kitagawa. Buenos Aires: Editorial Paidós, 116–39.

Emperaire, Joseph 1963. *Nómades del mar.* Santiago: Universidad de Chile.

Faron, Louis C. 1956. "Araucanian patri-organization and the Omaha system," *American anthropologist* 58/3: 435–56.

González, Ernesto 1986. "Vigencias de instrumentos musicales mapuches," *Revista musical chilena* 40/166: 4–52.

Grebe, María Ester 1973. "El kultrún mapuche: Un microcosmo simbólico," *Revista musical chilena* 27/123–124: 3–42.

   1974a. "Instrumentos musicales precolombinos de Chile," *Revista musical chilena* 28/128: 5–55.

   1974b. "Presencia del dualismo en la cultura y música mapuche," *Revista musical chilena* 28/126–127: 47–79.

   1974c. "La música alacalufe: Aculturación y cambio estilístico," *Revista musical chilena* 28/126–127: 80–111.

   1978. "Relationships between musical practice and cultural context: The kultrún and its symbolism," *The world of music* 20/3: 84–100.

   1980. *Generative models, symbolic structures, and acculturation in the panpipe music of the Aymara of Tarapacá, Chile* (PhD diss., Anthropology: The Queen's University of Belfast).

   1981. "Cosmovisión aymara," *Revista de Santiago* (Museo Nacional Vicuña Mackenna, Santiago de Chile) 1: 61–79.

   1986a. "Cambio sociocultural y bilingüismo Aymara-Español en Isluga," *Lenguas modernas* (Santiago de Chile) 13: 37–53.

   1986b. "El discurso chamánico mapuche: Consideraciones antropológicas preliminares," *Actas de lengua y literatura Mapuche* (Universidad de La Frontera, Temuco, Chile) 2: 47–66.

   1987. "La concepción del tiempo en la cultura mapuche," *Revista chilena de antropología* 6: 59–74.

   1989. "El tayil mapuche, como categoría conceptual y medio de comunicación trascendente," *Inter-American music review* 10: 69–75.

Grebe, María Ester, Sergio Pacheco, and José Segura 1972. "Cosmovisión mapuche," *Cuadernos de la realidad nacional* (Santiago de Chile) 14: 46–73.

Grebe, María Ester, and Blas Hidalgo 1988. "Simbolismo atacameño: Un aporte etnológico a la comprensión de significados culturales," *Revista chilena de antropología* 7: 75–97.

Gusinde, Martin 1931–1939. *Die Feuerland-Indianer.* Mödling: Verlag Anthropos, 3 vols. Volume I, *Die Selk'Nam,* translated and with commentary by Johannes Wilbert as *Folk literature of the Selknam Indians.* Los Angeles: UCLA Latin American Center, 1975 (Latin American Studies Series, vol. 32).

Hornbostel, Erich M. von 1936. "Fuegian Songs," *American anthropologist,* new series, 38/3 (July–September): 357–67; enlarged as "The music of the Fuegians," *Ethnos* 13/3–4 (1948): 62–102.

Isamitt, Carlos 1935. "Un instrumento araucano: La trutruka," *Boletín latinoamericano de música* (Montevideo) 1: 43–46.

   1937. "Cuatro instrumentos musicales araucanos," *Boletín latinoamericano de música* (Montevideo) 3: 55–66.

   1938. "Los instrumentos araucanos," *Boletín latinoamericano de música* (Montevideo) 4: 305–12.

Isbell, Billie Jean 1978. *To defend ourselves: Ecology and ritual in an Andean village.* Austin: Institute of Latin American Studies, University of Texas at Austin. Repr. ed. (Prospect Heights, Illinois: Waveland Press, 1985).

Massone, Mauricio 1987. "Las culturas aborígenes de Chile en el tiempo," *Hombres del sur.* Santiago: Museo Chileno de Arte Precolombino, 11–46.

   1989. "Historia de la ocupación indígena en el area septentrional de Tierra del Fuego," *Actas del II Congreso de Historia de Magallanes y III Congreso Regional de Chile.* Punta Arenas: Universidad de Magallanes, 129–30.

Mostny, Grete, Fidel Jeldes, Raúl González, and Fernando Oberhauser 1954. *Peine, un pueblo atacameño.* Santiago: Universidad de Chile, Facultad de Filosofía, Instituto de Geografía.

Oyarce, Ana María, and Ernesto González 1986. "Kallfulikán, un canto mapuche: Descripción etnográfica, análisis musical y sus correspondencias con el aspecto literario," *Lenguas modernas* (Universidad de Chile, Santiago, Chile) 2: 245–63.

Picón-Salas, Mariano 1966. *A cultural history of Spanish America.* Berkeley and Los Angeles: University of California Press.

Steward, Julian H., and Louis C. Faron 1959. *Native peoples of South America.* New York: McGraw-Hill.

Titiev, Mischa 1949. *Social singing among the Mapuche.* Ann Arbor: University of Michigan Press (Anthropological Papers, Museum of Anthropology, 2).

Tschopik, Harry Jr. 1946. "The Aymara" in *Handbook of South American Indians,* 7 vols., ed. by Julian H. Steward. Washington, D.C.: Smithsonian Institution, Bureau of American Ethnology, vol. 2, 501–73.

DISCOGRAPHY

C. Wellington Furlong 1907–1908. Recorded Edison cylinders of Selk'nam and Yámana songs, deposited in 1948 at the Library of Congress, Washington, D.C. Two of these songs are included in *The demonstration collection of Erich M. von Hornbostel and the Berlin Phonogramm-Archiv.* Ethnic Folkways Library, FE 4175.

Selk'nam chants of Tierra del Fuego, Argentina, compiled by Anne Chapman. Recordings of 48 shamanistic chants and laments. Ethnic Folkways FE 4176 (1972).

Grebe, María Ester 1974. For information about field recordings of Kawéskar, Yámana, and Selk'nam musics,* see Grebe, "La música alacalufe: Aculturación y cambio estilístico," *Revista musical chilena* 28/126–127: 81–83.

Amerindian music of Chile, compiled by Christos Clair-Vasiliadis, Rodrigo Medina, Adalberto Salas, and Mirka Stratigopoulou. Recordings of Aymara, Mapuche, and Kawéskar musics. Ethnic Folkways FE 4054 (1975).

Traditional music of Chile, compiled by Manuel Dannemann and Daniel Sheehy. It includes eight examples of Aymara music of Chile. ABC Command COMS-9003 (1975) [New Series Premiere Recording: Music of the Earth].

Selk'nam chants of Tierra del Fuego, Argentina, vol. 2, compiled by Anne Chapman. Ethnic Folkways FE 4179 (1977).

---

* On linguistic grounds, the indigenous group formerly called Alakaluf (Alacalufes) presently is called Kawéskar; the Yahgan now are called Yámana; and the Fuegian Ona presently are called Selk'nam.

Musical Culture of Indigenous Societies in Argentina

Irma Ruiz

The Mataco (Mataco proper or Wichí, Chorote and Chulupí or Nivaklé) and Guaycurú (Toba,
Pilagá, and Mocoví): Musical culture; Traditional beliefs and practices; Musical instruments;
The current situation of indigenous groups in the Chaco area—The Mapuche: Musical culture;
The current situation of Mapuche peoples—The Chiriguano-Chané: Traditional culture;
Musical instruments; The current situation of Chiriguano-Chané groups—The Mbyá:
Musical culture; The current situation of the Mbyá of Misiones—Conclusions

ARGENTINA'S INDIGENOUS POPULATION numbers approximately 350,000 persons, according to data gathered in 1976 by the Servicio Nacional de Asuntos Indígenas and the Asociación Indígena de la República Argentina (AIRA) (Hernández 1985: 62–63). Approximately half of these individuals still retain their native languages. Many of them preserved their cultural traditions until the 1950s, some even until the present day. This study is dedicated to all indigenous groups in Argentinian territory, with only brief mention of those that retained basic traits of their traditional practices only up to the first decades of the twentieth century.

We shall provide only an overview of the Northwest area because, although it is part of the ancient Andean culture, its strong and early cultural crossbreeding places it in a particular situation. This area comprises the provinces of Jujuy, Catamarca, La Rioja, Tucumán, and most of Salta and Santiago del Estero. Musical manifestations such as the reliance on tritonic and pentatonic pitch systems (the latter within a much smaller area in the North), are some of the indigenous residual strands lingering in this broad area, the only

one with a farming culture at the time of the Conquest and also the only one penetrated by the Inca empire. The tritonic system is still present in songs called *bagualas* or *coplas*, an old genre whose texts are based on traditional Spanish forms, and in religious instrumental music for *corneta* or *caña*, a very long transverse trumpet called *erke* in Peru. The pentatonic pitch system associated with the Inca is typical of the *siku*, a set of panpipes that must be played by a pair of musicians. Usually, many pairs form an ensemble or band. Several works by the Argentinian musicologists Carlos Vega and Isabel Aretz document this musical universe (Aretz 1946, 1952, and 1978; Vega 1946). Vega also carried out a systematization of mestizo musical expressions in the rural areas of this and other regions of the country (Vega 1944).

A panoramic view of indigenous societies from past to present shows, on the one hand, early transculturation processes in the Argentinian Northwest not devoid of fierce and bloody struggles, and the alienation of entire communities. On the other hand, it shows the virtual annihilation of aboriginal peoples in the Argentinian South, such as the Tehuelche of Patagonia and the Selk'nam of Tierra del Fuego. This dramatic decimation of Native American peoples in the South took place in areas conquered by white creole armies in the last decades of the nineteenth century, during the so-called "Conquest of the Desert" (1879–1880). For three centuries, the Mapuche—who influenced the northern Tehuelche—fought for their independence first in Chile and then in Argentina, demonstrating unusual warring skills by appropriating one of the enemy's most effective weapons: the horse. Even though they were eventually defeated, the Mapuche constitute today the only sizable indigenous group in southern Argentina (approximately 40,000 persons). The systematic slaughter of Indians and the diseases introduced by whites caused the near extinction of the Selk'nam (improperly called Ona), whose musical universe has been partially transmitted by only a scattered handful of descendants. Recordings of their music incontestably document a remote past, unique in its absence of Western influence (see Discography, Novati and Ruiz 1967; Chapman 1972 and 1977).

In the northeastern Chaco, a region less coveted by white settlers than southern Patagonia, the indigenous population was not annihilated but suffered many losses in armed conflicts resulting from their fierce opposition to the colonizing presence. "Resistance" is in fact the name of the capital city of the Chaco province. Comprising the provinces of Chaco and Formosa, the northeast of Santa Fe, and eastern stretches of Salta and Santiago del Estero, the Chaco area currently holds the highest density of indigenous groups (see Map). It is inhabited by the Mataco (about 32,000 individuals), Chorote (1,000), Toba (39,000), and Pilagá (3,000) communities, as well as individual Chulupí or Nivaklé (300), and Mocoví (9,000), all long-time dwellers. Furthermore, the area between the western Chaco and the Tucumán/Bolivian forest is home to Chiriguano communities (25,000 persons of Guaraní linguistic affiliation) who, in the sixteenth and seventeenth centuries, migrated there from the eastern jungles of Paraguay and areas further north. In particular, they moved into the Bolivian Chaco and, from that area, they reached Argentina. Attached to these groups and under their influence are also some 2,500 Chané persons linguistically affiliated with the Arawak.

The Argentinian Northeast, excluding the Chaco area, is a Guaraní zone. Until the expulsion of the Jesuits, decreed on February 27, 1767, this zone was part of the Jesuit Province of Paraguay and, even before that time, Guaraní groups had sailed down the Paraná River to approximately 30 kilometers from the capital city of Buenos Aires. Later on they were decimated by plagues, persecutions, and Portuguese traders from São Paulo who would hunt Indians to sell them as slaves. From the Guaraní linguistic group, the approximately 1,500 present-day Mbyá and Chiripá living in the province of Misiones came to Argentina from Paraguay in the last decades of the nineteenth century.

This brief historical sketch of indigenous settlements deliberately excludes areas where their presence is limited to a few and scattered families, as in the central provinces of Buenos Aires and La Pampa which are too rich in resources to allow more than small groups of descendants of the Mapuche. Present-day indigenous groups live mainly in borderline areas, where "civilization" has marginalized them; some wander about like pariahs, hoping the government will designate lands where they can settle permanently. With Argentina's return to democratic rule in 1983, several provinces such as Chaco, Formosa, Salta, Río Negro, and Misiones proposed legislation that addressed the critical situation of these indigenous groups. Vested interests, however, continue to block their implementation.

THE MATACO AND GUAYCURÚ

The Chaco, which is the area of maximum concentration of indigenous groups, is home to the Mataco or Mataco-Mataguayo (Mataco proper, Chorote and Chulupí) and Guaycurú (Toba, Pilagá, and Mocoví). The Mataco and the Toba are significantly more numerous. The Mataco have settled in western Chaco and the Guaycurú in the eastern part of the province, although small numbers of Mataco and Guaycurú are found in both areas. These are hunting-fishing-gathering groups with incipient horticulture who were considered typically Chaco dwellers in the 1930s because they were perceived as a partially homogeneous group. Subsequent ethnological studies, however, differentiated the Mataco as lower hunters, and the Guaycurú as higher or steppe-type hunters. While initial homogeneity cannot be assumed since substantial differences still can be identified (Cordeu and Siffredi 1971: 5–11), this differentiation probably

Map: Main indigenous settlements in Argentinian territory.

resulted from an impoverishment of the steppe-hunter layer and from inter-tribal transculturation, with some shared cultural traits.

In general, they have preserved their traditional economic base, gathering (wild fruits, tubers, and honey) and fishing by those who live along rivers. In several places, fishing is now a commercial activity. Prospects for hunting, especially big game, are increasingly slim, but they still hunt small land animals and birds. Sheep- and goat-raising, and increased horticultural activity (corn, watermelon, manioc, squash, soy, sweet potatoes, cotton), have brought about changes in their economy. Although most of these products are used for their subsistence, cotton is particularly important for the economy of the Toba. They mostly work as hired hands cultivating other people's lands, in lumberyards, on farms, and doing odd jobs (*changas*) in towns and cities. Matacos and Tobas regularly are hired to pick cotton and cut sugar cane. The cohabitation of culturally different groups in the large sugar plantations of Salta and Jujuy has been one of several factors contributing to transcultural processes affecting the traditions of these groups.

The missionary work of various Christian denominations, with their proverbial arrogance for "the truth" and their attendant scorn for traditional beliefs, has affected religious practices—to which music is closely linked—in a variety of ways. Some indigenous groups have stopped resisting conversion, others have completely abandoned their traditional beliefs, and some have created syncretic forms of worship in a desperate attempt to "recover a sense of belonging in the world" (Miller 1979), a feeling lost to the rigors of conquest and colonization. The process of substitution of traditional religious values, now under way for several decades, has significantly changed the musical patrimony of the Chaco's native peoples, especially in settlements dominated by Protestant sects whose missionaries prohibit singing not related to the adopted faith. Also forbidden were the traditional evening dances designed to encourage the meeting of prospective mates. In addition, some Protestant missionaries have forced those who own musical instruments to turn them over to the mission, thus symbolically renouncing their musical traditions and, consequently, their culture. Catholic missionaries, on the other hand, were characterized by excessive and pernicious paternalism, practicing a different form of indoctrination that circumvented the kind of repressive measures mentioned above. Even today, Catholic missions allow dancing and singing according to the traditional canon, although this only occurs in isolated groups. Catholic influence is minimal, while the outreach and relentless presence of the Protestant seed has yielded an abundant harvest. The Pentecostal faith has had the greatest impact, becoming a powerful factor of cultural change in the area.

One common goal pursued by both Catholics and Protestants was the eradication of shamanism, since in the person of the shaman were subsumed most of the spiritual powers of the religious structure (shared today with the minister) and the control over the population's health and well-being. For the missionaries, the shaman's leadership was the major obstacle to indoctrination. Other factors also reduced the shaman's power, such as a complex web of situations forced by the advance of white colonizers, and the indigenous peoples' need to redefine strategies in the face of new problems. Although weakened, the figure of the shaman has not disappeared altogether. This is the case even among the Toba, who are less attached to tradition than the Mataco. The different responses of these two groups in the face of subjugation became clear in the Toba's use of the horse in the seventeenth century, which significantly changed combat capacity and sphere of action as well as social structure. The Mataco never adopted the horse, although other Guaycurú groups did, including the Pilagá. Once whites had definitively conquered the area, the horse ceased to be a part of the indigenous cultural heritage.

Musical culture

Characterized by great intensity and considerable variability, indigenous musical practices in the Chaco area constitute the privileged language of communication between humans and deities. This ongoing dialogue with the sacred ensures preservation of the cosmic order, creates peace and balance with the natural environment, and secures the well-being of the individual and the community. In reference to the Toba, Elmer Miller notes that

> intimately related to direct communication between the individual and the spirits was the idea of power . . . and objects endowed with power, such as the gourd rattle. Besides the usual prayers and shamanistic activities, dance was another means of maintaining cosmic

harmony . . . . In addition to dance, music played a significant role in maintaining harmonious relationships with the natural order (1979: 46–47).

This general statement also can be applied to other indigenous groups.

The concept of power lies at the core of this cultural context, as it engenders the specific circumstances under which songs and certain musical instruments should be used to ensure optimum effectiveness. This also explains the existence of persons endowed with power, even beyond the shaman. Moreover, in the initiation rituals of indigenous peoples of the central Chaco, "acquiring song is decisive in obtaining power, and therefore assuming new status" (Ruiz 1978–79: 157). Although we agree with Miller on the importance of dance, it should be noted that the dancers always are singing: dancing and singing are univocal actions. With few exceptions that are part of the shaman's sphere of activity, dances are collective and gender specific, and songs invariably monophonic. Although under some circumstances the overlay of individual songs might produce a sonorous complex, there is no attempt to create polyphony or coordinate the monophonic songs engendering this multi-sonorous texture.

Another noteworthy characteristic of the musical life of these groups is that initiation rites—now extinct— provided pubescent youth with a point of entry into musical practices. The responsibility for teaching and transmitting the gender-specific musical traditions to the young rested on adult men and women.

Traditional instruments used in conjunction with song and dance, or only song, were in all the cases we observed used only to articulate the rhythmic pulses of the melody. This is the function of the sole membranophone, the water drum, and idiophones such as the gourd rattle and the *palo-sonajero de uñas*, a rattle made of hooves mounted on a stick which is stamped on the ground (Ruiz 1985).

Most of the traditional expressions of indigenous peoples of the Argentinian Chaco were limited to sacred ritual. Among the few exceptions were the nocturnal mating dances, a secular practice during which some measure of power also was summoned to achieve objectives. Another exception were lullabies, a genre we have documented only among the Toba.

Traditional beliefs and practices

The intensity and variability that characterize indigenous expressions in the Argentinian Chaco

underscore the different visions of the cosmos constructed by each of these groups. Although they share the belief in a world populated by animals conceived as animal/humans who control the cosmic whole or its parts, with multiple subdivisions that represent specific domains of power, they differ in their conception and classification of terrestrial, heavenly, aquatic, and sub-terrestrial space. Each of these elemental spaces is inhabited by a "Lord" who, in turn, rules over the "Owners," "Fathers," or "Mothers" that reside in each zone. These powerful beings are invoked in songs intended to summon supernatural intervention. More often than not, the narrative of ancient myths establishes the relationship between the mythic beings and the songs transmitted by them in mythic time.

Although the incidence of songs used for a single, specific purpose was high, we also found many instances in which the same song was utilized for a variety of purposes. The intention of the performance, depending on its purpose, also caused the song to be perceived differently. In addition, the perception of a given song changed when performed by different persons, given the importance assigned to vocal timbre and style of delivery.

A general distinction also can be made between shamanic and non-shamanic musical expressions, the latter being the domain of adult men and women who make up the communal group. Among the Chulupí or Nivaklé it also is possible to attain certain ranks of leadership without being a shaman.

The basic characteristics of shamanism as practiced among the Chaco indigenous groups replicate those of the Siberian model, as evidenced by the dual manner in which deities transmit knowledge about a specific realm of space, that is, through dreams or visions and through the empowered shaman. During the initiation period, the awakening to shamanic vocation among initiates was manifested by a constant intonation of songs. Those being initiated were isolated from social life, completed a lengthy period of fasting, and consummated their deaths as adepts by being reborn with a new status.

Through song and sometimes rhythmical shaking of the gourd rattle, the shaman, who performed many functions, controlled atmospheric phenomena, mediated for a plentiful hunt, and functioned most fundamentally as a healer. In traditional healing, still practiced occasionally, the shaman's repertoire of songs is varied and specific to the various diseases and situations. The concept of illness as "harm" caused by a hostile power, and—among some groups —as flight or kidnapping of the soul (or souls), requires action from the shaman to restore the sick person to health. Suction in the affected area and the restorative "magic flight" are the respective solutions. Only the Mataco danced to the curative singing. The Mataco also reinforced the power of healing by joining the action of several shamans, who danced and sang their individual songs simultaneously with the idiophonic support of jingle-like rattles. The shaman's capacity to sing independently from others during this joint performance displayed an extraordinary ability to sustain auditory self-reliance, an aptitude nurtured by the tradition of individual ownership of song.

The "magic flight," brought about by the shaman and his attendant spirits, assumed a series of actions and struggles with adverse, powerful entities. The Chorote shaman, for instance, performed seven songs to heal the ailing soul. The first three songs marked the journey on his mythical horse into the space where his attendants had discovered the diseased soul. The fourth song enabled the shaman to penetrate this domain, and the fifth signaled the point at which he overcame enemy powers. The sixth indicated his return, and the seventh marked the delivery of the restored soul to the ailing person. Relying only on vocal expression—without dance or instruments—the Chorote shaman performed his healing function amidst the rapt and silent attention of his assistants, who recognized the different phases of the process and marked the various songs. Particularly descriptive was the gallop of the mythical horse ridden by the shaman on his magic flight.

The expressive means used by the Toba shaman differed from those of other groups. Here, songs alternated with emphatic speech to establish a dialogue with the deity summoned to effect the desired change. The imperative tone of the dialogue made it explicit that he was confronting powerful forces.

Beyond the domain of shamanic expressions, other traditions observed included the *algarroba* ceremonies, the initiation of pubescent youths of both sexes, funeral rites, and the nocturnal mating dance. Most of these ceremonies involving musical performance would take place when fruits were ripe and nature was aplenty for the festivities and social gatherings, ending the trials of the dry season. The

festival of the *algarroba* (*Prosopis alba* or *nigra*) was a complex set of social events that gathered exogamous bands (in the case of the Toba), encouraged marriage, and built a sense of community. The *algarroba* festival was closely linked to the ritual function of inebriation. The preparation of beverages by fermenting various fruits and honey required constant intonation of men's songs, often with water drum accompaniment, to achieve the desired point of fermentation. An abundance of musical expressions accompanied the men's collective libations, as each intoned his song simultaneously and independently from each other. These included the adolescents' rites of passage whose different characteristics were regulated by gender, and the young males' nocturnal dances, performed to their own singing and in some instances supported by the rhythm of the water drum. The women observed the dances, selecting a temporary or permanent partner from among the young male dancers, and then joined the chosen mate.

Men and women are restricted to their own respective songs and dances, as there are no mixed expressions in these traditions. This feature, however, was not retained in rituals of Christian origin. With few exceptions, gender-specificity also extended to musical instruments. In the case of the Chorote, women's and men's musical activities would take place simultaneously during female initiation rites. The women sang and danced to the rhythm of the hoof-rattle (an instrument used only in this ritual), and men would surround the space where the women were singing while marking time with their water drums. The confluence of song and drumbeating was also present in traditional funeral rites, and in the shaman's journey to the underworld inhabited by the dead, who also sing and dance.

Musical instruments

The instruments most commonly associated with ritual are the gourd rattle or maraca—of wide diffusion throughout South America—and the water drum (a membranophone called *katakí* by the Toba and the Pilagá). This drum is used by men and women among the Toba; in all other cases, it is reserved for men. It is played by one person or several placed around a single drum, the latter in the case of the Toba and Pilagá. Different functions are represented by the position of the players (standing or crouching), with standing position used in ritual performances.

To the maraca and the water drum we must add the *palo-sonajero de uñas de ciervo* (a rattle made from hooves of deer or other forest animals, mounted on a stick), whose use in female initiation rites also has been documented among indigenous groups in northern California. Although use differs according to the tradition of each indigenous group, the function of these instruments in performance is almost invariably limited to marking the pulse of the vocal melody, both constituting a single expressive unit (Ruiz 1985).

Aerophones have not played a protagonistic role in the organology of indigenous peoples of the Argentinian Chaco. With some exceptions like the *kanojí*, a Mataco bone whistle used by the shaman in his "flight" to confront powers and restore health, aerophones have been used mostly as signaling instruments for hunting or war. In the twentieth century, a cane flute of Andean progeny has been adopted by some of these groups.

The current situation of indigenous groups in the Chaco area

Traditional culture has undergone drastic changes under the influence of such intrusive Christian sects as the Pentecostal church. In the paragraphs above, we have used the past tense to underscore the degree to which traditional practices have been truncated and disturbed by this relatively new Christian presence. A degree of identification with Pentecostal practices, especially among the Toba, could be explained by certain analogies between Pentecostal and traditional rituals. Song, prayer, preaching, dance, and healing are practices of the United Evangelical Church, founded and managed by the Toba.

Song is led by *cancionistas* or "songsters." According to Miller, the function of song "parallels [that of] the traditional song of the shaman, who acquired it from a kindred spirit. Similarly, *cancionistas* are eager to own their songs, a majority of which are learned from creole congregations in the Chaco's cities and small towns" (1979: 124). Analogies with traditional dance also facilitate syncretism, as "dance . . . starts with contortions and shaking . . . until the person . . . begins to jump rhythmically" (Miller 1979: 126). Then the participants join hands and dance until they reach ecstasy, with one or several individuals falling into a state of trance. Of the ancient traditional practices, now largely replaced, only a few isolated remnants survive.

THE MAPUCHE

Mapuche means "people of the land" (*mapu* = land, *che* = people). Some 40,000 Mapuche live in a vast area, ranging from the provinces of northern Patagonia (Neuquén and Río Negro) and Chubut, to some points in the southwestern part of La Pampa province, with scattered groups in the Buenos Aires and Santa Cruz provinces. Although they are called Mapuche, they constitute in fact a conglomerate of various indigenous groups whose roots are not always traceable to the Mapuche proper. These are the Pehuenche, Ranquel, Pampa, and Tehuelche, who came from the central pampa area and from northern Patagonia. Historical circumstances, however, have created sufficient sociocultural homogeneity to consider them as a unit (see also María Ester Grebe, ("Amerindian Music of Chile," in this volume).

Beginning in the sixteenth century and increasingly in the 1600s, indigenous groups in the western Andean Cordillera traded with those of the pampa (flatlands), giving the Mapuche livestock in exchange for fabrics and metals, and establishing wartime alliances. Considerable penetration of Mapuche groups from what is now Chilean territory into the present-day Argentinian side took place in the eighteenth century or even earlier. By the early 1800s, Mapuche was the lingua franca of the Argentinian pampa and northern Patagonia. This pampa teeming with horses was one of the major enticements that attracted migrations because, in addition to representing expansion, it allowed the Mapuche to raise their cavalry for their long war against the Spaniards. At the same time, indigenous groups in the pampa and Patagonia were being forced to organize their defense against relentless attacks from the creole Argentinian army bent on exterminating them. Alliances and contacts gradually modified the ethnic panorama from west to east and the weaker groups were overpowered by the Chilean Mapuche, whose subsistence was based on agriculture. A Mapuche coalition with the Guénaken or Günuna Kena (northern Tehuelche) conquered the Aöniken (another faction of the Tehuelche), driving them southward. Most sociocultural traits of today's Argentinian Mapuche can be traced to both terms of that coalition, with adjustments caused by the reservation system imposed upon them by the creole armies that defeated them, and by their confinement to lands most unsuitable for agriculture.

Musical culture

The most unusual characteristic of this indigenous conglomerate is the exclusion of men from the sacred domain of song. Although men participate in the annual fertility ritual (known as *nguillatún, nellipún, nguillipún* or *kamarikún* depending on the area) through dance and instrument playing (see Carol E. Robertson, "Fertility Ritual," in this volume), only the women can perform sacred song. Most musical instruments, however, are performed by men. Dances are ritualistic in nature and vary in male/female participation. Children do not have repertoires restricted to them.

Among all musical expressions, *tayil* clearly has received the most attention from ethnomusicologists (Robertson 1976, 1977, 1979). This is a female vocal expression, defined by Carol Robertson as the auditory component of the *kimpeñ* or soul shared by all living and dead members of a patrilineage. Every Mapuche belongs to a paternal lineage and therefore shares the *kimpeñ*, whose sound component is a specific *tayil* or—in Robertson's words—"pulling the ancestors." *Tayil* performances are prescribed for annual fertility rituals, before and after moving the animals to higher ground (summer season), before journeying to funerals, and during times of crisis, both individual and of the entire lineage (Robertson 1979: 408).

The sacred song that accompanies dances and supplications is known generically as *ül*, whereas non-ritual song (permitted for both men and women) is known as *ülkantún*. These expressions, which may be improvised, narrate a specific event and are sometimes associated with states of inebriation. Robertson points out that, while the Mapuche may use Spanish for texts of humorous compositions and parodies, their expressions of sorrow, reflection, or nostalgia always are performed in Mapuche (1977: 70). Although the term *kantún* suggests a corruption of *canto* (song = Spanish), Rodolfo Casamiquela has contributed an interesting interpretation. He suggests that *kantún* means "imitation" or "similar to" and, consequently, *ülkantún* could be translated as "imitation of the true or sacred song," that is, "profane song" (Casamiquela 1988, personal communication). Robertson designates vocal and instrumental improvisations simply as *kantún* and musics other than the traditional Mapuche, or "European," as *kantún winká* (1976: 39; 1979: 70), while we have registered the term *ülkantún* and a corruption, *elkantún*.

Dances are collective and circular, and take place during the *nguillatún* or *nellipún*, with dancers moving around the *rewe* or ceremonial center. *Purrún* means dance (both noun and verb) and thus the names of various dances include the term. There is, however, a tremendous difference between dances for an indeterminate number of women only, or women and men in separate formations, but never men alone (designated as *amupurrún, shafshafpurrún,* and *rinkürrinküpurrún*), and dances restricted to men (the *puelpurrún* or dance of the East) or *lonkomeo* (to move one's head). In the latter, male dancers are always five in number and the performance extends over long portions of the annual ceremony. The *puelpurrufe* (male dancers) wear ostrich feathers on their heads, accentuating head movements (*lonkomeo*). Each *lonkomeo* lasts about an hour or longer, depending on the endurance of the dancers, and consists of five parts that correspond to five rhythmic patterns sustained by the *kultrún* (the male Mapuche drum, a membranophone, which is larger than the type performed by female ritual specialists). To the sound of the *kultrún* are added bells, the women's voices performing *tayil*, and men's shouts encouraging the dancers. *Tayil*, however, is not to be considered a "melodic" component of the dance: there, women with knowledge of the lineage must intone the specific *tayil* of the *kimpeñ* of each of the dancers, in corresponding order.

The *amupurrún, shafshafpurrún,* and *rinkürrinkü-purrún* are dances restricted to women, or women and men in separate formations. Their music is the female song (*ül*). While the women sing, a female ritual specialist directs the dance, sings, and sustains the rhythm on the *kultrún* (the smaller, female-owned membranophone). The names of these dances refer to the steps used (*amu* = to walk; *shafshaf* = to shuffle along; and *rinkürrinkütún* = to jump). Although choreography varies greatly, some common features include joining hands, moving either in a line or in single-gender pairs, or moving in both formations at once.

In addition to the *kultrún*, a profoundly symbolic drum (Grebe 1978), the organology of the Mapuche includes aerophones such as the *pifilka* (a male-owned flute) and the *trutruka* (a male-owned natural trumpet used in the *nguillatún* or fertility ritual).

The *kaskawilla* (a corruption of the Spanish *cascabel* = pellet-bell rattle) is a significant idiophone in performances of the *nguillatún*. In addition to being worn by the *lonkomeo* male dancers, the *kaskawilla* is used by the *piwichén* (boys who represent the original male ancestor and are guardians of the *rewe* or sacred center) during *amupurrún*. *Kaskawillas* also are worn by the horses for the *awún* or circle of riders who delimit the sacred space within which the ritual is performed (see Robertson, "Fertility Ritual," Figs. 1–4, in this volume).

The current situation of Mapuche peoples

While older generations of Mapuche tenaciously continue to reaffirm their cultural identity, younger generations tend to integrate national society. This is most eloquently shown by the loss of the native Mapuche language among younger people. The performance of the annual fertility ritual may be the last bastion supporting their traditions. Although it strengthens social cohesiveness, performs religious beliefs, and transmits traditional musical expressions, the number of participants in this ritual is relentlessly declining and some groups have not performed it for many years. The musical instruments that are not absolutely essential for its performance (*pifilka* and *trutruka*) are also disappearing and sold as valuable arts and crafts. The possible extinction of the *nguillatún* or *nguillipún* may bring about the disappearance of Mapuche traditions, with the sole exception of *tayil*, which is inextricably linked to patriliny. In addition to their traditional practices, the Mapuche have partially adopted dances that are popular among *criollos* in the area, such as the *chamamé*, a dance from the northeastern coastal area in vogue throughout Argentina.

THE CHIRIGUANO-CHANÉ

The Chiriguano-Chané represent a special case in this panorama. They belong to different linguistic groups: the Chiriguano are Guaraní-affiliated, and the Chané are Arawakan. There is a master/servant relationship between them, possibly dating back to 16th-century Bolivia. The Chané adopted the Guaraní language of the Chiriguano. Both groups have exchanged cultural traits and speak with Kechua accentuation.

Although the Chiriguano and the Chané live today in separate settlements located on the western edge of the Chaco area, it is possible to speak of them jointly because of the extent to which Andean, Guaraní, and Arawakan cultural traits have integrated to become the patrimony of both ethnic groups. To this fusion we must add the geographic predicament that situates

them on the western boundary of the Chaco area, which is culturally alien to the Amazonian affiliation of the Chiriguano and the Arawakan origin of the Chané, while in close proximity to the Andes. Thus they are exposed to dual cultural pressure from both the Andes and the Chaco, which are areas of greater demographic density. The groups living in Argentina came from Bolivia, at first fleeing the ravages of the Chaco War (1932–35) and later in search of work. The sugar plantations in Salta and Jujuy provinces count them among a stable population of workers.

Traditional culture

Their musical heritage carries the imprint of constant adaptation to new situations over five hundred years. This began with the initial migration from the eastern jungles to the western Chaco, passing through almost futile resistance to Catholic missionaries, and concluding with the migration of some to Argentinian territory. Christianity left its imprint in their adoption of the celebration of Easter, St. John the Baptist, and the feast of the Annunciation of the Virgin Mary in which they express themselves vocally, instrumentally, and choreographically through specific manifestations which they consider to be their own. To the observer, however, traditional features are almost undetectable.

The *aréte aváti* (corn festival) is perhaps the most powerful cultural expression of the Chiriguano-Chané group. It has merged in recent times with the celebration of carnival, whose irresistible force is tenaciously retained in the Andes. Even in this instance it is difficult to identify traditional traits that are unique to the Chiriguano and Chané cultures. Those expressions that appear to retain some characteristics of their ancient practices include a few funeral songs intoned at the death of a close family member, the melodic structure of *tonadas* or tunes for flute and drum performed at carnival, and the style of delivery of certain vocal expressions with violin for Easter. Other expressions reflect traits adopted from Andean culture, or from European religious music, as in the predominantly pentatonic melodies for *pingüio* or *pinkullo* (flute) and in songs of praise to Jesus Christ, respectively. Choreographic gestures in the performance of traditional dances are, perhaps, the clearest remnants of ancient practices. These include men and women joining hands in circles, jumping while they raise and lower their arms in strong rhythmic movement, and foot-tapping (*zapateo*) with violin music.

Musical instruments

Flute and drum ensembles characterize most musical expressions at the present time. Except for the violin, which may be played by women, all other instruments are for male use. Called *turumi* or *miorí* (the latter a corruption of the Spanish term *violín*), this instrument retains the tuning of the European chordophone but, as it is built by local craftsmen, it has acquired some characteristics of its own.

Three double-headed drums of different sizes comprise a family of membranophones. These are, from largest to smallest, the *anguaguásu* or *angúa aretepe* (festival drum) played with a single stick, the *anguarái* (son-drum), and the *michirái* (youngest-son drum). The last two are struck with two sticks.

The current situation of Chiriguano-Chané groups

Although other indigenous groups have resisted participation of outsiders in their ceremonies and festivals, the Chiriguano-Chané have accepted such participation, perhaps because of the degree to which they have integrated Catholic religious feasts and the creole culture surrounding them into their traditional practices. Evidence of their adaptation to processes of change is the incorporation of the *aréte aváti* (the corn festival) into such explosive communal expression as carnival, where all kinds of participation are possible. This has taken place without any perceptible loss of the significance that the *aréte aváti* carries within their culture.

Carnival is a festival that brings together the living and the dead. Ancestors return each year, embodied in the *aña*, presently translated as devil, which are the "souls" of the dead. The bucolic overflow of alcohol (a remnant of the sharing of chicha that enhanced group cohesiveness); the exalted celebration of life in irrepressible circular dances moving in one direction, then the other; the final struggle of the Tiger (symbol of the Indian) and the Bull (the White Man) that always ends with the Tiger's victory, ritualizing a longed-for yet unattained conquest—these are ways in which these peoples persistently regenerate their cultural values, wisely mimicked in a collective orgy such as carnival.

At the same time, these groups have adopted creole repertoires typical of the area in their daily lives (such as *chacareras*, *takiraris*, and *bailecitos*). Some Chiriguano musicians even perform professionally at family celebrations in creole households. Perhaps this opening, resisted by a small conservative core that does not participate in the practice of creole traditions, explains their mixed culture and also its permanence.

THE MBYÁ

This Guaraní-affiliated group migrated to the northeastern province of Misiones from Paraguay, by all accounts their original habitat. The Paraná River forms their natural western boundary with that country, with the Uruguay, Pepirí Guazú, and San Antonio rivers on the east, and Iguazú to the north, bordering with Brazil. We point out their Misiones location, a wedge between Paraguay and Brazil (themselves contiguous) because it explains the presence of the Mbyá in the three countries. Their territory is relatively vast but they inhabit a few, scattered villages.

The current Mbyá population should not be considered a remnant of the Guaraní from Jesuit settlements in what is today the Province of Misiones, in part because the Mbyá were the most fierce in resisting that force. More fundamentally, the Guaraní indigenous groups brought by the Jesuits from Paraguay to the missions in present-day Argentina were driven back to Paraguay by the persecution of Portuguese traders from São Paulo (*mamelucos*), who would hunt Indians and then sell them as slaves. Others returned to Paraguay after the expulsion of the Jesuits in 1767, and those groups that remained and survived decimation and conflicts had finished migrating back to Paraguay by 1818 (Bartolomé 1969: 164–65).

According to some of our informants, the first Mbyá migrations to Argentinian territory took place slightly less than a century ago but the process continues, as does constant resettlement of small family groups and individuals from one village to another, and for long or short periods of time. As in the case of permanent migrations, personal or community circumstances determine the stability of these displacements. Although these are frequent within a country, displacements from one country to another occur less frequently.

The most significant cause of mobility is the relentless advance of the lumber industry, which takes their land and displaces entire communities, sometimes fragmenting them into small family groups that, even under these circumstances, retain a sense of identity and recognize their chief's authority. Migrations also are motivated by the search for *Yvy marã eỹ* ("Tierra sin mal" or Land purged of Evil, the Indestructible Land) that provides mythical support for their prophetic relocations. Some Mbyá informants attribute their migration from Paraguay to Argentina to this mythical search.

The Mbyá are subsistence farmers but hunting has always retained significance in their cosmovision, since it provides the meat to supplement their diet. Increased encroachment upon their land has hindered both activities. Although they rely less on fishing, they use the bow and arrow and the traditional technique of rendering the fish unconscious by placing pieces of *timbó* vine in the water.

Their main crops are corn, manioc, yams, squash, watermelon, beans, and rice. They plant citrus trees, grow tobacco for their own consumption, and have adopted onions and salt, which is strictly forbidden in the preparation of ritual meals. They use traps for hunting and own rifles. Birds are killed by a slingshot with mud balls hardened by firing. They also raise chickens and pigs.

Those villages farthest from towns, deep in the forest, are the most conservative and self-sufficient. The villagers need a small amount of money for clothing, machetes, lamps, rifles, and a few other basic necessities, and they procure it by selling baskets made by both men and women, mainly to tourists. Many visitors are drawn to the Province of Misiones by the Iguazú Falls, the Jesuit ruins, and the area's luxuriant vegetation.

Mbyá houses are made of mud and reed over a framework of posts, or merely pointed sticks, with a two-slope palm roof. They tend to be small, except for the dwellings of political and religious leaders. The house of the religious leader or *Pa'i* is the largest, being also the place of worship. Houses have a structure attached for cooking, where they have their meals when it rains or is very cold.

The chiefs are highly respected without being authoritarian, since all adults and even young people may express disagreement and be heard. This only applies to the political sphere, since in the spiritual domain no one may challenge the powers of the shaman and his control of the religious structure. Respect for the rights of individuals is reflected, for instance, in the fact that punitive measures are not imposed on those who miss religious rituals.

The following narrative is central to Mbyá cosmovision and essential for an understanding of their ritual practices.

Ñamandú Ru Eté (the primeval Being and true father, Ñamandú), the creator, before shaping the earth, "engendered the flames and the fine mist," "created the foundation of future human language," "conceived the basis of love (for one's neighbor)," and "gave birth to a sacred hymn." Only after that did he create those who would be his companions: Karaí Ru Eté, Jakairá Ru Eté, and Tupã Ru Eté and, subsequently, his wife and the wives of the others: Karaí Sy Eté, Jakairá Sy Eté, Tupã Sy Eté, and Ñamandú Sy Eté, the true mothers Karaí, Jakairá, Tupã, and Ñamandú respectively. He then engendered the Primal Earth (*Yvy tenondé*) and instructed the deities with regard to their respective tasks (Cadogan 1959: 13–33; Ruiz, unpublished field work).

The different musical expressions in performance of religious rites are dedicated to these deities (the only beings with no navel) and their progeny. Karaí, the god of fire who dwells in the East, cares for animals in the forest and controls agricultural production and crops. Jakairá is the god of mist and the source of wisdom he bestows upon the shamans. Jakairá also guards smoke and tobacco, and serves as foundation for the ritual smoke used in traditional healing and in the purification of food. Tupã, god of water, dwells in the West and engenders the rains and thunder. Ñamandú is the source of light, the Sun god who dwells in the East. During song and dance, men and women face the cardinal direction of the deity they are addressing.

The Primal Earth was destroyed by a flood caused by an incestuous relationship. Those who prayed, danced, and sang became indestructible. Those who did not were turned into animals. The New Earth was created (*Ivy Pyaú*, the present earth) and populated by beings who are images of those who lived in the mythical *Yvy tenondé* and now dwell in the celestial domain. Human beings lost their immortal condition and must endure hardship to secure their subsistence.

Musical culture

Mbyá practice of musical traditions is very intense in some villages, while less so in others. This intensity is unsurpassed by any other indigenous group in Argentina. Traditional practice among the Mbyá includes the appropriation of the rebec and the guitar, two musical instruments brought from Europe that they have assimilated fully into worship.

Their attitude toward tradition can be viewed as a paradox. On the one hand they have maintained almost intact their religious structure under the pressure of various religious congregations over the course of centuries; and, on the other hand, they adopted instruments brought from Europe, perhaps as early as the seventeenth century, and appropriated them to the extent that they are no longer considered exogenous. These instruments are a three-string rebec (*ravé*) and a five-string guitar (the *mbaraká*). The early adoption and persistence of these instruments also points to the Mbyá's strong sense of identity and cultural individuality. Although they are fully aware of the tuning and performance techniques of the widespread six-string guitar, playing with skill some of the "exogenous" creole dances they hear on the radio, they nevertheless retain the five-string instrument and its tuning for their own repertoire. These distinctive features allow them to clearly separate one guitar from the other and to claim the five-string chordophone as their own, along with the rebec. Both are unique to them in their environment. From this type of appropriation, we can infer that these instruments have been "traditionalized."

Almost all musical expression currently in practice is sacred, or at least associated with ritual. In addition, they sing lullabies and perform on two types of flutes, although this is less frequent.

Vocal music is the realm of men and women but the function they fulfill in joint performances varies according to the roles assigned to each gender in ritual. Paradoxically, and although the male plays the principal role, changes introduced in their ritual over the last four or five decades have silenced the communal male voices and only the religious leader or his assistant sing. By contrast, female participation is massive, although its role is limited to supporting the male function by reinforcing phrase endings or entire phrases at a range of two octaves above. Only under duress, such as the absence from the village of males who can lead the ritual, can this be taken over by a qualified woman and, in that instance, the collective ritual function of women remains unaltered (Ruiz, field work, 1977).

Instrumental performance is gender specific. The chordophones (rebec and five-string guitar) are played only by males. A vertical flute (the *mimby*, made of *takuapí*, a variety of bamboo), and a double-headed drum (*anguapú* or *mbaepú*), also are male instruments, now practically extinct. By contrast, only two female instruments are still in use. These are the *takuapú*, an indispensable stamping tube in ritual performances made out of *takuara* (*Guadua angustifolia*), and a panpipe, the *mimby retá*, made from *takuapí* (*Merostachys claussenii*, a type of bamboo).

Dances are mixed, and generally respond to two types: movement in circles, where the dancers maintain a distance and do not establish fixed exchanges; and line formation in facing rows of males and females, with minimum displacement forward of one row and backwards of the other, so as to also preserve a distance between them. Here, fixed exchanges also are avoided and only occasionally would a woman link arms with the female dancer on her left, as her right arm marks rhythmic pulses with the stamping tube. While displacement in circles can take place inside or outside the sacred space, the line formation is only restricted to the ceremonial site.

The vitality of traditional practices varies from village to village. In communities that can claim the presence of a prestigious ritual specialist, one or two daily ceremonies may take place. The main ceremony is held at dusk and may last for several hours. A shorter one may take place at dawn. In addition, the Ñemongaraí is an annual ceremony for the consecration of first fruits of the harvest which, held each January, also serves to name the children born during the preceding year. The *ára pyau* ceremony that marks the beginning of the new seasonal cycle each August, on the other hand, seems to be disappearing.

The daily ceremony at dusk is preceded by a dance performed in the *oká* or dance-space in front of the house of the religious leader, which is also the place of worship or *opy*. All participants meet there—men, women, and children—and dance for an hour or more until dark to rebec and guitar music, or guitar only if no rebec player is available. It is a counterclockwise circle-dance suggestive of aggression and resistance expressed by the subtle movements of the dancers. The presence of the religious leader, his wife, and the political chief lend an institutional character to the dance as preamble to the ritual.

The Mbyá people experience all ritual acts as earthly replicas of events in the heavenly domain or "the city of the gods." In the *oká*, the dancers represent the soldiers of the deities (Tupã *sondaro*, Karaí *sondaro*, and others, *sondaro* being here a Guaraní-speaker's adaptation of the Spanish term *soldado* = soldier). Just as the soldiers guard the deities, the dancers protect the sacred space (*opy*), thus dancing outside, in front of the house (*oká*). Their action signifies the daily renewal of a sense of respect for the gods and those who represent divine power on Earth. The rebec carries here the melodic line, and the guitar strumming on open strings underscores the rhythmic pulse. This dance is generically called *yeroky sondaro* (dance of the soldiers) and lasts until nightfall.

A hierarchical row is then formed at the door of the *opy*, led by the guitarist and followed by the rebec player and all other participants. The authorities mentioned have by then entered the *opy* and stand before the hearth (coals laid over bricks) to preside over the ritual. They accept the salutation of each participant (*aguyevete* = I am pleased, greetings), and answer likewise. Once salutations are completed, the religious leader takes the guitar, still strumming on open strings, and begins a narrative on the fundamental pitch of the guitar chord which he delivers in the style of a psalmodic recitation tone. In this narrative, which is improvised and lengthy, the shaman invokes the deities and thanks them for help that day. He also addresses special circumstances, admonishing those who ignore religious precepts and other standards of community ethics. Essentially, the ritual is a vehicle for achieving *aguyje* or fulfillment through song, dance, religious fervor, and compliance with the rigorous Mbyá ethical code, which is very demanding in the case of religious leaders. To "do" *aguyje* means to reach *Yvy mará eỹ* (Land purged of Evil) in body and soul, that is, attain the mythical domain without passing through the trial of death. The shaman's delivery, which teaches the children and preaches traditional religious values to young people and adults, takes on special meaning in conflicts with whites.

With no break at the end of the recitation, the shaman intones a song to Tupã Ru Eté and, after this point, the order of songs varies from ritual to ritual. When the leader has an apprentice (a youth), they alternate in leading the ritual actions. This allows the leader to rest from the exhaustion caused by the acceleration of song, dance, and instrumental performance that climaxes when he reaches a state of ecstasy.

Inside the *opy*, the rebec and guitar are joined by the *takuapú*, a sacred idiophone used exclusively by women. While its sonorous function is to keep a pulse, the *takuapú* carries transcendental meaning as the principal attribute of female deities and the

vehicle through which they communicate with male deities. In the context of ritual, the *takuapú* symbolizes the participation of women joined with men in all sacred action.

Songs follow no set order and they vary, although certain ones are always present. Each song is always specifically dedicated to a deity, either principal or secondary, female or male. Because mythical progenitors dictate actions carried out by their children on earth, songs address them, as well as the "soldiers" or the "soldiers' chief" who guard one or another deity.

Although there are specific melodies for the principal deities, other melodies can be dedicated to one of the secondary mythical beings. This is expressed by including the deity's name in the text and by phrases that contextualize the action. The words used are always improvised and comprise only a few, short phrases, or invoke the name of a deity between long sections intoned on an open vowel, particularly "a."

Because the shaman's performance mediates between the mythical and earthly domains, one of the basic expectations from religious leaders is their capacity for musical expression. Especially in song, changes to a melody are highly valued and perceived as displays of skill. By contrast, the assistants merely repeat the basic structure.

The length of the dusk ritual usually depends on the physical condition of the leader and the energy generated by the participants. It may last two or three hours, or even longer, or less than an hour. The shorter ritual at dawn, which consists of only three or four songs, is structurally similar to the evening ritual.

By contrast, the Ñemongaraí ceremony, which is celebrated each year, has its own special characteristics (Ruiz 1984: 45–102). Musical behavior is generally the same as in the dusk and dawn rituals but the objectives are different: to purify the first fruits of the harvest through male offerings (fruits of the *gwembé* or *Philodendron selloum*) and the female offering of corn breads (*mbytá* or *mboyapé*), and to name the children. The Mbyá believe that the soul of each child is sent by a specific deity. Consequently, the shaman must identify this deity before naming each infant, since the name depends on his or her mythical progenitor. Precisely because of its intimate relationship with the soul, the sacred name is not revealed and, in daily life, they adopt names commonly used among whites.

The Ñemongaraí ceremony, and the dusk and dawn rituals described above, subsume most of the musical traditions currently practiced by the Mbyá. In addition, they have a female panpipe (the *mimby retá*) and a male flute (*mimby*), both made of bamboo. Although the male flute is now rarely used, its main purpose is to announce a visitor's arrival at a village, so as to not take the hosts by surprise. At one time a complex welcoming rite included the "dance of the soldiers" (described above as preamble to the dusk ritual) with rebec, guitar, a double-headed drum (*anguapú* or *mbaepú*) and, according to some reports, the now rarely used male flute (*mimby*). Even today, they observe many rules of courtesy and welcome salutations, although without music. If the visitor holds one of the higher posts in the social hierarchy (which is similar to military hierarchies), he should carry the respective insignia and be greeted in accordance with his office. The vertical male flute (*mimby*) is said to be imbued with power to attract women.

The case of the *mimby retá* or female flute is unusual. It is a type of bamboo panpipe consisting of loose tubes (from 5 to 8, usually 7) on which two women play a single melody in interlocking fashion. They distribute among them the tubes of one panpipe according to the specifications of each melody (for instance, 4 and 3; 4 and 2; 5 and 2; 3 and 3). The second flute player is always responsible for a short repeated pattern of two, three, or four pitches, although one of these is a reiteration, creating with the first flute a composed, single melody in predominantly conjunct motion, or a diaphony. Although a *mimby retá* performance can be addressed to a deity, most women play it for entertainment (Recorded Ex. 1).

The melodies of sacred song, rebec tunes, and interlocking *mimby retá* melodies reveal interesting differences in structure. Sacred song, virtually the only vocal expression in current practice, follows a predominantly descending movement that significantly decreases in intensity, with overwhelming motion in minor thirds alternating with major thirds. This occurs over a wide melodic range of at least a minor sixth, but usually of an octave and even a twelfth. Also common are repetitions of phrase endings, as in refrains, which are linked to the women's supporting role in ritual, as discussed above. Perhaps we can attribute the reiteration of phrase endings in rebec and *mimby retá* instrumental performances to the protagonistic role of sacred song and the expressive force imprinted upon it

by the shaman and by the massive participation of women, who collectively repeat these phrase endings.

The repertoire of melodies for the rebec exhibits mostly conjunct motion as well as reiteration of phrase endings within the range of a major sixth. Other intervals used are major and minor thirds, with very sporadic use of perfect fourths and fifths. This is due to the fact that most melodies are played on the highest string, without displacement of the hand over the fingerboard, and in such a way as to produce most of the commonly used pitches without shifting the position of the hand. For instance, if the tuning is b', a', and e', which is one of the most common, the pitches used in the melody would be b', c#'', d'', e'', and f#''. Rebec melodies are pendular and composed mainly of short time values. It is interesting to note that this widespread rebec tuning (b', a', and e') corresponds with the following tuning of the five-string guitar of the Mbyá: c#', a, e', a, and e. The e', which is the pitch both tunings share, is then used as pitch reference to tune the rebec. The guitar is normally strummed on open strings, providing the rhythmic base of dances, songs, and rebec melodies. From village to village, the tunings of both chordophones preserve the same intervallic distances between strings but the concept of pitch is relative, not absolute. Example 1 includes standard tunings of the guitar and the rebec. Preceded by a seven-measure guitar introduction, the rebec melody proceeds in duple simple meter, while the guitar accompaniment continues its strumming on open strings, maintaining a rhythmic organization in triplets (Recorded Ex. 2).

The tunings of the *mimby retá* panpipe depart from any reference to the "tonal" tunings of the "European" rebec and guitar. While the second flute player repeats a pendular pattern, alternating conjunct with disjunct intervals, the first flute—freer than the second—plays short, repeated motives from its three or four tubes to jointly create a single, interlocking melody (Recorded Ex. 1). Examples 2 and 3 illustrate two standard tunings and three composite scales corresponding to three *mimby retá* interlocked melodies. It is interesting to note that, in both cases, only six of the seven pitches available to the players are used in actual performance.

The current situation of the Mbyá of Misiones
In villages that maintain greater contact with whites, young people play popular songs and dances

Ex. 1: Ritual dance of the Mbyá (*toque para danza*). Rebec and five-string guitar. Documented by Irma Ruiz in Fracran, Misiones (1977). Rebec, Mario Silva; guitar, Gervasio Martínez (Recorded Ex. 2).

practiced by their *criollo* neighbors on the six-string folk guitar. The Mbyá show great skill at singing in parallel thirds, another characteristic of creole folk music, and can imitate musical expressions they hear on the radio. They also participate in dances, enthusiastically joining in with the rural and townspeople, an act unthinkable for other indigenous groups in present-day Argentina (the Mataco, for example). Within the villages, the religious leader is a

moral impediment for performance of dances that are not part of their traditions. Young people are particularly attracted to mixed-couple dancing that involves embracing. The harp and the accordion also are occasionally played, especially among those Mbyá who live near urban centers.

In traditionally structured villages, that is, organized according to their own political and religious authorities, and with adequate space for

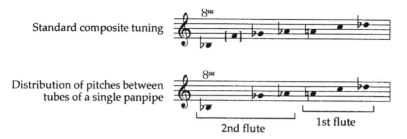

Ex. 2: *Mimby retá* tuning and composite scale, showing distribution of tubes between the two women players. Documented by Irma Ruiz in Colonia Gobernador Lanusse (1973).

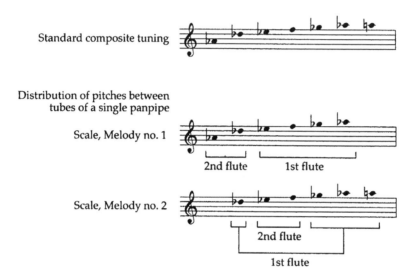

Ex. 3: *Mimby retá* tuning and two composite scales, showing distribution of tubes between the two women players. Documented by Irma Ruiz in Colonia 25 de Mayo (1977).

farming and hunting, exogenous cultural influences are scarce. This reflects a conscious decision by the Mbyá to reject exogenous influences, rather than a lack of knowledge on their part. Proud of their Guaraní origin, they view inter-marriage negatively and never assume positions of inferiority before whites. Although they value the traditions of their neighbors, they consider them foreign to their culture.

CONCLUSIONS

Strategies for preservation of traditional culture among Argentina's indigenous groups are diverse, as are the degrees of contact with national society and types of response to this contact. The strategy of the Mbyá has been to guard their rituals zealously, keeping them from the creole population living in those areas. The Mbyá withdrew, taking their acts of worship into the home of the religious leader. Documents from the last century show worship taking place outdoors, and women appear carrying their sacred stamping tube, the female-owned *takuapú*, which today cannot be removed from the *opy* or sacred space. When necessary, they raised the height of the fences that always surrounded the main house of worship. They resisted Christian indoctrination by feigning belief in Christianity. Today, they are friendly while very secretive about their religious tradition. Their resistance to observers makes the Mbyá the least studied indigenous group in Argentinian territory.

By contrast, evangelical activity in the Chaco area undermined traditional cultures and brought about significant changes in the musical practices of Mataco and Guaycurú groups. They have been constantly exploited in sugar plantations and in lumberyards. Driven into small spaces in a harsh, arid environment, this large population originally of hunters and gatherers has been reduced to hunger and poverty, and therefore dependence on whites. For survival in the face of anonymity and marginality, the Toba created a hybrid religion strongly based on the Pentecostal faith.

Being farmers, the Chiriguano found a more congenial place in the sugar plantations and, like the Mbyá (both linguistically affiliated with the Guaraní), they established a more egalitarian relationship with the creoles, even by participating in the official church's religious feasts, and in secular celebrations all around them.

As the last surviving indigenous group in the South, the Mapuche preserve their annual fertility ritual—the *nguillatún* or *nguillipún*—as a tenacious expression of their traditional beliefs. Precisely because it is inextricably linked to patriliny, the *tayil*, or auditory component of the *kimpeñ* or soul shared by all living and dead members of a patrilineage, carries its own capacity for permanence.

The Tehuelche contributed traits of their culture to the Mapuche and were—in turn—dominated by them. Of their culture, only traces have survived.

The Selk'nam of Tierra del Fuego were decimated but the songs preserved almost intact by a few individuals serve as testimony to the silent presence of an ancestral culture.

In spite of decimation and imposition of religious beliefs foreign to their own, these indigenous groups also have demonstrated resilience to the ravages of intrusion, and a tenacity to preserve some of their traditional practices. There is hope that governmental measures will respond to their greatest need, which is the ownership of land. Without territories in which they can settle and peacefully maintain their beliefs and ways of living, exploitation and extinction hover over their lives and cultures like giant shadows.

—*Translated by Mary Jane Wilkie*

REFERENCES

Ambrosetti, Juan Bautista 1894. "Los indios Cainguá del Alto Paraná (Misiones)," *Boletín del Instituto Geográfico Argentino* (Buenos Aires) 15/11–12 (November–December): 661–744.

Aretz, Isabel 1952. *El folklore musical argentino.* Buenos Aires: Ricordi Americana.

Aretz-Thiele, Isabel 1946. *Música tradicional argentina. Tucumán: Historia y folklore.* Tucumán: Universidad Nacional de Tucumán.
1978. *Música tradicional de La Rioja.* Caracas: Organización de Estados Americanos (OEA)—CONAC (Biblioteca INIDEF, 2).

Bartolomé, Miguel Alberto 1969. "La situación de los Guaraníes (Mbyá) de Misiones (Argentina)," *Suplemento antropológico de la Revista del Ateneo Paraguayo* (Asunción) 4/2: 161–84.

Cadogan, León 1959. *Ayvu rapyta: Textos míticos de los Mbyá-Guaraní del Guairá.* São Paulo: Facultade de Filosofia, Ciencias e Letras—Universidade de São Paulo (*Boletim* 227, Antropologia 5).

Casamiquela, Rodolfo M. 1964. *Estudio del nillatún y la religión araucana.* Bahía Blanca, Argentina: Instituto de Humanidades de la Universidad Nacional del Sur (Cuadernos del Sur).

Censo Indígena Nacional I–IV 1967–1968. Buenos Aires: Ministerio del Interior.

Cordeu, Edgardo J., and Alejandra Siffredi 1971. *De la algarroba al algodón. Movimientos milenaristas del Chaco argentino.* Buenos Aires: Juárez Editor.

Fischer, Erich 1908. "Patagonische Musik," *Anthropos* 3: 941–51.

Grebe, María Ester 1978. "Relationships between musical practice and cultural context: The kultrún and its symbolism," *The world of music* 20/3: 84–100.

Hernández, Isabel 1984. "Los indios y la antropología en la Argentina," *Los indios y la antropología en América latina,* ed. by Carmen Junqueira and Edgard Carvalho. Buenos Aires: Búsqueda-Yuchán, 11–46.
1985. *Derechos humanos y aborígenes: El pueblo Mapuche.* Buenos Aires: Ediciones Búsqueda.

Hornbostel, Erich von 1936. "Fuegian songs," *American anthropologist,* new series, 38/3 (July–September): 357–67; enlarged as "The music of the Fuegians," *Ethnos* 13/3–4 (1948): 62–102.

Hornbostel, Erich von, and Curt Sachs 1914 in 1961. "Systematik der Musikinstrumente," *Zeitschrift für Ethnologie,* 46: 553–90, trans. by Anthony Baines and Klaus P. Wachsmann as "Classification of musical instruments," *The Galpin Society Journal* 14: 3–29.

Huseby, Gerardo V. 1988. "El violín chiriguano como pervivencia del violín europeo temprano," *Primera conferencia anual de la Asociación Argentina de Musicología.* Buenos Aires: Asociación Argentina de Musicología, 52–58.

Lehmann-Nietsche, Robert 1908. "Patagonische Gesänge und Musikbogen," *Anthropos* 3: 916–40.

Melià, Bartomeu, Marcos Vinicios de Almeida Saul, and Valmir Francisco Muraro 1987. *O Guarani: Uma bibliografia etnologica.* Santo Angelo: FUNDAMES.

Métraux, Alfred 1948. "The Guaraní" in *Handbook of South American Indians,* 7 vols., ed. by Julian H. Steward. Washington, D.C.: Smithsonian Institution, Bureau of American Ethnology, vol. 3, 69–94.

Miller, Elmer 1979. *Los tobas argentinos. Armonía y disonancias en una sociedad.* México: Siglo XXI Editores.

Novati, Jorge 1969–1970. "Las expresiones musicales de los selk'nam," *Runa* (Buenos Aires) 12/1–2: 393–406.
1984. "El lenguaje sonoro común al hombre y a las deidades: Un estudio sobre las canciones de los mataco del Chaco argentino," *Temas de etnomusicología* (Buenos Aires) 1: 9–43.

Pelinski, Ramón, and Rodolfo M. Casamiquela 1966. "Música de canciones totémicas y populares, y danzas araucanas," *Revista del Museo de La Plata* (Argentina) 6: 43–80.

Pérez Bugallo, Rubén 1979–1982. "Estudio etnomusicológico de los chiriguano-chané de la Argentina. Primera parte: Organología," *Cuadernos del Instituto Nacional de Antropología* (Buenos Aires) 9: 221–68.

Robertson, Carol E. 1975. *Tayil: Musical communication and social organization among the Mapuche of Argentina* (PhD diss., Institute of Folklore: Indiana University).
1976. "Tayil as category and communication among the Argentine Mapuche: A methodological suggestion," *Yearbook of the International Folk Music Council* 8: 35–52.

1977. "Lukutún: Text and context in Mapuche rogations," *Latin American Indian literatures* 1/2: 67–78.

1979. "Pulling the ancestors: Performance practice and praxis in Mapuche ordering," *Ethnomusicology* 23/3: 395–416.

Ruiz, Irma 1978–1979. "Aproximación a la relación canto-poder en el contexto de los procesos iniciáticos de las culturas indígenas del Chaco central," *Scripta ethnologica* (Buenos Aires) 5/2: 157–69.

1984. "La ceremonia Ñemongaraí de los mbïá de la provincia de Misiones," *Temas de etnomusicología* (Buenos Aires) 1: 45–102.

1985. "Los instrumentos musicales de los indígenas del Chaco central," *Revista del Instituto de Investigación Musicológica "Carlos Vega"* (Buenos Aires) 6: 35–78.

1986. "Instrumentos musicales europeos en culturas indígenas de la Argentina, *Bulletin of The Brussels Museum of Musical Instruments* 16: 295–303.

1988. "1892–1987: Pasado y presente de un cordófono europeo en el ámbito indígena guaraní," *Primera conferencia anual de la Asociación Argentina de Musicología*. Buenos Aires: Asociación Argentina de Musicología, 59–70.

1996a. "Mito y música: El mito de la 'Tierra sin mal' y su expresión en los rituales de los mbyá-guaraní de Misiones (Argentina)," *Los mitos y su ámbito de expresión. IV simposio internacional sobre mitos*. Buenos Aires: Asociación Psicoanalítica Argentina, vol. 1, 91–98.

1996b. "Acerca de la sustitución de un idiófono indígena por un cordófono europeo: Los mbaraká de los mbyá-guaraní," *Revista argentina de musicología* (Córdoba, Argentina) 1: 81–92.

Ruiz, Irma, and Gerardo Huseby 1986. "Pervivencia del rabel europeo entre los mbïá de Misiones (Argentina)," *Temas de etnomusicología* (Buenos Aires) 2: 67–97.

Ruiz, Irma, Rubén Pérez Bugallo, and Héctor L. Goyena 1993. *Instrumentos etnográficos y folklóricos de la Argentina*, 2nd ed. Buenos Aires: Instituto Nacional de Musicología "Carlos Vega."

Ruiz de Montoya, Antonio 1639–1640 in 1876. *Vocabulario y tesoro de la lengua guaraní (ó mas bien tupi) por el P. Antonio Ruiz de Montoya. I: Vocabulario español-guaraní (ó tupi); II: Tesoro guaraní (ó tupi)-español*. Vienna: Faesy and Frick; Paris: Maisonneuve.

Setti, Kilza 1988a. "Relatorio científico presentado a la Fundação de Amparo à Pesquisa do Estado de São Paulo." Unpublished manuscript.

1988b. "O sistema musical dos indios Guarani do Estado do São Paulo: Hipótesis para estudo." Unpublished paper read at the Cuartas Jornadas Argentinas de Musicología, Buenos Aires.

Vega, Carlos 1944. *Panorama de la música popular argentina*. Buenos Aires: Editorial Losada.

1946. *Los instrumentos musicales aborígenes y criollos de la Argentina*. Buenos Aires: Ediciones Centurión.

Vignati, María Emilia 1979. "Fuentes bibliográficas de la música aborigen argentina," *Revista del Instituto de Investigación Musicológica "Carlos Vega"* (Buenos Aires) 3: 44–54.

Wright, Pablo 1979. "Apuntes para la comprensión de la música en una comunidad toba taksek." Unpublished manuscript.

Zavadivker, Ricardo A. 1988. "Los primeros grabados de la guitarra en la Argentina (1705)," *El mundo de la guitarra* (Buenos Aires) 3: 8–10.

DISCOGRAPHY

Música de los aborígenes, compiled by Jorge Novati and Irma Ruiz. Buenos Aires: Fondo Nacional de las Artes (Series Folklore musical y música folklórica argentina, VI). Qualiton QF 3000 (1967).

Música etnográfica mataco-chorote, compiled by Jorge Novati and Irma Ruiz. Qualiton QF 3008 (1972).

Selk'nam chants of Tierra del Fuego, Argentina, compiled by Anne Chapman. Ethnic Folkways FE 4176 (1972).

Selk'nam chants of Tierra del Fuego, Argentina, vol. 2, compiled by Anne Chapman. Ethnic Folkways FE 4179 (1977).

RECORDED EXAMPLES

1. "Arakú," *mimby retá* (panpipe) tune of the Mbyá, recorded in Cuña Pirú, Misiones. Performance by Agustina Cáceres and Luisa Ramírez (Irma Ruiz, field work, 1980).

2. Ritual dance of the Mbyá (*toque para danza*) for rebec and five-string guitar (see Ex. 1), recorded in Fracran, Misiones. Rebec, Mario Silva; guitar, Gervasio Martínez (Irma Ruiz, field work, 1977).

FERTILITY RITUAL

CAROL E. ROBERTSON

The nguillipún—*Ritual structures and worldviews—Performance as the enactment of belief*

THE NGUILLIPÚN

THIS RITE OF increase is currently celebrated by Native American peoples of southern Chile and Argentina (Patagonia). Variations of the *nguillipún* are practiced by Tehuelche, Pehuenche, Günuna-Kena, Huarpe, Ranquel, Puelche, and Mapuche. The Mapuche, an Araucanian people of central and southern Chile, assisted the peoples of Patagonia throughout the nineteenth century in their efforts to resist subjugation by the Argentine army. Today, the various indigenous groups of northern Patagonia usually are subsumed under the name of "Mapuche" (See Map).

In the past, the *nguillipún* could be celebrated several times during the year to increase animal and crop fertility, to mark a successful harvest, or to entreat the deities when a community was in crisis. The economic marginalization of the Mapuche in the twentieth century has limited these rites to an annual cycle, based on the completion of summer grazing and the marking of lineage flocks. The most impoverished communities seldom hold these rites, but families may travel many miles to attend the rituals of another community. If the lineage songs of visitors are known to women in the host community, newcomers may participate in most *nguillipún* activities.

This ceremony is known from the Andes to the pampas as *nguillipún, nguillatún, camaruco,* and *kamarrikún.* It is still practiced in the Argentine

provinces of Neuquén, Río Negro, and Chubut, as well as in Chilean lands south of the Bío-Bío River. The goals and ritual actions of the *nguillipún* reflect shared beliefs rooted in a worldview that predates the European invasion of Patagonia. According to Havestadt (1777 in 1883), documentation on the *nguillipún* tradition in Chile first appears in the writings of 16th- and 17th-century chroniclers such as Pedro de Valdivia, Luis de Valdivia, and Diego de Rosales. The military and ceremonial alliances between indigenous peoples on both sides of the Andes inform the ethnographic content of Alonso de Ercilla y Zúñiga's epic poem "La Araucana" (1569–1589). In Argentina, Jesuit priests kept records of the peoples they encountered in their incursions into the pampas and the Andes of northern Patagonia. Bernhard Havestadt, a meticulous early ethnographer and a Jesuit missionary, compiled linguistic and ceremonial data on people who called themselves Puelche and Pehuenche, whom he encountered between 1751 and 1752. Twentieth-century studies of the *nguillipún* include the accounts of Augusta (1910), Robles Rodríguez (1911), Groeber and Palavecino (1928), Cencio (1940), Zamorano (1949), Barreto (1959), Casamiquela (1964), and Faron (1964). Ethnomusicological studies of some of these ceremonies have been conducted by Lehmann-Nitsche (1908), Isamitt (1935), and Robertson (1975, 1977, and 1979).

The descriptions and interpretations of this rite come from the author's observation of and participation in the Eastern *nguillipún* tradition of Zaina

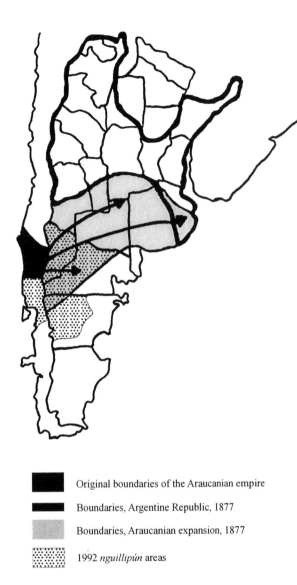

■ Original boundaries of the Araucanian empire

■ Boundaries, Argentine Republic, 1877

▨ Boundaries, Araucanian expansion, 1877

⬚ 1992 *nguillipún* areas

Map: Historical and contemporary areas of *nguillipún* performance.

Yegua, under the administration of the Ancatruz lineage; and the Western *nguillipún* rite of Malleo, under the leadership of the Painefilú lineage. Both communities are located in the Province of Neuquén, in western Argentina.

RITUAL STRUCTURES AND WORLDVIEWS

The goal of the *nguillipún* is to reach the inhabitants of sacred time through the performance of chants and dances that will fuse sacred and ordinary time. Once these temporal boundaries have been broken down, the supernatural beings can be brought to understand the

plight of their children on earth, and thus be moved to compassionate action.

Although the head of the cosmological pantheon is Ngeñechén (She/He Who Creates), ritual invocations are directed to deities who have ongoing influence and interaction with human beings. Ñuke Mapu (Earth Mother) and F'ta Chau (Great Father) are entreated during rogations to take on their sacred roles as Elchén Kushé (Venerable Old Mother) and Elchén F'Chau (Venerable Old Father); for it was in the latter capacity that they began to procreate and populate the earth. Ilche Dzomó (Young Woman) and Ilche Wentrú (Young Man), the offsprings of Elchén Kushé and Elchén F'Chau, are invoked as the original ancestors of all those peoples who today are known as Mapuche.

The *nguillipún* is led by two adolescent girls and two adolescent boys who embody the part-human, part-supernatural nature of the original ancestors. The girls, called *kalfumalén* (blue maidens), lead the women in dance, and remain in the custody of the female ritual leader, or *witakultruntufe* (she-who-carries-the-drum), during the entire ceremony (Figs. 1 and 2). The two boys, called *piwichén,* also are kept apart from the other celebrants. Although they lead the men in displays of horsemanship and in the *puel purrún* (dances to the East), they may not speak to anyone other than the chief and the female ritual specialist during the ceremony. This ritual isolation in time and space is a statement of the ancestral identity of the *piwichén* and *kalfumalén* (Fig. 3).

PERFORMANCE AS THE ENACTMENT OF BELIEF

Interaction with the beings of sacred time and space *(alüaluntu)* is established over a period of three days and two nights. The Mapuche name the day according to various manifestations of light (Waag 1982). The deities and ancestors are most available to humans during *epewun* (morning). Thus, at daybreak, men stand behind the altar *(rewe)* and invoke the inhabitants of *alüaluntu* through a form of ritual discourse called *lukutún.* Female deities and ancestors always are invoked first, for a great part of the *nguillipún* focuses on the life-giving power of female energy (Robertson 1989). These rogations cannot reach the beings of *alüaluntu* unless they are conveyed through the performance of the *tayil* or lineage song of each supplicant (Recorded Exs. 1 and 2). As men face East

Fig. 1: *Witakultruntufe* (left) drumming and chanting before the altar, accompanied by two *kalfumalén*. The carcasses of two sheep adorn the altar (Malleo, Neuquén, 1972). Photo by Carol Robertson, courtesy of the author.

Fig. 2: *Witakultruntufe* Carolina Milliapi (left) and two *kalfumalén*, resting between dances (Malleo, Neuquén, 1972).

and make their entreaties to the beings of *alüaluntu*, women of their lineages must stand behind them and sing, or "pull" the lineage soul out of the bodies of the supplicants, into the sacred ritual space, and into the time of sacred beings (Robertson 1979). Without such a performance, the supplications of the men are impotent. Only women may perform the *tayil* repertoire. Usually, only men recite the *lukutún*, although women are not forbidden to do so.

After the celebrants have established contact with the domain of *alüaluntu* through the performance of *lukutún* and *tayil*, they dance in honor of the ancestors. Men of the lowland or pampa areas dance *lonkomeo* (dance of the head movements), accompanied by male drummers and women who perform the lineage song of each dancer, so that the dance will be seen by the beings of sacred time. Usually each community has at least two alternating groups of five men who dress in loincloths, ponchos, *choike* (rhea) feathers, bells, and body paint. Each dance group performs five different dances, which represent different stages in the life cycle of the pampa bird known as *chegöl* (*tero* in Spanish). Some communities see the dance as a representation of the life cycle of the rhea (Groeber and Palavecino 1928;

Casamiquela 1964; Grebe, Pacheco, and Segura 1972).

Although *lonkomeo* dancing displays individual virtuosity, *puel purrún* dances, which are central to all *nguillipún* ceremonies, focus on community participation and cooperation. The *puel purrún* is organized by the female ritual specialist. In the *puel purrún*, the *kalfumalén* girls, representing the original female ancestor, lead the women clockwise around the altar, and the *piwichén* boys, representing the original male ancestor, lead the men counterclockwise around the altar. Women punctuate their dance with a song repertoire called *öl* or *nöl*. Men often play the *pifilka* as they dance (Fig. 4). The *pifilka* is played by blowing into a tube of bamboo or hollowed out wood, and can be tuned by pouring water into the bottom of the tube. Each man plays only one tube at a time, so that melodies are created by interlocking parts.

The clockwise and counterclockwise motion of the dancers, the texts and pathways or melodic contours of the women, and the punctuations of *pifilkas* played by the men work in concert to set in motion the same forces that were awakening at the moment of Creation. By these means, the Mapuche are both drawing on the *nguillipún* for survival and adding to the power of the

Fig. 3: Two *piwichén* mounted and preparing to lead the *awún* cavalcade (Malleo, Neuquén, 1972).

Fig. 4: *Piwichén* holding a *pifilka* during *nguillipún* (Malleo, Neuquén, 1972).

ritual, which grows incrementally with every generation of celebrants. In addition, the totality of these elements of performance combine to awaken compassion in the beings that inhabit sacred time, thus moving them to act in ways that benefit all living things.

REFERENCES

Augusta, Félix José de 1910. *Lecturas araucanas*. Valdivia: Imprenta de la Prefectura Apostólica.

Barreto, Oscar, S.S. 1959. "Nguillatún mapuche," *Boletín salesiano* (August) 183–184.

Casamiquela, Rodolfo 1964. *Estudio del nillatún y la religión araucana*. Bahía Blanca, Argentina: Universidad Nacional del Sur, Cuadernos del Sur.

Cencio, Luis 1940. "El 'villatúm': Fiesta indígena araucana," *Revista geográfica americana* 6: 13–77.

Ercilla y Zúñiga, Alonso de 1569–1589 in 1919. *La araucana*. Santiago: Editorial J. T. Medina.

Faron, Louis C. 1964. *Hawks of the sun: Mapuche morality and its ritual attributes*. Pittsburgh: University of Pittsburgh Press.

Grebe, María Ester, Sergio Pacheco, and José Segura 1972. "Cosmovisión mapuche," *Cuadernos de la realidad nacional* (Santiago de Chile) 14: 46–73.

Groeber, Pablo, and Eduardo Palavecino 1928. "Un nguillatún en el Lago Lakar," *Anales de la Sociedad Argentina de Estudios Geográficos* 3: 291.

Havestadt, Bernhard 1777 in 1883. *Chilidugu*. Leipzig: Julius Platzmann, 2 vols.

Isamitt, Carlos 1935. "Cantos mágicos de los araucanos," *Revista de arte* 1/3: 5–9.

Lehmann-Nitsche, Robert 1908. "Patagonische Gesänge und Musikbogen," *Anthropos* 3: 916–40.

Robertson, Carol E. 1975. *Tayil: Musical communication and social organization among the Mapuche of Argentina* (PhD diss., Institute of Folklore: Indiana University).

1977. "Lukutún: Text and context in Mapuche rogations," *Latin American Indian literatures* 1/2: 67–78.

1979. "Pulling the ancestors: Performance practice and praxis in Mapuche ordering," *Ethnomusicology* 23/3: 395–416.

1989. "Power and gender in the musical experiences of women" in *Women and music in cross-cultural perspective*, ed. by Ellen Koskoff. New York: Greenwood Press, 225–44.

Robles Rodríguez, Eulogio 1911. *Costumbres e creencias araucanas: Ñeigurehuen*. Santiago: Imprenta Cervantes.

Waag, Else María 1982. *Tres entidades "wekufü" en la cultura mapuche*. Buenos Aires: Editorial Universitaria de Buenos Aires.

Zamorano, Mariano 1949. "El nguillatún araucano y su sentido," *Boletín de estudios geográficos* (Mendoza) 1: 2–35.

RECORDED EXAMPLES

1. *Kawel tayil* (horse *tayil*), as delivered by Carolina Milliapi in Huilquimenuco, Neuquén, 1995.

2. Women during *nguillipún* performing for the saddling of ritual horses of the *piwichén*. *Kultrún* performance by Carolina Milliapi, Malleo, Neuquén, 1995.

MUSIC AND HEALING

CAROL E. ROBERTSON

*The power of song and the fabric of reality—Medical training and ritual
practice—Botanical and musical skills—Ritual as an agent for healing*

NATIVE AMERICAN HEALING is a complex science
rooted in ancient beliefs and practices. Archaeological
excavation sites from Illinois to Patagonia yield objects
related to healing rites and medical practices dating back
to the early migrations across the Bering Sea, sometime
between 40,000–50,000 and 12,000 B.C.E. Techniques
of shamanic healing, wherein the practitioner leaves
his/her body to travel in another dimension of time and
space, often are linked to hunting and gathering
cultures. Diaguita and Moche shamans documented
their discoveries by drawing on rocks (Donnan 1978).
Maya records, such as those held in the Madrid Codex
and the Codex Fejérvary-Mayer, allude to rituals and
beliefs that hold currency in contemporary traditions
throughout the continent (*Codex Madrid* 1882 and
1869–70; León-Portilla 1986). The Yucatec-Maya
manuscript known as the "Ritual of the Bacabs" is filled
with incantations, prayers, songs, and indigenous
medical prescriptions that present us with a firmly
established pre-Columbian medical tradition (Roys
1965). Though the last five hundred years of contact with
Europe and Africa have changed many aspects of
autochthonous medicine, healing and the rites in which
healing is contained and transformed date back to the
earliest attempts of indigenous peoples to come to terms
with their environment.

The 16th- and 17th-century priests and chroniclers
who recorded these practices in the Americas simply
did not understand indigenous concepts of wellness
and healing; nor could they grasp the power of sound in
such matters. Early ethnohistorians, such as Sahagún
(ca. 1558–ca. 1569 in 1956) and Garcilaso de la Vega
(1609) inform us about some of the beliefs that
undergird healing, but ignore the central place of
music in diagnosis and prognosis. European concepts
of wellness, cause and effect, cosmology, and
contamination, and the fanaticism spawned by the
Inquisition, relegated most shamanic healing to the
realm of heresy.

To this day, indigenous healing ceremonies use
many powerful devices to produce a catharsis that will
move the patient from disease ("dis-ease") into
wellness and full participation in the community. In
the healing traditions of the Americas, wellness is
perceived as a state that requires a delicate balance
between the individual, the community, and the
sacred. Physical, spiritual, psychological, and social
dimensions of illness usually are treated
simultaneously, for they are regarded as synchronous
expressions of personhood. Healing can be brought
about by community ritual, by prescribed vision
quests undertaken by individuals, by sessions in
which the patient's family takes an active role, or by
individualized work with a single healing specialist or
a group of specialists. The healer tends to be a person
who has inherited this role through his/her family,
who has been chosen by the spirit world as a
messenger to the human community, or who has

initiated contact with the spirit world through visions and pilgrimages to sacred grounds. Along the Venezuela/Brazil border, Yanomamö communities allow any adult male to become a healer and medium, and a village may have many such persons in its midst (Chagnon 1977). Among Araucanian speakers in the southern lands of Argentina and Chile, only women may take on the responsibilities of healing, and usually there will be only one *machi* per community. Mapuche men who wish to become *machi* must dress as women, for Mapuche healing is spun from the life-giving qualities of women (Faron 1964; Grebe, Fernández, and Fiedler 1971; Grebe 1973; Robertson 1987).

THE POWER OF SONG AND THE FABRIC OF REALITY

Healing with sound is particularly effective in many American cultures because of beliefs and experiences shared by healer and patient. First, sound and silence are both tools that can be used to structure reality. If a Tepehua (Mexico) violinist plays just the right combination of pitches and rhythms, he can cause the marijuana goddess, Lakatuhún Hatupasdíqal (known in Spanish as Santa Rosa), to bring wisdom to her followers. His melody is so precise in structure and intention, that even a small alteration in sequences can change the meaning and consequences of the "thought songs" he plays (Boilès 1967: 269–71).

Second, time is a multidimensional experience. Between the many layers of time are permeable membranes that are especially sensitive to sound. Held, but not trapped by these dimensions, are Creator deities; spirit guardians of trees, mountains, rivers, kin groups, or individuals; ancestors who once walked the earth and now live in ways that reflect the concerns of human beings; humans, who use sound to transform themselves simultaneously into all of these realms of time and space (Benson 1975). Among the Kalapálo (Brazil), these beings are called *itseke*, and carry out their activities through hyperactive uses of energy that are beyond the grasp of daily life among humans. Links with the *itseke* must be established through rituals that bring humans and hyperactive forms of energy into the same frequency (Basso 1985).

Third, sound, whether instrumental or vocal, can restructure the individual. On the physical plane, sound waves can alter the rhythms of the nervous system or can stimulate movement in specific areas of the body. In one form of the *machitún* healing traditions of the Mapuche in Argentina, expert healers are also skillful manipulators of sound. If energy is not moving in a particular area of a patient's body, healers will send sound through that part of their own body and into the inert part of the patient (Robertson 1989).

Fourth, sounds open the door to complex layers of association and meaning. An expert healer can sense intuitively the sounds, melodies, and timbres that will work best with each individual patient. In the city of Iquitos, in the Peruvian Amazon region, *ayahuasquero* healers use whistling to guide the patient through the paradoxical experience of *ayahuasca*, a potent hallucinogen used to help patients reconstitute reality and bring balance into their lives (Katz and Dobkin de Ríos 1971). Mazatec healers in Mexico might interweave powerful words, familiar and novel melodies, and invocations to multiple Mazatec and Christian forms of the sacred with copious nonverbal communication (Wasson, G. and F. Cowan, and Rhodes 1974). Until the twentieth century, Huarpe, Ranquel, Puelche, and Günuna Kena (northern Patagonia, Argentina) healers used sounds to reduce the size of tumors, fill empty or "dis-eased" places in the body, and transform the patient's relationship with the sacred. Some of these aural skills still are used by women and a few men among the Mapuche (Chile, Argentina) and Quechua (Peru) (Antigual 1978).

MEDICAL TRAINING AND RITUAL PRACTICE

Dis-ease usually poses a question for the healer, the patient, and/or the afflicted community. The significance of and answers to these questions can be assessed by moving beyond the boundaries that frame everyday experience. The boundaries of space and time are permeable. They are especially susceptible to sound. Thus, healers must be expert manipulators of time and space and must have complete mastery of those repertoires of sounds and movements that forge relationships between deities, forces of nature, plants and animals, and human beings. The healer must walk the path between these different realities so that the balance used in the healing journey will reflect balance back onto the circumstances of the patient (Myerhoff 1976).

Healers seldom are regarded as expert musicians in their communities, yet they have expertise in repertoires that are deemed central to the survival of the community. One of the tasks of the healer is to see objects and events of everyday experience within a different context of meanings. Thus, a Karajá healer (Brazil) might use the vibrant red tail feather of the macaw, used in the *aruaña* men's ceremony, to invoke the power and wisdom of his ancestors in a healing ceremony (Métraux 1944). An Otomí healer (Mexico) might take a grain of maize from a fallow field, sing the soul of Centeotl (god-goddess of maize) into it, and bury it in the ground to refertilize the land (Boilès 1971). An Aymara (Bolivia) healer's apprentice might spend many days blowing into his *siku* (panpipe) in search of the precise timbres and resonances that he will transfer to his patient (Ramos 1981).

Healing is a transformative art that must be performed with scientific precision. Entrance to the healing profession is usually dictated by the spirit world as well as by lineage. In areas where healing is a specialized task, initiates often receive signs in early childhood that indicate they are being courted by the spirit world. Dreams are interpreted as messages from realities that interface with daily living. Oracular dreams in a child are encouraged by Nahuatl and Mazatec (Mexico), Aymara (Chile, Bolivia), Mataco, Chorote, and northern Tehuelche (Argentina), and almost all other cultures that have individual healing specialists. Over time, the child whose dreams indicate a special connection with the spirit world will be apprenticed to a relative who has expertise in dream interpretation. As that child grows, he or she will learn to associate dream images with patterns and events in waking reality (Bourguignon 1973; Furst 1976; Grebe 1978).

In many areas of the Andes, seizures are also an indication that an individual is being contacted by the sacred. These seizures, which European medicine would classify as *grand mal* (epilepsy), indicate that the soul of the person afflicted is being removed from the body and taken into sacred time and space. The initiate will return from that place with visions, chants, or other messages from the sacred. Eventually, if put under the guidance of an expert healer, the person chosen by the spirits as a medium will have to learn how to enter and leave the domain of the sacred. Traveling between these realities is one of the most difficult tasks of the healer, for it makes extraordinary demands on the body and soul of the practitioner.

The main guideposts for these journeys are put into place by sound. One of the most common techniques of the shaman is soul retrieval, wherein the healer uses sound to enter a trance state that will expose the soul of the patient to shamanic scrutiny. Drumming and rattling are especially effective in inducing and guiding this kind of journey. In the *ülutún* rite of the Chilean Mapuche, the healer or *machi* beats a frame drum to enter, negotiate with, and leave the spirit world. The shamanic drum, or *kultrún*, symbolizes the elements and forces of the universe, even in the way it is painted. Its sound opens the gateway to the cosmological forces portrayed on the drumhead (Grebe 1979–1980). The gourd-rattle, usually made from the dried fruit of the *Lagenaria vulgaris* or the *Lagenaria siceraria* vines, is one of the most sacred objects of rain-forest cultures. Among the Guaraní (Brazil, Paraguay) the *mbaraká* rattle is a paradigm of the cosmos. It is likened to a womb that contains the primordial ingredients of sound and power, and gives birth to transformation (Nimuendajú 1978).

Mapuche healers in Argentina speak of their chants as trails that take them through uncharted lands (Robertson 1979). Those who travel into the dimensions of the extraordinary also must be able to hear the frequencies that emanate from plants, rocks, and different densities of matter. The hearing of a Mapuche *machi* becomes so acute that she can differentiate the frequencies produced by the same plant at different times of the day or during different phases of the moon. Along the upper Amazon, the Desana (Tukano) healer or *payé* uses chants to communicate with animals and colors. His keen memory and knowledge of mythology, ritual, and the "voicing" of different beings allows him to conduct lengthy healing sessions (Reichel-Dolmatoff 1971 and 1975). Thus, drums, rattles, and song are the central aural components of Native American healing.

BOTANICAL AND MUSICAL SKILLS

The skills developed by healers are many, and they vary from culture to culture. In most instances, the healer must become a skilled biochemist, for plants are an important part of prognosis (Spruce 1908; Lastres 1951; Dobkin de Ríos 1984). Most healers, from the Peruvian *ayahuasquero* to the Mazatec (Mexico) *curandera* who induces her healing trance through the ingestion of hallucinogenic mushrooms, learn the effects of different plants by testing them on their own bodies. In this process, they build up an immunity to many of the poisons and diseases with which they will come into contact. Though the basic inventory of pharmacology is acquired during apprenticeship, healers continue to add to their repertoire of remedies, and often guard their individual discoveries from other healers. The element of secrecy so often associated with traditional healing is usually a means of ensuring that potent botanical substances will not be misused by amateurs.

Some of the most effective substances used in healing rites in conjunction with sound are of an alkaloid nature. Botanical substances have been used in the Americas for many centuries. The coronation of Moctezuma in 1502 was described by a Spaniard named Durand, who reported that mushrooms were ingested so that oracular visions could be received by the celebrants (cited in Heim 1969: 203). Lastres (1951) lists many substances used in the Andes to focus the attention of the healer on the supernatural. Among the alkaloids most commonly used today are black henbane (*Hyoscyamus niger*); various derivatives of belladonna (*Atropa belladonna*); *ayahuasca* vines belonging to various species of *Banisteriopsis*, which are commonly mixed with psychedelics containing *Datura* (*Datura brugmansia*) and/or indolic substances; varieties of *Brugmansia aurea*; psilocybine; mescaline; and varieties of *Cannabis*. Potions made from these substances are used to induce an altered state in the healer or the patient, and sometimes in both.

The Wixárika, or Huichol (Mexico), use the hallucinogenic cactus peyote *(hikuri)* as a sacrament that brings visions and songs into relief (Myerhoff 1974). In community healing rites, the shaman, or *mara'akáme*, often uses the chants that come to him through the drug to guide other members of the community through their visions, and to put them in direct contact with the sacred nature of peyote. Among the shaman's gifts is the ability to negotiate the difficult and sometimes rather confusing sacred path of hallucinogenic visions for his patients as well as for himself.

The psilocybine mushroom, known among the Mazatec (Mexico) as *teo-nanacatl*, is a vegetable form of the sacred. Sometimes it is referred to as the body of the snake-serpent god Quetzalcoatl. In more recent times, it is equated with the body of Christ. Thus, many of the incantations that come to the healer during her *velada*, or healing session, are aural manifestations of god incarnate (Wasson, G. and F. Cowan, and Rhodes 1974). The mushroom takes a person's soul where it needs to go to receive the information that will induce physical, psychological, and spiritual catharsis. The journey is made through song, the messages of the sacred are communicated to the patient through song, and the identity of the healer as medium is revealed through song.

Along the border shared by Brazil and Venezuela, Yanomamö shamans, or *shabori*, specialize in contacting *hekura*, the demons that dwell in mountains or on rocks. The shaman must entice these spirits to enter his body, so that he can control them and then cast them out of the village. Contact with the spirit world is made by taking the drug *ebene*, combined with other hallucinogens. The drug instructs the shaman on how to reach and address the *hekura* spirits, as well as how to dance so that the spirits can be attracted or repelled (Chagnon 1977).

Among the Warao (Venezuela), tobacco is used to induce trances that connect the healer, or *bahanarotu*, to specific areas of the cosmic vault. Although some *bahanarotu* are known to kill through their manipulation of negative forces in the cosmos, the benevolent *bahanarotu* blows tobacco smoke over his patient to remove evil spells and sucks arrows out of the patient's body as a means of removing poisons. He also uses his vast knowledge of sacred chants to travel to the dwelling of the eastern Supreme Spirit, or Bahana, to bring back peace and prosperity to his community. Tobacco smoke, when exhaled, creates a bridge that rises from the earthly plane to the realm of the sacred. The songs that the shaman must use in his dialogue with Bahana ride upwards on the trail of smoke (Wilbert 1975).

Not all shamans use hallucinogens or other mind-altering drugs to achieve their goals, but they all use sound. Among the Tukano of Colombia, the *payé* often goes into retreat before a healing ceremony, bracketing his ritual and the music essential to healing with silence (Reichel-Dolmatoff 1975). The Andean Mapuche *machi* frames her vocalization of the lineage soul, or *tayil*, through silence (Robertson 1979 and 1989). In healing, silence and sounding are part of a continuum of communication that shatters the parameters of everyday experience in order to introduce a new sense of order—one that will transform dis-ease into harmony within the universe, the individual patient, and the community.

RITUAL AS AN AGENT FOR HEALING

Most of the healing specialists described above are shamanic practitioners, that is, they use their skills and powers to travel through different domains of reality and accomplish tasks that cannot be done in ordinary time and space. The primary vehicle for their journey is song, for the chants and sacred words they use have linked their ancestors to the sacred for many centuries.

Many communities maintain their balance or "wellness" through regular ceremonies that keep them in touch with the sacred elements of the universe as well as the sacred that dwells in each individual. These rites link entire kin groups or entire settlements to one another, and they raise the individual from the drudgery and burdens of everyday experience into the concert of the cosmos. Mapuche speakers of Argentina and Chile accomplish this form of community regeneration through the *nguillipún* (see Carol Robertson, "Fertility Ritual," in this volume), wherein ritual actions and sacred chants combine to remind the deities that they too are parents. Through the dances, rogations, and chants of the *nguillipún* the deities are moved to compassion. It is compassion that ultimately brings fertility, good weather, abundance, and health.

Health also depends on passing successfully from one phase of life into another. Suyá (Brazil) men mark entry into adulthood by separating from the sisters who raised them and moving into a men's hut in the center of a village. Thereafter they are allowed little contact with their sisters, with whom they have formed a primary psychological bond. This relationship can be acknowledged in adult life when men sing songs (*akia*) that are shouted from the vicinity of the men's hut so that they can be heard by sisters dwelling on the periphery of the village (Seeger 1987 and 1988).

The inevitable change of status for all individuals comes at death. The final exhalation of breath is an ordered sound that signals not a loss of health, but a transition from one mode of being to another. Thus, exhaling breath through song often accompanies mourning and the final rite of transition. Among Apapocuvá (Brazil) kin, death is a group effort that is faced peacefully. While the shaman keeps watch over subtle changes that begin to overtake the body of the person in transition, neighbors and family of the patient gently sing the songs acquired by that person during initiation. When the shaman signals that the next change will be fatal, the community shifts to a repertoire that will enable the soul of the beloved to move into another form—a form that can return to dwell in the community in a different way. The melodies and rhythms of this transition change as the condition of the patient changes. At the precise instant of death, the healer intones the solemn *ñeĕngaraí*, a delicate melody with which the shaman accompanies

the deceased on the journey to the next world (Nimuendajú 1978).

Healing in the Americas is clearly a complex, sacred process in which music plays a central role. Understanding that role requires a grasp of the nature of sound as a sacred, transcendent phenomenon. Understanding the power of sound to heal also requires an acceptance of the capability of human beings to embody and respond to sound. Native American systems of healing have survived many centuries of cultural upheaval. The ability of these traditions to grow, change, and assimilate new ideas bears witness to their resilience and wisdom.

REFERENCES

Antigual, Carmen "Kushé Papai" 1978. Field interview conducted by Carol E. Robertson, Las Negras, Neuquén, Argentina.

Basso, Ellen B. 1985. *A musical view of the universe.* Philadelphia: University of Pennsylvania Press.

Benson, Elizabeth P., ed. 1975. *Death and the afterlife in pre-Columbian America.* Washington, D.C.: Dumbarton Oaks Research Library and Collections.

Boilès, Charles L. 1967. "Tepehua thought-song: A case of semantic signaling," *Ethnomusicology* 11/3: 267–92.

———. 1971. Personal communication.

Bourguignon, Erika 1973. "Introduction: A framework for the comparative study of altered states of consciousness" in *Religion, altered states of consciousness, and social change,* ed. by Erika Bourguignon. Columbus: Ohio State University Press.

Chagnon, Napoleon 1977. *Yanomamö: The fierce people.* New York: Holt, Rinehart and Winston.

Codex Fejérvary-Mayer 1971. Pre-Columbian manuscript in the Free Public Museum of Liverpool, M 12014, facsimile edition with commentary by C. A. Burland. Graz: Akademische Druck- und Verlagsanstalt.

Codex Madrid (Cortesian section) 1882. *Códice maya denominado Cortesiano que se conserva en el Museo Arqueológico Nacional* (Madrid), facsimile ed., by J. de D. de la Rada. Madrid.

Codex Madrid (Troan section) 1869–70. *Manuscrit Troano: Études sur le système graphique et la langue des Mayas,* ed. by C. E. Brasseur de Bourbourg. Paris, 2 vols.

Dobkin de Ríos, Marlene 1972. *Visionary vine: Hallucinogenic healing in the Peruvian Amazon.* Prospect Heights, Illinois: Waveland Press.

———. 1984. *Hallucinogens: Cross-cultural perspective.* Albuquerque: University of New Mexico Press.

Donnan, Christopher 1978. *Moche art of Peru.* Los Angeles: Los Angeles Museum of Cultural History, University of California.

Faron, Louis C. 1964. *Hawks of the sun: Mapuche morality and its ritual attributes.* Pittsburgh: University of Pittsburgh Press.

Furst, Peter T. 1976. *Hallucinogens and culture.* San Francisco: Chandler and Sharp.

Garcilaso de la Vega 1609. *Primera parte de los comentarios reales.* Lisbon: Pedro Crasbeeck.

Grebe, María Ester 1973. "El kultrún mapuche: Un microcosmos simbólico," *Revista musical chilena* 27/123–124: 3–42.

———. 1978. "Relationships between musical practice and cultural context: The kultrún and its symbolism," *The world of music* 20/3: 84–106.

1979–1980. "Relaciones entre música y cultura: El kultrún y su simbolismo," *Revista INIDEF* 4: 7–25.

Grebe, María Ester, Joaquín Fernández, and Carlos Fiedler 1971. "Mitos, creencias y concepto de enfermedad en la cultura mapuche," *Acta psiquiátrica y psicológica de América Latina* (Buenos Aires) 17/3: 180–93.

Heim, Roger 1969. *Les champignons toxiques et hallucinogenes*. Paris: Éditions du Musée National d'Histoire Naturelle.

Katz, Fred, and Marlene Dobkin de Ríos 1971. "Hallucinogenic music: An analysis of the role of whistling in Peruvian Ayahuasca healing sessions," *Journal of American folklore* 84: 320–27.

Lastres, Juan 1951. *Historia de la medicina peruana*. Vol. 1, *La medicina incaica*. Lima: Universidad Nacional Mayor de San Marcos.

León-Portilla, Miguel, ed. 1986. *Tonalamatl de los Pochtecas*. México: Universidad Nacional Autónoma de México.

Métraux, Alfred 1944. "Tapirage, a biological discovery of South American Indians," *Proceedings of the Washington Academy of Sciences* 34/8: 252–54.

Myerhoff, Barbara G. 1974. *Peyote hunt*. Ithaca, New York: Cornell University Press.

1976. "Shamanic equilibrium: Balance and mediation in known and unknown worlds" in *American folk medicine: A symposium*, ed. by Wayland D. Hand. Berkeley: University of California Press, 99–108.

Nimuendajú, Curt 1978. *Mitos de creación y de destrucción del mundo como fundamentos de la religión de los Apapokuvá-Guaraní*. Lima: Centro Amazónico de Antropología y Aplicación Práctica.

Ramos, Independencio 1981. Field interview conducted by Carol E. Robertson. San Juan, Argentina.

Reichel-Dolmatoff, Gerardo 1971. *Amazonian cosmos: The sexual and religious symbolism of the Tukano Indians*. Chicago: University of Chicago Press.

1975. *The shaman and the jaguar: A study of narcotic drugs among the Indians of Colombia*. Philadelphia: Temple University Press.

Robertson, Carol E. 1979. "Pulling the ancestors: Performance practice and praxis in Mapuche ordering," *Ethnomusicology* 23/3: 395–416.

1987. "Power and gender in the musical experiences of women" in *Women and music in cross-cultural perspective*, ed. by Ellen Koskoff. New York: Greenwood Press, 225–44.

1989. "Coming to grips with songs of power," panel on Music and Healing, Society for Ethnomusicology Annual Meeting, Massachusetts Institute of Technology.

Roys, Ralph L., ed. 1965. *Ritual of the Bacabs*. Norman: University of Oklahoma Press.

Sahagún, Bernardino de ca. 1558–ca. 1569 in 1956. *Historia general de las cosas de Nueva España*. México: Porrúa Hermanos.

Seeger, Anthony 1987. *Why Suyá sing*. Cambridge: Cambridge University Press.

1988. "Voices, flutes, and shamans in Brazil," *The world of music* 30/2: 22–39.

Spruce, Richard 1908. *Notes of a botanist on the Amazon and Andes*, 2 vols. London: Macmillan, vol. 2.

Wasson, R. Gordon, George Cowan, Florence Cowan, and Willard Rhodes 1974. *María Sabina and her Mazatec velada*. New York: Harcourt Brace Jovanovich.

Wilbert, Johannes 1975. "Magico-religious use of tobacco among South American Indians" in *Cannabis and culture*, ed. by Vera Rubin. The Hague: Mouton, 439–61.

The Fundamental Role of Music in the Life of Two Central American Ethnic Nations: The Mískito in Honduras and Nicaragua, and the Kuna in Panama[*]

Ronny Velásquez

The Mískito in Honduras and Nicaragua: Musical traditions of the Mískito; Mískito song; European elements in the music of the Mískito—The Kuna in Panama: Decoding the meaning of Kuna chant; The world of Kuna chant; Instrumental music of the Kuna—Conclusions

THE CHOICE OF THESE two indigenous groups, separated in time and space, is not fortuitous and responds to reasons of a conceptual nature. Not only do these groups share the practice of a universe of shamanic song, but they also have constructed systems of explanation about their musical worlds. Through our studies of both cultural groups, we have identified points of convergence. An ethnographic fact that carries great significance in the explanation of shamanic song was given to us by several *sukias* or Mískito shamans: they receive their shamanic information, and even learn the shamanic songs, during their daily sleep. This would appear to be "normal" information and applies to all central types of shamanism, but the significant difference is that the "dreams" of the Mískito describe exactly what is taking place in the now-called daily "meetings of the Kuna

congress." That is, the dreams received by one cultural group describe proceedings at meetings of leaders of the other group. The daily reunions of the "Kuna congress" serve as a means to convey information to the people about the origins of the culture, diseases, dangers, and rejoicements. The Mískito's dreams describe this daily meeting that takes place in *Ibeorgun Nega*, or "House of Grandfather Sun" of the Kuna.

Although the distance that currently separates the geographic settlements of these groups may appear to be considerable, this was probably not a factor before the arrival of Europeans. The Mískito attacked the warring Guaymí peoples of Panama but it seems that they learned much from the Kuna, who have been a peaceful people devoted to daily communication with the supernatural. According to the recollections of Sam Archibold, a Kuna from the island of Ustupo, those Kuna who practiced traditional medicine used to travel to the Mískito areas of present-day Honduras and Nicaragua. They did so on foot along the beach, and also in small vessels. The same Sam Archibold, then 76 years old, used to speak some Mískito when

* The author wishes to express his gratitude to Luis Felipe Ramón y Rivera, María Teresa Melfi, and Elena Hermo for their invaluable help with the musical transcriptions and critical comments. We also wish to thank Mískito professor Nathan Pravia Lacayo for correcting translations from Mískito, and to the Kuna professors Jesús Smith Kantule and Filemón Herrera for their invaluable assistance in the interpretation of Kuna symbolic language.

we interviewed him in 1976 and had traveled to the Mískito region in his youth.

Other points of convergence link the cultural practices of these two groups. These include the performance of songs for the woman in labor; songs to protect a community from the danger of epidemics; exorcisms to pacify hurricanes; the practice of magic to master the forces of fire; similar conceptions of the origin of diviners and how to prepare them; similar rites of initiation; and the existence of "special houses" for the menstruating woman and for the woman in labor. These two groups also share similar conceptions of the power of wood carvings to purge communities from evil spirits, as well as the belief in the powers of some woods that are used in shamanic practices. There is a universe of similarities between conceptions of the afterlife and, in shamanic practice, between the paths that souls follow on their journey to their final dwelling. Linguistically, however, the Mískito and Kuna appear to be unrelated, although they have been tentatively affiliated with the great Macro-Chibcha family of South American provenance.

The foregoing explains the reasons that have prompted us to focus on the Mískito and Kuna in this essay. As limited as this study may be—given the wealth of cultural aspects excluded here—it is intended to provide a point of entry into the musics of these two ethnic nations. Our tentative hypothesis is that, although many facts remain unknown concerning the Mískito-Kuna relationship, the subjacent layers of symbolic behavior exhibit striking similarities.

THE MÍSKITO IN HONDURAS AND NICARAGUA

The Mískito inhabit a part of the Caribbean coastal area of Honduras and Nicaragua in Central America. Although demographic data cannot be supported by a recent census, the Mískito population had been estimated roughly at 60,000 to 70,000. From our own observation and demographic analysis conducted in July and August of 1986, however, it can be concluded that the Mískito are an ethnic nation of about 90,000 to 100,000 persons. Both Nicaragua and Honduras report the same figures. Contrary to the belief held in the 1970s, that the Mískito were on the way to extinction, they have increased numerically in recent years and have strengthened their belief in the value of their culture (see Map 1).

Some distinguished linguists support the affiliation of the Mískito language with the Chibcha family of Central America. Although only hypothetical, this affiliation also considers Mískito as part of the Misumalpa branch, that is, Mískito-Sumo and Matagalpa (Tovar 1961: 185; González de Pérez 1980: 183). The language presents heterogeneous elements whose origin can be traced to different linguistic branches of possibly a single and dynamic linguistic source that could have been Chibcha or another South American language spreading from the south toward Central America, and passing through the Isthmus of Panama. It is quite likely that the Mískito language, as part of its own dynamic processes, nourished itself from various sources, taking perhaps words from extinct languages or protolanguages that converged in this territory, which currently extends through Caribbean coastal lands, great plains toward the interior of Honduras and Nicaragua, and tropical rain forests toward the mouths of the great rivers of the area.

"Mískito" is this ethnic nation's self-denomination. According to our research, the term is derived from *musi*, meaning "people" or "human beings," but alludes also to the origin of the Mískito and bears a cosmogonic connotation. In Chibcha, *muisca*, *muexka*, or *mosca* also means "people" or "human beings" (González de Pérez 1980: 21). A majority of ethnographic and ethnohistorical sources on American aborigines points to the fact that natives called themselves "people" or "human beings." Lacking linguistic training, the conquistadores did not understand the native words and recorded approximations of these terms in their diaries. With the passage of time, however, these misnomers became the most frequently used terms to designate specific human groups. The conquistadores called the Chibchas "Indios Moscas," the Mískito "Moscos" and "Mosquitos," and the region they inhabited was called "La Mosquitia." These designations continue to be used by the creole population of Honduras and Nicaragua to refer to the Mískito, and the geographic area they occupy is still called La Mosquitia.

During the colonial period, the Mískito allied themselves with the British against Spaniards in a struggle over Mískito territory in the Caribbean coastal area. Several factors favored Mískito-British relations, such as the fact that the Mískito were always warriors. On the other hand, Spanish settlers never gained absolute control of the area, but they attempted

Map 1: Mískito territory in present-day Nicaragua and Honduras.

to convert natives by force. Because they live along an extended coastal area, the Mískito are "canoe people" and were always expert navigators who could control the swamps, aquatic labyrinths, the Caribbean Sea, and the riverine networks. They also knew the Central American area, specifically toward the south, between Honduras and Panama. It is worth noting that the Mískito region never had precious metals, which was one of the magnets luring Spanish conquerors. (The Bonanza and La Luz mines in Nicaragua were not discovered until the nineteenth century.)

The first Europeans with whom the Mískito established friendly contact were buccaneers and English pirates, around 1600. They took advantage of the Mískito's knowledge of the water labyrinths to penetrate the territory with their galleons, instill more hatred toward the Spaniards, and push for an

independent territory called La Mosquitia, a kind of nominal Mískito kingdom that would be protected by the British crown.

Although Spanish chroniclers did not leave detailed descriptions of the Mískito, we can surmise some attitudes of Spanish missionaries toward them from the notes of Columbus and his son Fernando, who observed the Indians in this region during Columbus's fourth voyage. According to George Squier (1855 in 1965: 336),

Columbus describes these inhabitants as fishermen and as terrifying sorcerers. Fernando Colón is more explicit. He says that they were dark-skinned, beastly, rough in every respect, anthropophagous creatures who walked around naked and devoured raw fish as soon as they caught it.

Present-day Guaymí Indians of Panama, who live by the Cricamola River, describe the historical Mískito as fierce and vengeful warriors, and it is among the Guaymí that the Mískito have preserved their old denomination, Musiguí. In their legends, the Guaymí tell of the Musiguí springing from the earth like rabbits.

We are certain that the information given by present-day Guaymí on the Mískito subsumes two historical processes: precontact and colonization. From a cultural perspective, this information retains its viability because, before the Mískito migrated during the colonial period, they had settled in what is today Panamanian territory and implanted there several aspects of their culture, such as beneficial and harmful shamanic practices. The Guaymí of the Cricamola region of Panama report that only the force of their protective spirits could shield them from the magical powers of the vandalic and destructive Mískito, who were turned to stone by the strength of Guaymí creation gods.

Historical data on Panama confirm the presence of the Mískito in that territory. Rubén Darío Carles (1963: 19–20) writes that,

On the Nicaraguan coast, the British were presented with a magnificent opportunity. The cacique of the Mosquito Indian tribe, attracted by the gifts and offerings of the British, placed himself under their protection and became hostile to Spanish authorities, disclaiming their rights and government. One of the chief's sons was sent to study in Belize and Jamaica and, upon his return, the British crowned him king of the Mosquito Indians. Vanity compelled the Mosquito king to reclaim the entire northern coast, from Honduras to Punta Valiente, comprising the Chiriquí Lagoon, as lands of his domain [in the Province of Bocas del Toro]. . . . Even the people of Chiriquí [a Panamanian province on the Pacific] and Bocas del Toro [on the Caribbean] shook in terror on several occasions upon hearing about the approaching Mosquito Indians (see also Castillero 1968: 22–24; and Carles 1969: 290).

The Mískito, however, have not been just a warlike nation, but also travelers and masters of the river, sea, and land routes who contributed many cultural elements while assimilating others that are now an integral part of their culture. All indigenous peoples of Central America have exchanged cultural traits. In certain areas, the Mískito have imposed their culture to such an extent that the Sumo and Paya ethnic groups speak the Mískito language, which is the lingua franca of that entire coastal and partly forestal area. A quote from Edward Conzemius illustrates this point:

The Mískito do not oppose intermarriage with foreigners. They assimilate all races; children always speak the language of their mother and grow up as Mískito, even if their father is creole, ladino, Carib, Black, Sumo, Rama, Paya, North American, European, Syrian, or Chinese . . . . Consequently, the Sumo, Paya, and Rama Indian tribes are rapidly dwindling, while the Mískito thrive due to their capacity to assimilate the influx of new blood.

In spite of their contact with pirates, merchants, and English colonists, mahogany cutters, rubber extractors, and Moravian missionaries since the seventeenth century, the Mískito have not changed their way of life in any substantial manner (Conzemius 1932: 13).

Although Conzemius made these observations in the early twentieth century, they continue to represent the pattern of lineage relations among the Mískito. This pattern has led some scholars to the erroneous conclusion that the Mískito are partly Black or descendants of Africans. In some demographic classifications of Honduran society, for instance, the Mískito have been called *zambos*, that is, mestizos of Indian and African descent. Even Elisée Reclus (1881), who mastered this subject, succumbed to this temptation, as evidenced in this quote from Roger Bastide:

. . . 5,080 Black Caribs were deported to the beaches of the Bay of Honduras. At present their descendants occupy a long and narrow strip of land which extends the length of Central America, from the Yucatan Peninsula to the swamps of La Mosquitia. According to Elisée Reclus, in the *Geographie universelle*, Black Caribs also can be found in Nicaragua. Consistent with this opinion, the Moscos or Mosquitos of that country are descendants of mixed Indians and Africans, and not of pure Indians (1969: 76).

Reclus is correct with respect to the Black Caribs, who were deported from San Vicente and reached Roatán in 1797. This population now makes up the Garífuna ethnic nation in Belize, Guatemala, Honduras, and a part of Nicaragua. On the one hand, however, much of the crossbreeding between Black Caribs and Mískitos already had taken place in the Lesser Antilles. On the other hand, the Mískito were settled in the coastal area of Nicaragua and part of Honduras by the time of Conquest or even earlier.

Let us consider a quotation from Ricardo Beltrán y Rózpide (1937: 6): "From Talamanca to the Gulf of Honduras, there were a large number of independent indigenous groups, such as the Votos, Ramas, Cuevas, Ulúas, Toacas, Sucus, Payas, etc., that is, Indians with whom Blacks from the Antilles intermixed to produce Moscos, Mosquitos, or *zambos.*"

Historically, we have to consider that the ethnic origin of the Mískito remains an unknown factor; this should be a matter of some interest, given the fact that the Mískito are a thriving ethnic nation. We also know that this uncertainty has affected the actions of political leaders in both Honduras and Nicaragua. We believe that this way of thinking is one reason why the ethnic groups in this region have been treated generally with contempt and have been deprived of protection owing to, among others, the fact that the region they occupy is not fit for economic exploitation.

Moreover, the term *zambo* carries pejorative connotations lingering from colonial times in both Honduras and Nicaragua. Although it is true that present-day Mískito have intermarried with Garífunas, what has weighed most negatively on them is a repertoire of designations such as "sorcerers," "cannibals," "lazy," "indolent," and—above all—"lacking love for their country." This generalized attitude has caused these indigenous communities of the Caribbean coast of Honduras and the Atlantic coast of Nicaragua to take control of their own destiny. This is how we arrive at the present state of political affairs, which is seen as destabilizing their internal systems. Shielding its own guilt, national society sometimes expects these groups to eradicate their entire historical past and start anew, without considering that such a past followed its own independent course and had little to do with colonization and Hispanic dominion, which these indigenous groups rejected. After independence from Spain, the reins of power fell into the hands of creoles who perpetuated the colonial contempt for societies opposed to the teachings of the Catholic missionaries.

In this manner, Honduras and Nicaragua, which are predominantly Catholic, turned their backs on the ethnic nations of the coast and delivered—even with

contempt—these *zambos* or "Indians" or "rebels" or "blasphemers" to the Protestant Moravian priests who indeed knew how to infiltrate them and took advantage of their historical predicament to change their mentality. Of course, the great majority of the Mískito who converted to the Moravian religion do not conceive their "native territory" to be the boundaries of Honduras or Nicaragua. They would not "defend" these as their national territories because, from a civic viewpoint, these values do not exist for them. Rather, they express nostalgia for the bygone days of British occupation, hope for the return of the Mískito kings, and—under Moravian religious rule—identify themselves with economic, political, and ideological trends in the United States (Figs. 1 and 2).

This set of circumstances explains the present situation of the Mískito in Nicaragua and calls for clarification of charges that the Sandinista government had destroyed entire Mískito towns and driven out many Indians into Honduras. With knowledge of the facts, we can ascertain that this information was manipulated to discredit the Nicaraguan government, which in fact convened in July 1986 an international symposium on the state, autonomy, and rights of the indigenous peoples in its territory. Moreover, the plan of action recognizing their autonomy was fully implemented on October 12 of that year. This project can succeed only within the context of dialogue between the central government and the ethnic nation. Nicaragua, which is a multiethnic, multilingual, and multicultural nation, has recognized the right of self-determination of indigenous groups, and has created an opening for a democratic process that demands recognition and respect for their languages and traditional culture.

Musical traditions of the Mískito

The term "music" does not exist in the Mískito language. There is only the concept of "song" or *láwana*, in the sense of "detaching a part of oneself and directing it to fulfill a certain task." It is voice and word, but imbued with ritual meaning. The word for the voice itself is *bila*, which also means mouth, road, or path in the physical sense. *Láwana*, however, carries the sense of "road," but as a spiritual path that can lead toward the unknown.

Shamanic practices are integral to the culture. Traditional Mískito song is intimately linked to shamanic practices, given that the *sukia* or shaman is

Fig. 1: Mískito of the Kruta River (Honduras, 1973). Photo by Ronny Velásquez, courtesy of the author.

the one entrusted with acquiring the knowledge of songs to fulfill the tasks of healer, priest, teacher, and leader of souls in Mískito society. To a certain degree, it could be said that the Mískito shaman is self-elected. Divine intervention occurs, however, when "lightning strikes" a Mískito man. It can strike the house where he lives or a tree where a storm releases its force, or the *cayuco* (canoe used for fishing) in which he is traveling, or a tree close to where he is standing. They consider this as a sign of divine selection, and a shaman chosen in this manner is the one who reaches the highest rank in Mískito society. There are other ways of recognizing shamanic vocation among the Mískito, such as expressing that a spiritual selection has been perceived through dreams or the presence of spirits during waking hours. In addition, the Mískito shaman must possess great oral skills, a capacity to learn songs and magic formulas, a talent for applying the principles of traditional medicine, and physical strength to project the power and resilience of his body, something he does during his apprenticeship and at the moment of shamanic

initiation. Endurance also is put to a test during the performance of specific rituals such as healing, when the shaman has to struggle physically with an evil spirit harming the Mískito society he represents. The term *sukia* derives possibly from the verb *utkaia* which means "to suck," since suction of the illness of a patient is a frequent therapeutic practice. One of the first written descriptions of a *sukia* appears in the memoirs of an English traveler identified only by the initials M. W. and published in 1699.

Among the Mískito there are female shamans whose descriptions of their experiences and ecstatic flights are identical to those offered by males. We were unable to determine how far back women became part of the shamanic experience, but they say that this always has been so. Among the Mískito, women go through a period of impurity which is linked to the menstrual cycle. They explain that the menstrual cycle is released by a spiritual force in direct opposition to the powers of the *sukia*. If a woman is in a period of *kati sikniska* (moon illness equivalent to menstruation), she tacitly understands

Fig. 2: Mískito of the Laka-Tuntuntara River area, La Mosquitia. Father and sons in their fishing canoe (Honduras, 1973). Photo by Terry Agerkop, courtesy of Ronny Velásquez.

that she cannot pass between the shaman and the eastern cardinal point if he is performing a cure or any other ritual. Were she to do so, evil spirits immediately would enter the body of the *sukia*, engaging him in a destabilizing struggle between benefic spirits and pernicious ones emanating from the menstrual flow.

In spite of restrictions that apply only to women, there are *sukias mayrin* or female shamans among the Mískito who reach a high rank in the religious structure. When we asked them about the source of their power, all those we interviewed responded that they did not want to be *sukias* but "they were chosen," meaning that the spirits had found them susceptible and had taken possession of them. In such cases, they devote themselves to training for the task, just like the men, in order to be good spiritual leaders of their society.

In *Waikna: Adventures on the Mosquito Shore*, published in 1855, the traveler George Squier describes in minute detail how a female *sukia* steps into a bonfire prior to commencing a cure. This is also a practice among male *sukias*. Due to several factors inhibiting cultural practices among the Mískito in present-day Honduras, this is no longer done publicly,

but the Mískito continue to control fire in their healing ceremonies, although in a less evident manner (Squier 1855 in 1965: 239–40; Velásquez 1982: 104–5).

Mískito song

There are two types of songs: laments (*inanka*) and shamanic songs (*sukia láwana*). *Inanka* derives from the verb *inaia*, to weep, and most of the Mískito song repertoire is of this type. Under *sukia láwana* are subsumed the shaman's ritual and spiritual songs that traverse the roads of the life cycle and the paths of death.

Inanka. The lament, sorrowful song, or wailful singing is intimately related to the sound of thunder accompanying the great tropical storms that beseech La Mosquitia for eight months of the year. The expression *alwani inaia* means "to thunder" or—literally translated—the weeping of Alwani, which is thunder understood in the sense of a mythical figure that dwells in *Kásbrika-pura* or the infinite, the canopy of heaven, which religious leaders translate as "sky." *Inankas* express the deepest emotions: sorrow, hope, resignation, supplication, gratitude, indignation, hatred, curses, joy, and personal exaltation. The singing of *inanka nani* is more frequent during days of rain, thunder, and lightning (*emiula*), as an event that links symbolic beliefs, because the Mískito experience the relationship earth–water with great intensity, and also because the songs establish a spiritual communication with the supernatural world at dawn, before sunrise. In this manner, and even when it does not rain, dawn carries to the spirits of the dead the messages of their relatives on earth. The *inanka nani* are performed by men, women, youth, and adults who have dead relatives. The messages are addressed to the spirits of those who may have died recently or may have been dead for a long time. All the Mískito who live on earth will perform their *inanka nani* for the rest of their lives and thus keep an uninterrupted spiritual communication with the spirits of their dead. Consequently, these *inanka* will survive among all Mískitos who respect and love their cultural legacy, as preserved in their oral tradition. As a society, the Mískito have remained outside the parameters of the most orthodox type of Moravian religion and do not answer to the God of the Protestant faith. The most introspective Mískito believe in an omnipotent creator who guides their actions and whom they refer to as

Won-yu and Won-Aisa. (*Yu* is sun in shamanic language; in everyday language, sun is *lapta*, which—by extension—also means day.) The first compound stands for "our sun," the second for "our father," because Aisa is the Great Father. This belief is quite formal and never appears in the texts of the laments (*inanka*), although it is part of shamanic knowledge.

Normally, *inanka* texts only make reference to the spirits of ancestors. This is an important criterion because the *inanka* reaffirm and establish earthly as well as spiritual communication with a world that the spirits of the dead already have experienced, that is, the world they shared with their living relatives. Death is the start of a journey to the unknown; the road is dark and yet conceived as an intangible representation of the world on earth. Through this road, the spirits of the dead will travel the same path they followed during their lifetime. Moreover, these spirits do not relinquish their responsibilities toward their living relatives left behind. They travel toward a final dwelling place, known as *Yapti-misri*, or "great ancestral mother" who welcomes to her bosom all the spirits of the Mískito. In order for the spirits of the dead to reach her, however, both the shaman and the living relatives have to perform various rituals, among them the *kwal taya*, which is compulsory. In this ritual, the shaman assumes the responsibility for leading the souls to their afterlife.

The laments or *inanka* of the Mískito vary according to thematic categories. These include *sary inanka*, or mournful weeping; *aikulki inanka*, or the weeping of sons who have lost their father; *aimasihbi inanka*, or laments of childless adults; *lahtubi inanka*, or wailful curses; *inanka upla pruan bara*, or laments for the dead; and *ihbaia láwana*, for exaltation of the ego.

Sary inanka is a generic term for sorrow and alludes to all types of recollections of past grief. These laments include the theme of death of relatives, and their narrative refers to episodes that occurred during the lifetime of the person invoked. Within this category we also find narrations describing the poverty and misery of those who sing them, or misfortunes that befell them as, for instance, the involuntary fire that burned a house; the flood that destroyed the cultivated fields; the death from pestilence of penned animals; the devastation of a community from a hurricane; dearth of food, fishing, hunting, or harvest; and droughts due to late first rains. In general, all *sary inanka* dedicated to ancestors or to dead children, when they are remembered, avoid exteriorizing grief except for sobbing at the end of each melodic phrase. We have purposely chosen an example of a *sary inanka* that shows this characteristic. The song, notwithstanding its mournful nature, denotes control and is performed with the utmost devotion. The singer intones this invocation firmly, tuning the song to pitches that only occasionally depart from the tempered scale. In the final segment, a registral and tonal change enriches the song. The song is repeated with variants and, at the end of some of these repetitions, the singer adds an "F" (notated at the end of the transcription) (Ex. 1; Recorded Ex. 1). The following is a free translation of the text:

> Mother, your daughter, an orphan woman, went up to the mountain (to work) and is pregnant. You can see her from your darkness, you can see her. The dead relatives of her husband should see her. Where are they? Are they far? I have a son, he is mine, I already told you . . . etc.

Ex. 1: *Sary inanka* of the Mískito transcribed by Ronny Velásquez (Recorded Ex. 1).

The *aikulki inanka* are nostalgic songs performed by young orphans to communicate with their dead parents or with one of them. The texts inform his or her progenitors' spirits of the suffering in life because of their absence. He or she says that nobody will be able to care for him or her better than his or her own parents. The texts also make reference to the sadness caused by the lack of guidance, love, and teaching that parents would have provided.

The themes of *aimasihbi inanka* allude to the sorrow of childless parents (the singer in this case) and evoke the emptiness of living without the support of offsprings. Laments explain the reasons for not having them: either they were never born or they died; if so, they explain why they died; if they are alive and have left the place, the singer evokes a feeling of abandonment. If the singer is a woman and never had any children because of physical impediments, she then alludes to what she calls a "personal misfortune" and identifies herself as a *kuka o mayrin biarpara*, which means "old woman" or "barren womb woman," and accuses herself in a dramatic manner because children, according to Mískito beliefs, are the wealth of the family and the stability of the home.

The category of laments addressed to harmful persons are called *lahtubi inanka* or "cursing a devious or slippery one." This is a broad interpretation because it corresponds to the belief that death is not a natural occurrence but one caused by pernicious humans. Thus, the *lahtubi* are performed every time a relative of the deceased sees the person who, according to divination practices, has been identified as the spiritual murderer of the person evoked. Possibly it may not be him or her, but instead a person exhibiting similar features and behavior. This person is then blamed for all the misfortunes of the family performing the *lahtubi inanka* and—through song— the Great Father is asked to hurry and take "the devious one" so that his or her family also will suffer. If the family of the deceased happens to be powerful and forceful, it can gain access to sorcery and thus avenge the death of the relative or life companion. The following free translation of the text of a *lahtubi inanka* conveys the vengeful tone of these songs:

Wihta-bila karhnira
siam aidaukikán
wihta-bila karhnira
wihta tait nani
pruwi warasia saura

klah-klah bila laptira nani,
ah, ah, ay.
Wihta bila tait nani
wihta bila tait nani
wihta bila karhnira nani
wihta bila karhnira nani
siam uba aidaukan
aiura prauramba
tingki pali, ah, ah, ay.
Wihta karnira nani
kau luhpia wal raya kirhbisma ba
yang rau aisauhkaia kirhbisma
wihta karhnira priwi waras ya
ibo wihta nani, wihta tait nani, aja, ah, ah, ay, etc.

Accursed, immortal, devious one, I loathe you.
Accursed, immortal, devious one, of hard life
you would not die, of hard life, of hot fists,
ah, ah, ay.
You had a long life, hard life.
You displeased me very much, you mistreated me.
. . . Your children who are still alive
survive to mistreat me,
of long life, immortal, devious one,
of slow death of *yagua* wood (a very hard palm),
of long life . . .

The *inanka upla pruan bara* is the vehicle through which the entire community weeps at wakes in the presence of the body of a deceased (Recorded Ex. 2). Though these performances assume a very dramatic character, the *inanka* are more powerful when only the spirit of the deceased is invoked. Informants confirm that the most important *inanka* are about remembrance and not about the actual farewell. It becomes evident that, when bid farewell, the dead are given instructions about the long journey he or she is about to initiate, and at the same time he or she is entrusted with special requests and asked not to forget relatives on earth. The soul also is asked to greet other dead relatives or friends whom he or she may meet. It is somewhat like preparing the behavior and guiding the spirit to its proper place in the afterlife. Death among the Mískito is a social event, grieved by the whole community and those who live in neighboring villages. Therefore, the collective weeping is performed by almost the entire population. This creates a heterophonous texture that makes it nearly impossible to follow a single text, given that communal singing results in an intersecting network of multiple messages.

The *inanka* of remembrance, however, are sung individually and, as noted above, are performed when it rains and at dawn. Here, each singer narrates a particular memory of the deceased, informs him/her about current events, requests favors, and acknowledges with thanks those that were granted. This type of communication carries great intensity and is performed with boundless devotion. Moaning is especially significant in these songs, whose vocal range is restricted to the interval of a perfect or augmented fourth within which the singer elaborates melodic phrases (Ex. 2). The vocal fluctuations that characterize the delivery of these songs do not seem to be restricted to laments for the dead but constitute a generalized trait of the musical language.

As a collective experience, the sung-weeping of *inanka upla pruan bara* at wakes results in a cumulative type of cantillation that mixes weeping with song and brief conversation among the participants, whose voices do not lose their individuality (Recorded Ex. 2). At times there are shouts, weeping proper, and strong oscillation in long sounds that lend great pathos to this vocal expression. The participation of many women in this type of singing is totally free.

Ihbaia láwana, the songs for exaltation of the ego, can be translated literally as "the roar of the tiger" or song about "the neighing of wild colts." This general topic is subsumed under the category of *inanka* because it shares melodic patterns with the repertoire of *inanka nani*, though differing from these in their powerful delivery and expressive force. The designation itself points to their content: *ihbaia* derives from *ihbi*, which represents the roar of the tiger and, at the same time, it is related to the verb *ihibaia*, which means the neighing of wild colts. The songs narrate the epic of their singers who, as a rule, are male, and the message is not directed exclusively to the spirits of their dead but to Mískito society in general. The texts dwell on the strength of the ancestors' perpetuation within their own microcosm, namely the body of the singer. The *ihbaia láwana* are fundamental and necessary for a number of social, religious, and ritual practices of the Mískito. Normally, these accounts exalt the fierceness, ability, and dexterity of each singer, this strength being the spiritual shield that makes him invulnerable to the negative forces that may emanate from his enemies or those who envy him. This is because, as we have noted above, all Mískito people protect their lives from negative influences and resort to the artifices of sorcery and magic to achieve this objective.

Terry Agerkop (1977: 13) identified two styles of delivery in the repertoire of laments (*inanka*) discussed so far. Under the first type are phrases built on a nuclear pitch that are delivered in a syllabic style, thus clearly articulating the semantic content of the text. The second type is a chant in melismatic style whose phrases do not articulate a defined semantic content, but rather consist of interjections typical of the Mískito language. Syllabic delivery predominates in the repertoire of *ihbaia láwana*, or songs of exaltation, a style in which phrase articulation is more precisely defined.

Each lament or *inanka* is composed of melodic segments that can be analyzed as units similar to those in centonized plainchants. In a majority of laments, the syllabic phrases carrying semantic content alternate with elongated weeping tones of almost unintelligible text, although this is only characteristic of *inanka* performed by women. Those performed by men tend to align themselves with the syllabic style of delivery that fundamentally emphasizes the text, in alternation with brief tones of interrupted weeping. The melodic range of the laments is always smaller than an octave and most frequently limited to a sixth. The melodic intervals used in vocal phrases never exceed a fourth, with predominance of major and minor thirds. Agerkop also noted that the melodic direction of the larger melodic units or "periods" in an *inanka* generally follows a descending tendency.

In Mískito, word accentuation always falls on the first syllable as, for instance, in the terms *kásbrika* (firmament), *ínanka* (weeping), and *ânira* (where). The same principle is mirrored in a motivic conception that assigns higher pitches to the beginning syllable of a word, as illustrated in Example 3. Here, the first syllables in utterances like Luhpi ba, naiwa, maikaikan, aidauki, luhpi, anira waranki (. . . that son, now before me, my dear son, where did you go?) are musically stressed by means of a higher pitch.

Ex. 2: Vocal range of the *inanka upla pruan bara,* or laments for the dead.

Ex. 3: Prosodic accents reflected in the motivic structure of Mískito laments or *inanka*.

The *inanka* are a form of free communication and cannot be confined to narrow definitions of "singing," exceeding such boundaries in their exteriorized sobbing and other expressions of "volumes of woe in me" or "ajaay," as noted by the ethnomusicologist Luis Felipe Ramón y Rivera. Each *inanka* or spiritual communication lasts no less than one hour and it is the women who can sustain it for the longest periods of time. Women also can maintain the vocal fluctuations and the fixed tones that articulate the endings of phrases and longer sections of each song. Just like the melodic contours mirror the prosody of the Mískito language, the laments' range of loudness mirrors the ample dynamic range of the language, which can be construed as characteristically extroverted.

Sukia láwana. The songs of the *sukia* or shaman serve him or her to mediate in his/her role as teacher, healer, priest, diviner, and leader of souls. The *sukia* is the owner and keeper of traditional knowledge and therefore has the obligation to transmit it in order to perpetuate the tradition and ensure the presence of a spiritual leader who always will defend Mískito society. As such, the *sukia* must learn the specific repertoire for rituals, ceremonies, and medical practices. Shamanic songs can be learned from another shaman, or—according to our informants—can be taught by spirits through dreams that are interpreted as voyages into the spirits' domain, which can be the infinity of space, the heart of a rain forest, the depths of mountains and swamps, the sources of rivers and caves, or the depths of water where the *liwa* or aquatic spirits dwell.

The *sukia* must be in permanent contact with protective spirits and know the adverse ones in general. He or she also must know the woods with which to carve canes (*kinka*) to control evil. It is the *sukia*'s responsibility to watch over the health of the community and apply the therapy required for each illness. In the practice of healing, the shaman extracts various objects through suction, explaining that the spirit in the form of that object intended to take possession of the soul of the patient. In reality, the element that determines the cure is not the object, but rather the shaman's identification of the spirit ailing the patient. There are cases in which shamanic song is not sufficiently powerful to cure a specific illness and, in those instances, it is necessary to resort to material representations of auxiliary spirits, such as anthropomorphic figures of *balso* wood, healing stones, and knots and roots of trees, among others.

It is through his or her ecstatic flights or voyages that the shaman encounters the various divinatory spirits, explaining that he/she discusses with them problems about health, illness, and death in Mískito society. This information almost always refers to tempests and cyclones, because the zone where the Mískito live is very vulnerable to this type of inclemency. Thus, one of the basic activities of the *sukia* is to divert natural disasters. Traditional Mískito society places its trust in the *sukias* and rewards their services by supporting them, only occasionally giving them money.

In the role of healer, the shaman classifies illnesses into three categories: (1) *iumu* or minor ailments that include subtypes normally associated with stomach problems and other uncomplicated illnesses; (2) *isingni ulan*, translated as "mounted or ridden soul," or serious illnesses; and (3) extremely serious ones because their origin is unknown and caused by harmful spirits. Usually incurable, a person in this state of *paun* has no control, and this can be perceived from the shaman's actions and the advanced degree of the illness.

The shaman's specialized knowledge is not strictly required to attend to the illnesses of the first category (*iumu*). In present-day Mískito communities where no shaman is available, there are *maestros del soplo* or exhalation experts (*iumu yayabakara*) who—although they are not strictly shamans—can apply exhalation or curative blowing to water, with verbal formulas addressed to the spirits considered to be causing the illness. *Iumu* are illnesses associated with abdominal problems, such as acute stomachache, diarrhea, and vomiting, but also extend to skin eruptions, rheumatic pains, headaches, nervous twitches manifested in some parts of the body, and others. Treatment consists of taking medicinal waters that have been prepared by the power of the healer's word. These are formulas that penetrate the water through a small cannula introduced by the shaman or specialist and through which he speaks to the water, whispering phrases of indefinite semantic content but of symbolic and practical effectiveness for the users.

The following *iumu* or "preparation of the water" to heal minor illnesses is characterized by an intermittent emission produced by the percussion of blowing on the water in a container. The healer uses a hollow reed, which serves as a kind of mirliton through which he intones a shamanic melody whose semantic content he develops mentally (Ex. 4; Recorded Ex. 3; Figs. 3 and 4).

The songs for the *isingni ulan* or more serious illnesses are more specific and this healing can be performed only by the *sukia*, as it involves a struggle with the evil spirit that is attempting to take possession of the patient's soul. In order to heal the

patient, the *sukia* must capture this harmful spirit, which he will try to destroy through fire. The treatment may last several days, until the spirit is caught. The shaman sings and blows over the body of the sick person, spits, drinks especially prepared ritual water, and periodically makes gestures over the body of the patient that signify his attempt to capture the *isingni* but never manages to accomplish this easily. Because the ritual is long, the shaman rests in a hammock and keeps singing, shaking a small calabash rattle and sometimes also playing the *lungku*, a musical bow, in order to attract the spirits to whom he offers chicha, to make them friendlier and more accessible. According to his understanding, the evil spirit is there, together with other good and evil spirits, and he will try to identify it, lure it through inebriation, and capture it. At the end of the treatment, when the shaman considers his work finished, he will show the family or the participants before dawn an intensely green light, shining from a piece of wild cotton wool, and this is when he announces that the spirit causing the harm finally has been captured. Later on, in the course of the same song, he performs a divination rite. Before dawn, the *sukia* burns the evil spirit with kindled wood from the *labín* tree. This act, however, does not indicate the final destruction of the spirit, but rather its transformation. The *sukia* causes the spirit to reconsider, after giving it

Ex. 4: *Iumu* of the Mískito transcribed by Ronny Velásquez (Recorded Ex. 3).

Fig. 3: Elerio Pederek performing an *iumu*. One of the youngest *sukias* of the Kruta River region, he lost his sight during one of his shamanic tests in 1981. He treated it himself and, in 1986, when we saw him again, he had recovered it completely. Photo by Ronny Velásquez (1973), courtesy of the author.

a good lesson so that it will not continue to harm members of the society.

In shamanic sessions dealing with the most serious illnesses, described as "being in a state of *paun*," the *sukia* will not show a live spirit like the green shining light he had "extracted from the body of the sick person," but will display other inert objects such as small pebbles and hair knots, or throw blood sputum and even dead insects to which the shaman attributes the cause of the illness. These objects too will be burned and thrown into the underworld of harmful spirits, so that they will no longer harm society. Should the sick person die, the shaman excuses him/herself by saying that the disease was too

advanced and its exact origin could not be determined, or admit publicly that the person who sent the disease to the patient was, at that moment, more spiritually powerful. This greater power may be attributed to age, seniority, or newly acquired powers. That person may be another *sukia*, because powers can be used for beneficial or harmful purposes. This is a fundamental principle that ensures the continuity of shamanic practices. When the Mískito shaman fails to heal, he/she must abandon the practice of the profession and retreat into sacred places to reinvigorate and acquire new powers according to the needs of the latest experience. In Mískito shamanic practice, and under normal circumstances, *sukias* reinforce their powers every seven years.

As the spiritual leader of the community, the *sukia* also is responsible for rituals to guide the souls of the dead to their final dwelling. *Kwal taya* ("that which encloses") alludes to this ritual, and the final abode is described by the Mískito as *Yapti-misri* or ancestral mother who shelters all the souls of the Mískito. One of the most important phases of the ritual is the capture of the soul because, consistent with its nature, it struggles to remain on earth and the *sukia* must master its arbitrary will. The shaman has special soul-capturing songs for the *kwal taya*, many of which are based on improvisations that the shaman performs outdoors, across the fields, entering swamps, in the rivers, and running through plains, while using chicha, lianas, ropes, and baskets, always carefully searching for the soul that refuses to be found. The capture, which involves the entire community, only can take place between the hours of the afternoon and evening. When the *sukia* finally captures the soul or *lilka*, the shaman shows the relatives a living light, intensely green and similarly wrapped in wild cotton wool as the *isingni ulan*, assuring them that it is the spirit of the deceased. Soon thereafter the shaman ties it with cloth, which is usually smeared with *onoto* (*Bixa orellana*) and takes it to the house of the deceased. This is when the appropriate rituals and ceremonies begin and, after four days of wake, the spirit is buried alongside the body of the deceased, which had been interred twelve days earlier. It is then that the soul initiates the great voyage to the afterlife (Figs. 5 and 6).

In the example chosen to illustrate the peculiarities of songs to capture the soul of the dead (Ex. 5; Recorded Ex. 4) we can observe the fluctuations characteristic of long sounds, the very slow ascending and descending glissandos, and only slight increases

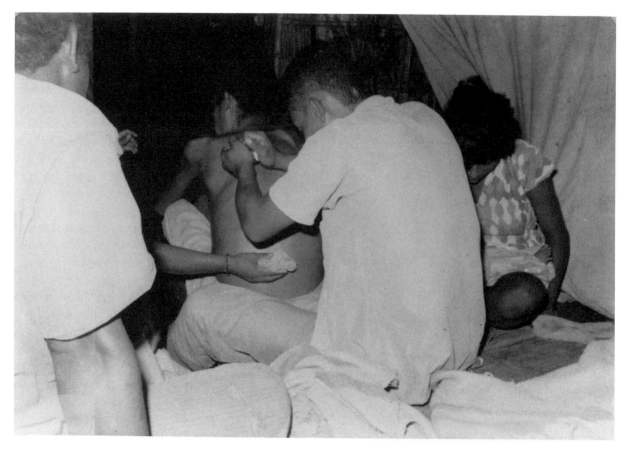

Fig. 4: Elerio Pederek during a healing session. Photo by Ronny Velásquez (1973), courtesy of the author.

in sonority. We can identify six gestures in the course of this song: (1) puffing; (2) the repetition of a similar gesture; (3) sung text; (4) recitation; (5) sung text with puffing; and (6) singing that ends with recitation.

> U,u,u,u,u,u,u,u,u,u,u, listen, listen,
> I wish to talk to you (coughs three times)
> my fellow man, to you I am talking,
> man, you left at the hour of death,
> the day came and you went,
> thus you left on the appointed day,
> you penetrated the reeds and the earth,
> with other legs you walk, come and share my drink,
> I am your paternal uncle . . .
> (shakes a small rattle)
> listen to my sounds, I know you are watching,
>   I know it
> my fellow man, come and share my food.
> You, *Isingni* misbehave and run too much,
> you can see that I am your companion, recognize my
>   voice (coughs).
> (Speaks) *Isingni*, I will take you slowly, I will not hurt
>   you,

> look, slowly, slowly I am penetrating the earth, come
>   lianas because I brought you (to capture the soul)
> (coughs) . . .
> (puffs forcefully).
> (Speaks) *Isingni*, you misbehave, you run too much,
> you moved toward the mouth of the river, but I am
>   going slowly, slowly.
> I know you dislike the smell of humans, but my
>   spirits will lure you . . .
> here I have chicha and toast you with each puff,
> here I have chicha also for your dog (in spirit, his
>   companion)
> fellow man, now you are man (turned into)
>   shreds,
> you walk and rise, and I feel you brushing against my
>   skin lightly,
> you went downriver, now upriver, you changed places,
> look, I have cotton wool to capture you . . .
> the cotton wool makes up the net, I have the cotton
>   wool,
> but now you hid amidst the grass, you are very
>   naughty, very naughty.
> Now I will go downriver blowing on the water so you
>   will rise . . .

Fig. 5: *Sukia* Dorialina, Uhnuya, La Mosquitia. Photo by Ronny Velásquez (1973), courtesy of the author.

. . . Do not go into that mud, it is very deep,
surrender, surround him . . .
ready, I caught him in the grama grass, you have the
   strength of a horse
but I have lianas, ropes to stop you, by the neck,
. . . do not open it (the cotton wool), I already got you,
let us go . . .

European elements in the music of the Mískito

Although the indigenous traditions (*inanka* and *sukia láwana*) are firmly established among a majority of the population, the younger Mískito have adopted the guitar to accompany what they call the *tiun* (from the English, tune), which denotes sound, tune, tuning, concordance, harmony. *Tiuns* are songs about love, and also about sadness or other types of nostalgic evocations of nature. They frequently allude to death and the supernatural world, which is the reason why we consider them significant in this context, given that there is no total separation (yet) between a lament (*inanka*) and a *tiun*. That is to say, *tiuns* are constructed according to the melodic principles of *inankas*, with weeping and communication with the spirits. *Tiuns*, however, can be danced.

Another recent phenomenon among younger Mískito is that they talk freely about the *sitan láwana*, translated as "songs of the demons" (Sitan = Satan), as they are called by the Moravian priests. These are, in fact, the same *tiuns* that have acquired characteristics of Mexican music heard on the radio in La Mosquitia. Another designation for the same songs is *tasba láwana*, which means "secular" or "earthly" songs, which young Mískito sing during moonlit nights. The *tiuns*, also called *kitar láwana* (songs with guitar), *sitan láwana*, or *tasba láwana*, rely on the same simple harmonic principle of rhythmic strumming on dominant and tonic chords. To the voice and guitar they normally add other instruments, including maracas and *aras napat* (horse jaws), used as scrapers. Another accompanying instrument is the *tina*, a kind of monochord made of an upside-down tub to which a string is attached, which is played as a "string bass" to mark the rhythm of the melody. In a Mískito community it is not uncommon to find a duo of guitars playing "mazurkas."

The Mískito texts of the *tiuns* are sung to periodic phrases of two or four measures each, in ternary or

Fig. 6: Shaman Dama Prapit, Puerto Lempira. Photo by Ronny Velásquez (1973), courtesy of the author.

Ex. 5: Song to capture the soul of the dead (Recorded Ex. 4).

binary meter (¾ or ⁴⁄₄). The melodies are always in a major key and reflect Hispanic influence (Recorded Ex. 5).

The creole music of the Mískito includes children's games or *pulanka*, which take place during periods they define as special. *Pulanka*, a term derived from the verb *pulaia* which means "to play," designates all types of games and rounds. There are two types of *pulanka*: *Krismes*, also called *órale*, and *tuktan-pulanka*. *Krismes* is a round dance, which, as its name indicates, is performed at Christmas and involves responsorial

singing. *Tuktan-pulanka* is the favorite entertainment of children ages 6 to 14 and its repertoire is shared by the Mískito in both Honduras and Nicaragua, as are the *tiuns*. *Tuktan* (children)-*pulanka* (game) is a combination of song, dance, and play performed on full-moon nights as well as consecutively during the Christmas season.

The melodies and structure of *pulankas* show a clear influence from the traditional English repertoire. The dances have fixed meters and are accompanied by hand clapping; songs are performed in chorus with or without soloists, although many *pulankas* require the presence of a soloist to lead in the game. In the majority of *pulankas*, the participants form a circle, everybody dances, and, at a signal from the leader, a couple moves to the center of the circle and performs a dance displaying individual ability. Thus, all participate in the dance and get their turn in the circle.

The texts of *pulankas* display an interesting mix of Mískito and English terms, the meaning of which in general is neither known by the participants nor understood by the adults. They assert that the song is like that, and that they learned it that way because the grandparents sang it in this manner. One of the most widespread songs throughout La Mosquitia of Honduras and Nicaragua is "Awbia daktar," undoubtedly a variant of "Yankee Doodle," which was sung by North Americans during the war of independence (Ex. 6).

Awbia daktar koñote
Ose sika Vilma win
Vilma sika rikaya laya
dokto lo meko mama krais
sika wai leiwra wama sika lusi anda
Guivara sika, Guivara plapan tala lusi anda.
Awbia daktar koñote
Ose sika Amplin win
Amplin sika rikaya laya
dokto lo lika mama krais
sika wain
Blupil ra wama sika lusi anda

Guivara plapan
Guivara plapan tala lusi anda.
Ose sika Vilma win, etc.

Most of the texts underwent many changes and acquired particular phonetic variants when adapted to the Mískito language. It is also important to consider that a relatively long period of time might have elapsed between the introduction of these songs and their survival in children's games and round dances. *Pulankas* are part of a tradition maintained in all Mískito communities, which explains their strength and resilience to change. In some villages, heads of families encourage the performance of *pulankas*, sometimes linking one melody to another, and performing, of course, various actions corresponding to each musical unit. Example 7 is a children's game-song whose melodic profile clearly suggests "The Muffin Man," which can be translated loosely as follows:

Brit ayang-kra ba kaikisma ki
kaikisma ki, kaikisma ki,
aw yang nani kaikisni brus ra iwi yaba.

Perhaps we can make corn bread,
with pleasure, with pleasure,
we knead and it is your turn, and it is my turn.
With a brush let us make it round.
Let him make it, let her make it, let this one make it,
and so on.

Ex. 6: "Awbia daktar," a widespread *pulanka* sung by the Mískito in Honduras and Nicaragua, which is clearly a variant of "Yankee Doodle."

Ex. 7: "The Muffin Man," sung to the words "Brit ayang-kra ba kaikisma ki," *pulanka* of the Mískito in Nicaragua and Honduras.

The teachers in the state schools, who are not Mískito and come from other parts of Nicaragua and Honduras, show little interest in the language and the rich musical repertoire of Mískito children, as in the case of *pulankas*. During each school break or free time from activities, however, children sing and play these games on their own initiative.

THE KUNA IN PANAMA

The Kuna Indians live on some forty-five islands, which are part of a coral archipelago known in Panama as the Archipiélago de las Mulatas. It stretches along the Panamanian coast on the Caribbean Sea from Cabo Tiburón, which borders with Colombia to the east, to the Golfo de San Blás on the Caribbean, and to the Mandinga River in the area bordering with the provinces of Colón and Panamá.

The Comarca de San Blás, or Kuna Yala, was created by an ordinance called "Ley Segunda" or Second Law of 1938. Kuna Yala is the indigenous name for Comarca de San Blás, a Castilian denomination that the Kuna do not use because it was imposed by *wagas* or foreigners. San Blás or Kuna Yala emerged after a successful Kuna revolt against Panama's central government in February 1925. The leader of the revolt, Nele Kantule of Ustupo, continued his struggle for the preservation of Kuna traditional culture and the consolidation of this territory for future generations of Kuna. This ethnic nation extends over an area of 3,260 square kilometers (see Map 2). Its population of 30,000 persons resides on forty-five islands (Figs. 7 and 8) and also fifteen villages located in the mainland. In addition, approximately 5,000 Kuna Indians live in Panama City.

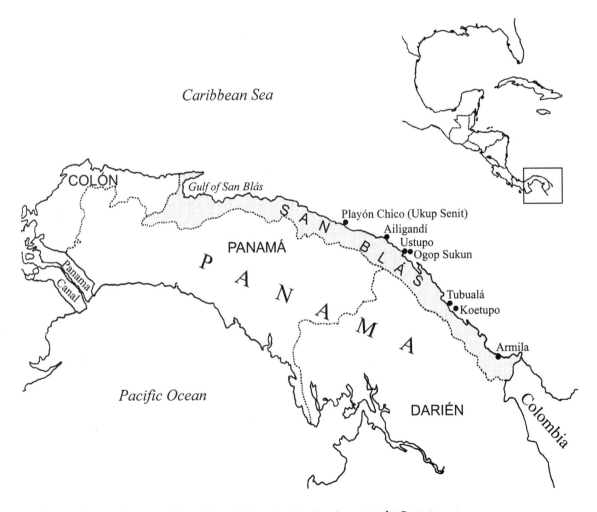

Map 2: Kuna ethnic nation's territory in present-day Panama.

Figs. 7 and 8: Typical scenes of life in Kuna villages on the islands. Photos by Ronny Velásquez (1984), courtesy of the author.

The Kuna language is affiliated with the Chibcha family of Central America (Tovar 1961; Kramer 1970; González de Pérez 1980; and Constenla Umaña 1985). Several authors refer to this language as Carib-Cuna because of the Carib linguistic elements found in the Kuna language (Puig 1944; Prestán n.d.).

The Kuna have established one of the strongest ethnic nations on the continent. They are part of a traditional power structure that has remained resilient to changes proposed by governmental programs. They have fought not only the Spanish colonists but also the Panamanian creoles, and thus preserved their culture as well as their dignity and freedom. Their traditional structure is respected to such a degree that, in present-day Panama, one principal Kuna chief and three regional chiefs represent the Kuna ethnic nation in the political structure of the country. The leading figure of this successful political movement was the great sage Nele Kantule (1868–1944), whose wisdom continues to guide the destiny of the Kuna nation. One of the principles guiding the political survival of his culture is summarized in the following statement:

> I would like the culture of my race to survive within the universal framework of world cultures, because only in the cultural expression of a people can one define the lasting legacy of the essence of their liberty, dignity, and respect as a nation (Nele Kantule, in *Boletín Nele Kantule en marcha*, Ustupo, Kuna Yala, Órgano informativo, 1976).

This principle guides and inspires most of the actions taken to preserve, disseminate, and project the millenarian Kuna culture, which stands as an extraordinary example of a people fighting for their sovereignty, their rights, and their dignity. Before national society, and before the peoples of the world, the Kuna have asserted their historical patrimony and the legacy of their forebears whom they evoke daily in traditional songs. These, in turn, transmit teachings from the time of their mythic origins.

Decoding the meaning of Kuna chant

The term *namake* refers only to the action of singing without connoting other meanings, images, or symbols. For Kuna chant, the most important term is *ígala*, which means path, road, "the way" to the known and the unknown through song. This is why all Kuna chants are identified by the term *ígala*.

The concept of "music" exists in Kuna language, but it is expressed in a composite formulation that names a dynamic process, as opposed to a static object: *Núe igar ba namake* (beautiful "way," according to song); and also *Oturdaket ígala* (the "path" of teaching). *Ígala* is thus the path traveled by Kuna song. Orally transmitted, it is based on symbolic and traditional principles and structures that are defined by the Kuna as a secret language.

One of the fundamental forces that maintains this millenarian culture so alive is the native literature expressed through narrative chant, which is a daily reality in *Ibeorgun Nega* or "the House of Grandfather Sun," also called *onmaket nega*, the "House of Reunions" or "the meeting house." At present, both designations are translated as "house of congress" by association with the Congress of the Republic. The *sailas* or leaders and the people meet daily in *Ibeorgun Nega* to hear the teachings of the ancestors, which are transmitted through song. The entire network of relationships among the Kuna is guided by these teachings and their implementation is demonstrated in each Kuna song. Shamanism is fundamentally based on secrecy and on the efficacy of shamanic chant: there is no therapeutic practice that does not involve the intervention of healing chants that reenact the great mythic events.

There exists, therefore, a world of creation chants that constitutes the core of the Kuna symbolic universe. Songs reenact creation myths and recount the origins of humans, the birthing of elements of nature, the source of traditions populated by cultural heroes, the origin and possession of fire, and also a wide variety of songs self-classified as belonging to their history. These allude to a magical and religious world of key historical figures who established the foundations of Kuna culture. There are also songs that serve a socioeconomic purpose, such as those that propitiate good hunting of wild or marine animals and good fishing. Other chants manifest the powers of the shaman to hold a red hot iron in the hand; to let wasps sting without being stung; to fell a tree with the power of the mind; to hold a rattlesnake with the hand; to attract thunder and cause rain to fall; and to drink water or chicha from a calabash strainer. The social function that these songs fulfill is also an incentive that encourages their learning and practice.

In short, the entire universe of Kuna beliefs is narrated extensively through chant. We will refer here only to chants that bear a relation to the life cycle requiring the direct participation of the shaman. We also will mention the instrumental *toques* of the young Kuna, which fulfill an eminently festive role and adhere to traditional melodic patterns transmitted with devotion by the old masters of the instruments.

The extraordinary system of Kuna chant is embedded in a broad symbolic structure. Each chant represents a totality within the specific phase of the ritual of which it is a part, and the same chant then refers the performer to other chants of the same type. Only all of them constitute the essence of the efficacy being sought, because the magic formulas, secrets, and history of each chant are intimately related to a symbolic network known only to the chant specialist. Each Kuna chant is thus a part of an enormous mental structure that corresponds with a codified system to which only the chant specialists have access, since they are the ones who know their applications to ritual, needs they fulfill, and teachings they are meant to transmit. Consequently, an isolated chant cannot account for the entire system and, conversely, an understanding of the system results only from specific analyses of each chant.

We observed, however, that the chant specialists do not analyze the linguistic content of the formulas used because they are part of the mystery that surrounds each chant. In practice, however, they told us that it was during their apprenticeship that the secret of each song was revealed to them, and that it must be mastered in order to ensure efficacy in its application. The specialist believes that each chant he knows is exactly as it was sung at the beginning of creation, and he insists that it is the same as taught to him by his master, and as he will teach it to his apprentices. An important aspect discussed with precision by the practitioners is the existence of twelve different formulations of the same semantic content representing the twelve paths to reach the same objective. At the present time it is very difficult to witness the practice of these twelve variants because either the shamans or chant specialists who knew them have died, or their students did not fully learn them before the master's death. Also, it is possible that those who were taught did not learn them properly because of a failure in the teaching–learning process.

The person who wishes to study one of the Kuna chants must enter into an agreement with one of the masters, who does not ignore the remunerative aspects of this transaction, and establishes the time that can be dedicated to the task. An authentic Kuna shaman cannot transmit knowledge on the basis of any deceit. For this reason, the "Kuna university of traditional chant" graduates its students in a public exercise, and once the community is informed about the graduation of a new specialist, it treats him with respect and turns to him for consultation.

Traditionally, the students of a particular teacher would work in the fields as part of payment. In addition to the agreed-upon price in currency, a substantial part of which is paid in advance, gifts such as tobacco, pipes, shirts, and hats are expected. We interviewed apprentices who had worked up to twenty years for their teacher during the period of instruction because the price in local currency, which is the U.S. dollar, had taken that long to be gathered. Given that this system of learning does not set time limits on completion of the instruction, some students have devoted from twenty-five to thirty years to this process. There are also those who never complete it because the master dies before graduating them. The *absoguedi*, for instance, which is the longest of the shamanic chants, contains more than 5,000 verses, each of about the following length:

Nele Wala lele Kana naka pe uhua na-ali. Nui take coati yala bali naka pe ua naie ye mala ini-yee.

It can be translated as follows: The *abisúa* or great shaman has commenced his action to instruct *Nele Wala* (*balso* spirit). He has started to tell him: "I must give you all the necessary directions and you must receive them properly." The master of *absoguedi* (this longest chant) sings a complete verse and the student must memorize it and learn it exactly as the teacher sang it. For that reason, the *absoguedi* is one of the chants studied over a period of twenty-five to thirty years. Then, it has to be taken into account that the apprentice cannot start his studies before the age of 30, except in the case of chants that can be learned at a younger age. One exception to the rules of shamanic instruction are the *neles,* who are diviners or shamans by birth. In general, shamans are not considered valued masters until late in life. They can, however, master knowledge of less complex chants and thus attain prominence at approximately the age of 45.

The system of cash payment for the teaching of shamanic chant only began in the early twentieth century, with the arrival of U.S. ships seeking precious wood, tortoiseshell, and other resources of the region.

The Kuna learned to sell the product of their work and, by extension, to expect remuneration in currency for the teaching of their shamanic knowledge.

When describing the life of Nele Kantule in his 1938 book, *An Historical and Ethnological Survey of the Cuna Indians*, Erland Nordenskiöld writes: "[Nele] was also three times with the *absoguedi* who sang his chants for him. Nele spent his money on these chants" (1938: 89–90). The quote eloquently illustrates that the ideologue of the Kuna revolution also paid to acquire part of the traditional knowledge that was subsequently institutionalized and is now understood, respected, and projected toward a future that almost guarantees its survival.

Modern technology has had its impact on the process of acquiring traditional knowledge. At the present time, those apprentices who live in Panama City record a part of the chant sung by their masters on the islands, memorize it, then return to Kuna Yala to clarify points with the shaman, who proceeds to record another section of that particular chant. This system works because of the mnemonic nature of the teaching method, which circumvents the meanings of symbolic structures because shamans consider them secret (*inmal tukwaledi*). Usually, the complete meaning of a Kuna chant is not learned until the end of the studies because its secret or *epurba*, containing all the symbolic elements of the origin of that chant, cannot be revealed until all its parts have been learned. The underlying principle is that the shaman cannot be effective until he has gained knowledge of this origin (Fig. 9).

If an apprentice resides in Panama City and wants to devote himself to this profession, he will have to return to his community and be near his master, at least during the final stages of learning, to also acquire knowledge of the paraphernalia used in rituals, the profound secrets of the woods he will use, not only for the canes he needs, but also of the trees, bushes, and roots from which he will carve the *nuchu-gana*. These are anthropomorphic figures representing the auxiliary spirits (*nele-gan* or sages, diviners) that aid the great shaman in any given ceremony. He also needs to prepare his special zoomorphic chair; the clay censers

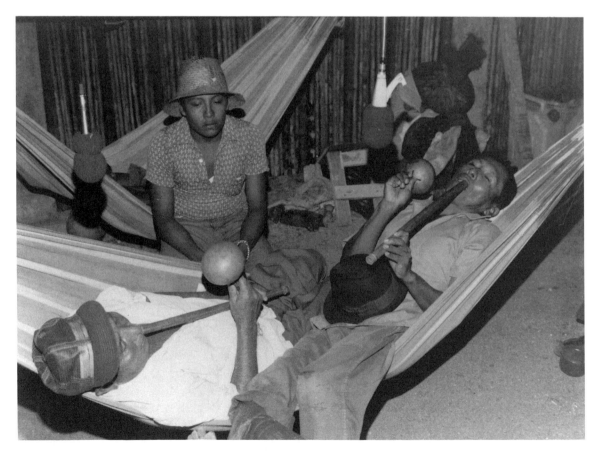

Fig. 9: The *kandur*, Mr. Colombia (recently deceased), teaching the *kammu ígala*. Photo by Ronny Velásquez (1976), courtesy of the author.

and typical Kuna incense of pepper, cacao, and tobacco; he will have to know the healing power of plants, tree barks, special tree burls, roots, reeds, healing stones, and the like. Each of these elements has its chant and its secret, which the shaman must master, along with all the behavior related to healing, initiations, and times of crisis in the community.

As noted above, the *epurba* or profound secret of the origin of the chant at that primordial moment of creation of life and the elements of nature, is the most difficult phase of the learning process because it is not revealed until the master considers that the apprentice is mentally and physically prepared to receive it. Kuna chant requires precision and no structural departures are possible without affecting its transformative power and effectiveness. Each chant must follow a strict internal order because that is the path followed and the example set by the primordial ancestors. This internal order is always the chant's guiding principle. In the person of the shaman coalesce two simultaneous actions: the sung-speech delivery of the chant, and the mental reiteration of the *epurba* or secret that ensures the chant's effectiveness. The simultaneous performance of this dual role only can be achieved through exalted communication with the divine.

The Kuna Congress. General teaching is transmitted daily to the people at the House of Grandfather Sun or *Ibeorgun Nega*, also called *onmaket nega* (meeting house). The *sailas* are those in charge of singing the narratives, organizing them according to theme, day, and whether only for men, women, children, or for everyone. Although these chants permit improvisations, there are basic patterns that must be respected and the chant must be performed as learned. The *sailas*—who may or may not be shamans—are community leaders and specialize in healing chants. In Ustupo, for instance, the *saila* Odis Navas is also a shaman who specializes in *absogued* (or paths of knowledge). *Sailas* are respected for their knowledge of the people's history and, when they are not shamans, they understand shamanic practices. As a rule, the chants performed by the *sailas* in *Ibeorgun Nega* regulate all the economic, political, juridical, and cultural activities of Kuna society.

At the meetings that take place in *Ibeorgun Nega*, there are only two hammocks, occupied by the chant leader (*saila namakoedi*) and by the receiver of the chant (*saila abinsuedi*). The leader always sits to the right of the receiver. Both face West, where the sun sets. The receiver listens attentively to what the leader sings and, at the end of each long verse, utters words of approval such as "it is so," or *eye* (yes). The receiver of the chant must know the same narrative and confirm the truth of the delivery, instilling confidence in those present who are taught through the voice of the *saila* representing the great mythical figures. Native policemen (*suaribedis* or "keepers of the club of order"), strategically placed among the audience, take advantage of the pauses during the chant to shout "listen very carefully," "do not fall asleep," and other expressions when listeners doze off or snore. When the leader completes his chant, which can last from one to three hours, the spokesman or *árgala* rises to his feet and translates into everyday language a synthesis of the chant just heard. It is then that the audience may participate with comments and express approval of the facts that have been narrated.

Most Kuna singers and shamans record chants in an ideographic system that may be used as a mnemonic device because it also conveys intonation. These are color drawings or "pictures" that outline each chant and thus record great narratives, mythical concepts, origins of the various elements of nature, the secrets of medicines, the history of the great Kuna sages, the origin of the *kalus* or natural fortresses that birthed animals, minerals, and fluids, and also the origin of harmful spirits that prey on Kuna communities. Traditional writing is used in the teaching of chants to preserve a memory of the secret magic formulas contained therein. This writing, transmitted from generation to generation, strengthens the process of learning and preserves the chants' traditional structure.

The ideographic representation of chants follows the trajectory of the sun, from east to west, and returning to the east. Chants are like an endless thread of beads (a metaphor for each word) unfolding the structure of these long, symbolic narratives. The following diagram illustrates the scheme followed by this ideographic representation (Fig. 10). The hypothetical numbers 1 through 11 represent the east-west movement of the sun (with the shaman facing North or *Yol purwa sik-ki*). The curve between numbers 11 and 12 is the resting place (*tada arguane* or *nega*, the "house" where the sun sets). Numbers 13 to 21 represent the reversal of the trajectory, or nightly return, and 22 to 23 the sun's rebirth and its light, continuing in this manner ad infinitum. The East (*Tada Nakwe* or *Tada Ainakwa nega*) is the eternal "House of the Sun" (Ibelele).

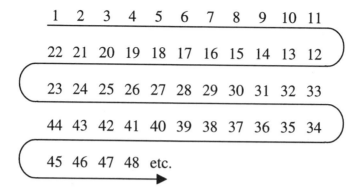

Fig. 10: Diagram of the trajectory followed in ideographic writing of Kuna chant.

Currently, many Kuna singers who can read and write (or whose children do) record the chants and historical narratives phonetically, using the Roman alphabet. Consequently, their traditional ideographic system is being abandoned or replaced. Some younger apprentices format their drawings in Western style, representing the main scenes of the chant's narrative, but no longer use the thousands of characters required to depict a shamanic chant in its entirety.

Just as all Kuna teachings are transmitted through chant, Kuna cosmovision is taught not only through chants and explanations of the origins of chants, but also through the actual performance of rituals. The Kuna distinguish two principal elements in human beings: *niga*, or the life force emanating from Muu, the deity of creation who engenders movement; and *purba*, or the breath of life and guardian of *abargana*, the body. *Purba* is not exclusive to humans; all other animate and inanimate elements of nature possess *purba*. Kuna shamanism conceives the human body as a microcosmos and, therefore, each body is a representation of nature. Each of the principal vital organs of the body possesses its own soul, but one of them rules over the others, and this predominant soul is the life force of Muu. When the body dies, the *purba* carrying the strength of *niga* initiates a voyage to the final domain of Kamibe, who inhabits *Olo nibdur Nega*, or the blue sky. To lead the soul, the *massar tuledi* or song specialist will chant and perform the appropriate rituals to guide the soul on this long journey. Were the shaman not to do so, the soul could become a harmful spirit or *kilu kalu dola*.

The ancient world of the Kuna has a long history, rich in mythical images. We shall focus here on a more recent history to highlight some significant aspects that are relevant to the tradition of Kuna chant.

Present-day Kuna consider themselves protected and guided by the spiritual presence of eight great sages, or *neles*, who descended upon their people through eight great spiritual rivers conceived as streams of gold. The *neles* taught the people and led them on material as well as spiritual matters to ensure that the principles and values of traditional culture would continue to be preserved in the social structure, and transmitted from generation to generation.

The Kuna assert that the earth was impregnated by the Sun, called Ibelele. The spiritual creator, *Dada saila tummadi*, sent four generations to populate the earth, which was ruled by *neles* or sages, but, as many of them failed to fulfill their assigned mission, they were punished by the creator and banished to the underlayers of the earth which they currently inhabit. Chants make reference to the "layers of the earth" through which the shamans travel in their spiritual voyages or "flights." The creator transformed other *neles* into vegetables, animals, and minerals. At the same time, the creator or Great Father brought decimation and destruction to almost entire populations through four main elemental forces: hurricanes, darkness, fire, and water. Thus, the four worlds were successively destroyed. Ibelele, the Sun, however, was more benevolent than the Great Father or *Dada saila tummadi*, and made the world in which humans live today rise from the waters. This world had its origin in the great mountain Takarkuna, located toward the southeast (in Colombia, according to the narrative), and it was saved because it was the spiritual fortress inhabited by the eight great sages or *neles* who subsequently founded Kuna culture. In the mountain, Takarkuna, there lived a great chief called Ibeorgun, who sent diviners to teach all the new Kuna the wisdom of their ancestors; this is the culture that has survived to the present day. According to several descriptions we have gathered, Ibeorgun is the son of Ibelele. Both, however, represent the Sun. Other explanations assign the derivation of "Kuna" to Takarkuna, the dwelling of Ibeorgun.

The great *neles* trained students, and these in turn transmitted their knowledge to other *neles*, diviners, and shamans (*inatuledis*, or "owners of medicines"; *kantules* or *kandur*, "specialists in the ritual cutting of women's hair"; *absoguedis*, owners of chants to exorcise the spirits that cause epidemics; and *massartuledis*, specialists in chants about the paths of death). Knowledge also was transmitted to the *sailas* and *sailas tummat*, chieftains, leaders, community leaders, administrators of collective property, and specialists in the transmission of other Kuna traditions through chant.

The world of Kuna chant

Muu *ígala*, or, through the paths of the divinity of creation. This is a therapeutic chant that the great shaman performs to aid in the birth of a child during difficult labor. The shaman comes to the house only if he is called by the midwife (*muu-koe siket*). Muu is the force that breathes life into the fetus and inhabits the depths of the maternal uterus, accompanied by her twelve daughters who preside over the development of the new being and confer upon it his or her attributes (*kurkin*). Because Muu is responsible for the gestation and birth, at this time she is causing a disturbance in the mother-to-be, has captured her *purba*, and has sapped all her strength. Muu is being rebellious and is using her power to interfere with the birth. The shaman's interpretation of this behavior is that Muu is possibly reacting to some offense to her honor during one of the rituals that Kuna women must undergo from early childhood. This explains why the Kuna believe that all rituals must be performed with the utmost knowledge and devotion, namely to avoid the anger of deities. (The chicha celebrations dedicated to the ritual cutting of the Kuna girl's hair, for example, are performed with absolute rigor and each ceremonial phase must be carried out with precision and profound wisdom.) Only the great shaman, who knows the ways of Muu, can confront her. He is ready to engage in a difficult struggle, but the shaman is also powerful. He prepares a legion of *nuchus* or anthropomorphic figures carved in special woods, in this case cacao (Fig. 11). These figures—transformed into *nelegan* or sages, healers, powerful assistants of the great shaman—will penetrate the paths of Muu. The Muu *ígala* chant,

composed of approximately six hundred verses, describes in rich detail all the actions taking place on that long path. The verses of the *kanalekwa* or specialist describe in beautiful metaphors the internal world of the maternal uterus and all he can see along the path that he and his *nelegan* are traversing. When they are near the silver *kalu*, a kind of castle where Muu and the Muugan live, the *kanalekwa* exhorts his *nelegan* to use their strategy and give Muu and the Muugan sacred chicha to confuse them, and not to rest until they have stripped all the strength from their mouths, throats, and eyes. Also, the *nelegan* should try to break the *kanalekwa*'s staff so that the ripe fruit (the unborn) can come out of its *kalu* and descend to the seat of gold.

When the *kanalekwa* and *nelegan* have defeated Muu and the Muugan, and emerged victorious from the confrontations with the ferocious animals guarding Muu's path, the great shaman bids Muu farewell and she reciprocates, asking if they will meet again. "Of course," answers the shaman, "every time Muu wishes to deny spiritual force or *niga purbalele* to the *walepungua* or young woman who is giving birth to her firstborn." This exchange appears in all versions of this chant. From the farewell onward, the chant describes how the child descends through the paths of Muu, guided by the *nele tetekwalele* or armadillo spirit who opens the way until birth takes place. Example 8 (Recorded Ex. 6) illustrates a Muu *ígala*, whose text is reproduced below:

> I see that my *walepungua* is wrapped in warm cloths
> and begins to travel the paths of Muu.
> I see that she begins to feel that her sight is straying,
> her sight is straying on the path, this is how
> *walepungua* feels.
> I see that *walepungua* feels pains and tries to see in all
> directions of the path.
> I see that *walepungua* feels the heat of the illness and
> wets herself with the pain.
> I see that the fruit of her womb has not descended,
> has not made any noise, nor has it called,
> she begins to be ill.
> I see that *walepungua* is only looking toward the East
> ... etc. (there follow about six hundred more verses).

This tritonic chant, as performed by shaman Milceades Gómez on the island of Tubualá, unfolds at two pitch levels contained within a minor third (Ex. 8).

Nils M. Holmer and Henry Wassen published the first investigation of this chant (*Muu-ígala or the Way of Muu, a Medicine Song from the Cunas of Panamá* [Göteborg: 1947]). Their research served Claude Lévi-

Ex. 8: Muu *ígala* or chant to assist in the birth of a child during a difficult labor (Recorded Ex. 6).

Strauss as a basis for his detailed analysis, which, initially published in the *Revue de l'histoire des religions* (135/1, 1949: 5–27), was included as chapter ten, "The Effectiveness of Symbols," in *Structural Anthropology* (1958 in 1967: 181–201). In 1953, Holmer and Wassen also published *The Complete Muu-ígala in Picture Writing* (Göteborg).

***Kammu ígala,* or through the paths of the sonorous reeds.** This is a ritual chant that, performed by the great shaman or *kandur*, is dedicated to the ceremonial cutting of hair of the Kuna girl at the three fundamental stages of her life. These age groups are known as *Yaidula* (three-year-old girls), *Yainúa* (six-year-old girls), and *Iguayay* (twelve- to thirteen-

Fig. 11: *Nuchus* or powerful auxiliary spirits who help the great shaman to conquer the will of Muu by struggling with legions of harmful spirits. Photo by Ronny Velásquez, courtesy of the author.

year-old girls). This last ceremony follows the onset of the first menses and represents the initiation into womanhood, as she now begins to give life and perpetuate the vital cycle.

There are three types of hair-cutting ceremonies: *Inna mutikit*, the one-night chicha ceremony; *Inna tutsikaledi*, the two-night chicha ceremony; and *Inna suid*, also known as *Inna wil'la*, which lasts three days and three nights. *Inna suid* means long chicha, and *Inna wil'la* means deep chicha. This is the longest and most splendid ceremony of the Kuna.

We can hypothesize that the *kammu ígala* subsume the most traditional religious structure of the culture because, as the ceremony of initiation of Kuna women is marked by the onset of menses, it represents their life-giving powers in an eminently matrilineal society. Each head of a family has an obligation to perform the ceremony of menarche with all due formality, because it is believed that the *Inna wil'la*, or deep chicha, for instance, marks a return to the origins of the world, when Ibelele, the Sun, lived among the Kuna.

A complex hierarchical structure is set in place for the performance of this ceremony, which is entrusted to thirty-two specialists. They are responsible for their

organization and for maintaining the integrity of the rituals. They are also the guardians of the girl's future, as well as circumstances that might befall her, her family and, in turn, Kuna society, which experiences intensely whatever happens to each of its members.

Kuna specialists explain that, if the hair of a Kuna girl is not cut, all cultural precepts are transgressed. She could not marry and, therefore, would not be prepared to procreate. Were she to give birth without undergoing initiation, her life would be imperiled when giving birth. As this is socially sanctioned and a majority of Kuna respect traditional behavior, no man would marry her and, were one to do so, he would suffer the consequences in his afterlife. According to Kuna mythology, the hair of the woman is an enormous tree whose entanglement is symbolic of an impenetrable, virginal jungle. This symbolism carries great significance within the conception of the body as a microcosmos of nature. When the body dies, the soul begins the great voyage through the paths of the *massar*, which are also reeds but more slender than the *kammu*. Within this system of beliefs, the hair of each woman represents the enormous entangled tree that the soul or *purba* of her husband must climb when he dies. If her hair is not cut according to all the corresponding rituals, the branches, trees, lianas, tangles in general, the great rivers in that symbolic "jungle," and all the other elements of that great world, will not let the husband's soul get through to rise to the top and then climb to his final abode in the heaven of Kamibe. Instead, his soul would die asphyxiated by the tree which is his own wife's hair.

The chant, or *kammu ígala*, generally is composed of fourteen sections, each identified by name. Depending on the type of ceremony being performed, some sections may be omitted without any virtual change in the ritual's structure. However, in the central ceremony or *Inna wil'la* all fourteen sections are included and two more are added. The entire chant consists of 3,584 verses, each of which is sung twice, first by the *kandur* or ritual specialist, and then by his principal assistant, who repeats each verse. Both accompany themselves with flutes of two finger holes, and with two rattles that are shaken throughout the delivery of the entire chant.

The sections of the *kammu ígala* chant describe in minute detail each step of the ritual, and its text—for those versed in symbolic language—constitutes the core of the performance. The fourteen sections and the two additions mark the following steps:

(1) *Napa nega.* This is the chant that narrates everything pertaining to the construction of the *inna nega*, or the house of chicha, which is associated with the creation of the world and therefore with the divine origin of the *inna nega*, the sacred space where this ceremony takes place.

(2) *Inna saed ígala.* It narrates in detail the search for the ingredients to produce chicha. The Kuna explain it as "the sacred paths to make chicha."

(3) *Binye ígala.* This chant describes the end of the first life of a Kuna girl (organic birth) and the final birth of a new woman, fit to procreate.

(4) *Obed ígala.* It unfolds the paths of the origin of ritual baths to which the Kuna girl is constantly subjected.

(5) *Kabed ígala.* This chant describes the paths of dreams requiring the greatest attention because in them powerful spirits are encountered, including destructive ones for Kuna society in general.

(6) *Purba ígala.* This is the chant that penetrates the paths of the soul.

(7) *Ibarkuane ígala.* In beautiful metaphors, this chant narrates the setting of the sun and the entry of the *kandur* into the nocturnal world.

(8) *Ibenakued ígala.* This is the chant of dawn, describing how the sun vanquished the night.

(9) *Ied ígala.* This chant guides women specialists in the paths they must follow when they cut the girl's hair.

(10) *Onakued ígala.* On the paths of changing the garments, the chant announces that the specialists must change clothes at the beginning of the second day of the ceremony.

(11) *Tiamma ígala.* This chant travels the path of the tree (*tiamma*) symbolized in the hair of the young Kuna girl through which souls will climb when they travel to Kamibe's heaven.

(12) *Nuga ígala.* This is the path toward the name. The Kuna girl will be given a secret name by the *kandur*. Created by the ritual specialist, it joins the roots or endings of the names of prominent figures in traditional culture. Sometimes it is linked to the skills of the young Kuna girl, other times it is based upon some characteristic of her behavior that identifies her with a mythical figure. This name only is revealed to her parents and will be invoked solely during rituals, or at critical times like a difficult labor.

(13) *Kinki turkan ígala.* This chant marks the paths of the great hunters. It describes the difficult art of hunting in the jungle. It compares hunters with wasps and metaphorically extols the power of the sting, comparing it to the weapons of the hunters.

(14) *Obed ígala kiakwa.* This describes the short baths in salt water that all participants in the great ceremony must take.

To these fourteen sections, two chants are added. These are:

(15) *Nega ígala.* This chant describes the sacred places of *inna nega*, such as the special house or isolated enclosure (*surba*) where the initiate is confined, and the house where the tobacco smokers gather before the beginning of the ceremony. It goes on to describe each object in particular, its specific use, and the meaning it carries within the great ceremony. These include the place of the chicha pots, the containers from which people drink, the walls of the house, the location of the specialists, and so on.

(16) *Sohu igar.* This chant explains the origin of fire and its meaning within the great ceremony.

Several Kuna specialists report that the great *Inna wil'la* ceremony and the chants that make up the ritual were taught by the great sage (Kamibe), who was sent to earth by the great creator. His earthly name is Olourgunaliler. His divine name, Kamibe, derives from the combination of the words *kammu* and *ibe*. *Kammu* means reed, hollow reed, sonorous reed, and flute, and also means throat. *Ibe*, in its mythical sense and in symbolic language, means sun.

Our research on Kuna chant enabled us to identify four variants of the *kammu ígala*: *Wibudur kandur*, a type of *kammu ígala* taught by a mythical figure called Wibudur; *Sulu kandur*, another type taught by an ancestral monkey that is part of Kuna mythology; *Nía kandur*, a variant of *kammu ígala* taught by Nía, a hostile but necessary spirit in Kuna culture; and *Ibe kandur*, taught by the Sun. Of the four that are still mentioned, only two are in current use: the *Wibudur kandur* practiced among the Kuna who live on land toward the area of the upper Chucunaque River and the Bayano River; and the *Ibe kandur*, the most widespread on all the islands of Kuna Yala.

From the practices of different *kammu ígala* specialists, we observed that the order of the sections is maintained rigorously until section or "lesson" 10. The ritual sections 11–14 can vary, and may be omitted without affecting the ceremony. As we have noted above, the presence of all sections depends exclusively on whether the ceremony is performed for the *Yaidula* (three-year-old girls), *Yainúa* (six-year-old girls), or *Iguayay* (twelve-year-old girls, Fig. 12). Example 9 illustrates a section of the *kammu ígala* (Recorded Ex. 7). Two flutes alternate with the chant, accompanied by maracas. The deepest flute sets the tonal base for the first male voice. The text can be translated as follows:

> In the *inna nega* (the ritual house of chicha) the earthenware jars will be placed properly in the holes dug in the earth. The holes have been made in a round shape for the young woman. The holes can be seen through the young woman's haircut . . .

Akwa nusa ígala, or the paths of the stones that hold the power to heal. The Kuna healers or *inatuledis* (owners of the medicines) use various stones in their medical practices. According to traditional beliefs, these stones are of divine origin because they are the *neles* or great sages who were transformed into stone and sent to live on the various layers of the earth. The stones are found on the banks of prestigious rivers, some of which may

no longer exist. These semiprecious little stones of different colors only can be in the possession of a shaman and, if an ordinary person finds them, this individual must inform the *inatuledi* of his choice, and he must go to that place and bring them to his home. They then become auxiliaries in the practice of his profession. The *inatuledi* goes to the place—prepared with all the indispensable tools that include a censer, incense, and special plants to perform all the appropriate rituals—to invite the *nele* transformed into stone to come and live in his house. The *inatuledi* performs the corresponding songs in the very place where the stones have been found.

The manner in which the power of these stones is used varies according to the type of illness the shaman diagnoses. Some are introduced into the water that the sick person will drink, others are placed where the pain is localized, and some are steamed in burning aromatic herbs or incense and the vapor exuded is smeared over the parts of the body being treated. Consistent with all other shamanic practices of the Kuna, the various stones, or *akwa nusa*, will be effective only if the secret of their origin is known,

Ex. 9: *Kammu ígala* transcribed by Ronny Velásquez (Recorded Ex. 7).

Fig. 12: Young Kuna woman, after she has completed all the rituals appropriate to her gender. *Icco inna* is the first ritual to which the Kuna girl is subjected ten days after birth. It involves the perforation of the nasal septum to place the golden ring (*olasu*), which is a distinctive symbol of her sex and one of the principal characteristics of her beauty. Photo by Ronny Velásquez (1976).

and if the corresponding chants to empower them are performed, leading the *akwa nusa* and the patient through the paths of their incantation.

The musical characteristics of the *akwa nusa ígala* are illustrated in Example 10 (Recorded Ex. 8). A male voice delivers the text syllabically, over two descending recitation tones that occasionally are reinforced by appoggiaturas:

> The Great Father created rivers everywhere for the *akwa nusa*, and in the midst of rivers He built their spiritual fortresses or castles (*kalus*). The *Abisúa* or specialist says to the stones: "Nele Nusaga Lele, Akwa Lele and Puna Kallele" (Just as the Great Father instructed you at the dawn of creation, I also will instruct you in the ways of healing). The *Abisúa* is amidst the raw tobacco chicha (*war suid*) to give you the necessary advice. Kana, the *Abisúa*, is amidst the cacao chicha (*puna kelikwa*) so that you can receive its nourishment . . . .

***Sia ba kabur unaedi*, or giving advice to the cacao and the hot pepper.** This chant searches for the soul of a patient that has been captured by an evil spirit. The *sia* (cacao) and *kabur* (hot pepper) play an extremely important role in healing practices of the Kuna because they never fail to assist in every medical treatment. Both are used as incense. The smoke of cacao nourishes the benefic spirits, and the smoke of hot pepper drives away the evil spirits and controls those that are holding the soul of the patient captive. There are also separate chants for *sia* and *kabur*. *Sia* always is present in healing rituals, and *kabur* carries more specific applications, such as fighting harmful spirits that injure humans, and keeping away those causing hurricanes, floods, and epidemics.

For specific cases, shamans explain that the joining of *sia* and *kabur* creates an indestructible formula. They state that *sia* is the diplomat and politician that enters into a dialogue with the spirits, and *kabur* is the warrior that attacks. If both travel to the world of the spirits where the soul of the patient is trapped, they believe that soon the afflicted person's soul will return to his or her body. Shamans explain that there are special phrases in the chants to distract and even entertain the adverse spirits because at those times it is easier to catch them. They also informed us that it is necessary to amuse the benefic ones because, if they are upset for any reason, they will not effect the desired cure. According to traditional beliefs, the cure does not depend on the intrinsic properties of the medicinal plants, but on the transformative mediation of the chant that leads the curative plants through the appropriate path. The path marked by the chant, then, is where the mystery of their efficacy rests.

The same plant, seed, fruit, stone, or wood may be used to cure various illnesses. Their effectiveness depends on the chant applied to them, or the path on which they are sent. Medicines receive "instructions" (*unaedi*) and their behavior must follow the advice of the shaman. The smoke of cacao, for instance, plays a fundamental role in aiding during a difficult birth when sent on the paths of Muu because it lubricates the uterine passages. It is also the principal nourishment of the benefic spirits inhabiting the *nuchus*, which are the anthropomorphic figures or *nelegan* assisting the shaman. Cacao also opens the paths of understanding in initiates into the practice of shamanism, and dialogues with the *poni*, or adverse spirits causing epidemics, and in this case advises and almost begs them to withdraw from the

Ex. 10: *Akwa nusa ígala*, healing chant of the Kuna transcribed by Ronny Velásquez (Recorded Ex.8).

community or else they will have to face the powers of the shaman. Most of all, *sia* (cacao) sets out to search for the captured soul of a sick person and is instructed to find it and restore it to his or her body.

The following text (Recorded Ex. 9) is an example of a shamanic *Sia ba kabur unaedi*, instructing cacao and hot pepper to search for the soul of a patient, which he lost in the mountain where he was working. The sick person is not present; he is lying in his hammock, "burning with fever," in the neighboring community of Coetupo while the chant is being performed in Tubualá. The family approached the shaman and asked for his help, bringing to him eight peppers and eight grains of cacao. Through the chant, the shaman transferred his powers to the peppers and the cacao, and sent them back to be burned in a censer placed under the sick person's hammock. The shaman, in turn, continued the chant from his village, leading the trajectory of the assisting spirits through the path that restored the soul to the body of the sick person. In this manner, shamanic chant invests healing with a particular solemnity because it holds the incantatory and religious secret whose power will mediate in attaining the desired objectives. The text of *Sia ba kabur unaedi*, or "instructing the cacao and hot pepper," is reproduced below (Recorded Ex. 9):

At the time of the creation of the world, all the elements were placed everywhere. The creator made the earth and all the humans everywhere. The creator made plantain groves everywhere, and in their midst made you (cacao and hot pepper). Amidst the plantain groves live *Sia* and *Kabur*. In the East, where the Sun is born, women were created and, from the house of the Sun, women came cutting the plants of *Sia* and *Kabur* with their hands, to bring them to humankind. Our women cut the medicinal plants, breaking their branches in the East and then in the four cardinal points . . . .

Ukku naibe ígala, or through the paths of the serpent. This chant describes the origin of the rattlesnake. It extols its particular characteristics and describes the powers given to it by the divine ancestors, when these snakes were humans. In general, the Kuna believe that animals were prestigious humans in primeval times. *Ukku naibe* was the great healer who specialized in the cure of snakebites. The *Ukku naibe* chant also describes the origin of other poisonous snakes, their strength, their poison, their wickedness, and gives minute detail about where they live, depicting the stones and caves where they are curled up, sleeping or lying in ambush. Then it narrates that a poisonous serpent (Kirpali), an enemy of humankind, bit one of his patients, causing acute pain and blood sputum. The chant travels the path of enchanted riverbanks, meticulously describing all kinds of plants, bushes, and reeds displaying the same designs and colors as rattlesnakes. The chant awakens the sleeping spirits of these plants, which then join *Ukku naibe* in his path to defeat the malignant spirits of the snakes that bit the patient. The battle is won toward the end of the chant, and here appears the mythical bird, Wekku, who devours poisonous snakes and is a friend of *Ukku naibe*. Thus, the earth joins the forces of heaven in a struggle to defeat Kirpali, the venomous serpent, and return the soul to the affected patient.

Kuna communities maintain a special house for the treatment of this type of problem, where the necessary healing takes place. In the continent, more than on the islands, there are many cases of snakebites. If the patient dies, the chant ends by saying "The patient has fallen asleep forever, has fallen asleep never to wake up again." If, however, the patient recovers, the chant says: "The yellow fluid is leaving the body, it comes out of the mouth, through the eyes, through the ears, the reed and great fresh tree have protected him/her, *Ukku naibe* has won." Recorded Ex. 10 illustrates an *Ukku naibe ígala* whose text is given below:

Aieeee . . .
Nele papa dio kwa Nele Uku bankana
ala gate kalu kana tirbi deye
ala diwala pali pe gunder
ti wala ki.
Dre nuku dre nuku, dre gine-ye.
Nele uku bana manayla pile ye
nega ter pali deye-a-
Paba dio kwa Nele ukku ban gana ga
idre paba dio kwa di nele
ukku banka ala ipeka lugana irbeda
ala diwala drepa li begun di-wala
dre nuku, nuku gine-ye.
Nele ukku ba nega der bali deke sía
manayla dre pili gine-ye
Nele ukku bana
yarmake ma, Nele ukku bana
irmake ma iye
olo diwala pali pe gundiwala
dirbali-e ti baba di akwa
Nele ukku bangala, olo wachi kalu gana urbi-de.
Olo der tiwala pali be gundiwala
pe nuku de nuku gine ti-de.
Nele ukku bana di
ma-nayla pili gui nega
pali daydi olo diwala der pali
pe gun-diwala der pali-e- . . .

The great Creator began to place spiritual fortresses (*kalus*) for *Ukku naibe*.
His first *kalus* were placed in infinity, where the Creator dwells.

Ukku naibe is in heaven, in *Manayla pili*, and from there he looks down in all directions;
from there he sees the rivers and from there he sees the reflection of the waters.
Ukku naibe is in *Manayla* and walks in a slithering way, descends from *Manayla*
and goes toward the great river of gold; now he is looking around him,
at all that the Creator has given him . . .

Absogued ígala, or through the paths of knowledge. This chant serves to defeat harmful spirits (*poni*) causing illnesses and epidemics in Kuna communities. As noted above, the narrative of the great shaman is the longest of the Kuna chants. This narrative describes, step by step, the creation of the world, its plants, animals, minerals, and marine flora and fauna. It explains in minute detail the origin of *ukur war*, or *balso* wood, which is the main powerful spirit who will multiply into legions of supernatural beings to assist the great shaman in his struggle against the adverse spirits, called *kilu gana* in shamanic language. According to traditional beliefs, *kilu gana* bring epidemics and attract poisonous snakes that bite workers in the fields.

The voyage of the great shaman starts in *Tada ainakwa nega*, the birthplace of the sun in the East, and traverses the cosmos describing it with innumerable symbols and beautiful literary images. Subsequently, the narration indicates that his spirit has commenced the descent through the layers of the earth or layers of the world, and toward the fifth layer, where the great shaman of evil dwells in the company of a legion of harmful spirits. Here is where the spirit of the *absoguedi*, or great shaman, will apply his power, unfolding his net to seize all the evil spirits that he later will transport to the eighth layer, under the earth, and there they must remain captive, tied with reeds.

Once the struggle is over, the chief of evil asks the great Kuna shaman: "When will you visit me again?" and he answers: "When you again harm my community." Now they bid farewell and the great shaman returns to the world of humans, *Nekas pili*, where his body has remained in his hammock, singing, until his powerful spirit again is reunited with his body after the spiritual flight.

Among the actions required in advance of the ritual, or *absogued*, the preparation of chicha made of corn, cacao, and sugarcane occupies a prominent place because, according to belief, it will be consumed only by the spirits.

The great shaman and his helpers smoke raw tobacco during the eight days of the ceremony. At the same time, the shaman carves the *ukur war* or anthropomorphic figures of *balso* wood, of the same size or larger than a human shape. He places these figures, sometimes hundreds of them, in strategic places. According to belief, these will multiply into thousands of benefic spirits and form a powerful army of *nele-gana* to assist the great shaman.

As noted above, the text of the *absogued* consists of over 5,000 verses and belongs to the tradition of Ibelele, the Sun, one of several types of *absogued*. The apprentices of the tradition might spend twenty or more years learning this chant. Recorded Example 11 illustrates the *absogued ígala*, the chant of the great shaman that penetrates the paths of knowledge and powers of *balso* spirits:

> Yeii-ai-ea-ie. . . .
> Dada Lele eye nega targana ye
> obeye naga mala dio muchupi-e,
> ama saila ya mola ya sese
> gi mola ye nega ulu ye eke.
> Tuena sa mala ti muchipi-e,
> ama saila ye mola chichi mola
> ye nega ulu ye somorro eye
> na ya mala ti muchipi-e,
> Nela Wala Nele Kana
> ye naga sunna ogole yola gui, gu eye
> Nele Wala lele kana yena kape
> una iya le iye no e dake wati yala bane
> kape uana e mala ini-ye.
> Kebe aguti yala bali yana kape uana
> e mala ye ibi sogue gude eye
> igui nu itake goati gine ye nega, peu uana e mala di
> deye . . .

The sun rises at dawn and traverses the day going through the clouds of the firmament that take shapes in groups. There are various types of clouds, white clouds, black clouds. The sun traverses the world until it hides behind the mountain and then the night arrives. Light fades, there are no more reflections or sunrays, night falls after the sun has passed, illuminating the earth. Now, the *Nele Ukur Wala* (*Nele Balso*) appear, they have life and are going to represent humans. The *absogued* calls the *Ukur Wala* and tells them: "Already in the times of *Tad Ibe*, you labored to encircle the spirits of evil, now I summon you and will give you instructions, and will give you the powers to help humanity. This is not the first time I have summoned you; I call you now in full possession of my mental faculties to instruct you and tell you that you will have to begin transforming yourselves to travel to the domain of the spirit of evil (*Nía*) . . ."

Massar ígala, or through the paths of the solid reeds. This expression is interpreted as "through the paths of the sacred reeds," or "journey of the dead." In everyday language, *massar* means "bristly reed," but shamanic interpretation links it intimately to the world of the dead. This chant's specialist is called *massar tuledi*, or owner of the *massar, massar kadet, massara*, or, in shamanic language, *Nele tulu balikwa*.

This specialist is called upon when a person dies. He brings eight solid reeds cut from the top of the *massar*, which he himself has prepared, each with four colored feathers, wild cotton, small glass beads, and pieces of wood. These eight reeds are entrusted with the difficult task of guiding and defending the *purba*, the soul of the deceased. Four of them will accompany the soul up to the Takarkuna, the sacred mountain of the Kuna. The other four will guide it until it reaches the house of the *Paba saila tummadi*, or heaven of Kamibe, the Sun and great mythical god of origins.

The specialist nails the eight reeds to the floor under the hammock where the body of the deceased is lying, and places a censer in their midst (*sia nala*) where he burns eight cacao seeds as he delivers the chant. The beginning narrates the confusion that befalls the family at this difficult time. Then it goes on to describe in great detail the tomb where the deceased will be buried, and explains that this will be only the earthly house for eight days, before the start of the great voyage. The journey should not be feared because the great shaman and leader of souls will accompany him or her to the final dwelling. It further explains that, after the eight days of entombment, the soul of the deceased will leave the burial hammock to start the great voyage. The chant guides the reeds accompanying the *purba* and instructs them about their behavior and care they must exercise along the difficult roads of penance they must traverse. As he performs the chant, the specialist places around his neck an instrument called *ted-nono*, or armadillo head, a kind of flute made out of an armadillo skull and a tiger bone. These animals also will be spirits protecting the soul on its long journey. The armadillo, because it burrows in the earth, is quick and astute; the tiger represents strength and agility. The *purba* must climb up the *palu wala*, the mythical tree of death, navigate through swollen rivers, and cross over wells of boiling water, swamps of hungry alligators, oceans filled with enormous sharks, mountains infested with snakes, and precipices crossed by turbulent waters. The *purba* also will have to overcome other dangers in places where other souls have been trapped and will try to stop it.

The spirit of the great shaman travels with the *purba* and, in addition to the reeds, brings along the sacred fruits of the *sabdur* (*Genipa americana*) that will be used to paint the soul black at some critical point so that the trapped souls will not see it. He also carries annatto seeds (*nisar*) to paint the face at the end of the voyage. When the soul has passed through all the possible ordeals, it will disappear into an immense abyss for a long time until it finally emerges cleansed and prepared to dwell in the eternal world of the dead. There, the soul may or may not become a powerful spirit, depending on the attributes that the person possessed during his or her lifetime. In either case, the spirit becomes a superior being, higher in status than mere mortals, and now will assist in ruling the destiny of beings left behind in the material world. It will have this power because it now lives next to *Tad Ibe*, the sun, a kind of ancestral Father to whom it is necessary to return in order to reach eternal life. Example 11 illustrates a *Massar ígala*, or chant of the great shaman to lead the soul of the dead to the afterlife (Recorded Ex. 12). The cantillation proceeds in conjunct motion, with occasional intervals of a minor third and descending half steps.

Kía daka Lele nega, drewi make uni guaye,
kía daka Lele nega, drewi may de uaye.
Dío Lele du iwala gua duba durba bali daysa ye,
baga derbíe yola guíe nega ili wa yola,
bo nega der tubyola barguiné.
Dio Lele bali tulanka sogue bagana pie yola guie
nega ilikwa ya la ba nega der tubya la barye
wegui naguibe gana kunnuy de malati pali ona kue ka
Dio Lele petula di oguichi deye nega ilika yala ba nega
dubyala barguiné, wegui naguibe gana,
aba gala aisaki de mala ti
bali ona kwe ga, Dio Lele der pe tula dio guichi de nega
ilikwa yala ba nega der tub yala bar-yie . . .

At the beginning of the world when you, *Kia daka Lele* (the Sun), came to the world, I also arrived at the same time. When you created everything, I also was there and now, as I have also seen your creation, now I summon you to guide me in my work. When the Sun was created, I too was created, therefore we were both made at the same time. When the sick person was taking leave of the world, I made you (the *massar*); we mourned but we must use the last breath of life to guide *Naguibe* in the voyage to the other world. When I make you (the *massar*), under the hammock where *Naguibe* lies, I prepare you mentally and I also prepare your dressed bodies; I will transform you into purified specialists so that you can prepare yourselves there, under *Naguibe*'s hammock . . .

Instrumental music of the Kuna

There exists among the Kuna an important musical world linked to panpipes or *kammu purwi*, which

Ex. 11: *Massar ígala*, chant of the great shaman to lead the soul of the dead to the afterlife (Recorded Ex. 12).

are performed daily in each community. Although young people play this instrument, the traditional knowledge required is transmitted by specialists. The *kammu purwi* always are played accompanied by maracas, or *násisi*. In ritual contexts, the panpipes are played by males, and the maracas by females. In secular contexts, both men and women play the panpipes.

The reeds are obtained by the *kamsuedi*, or seekers of cane. They go to special places in the jungle and bring with them cacao incense and raw tobacco (*war suid*) to make an offering to the *kammu* spirits, because otherwise the "sonorous" reeds cannot be found, or permission is not given for them to be cut. At the *kamsuedi*'s home the cut reeds also receive the smoke of special aromatic herbs to preserve their magical powers.

The *kamsuedi* makes the male and female *kammu purwi*. The male consists of four tubes, cut from large to small, with a difference in tube length of one third. The female instrument has three tubes. Each group of tubes is tied with plant fiber, and both groups are joined by a rope that the player hangs around the neck for the instruments to reach breast level. The performer will join the two smallest tubes to form a composite instrument. Moreover, the performance of melodies requires two interdependent sets of male and female instruments, namely a pair of musicians, who alternate and combine the pitches of a complete melody. Each "set" of four and three tubes also is conceptualized as male and female. In performance, the female and male sets produce most of the time a melodic texture in parallel fifths between the leader or female set of panpipes, and the follower or male set of panpipes. The sets also can be conjoined to blow on two tubes and produce a harmonic interval of a fifth with a single emission of air. A *toque* or performance usually involves several pairs of panpipes, with maracas (*násisi*) marking the pulse of the melody. These performances always are danced, and this tradition also is observed when a youngster is being taught how to play the instrument (Fig. 13).

We are including only one example of secular music of the Kuna in this essay. This is the *Mete sikwi uurma kali*, a melody for a festive dance that, according to explanations given by those who cultivate this genre, imitates the song and movements of a bird. In general, all the instrumental *toques* and dances imitate the various animals in nature. Occasionally, *toques* represent hunting and other activities of daily life (Ex. 12; Recorded Ex. 13). In this *toque* or instrumental performance, the panpipes play harmonic fifths, and the passing tones of the first flute make the melody more conjunct. The basic binary meter is marked by the isochronous pulse of the rattle (*násisi*). These performances are a part of daily activities in all Kuna communities.

Fig. 13: Young Kuna playing the *kammu purwi* and dancing. Photo by Ronny Velásquez (1976), courtesy of the author.

Ex. 12: *Mete sikwi uurma kali*, festive dance played on Kuna panpipes (*kammu purwi*) (Recorded Ex. 13).

CONCLUSIONS

The musical practices of these two Central American ethnic nations leave little doubt about the prominent role of chant or song in the enactment of their beliefs. Although music may be intangible, this form of representation of the people's vast cultural knowledge is highly institutionalized in norms and rules of behavior that, one way or another, regulate the social life of the practitioners.

In order to consolidate their powerful world—filled with images, symbols, and messages from the gods of creation that strengthen cultural canons—the Mískito and Kuna have formulated concepts and practical theories about their music. Moreover, these forms of conceptualizing musical practices open new roads to scientific interpretations of the field of music in general.

The frequent and necessary presence of song at various junctures in the life cycle of the Mískito and Kuna, to which we must add the extraordinary length of Kuna chants, cannot be understood only as a linguistic message, because it alludes to a symbolic domain that, in both cases, harks back to mythical paths of profound significance for each of these two societies. As in the case of other indigenous groups, it is essential to analyze the symbolic domains because these networks of meanings are embedded in the deepest recesses of the practitioners' minds. For the Mískito and Kuna, chants hold a symbolic value that takes shape through linguistic sound, or sung speech. In the rituals and ceremonies of both ethnic nations, we can identify tacit and unspoken conventions that, carrying transcendental significance, are integral to a cognitive structure that requires no verbal formulation. Rather, these are attitudes that are shared, accepted, and tacitly understood by the members of these societies.

Particularly in the case of the Kuna, there exists an underlying theory in the practice of the system of chants that is intimately linked to long and mythical, yet concrete and explicit, explanations of each linguistic sign. This is because, although the explanations of each chant's origin and path summon mythical, oneiric, or literary formulations, nature provides a frame of reference that makes these symbols concrete. It is through the terms of nature that the symbolic path of each *ígala* or chant is represented, and it is in nature that the symbolic effectiveness of each shamanic chant is manifested.

The members of these two ethnic nations have constructed an array of paths that, as noted above, are built into the deepest recesses of their mental structure. At an abstract level, these paths guide their behavior. The actions of individuals are thus circumscribed to practices implicit in the theory underlying their respective musical universes. For each actual human need there is a mythical explanation, which is received as truthful and worthy of respect. Each shamanic act involves direct or indirect social participation, and the enactment of each religious ritual induces the people to reflect upon and become increasingly aware of their millenarian cultures.

Both the Mískito and Kuna have suffered attacks of all kinds. The Mískito have had to protect their territory, which is strategically located. The Kuna have had to endure an image of exoticism built on their women's dress and habitat on islands of coraline origin, and they have been exploited by tourism. Mískito shamans have suffered imprisonment and have been accused of witchcraft. They also have been forced to enter bonfires in a conscious state, not in a trance, to expose their vulnerability. In both cases, but particularly in the case of the Mískito, Protestant denominations, such as the Moravian Church in Honduras and Nicaragua, have ravaged them culturally. However, and notwithstanding all the contempt they have had to endure from creoles holding the reins of power who lacked awareness of native cultures inhabiting their own territories, and the harassment suffered at the hands of foreign powers bent on economic and ideological domination, neither of these ethnic nations has undergone radical changes in the deep structure of their shamanic worlds. This is because their symbolic universe is a social institution shared by all members of each ethnic nation. An impenetrable bond, created by shared meanings and the understanding of shamanic terms, transcends the surface level and unites them in a symbolic metalanguage that cannot be eradicated from their mental structure.

All the constitutive elements of a shamanic chant are arranged according to an internal logic that creates its own structure. In turn, meaning unfolds from this structural ordering. This meaning, however, proves resistant to verbal explanations; it only begins to emerge fully with the actual experience of each ceremony, and by direct contact with the reality of the symbolic universe that lives in the minds of shamans, *sailas*, *neles*, and *sukias*. Only under these conditions can we penetrate the fact that each shaman, as a representative of the society, broaches speculative issues concerning the shamanic profession, and partakes in a theory that is inherently spiritual.

REFERENCES

Agerkop, Terry 1976. "Lunku, el arco musical de los Mískitos," *Revista INIDEF* (Caracas) 2: 28–42.
1977. "Música de los Mískitos de Honduras," *Folklore americano* (México) 23: 7–37.
Bastide, Roger 1969. *Las Américas negras: Las civilizaciones africanas en el Nuevo Mundo.* Madrid: Alianza Editorial.
Beltrán y Rózpide, Ricardo 1937. *Algunas notas documentadas para escribir la historia territorial de Centro América.* Tegucigalpa: Talleres Tipográficos Nacionales.
Carles, Rubén Darío 1963. *A través del istmo.* Panamá: Impresora Panamá.
1969. *220 años del período colonial en Panamá.* Panamá: Escuela de Artes y Oficios "Melchor Lasso de la Vega."
Castillero, Ernesto 1968. *Chiriquí, monografía de la Provincia de Chiriquí.* Panamá: Impresora Panamá.
Chapin, Mac 1978. *Pab ígala: Historias de la tradición Kuna.* Panamá: Universidad de Panamá.
Constenla Umaña, Adolfo 1985. *Clasificación lexicoestadística de las lenguas de la familia Chibcha.* Costa Rica: Universidad de Costa Rica (Estudios de lingüística Chibcha, 4).
Conzemius, Edward 1932. *Ethnographical survey of the Mískito and Sumo Indians of Honduras and Nicaragua.* Washington, D.C.: Government Printing Office.
1984. *Estudio monográfico sobre los indios Mískitos y Sumos de Honduras y Nicaragua.* Costa Rica: Editorial Libro Libre.
Floyd, Troy S. 1967. *The Anglo-Spanish struggle for Mosquitia.* Albuquerque: University of New Mexico Press.
González de Pérez, María Stella 1980. *Trayectoria de los estudios sobre la lengua Chibcha o Muisca.* Bogotá: Instituto "Caro y Cuervo."
Holmer, Nils M. 1954. "Apuntes comparados sobre la lengua de los Yaganes," *Revista de la Facultad de Humanidades y Ciencias* (Montevideo, Universidad de la República del Uruguay) 12: 121–42.
Holmer, Nils M., and Henry Wassen 1947. *Mu-Ígala or the way of Muu, a medicine song from the Cuna Indians of Panama.* Göteborg: Elanders Boktryckeri Aktiebolag.
1953. *The complete Mu-ígala in picture writing.* Göteborg (Etnologiska studier 21).
Howe, James 1979. *Cantos y oraciones del Congreso Cuna.* Panamá: Editorial Universitaria.
Jenkins Molieri, Jorge 1986. *El desafío indígena en Nicaragua: El caso de los Mískitos.* México: Editorial Katún.
Kramer, Fritz 1970. *Literature among the Cuna Indians.* Göteborg (Etnologiska studier 30).
Lévi-Strauss, Claude 1958 in 1967. *Structural anthropology.* Garden City, New York: Anchor Books—Doubleday and Co.
M. W. 1699. *The Mosqueto Indians and their golden river.* London (Collection of Voyages and Travels, 6, 1732).

Nordenskiöld, Erland 1938. *An historical and ethnological survey of the Cuna Indians*, translated by Mary Frodi. Göteborg: Göteborgs Museum, Etnografiska Avdelningen (vol. 10 in the series Comparative ethnographical studies, edited by Henry Wassen).

Prestán, Simón A. n.d. *Ensayo monográfico sobre los Caribe-Cuna.* Bogotá: Universidad de San Buena Ventura.

Puig, Manuel María 1944. *Diccionario de la lengua caribe-cuna.* Panamá: Editorial La Estrella de Panamá.

Reclus, Elisée 1881. *Geographie universelle: La terre et les hommes.* Paris: Hachette.

Sherzer, Joel, and Sammie Ann Wicks 1982. "The intersection of music and language in Kuna discourse," *Latin American music review* 3/2: 147–64.

Squier, George 1855 in 1965. *Waikna: Adventures on the Mosquito shore.* Gainesville: University of Florida Press.

Taussig, Michael T. 1993. *Mimesis and alterity: A particular history of the senses.* New York: Routledge.

Tovar, Antonio 1961. *Catálogo de las lenguas de América del Sur.* Buenos Aires: Editorial Sudamericana.

Velásquez, Ronny 1982. "El chamanismo Mískito de Honduras," *Revista INIDEF* (Caracas) 5: 102–20.

1987. *Chamanismo, mito y religión en cuatro naciones étnicas de América aborigen.* Caracas: Academia Nacional de la Historia (Colección Estudios, Monografías y Ensayos 97).

AUDIOVISUAL MATERIALS

Ronny Velásquez and Terry Agerkop 1979. "Mískitos, Honduras," *Cajas audiovisuales INIDEF 2.* Caracas: Instituto Interamericano de Etnomusicología y Folklore.

RECORDED EXAMPLES

1. *Sary inanka*, or lament (Mískito) (see Ex. 1).
2. *Inanka upla pruan bara*, or collective laments for the dead (Mískito).
3. *Iumu*, or preparation of the water to heal minor illnesses (Mískito) (see Ex. 4).
4. Song to capture the soul of the dead (Mískito) (see Ex. 5).
5. *Tiun* (tune), creole music of the Mískito accompanied by guitar illustrating Hispanic influence.
6. *Muu ígala*, or through the paths of the divinity of creation. Therapeutic chant that the great shaman performs to aid in the birth of a child during difficult labor (Kuna) (see Ex. 8).
7. *Kammu ígala*, or through the paths of the sonorous reeds. Ritual chant of the great shaman (*kandur*) that marks the path of the ceremonial cutting of hair of the Kuna girl. Two flutes alternate with the chant, accompanied by maracas (see Ex. 9).
8. *Akwa nusa ígala*, through the paths of the stones that hold the power to heal (Kuna) (see Ex. 10).
9. *Sia ba kabur unaedi*, healing chant instructing the cacao and hot pepper to search for the soul of a patient (Kuna).
10. *Ukku naibe ígala*, or through the paths of the serpent. Chant describing the origin of the rattlesnake (Kuna).
11. *Absogued ígala*, the chant of the great shaman through the paths of knowledge and the power of *balso* spirits (Kuna).
12. *Massar ígala*, or through the paths of the solid reeds. Chant of the great shaman to lead the soul of the dead to the afterlife (see Ex. 11).
13. *Mete sikwi uurma kali*, instrumental performance on panpipes (*kammu purwi*) accompanying a festive dance of the Kuna (see Ex. 12).

MEXICO'S INDIGENOUS UNIVERSE

MARINA ALONSO BOLAÑOS

Ancient and present-day Mexico—Languages—Regions and cultures: The northwestern region;
The eastern region; The western region; The central region; The southern Pacific region;
Transisthmus region; The central valleys and northern Oaxaca; The southeastern region

WHEN WE SPEAK of contemporary indigenous peoples, we tend to disassociate them from their history by creating a hypothetical line of continuity between them and their also hypothetical pre-Hispanic past that reduces them to the condition of mere remnants of ancient civilizations. Although we can identify certain linguistic, social, and cultural continuities between present-day groups and ancient Mesoamerican civilizations, it is important to keep in mind that the nature of such links is the result of highly complex historical processes.

ANCIENT AND PRESENT-DAY MEXICO

As a historical concept, ancient Mexico refers to a time-span of some 35,000 years, beginning with the arrival of groups of hunter-gatherers, and ending with the Spanish Conquest (1521). It was never a single historical entity but rather a conformation of three macrocultural areas that extended beyond the borders of contemporary Mexico: Aridamerica (comprising the Northeast and the Baja California Peninsula); Oasisamerica (the Northwest); and Mesoamerica in the southern part of Mexico. Regional subdivisions correspond to each of these macrostructural areas. The boundaries of ancient Mexico comprised a major part of the United States, Mexico, Guatemala, Belize, Honduras, El Salvador, Nicaragua, and Costa Rica (López Luján and López Austin 1996: 15) (Map 1).

The concept of Mesoamerica was proposed by Paul Kirchhoff in 1943 and resulted from an attempt to reconstruct the ethnic composition of southern Mexico at the time of Conquest. Kirchhoff maintained that the ancient and recent inhabitants of this macrocultural area were linked by a common history that set them apart from other indigenous groups on the continent (1949: 4).

At the time of Conquest, Mesoamerica was populated by numerous indigenous groups whose languages have been associated with one of the following five linguistic families: (1) Tarasco, Cuitlatec, Lencan; (2) Zoquean-Mayan; (3) the Oto-Manguean group; (4) Uto-Aztecan group; and (5) Hokan (Kirchhoff 1949: 3).

In order to establish the boundaries of Mesoamerica as a cultural area, Kirchhoff identified the following three main categories, based on the principle of distribution of shared traits:

(1) Elements exclusive to, or at least typical of, Mesoamericans, such as the staff used for planting (*coa*); the use of agricultural plots on soil reclaimed from lakes (*chinampas*); the cultivation of lime-leafed sage seed (*chía*) and its use in making beverages and for oil; the cultivation of maguey for making sweet beverages, such as *aguamiel* and *pulque*, syrup (*arrope*), and paper; the cultivation of cacao; the grinding of boiled

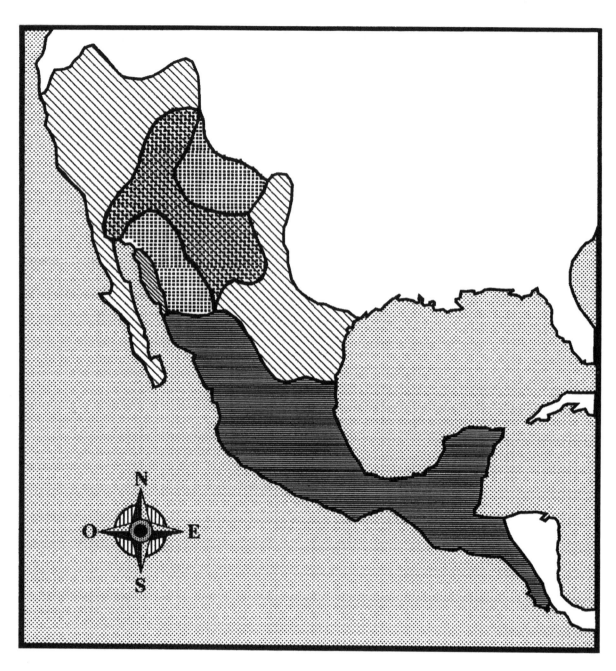

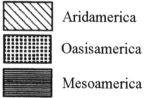 Aridamerica

Oasisamerica

Mesoamerica

Map 1: Macrocultural areas of ancient Mexico: Aridamerica, Oasisamerica, and Mesoamerica.

corn with ashes or lime; the polishing of obsidian; the construction of stepped pyramids; stucco floors; patios with rings for ball games (*juego de pelota*); writing systems; books folded or pleated in accordion style; the keeping of historical records or annals, and maps; a system of specialized markets, or markets with specialized subdivisions; the practice of warfare; and the assignment of military ranks, among many other shared traits (Kirchhoff 1949: 9).

(2) Elements common to Mesoamericans and groups in other American macrocultural areas, such as the cultivation of corn, beans, and squash; the practice of human sacrifice; terrace agriculture; the weaving of different types of baskets; the construction of underground ovens; and the use of steam baths, to name but a few (Kirchhoff 1949: 9–10).

(3) Elements that are conspicuous for their absence in Mesoamerica, such as the practice of decorating the ear observed in Chibcha culture; the presence of matrilineal clans; the use of poison-bearing weapons; the cultivation of coca leaves; and the cultivation of palm trees, among others (Kirchhoff 1949: 10–13).

The northern border area of Mesoamerica, which was the last link in a northward chain of advanced farmers, differed from the southern border area in its greater degree of migration and mobility. With the exception of two small areas, one in Sinaloa and the other on the Gulf, Mesoamerica bordered directly on territories of hunter-gatherers. The southern boundary was adjacent to the land of another group of agricultural peoples, the Chibcha.

Aridamerica was characterized by a certain degree of isolation and by settlements of mostly hunter-gatherers who lived under harsh environmental conditions. These groups were highly differentiated due to the enormous distances that separated them. There was never as much contact between these groups as there was between those in the other macrocultural areas. In Mesoamerica there was constant communication among the different settlements and, to a lesser extent, between them and other, more distantly located groups. As in the case of Mesoamerica, Oasisamerica comprised indigenous groups that shared a fair number of cultural traits (López Luján and López Austin 1996: 273).

Recent studies have confirmed the viability of Mesoamerica as a concept on the basis that, alongside the many different historical paths that distinguish each contemporary indigenous society as a unique cultural group, similarities have been identified that apply to the present-day inhabitants of the region (Bonfil 1990: 23–39). According to the anthropologist and historian of Mexican religions Alfredo López Austin, this can be explained by the existence of a core system of thought in Mesoamerican cultures. This core subsumes elements that are more resistant to change than others. When added to new and more recent traits, the core then reconstitutes a traditional legacy that vests these elements with meaning within a particular social context (López Austin 1990a: 25–42).

Although colonization had a devastating impact on all aspects of indigenous life and attempted to eradicate some of its fundamental core values by prohibiting or inhibiting cultural practices, the indigenous peoples continued these practices clandestinely, or openly when these were tolerated by the Church. For instance, they were allowed to retain their languages (Ricard 1947 in 1986: 121–22).

Among the identifiable characteristics shared by indigenous groups in Mexico today that have their roots in Mesoamerican thought are the concept of time and space in relation to nature, and the place of human beings in nature:

> The obsession with the flow of time [in Mesoamerica] . . . was part of a cosmovision forged throughout the centuries in normal daily interactions, as well as in the transformative action of humans upon nature (López Austin 1990a: 28).

Summarizing the achievements of Mesoamerican civilizations in "Introduction: The Dance of Conquest," ethnomusicologist Carol E. Robertson reminds us that,

> As early as the 4th century C.E., the Maya had produced inscriptions based on a partly ideographic, partly phonetic code. Through this literature and later murals and stone carvings we know that, throughout Maya lands, astronomy laid the foundations for the concept of cyclical time. The time spiral in which events cyclically replicated variants of themselves was kept in motion by complex ceremonial performances. Music, dance, and drama provided the means by which humankind could move through this multilayered model of time and space (1992: 14–15).

The concept of cyclic time is a fundamental link between ancient and present-day indigenous groups.

The Mesoamerican calendrical system and its main variants have existed, according to López Austin, at least since the seventh century C.E. (1990b: 28). Time was organized according to dimensions related to the cycles of nature, that is, 360 days apportioned between rainy and dry seasons, diurnal and nocturnal parts of a day, and by the movement of the heavenly bodies, especially the phases of the moon. These cycles were complemented by others:

> . . . the 9 days of the lords of the night; the 360-day cycle . . . or 18 months of 20 days each; and one of the most significant, the calendrical cycle of 260 days, whose origin is attributed to the combination of two fundamental numbers in the cosmic order, 13 and 20. There were others as well, but the most basic was the combination of two of them: the ritual calendar, and the cycle of 260 days that established an order to the destiny ruling the lives of human beings. In the Maya world, these were further combined with the 360-day cycle, whose main function was to record history (López Austin 1990b: 29).

Other elements of that resilient core that links past and present indigenous life include a holistic conception of the agricultural system and its complete harmony with all aspects of communal life; the wide variety of agricultural techniques, including the use of small plots on the shores of lakes (chinampas) (Bonfil 1990: 23–39); polycultivation in the same plots of corn, beans, squash, and chilies; the adaptation of house building to the conditions of the terrain; and the use of various textile techniques for the production of necessary goods, such as clothing. Dress varies not only between ethnic groups, but within them as well, as clothing is used to distinguish one group of villagers from another (Lechuga 1986: 24). Present-day indigenous groups are linked also by the practice of religious traditions that are syncretic products of Mesoamerican beliefs and Christianity (López Austin 1990a: 38); the ritual use of psychoactive plants and shamanic practices; the knowledge and application of traditional medicine; the concept of communal work as an axis of historical continuity; the observance of complex ceremonial calendars; and the ritual exchange of goods and symbols.

In this context, it is important to emphasize that the fiesta or celebration serves as the principal venue for symbolic exchange. The social life and identity of indigenous peoples are defined mainly in relationship to the celebrations of the ceremonial cycle, in turn determined by agricultural activities and the life cycle rituals (birth, baptism, weddings, and funeral ceremonies). Music is not only integral to the sacred and secular aspects of life, and as essential to ceremony as are food, drink, and dance, but also transformative because it mediates in the communication between humans and supernatural beings.

The organization of different types of ceremonies, although they vary greatly, is linked to a system of civic duties and responsibilities placed in the hands of individuals who govern the public life of the communities. Participation in the ceremonies is obligatory for all members of the community, although the type of participation differs between men and women (Millán 1993: 121). The ceremonies are centered on the worship of Catholic saints (Thomas 1974: 15) and are organized by individuals who hold rotating posts instituted by the Catholic Church during colonial times. These posts are clearly defined and ordered according to a ranking system whose hierarchy is commensurate with responsibility and prestige (Fábregas 1982: 1).

Most importantly, these groups' sense of history and cultural survival are themselves anchored in the practice of these celebrations, which respond to a set of norms based on reciprocity. Catharine Good (1994: 140–48) documents how "maintaining customs"—or reenacting cultural practices—constitutes such an anchor for the Nahua of the Balsas basin in the State of Guerrero. For instance, Good finds that they use highly developed concepts to refer to the preservation of continuity. Cotona, for example, means to pull a rope, string, or thread until it breaks. It is used figuratively to mean a definitive break with tradition, leading to the expression "xticotoniskeh, no romperemos la tradición" (we will not break the thread). This expression is used when a person agrees to participate in a ceremony and in this manner contributes to communal life when a fiesta is being prepared.

Present-day indigenous societies in Mexico are distinct historico-cultural entities that do not merely represent coexisting historical epochs (the old and the new). Rather, they are dynamic social groups constantly engaged in the procreation of beliefs. From each of their own respective and unique histories, these societies have appropriated a number of elements to continually renew their worldview. In the same manner, new expressive forms emerge that retain the main principles of lost, ancient practices (Collin 1994: iii). In this process, the historical memory of indigenous peoples, tenaciously protected by their oral traditions and all other elements of their culture, plays an essential role when these groups have to face new situations or adapt to changing circumstances.

LANGUAGES

Ethnic groups generally are identified by the name of their language. Although language does not constitute the only defining factor of ethnicity, language and culture mutually interact to construct unique ways of representing views of the cosmos, nature, space, and time.

According to Leopoldo Valiñas, there are—in the late 1990s—sixty-two identified names of languages spoken in Mexico (1993: 165). Most of these languages, however, branch out into at least two dialects. Some dialects are divergent enough to be considered distinct languages. Zapotec, for example, has six dialects; Nahuatl, the Uto-Aztecan language spoken by descendants of the Aztecs, is diversified into at least ten dialects. Conversely, some languages with different names could be considered as a single linguistic unit, as, for instance, Mayo and Yaqui. From this we can infer that the number of indigenous groups living in present-day Mexico approximately doubles the number of identified linguistic designations.

Native languages were challenged and outweighed by Spanish during colonial times, even during the period when Nahuatl was used as a lingua franca. For supporters of independence, Spanish was the national language in spite of the fact that, toward the end of the nineteenth century and during the first decade of the 1900s, 38 percent of the population spoke an indigenous language (Manrique 1988: 7). We include below a list of indigenous languages currently spoken in Mexico, classified according to linguistic group affiliation (Valiñas 1993: 186), and a map of their geographical distribution (Map 2).

Hokan family
1. Cucapá
2. Cochimí
3. K'mai
4. Kiliwa
5. Paipai
6. Seri

Uto-Aztecan family
7. Cora
8. Huichol
9. Guarijío
10. Mayo
11. Nahuatl or Mexicano
12. Pápago
13. Pima
14. Tarahumara
15. Tepecano
16. Northern Tepehuan
17. Southern Tepehuan
18. Yaqui

Mixe-Zoque family
19. Mixe
20. Popoluca
21. Zoque

Totonacan family
22. Totonac
23. Tepehua

Unknown affiliation, isolates
24. Kikapú
25. Tarasco or Purépecha
26. Chontal of Oaxaca
27. Huave

Oto-Manguean family
28. Amuzgo
29. Chatino
30. Chichimec (Jonaz)
31. Chinantec
32. Chocho
33. Cuicatec
34. Ixcatec
35. Matlatzinca
36. Mazahua
37. Mazatec
38. Mixtec
39. Ocuiltec
40. Otomí
41. Pame
42. Popoloc
43. Tlapanec
44. Trique
45. Zapotec

Mayan family
46. Chol
47. Chontal of Tabasco
48. Chuj

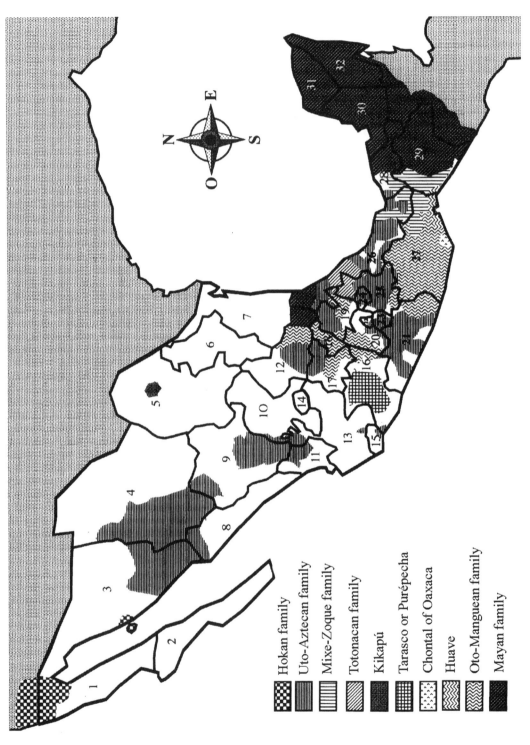

Map 2: Geographic distribution of linguistic families and isolates. Numbers refer to states in present-day Mexico.

Hokan family
Uto-Aztecan family
Mixe-Zoque family
Totonacan family
Kikapú
Tarasco or Purépecha
Chontal of Oaxaca
Huave
Oto-Manguean family
Mayan family

1. Northern Baja California	5. Coahuila	9. Durango	13. Jalisco	17. Guanajuato	21. Guerrero	25. Puebla	29. Chiapas
2. Southern Baja California	6. Nuevo León	10. Zacatecas	14. Aguascalientes	18. Querétaro	22. Federal District	26. Veracruz	30. Campeche
3. Sonora	7. Tamaulipas	11. Nayarit	15. Colima	19. Hidalgo	23. Morelos	27. Oaxaca	31. Yucatán
4. Chihuahua	8. Sinaloa	12. San Luis Potosí	16. Michoacán	20. State of Mexico	24. Tlaxcala	28. Tabasco	32. Quintana Roo

49. Huastec
50. Ixil
51. Jacaltec
52. Kanjobal
53. Kekchí
54. Lacandón
55. Mame
56. Mayan Yucatec
57. Mochó (Motozintlec)
58. Quiché
59. Teco
60. Tojolabal
61. Tzeltal
62. Tzotzil

REGIONS AND CULTURES

We have addressed above the characteristics that identify three macrocultural areas within the boundaries of ancient Mexico, with special emphasis on Mesoamerica. Moreover, the original geographic distribution of indigenous settlements in this territory was profoundly altered by the process of colonization (Bonfil 1990: 51), which superimposed its own demographics over the Mesoamerican distribution.

During the seventeenth century, the territory was regionally subdivided into Nueva España, Nuevo León, Nueva Vizcaya, and Nueva Galicia. These were settled not only by Spaniards and Native Americans, but also by Africans and their descendants, giving rise to mestizo communities. This regional reconfiguration was determined mainly by economic and political factors driven by trade routes, which is why these divisions do not coincide with the borders of the current states. A majority of the indigenous population is now concentrated in the diverse ecological environments of the central, southern, and southeastern parts of the country (Bonfil 1990: 52).

We present below a brief survey of indigenous groups that includes historical and ethnographic data based on information compiled by the Instituto Nacional Indigenista. It is important to note that the Instituto Nacional Indigenista has identified the existence of only fifty-six indigenous groups. As mentioned earlier, however, recent studies indicate the presence of at least twice that number. We have included some statistics, in spite of their imprecision, because they provide a useful reference to the minimum number of people of indigenous descent in the different regions. The Instituto Nacional Indigenista

relies on demographic information based on the *XI Censo de Población y Vivienda* (population and housing census) compiled in 1990 by the Instituto Nacional de Estadística, Geografía e Informática (National Institute of Statistics, Geography, and Information Sciences). According to Miguel León-Portilla (1997: 8–9),

The descendants of the original inhabitants, as history has demonstrated, have in some cases lost and in others maintained forms of cultural continuity or differentiation, irrespective of the state of dependency which they may have maintained in relation to other groups, and in spite of having had all or part of their territory wrested from them.

Although this population always has been highly mobile due to many factors, migration has become an important resource for survival, because of the level of poverty and marginalization in some communities. Nahuas, Mazahuas, Triques, P'urhépechas, and especially Mixtecs are among those who migrate to Mexico City and northern towns that serve as bridges for entry into the United States, where they hope to find work. We also should note that indigenous groups live in the close proximity of mestizo and Afromestizo communities, maintaining with them a type of uninterrupted contact that is reflected in their culture.

Cultural boundaries—a fragile concept to begin with—have both expanded and contracted, creating areas that defy demarcation because, aside from the particularities of each group and the multiple influences that have configured their identity, many similarities also link groups in surrounding areas. A clear example of this is the impossibility of assigning boundaries to cultural practices in the northern and southern border regions.

The northwestern region

Before the Conquest, what became Nueva Vizcaya was home to over one hundred indigenous groups, with an estimated population of 540,000 persons (Hu-DeHart 1995: 15). During the sixteenth century, there were constant expeditions to the territory that is now Sonora, in search of mythical cities, gold, and slaves. The first expedition (1521–31) was led by Nuño Beltrán de Guzmán, who commanded an army of 300 Spaniards and 6,000 Tlaxcaltecs. The Lienzo de Tlaxcala battles stand as testimony of this enterprise (Radding 1995: 51).

This region, which was colonized later than most, is known for its large number of indigenous uprisings. The Kikapú, for example, after suffering a long process of genocide and territorial dispossession, resisted the domination of France, England, and the United States during the nineteenth century and perhaps earlier (Rodríguez 1995: iii).

Soldiers and missionaries shaped the profile of the Northwest by establishing complex socioeconomic structures around mining centers, with the stated objective of "taming the Indians." According to the distinguished historian Miguel León-Portilla, the fact that the indigenous groups in the area maintained substantial cultural differentiation in spite of profound changes in their traditional ways of life, proves that the process of mestizaje failed to eradicate their sense of identity (1997: 22).

The present-day Northwest—a region of deserts, mountains, and plains—covers nearly a third of Mexico, including the states of Baja California, Sonora, Chihuahua, Sinaloa, Durango, and Coahuila. The indigenous groups that inhabit this region are the Guarijío, Kikapú, Pápago, Pima, Seri, Tarahumara, northern Tepehuan, southern Tepehuan, Yaqui, and Mayo. With the exception of the Kikapú and Seri, all these indigenous groups speak languages of Uto-Aztecan affiliation, which means that they are culturally related as well.

The main form of social organization is the nuclear family and the division of labor within it according to age and gender. Like their ancestors, these groups are mainly hunter-gatherers and practice agriculture to a limited extent. Some groups, such as the Guarijío, Mayo, and Yaqui, engage in some forms of economic activity, such as the use of palm leaves, branches, and different types of plant fibers to make baskets (mats and hats in the case of the Guarijío), and the use of wood to make masks for ceremonial dances and musical instruments. The Kikapú make traditional clothing from cured deer hides. They also make *tehuas* (moccasins) and *mitazas* (pants decorated with beads).

Guarijío or Macurawe, also Macoragü, "those who cling to the earth" or "those who roam the earth." The Instituto Nacional Indigenista estimates the population of this group at around 1,000 in the mountainous area that extends from the southeast of Sonora to Chihuahua. There is little information about their pre-Hispanic past, although scholars believe that their territory remains "unspoiled." They live in dispersed settlements and their adobe houses are found in the high mountainous areas, near small streams and other water sources (Aguilar Zeleny 1994: 8, 13).

Kikapú or Kikaapoa, "those who roam the earth." The Kikapú language is not part of the Uto-Aztecan phylum that relates other indigenous groups in the region. The Kikapú inhabit Nacimiento de los Kikapú, a village located in the municipality of Múzquiz, Coahuila. This group maintains contact with mestizos in the region and with a small community of African descent whose inhabitants are called *negros mascogos*.

Pápago or O'tham. The Pápago inhabit the Altar-Yuma or Sonora Desert. The establishment of the border between Mexico and the United States cut their territory in half, making this a binational group.

Pima. The Pima call themselves O'ob, "the people, the villagers," and their language O'ob no'ok. They live in the western Sierra Madre mountain range, where their territory borders with the southeastern part of Sonora and the southwestern part of Chihuahua.

Seri or Konkaak, "the people." The term *seri* probably comes from the Yaqui "men of the sand." The Seri language is part of the Hokan linguistic family. The Seri inhabit the desert area of the State of Sonora, and their population is estimated at 500 individuals.

Tarahumara or Rarámuri, "those who run on foot." This name comes from the fact that the Tarahumara roam great distances in the eastern part of the Sierra Tarahumara in Chihuahua. Their current population is estimated at 95,000 persons.

Northern Tepehuan or Ódami, "the people of the mountains," and **southern Tepehuan.** The colonization process split a single cultural group into two that have become differentiated to the point of being considered as two groups speaking different languages. They inhabit the southern part of Chihuahua. The southern Tepehuan also are found in parts of Nayarit, Jalisco, and Durango.

Yaqui or Yoreme, "person," "man." The term *yoreme* is used to refer to both the Mayo and the Yaqui. The European missionaries chose the native term *cahíta* to designate both languages. The population currently is concentrated in eight settlements, from the southern to the northern end of the Yaqui Valley, in the municipalities of Guaymas, Bácum, Cajeme, Empalme, and Hermosillo. The population is estimated at 25,000 persons.

Mayo or Yoreme, "he who respects [tradition]." This group inhabits the northwestern part of Mexico between the states of Sonora and Sinaloa on the Pacific coast (Fig. 1).

The eastern region

The Huasteca, a region located in the lower basin of the Pánuco River, was of enormous importance in pre-Hispanic times and has been historically inhabited by a number of ethnic groups. The area includes parts of the present-day states of Tamaulipas, San Luis Potosí, Guanajuato, Querétaro, Hidalgo, and Veracruz. It was inhabited since ca. 2500 B.C.E. by agricultural peoples and is the birthplace of rich cultural traditions that still exist today.

The main economic activity is agriculture and parallel activities include basketry, pottery making, and the sewing of traditional clothing. Characteristic of the region is the confluence of groups from the entire area on market days for the exchange of goods. Like all indigenous groups in Mexico, their social organization is based on the nuclear family as core from which its members create a network of social relationships.

This region is inhabited by different groups of Huastecs or Teenek, "those who live in the land with their language and their blood, and share the idea," from San Luis Potosí and Veracruz, with a population of over 100,000 individuals. The Teenek come from a migration of Mayan population along the Gulf coast, which was interrupted by the arrival of Totonacs and Mexicas toward the end of the preclassic or formative period (Ávila 1993: 7). This explains their linguistic affiliation with the Mayan family, though they separated from that group over 3,000 years ago (Ruvalcava 1995: 63).

Nahua. The Nahua population (of Uto-Aztecan linguistic affiliation) of the huasteca veracruzana area live in municipalities of northern Veracruz, especially Chicontepec. The Nahua of the northern sierra of Puebla inhabit sixty-eight municipalities of that mountain range with an approximate population of 259,756 Nahuas, Totonacs, Otomíes, and Tepehuans (Fig. 2).

Pame. The Pame of Querétaro and Pame of San Luis Potosí, of the Oto-Manguean linguistic family, call themselves Xi'úi or "indigenous," that is, "all those people who are not of mestizo descent" (Nava López 1995b: 283). They currently occupy a part of San Luis Potosí and a small part of Querétaro.

Totonacs. The Totonacs, of the Totonacan linguistic family, are estimated at 207,876 persons living mostly in Puebla and Veracruz, in the State of Mexico, in Mexico City, and, as a result of migration, in Quintana Roo, Tlaxcala, Tamaulipas, Campeche, Hidalgo, and Jalisco.

The western region

The indigenous inhabitants of southern Sinaloa, Nayarit, and Jalisco are affiliated linguistically with the Uto-Aztecan group. The Cora, Huichol, and Mexicaneros share traits with the peoples of the Northwest insofar as living in extremely dispersed settlements and practicing belief systems that are closely linked to surrounding nature.

Agriculture and gathering are the main subsistence activities, although some families also hunt and tend small gardens (Grimes and Hinton 1972 in 1990: 73).

Fig. 1: Mayo dancer of *pascola*, or *pascolero*. The *pascola* dance is traditionally performed during Holy Week. Photo by Marina Alonso Bolaños, courtesy of the author.

Fig. 2: Nahua child of the Sierra de Zongolica, Veracruz. Photo by Marina Alonso Bolaños, courtesy of the author.

Some settlements also raise sheep for wool and sew cotton pouches or bags that they decorate with embroidered symbolic representations of their worldview.

Cora or Nayeri. They inhabit the highland of the western Sierra Madre mountain range (the ancient Sierra de Nayar) and the coast of Nayarit. Their population is estimated at 11,434 in the municipalities of El Nayar, Rosamorada, and Ruiz.

Huichol or Wirr'arika. A majority of Wirr'arika live in northern Jalisco, a smaller number in Nayarit, and a few small groups in Zacatecas and Durango. Their approximate population is 19,000.

Mexicaneros. This group speaks Nahuatl, the language of the descendants of the Aztecs, or Mexicano. Unlike the Nahuatlatos or "owners of the word," those Nahuatl-speakers living in the western states of Durango, Nayarit, Jalisco, and Zacatecas are called Mexicaneros.

The central region

Mexico City and the greater metropolitan area currently have a large concentration of indigenous peoples from all over the country, which represents a mosaic of diverse cultures created by the large waves of migration to urban centers. The states that make up the central region are Querétaro, Guanajuato, Hidalgo, the State of Mexico, Morelos, and Puebla.

The languages spoken in this region are of Oto-Manguean affiliation, with the exception of Nahuatl, which belongs to the Uto-Aztecan linguistic group, and Purépecha or Tarasco, an isolate. While some of the inhabitants of the region work in agriculture and make handicrafts for their own use and for sale in tourist areas, others work as laborers and domestics in the major cities.

Chichimec. This group uses the term Úza ("Indian") to refer to all people of indigenous descent, including themselves. The Chichimecs live in only one community within the municipality of San Luis de la Paz in the State of Guanajuato, in a territory bordering with settlements of Otomíes and Pames (Nava López 1995a: 12–13).

Matlatzinca. This is a Nahua word that means "the lords of the net" or "those who make nets," referring to the mesh nets they made for carrying corn. There is only one remaining Matlatzinca community of 1,576 persons. Called San Francisco Oxtotilpan, it is located in the municipality of Temascaltepec in the State of Mexico (Vásquez Rojas 1995: 49).

Otomí. The Otomí of the State of Mexico and the Otomí of the Mezquital Valley of Hidalgo call themselves "Hña hñu" (and variations by dialect) or "those who speak the nasal language." Otomí is the main language spoken in 15 of the 121 municipalities of the State of Mexico and in 28 municipalities of the Mezquital Valley of Hidalgo. As a result of migration, there are Otomíes in eight Mexican states.

Purépecha (P'urhépecha) or P'urhé. Formerly called Tarascos, this group occupies 22 municipalities of the lakeside and mountain regions of central Michoacán.

The population is estimated at 100,260 individuals. The uniqueness of their language places them in a group by themselves. The Purépecha culture is considered a part of western Mesoamerica. (See E. Fernando Nava López, "Musical Traditions of the P'urhépecha (Tarascos) of Michoacán, Mexico," in this volume.)

The Nahua of Morelos. There are 35 Nahua communities in 16 municipalities in Morelos (Saldaña Fernández 1995: 88). Nahuatl is spoken mainly in Hueyapan, Tetelcingo, Xoxocotla, Santa Catarina, and Cuentepec.

The Mazahua. Affiliated with the Oto-Manguean linguistic group, the Mazahua occupy 10 municipalities in the northwest of the State of Mexico, and one in eastern Michoacán. A large percentage of the population has migrated to Toluca, the capital of the State of Mexico, and to Mexico City.

The southern Pacific region

This area includes indigenous groups in the states of Colima and Michoacán, and in the western parts of Guerrero and Oaxaca. With the exception of Nahua groups, all others speak languages of Oto-Manguean affiliation. Because of the social complexity of this region, the application of the concept of "cultural area" has been questioned in this case. One important factor that cannot be overlooked is the contribution of Afromestizo influence in the area of Costa Chica of Guerrero and Oaxaca that is home to many different ethnic groups. The indigenous groups living in this region are highly differentiated, although they share the "Mesoamerican core system of thought" described above.

The Amuzgo or Tzjon Non, "weavers, or thread-spinners." This group inhabits two of the three zones that make up the Mixteca, another important multiethnic area in the states of Guerrero and Oaxaca.

The Chatino. The members of this group call themselves Kitse cha'tnio, Cha'tña, or Tsa'jnya. The majority live in the southern Sierra Madre mountain range in Oaxaca. Their language is called "hard-work word" or "difficult word" (Sesia 1995: 9).

The Mixtec inhabit the mountainous region of northwestern Oaxaca, southern Puebla, and eastern Guerrero. This area is known to its inhabitants as Ñuu Savi or "village of the rain or the clouds." This is a multiethnic area inhabited by Amuzgos, Triquis, Ixcatecos, Popolocas, Chocholtecas, Nahuas, and Tacuates (a subgroup of Mixtecs), as well as Afromestizos. The Mixtec population is estimated at over 240,000.

The Nahua of Guerrero. This group inhabits the subareas of the Central Sierra and the upper basin of the Balsas River, Sierra Norte, and Tierra Caliente in Guerrero (Villela 1995: 189) (Fig. 3).

Tlapanecos or Mbo me'phaa, "he who inhabits Tlapa." This group is concentrated on one slope of the southern Sierra Madre and on the coastal plains of the State of Guerrero (Carrasco Zúñiga 1995: 251).

Trique. They inhabit a lowland area whose major center is San Juan Copala, and a highland area in San Andrés Chicahuaxtla in eastern Oaxaca. Although there are variations in the dialects of these two areas, these two groups speak mutually intelligible languages.

Transisthmus region

This region includes Oaxaca, Veracruz, and a small part of western Chiapas. The Tehuantepec Isthmus has a large population of Zapotecs, Huave, Mixe, and Chontal. The main activities of coastal groups are related to sea and lake products, while the mountain groups subsist on agriculture. Both modes of subsistence are closely linked to each group's religious practices. The close contact these groups have maintained has allowed for economic and especially cultural exchange among themselves and with the inhabitants of the central valleys and northern Oaxaca, in particular the Zapotecs.

The Huave. Also known as Mareños ("sea dwellers"), the Huave speak an unaffiliated language. They inhabit the coast of the Gulf of Tehuantepec. Scholars continue to investigate their linguistic roots (Valiñas 1993: 186).

The Chontal of Oaxaca. The Chontal inhabit the municipalities of Santiago Astata and San Pedro Huamelula on the coast of Oaxaca. Like the Huave, they speak an unaffiliated language.

Mixe. The Ayukk or "people of the elegant language" live in 19 municipalities of northeastern Oaxaca and in the Serranía del Zempoaltépetl. Their language belongs to the Mixe-Zoque family.

Fig. 3: Nahuas of Guerrero. Dance of *tlacololeros*. Photo by Marina Alonso Bolaños, courtesy of the author.

Popoluca. This group is now very small and there are few Popoluca-speakers. Their language is part of the Mixe-Zoque family. They inhabit the border region between the states of Veracruz and Tabasco.

Zoque, O'de püt, or "people of language." This group inhabits northwestern Chiapas, the Chimalapas area of Oaxaca, and a part of southern Veracruz and Tabasco. Their language belongs to the Mixe-Zoque family (Fig. 4).

The central valleys and northern Oaxaca

Many different ethnic groups are found in this region, living in close proximity to the mestizo population. The central valleys and northern Oaxaca always have been areas with high levels of migration. Oaxaca is one of the states with the largest indigenous population. A majority of them are farmers who cultivate corn, beans, small vegetable plots, maguey for *mexcal* (an alcoholic beverage), and alfalfa.

The Zapotec culture extends throughout the entire area, and provides the context for interaction between those groups that are culturally and economically subordinate to the Zapotecs (Millán 1993: 26). An example of this is the complex system of Zapoteca markets where people converge from different areas to buy, sell, or trade goods. All the languages spoken are of Oto-Manguean affiliation.

The Chinantecos call themselves Tsa ju jmí or "people of the ancient word," although each settlement has its own name. They inhabit the northern part of the State of Oaxaca.

Mazatecs or Ha Shuta Enima, "we who work the mountains, humble people of tradition." This group is concentrated in the Cañada and the Papaloapan-Textepec Valley in the State of Oaxaca.

Chochos or Chocholtecas, Runixa ngiigua or "those who speak the language." This group inhabits 13 municipalities in the district of Coixtlahuaca in Oaxaca. Textile work was their primary means of subsistence but this activity has declined substantially (Jiménez 1994: 12).

Fig. 4: The Zoque of Chiapas. *Danza de San Lorenzo*. Photo by Marina Alonso Bolaños, courtesy of the author.

Zapotecs. After the Nahua and the Maya, the Zapotecs are the largest indigenous group in Mexico (341,583 persons). Their name comes from the Nahuatl word Tzapotecatl, "people of the zapote" or Ben 'zaa, "people of the clouds." They inhabit the central valleys, the Sierra Juárez, and the Isthmus of Tehuantepec.

The southeastern region

This region comprises the states of Campeche, Yucatán, and Quintana Roo, and also includes the Maya groups in the State of Chiapas. The area was conquered relatively late, which meant that it remained isolated from other parts of Mexico for a long time. Consequently, it underwent a very different type of cultural evolution. With the exception of Zoque, the large number of indigenous groups in this region speak Mayan-affiliated languages.

Because the Maya live in diverse environments, they have developed different means of subsistence related to the ecology of the area and a vast array of expressive forms, including well-differentiated

ceremonial practices (Marion 1994: 11). The State of Chiapas is one of the poorest and most marginalized areas of Mexico. Since the colonial period, the area has been characterized by constant rebellions on the part of the indigenous peoples, the most recent of which were the uprisings of the Zapatista Army of National Liberation in the 1990s.

Peninsular Maya. This designation probably is derived from Maya or Mayab and refers to the name of the territory. These groups inhabit the territory where the ancient Maya culture flourished, namely Quintana Roo, Campeche, and Yucatán. The language is currently spoken by over 700,000 people (Bastarrachea 1994: 5–6).

Ch'oles or Winik, "hombre," "los hombres creados del maíz," "man," "men created from corn." This group is located in northwestern Chiapas.

Lacandón or Hach winik, "hombres verdaderos" or "true men." This group inhabits the jungle region of northern Chiapas in the municipality of Ocosingo.

Tojolabales or Tojolwinik'otik, "hombres verdaderos" or "true men." This group is located in the municipality of Las Margaritas, in Chiapas.

Tzotziles or Batsil winik'otik, "hombres verdaderos" or "true men"; **Tzeltales** or Winik atel, "hombres trabajadores" or "hardworking men." Both these groups live in the highlands of Chiapas.

Mames or "father, grandfather, or ancestor." This group inhabits Campeche, Quintana Roo, Chiapas, and Guatemala.

Mochó or Motozintlecs. This group inhabits the areas surrounding Motozintla de Mendoza in the Sierra Madre in Chiapas. Although the Zoque of Chiapas belong to the Mixe-Zoque family, they also can be included in the southeastern region because they share many cultural traits with their neighbors in the highlands of Chiapas and the northwestern mountains.

The ethnic composition of Chiapas is very complex. It is important to take into account the high level of migration to the Lacandón jungle leading to the establishment of new settlements, as well as the constant waves of Chuj, Kanjobal, Cakchikel, and Quiché refugees from Guatemala who have settled in the State of Chiapas.

—*Translated by Nancy K. Hand*

REFERENCES

Aguilar Zeleny, Alejandro 1994. *Guarijíos.* México: Instituto Nacional Indigenista (Series Pueblos indígenas de México).
    1995. "Guarijíos" in *Etnografía contemporánea de los pueblos indígenas de México: Región noroeste.* México: Instituto Nacional Indigenista—Secretaría de Desarrollo Social, 13–51.
Ávila, Agustín 1993. *Huastecos de San Luis Potosí.* México: Instituto Nacional Indigenista (Series Pueblos indígenas de México).
    1995. "Huastecos de San Luis Potosí" in *Etnografía contemporánea de los pueblos indígenas de México: Región oriental.* México: Instituto Nacional Indigenista—Secretaría de Desarrollo Social, 9–59.
Bartolomé, Miguel Alberto, and Alicia Mabel Barabas 1996. *La pluralidad en peligro: Proceso de transfiguración y extinción cultural en Oaxaca (chochos, chontales, ixcatecos y zoques).* México: Instituto Nacional Indigenista.
Bastarrachea Manzano, J. Ramón 1994. *Mayas de la península de Yucatán.* México: Instituto Nacional Indigenista (Series Pueblos indígenas de México).
Bonfiglioli, Carlo 1995. *Fariseos y matachines en la sierra tarahumara: Entre la pasión de Cristo, la transgresión cómico-sexual y las danzas de Conquista.* México: Instituto Nacional Indigenista—Secretaría de Desarrollo Social (Series Fiestas de los pueblos indígenas de México).
Bonfil, Guillermo 1990. *México profundo: Una civilización negada.* México: Consejo Nacional para la Cultura y las Artes—Grijalbo.

Carrasco Zúñiga, Abad 1995. "Tlapanecos" in *Etnografía contemporánea de los pueblos indígenas de México: Región Pacífico sur.* México: Instituto Nacional Indigenista—Secretaría de Desarrollo Social, 251–89.
Collin, Laura 1994. *Ritual y conflicto.* México: Instituto Nacional Indigenista—Secretaría de Desarrollo Social (Series Fiestas de los pueblos indígenas de México).
De Vos, Jan 1994. *Vivir en frontera: La experiencia de los indios de Chiapas.* México: Centro de Investigaciones y Estudios Superiores en Antropología Social——Instituto Nacional de Antropología e Historia, Universidad Nacional Autónoma de México (Series Historia de los pueblos indígenas de México).
Fábregas, Andrés 1982. *Notas sobre las mayordomías zoques en Tuxtla Gutiérrez.* Tuxtla Gutiérrez, Chiapas: Secretaría de Educación Pública del Estado de Chiapas—Gobierno del Estado de Chiapas (Cuadernos culturales no. 5).
Florescano, Enrique, and Isabel Gil Sánchez 1976. "La época de las reformas borbónicas y el crecimiento económico, 1750–1808" in *Historia general de México,* 4 vols. México: El Colegio de México, 1976–1977, vol. 2.
Good, Catharine 1994. "Trabajo, intercambio y construcción de la historia: Una exploración etnográfica de la lógica cultural nahua," *El tiempo y las palabras* (Cuicuilco, nueva época) 1/2: 140–48.
Grimes, Joseph E., and Thomas B. Hinton 1972 in 1990. "Huicholes y coras" in *Coras, huicholes y tepehuanes.* México: Consejo Nacional para la Cultura y las Artes—Instituto Nacional Indigenista.
Hu-DeHart, Evelyn 1995. *Adaptación y resistencia en el Yaquimi: Los yaquis durante la colonia.* México: Centro de Investigaciones y Estudios Superiores en Antropología Social—Instituto Nacional de Antropología e Historia, Universidad Nacional Autónoma de México (Series Historia de los pueblos indígenas de México).
Instituto Nacional de Estadística, Geografía e Informática (INEGI) 1993. *XI censo general de población y vivienda 1990: Indicadores socioeconómicos de los pueblos indígenas de México 1990.* México: Instituto Nacional Indigenista.
Instituto Nacional Indigenista 1994. *Etnografía contemporánea de los pueblos indígenas de México: Región occidental (Huicholes, Coras, Tepehuanes del sur, Mexicaneros).* México: Secretaría de Desarrollo Social.
Instituto Nacional Indigenista 1995. *Etnografía contemporánea de los pueblos indígenas de México: Región centro.* México: Secretaría de Desarrollo Social.
    1995. *Etnografía contemporánea de los pueblos indígenas de México: Región noroeste.* México: Secretaría de Desarrollo Social.
    1995. *Etnografía contemporánea de los pueblos indígenas de México: Región oriental.* México: Secretaría de Desarrollo Social.
    1995. *Etnografía contemporánea de los pueblos indígenas de México: Región Pacífico sur.* México: Secretaría de Desarrollo Social.
    1995. *Etnografía contemporánea de los pueblos indígenas de México: Región sureste.* México: Secretaría de Desarrollo Social.
    1995. *Etnografía contemporánea de los pueblos indígenas de México: Región transístmica.* México: Secretaría de Desarrollo Social.
    1995. *Etnografía contemporánea de los pueblos indígenas de México: Región valles centrales y norte de Oaxaca.* México: Secretaría de Desarrollo Social.
Jiménez, Dionisio 1994. *Chochos o chocholtecas.* México: Instituto Nacional Indigenista (Series Pueblos indígenas de México).
Kirchhoff, Paul 1949. *Mesoamérica: Sus límites geográficos, composición étnica y caracteres culturales,* 2nd ed. México: Ediciones Aguirre y Beltrán—Escuela Nacional de Antropología e Historia.
Lechuga, Ruth D. 1986. *La indumentaria en el México indígena,* 2nd ed. México: Fondo Nacional de las Artesanías.
León-Portilla, Miguel 1997. *Pueblos originarios y globalización.* México: El Colegio Nacional.
López Austin, Alfredo 1990a. *Los mitos del Tlacuache.* México: Editorial Alianza.

1990b. "El tiempo en Mesoamérica," *Ciencias* (Revista de Difusión, Facultad de Ciencias, Universidad Nacional Autónoma de México) 18: 28–33.

López Luján, Leonardo, and Alfredo López Austin 1996. *El pasado indígena*. México: El Colegio de México—Fondo de Cultura Económica.

Manrique, Leonardo 1988. *Atlas cultural de México: Lingüística*. México: Secretaría de Educación Pública—Instituto Nacional de Antropología e Historia—Editorial Planeta.

Marion, Marie-Odile 1994. *Identidad y ritualidad entre los mayas*. México: Instituto Nacional Indigenista—Secretaría de Desarrollo Social (Series Fiestas de los pueblos indígenas de México).

Millán, Saúl 1993. *La ceremonia perpetua*. México: Instituto Nacional Indigenista—Secretaría de Desarrollo Social (Series Fiestas de los pueblos indígenas de México).

Nava López, E. Fernando 1995a. "Chichimecas" in *Etnografía contemporánea de los pueblos indígenas de México: Región centro*. México: Instituto Nacional Indigenista—Secretaría de Desarrollo Social, 11–46.

1995b. "Pames de San Luis Potosí" in *Etnografía contemporánea de los pueblos indígenas de México: Región oriental*. México: Instituto Nacional Indigenista—Secretaría de Desarrollo Social, 283–319.

Radding, Cynthia 1995. *Entre el desierto y la sierra: Las naciones O'odham y Tegüima de Sonora, 1530–1840*. México: Centro de Investigaciones y Estudios Superiores en Antropología Social—Instituto Nacional de Antropología e Historia, Universidad Nacional Autónoma de México (Series Historia de los pueblos indígenas de México).

Ricard, Robert 1947 in 1986. *La conquista espiritual de México*. México: Fondo de Cultura Económica (Colección "Quinto Centenario").

Robertson, Carol E. 1992. "Introduction: The dance of Conquest" in *Musical repercussions of 1492: Encounters in text and performance*, ed. by Carol E. Robertson. Washington, D.C.: Smithsonian Institution Press, 9–30.

Rodríguez, Martha 1995. *Historias de resistencia y exterminio: Los indios de Coahuila durante el siglo XIX*. México: Centro de Investigaciones y Estudios Superiores en Antropología Social—Instituto Nacional de Antropología e Historia, Universidad Nacional Autónoma de México (Series Historia de los pueblos indígenas de México).

Ruvalcava Mercado, Jesús 1995. "Huastecos de Veracruz" in *Etnografía contemporánea de los pueblos indígenas de México: Región oriental*. México: Instituto Nacional Indigenista—Secretaría de Desarrollo Social, 63–102.

Saldaña Fernández, María Cristina 1995. "Nahuas de Morelos" in *Etnografía contemporánea de los pueblos indígenas de México: Región centro*. México: Instituto Nacional Indigenista—Secretaría de Desarrollo Social, 87–137.

Sesia, Paola 1995. "Chatinos" in *Etnografía contemporánea de los pueblos indígenas de México: Región Pacífico sur*. México: Instituto Nacional Indigenista—Secretaría de Desarrollo Social, 9–77.

Thomas, Norman 1974. *Envidia, brujería y organización ceremonial: Un pueblo zoque*. México: Secretaría de Educación Pública (Series Sep-Setentas, no. 166).

Valiñas, Leopoldo 1993. "Las lenguas indígenas mexicanas: Entre la comunidad y la nación" in *Antropología breve de México* ed. by Lourdes Arizpe. México: Academia de la Investigación Científica—Centro Regional de Investigaciones Multidisciplinarias, UNAM, 165–87.

Vásquez Rojas, Gonzalo 1995. "Matlatzincas" in *Etnografía contemporánea de los pueblos indígenas de México: Región centro*. México: Instituto Nacional Indigenista—Secretaría de Desarrollo Social, 49–84.

Villela, Samuel 1995. "Nahuas de Guerrero" in *Etnografía contemporánea de los pueblos indígenas de México: Región Pacífico sur*. México: Instituto Nacional Indigenista—Secretaría de Desarrollo Social, 187–247.

Musical Traditions of the P'urhépecha (Tarascos) of Michoacán, Mexico

E. Fernando Nava López

DURING THE SECOND decade of the sixteenth century, Tzintzicha Tangaxoan, the last *Cazonci* or cacique of the ancient kingdom of Tzintzuntzan located in the general area that is now the State of Michoacán, ritually sacrificed several Spaniards. In accordance with tradition, the Spaniards were skinned and their hides were used as costumes for the dances held to celebrate the military victory. The prisoners themselves had participated in three ritualistic dances: they danced with the warrior who had captured them; they danced with the governors on the eve of their sacrifice; and they danced alone in the state of inebriation that prepared them to meet their death. This fervent cult of war included such practices as the use of conch-shell trumpets (*caracoles*) for troop mobilization, and the ruckus produced by a conglomerate of trumpet calls and yelling that signaled an attack. Singing was part of many military missions: included in military contingents were *pregoneros* (criers) who would sing to guide captives on the way back from battle; at the village entrance, leaders would greet their soldiers with songs; and the victims themselves sang and danced during the vigils preceding their sacrifice and even just before their deaths.

Peacetime celebrations were characterized by ritual inebriation of the population as a whole, lasting five days in the case of minor feasts and ten days for the most significant ones. The high priest, however, remained sober. Upon the death of a nobleman, each of his heirs would hold a celebration in which the "Danza de la flor" (Flower dance) was performed. The ritual calendar dictated performance of particular artistic practices. Trumpets were heard sounding in the temples. The journeys the priests made to celebrations in other villages, carrying their gods with them, were accompanied by music. Singing also summoned the presence of the gods. One of these songs was called a *canajqua* (*kanákwa*) or "La corona" (The crown). However, the singing in which both men and women participated was only one part of the tribute paid to the gods. The other was wood for offerings of fire. These customs differed from those of the Aztecs—the enemies of the ancient people of Michoacán who were never successful in subjugating them and worshiped their deities only with song. The *Cazonci*'s people did not believe the gods would be satisfied with songs only, and they demanded of the Spaniards the death of the Aztecs for failing to make offerings of fire to the gods.

The instruments used in the practice of their arts included *caracoles* and trumpets (probably made of clay) for a system of calls; turtle shells; the *kiríngwa* (an idiophone similar to the Mesoamerican *teponaztli*); and a *raspador* (scraper) made from a striated stick, which accompanied dances and songs. In terms of other aerophones, primary sources only mention a *silbatillo* (small whistle) and make no reference to flutes, in spite of archaeological evidence suggesting that they were, in fact, present. People also carried bells during the celebrations: women wore ordinary bells on their wrists and men wore gold bells on their calves, as well as snake rattles on their temples.

Certain events in the cycle of human life also were marked by specific sounds. When a man died, the trumpet would be played during the burning of his insignia and his widow would sob loudly. The texts of the songs sung at the funeral of the last *Cazonci* were unintelligible, probably in an archaic language. In fact, the murder of the last *Cazonci*, ordered by Nuño de Guzmán in 1530, symbolically marked the end of the Indian era.

The new age had begun in 1521, when the first Spanish soldier appeared on the western border of the Kingdom of Tzintzuntzan. Franciscan missionaries also arrived during the same decade, followed soon thereafter by the Augustinians. Both mendicant orders played important roles in shaping the new musical culture of the indigenous people who, from that point on, were referred to as "Tarascos." It was in this context of conquest that the "Danza de moros y cristianos" (Dance of the Moors and Christians) began to be enacted by the Tarascos. This is an ancient dramatization of Mediterranean origin that "commemorates"—through a Christian lens—the political and religious confrontation between Spaniards and Moors (former Muslims of Spain). In the Americas, the drama has survived in relatively complete versions, as well as in syncretic forms that blend it with other ritualized combats of local or European origin (see Gerard Béhague, "Music and Dance in Ritual and Ceremony," in these volumes). The "dance of conquest" was not entirely foreign to the Michoacaners, however, because they already were enacting a type of warfare drama in which they battled the Chichimecas.

Within the framework of an imposed Christian way of life, the Indians immediately began playing European trumpets, *chirimías* (shawms), and—the novelty—string instruments. They also sang *canto de órgano* (polyphony) and mastered counterpoint. New spaces for music making and dancing unfolded with the new calendar of celebrations. The arrival of a religious or civic authority in a community, or even just a visit, was greeted with festivities. The rapid adoption of Western traditions has been explained in a variety of ways, from the fact that ancient Michoacán society already possessed a fully developed tradition and musicians were open to new experiences, to the perception of the first chroniclers, who wrote that the Indians by nature imitated the customs of other peoples to avoid being considered un-Christian or uncivilized. At least up until the beginning of the eighteenth century, there are references to celebrations in which Tarascos participated alongside the Spaniards with dances, costumes, and instruments typical "of their ancient ways."

For this indigenous group whose present self-denomination is P'urhépecha, music is the exclusive domain of human beings. Birds only metaphorically are said to "sing," but neither birds nor any other living beings are capable of generating music. The P'urhépecha concept of music centers on pitch fluctuations, that is, melodic series of consecutive sounds of equal or different duration that—in alternation with periods of silence—present deliberate changes in pitch. Consequently, all musical expressions of the P'urhépecha require a melodic component, regardless of the presence or absence of a rhythmic accompaniment. No rhythmic pattern or percussive practice is considered "music." Rather, these are viewed as subordinate elements that form part of the accompaniment. According to this conception, the human voice and melodic instruments perform the function of singing or carrying a melody, while percussion instruments and those that provide a harmonic/rhythmic complement are relegated to an accompanimental role. In the worldview of the P'urhépecha, there are only two types of music: their own, and that of the mestizos (people of mixed race). They define their own music in the following terms: it is the oldest, situated mythically in the pre-Hispanic era; it belongs to the traditional inhabitants of the region of the Meseta Tarasca (plateau), the Cañada de los Once Pueblos (ravine), the Ciénaga de Zacapu (marshland), and Lake Pátzcuaro in Michoacán; it is the music associated with specific rituals within the cycle of religious celebrations, and with weddings; and it is sung in the P'urhépecha language, always in ternary subdivisions of time. Figure 1 illustrates the native taxonomy of musical genres of the P'urhépecha.

The genres called simply *son* and *abajeño* (not danced)—the only two vocal categories—offer unlimited possibilities for the display of musical and literary creativity. These genres are not only cultivated by dedicated musicians, but also by men and women who are not members of musical groups and make use of these creative opportunities by adapting a text or composing a melody in their everyday lives. Their structure is very distinct from all other indigenous and mestizo musical traditions in Mexico. *Son* is unique to the P'urhépecha. It did not derive from the *vals*, nor is there any other musical expression

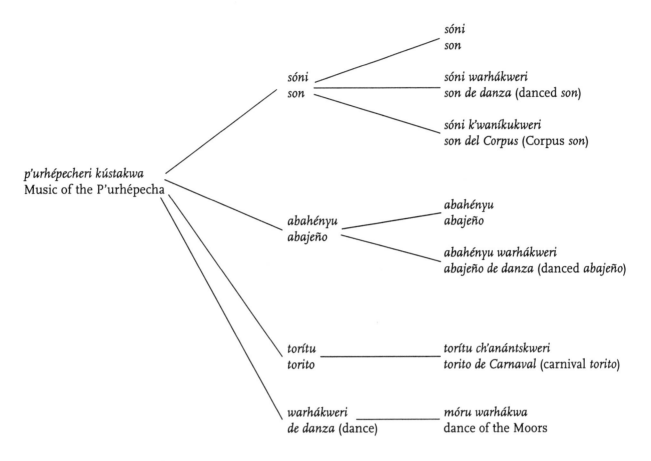

Fig. 1: Native classification of culture-specific musical genres.

that resembles it. *Abajeño*, a term that alludes to the low-lying geographical area called Tierra Caliente, has clear ties with mestizo genres from western Mexico, including mariachi music. Some of these mestizo genres are characterized by a syncopated bass of possible African origin. Regardless of its associations with other Mexican traditional musics, the *abajeño* remains a typically P'urhépecha musical expression. The characteristic treatment of the bass (*bajeo*) in the *son* and *abajeño* consists of an improvised line imbued with a highly developed sense of the intricacies of counterpoint. The correct performance of a *son* requires a "singable" *bajeo*. It must not follow the simple sequence, typical of the waltz, of one strong beat followed by two weak pulses.

Sones and *abajeños* follow generally a two-part, binary structure (A B). Each of the two parts is relatively long and hardly ever contains the same number of measures. The essential difference between *son* and *abajeño* is the tempo. The *son* is particularly slow and *abajeño* is decidedly quick, and each reflects the choreographic steps of the respective danced forms (*son de danza* and *abajeño de danza*).

Torito (little "bulls") is a genre with several specific functions, but only the *torito* related to carnival is considered P'urhépecha; the rest are mestizo. The *torito*'s structure is also binary, although its parts tend to be shorter than in the *son* and *abajeño*. The music for the dance of the "Moors" follows the scheme that characterizes the cycle of Conquest dances, namely a set number of sections in binary structure alternating with a "bridge" in very free rhythm.

Although the only vocal genres are the "simple" (not danced) *son* and *abajeño*, singing holds the place of privilege in the musical life of the P'urhépecha. *Pirékwa* is the generic term for songs sung in their language, albeit with a greater number of borrowings from Spanish than in common speech. Songs are learned and transmitted by oral tradition. The process of becoming a singer—mostly a male activity—involves imitating the vocal style of singers, memorizing the texts, and learning to reproduce the guitar accompaniments.

The essence of the tradition of P'urhépecha song rests on the themes of the texts and the creativity displayed in their linguistic turns; the music remains somewhat secondary. Recurring themes are the love and beauty of women, metaphorically represented by images of flowers, birds, stars, the moon, the mist, and the rain. This imagery surfaces in the titles of songs, such as "Klabéli tsïtsïki" or "Flor de clavel" (carnation) (Recorded Ex. 1) (Fig. 2). The poetry often includes expressions such as *tsïtsïki sapíchu* (little flower) and *xáni sési hásï* (how beautiful), as well as the term *mále*, borrowed from Spanish, which means "beloved, cherished, dear."

Weeping is also a recurrent theme. Often associated with states of inebriation, it appears in the context of rupturing love ties or feelings of disdain, abandonment, solitude, and when addressing the critical subject of death. The poetry, often stingingly nostalgic, creates a depressive state in the listeners, which the P'urhépecha use to further inebriation.

Other topics are personal narratives dealing with emigration or education, alluding equally to some form of disengagement. Emigration can inspire songs on farewells and feelings of abandonment while also denouncing exploitation and mistreatment; education implies leaving the community for a mestizo town, where middle schools and institutions of higher learning are located. Songs also tell stories of frustration with impediments to advancement, such as having to abandon education for the responsibilites of marriage at a young age. Other themes addressed are the desire to fulfill personal ambitions and regrets surrounding thwarted expectations.

Historical narratives also are sung. These texts "com-memorate" social struggles and pronounce judgments on the actions of leaders. The most salient in this category are songs about Vasco de Quiroga (ca. 1470–1565), the Bishop of Michoacán (1538–1565) also known as "Tata Vasco," one of the most influential figures in the shaping of colonial Michoacán whose memory remains alive in Indian history. A staunch protector of the Indians, the indefatigable bishop envisioned the construction of a "tradition-defying" cathedral in Pátzcuaro, architecturally conceived with

Fig. 2: Trio Los Chapás. From left to right, Victoriano Sebastián Apolinar (second voice); the trio's director, Ismael Bautista Rueda (lead voice and guitar); and Filemón González Sánchez (*requinto*). Comachuén, Michoacán, 1992. Photo by Fernando Nava, courtesy of the author.

five naves converging on a single sanctuary to hold his entire Indian congregation under one roof, rather than force Indians to attend Mass in the outside atriums, as in other Mexican churches (McAndrew 1965 in Kuss 1992). The Bishop also inspired an opera, *Tata Vasco* (1941), by the Morelia-born composer Miguel Bernal Jiménez (1910–1956).

There are also historical narratives about General Lázaro Cárdenas del Río, a Michoacaner and former president of Mexico (1934–1940), who is recalled with loyalty and affection by the P'urhépecha because of his commitment to the social betterment of the lower classes.

Lastly, what is now called "ecology" has been the theme of P'urhépecha songs for many years. They denounce unreasonable exploitation of natural resources, generally by mestizo interests, and express anguish about contamination of the environment.

It is interesting to note the ephemeral nature of most of these songs. New songs do not become part of a cumulative repertoire. Instead, the P'urhépecha substitute older songs with new ones, as is the case also with the music for certain dances. Today's songs will be replaced by tomorrow's creations and soon will be forgotten because not even their authors continue to sing them, although some do record their songs in writing. The songs most susceptible to replacement are love songs with floral metaphors.

The creation of new texts presently outnumbers the composition of new melodies. The tendency among songwriters is to adapt new texts to existing music, demonstrating by this strategy the vitality of the language. Songs generally consist of two strophes that correspond to the binary structure (A and B) of the music. Some songs exhibit a similarity with the so-called "structure of Mexican song," that is, a musical correspondence—and, occasionally, literary parallelism—between the second phrase of section A and the corresponding second phrase of B. The poetic meters, as well as the rhythmic patterns, are clearly asymmetrical. In performance, the delivery of the texts adheres to musical, rather than prosodic, accentuation. These texts generally are constructed in the first person. The dialogue form also is used, but in such cases songs are performed by one singer. The style of singing is shrill, resorting to falsetto especially in the second voice. Songs are performed by one singer or in duo, trio, or chorus. However, the P'urhépecha do not resort to responsorial singing or to other types of textural contrasts. Songs without

instrumental accompaniment are rare. In a majority of cases they are accompanied by string instruments, especially the guitar, which is played by the singer.

All forms of P'urhépecha music include some type of instrumental performance. There are several types of ensembles. Some are made up exclusively of chordophones and consist of one or two compulsory violins, plus guitar, *vihuela*, and a string bass. The other traditional ensembles of the P'urhépecha combine different categories of instruments, such as the ubiquitous fife and drum combination. Another very traditional combination is that of *chirimías* (shawms) and membranophones. String ensembles tend to play dance music, specifically danced *abajeños*. Aerophones and percussion often are used to perform simple (not danced) *sones* and *abajeños*.

The most important post-Conquest ensemble of the P'urhépecha is the *orquesta*, which is made up of approximately eight musicians (Recorded Ex. 2). This is an ensemble of chordophones and aerophones whose leader is always one of the musicians, generally a violinist or saxophone player. The *orquesta*'s repertoire is basically the same as that of smaller ensembles, although it occasionally plays the *torito* of carnival and the Corpus *son*. Only occasionally are songs accompanied by the *orquesta*, which then requires the preparation of musical arrangements, the coordination of voices and instruments, and rehearsals.

The largest ensemble is the *banda* of aerophones ("wind" instruments) and percussion with an average of twenty musicians. The leader of the *banda* may play the trumpet or trombone, or may stand apart from the band, conducting with a baton. This is the only ensemble that plays all the types of music included in the native taxonomy of P'urhépecha music. There is a trend among *bandas* toward favoring performances of the Corpus *son* and the carnival *torito*. In addition, the *banda* is the only ensemble that provides the instrumental accompaniment for the "Dance of the Moors." Unlike vocal music, whose poetry and music remain in the domain of oral tradition, the compositions for *orquesta* and *banda* require musical notation.

Instruments are known by their Spanish names. The guitar, which is never a solo instrument, is called a "sétima" or "séptima" ("seventh" referring to a seven-course guitar of three single and four double courses that has been replaced by the six-string instrument).

The *kiríngwa* is the only pre-Columbian instrument still in use. It is an idiophone similar to the Meso-american *teponaztli*, a "hollowed-out wooden cylinder laid sideways that could produce two pitches sounded by striking the two tongues of a horizontal H-shaped incision, played with two rubber-tipped mallets" (Stevenson 1968: 63). The *kiríngwa* lacks the tongues of the *teponaztli*—the only difference between the two instruments—and it is built in a zoomorphic shape. Most of the other instruments used by the P'urhépecha are of Western derivation. However, these instruments often differ from their European counterparts in function and playing technique. The guitar, for instance, fulfills two functions in relation to the singing: it accompanies and complements. The trombone, both in *orquestas* and *bandas*, carries the improvised counterpoint characteristic of the bass part (*bajeo*) in performances of *sones* and *abajeños*.

The music categories that the P'urhépecha classify as "mestizo" (that is, not their very own), include a long list of genres of very diverse origins and structural characteristics: *alabanzas*, shepherds' songs, the *corrido*, *cumbia*, *mañanitas*, songs for the celebration of Christmas, polkas, *danzón*, marches, overtures, *pasodobles*, and some specific types of *toritos*. These are the *toritos* performed during pyrotechnical displays, inaugurations, weddings, and a few other occasions. Although the P'urhépecha simply imitate these genres, they imbue them with a distinct indigenous feeling through the character of their arrangements. They rarely, if ever, compose new pieces in these generic categories. Along the same lines, they seldom adapt the original Spanish text of some of these genres to their native P'urhépecha language, in spite of a high rate of bilingualism. In the context of the relationship between P'urhépecha and mestizo traditions, it is important to note the P'urhépecha tendency to solemnicize events through music, and their reliance on mestizo genres that were historically associated with cattle-raising activities. This also reflects the high social value assigned to cattle raising as an imposed economic activity during the colonial period. The incorporation |of mestizo genres into their repertoire also depends on the degree to which each genre lends itself to appropriation. For instance, from the time the P'urhépecha incorporated the style of song known as "Tambora sinaloense" (or *tambora* from the northwestern State of Sinaloa), they began to use *bandas* to accompany P'urhépecha songs, appropriating for their own vocal repertoire a common practice in Sinaloa, which is the performance of songs accompanied by *bandas*. This was only possible with sound amplification, which raises the volume of the vocal

performance. Since that time, *bandas* also are used to accompany *pirékwas* (songs that the P'urhépecha compose and perform in their language).

Dance occupies a central place in the constellation of P'urhépecha arts. Five among the seven categories in the native classification of P'urhépecha music are always necessarily danced. The remaining two, the simple *son* and *abajeño*, also might be danced. However, from the native viewpoint, there are dances with music and dances without music. The latter are performed to the rhythms of guitar strumming, that is, without the "melody" that must be present for the P'urhépecha to think of these as "music." Meanwhile, dancing and singing do not overlap: when they perform sung dances that obviously involve texts, the dancing stops during the sung sections. Most dances have musical accompaniment and a repertoire of melodies. Moreover, the contrast between the *son* and *abajeño*—as pointed out above—is inextricably bound to the dance, as reflected in the tempo and choreographic style that correspond to each. On the one hand, the choreographic style of the *abajeño* involves *zapateo* (footwork that itself creates a rhythmic line); *son*, on the other hand, requires a smooth, sliding movement of the feet. The musical repertoire of these danced forms favors *abajeños*, precisely because inherent to this genre is the *zapateo* (or, the action of *zapatear*, tap dance), characteristic of traditional P'urhépecha dance.

The simple *son* and *abajeño* can be danced by women only in groups of up to six, or in pairs, and occasionally alone. Men do not dance in gender-exclusive groups, although they occasionally may dance alone. The *son* and *abajeño* also are danced by couples of men and women. The dancing of *sones* and *abajeños* is based on a set choreographic discourse, and involves a fixed number of participants determined by traditional rules, each fulfilling a particular function. For instance, tradition dictates whether only women, men alone, or women and men should participate, and in what proportions. In several dances that involve participation of men and women, the men perform more complex gestures while the women's movements are more subdued. In these instances, the women generally bring trays of fruit and bread that they distribute after the dancing is over. These mixed-gender dances might mirror the marked differences between gender roles in P'urhépecha society and symbolically project gender-specific characteristics. For instance, the symbols of abundance displayed in the women's headpieces and other elements of their costumes, as well as the food they distribute, may allude to fertility. The music for these dances follows a set sequence whose duration depends on the choreographic requirements. Among these dances, "Los moros" presents the most stable choreographic structure. By contrast, some dances require renovation of the musical repertoire. As in the case of the *pirékwas* (traditional songs), new melodies replacing older ones are created for dances such as *viejitos*, *cúrpites*, *uananchas*, and *negritos*, among others. The choreography of these dances, however, remains relatively unchanged.

The world of music and dance of the P'urhépecha is manifested in two contexts: festive celebrations and everyday life. The latter is limited to a few occasions, such as evening gatherings of friends for the purpose of singing, or the young suitor who visits his sweetheart on her birthday to woo her with songs. *Pirékwas* with floral metaphors are sung in most of these cases. The figure of the flower, which symbolizes woman and affection, seems to be related to an ancient web of associations with beauty anchored in Mesoamerican thought. This is evidenced by the expression "flor y canto" (flower and song) from the refined and "musicalized" poetic language of the pre-Hispanic Aztecs, and by the presence of musical genres known as "de flor" (floral), cultivated—among other contemporary practices—by several indigenous groups in Oaxaca. Sometimes on Saturday evenings, two or more singers will get together on a street corner for a sort of poetic confrontation that serves to exchange and disseminate *pirékwas* on a broad range of subjects. In some villages, afternoon serenades take place in the plaza, where a *banda* plays *valses*, *danzones*, marches, and polkas, as well as *sones* and *abajeños*.

The celebrations, in turn, are occasions to display the full range of artistic expressions in a manner consistent with the indigenous peoples' identification with ritual. Music and dance, together with processions, are themselves the most important forms of prayer for the P'urhépecha. These celebrations are organized by individuals who take responsibility for particular elements of the ceremonies. For instance, one person hires the bands and oversees the performances, which must take place in accordance with tradition, that is, where and what the band will play. These organizational posts serve as a link between the religious meaning of a celebration and the political leadership of the community, because any man who seeks employment

in public administration must have participated in these ceremonies. The rituals and values enacted on these occasions are factors that differentiate the P'urhépecha from the mestizos, in particular the deep sense of religiosity expressed in a kinetic/sonorous form of prayer. Among these rituals, one of the most powerful is the feast in honor of the Cristo de los Milagros that involves a multitude of pilgrims who pray by dancing. Carl Lumholtz observed it toward the end of the nineteenth century in the ancient village of Parangaricutiro, the mainstay of this traditional ritual, which was destroyed in 1943 by Parícutin's volcanic eruption. Lumholtz described the experience as follows:

> I found out later that several priests and bishops from the diocese had made efforts to do away with this extravagant religious tradition, but found themselves up against the unflappable resolve of the people, who insisted that the religious icon "must see them dance". . . . It is said that one [mestizo] priest resolved to put an end to the pagan worship and when the people went to the church, they found its doors closed. However, it was not even dawn yet when the sexton woke the priest to tell him that, in spite of everything, the dance was taking place. The two went to the church, where they were utterly astonished by the sight of hundreds of moving lights accompanied by the familiar dust cloud and the sound of stomping feet, but they saw no one. Scared, the priest ordered that the doors of the church be opened at the normal time. Since then no other priest has attempted to abolish the ritual and, in the opinion of the natives, this could never come to pass (Lumholtz 1902 in 1981, II: 372–73).

To this day, in what is now a new site called Nuevo San Juan Parangaricutiro, the people continue to pray with their feet.

There are three types of fiestas: regional, communal, and those related to the life cycle. The first two types follow the Christian calendar and are held at the same time throughout the region. Three of these are of particular importance. First and foremost is the Christmas cycle, during which shepherds' songs (*cantos de pastores*)—some in P'urhépecha—are sung before home altars or in the church. Instrumental *tonadas* (or "songs") also are performed as part of the worship. During this period, which includes Epiphany or "Día de los Santos Reyes" (January 6), various dances are performed. Among the most salient are the jocular "Los viejitos," widespread within and beyond P'urhépecha territory, and "Los

Fig. 3: Musician playing the *kiríngwa* during carnival, Ahuiran, Michoacán, 1992. Photo by Fernando Nava, courtesy of the author.

cúrpites," which means "grouped together," a competitive dance that provides an outlet for rivalries between barrios of the same village. The Christmas cycle ends the day of Purification or "Fiesta de la Candelaria" (Candlemas Day), on which *toritos de levantamiento* are played for the visit of the Virgin Mary to the church to present the Holy Child. Candlemas is also a day of pilgrimages to springs, among which the most notable is the journey of the people of Ahuiran to a spring, accompanied by the sound of the *kiríngwa*.

The second major fiesta is carnival. The P'urhépecha call it *ch'anántskwa*, "the great game," because people play with bulls (*toros*) made of reed frames covered with cloth. There is a mock sale, after which the figures are paraded through the streets, simulating bullfights to the sound of the "Torito de Carnaval." Women dance alone or in small groups. Ritual inebriation, especially among women, reaches its peak during these days. The *kiríngwa*, incorporated into the wind ensemble (*banda*), is played by both men and women during carnival. Only two communities retain this tradition (Fig. 3). The

kiríngwa is an idiophone shaped like a bull; it is made by local craftsmen and replaced when considered worn-out. During carnival, water is worshiped mainly in the mountainous areas. This ritual consists of journeys to springs outside the community, in the course of which people play with the bulls (*toritos*) to the sound of a *banda*.

The third regional fiesta is Corpus Christi, called *k'waníkukwa* or "the act of tossing" because workers—carpenters, hatmakers, farmers, and others—distribute their products, or small replicas of them, by tossing them to the people assembled. This gift from the workers symbolically summons abundance of production. In several towns, the trunk of a large felled tree is erected in the plaza. A honeycomb is placed at the top, which must be reached in the "greasy pole" manner (*palo encebado*). For this reason the fiesta also is called *k'wípu akúri* or "the one who eats the honeycomb," referring to the person who reaches the trophy. The melody for the *son del Corpus* is believed to be very old. It is said also that this ritual antedates the arrival of the Spaniards.

At the community level, a large fiesta dedicated to the local patron saint is held each year. Annual celebrations include minor fiestas, and there are also occasional rituals that carry religious significance. An air of rivalry surrounds the large festivals, because they are organized by people who belong to different sectors of the population. These divisions can be territorial (barrios), occupational (potters, carpenters, etc.), or administrative (municipality, county), and they all jockey to play a bigger or better part. This competitiveness is played out at different levels, including proficiency in musical performance, dance, and pyrotechnical displays.

The musical competition symbolically enacts a power struggle that generally reflects real community conflicts. In fact, the first half of the twentieth century witnessed a clash between two groups: the "conservatives," who advocated a traditional way of life based on Catholic ethics, and the "agrarianists" (traditionally supporters of land reform), with an anticlerical bent that has stunted several artistic traditions. This musical competition does not form part of the expressive ritual prayers. It involves two opposing *bandas* that compete from the afternoon until dawn, although the encounter may last one, two, or three nights. The *bandas* must play the pieces considered to be most difficult, especially works from the so-called classical music repertoire. The performance of works by Tchaikovsky, such as the *Capriccio italien*, is considered a show of prowess worthy of great respect. Often played are overtures by Franz von Suppé, Mozart, and Rossini. Technically demanding marches, *pasodobles*, and waltzes also are included, as, for instance, those of Johann Strauss. This repertoire reflects the taste of older generations, which the *bandas*—in the course of the competition—mix with *cumbias*, *corridos*, and *música norteña* with sound amplification to please the younger people. During the late evening the *bandas* may play *sones*, although the end of the confrontation at dawn is always marked by the performance of *abajeños*. This is the perfect occasion to introduce new compositions with the traditional, complex contrapuntal treatment of the bass in fast tempos and sections of more than twenty measures that are meant to provoke the opponent. The competition reaches its climax around midnight, during the series of "castle burnings" from each part of the community. Each respective *banda* must then play "Toritos de quema de castillo,"

which tend to be compositions of recent vintage (Recorded Ex. 3).

In addition to the breadth of the repertoire, judgments on which band should win the competition are based on resistance or the ability to play for the longest period of time, and on the capacity to produce the loudest sound. The *bandas* are submitted to a true endurance test: they play for many hours during the day, either standing or walking, before the competition, which is carried out without breaks, and they may not repeat a piece. After a collective evaluation of the groups, in which the women's opinions hold a great deal of weight, a decision is made as to which *banda* was the best, that is, which band "made a racket until they successfully drowned out their opponent." The stridence of these *bandas* might explain why they are displacing the *orquestas*, which are more subdued. The symbolic prize for the winner is added prestige.

In the few communities that still practice the "Danza de los soldados" (Dance of the soldiers) in addition to its counterpart, the "Danza de los moros" (Dance of the Moors), these dances mask the rivalry between two factions. Unquestionably, the "Danza de los moros" is the most significant vehicle for ritual prayer among the P'urhépecha. This dramatic dance marks the pivotal point of the ritual—the procession of the entire community with the patron saint—and is performed from beginning to end at least four times during the procession.

An important component of these large celebrations is the *jaripeo*, a "rodeo" that takes place in the afternoon on the outskirts of the village. When leaving and reentering the community, "Toritos de jaripeo" are played and the contingent is led by a group of dancing women.

For large festivals, people are invited from outside the community. This custom encourages intraethnic relationships with other P'urhépecha communities as well as with mestizos in the region. These festivals are devotional, recreational, and transactional in nature: the participants make a pilgrimage, carrying images of their respective local religious icons to "visit" the saint being worshiped; they also intend to have fun, and do not miss the opportunity of trading in goods.

The minor celebrations differ in that they are limited to the community or to one group within it, which then fosters internal relationships. This is the case, for example, when a ritual is performed to mark the replacement of *cargueros* ("in-charge"), that is, those responsible for organizing the fiestas. In some villages this takes place during the regional celebrations, such as carnival; in others, this event is held during a communal fiesta. In still other villages there is a special date for this "changing of the guard." "Toritos de cambio de autoridades" (*toritos* for changing authorities) are played on these occasions. In some places the "Danza de la flor" or *tsïtsïki warhákwa* (flower dance) is performed, whose function is to conciliate and relieve tensions created by the election of a new *carguero*. In other places a ceremony called *sïrángwa* or "la raíz" (the root, or core) is held in honor of outgoing *cargueros* who have served with distinction. Communities also tend to organize a warm welcoming celebration especially for the arrival of new religious authorities, and offer a grateful farewell for outgoing leaders. On these occasions, women dance adorned with headpieces, toss confetti, and share the gift of fruits and sweets to the musical accompaniment of a *banda* (Fig. 4).

In some communities, the largest fiesta is not dedicated to the patron saint, but rather to a religious symbol of the power to perform miracles. Civic holidays also are observed, such as the anniversary of the Mexican Revolution on November 20, which also is celebrated by mestizos who live around the P'urhépecha area. Each community celebrates more than one fiesta every year—one large and a few smaller ones—in addition to the regional celebrations. In all of these, music and dance provide the essential means to enact the system of beliefs that defines the P'urhépecha as a distinct cultural group.

Among the observances related to the life cycle, weddings merit special attention because they include several elements of pre-Hispanic origin. One of these is the dance performed by relatives and godparents of the newlyweds while carrying their gifts to the couple on their backs—items such as dishes, *metates* (a stone mortar and pestle for grinding corn), and blankets, among others. A *banda* accompanies the different stages of the wedding ritual with specific pieces, as, for instance, during the *enlace* or joining of the couple, when bride and groom are tied together with a rope. There are also wedding *toritos* played in the street to invite people to the festivities that may last for several days and take place in the homes of the groom's parents, the bride's parents, and the godparents. Altogether, wedding ceremonies are community events. In several mountain villages, a large number of participants in the celebration journeys with the *banda* to the springs outside the village the day after the

wedding to collect water and then return to continue their merrymaking.

When a person finishes the arduous task of building a house, he holds a celebration called "El combate" (the battle). The owner of the house solicits the unpaid help of a large number of men, who complete the task in the space of one day. Today, this type of support is mobilized to pour cement roofs. In the afternoon, when the work is finished, there is music, dancing, and food. This is a well-attended event that celebrates communal cooperation.

During the last few days of October and the first few days of November, a ritual is held to pay homage to the deceased. It is called "Ofrenda" (offering) or "La fiesta de las ánimas" (souls). It is a family gathering and, in some homes, activities shared by the relatives of the deceased include music and singing. If a family has lost a child or a young and unmarried person during the year, the music recreates the environment of a wedding because the P'urhépecha believe that the deceased will marry in the afterlife and that this bond should be celebrated by his or her relatives here on earth.

P'urhépecha society is predominantly rural, and this is also the context in which the art of ceremonial prayer takes place. According to the traditional social roles of men and women, men perform all types of songs, while women are limited to church songs and to the singing of lyric compositions in public only during competitions. Playing musical instruments is the exclusive domain of men. Some women play the guitar and, spurred by the spirit of competition, young women have learned only recently to play the violin, the clarinet, and other instruments.

Most of the musicians and singers do not make their living from musical performances. Their occupation is farming, fishing, or pottery making. In very few communities is music an economic activity. Music and dance are valued highly by the P'urhépecha because they recognize the power of expressive behavior to create communal bonds. Learning music, for example, brings together children, teenagers, and adults. Also highly valued by the P'urhépecha is the reciprocity underlying their traditions. The "Danza de los negritos," for instance, is performed by unmarried men who carry pledges (*prendas*), or objects loaned to them by their girlfriends; as a gesture of reciprocity, the dance is then held in the homes of the respective young women and these are occasions for the performance of newly composed *abajeños*.

Dance is practiced widely by both men and women. In several instances dance carries community responsibilities, in addition to religious meaning. In the "Danza de los moros," the performers who play the parts of the Moorish captain (Moro Capitán), Mesa de campo, second lieutenant (Alférez), and sergeant (Sargento) are also those who organize the festival. In some villages, the responsibility for the organization of patron saint celebrations rests with one married couple. They live for a year in the place of worship where the image of the saint is kept, in order to offer their prayers and care for its vestments. Each social subgroup—older married couples, newlyweds, single people—has to participate in the performance of a dance, and also has certain concomitant responsibilities that may be carried out within or beyond the context of the patron saint fiesta. For instance, the single young men who participate in the "Danza de los negritos" mentioned above must observe a measure of abstinence and remove themselves as a group from community life, until they reenter the village carrying the great tree trunk that will be used in the plaza for celebrations such as Corpus Christi.

National society is increasingly suffocating indigenous culture. The P'urhépecha have begun to incorporate their various art forms into contemporary society and culture. This process began in earnest during the 1970s, as part of a process of cultural reevaluation. The main agencies of change have been P'urhépecha professionals in the fields of education, tourism, culture, and public administration. Financial support has been provided, for example, to hold contests and award prizes to traditional artists. Major books have been published about the P'urhépecha. At the Universidad Michoacana de San Nicolás de Hidalgo, indigenous intellectuals have established the P'urhépecha Cultural Research Center (Centro de Investigación de la Cultura P'urhépecha), which has a division dedicated to music and dance. Together with these professionals, P'urhépecha priests who follow the indigenous pastoral traditions have created the most important new venue for the preservation of P'urhépecha cultural traditions: "The P'urhépecha New Year." This is a festival whose express purpose is to reclaim ethnic identity in the context of a search for ideological, political, and economic autonomy.

In addition to the P'urhépecha New Year celebration, there are similar events promoted as part of the major festivals in several villages, such as "The P'urhépecha Artistic Contest" (Concurso Artístico de la Raza P'urhépecha) in Zacán, which has been taking place since 1971. The purpose of these events is to reinforce the festival traditions by providing an economic incentive to the musicians and dancers. This has brought many previously unknown composers to public attention. Among the most important results are the opening up of music-making to women, and a surge of new songwriters, including women.

Another venue that furthers preservation of the musical creativity of the P'urhépecha emerged within the larger festivals, when Masses began to be celebrated in the P'urhépecha language. During the 1970s, songs called "Canciones del Señor Dios"—corresponding to the sung portions of the Roman Catholic Mass—were composed for this purpose. The archdiocese of Michoacán has designated certain dates for the celebration of the P'urhépecha Mass outside of the indigenous area, in the cathedral of Morelia, capital of the State of Michoacán, and in the famous sanctuary of the Virgin of Guadalupe, Patron of Mexico, in Mexico City.

A radio program was initiated during the 1970s in the mestizo city of Zamora. Called "Mañanitas P'urhépecha," it featured live performances by invited musicians. The years during which the program was broadcast stimulated a genuine surge of interest in P'urhépecha music and many groups wanted to record albums, not for economic gain, but rather to hear themselves and be heard. The high point of this recording activity came during the 1980s, particularly among singers of *pirékwas* on love themes, accompanied by guitar. *Bandas* and *orquestas* also made recordings, but they were fewer in number. There were problems with plagiarism, however, and false attributions, which led to friction. Another outlet for the dissemination of P'urhépecha music was created by the radio station of the University of Michoacán, established in 1979. The Instituto Nacional Indigenista's radio station, XEPUR, "The Voice of the P'urhépecha," is also an important center for P'urhépecha musical life. Located in Cherán, it houses the largest collection of sound recordings of P'urhépecha music, with over 10,000 items. In addition, every May 24, the "Day of the P'urhépecha Composer" is celebrated in Cherán, drawing a large number of musicians, dancers, and spectators.

Certain types of P'urhépecha music and dance also are joining the traditional repertoires performed in the broader context of national society. *Pirékwas*, for instance, are the music most often performed by mestizos. They are known outside the P'urhépecha area through folk groups and recordings of traditional music that have been in circulation since the 1960s. The best-known *pirékwas* are *tsïtsïki urápiti* or "Flor de canela" (cinnamon flower) and "La Severianita." The former is sung in a "semblance" of Spanish translation. As part of school festivals throughout Mexico, children present "regional dances" from the country's traditional repertoire. The P'urhépecha dances most often performed on these occasions are "Las uarecitas" (from *wárhi*, the P'urhépecha word for woman), which makes reference to the ritual greetings from young girls wearing headpieces; and "La danza de los viejitos" (the diminutive for old men), whose masks and costumes are sold in community marketplaces. P'urhépecha musicians and dancers also perform for tourists in the larger cities of Michoacán, though often under conditions of severe exploitation. Under very different circumstances, the P'urhépecha who have migrated to Mexico City enthusiastically invite musicians and

dancers from Michoacán to participate in their traditional festivals, also ensuring in this manner the transmission of traditions to their children, who participate in these events. These are enjoyed not just by the visitors from Michoacán, but also by a large number of mestizos who are friends of the P'urhépecha. The guitars and other instruments built in the villages of the P'urhépecha mountain range are sold throughout Mexico as well as in a few foreign countries.

In the 1990s, the characteristics of P'urhépecha music appear to be eminently Western. This indigenous group exhibits a high degree of acculturation, and many of their patterns of behavior, habits, and lifestyle follow the norms of the larger mestizo culture. However, it is equally clear that, over the years, P'urhépecha society has not merely adopted exogenous norms, whether in art or other aspects of culture. In the case of their music, the process of appropriation has resulted in a mastery of form and in assignment of functions that project musical

Fig. 4: Girls dancing to greet the arrival of visitors to the village for the celebration of the 50th anniversary of Parícutin's volcanic eruption. Angahuan, Michoacán, 1993. Photo by Fernando Nava, courtesy of the author.

performance into multiple domains of meaning. The structure of the *son* and *abajeño*, for example, provides the perfect framework for the delivery of sung expression in the P'urhépecha language. In addition, the contrast between the gentle feel of the *son* and the dynamic nature of *abajeños* serves to emulate competition, both musical and choreographic. The fiestas also display the presence of other complementary elements: while in patron saint fiestas the competition between *bandas* and dancers remains the domain of men, other celebrations emphasize choreographic competitions and dances that require greater participation of women.

One of the most significant characteristics of P'urhépecha musical culture is the ephemeral nature of the musical repertoire, which is imbued with a strong sense of renovation and rejects the concept of "aging" or the cumulative effect of "history." This process of substitution affects, for instance, many of the "flower" songs and the new *abajeños* needed for the competitions or to update the dance repertoire. Thus, it would seem that love, life, and passion, as well as changes in administrative authorities and fiesta organizers, are all permeated by a sense of continuous renewal, mediated by an attitude toward music that creates no "classics."

Heeding the challenge of interpretation, it could be said that the P'urhépecha enact two simplified versions of the traditional drama of Moors and Christians. One of those is the "Danza de los soldados," still practiced in just a few places, in which only the Christian contingent is represented. The other is the flamboyant and widespread "Danza de los moros," in which only the mythical infidels take part. Each of these is completely independent of the other and has its own traditional music and choreography. The P'urhépecha see no relationship between these two enactments and the "culture of Conquest." In fact, they do not even perceive each of these dances as one of the two parts within a thematic whole. The elements with which they identify seem clear, however: there is a certain rejection of the evangelizers and outsiders, as well as a clear identification with the non-Christian group, the native group. In this manner, and beyond acculturation, the P'urhépecha maintain a musical and choreographic discourse—in addition to their language and culture in general—that defines them in relation to the rest of the world as a tenaciously vital indigenous culture.

REFERENCES

Alcalá, Fray Jerónimo de 1540 in 1988. *Relación de las ceremonias y ritos y población y gobierno de los indios de la Provincia de Michoacán*, ed. by Francisco Miranda. México: Secretaría de Educación Pública.

Ávila, Patricia, and Aída Castilleja 1992. "María Valdez . . . María Kachacha: Las fiestas del agua en dos comunidades de la cuenca del Lago de Pátzcuaro," *Anales del Museo Michoacano*. Morelia, Michoacán: Centro Regional Michoacán—Instituto Nacional de Antropología e Historia, 135–47.

Brandes, Stanley 1990. *Power and persuasion: Fiestas and social control in rural Mexico*. Philadelphia: University of Pennsylvania Press.

Brody Esser, Janet 1984. *Máscaras ceremoniales de los tarascos de la Sierra de Michoacán*. México: Instituto Nacional Indigenista.

Carrasco, Pedro 1976. *El catolicismo popular de los tarascos*. México: Secretaría de Educación Pública.

Chamorro Escalante, Jorge Arturo 1992. *Universos de la música purhépecha*. Zamora, Mexico: El Colegio de Michoacán. 1994. *Sones de la guerra. Rivalidad y emoción en la práctica de la música p'urhépecha*. Zamora: El Colegio de Michoacán.

Dimas Huacuz, Néstor 1995. *Temas y textos del canto p'urhépecha. Pirekua: nirasïnkani ma pireni*. Zamora: El Colegio de Michoacán.

García Canclini, Néstor, and Amparo Sevilla Villalobos 1985. *Máscaras, danzas y fiestas de Michoacán*. Morelia: Gobierno del Estado de Michoacán.

Gómez Bravo, Lucas, Ireneo Rojas Hernández, and Felipe Chávez Cervantes 1987. *Pirecuecha*. Morelia: Universidad Michoacana de San Nicolás de Hidalgo.

Granados Ascencio, Julio 1988. *Ichani anapu kustakuecha: Sones y abajeños p'urhépecha de Ichán, Michoacán*. Morelia: Universidad Michoacana de San Nicolás de Hidalgo.

Kuss, Malena 1992. "Identity and change: Nativism in operas from Argentina, Brazil, and Mexico" in *Repercussions of 1492: Encounters in text and performance*, ed. by Carol E. Robertson. Washington, D.C.: Smithsonian Institution Press, 299–335.

Lumholtz, Carl 1902 in 1981. *El México desconocido: Cinco años de exploración entre las tribus de la Sierra Madre Occidental; en la Tierra Caliente de Tepic y Jalisco, y entre los Tarascos de Michoacán*, Spanish translation by Balbino Dávalos of *Unknown Mexico: A record of five years' exploration of the Western Sierra Madre; in the Tierra Caliente of Tepic and Jalisco; and among the Tarascos of Michoacán* (New York: Charles Scribner's Sons, 1902), facsimile ed. México: Instituto Nacional Indigenista.

Márquez Joaquín, Pedro 1986. "El casamiento en Cherán Atzicurín," *Relaciones* (Zamora) 7/28: 111–25.

McAndrew, John 1965. *The open-air churches of sixteenth-century Mexico*. Cambridge, Massachusetts: Harvard University Press.

Nava López, Enrique Fernando 1999. *El campo semántico del sonido musical p'urhépecha*. México: Instituto Nacional de Antropología e Historia (Series Lingüística).

Ochoa Serrano, Álvaro 1992. "Agustinos: Bandas y orquestas. Notas para tocar una tradición musical en Michoacán" in *Mitote, fandango y mariacheros*, ed. by Álvaro Ochoa Serrano. Zamora: El Colegio de Michoacán, 13–24.

Próspero Román, Salvador 1984. *Costumbres festivas de los p'urhépecha en Michoacán*. Morelia: Universidad Michoacana de San Nicolás de Hidalgo.

Ramos Felipe, Domingo 1988. *K'umajchuni anapu kustakuecha: Sones y abajeños p'urhépecha de Comachuén, Michoacán*. Morelia: Universidad Michoacana de San Nicolás de Hidalgo.

Roth Sneff, Andrew 1993. "Región nacional y la construcción de un medio cultural: El Año Nuevo P'urhépecha," *Relaciones* (Zamora) 14/53: 241–72.

Salmerón Equihua, Francisco 1992. *Kintsio anapu kustakuecha: Sones y abajeños p'urhépecha de Quinceo, Michoacán*. Morelia: Gobierno del Estado de Michoacán.

Secundino, Agapito 1976. *Tatá Diósīri Pirékuicha*. Comunidad Indígena de San Andrés Tziróndaru, Michoacán: Fímax Publicistas.

Stevenson, Robert 1968. *Music in Aztec and Inca territory*. Berkeley and Los Angeles: University of California Press.

Yurchenco, Henrietta 1983. "Estilos de ejecución en la música indígena mexicana con énfasis particular en la pirecua tarasca" in *Sabiduría popular*, ed. by Jorge Arturo Chamorro Escalante. Morelia: El Colegio de Michoacán—Comité Pro Sociedad Interamericana de Folklore y Etnomusicología, 248–60.

Zantwijk, Rudolp van 1965 in 1974. *Los servidores de los santos: La identidad social y cultural de una comunidad tarasca en México*. México: Instituto Nacional Indigenista.

DISCOGRAPHY

Música P'urhépecha. Antología Vol. 1: Orquesta de Cámara "Kuerani"/ Rocío Próspero Maldonado, compiled by the Centro de Investigación de la Cultura P'urhépecha. CD and notes. Discos Pentagrama, PCD 218. Morelia: Universidad Michoacana de San Nicolás de Hidalgo.

Música P'urhépecha. Antología Vol. 2: Orquesta de Quinceo/Los Hermanos Dimas, compiled by the Centro de Investigación de la Cultura P'urhépecha. CD and notes. Discos Pentagrama, PCD 219. Morelia: Universidad Michoacana de San Nicolás de Hidalgo.

Música P'urhépecha. Antología Vol. 3: Trío "Los Chapás" de Comachuén/Banda Juvenil "Ecor," compiled by the Centro de Investigación de la Cultura P'urhépecha. CD and notes. Discos Pentagrama, PCD 220. Morelia: Universidad Michoacana de San Nicolás de Hidalgo.

Danzas de la región lacustre del estado de Michoacán, field work directed by Josefina Lavalle. LP recording and notes. México: Fondo Nacional para el Desarrollo de la Danza Popular Mexicana (Series Música de las danzas y bailes populares de México, 1).

Música indígena purépecha, compiled by Arturo Macías. LP recording and notes. Peerless LP 1663 (México, 1973) (Series Maestros del folklore michoacano, vol. 1).

Abajeños y sones de la fiesta purépecha, compiled by Arturo Chamorro and María del Carmen Díaz de Chamorro. LP recording and notes. México: Instituto Nacional de Antropología e Historia—El Colegio de Michoacán, 1983 (Series INAH, 24).

24 de mayo: "Día del compositor p'urhépecha." Pirekuas, sones y abajeños, compiled and selected by radio XEPUR, "La Voz de los P'urhépechas," Cherán, Michoacán. One cassette with notes. México: Instituto Nacional Indigenista, 1997.

RECORDED EXAMPLES

1: "Klabéli tsïtsïki–Flor de clavel," *pirékwa* in *abajeño* style performed by the trio Los Chapás from Comachuén, Michoacán (see Fig. 1) in *Música P'urhépecha. Antología Vol. 3: Trío "Los Chapás" de Comachuén/Banda Juvenil "Ecor,"* compiled by the Centro de Investigación de la Cultura P'urhépecha. CD and notes. Discos Pentagrama, PCD 220. Morelia: Universidad Michoacana de San Nicolás de Hidalgo. Used by permission.

2: "Flor de chicalote" by Francisco Salmerón Equihua, performed by La Orquesta de Quinceo conducted by Francisco Salmerón Equihua (saxophone) (founding director, Juan Crisóstomo Valdés, violin) in *Música P'urhépecha. Antología Vol. 2: Orquesta de Quinceo/Los Hermanos Dimas*, compiled by the Centro de Investigación de la Cultura P'urhépecha. CD and notes. Discos Pentagrama PCD 219. Morelia: Universidad Michoacana de San Nicolás de Hidalgo. Used by permission.

3: "Torito 'para castillo,'" performed by the *banda* La Michoacana of Ichán conducted by Argemiro Ascencio (recorded in Tzintzuntzan during the feast of the Señor del Rescate, 1981) in *Abajeños y sones de la fiesta purépecha*, compiled by Arturo Chamorro and María del Carmen Díaz de Chamorro. LP and notes. México: Instituto Nacional de Antropología e Historia—El Colegio de Michoacán, 1983 (Series INAH, 24). Used by permission.

AEROPHONES OF TRADITIONAL USE IN SOUTH AMERICA, WITH REFERENCES TO CENTRAL AMERICA AND MEXICO

DALE A. OLSEN

Criteria for classification—Sources—The nature of aerophones: Physical materials; Musical instruments: Do they measure cultural complexity?—Musical materials, performance techniques, symbolism, and aesthetics—Ensembles of aerophones—Representative instruments and families of instruments of current practice:

Edge aerophones: end blown, ductless, one or more simple tubes without finger holes (*pifülka; flauta de chino* or *flautón; guli; mimby retá;* the *siku* and its variants; *kammu purwi and carrizo; antara and kanchis sipas; rondador*);
Edge aerophones: end blown, ductless, simple tube with finger holes (*gammu suid* or *kammu suid*);
Edge aerophones: end blown, ductless, notched tube with finger holes (*muhusemoi; kena; pina pinkulucha; tura*);
Edge aerophones: side blown, ductless, globular (*cacho de venado; naseré; tsin-hali*);
Edge aerophones: side blown, ductless, single tube with finger holes (*pitu, pfala,* and other transverse flutes; *tunda; pinkulwe; pífano*);
Edge aerophones: end blown, detachable duct (*atuñsa and kuizi; gaita*);
Edge aerophones: end blown, built-in duct (*uru'a; pito; yaku'i; pinkullo* and its linguistic variants; *tarka; pingullo, cajero,* and *roncadora*);
Lip concussion aerophones: end blown, coiled (*pututo, kepa, and heresemoi; wak'rapuku; trompeta*);
Lip concussion aerophones: end blown, straight (*trutruka; pututu*);
Lip concussion aerophones: side blown, straight (*clarín*);
Single-reed concussion aerophones: idioglottal and heteroglottal, without finger holes (*erke; tekeya; tarawi and takwara; isimoi*);
Single-reed concussion aerophones: idioglottal and heteroglottal, with finger holes (*totoy and massi; caña de millo; clarinete* and *saxofón*);
Multiple single-reed concussion aerophones (*acordeón; rondín*);
Double-reed concussion aerophones (*chirimía* and *chirisuya*);
Free aerophones (*aiğe; nurá-měe*)

—Conclusions

AN AEROPHONE IS defined as "a wind instrument . . . whose sound is caused by the vibrations of a column of air" (May 1980: xii). Within the rich musical universe of peoples who represent a complex, pluralistic mixture of many ethnic and linguistic groups—extending throughout a vast geographic area that includes topographies of extreme contrast, from the world's largest rain forest (Amazon) to the driest desert (Atacama), and from lowland basins (Orinoco) to frigid highlands and glacial peaks (the Andean mountains, including Aconcagua, the highest mountain in the Western Hemisphere)—Native

Americans and their descendants developed the largest number and greatest diversity of aerophones (see Map). More difficult to define is the concept of "traditional." Although some explain it as the "continuation of pre-immigrant . . . forms" (Nettl 1985: 27), we will define "traditional" as that which a particular group of people (a culture or subculture) calls its own. By broadening the concept of "traditional" we imply inclusion of instruments that, although not developed by Native Americans, have been appropriated by them to the extent that they are perceived as native or autochthonous, as in the case noted by José María Arguedas:

> Harp, violin, transverse flute, and *chirimía* are Indian instruments in the Peruvian mountains . . . . I remember with special . . . sentiment the expression of amazement of some of my friends, well known *mistis* or men of the village, upon finding that the harp, violin, and flute were not Indian instruments, but European ones (1977: 16).

Indeed, attempting to decipher the ethnic origins of many aerophones is very difficult and often evades the more important questions that relate to their current use within particular cultures. This essay, then, is a study of wind instruments accepted by native peoples themselves as their own, and for their own music making. Numerous subgroups are included in this category, and those covered in this chapter are presented in Table 1.

According to Cestmír Loukotka (Wilbert in Loukotka 1968: 17), 1,492 native languages were spoken in South America from pre-Columbian times to the present. If one assumes that each of these language groups had some type of aerophone for which there was a particular name, the list and description of each instrument alone would require a lengthy treatise. Although it is believed that some of the now extinct Native American cultures did not possess aerophones, either because they were not reported or because present cultures such as the Yanomamö (Wilbert 1972: 31) and Suyá (Seeger 1987: 80) do not have them, still the number of wind instruments studied in this century alone is very extensive (see Izikowitz 1935 in 1970). In addition to South America, a consideration of the musical material cultures of ancient, pre-contact peoples from Central America and Mexico leads one to justifiably refer to Native America as a geographic unit dominated by aerophones as the major nonvocal, melodic sound makers.

CRITERIA FOR CLASSIFICATION

It will not be the nature of this essay to list all of the diverse Native American wind instruments known to us, since such attempts have been made for South America (Izikowitz 1935 in 1970) and for particular countries (Aretz 1967, Venezuela; Bermúdez 1985, Colombia; Coba Andrade 1981 and 1992, Ecuador; Díaz Gainza 1962, Bolivia; Eli Rodríguez 1997, Cuba; for Peru, *Mapa de los instrumentos musicales de uso popular en el Perú*, 1978; Roth 1924, Guiana Indians; Ruiz and Pérez Bugallo 1980, and Vega 1946, Argentina; and others). Instead, the present essay will introduce aerophones in a systematic manner by studying them cross-culturally, geographically, and ecologically. Second, it will present an in-depth cultural analysis of a number of aerophones that pertain to particular groups, placed within a classification scheme that is a slight revision of the Hornbostel-Sachs system (1914 in 1961). This analysis will include such parameters as function, physical and aural symbolism, the extent to which aerophones project cultural beliefs, construction techniques, and other aspects that relate the instruments to the people who build them for their own musical practices.

Karl Gustav Izikowitz, a leading authority on traditional instruments of the South American native peoples, first published his monumental work on *Musical and Other Sound Instruments of the South American Indians* (Göteborg, Sweden) in 1935. His study is based on the descriptions of musical instruments published by anthropologists and other researchers. Izikowitz's comprehensive study of aerophones covers more than 200 pages in the 1970 reprint of his book. Many of the current studies of aerophones of traditional practice in specific countries of this region follow Izikowitz's outline. This study also will use his book as a working model, although we have introduced variants in Izikowitz's terminology. His initial definition of aerophones, for example, reads:

> Aerophones are instruments which are made to sound by directing a jet of air against the edge of an orifice, or through a valve, in such a way as to set up vibrations producing musical tones (1935 in 1970: 207).

This definition, cited from Henry Balfour, uses the term "valve" instruments for what we will call "concussion" instruments. Therefore, our two subgroups of aerophones will include "edge instruments" and "concussion instruments" for what Izikowitz calls "flutes and valve instruments" (1935 in 1970: 207). We do this in order to refrain from employing terms that are derived from the Western European instrumentarium. Both categories can be further subdivided. For example, edge instruments will include those that are ductless and those with a duct. Concussion instruments will include lip concussion and reed concussion, and the latter grouping will be further subdivided into single reed and double reed. Our classification of aerophones of traditional use in the whole region appears in Table 1 below.

TABLE 1

I. Edge aerophones
  A. Ductless
    1. End blown
      a. One or more simple tubes without finger holes
      b. Simple tube with finger holes
      c. Notched tube with finger holes
    2. Side blown
      a. Globular
      b. Tubular
  B. Duct
    1. Detachable
    2. Built-in
II. Lip concussion aerophones
  A. Coiled
    1. End blown
    2. Side blown
  B. Straight
    1. End blown
    2. Side blown
III. Reed concussion aerophones
  A. Single-reed
    1. Idioglottal and heteroglottal, without finger holes
    2. Idioglottal and heteroglottal, with finger holes
    3. Multiple single-reed
  B. Double-reed
IV. Free aerophones

SOURCES

Many primary sources reveal information about the development of aerophones in this region. We will call these artifactual and literary. Artifactual sources include pre-Columbian objects closely related to the actual instruments themselves, as well as artifacts brought to the Americas. Literary sources include mythological and historical sources that appear through oral or written communication.

Pre-contact artifactual evidence for edge aerophones is abundant. For instance, globular, tubular, and multiple flutes of numerous cultures have been discovered and are available for study. These provide invaluable information about musico-cultural continuity, discontinuity, borrowing, and isolationism, as well as musico-cultural complexity, symbolism, and context. Studies by Martí (1968), Stevenson (1968), and Olsen (1987 and 2002), for example, present evidence of cultural continuity between ancient peoples and their descendants. Likewise, much pre-contact artifactual evidence exists to prove that lip concussion aerophones have continued since antiquity, although the materials often have changed from ceramic and wood to cow horn and sheet metal.

Evidence for the existence of single- and double-reed concussion aerophones in pre-contact America, however, does not exist, as Izikowitz writes: "In South America the clarinet is never found archaeologically. . . . It is therefore possible that the clarinet is a post-Columbian instrument in South America" (1935 in 1970: 262). This analysis, however, does not consider the fact that perishable materials (until the plastic age) almost always have been used for reeds throughout the world, and these disappear over great periods of time when buried in the earth. For example, tubes that are classified as bone or wooden flutes or trumpets in some cases (such as Tiwanaku wooden trumpets and Nazca ceramic trumpets), could just as likely be single- or double-reed aerophones whose reeds have perished. Greek and Etruscan *auloi*, for example, have never been unearthed with their reeds intact. Why should the same argument not hold for pre-contact America?

Imported artifacts reached the Americas from Europe and Africa, and surviving evidence is available for study in the form of museum holdings, replicas, musical iconography, and current use of recent importations. Collections such as those of Perdomo Escobar (1986) and others found in national museums provide evidence for the cultural dynamics of aerophones in this region. Many instruments in current use are replicas of importations, such as the *chirimía* and *chirisuya* double-reed concussion aerophones, whose prototypes also can be seen in musico-iconographic sources (Chamorro 1982: 179). Recent importations in current use are the *rondín* (harmonica), accordion, clarinet, saxophone, and other aerophones that form a part of the instrumentarium of contemporary Latin America.

The oldest "literary" sources for the study of musical instruments of Native Americans are myths. While not empirical, myths often provide the only access to contextual associations that musical instruments may carry, as well as native explanations of their origins, symbolism, power, function, and taboos that emanate from the cultures themselves. Myths about instruments may be ancient or recent; they may be unacculturated, or they may reflect cultural borrowings. Nevertheless, they are of the utmost importance because, through them, native (or emic) views are expressed. A vast amount of information about wind instruments stems from historical evidence (i.e., written documents). Within decades of the "discovery" of the New World, chroniclers penned their impressions of the Indians, describing them and their habits as best they could from their own, European worldview. The accounts by 16th-century writers, such as Bernal Díaz del Castillo for Mexico and Gonzalo Fernández de Oviedo for South America (cited in Stevenson 1968: 12–14, 261; and Girard 1980: 1), contain very little descriptive information about the aerophones of Native Americans, but are important for an understanding of their contextual function shortly after European contact. Invaluable information about contexts within which aerophones were used appears in the writings of Garcilaso de la Vega, who, in the late sixteenth century, wrote about the Peru he remembered as a youth, growing up as the son of a Spanish captain and an Inca princess. Seventeenth- and 18th-century writers, such as Joseph Gumilla (cited in Girard 1980: 2–3; and Roth 1924: 451–54, 459–60) and Huamán Poma de Ayala (cited in Stevenson 1968: 262–63, 265–68) provide important descriptions and even drawings of Native American aerophones. Likewise, the late 19th- and early 20th-century studies by Im Thurn (1883), Koch-Grünberg (1923), and Roth (1924) are valuable because they offer information about Native American cultures at or near their first contact by scholars. Finally, ethnomusicological studies in the twentieth century are fundamental because many of them are the first of their kind. Although such scholarship may be categorized as a "secondary" source (because it is literature about the musical evidence itself), it constitutes—in fact— a body of primary sources of recent accumulation that often is based on oral histories of particular cultures.

THE NATURE OF AEROPHONES

Physical materials

Theodore Grame, in 1962, presented an argument for approaching organology from the standpoint of bamboo as basic material. Although bamboo might well serve for the ordering of musical instruments in Asia, Southeast Asia, India, and other parts of the Orient, one could similarly approach the classification of ancient aerophones of the Americas (excluding the Amazon basin) with fired clay (ceramic) as the major medium. The abundance of extant ceramic exemplars that have been excavated by archaeologists and grave robbers (pictured in d'Harcourt 1925: vol. 2, plates 10, 12, 16, 17, 26, 29–32) suggests that fired clay was the most frequently used material. This suggestion can be challenged, however, by considering the probability that ceramic simply has been the material that has survived the effects of prolonged burials in earthen tombs, pot sherds, or temple sites. Other, more perishable, natural materials probably have not withstood the ravages of time. Pre-contact aerophones, for example, also were constructed from bone, stone, wood, cane, silver, and gold. Bone was a common medium for single tubular edge aerophones (pictured in d'Harcourt 1925: vol. 2, plate 24), and human bone was not uncommon. Other types of bone used were llama, puma, pelican, condor, and possibly deer. Some aerophones were painstakingly hewn from stone, such as the stone panpipes of the Moche culture (pictured in d'Harcourt 1925: vol. 2, plate 15). Wood was seemingly not very common, although several wooden lip concussion aerophones have been found that pertain to the Andean Tiwanaku, Pachacamac, and Cajamarquilla cultural areas (pictured in d'Harcourt 1925: vol. 2, plate 13). Cane instruments (pictured in d'Harcourt 1925: vol. 2, plates 20 and 23) were undoubtedly frequent, but most have deteriorated over great periods of time. Silver and gold occasionally were used for instruments that were probably very powerful, because silver was the metal of the Moon goddess, and gold that of the Sun god, according to Inca belief. Most of the aerophones made from precious metals were melted down by the Spanish conquerors and sent to Spain in bullion form, although several can be seen in the Gold Museum in Bogotá.

Today ceramic is rarely used for musical instruments, except for small ocarinas (globular aerophones) used for tourism in Chile, Peru, and

Map of Native American cultures discussed in the text (in order of presentation).

Key:

1. Mapuche
2. Kuna
3. Mbyá
4. Aymara
5. Kechua
6. Chipaya

7. Moche
8. Nazca
9. Carib
10. K'ero (Kechua)
11. Warao
12. Ayomán and Hirahara

13. Guahibo
14. Pilagá
15. Nambikwára and Paresí
16. Yuko and Yupa
17. Kogi
18. Kamayurá

19. Yekuana
20. Wayúu
21. Bororo
22. Desana

other Andean countries. Similarly, bone is not often used today except by remote tropical forest cultures (such as the Warao, Yekuana, and Tukano), while stone is not used at all. Instead, 20th-century aerophones could be studied from the viewpoint of cane, of which there are many varieties. Although it is similar to bamboo in many ways, cane *(Arundo donax)* has the unique difference of being thinner walled with greater distances between nodes, thus offering perfect conditions for the construction of aerophones of many types. Three edge-aerophone groups from the Andean region of South America that owe their greatest modern developments to cane are panpipes, notched flutes, and duct flutes. (The term "panpipe" is more legendary than scientific—somewhat like the term "Gregorian" chant—since Pan, the Greek lesser deity, had nothing to do with the development of instruments we may more scientifically designate as "raft pipes." Given the widespread use of the term "panpipe" in organological terminology, however, and considering the fact that not all pipes of this type assume the shape of a raft, we are retaining—with some reluctance—the commonplace designation in this essay.) The most common panpipes in the Andes are the *siku* (Aymara term), the *antara* (Kechua term), the *zampoña* (Spanish term), the *rondador* (Spanish), the *capador* (Spanish), and the *carrizo* (Spanish term). The most common notched flute is the *kena* (Aymara term), whose distribution is the central Andes; and the most common duct flutes are the *pinkullo* (Kechua and Aymara term) and its many linguistic variants.

Musical instruments: Do they measure cultural complexity?

The correlation between the technological complexity reflected in the construction of a musical instrument and history (or change over time) as a process that often assumes (rightly or wrongly) an evolution or "development" from simple to more complex technologies, is a concept that stems from studies of European instruments in their "art" (from artifice) musical contexts. Consistent with this correlation would be a historical model that presents the recorder, most in vogue during the European Renaissance, as a predecessor of the 1832 Boehm flute, and the assumption that each reflects a different technological stage and degree of "cultural complexity." Such correlation and assumptions, if applied to musical instruments whose use is determined by symbolic

associations, as are most of the aerophones treated in this chapter, would be woefully inadequate and totally misleading. How Native American musicians made their cane tubes to sound is a study in the development of edge-instrument mouthpiece types on the one hand, and single-reed concussion mouthpiece types on the other. This also applies to tubes made from other materials. Since we only can speculate about attaching time periods to the developmental process of aerophones in current, traditional use, setting up a chronological hierarchy or one that pertains to cultural evolution is foolhardy at best. Many cultures possess almost all types of aerophonic instruments and often use particular types for particular functions (such as the Warao of Venezuela, the Kuna of Panama, and the Chipaya of Bolivia), while other cultures have none (such as the Yanomamö of Venezuela and Brazil). Thus, we must not think that panpipes are older than single pipes with finger holes, for example, or that notched mouthpieces are older than duct mouthpieces, because each has its role in lifecycle events that oftentimes are dictated by the seasons (Baumann 1981; Turino 1989). Consequently, and given the irrelevance of technology to contextual association, instruments should not serve as measures of cultural complexity. Instead, and for purposes of comparison only, we will place edge-instrument mouthpiece types and single-reed concussion mouthpiece types and their characteristics of construction on two unrelated technological scales, avoiding any chronological or hierarchical implication.

The most common edge-instrument mouthpiece types can be grouped into the following technological scale:

(1) flat edge, single closed pipe without finger holes *(pifülka = pifilka)*;

(2) beveled edge, single closed pipe without finger holes *(chino* flute);

(3) flat edge, joined set of closed pipes without finger holes *(siku, antara* in southern Peru);

(4) beveled edge, joined set of closed pipes without finger holes *(antara* in northern, coastal Peru);

(5) flat edge, single open pipe with finger holes *(kammu suid* or *gammu suid*, an important ceremonial instrument of the Kuna in Panama and Colombia, used in female initiation rituals; *pitu, pfala, tunda,* and other transverse flutes);

(6) beveled edge, single open pipe with finger holes *(muhusemoi, wara,* the latter a Warao hollowed

plant stalk version of the former, but of greater length);

(7) notched edge, single open pipe with finger holes (*kena, tura*);

(8) detachable duct, single open pipe with finger holes (*kuizi, atuñsa, gaita*);

(9) built-in duct, single open pipe with finger holes (*pinkullo, tarka, roncadora*).

While some less common combinations are omitted, such as flat edge, single closed pipe with finger holes (the Warao *harehare*), or the built-in duct, single closed pipe with finger holes (the Yekuana *hito* or *wichu*), the categories mentioned above constitute the most frequent types. The mouthpiece scale includes no special category for transverse flutes, and for that reason they are included in group 5. Although it may be tempting to compare groups 7 and 9 in evolutionary terms, with the latter developing out of the former (because, for example, cutting off the built-in duct in group 9 just above the window or rectangular air hole would result in an aerophone of group 7), the great number of edge aerophones with built-in ducts fabricated in ancient Mexico (Martí 1968) and Colombia (Olsen 1986, 1987, 1990) rules out "evolution" as a possibility. The most common single-reed concussion mouthpiece types can be grouped into the following technological scale:

(1) idioglottal (i.e., the reed is built-in), single open pipe without finger holes (*erkencho, tekeya*);

(2) idioglottal, single open pipe with finger holes (*caña de millo, massi, totoy*);

(3) heteroglottal (i.e., the reed is detachable), joined set of single reeds (*acordeón, rondín*);

(4) heteroglottal, single open pipe without finger holes (*isimoi*);

(5) heteroglottal, single open pipe with finger holes (*clarinete, saxofón*).

MUSICAL MATERIALS, PERFORMANCE TECHNIQUES, SYMBOLISM, AND AESTHETICS

As there is a wealth of spoken languages among Native Americans, so there are different tunings for their aerophonic instruments in traditional contexts. Even within a particular culture the melodic aerophones often have differing tuning systems than the vocal musics they may accompany or emulate.

This strongly suggests that aerophones are extensions of the voice, an idea often expressed but seldom proven. Among the K'ero in Peru, for example, a *kanchis sipas* panpiper will play a song with the particular tuning system of the pipe, to be immediately followed by a singer who uses a slightly different tuning system (Cohen 1966: side 2, band 1/C, see Discography). If we ask which is correct we would be posing the wrong question. Both are "correct" because both are accepted. Which came first? There is not enough information to tell. Among the Warao in Venezuela, however, there is enough evidence to suggest that the *muhusemoi* bone flutes imitate the tuning system of Warao shamanistic singing for curing, although they do so within a rather flexible parameter that may be referred to as "folk intonation." Turino (1989: 13) refers to a flexible tuning parameter that he calls "dense unison," whereby—on unisons and octaves—pitch variations of up to forty cents (about twenty cents sharp and flat) are common in a given *siku* within a tuned ensemble, thus helping to create density of sound (see also "Local Practices Among the Aymara and Kechua in Conima and Canas, Southern Peru," in this volume). This is an acceptable performance technique in traditional practices of many cultures. Even with the introduction of European aerophones throughout Latin America, such as the brass lip concussion instruments used in military bands, the folk intonation and "dense unison" performance techniques continue as forms of traditional expression.

A performance technique related to dense unison is heterophony or melodic group variation. Aerophones with finger holes have the capability of producing rapid ornaments, and many melodic ensemble performances are based on numerous "individual" expressions sounding simultaneously. Sets of aerophones without finger holes, such as the *sikuri* panpipes of the Aymara, however, perform together with an overlapping technique used to avoid "gaps, or periods of silence in an ensemble's music" that Turino has called "dense sound" (1989: 13). The overall effect is still one of slight heterophony. When the melodic variations of multiple performers are separated by slight differences in points of time, as during performances by Warao *muhusemoi* flute players, the texture can be referred to as "free imitation." It is, perhaps, but a fine line between melodic heterophony and free imitation, and both can be seen as individual expressions within group cohesion. When several aerophones perform a melody simultaneously at several pitch levels, the technique can be termed "parallelism," and this is commonly found in ensemble performances in southern Peru and Bolivia. Among the Aymara and Kechua, for example, parallel melodies at the intervals of the fourth and fifth are rooted in ancient practice, while the use of parallel thirds may reveal Spanish influence.

Another group practice found in the Americas (and many other parts of the world) is the technique of interlocking parts, commonly called "hocket." (Because "hocket" is derived from *hoquetus,* a practice identified with the European Middle Ages, this term will not be employed here; "interlocking parts," on the other hand, implies no European point of reference.) Musicians who use the technique of interlocking parts each play the fraction of a melodic range to which their instruments are restricted. The mestizo *chino* flutes of central Chile, for example, include two instruments, each capable of one-half of the melodic whole; the *siku* panpipe of the Aymara (Bolivia, Peru, Chile, Argentina), comprises two complementary parts, each capable of six or seven notes spaced stepwise; and the *tule* single-reed concussion aerophones of the Wayãpí (French Guiana, Brazil) include four instruments, each capable of one note (Beaudet 1997). In all of these ensembles, the melodic whole requires the strictest form of musical cooperation among the players, and the performance event is similar to other traditional forms of communalism, especially the labor force.

The concept and practice of dividing the musical whole into halves or quarters is often related to native cosmology, such as the duality of the natural, physical world (day and night, summer and winter, man and woman, up and down, etc.). Four is often powerful in itself because of its relationship to the four cardinal points (among the Warao), the four seasons in some regions, and as the double of two. Thus, in specific cultures of this region, the symbolism of duality and complementation of opposites is mediated by aerophonic practice, as well as reflected in other aspects of life. (See Max Peter Baumann, "Music and Worldview of Indian Societies in the Bolivian Andes," in this volume.)

Another practice that may be related to dualism, but actually is manifested in the joining of opposites rather than the separate parts of a whole, is the use of percussion accompaniment to aerophonic performance. The Tukano of the Amazon basin

(Colombia), for instance, attach sexual symbolism to the sounds of their instruments: the whistling sound of edge aerophones (flutes) symbolizes sexual invitation; the buzz of single-reed concussion aerophones (clarinets) symbolizes male aggressiveness; and the percussion sounds of membranophones and idiophones symbolize "a synthesis of opposites . . . , an act of creation in which male and female energy have united" (Reichel-Dolmatoff 1971: 115–16). In other instances (less well documented with regard to their meaning), percussion accompaniment provides energy and pulse for dancing or parading. Commonly found throughout this region are individual aerophones performed with a percussive sound maker, or groups of aerophones accompanied by several membranophones or idiophones. In the Andes, from northern Chile to Ecuador, and in many regions of Central America and Mexico, dualism is individually expressed as a synthesis of opposites by several types of aerophone and membranophone combinations played by one person. In this "one-man-band," a detachable or built-in duct-edge aerophone is played with the musician's one hand while his other hand plays a drum or a rattle. This combination may have Spanish roots, as the pipe-and-tabor was very common in the European Middle Ages and Renaissance. The technique, however, also was known and practiced in pre-contact America, although all the evidence depicted on pre-Columbian Andean effigy jars reveals a panpipe and drum, rather than a duct flute and drum, played by one person (the notched flute and drum player depicted on a Peruvian effigy jar, pictured in Diane Olsen 1978: 104, is believed to be a post-Columbian replica; see Dale Olsen 1992: 78–79). Nevertheless, in ancient Middle America (Mesoamérica), gold effigy figurines of one-handed flutists who are playing a rattle with the other hand are common (Boilès 1966). Cultural continuity of that practice is seen today with the Colombian *gaita macho* player, and also among the Kuna in Panama. This similar ancient practice is perhaps one reason why the Spanish pipe-and-tabor may have replaced or fused with the pre-Hispanic usage fairly quickly, causing widespread diffusion throughout much of the Americas. While one-person combinations of panpipe and membranophone have been depicted on ancient ceramic pottery from Ecuador to southern coastal Peru, the practice continues in the central Andes of Peru and Bolivia.

Aerophones often carry symbolic significance associated with their physical shape, both internal and external. In many Native American cultures, for example, tubular aerophones (especially flutes) are phallic symbols and are restricted to male use (Olsen 1980b: 377). The conch shell and other spiral trumpets are, by contrast, female symbols, although their "masculine" sound gives them authoritative power and their use also is restricted to men. The Colombian *capador*, a panpipe used by mestizos, is the instrument of pig gelders, and it is played by males. In fact, almost all aerophones of traditional use in this region, especially among indigenous groups, are restricted to men. There is a paradox, however, in the confinement of aerophonic performance to males since, in Kechua and Aymara aesthetics, high sounds are the most valued. The preferred style of singing is high pitched, performed by females, and the preferred aerophonic style is high pitched, performed by males. Within ritual contexts especially (planting and harvest festivals, animal marking, and weddings), this again can be interpreted as a dualistic quality symbolizing fertility, procreation, and power.

ENSEMBLES OF AEROPHONES

The dualistic nature of many aerophones requires ensemble playing. Other performance groups of aerophones are found, however, that seem unrelated to the dualistic concept. Foremost among these are wind ensembles or bands, the result of the early 19th-century presence of military bands in Latin America. Although ensembles of war instruments, such as groups of *kepas* (conch shell trumpets) and *wankaras* (membranophones), were employed by the Inca, the use of European lip concussion (trumpets, trombones, baritone horns, tubas) and single-reed concussion instruments (clarinets and saxophones), accompanied by snare and bass drums, developed with the expansion of military and civilian bands throughout Latin America (see José Peñín, "Bands in Venezuela," in these volumes). The entry on "Bandas" in the 10-volume *Diccionario de la música española e hispanoamericana* (Plesch *et al.* 1999: 137–60) provides the most comprehensive history of bands to date in fourteen Latin American countries. Information on bands surfaces in national histories, as well as in studies by Egberto Bermúdez (1985) and Marcos A. Salas Salazar (1998), whose monograph traces the history of a single band in Nariño (Colombia). In 1981, Bermúdez (1985: 74) documented the presence of 89 bands in Colombia.

They are used during religious festivals, and for parades, outdoor concerts (*retretas*), and dancing, the common contexts for bands throughout the region.

Bermúdez documents another type of ensemble in Colombia that is known as "La Banda de los Borrachos." In addition to two transverse flutes, two chordophones, and six idiophones, this ensemble comprises four vegetable lip concussion instruments called trombone, saxophone, trumpet, and tuba, all made from calabashes. "They do not have a system with which to produce different sounds except to vary the position of the player's lips" (1985: 107). A similar ensemble is documented for Ecuador, which is composed of musicians of African descent living in the Chota Valley, as Carvalho-Neto writes:

> Except for the *bombo*, all the other instruments were the most primitive that you could imagine: an empty oil tin for a drum; some of the musicians played pieces of banana leaves, imitating quite well the sound of flutes, of the *pífanos*, and of the *clarines*; others, playing into empty calabashes, imitated the sound of the cornets and trombones (1964: 94).

Whereas the term "band" usually refers to ensembles of aerophones, and "orchestra" often implies the presence of bowed chordophones, the typical orchestra of central Peru includes several clarinets and saxophones, accompanied by violins and a harp. This ensemble will be discussed below.

REPRESENTATIVE INSTRUMENTS AND FAMILIES OF INSTRUMENTS OF CURRENT PRACTICE

Edge aerophones: end blown, ductless, one or more simple tubes without finger holes (see Table 1, IA, 1a).

Pifülka **(Mapuche: Chile, Argentina).** The *pifülka* (also transliterated as *pifilka* in current literature) is a small end-blown tubular aerophone without finger holes belonging to the Araucanians of south-central Chile and central-western Argentina, more properly known as Mapuche (people of the land). The *pifülka* may be compared to a single closed pipe of a panpipe, with the only difference being that today's *pifülka* is made from a single piece of hard wood that has one or, occasionally, two tubes bored into it (Carlos Vega, however, has documented flat, wide, wooden *pifülkas* with three and five internal tubes among the

Mapuche in Argentina [1946: 211]). Old one-tubed examples of *pifülkas* made from bone (perhaps human bone according to Merino 1974: 81), ceramic, and stone, however, have been excavated, making those instruments similar to archaeological exemplars of panpipes from Ecuador to northern Chile.

The *pifülka* appears to be an instrument of great antiquity because of archaeological specimens that have been found in northern Chile. Long before the 16th-century Spanish conquest (Pedro de Valdivia first set foot in Chile in 1540, founding Santiago in 1541), people known as the Pikunche who inhabited the northernmost extension of the Araucanian empire had established a culture that perhaps had contact with other pre-contact civilizations, such as the Diaguita. Numerous stone and ceramic artifacts that closely resemble present *pifülkas* have been excavated, some with anthropomorphic and zoomorphic designs or shapes that resemble stylized humans or fish (Grebe 1974b: 39; Isamitt 1937: 59). In most cases the archaeological exemplars (Fig. 1) have the same basic shape as modern *pifülkas* (Fig. 2).

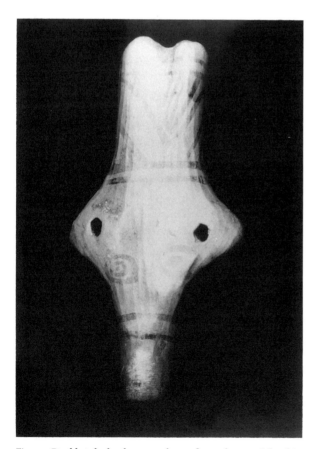

Fig. 1: Double-tubed edge aerophone from the pre-Columbian Diaguita culture, northern Chile. Olsen Collection.

Modern instruments are made from oak or a Chilean wood known as *lingüe,* and their external measurements are approximately 25 cm in length and 6 cm in width (Isamitt 1937: 59). The central tubes are made with a red hot poker, which does not completely pierce the wood, leaving one or two closed tubes. The typical *pifülka* has two pierced ear-like protrusions through which the musician attaches a string for carrying the instrument around his neck.

The simple concept of this small musical instrument suggests that only one pitch can be produced by each tube; this is, however, an incorrect deduction because, in fact, the musician often blows to produce the fundamental tone and one overtone, such as a twelfth higher, as indicated in several musical examples notated by Carlos Isamitt (1937: 60).

Isamitt (1937: 60), Juan Orrego-Salas (1966: 51–52), and Samuel Claro (1971: 30) have suggested that a two-tubed *pifülka* can produce from 24 to 26 pitches, arranged chromatically. Orrego-Salas even notates the chromatic scale of a single-tubed *pifülka* beginning on B-flat and descending to E-flat. Even though it is possible to produce a microtonal glissando (or gliding effect) on the *pifülka,* the instrument is never performed in this manner by the Mapuche themselves, thus diminishing the value of such analyses and conclusions by these Chilean researchers. Further accounts by anthropologists and ethnomusicologists who have lived and worked with the Mapuche verify the playing techniques of the *pifülka.* Titiev (1949: 33), for example, writes: "The new kinds of *pifülkas* may be blown on any occasion, but the old-fashioned instrument is reserved for ceremonial events. It is blown in conjunction with dancing, its higher note signifying fast time, and the lower one a slower tempo." Another performance technique whereby two male performers alternate their single notes is explained by Grebe (1974a: 74–75), who writes: "It is common practice for *pifülkas* to be played by two men who alternate their sounds in a measured manner. According to custom, these musicians play their respective instruments in alternation, with the ideal musical relationship being the distance of a minor or major third between them." Example 1 illustrates this technique, as transcribed by Grebe (1974a: 75).

In a typical performance numerous *pifülka* players gather together and form into two large groups to play their alternating notes, "the resulting sounds being equivalent to two alternating sonorous clouds of

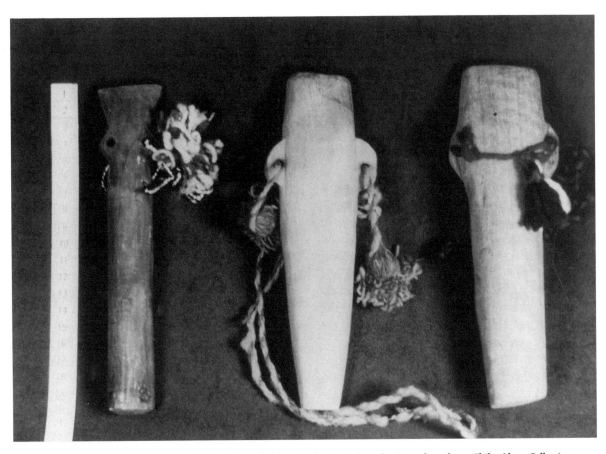

Fig. 2: Three *pifülkas* (left, single-tubed; middle and right, double-tubed) from the Mapuche culture, Chile. Olsen Collection.

richly colored aleatoric timbre" (Grebe 1974a: 75). In these instances of communal performance practice on the *pifülka*, the instruments are supporting or underscoring the rhythmic pulse of the *kultrún* (the shaman's kettledrum). In such ritual dances as the *choike-purrún* (dance of the rhea ostrich), *nguillatún* (fertility ritual), *ngeikurrewén* and *eluwün* of the *machi* or shamaness, Mapuche ensembles composed of groups of *pifülka*, bell rattles *(kaskawilla)*, rattle *(wada)*, and drum *(kultrún)* perform their percussive sounds, providing a rhythmic base for the improvisations on the *trutruka, lolkiñ,* and *corneta,* which are Mapuche lip concussion aerophones (Grebe 1973: 21, 24). (See Carol E. Robertson, "Fertility Ritual," and María Ester Grebe, "Amerindian Music of Chile," in this volume.)

Flauta de chino or *flautón* (mestizo: Chile). This end-blown tubular aerophone without finger holes is very common in religious festivals of central and northern Chile. Known as *flautón* (big flute), *pito* (whistle), and *flauta de chino* (chino flute), the instrument is very similar to the Mapuche *pifülka* and the Diaguita prototypes of the *pifülka,* from which it possibly derived. Since this aerophone occurs in various sizes, from over three feet in central Chile to under one foot in the north, the term "chino flute" is more accurate than *flautón* or *pito,* and also because the musician/dancer who plays the instrument is called a *chino.* This term has nothing to do with Chinese (English for the Spanish *chino*), but it is used in Chile to mean "humble servant" of the Virgin or another saint (Urrutia Blondel 1968: 59), in this case the devoted performer who is a

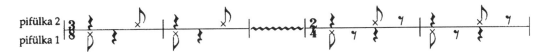

Ex. 1: Typical music of two *pifülkas* (Grebe 1974a: 75).

faithful participant in the Catholic patronal festival. *Chino* flutes can be made from wood or bamboo, and both types can be found at the same Chilean religious festival, as experienced by this author in Andacollo, north-central Chile, in 1969. The instruments made from bamboo are longer than those made from wood. Henríquez (1973: 30) gives a detailed description of the construction of a bamboo *flautón,* explaining how one piece of cane is fitted within another, leaving one end open and the other closed. The proximal or mouth end is cut until it is the proper length to produce the desired pitch, and a putty mouthpiece (simply a reinforcement of the open end) is made to flare out wider than the cane. The final product is then wrapped with colorful cloth and plastic, adorned with mirrors and abalone shells, and the mouthpiece painted with enamel. The *chino* flutes we observed in Andacollo also were made from bamboo; however, a distinctive feature was the addition of an outer frame of split bamboo around the inner bamboo tube, creating the shape of an elongated V. The upper part of the V was fashioned out of wax into a wide, concave notch. The proximal end of the bamboo itself was obliquely cut on each side, with the side closest to the musician more deeply cut than the back side against which the musician directs his air stream. The entire body of the instrument was wrapped in cloth and adorned with mirrors (Fig. 3). This V-shaped widening is referred to as "butterfly wings," according to Pumarino and Sangüeza (1968: 30), who give the following account of the wooden *chino* flutes from Limache:

> The flutes are characterized by a widening in both sides of their outer parts, called "butterfly wings." In some instances, these wings can be double, as in the case of the flutes for the dance of the Maitenes of Limache. They are painted in diverse colors and often appear ornamented with ribbons . . . or small mirrors that produce strange sunlight reflections or shine with the lights of the evening's presentations.

The wooden *chino* flutes from Limache are hollowed out by piercing the wood (poplar or *lingüe*) with a drill or several red hot pokers of different sizes. The first hole is 1/4 inch in diameter and made with a drill (Garces 1968) or a red hot iron (Pumarino and Sangüeza 1968: 30) forced completely through the wood from top to bottom, as is the second hot poker, measuring 5/16 of an inch, which is meant to polish the tube. The third iron, however, measuring 1/2 inch in diameter, burns to only half the length of the

others, until it is at the place where the proper pitch or tone can be produced, the "goose's throat, so it does not sound like a bottle" (Pumarino and Sangüeza 1968: 30). When that sound is found, the distal end is permanently plugged with a cork or piece of wood. Finding the proper pitch is of utmost importance, because the *chino* flutes are tuned in pairs. Like the Mapuche *pifülka,* two instruments alternate their individual notes, which are usually from a minor second to a major third apart, depending on the dancing group. The proper pitch of each is important because many *chino* flutes play together with those of the higher pitch in one dancing line, and those of the lower pitch in another parallel line. The precision playing of the musicians is accompanied by several membranophones, namely *tambor* and *bombo.* The smaller, wooden *chino* flutes do not play overtones as do the Mapuche *pifülkas.* The larger bamboo flutes from Andacollo, however, must produce overtones. Because the tube of the Andacollo *flauta de chino* is about two feet long, the fundamental pitch is too low, soft, and difficult to produce to be effective. Thus, the flutist must blow an overtone by making a hard breath accent. Each row of flutists must play overtones in nearly perfect unison,

Fig. 3: Single-tubed *flauta de chino* (an edge aerophone), being performed at the patronal festival of the Virgen del Rosario in Andacollo, north-central Chile. Olsen Collection.

and the two rows of musicians/dancers alternate their notes at the interval of a minor second. The "Chinos de Andacollo," for the 1968 festival of the Virgen del Rosario, included sixteen flutists who danced and played in two parallel rows of eight people.

The materials, colors, and sizes of the *flautas de chino* are related to their place of origin and their placement in dance sequence, as in the following description of the 1968 "Bailes chinos" in Limache (Garces 1968):

> In the dances performed at the event organized in Limache, one could see the differences in their flutes. The dance of Puchuncaví had blue flutes. That of Granizo had flutes wrapped in plastic ribbons with mirrors attached. The dance of La Quebrada used wooden flutes of distinct colors, such as light blue, red, green, and rose with white. Those for the dance of Tabolango were wrapped in tricolored plastic ribbons. For the dance of Maitenes, the dancers played on wooden flutes, painted red. A general practice for all the dances is the placement of the flutes, which corresponds to the placement of the dancers, who play while they dance; they are distributed from greater to lesser stature. The first ones use the longest flutes, which are called *punteras* [leaders of a parade] (made from bamboo); in the second place are the *secunderas,* followed by the *terceras,* and finally the *coleras* [tail] or *chicharras* [cicadas, or harsh sounders], which usually are played by children.

The dances, colors, instruments, method of performance, and hierarchy of elements of the *chino* dancers are perhaps imbued with symbolism whose roots are shrouded in the past. When asked how long has this tradition existed, the musicians/dancers invariably answer "desde siempre," or since always (Garces 1968). The bonding between indigenous material culture and Catholic religious practice is typical of Andean musical syncretism.

Guli **(Kuna: Panama and Colombia).** The *guli* (Smith 1984: 156–61) or *kuli* (Tayler 1972: 56–57) of the Kuna Indians of the Caribbean coastal portions of Panama and Colombia is a set of separate but complementary tubes conceptualized as masculine and feminine,

with external lengths varying from 40 to 65 cm (Smith 1984: 156). In the past, the tubes ranged from 50 to 150 cm and even two meters in length (Ronny Velásquez, personal communication to Kuss). A *toque* or performance requires a minimum of two tubes, but normally involves three pairs or six tubes and, optimally, six pairs or twelve tubes, each played by a single musician/dancer. These musicians perform melodies and clusters of notes by interlocking the individual pitches of the end-blown pipes. The Kuna have devised a unique technique for producing the fundamental and first overtone (interval of a twelfth) on the rather large *guli* pipes (Smith 1984: 158): the musician turns his right hand toward his face and drapes his first two fingers in a clawlike fashion over the top of his pipe, leaving an opening between them. Using the first knuckles of each finger as an embouchure rest, he blows into and slightly across the top of the tube to produce his tones. This is the only way in which a large ductless stopped pipe can be sounded. The repertoire of the male musicians/dancers who perform the *guli* consists of melodies, snaps, clicks, huffs, shouts, and dances that imitate birds and animals (Smith 1984: 159). At times the men are accompanied by women who play rattles. Example 2, from a portion of a *guli* performance by six musicians, illustrates an interlocking melody and note clusters. (See also Ronny Velásquez, "The Fundamental Role of Music in the Life of Two Central American Ethnic Nations: The Kuna in Panama," in this volume.)

Mimby retá **or** ***mimbü-eta*** **(Guaraní-affiliated Mbyá: Argentina).** The *mimbü-eta* (Locatelli de Pérgamo 1975) or *mimby retá* (a composite name that means "many flutes") (Ruiz and Pérez Bugallo 1980: 16–17), is a set of seven loose bamboo panpipes of the Mbyá, a Guaraní-affiliated group who live in a few and scattered villages in the Province of Misiones (Argentina). The varying lengths of the *mimby retá* tubes rarely exceed 20 cm and are made from *takuapí,* a type of bamboo (Ruiz 2000: 585–86). Whereas each of the large tubes of the Kuna *guli* is played only by a man (six men for six tubes, etc.), the much smaller pipes of the *mimby retá* are played solely by two

Ex. 2: Music by six *guli* musicians (Smith 1984: 161).

women, who divide their seven tubes in a variety of ways, depending on the melody. At times, only six or five tubes are shared. Generally the woman who plays the lower pitched pipes (often three tubes) plays an ostinato, while her female partner performs varying pitches or melodic patterns that may interlock, overlap, sound simultaneously, and even cross in pitch with the notes of the ostinato pattern. The repertoire played on the *mimby retá* includes pieces whose titles relate them to animals and birds of the forest. The musicians do not dance while they play, and the performances take place within the context of entertainment rather than ritual. (See Irma Ruiz, "Musical Culture of Indigenous Societies in Argentina," in this volume.)

The *siku* and its variants (Aymara, Kechua, Chipaya: Peru, Bolivia, and Chile). One of the most important identifying characteristics of the Chilean *pifülka* and the *flauta de chino* is that two instruments must perform together in an interlocking fashion to comprise the whole of the melody. Nowhere in South America is this emphasis on dualism more prevalent than with an instrument whose most common name is *siku*. (See Max Peter Baumann, "Music and Worldview of Indian Societies in the Bolivian Andes," in this volume.) The *siku* (Fig. 4), an end-blown tubular aerophone without finger holes, consists of numerous closed pipes rafted together (hence, "raft pipes," also panpipes), and requires two interdependent parts, each of which is played by a different musician (pictured in Buchner 1972: Fig. 116). These parts also can be conceptualized as two instruments, "each of which is able to play only a part of the pitches necessary to perform the music of *sikuris*" (Romero 1985: 238–39). The *siku* has a wide distribution in the central Andes of South America and also is known by a variety of names. Among the Aymara people of Peru and Bolivia it is called *siku*; among Aymara descendants in northern Chile it is known as *pusa* or *laka* (Dannemann 1977: 106; Yévenez Sanhueza 1980: 54); the Spanish speakers of northern Chile call it *zampoña*; among the Peruvian Aymara one also finds the term *chiriwano* (Turino in Romero 1987: 20) for a similar instrument used for a particular

Fig. 4: *Siku* panpipes (left, *arka*; right, *ira*), performed by the Grupo Aymara in concert at Florida State University in Tallahassee. Olsen Collection.

function; also in Peru, but among the Kechua of Paratía, it is called *phuko* for their *ayarachi* ceremonial music (Valencia Chacón 1989: 70). Other names also can be found. The important distinguishing feature of all these aerophones is the complementarity of the two parts of a set, each of which most commonly is called *ira* (the leader) for the part with six tubes, and *arka* (the follower) for the part with seven tubes (see Fig. 4).

In number notation (using a Western diatonic scale as the basis, where ♭ equals the flat seventh tone, 1 is equivalent to the tonic, ♭ corresponds to a flat third, 5 to the fifth, i̇—with an upper dot—to the octave of 1, etc.), the *ira* has pitches 1 ♭ 5 ♭ 2̇ 4̇, and the *arka* has pitches ♭ 2 4 6 i̇ ♭ 5̇. This also is expressed in Example 3. The *ira* and *arka* "halves" of a set of *siku* panpipes (theoretically one instrument) are meant to be played by two men in a musically interlocking fashion, called in Aymara *jjaktasina irampi arkampi,* or "to be in agreement between the *ira* and the *arka*" (Valencia Chacón 1989: 34).

A group of *siku* instruments is called a *sikuri,* as are the musicians/dancers who play them; and the most common type of music played by a *sikuri* ensemble is a *sikuriada* (literally, music for *sikuri*), although there are also numerous religious and ceremonial forms that have different names. In addition, many *sikuri* groups play marches, *waynos* or *huaynos,* and other popular Andean dance forms. The present dispersion of the *siku* is in southern Peru and western Bolivia, in a region known as the Altiplano, a high plateau between the eastern and western cordilleras of the Andes, also called Puna, that extends southward from Lake Titicaca to Lake Poopó and the Coipasa and Uyuni salt flats. Lake Titicaca, the highest navigable lake in the world, is at the heart of the cosmological world of the Aymara and Kechua. This lake's surrounding areas, and the islands and peninsulas within it, are also at the center of the largest dispersion of the *siku* in Peru. At the present

time, the city of Lima has become another center of *siku* activity because of the large number of migrants from the Altiplano who have moved to the capital (Turino 1988: 144).

Aerophones related to the *siku* are found archaeologically in coastal Peru, especially in the pre-Columbian Moche culture in the North and Nazca in the South. Whether these ancient panpipes made from ceramic, stone, cane, silver, and gold were of the type like the *siku* (i.e., two parts or instruments played in interlocking fashion) is not known for sure, but there is strong evidence to support that they were performed in that manner among the Moche (Olsen 2002: 72–74). Iconographical evidence of dual panpipe players whose instruments are joined by a string can be seen on Moche pottery (see Figs. 7 and 11 in Valencia Chacón 1989), and there is strong physical and acoustical evidence that Nazca panpipes were played in groups, as Bolaños (1981: 24) writes:

> The important conclusion of the study of the [Nazca] *antaras* from this tomb is that all of their sounds were interrelated. It is as if all the *antaras* had pertained to an instrumental ensemble that was very similar to the present *sikuri* groups of the Aymara, who are accustomed to organizing their cane instruments . . . in groups of two or more pairs of players, sometimes forming large ensembles in which each person, with his *siku,* has only a portion of the pitches of the musical scale.

Valencia Chacón (1989: 85–93) arrives at similar conclusions about possible dualistic and collective uses for Moche and Nazca panpipes, and sees the musical practices of both cultures as prototypes for the present performance techniques of the Andean *siku,* as did Izikowitz decades before for the Moche (1935 in 1970: 396). Today, Andean *sikus* are made from a cane known as *chocclla* (Vargas 1928: 6) or *chuqui* (Jiménez

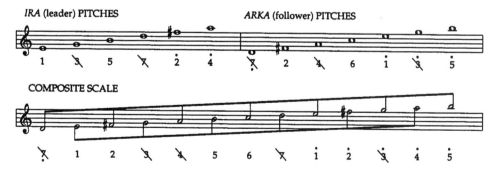

Ex. 3: The tuning system of a dualistic set of *siku* panpipes in the middle (*malta* or *ankuta*) register (Bolaños 1988: 115).

Borja 1951: 40), growing on the eastern slopes of the Andes, whose scientific name is *Arundo donax*. Raoul and Marguerite d'Harcourt (1925: 49), however, write that the cane comes from the region of Lake Titicaca, and that it is "exceptional for its dimensions." Since the dispersion of the *siku* type of panpipe is wide, differing natural tubes can be found to construct them, such as certain types of bamboo in northern Chile. Additionally, experiments with materials other than natural ones, such as PVC tubing, have been undertaken by Valencia Chacón (1989: 103) and by Olsen and Ahyoung (1989: 86–87) for use in public school teaching.

Sikus are constructed in the form of a raft, with the pipes of each part of the set placed in a stepped arrangement, like organ pipes, as described by Garcilaso de la Vega (1609 in 1961: 79):

> The Colla Indians and all those in their district had a certain knowledge of music. They played reed or cane instruments, made by joining four or five tubes together, each one of which furnished a higher or lower note than the preceding one, as in the case of organ pipes. (Cf. quote from Garcilaso de la Vega 1609 in Max Peter Baumann, "Music and Worldview of Indian Societies in the Bolivian Andes" [Panpipe representations in pre-Columbian times], in this volume.)

The nodes of the cane serve as the ends of the *siku*'s closed tubes, giving the raft an externally stepped form. The Aymara call this type of instrument *ch'aka siku*. In some regions, instrument makers cut cane tubes into equal lengths, although the nodes of the cane are still calculated into an internally stepped form. These tubes are rafted together into a rectangular form, which the Aymara call *tabla siku*; this type of instrument construction is more durable than the *ch'aka siku* (García 1979: 13). In both types of *siku* construction, the pipes are placed within several split pieces of cane that are either perpendicularly affixed in parallel on both sides of the tubes, or wrapped around the tubes several times, then lashed with string. This stabilizing mechanism is called a "ligature" by Izikowitz (1935 in 1970: 388–90), who provides several informative drawings of the most common varieties.

Sikus can be constructed in single rows of closed tubes, or in double rows, with the second row always an octave higher in pitch than the first. The second row, which is lashed exactly in parallel to the closed row, can be either closed or open (pictured in Buchner 1972: Fig. 114). In both cases, it always produces a resonated octave, since it is not blown directly into, but it is there simply to pick up escaped air from the musician's air stream. When the flutist blows across the closed tube of his choice, the adjacent parallel tube resonates slightly, giving the instrument its characteristic timbre.

A complementary set of *sikus* can be played by two men, or several *sikuri* can be played in multiples of two performers. Only recent nightclub usage has allowed one *siku* to be played by one person (male or female), and this is done by placing the two members of a pair back to back, with the *ira* closest to the player. In the traditional Aymara manner, these instruments are constructed and performed in *familes* of different sizes, occasionally corresponding (by way of analogy only) to Western soprano, alto, tenor, and bass (Bustillos, Oporto, and Fernández 1981: 5); or, more commonly, to soprano, alto, and tenor. The acoustical properties of the three-member families have been studied by many scholars (Bolaños 1988: 114–16; Turino 1989: 10–11; Valencia Chacón 1989: 44, 48–53, 58–59, 65–66, 70–72, and 78–79), and *sikuri* group characteristics depend on the particular tradition of the users. Generally, the three fundamental registers of the *sikuri* panpipe family members are an octave apart. Within each of the family member groups, however, there can be three additional divisions of *sikus* at intervals of major and minor thirds, totaling nine pairs (18 performers) who play in parallel texture (Turino 1989: 10). Additionally, some *sikuri* are ordered in such a way as to perform in parallel fourths or fifths within octaves, and the part providing the intermediate register is referred to as *contra* (García 1979: 12).

Among the most important traditions in Peru are the Aymara *sikuri*, the Kechua *sikuri* from Taquile Island in Lake Titicaca, the Aymara *chiriwano* from Huancané, the Kechua *ayarachi* from Paratía, and the mestizo (mixed Aymara and Spanish) *pusamoreno* or *sikumoreno* (Valencia Chacón 1989). Significant in Bolivia are the Aymara, Kechua, and Chipaya traditions (Baumann 1981: 189–92). Many varieties of nomenclature for the instrument are found within the Aymara *sikuri* tradition, as Valencia Chacón (1989: 48) writes: "The different ensembles in the Aymara *sikuri* tradition are actually complex orchestras with specific and distinctive structures. The ensembles are composed of different groups according to the sizes of the *sikus*." Table 2 lists the most common names for the members of *sikuri* families, as they pertain to the major traditions in use today.

When *sikuris* perform together for festivals their numbers are greatly increased, but usually the middle or alto voice (the *malta* register at the center) is given prominence by increasing the number of instruments (Turino 1989: 11). Likewise, an ensemble may use a large number of *sikus* in the "tenor" register, so that their soft sound will not be overpowered by the other, stronger voiced instruments.

As the names of the instruments often vary within the major traditions, so do the scales employed in the music. The following observations generally pertain: Peruvian Aymara *sikuri* music is pentatonic, hexatonic (1 ♮ 4 5 ♭ ♭ 1̇), or heptatonic (1 2 ♮ 4 5 6 ♭ 1̇); Kechua *sikuri* music from Taquile Island in Lake Titicaca is heptatonic (1 2 ♮ 4 5 ♭ ♭ 1̇); Aymara *chiriwano* music from Huancané is hexatonic (1 2 4 5 ♭ ♭ 1̇) and heptatonic; Kechua *ayarachi* music from Paratía is pentatonic (1 2 4 5 6 1̇); and the mestizo (mixed

Aymara and Spanish) *pusamoreno* or *sikumoreno* music is heptatonic (1 2 ♮ 4 5 6 ♭ 1̇) (analyses from transcriptions in Valencia Chacón 1989). The Chipaya *sikuri* tradition in Bolivia has borrowed greatly from the neighboring Aymara (Baumann 1981: 190–91), although Chipaya music also makes use of a major heptatonic scale (1 2 3 4 5 6 7 1̇).

Sikuri traditions also vary in ensemble size, performance practice, styles of dancing, and cultural context. The largest ensemble is the *chiriwano*, which has been documented with as many as 500 performers on special occasions (Bellenger 1981; Valencia Chacón 1989: 64). Usually, *sikuri* ensembles or *tropas* (troops) include from about twelve to over fifty musicians. Many *sikuri* players are dancers who perform while they play their instruments. Among the *sikuri* of Taquile Island, women join in the dancing, forming couples (Valencia Chacón 1989: 57). Some *sikuri* groups, such as the *pusamorenos*, also parade down streets during patronal festivals,

TABLE 2: *Sikuri* family names within documented Andean traditions.

Name of tradition	Region	Soprano	Alto	Tenor	Bass
Aymara *sikuri* (Turino 1989: 10)	Conima, Peru	suli bajosuli contrasuli	malta bajomalta contramalta	sanja bajosanja contrasanja	
Aymara *sikuri* (Bolaños 1988: 115)	Peru	chili (suli)	malta (ankuta)	sanja (bajo, basto)	
Aymara *sikuri* (Valencia Chacón 1989: 50)	Rosaspata, Peru	suli sulfa	ankuta ankuta dúo cantante	tayka tayka dúo barretón	
Kechua *sikuri* (Valencia Chacón 1989: 58)	Taquile, Peru	auka (chuli)	liku	maltona	mama
Aymara *chiriwano* (Valencia Chacón 1989: 65)	Huancané, Peru	chili	ankuta	tayka	
Kechua *ayarachi* (Valencia Chacón 1989: 71)	Paratía, Peru	suli	wala	lama	mama
Mestizo *pusamoreno* (Valencia Chacón 1989: 78)	Peru	ñaño (chili, requinto)	cantante (chaupi, maltona)	bajo (bastón)	
Chipaya *sikuri* (Baumann 1981: 189)	Bolivia	sanja	taipi (malta)		
Aymara *sikuri* (Bellenger 1981)	Bolivia	chehuli	likhu	malta	taika
Aymara *sikuri* (Díaz Gainza 1962: 186)	Bolivia	chchulis	likus	malta	taika
Aymara *sikuri* (Paredes 1936: 80)	Bolivia	chuli	mahala	tayka	
Aymara *sikuri* (Paredes 1936: 80)	Bolivia	tuto	chuli	liku	mahalta
Kechua *antara** (Bellenger 1981)	Bolivia	chilu	iskay	mamay	altu mamay

* *Antara* is the Kechua term for panpipe. The Bolivian tradition is referred to here because it follows closely the Aymara performance practice of interlocking parts, called *kkatik* for the follower and *pussak* for the leader. Notice that Valencia Chacón uses *sikuri* rather than *antara* for the Taquile Kechua. This interchange of nomenclature is currently common among Altiplano cultures who live close to each other.

breaking into circle dances at street corners, whirling while playing. In several of the traditions, such as some of the Aymara *sikuri* and the Kechua *ayarachi,* the *sikuri* musicians play drums while blowing their panpipes, a tradition spanning over a thousand years, as evidenced by similar playing techniques depicted on ceramic pottery of the Nazca civilization (Olsen 2002: 96). On the other hand, the *chiriwanos* use no percussion instruments whatsoever (Valencia Chacón 1989: 64). The method of blowing the pipes together as a single unit is another playing technique that requires careful attention. Turino (1989: 12) explains that the Aymara musicians themselves express how important it is to play as one, or to sound like one instrument: "No individual's instrument should ever stand out . . . from the integrated fabric of the ensemble's sound." The style should be "legato" and slightly overlapping, and never should the musician blow so hard that an overtone is produced (1989: 12–13); this is quite the opposite of the Chilean *chino* flute and the *pifülka* of the Mapuche. (See Thomas Turino, "Local Practices Among the Aymara and Kechua in Conima and Canas, Southern Peru," in this volume.)

Andean *sikuri* traditions often are imbued with symbolism, as expressed by the elaborate costumes of the musicians/dancers on particular occasions. One of the most symbolic is the Kechua *ayarachi* tradition, which "is related to the cult of the condor, considered a totemic bird among Andean cultures. The garments of *ayarachis* and a ceremony alluding to this bird are indications of this character" (Valencia Chacón 1989: 69). Not all the symbolism, however, is mythological or cosmological. It also can be sociological, as among the Aymara *chiriwano* groups, where two subgroups from neighboring communities musically interact in competition (Turino, cited in Romero 1987: 20). This once again returns to the symbolic concept of dualism, so important in the Andean worldview (Grebe 1974a: 47–50), which, when combined with the long-standing system of communal work effort, helps us to understand Andean musical expressions, so deeply rooted in ancient traditions.

Kammu purwi (Kuna: Panama) and *carrizo* (indigenous and mestizo: Venezuela). Numerous indigenous cultures other than the Aymara make use of panpipes in a dualistic manner. While the Aymara *siku* tradition thrives, performances on the *kammu purwi* by musicians / dancers are daily occurrences in all Kuna communities, and the *carrizo* tradition—which has lost some of its former vigor—maintains its currency among specific groups in Venezuela.

The definitive studies of *kammu purwi* Kuna panpipes (also known in the literature as *gammu-burui, kamu-purrui,* or *kammupurui*) are by Sandra Smith (1984) and by Ronny Velásquez (1992). Smith carefully integrates their uses into two categories: for power and for entertainment. Velásquez explains that, for the Kuna, the term *kammu* functions as an archetype whose meanings are submerged in mythical beginnings and transcend any literal translation. *Kammu* means hollowed cane (and therefore sonorous cane), tube, passage (metaphorically, the vaginal canal), the throat of the *kantule* (or *kamtule,* from *kammu* and *tule,* i.e., man) or specialist who knows the paths of the *kammus* and their secrets, and the singing of the shaman who knows the chants through which he communicates with the spirits of these canes. In essence, the term is perceived as a metaphor for a hollowed path of communication between the real world and the mythic time within which all the rituals and ceremonies presently practiced by the Kuna are situated (1992: 12).

The festive use of the *kammu purwi* panpipes derives from one of the longest and most splendid ceremonies of the Kuna. This is the *Inna suid* (long chicha) or *Inna wil'la* (deep chicha), the celebration that marks the onset of the Kuna girl's first menses and includes the ceremonial cutting of her hair. The ritual chant performed by the great shaman during this celebration, the *kammu ígala,* subsumes perhaps the most traditional religious structure of the Kuna because the ceremony of initiation of a Kuna woman is held when she reaches menarche and thus represents the birth of her life-giving powers. *Kammu ígala* means "through the paths of the sonorous canes," which are symbols of the paths of her uterus. Ceremonial actions allude to the origin of life, represented in offerings to the spirits of the flutes, which in mythic time were primordial beings living with the Sun (Ibelele or Kam-Ibe, from *kammu* and *ibe*) in the homeland of the Kuna. In anticipation of this ceremony, the *kamsuedi,* or "owner of the flutes," must select the canes, cut them, prepare them ritually, build the instruments, and make offerings to the spirits of the *kammus,* otherwise they will not lend their voices to the *kamsuedis* or bring fertility to the young woman (Velásquez 1992: 12–13).

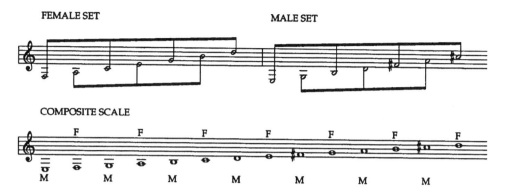

Ex. 4: Tunings of two complementary pairs of *kammu purwi* panpipes (Velásquez 1992: 14–17). Male tubes are identified by upward stems, and female tubes by downward stems. In the composite scale, M indicates pitches of the 7-tube male set, and F the pitches of the 7-tube female set.

The male *kammu purwi* has four stepped tubes, and the female has three stepped tubes. Each of these groups is rafted together, and both instruments are connected by a string that one musician hangs around the neck for the panpipes to reach breast level. The musician holds the male and female instruments in each hand, and brings the smallest pipes together to form two right-angled triangles joined at their points, as pictured in Izikowitz (1935 in 1970: 397) and Keeler (1960: Fig. 4). Moreover, the performance of melodies requires two interdependent sets of male and female instruments, namely a pair of musicians, who alternate and combine the pitches necessary to complete a melody. In the early twentieth century, Frances Densmore described this tradition of performance as follows: "Two sets are usually played together, one player sounding one tone and the other the next tone, alternating in this manner throughout the performance" (1925: 123). Each "set" of four male and three female tubes also is conceptualized as male and female. At this level, the gender of the composite instruments is defined by their different and complementary tunings, as well as by other characteristics. Both composite instruments are tuned on the basis of perfect fifths, maintaining a distance of a semitone between the lowest pitch of the male instrument ("e," for instance), and the lowest pitch of its female counterpart ("f"), the latter being a semitone higher (Ex. 4). Corresponding to the male and female tubes, the six perfect fifths of each composite instrument are divided into two cycles of four and three pitches each, which, when interlocked, define a sequence of minor and major thirds. When the pitches of both composite instruments are interlocked, they form a diatonic series over a two-octave range in which male and female pitches alternate (Ex. 4) (Velásquez 1992: 14–17). From the complementarity of tunings associated with gender at two levels, it can be surmised that the Kuna conceptualize each pitch as male or female. In performance, the female and male sets produce in a majority of cases a melodic texture in parallel fifths—and occasionally, other harmonic intervals—between the leader or *kamtule* who plays the female or "first" set of panpipes, and the follower or *kamtule* who plays the male or "second" set. Occasionally, a single musician can consolidate the role of both sets by conjoining the instruments to produce harmonic intervals of perfect fifths (and thirds) with a single emission of air. Most of the repertoire is performed by several pairs of male and female instruments, accompanied by an equal number of maracas (*nási* or *násisi*) that maintain an isochronous rhythmic pulse, and whose construction also is imbued with symbolism. (For an illustration, see Ex. 12 and Recorded Ex. 13 in Velásquez, "The Fundamental Role of Music in Two Central American Ethnic Nations: The Kuna in Panama," in this volume.) This perfect example of dualistic complementarity at two levels also can be conceptualized as quadripartition, with the male and female composite instruments as a holistic unit, itself divided into male and female parts, but this representation probably would not conform with how the Kuna themselves perceive the instrument(s).

These panpipes never are played in a static position, but by musicians / dancers. This is because the dancers embody the ancestral spirits that come to participate in a celebration, mimicking their gestures according to the occasion, and requiring—as do the spirits of the *kammu*—corn and cacao chicha (Velásquez 1992: 12–13). In ritual contexts, the panpipes are played by men and the maracas by women. In social contexts that are a part of everyday life in all Kuna communities, both men and women play the *kammu purwi* panpipes. Sandra Smith McCosker (1974: 20) recorded the following observation:

> It is heard at night when men come back from their work or when the village is celebrating a girl's puberty rites. On the last night of the four-day rites, when most of the villagers are quite intoxicated from their fermented cane [beverage], dancing and playing of flutes culminates the celebration.

Present-day youngsters also cultivate the skills required to play these instruments as a form of artistic expression. Although widespread in secular contexts, the *kammu purwi* retains the magico-religious character inherent to its tradition. It is played to establish relations between an individual and his/her sociocultural matrix, and the Kuna encourage the presence of specialists who teach young people the narratives describing the origin and secrets of the "sonorous canes" (Velásquez 1992: 20).

Venezuela has several panpipe traditions that are based on the concept of dualism, although some are on the verge of extinction. The most common name for panpipes in Venezuela is *carrizo*—a Spanish term for the cane that grows on river banks and is used to fabricate the instruments—and the major studies of them are by Isabel Aretz (1967). Chroniclers and travelers have documented the use of panpipes among Carib-affiliated groups, and from these references it can be surmised that present-day traditions practiced by *criollos* in eastern Venezuela are related directly to those of the Carib who inhabited the same areas in the past (García 1998: I, 330). Among some descendants of the Carib, the instrument is called *caramillo* (also referring to the cane). Moreover, one of its most widespread names is *mare-mare*, the term used not only for the cane itself (*mare*), but also for the indigenous dance-genre linked inextricably to panpipe music in its original context. Aretz points out that, from the eastern plains to the Orinoco River, the Carib sing and dance the *mare-mare* to music played on instruments of the same name (1967: 248). In Venezuela, all the panpipes—whether they are monistic, dualistic, or pluralistic—are played by men; only among the Macoa in northwestern Venezuela are panpipes played exclusively by women. At the present time, the panpipe tradition survives among several indigenous groups, including the Guahibo, Kariña, Panare, and Yekuana, who call these instruments *jiwa*, *verékushi*, *are're*, and *suduchu*, respectively; and among *criollos* in the states of Guárico, Sucre, and Monagas (Aretz 1967: 227; García 1998: I, 330).

Among present-day Guahibo living in the Federal Territory of Amazonas (Bolívar State), the panpipes have five rafted tubes, the longest of which remains loose. Melodies are played by pairs of female (*hembra*) and male (*macho*) instruments in an interlocking, complementary fashion, and the pair of musicians usually leads dancers who advance westward in circle formation (Alemán 1998: I, 331). The panpipes of a Guahibo-affiliated group studied by Aretz, however, are monistic, and several instruments perform simultaneously, creating heterophony, or two instruments overlap their respective motifs (1967: 240–43). In Kariña communities (Anzoátegui State), such as Cachama, Santa Clara, and Guanipa, the *mare-mare* is danced to the melodic and rhythmic richness of music played on panpipes they call *verékushi*, accompanied by creole instruments, such as the *cuatro* (a chordophone) and a drum. There are four types of *verékushi*: two are female, and two are male. The main panpipe (*prima*) is female, has three small tubes, and is the leader of the group; the *segundas* ("second" ones) are a six-tube male panpipe that follows the *prima*, and a five-tube female panpipe that guides the *tercera* ("third"), which is a six-tube male panpipe and the largest of the four instruments (Alemán 1998: I, 331).

The *carrizo* tradition maintains its currency among *criollos* in several communities in northern Guárico State (San José de Guaribe and Río Negro), and in the eastern states of Sucre (in the Valley of Cumanacoa) and Monagas (San Antonio and Ipure). In 1957, Aretz studied numerous *carrizos* among *criollos* in Cumanacoa, where a pair is conceptualized as female and male. The female member of a pair leads, and the male follows. These *carrizos* have five tubes, the largest male tube measuring about 15 cm in length, the largest female 14 cm, and the smallest about 5 cm (1967: 232–33). The tubes of the male instrument are slightly longer and tuned an approximate minor second higher than the female tubes, as seen in Example 5. The fourth and next to smallest tube of the

Ex. 5: The tuning system of a dualistic set of *carrizo* panpipes, recorded in 1957 by Aretz in Cumanacoa (1967: 234).

female instrument is called *prima*, and it is used to tune the panpipes to the *cuatro* or vice versa, depending on the key of the music.

Among *criollos*, Carlos García (1998: I, 330) identifies two techniques of performing melodies on sets of two or three basic *carrizos*, which are the most common groupings. In general terms, playing the pitches of a melody in an interlocking fashion—as do the Andean *siku* players—prevails in the Valley of Cumanacoa (Sucre), while in San José de Guaribe and Río Negro (Guárico State) the musicians play independent melodic motifs in juxtaposition. Regarding the dualistic *carrizos* that Aretz studied in Cumanacoa (Sucre), she explains that the members of a pair of instruments complement each other in their tuning, but in performance most of the time they play their motifs in juxtaposition, only occasionally interlocking their pitches. She also adds the following about the traditional form of playing:

> The *carrizo* called female carries the melody and the males follow her. Sometimes there are two female instruments; in that case, only one plays and the second replaces the first when it takes a rest from playing, because the female instrument is that which "does more work" (1967: 232).

Through this description it is clear that, although three panpipes are involved, the concept is still dualistic because the primary female instrument—which leads and carries the melody—is only assisted by the other female panpipe. (Aretz adds that the male part can involve from three to ten musicians who reinforce each other, playing what the practitioners themselves call the "accompaniment" in either unison or, more exceptionally, chords.) There is another tradition, however, that requires three basic instruments interlocking their parts in such a way that the dualistic concept is replaced by a pluralistic one. This is the case of the *mare-mare* panpipes recorded by Juan Liscano in Cantaura (Anzoátegui State), whose three members are named *mare prima* (or "first," with three tubes), *mare hembra* (the female, with five tubes), and *mare macho* (the male, with six tubes) (Aretz 1967: 237). The partial tunings of this set of pluralistic panpipes are provided in Example 6.

At the risk of confining living traditions to procrustean beds, Carlos García (1998: II, 176) has identified three categories of *mare-mare* performance traditions in Venezuela: indigenous, mestizo, and creole. The indigenous tradition is still retained by the Kariña, a group that has preserved its language, rituals, and principles of social organization, along

Ex. 6: Partial tunings of a set of pluralistic *mare-mare* panpipes: the *hembra* has five tubes, and the *macho* has six tubes. When these tunings were recorded, the musicians did not blow on all the tubes. The composite scale includes all the pitches that these panpipes should produce (cf. Ex. 7) (Aretz 1967: 237–38).

with their *verékushi* panpipes for performances of the *mare-mare*, of which Gustavo Martín has identified eleven types (cited in García 1998: II, 176). The mestizo *mare-mare* tradition is practiced mostly by *criollos* and preserves the panpipes; most likely it is accompanied by *cuatro*, maracas, and drum; and its music reflects an overlapping of indigenous and creole elements. The creole tradition is the most vigorous and widespread, and stands as one of the few expressions of indigenous origin that has become a part of the nation's cultural patrimony. The *mare-mare* tradition practiced by *criollos* may or may not include the panpipes; it is accompanied by *cuatro*, maracas, and a drum, to which other instruments can be added; and its musical characteristics—namely the use of periodic phrases within a sectional structure and a reliance on folk poetry in octosyllabic quatrains—are clearly of Hispanic provenance.

Aretz's transcription of the indigenous *mare-mare* recorded by Juan Liscano in Cantaura was performed by the three basic *mare-mare* panpipes whose partial tunings are provided in Example 6, with the male instrument duplicated, as is traditional among some indigenous groups. Each basic instrument plays its own motif, and the resulting music—particularly through the motif played by the male instruments, which adjust their D natural to a sharp—suggests Hispanic influence. The instrumental introduction to this *mare-mare*, preceding the entrance of the voice, is presented here as Example 7.

The symbolic significance of the Venezuelan *carrizo* and *mare-mare* is not known. Among *criollos*, performances nowadays take place on festive occasions throughout the year and are not associated with rituals. However, we can hypothesize that the use of pluralistic (rather than dualistic) sets of panpipes, as seen in the *mare-mare* from Cantaura, suggests a weakening of the Native American dualistic concept, which was undoubtedly pervasive in the instrument's autochthonous context.

The *antara* and a specific survivor from the past, the *kanchis sipas* (Kechua: Peru, and, specifically, the K'ero). While the *siku*, the *kammu purwi*, and other dualistic panpipes carry cosmological associations, some panpipes of a monistic nature also are imbued with great significance. Foremost among these single-unit instruments is the *antara*, an important instrument of the Kechua-speaking Inca, who often made it from human bones. Musical instruments made from human parts had great power, as Jiménez Borja (1951: 39) writes:

> The Incas, more than cane, metal, and ceramic, used bones to make tubes [for their flutes] . . . . These [*antara*] flutes made from human bones, just like the drums from human skin, most likely were not meant to be ordinary musical instruments. Instead, considering the infusion of the essence of the whole into the parts (bones, skin), their voices must have been perceived as something alive.

Today Kechua speakers and mestizos play *antaras* made from cane *(Phragmites communis)*, known as *carrizo* in Spanish. On the coast and in the Andes of Peru they are found in and near Trujillo in the north, and in the vicinity of Cuzco in the south, respectively.

Ex. 7: Introduction to a *mare-mare* song from Cantaura performed on a set of pluralistic panpipes (Aretz 1967: 246).

The monistic panpipe in northern Peru is pentatonic, has a primarily solo entertainment function, and often it is played by beggars. In southern Peru its use can be more ceremonial and it is associated with the communal aspects of rural life, as Jiménez Borja writes:

An *antara* from Sallaq Urcos [Quispicanchi, Cuzco] . . . is composed of four tubes of 28, 27, 25, and 24 cm in length. The tubes are joined by a fiber of agave plant and pitch, forming only one very rigid row. One of the tubes, the longest, has various turns of a white woolen thread around its bottom end, and also has an engraving of a cross in the cane. This tube is not played because it would bring bad luck to the community; therefore, the *antara* has only three useful tubes. The *cañari* functionary in charge of playing this *antara* walks around the roads and streets of the village from the early morning. The voice of the flute calls together the peasants to harvest the wheat. This is the mission of the *antara* (1951: 39).

The *antara* has been well preserved as an instrument of power among the K'ero, isolated Kechua speakers who live high in the eastern Andean cordillera in southern Peru at altitudes up to 16,000 feet above sea level. John Cohen writes the following: "Panpipes also are used by the K'eros. This instrument consists of a double row of seven tubes of cane, roughly one inch in diameter, ranging from 6 to 14 inches long . . . . The K'eros' name for these pipes is Kan chi si pas, which means 'Seven years an unmarried woman'" (Cohen in Holzmann 1986: 213). Rodolfo Holzmann (1986: 219) elaborates on this: "*Kanchis:* seven; *sipas:* unmarried girls. This *antara* has seven cane tubes, in a double row." The *kanchis sipas*, or K'ero *antara*, therefore, has only one row of seven tubes that can produce audible pitches; the second row consists of seven open tubes that function as resonators and are never directly played because of taboos attached to them (Cohen 1966: 5). Cohen also states that each playable tube "represents luck in a different area of life" (1966: 8). The *kanchis sipas* are so imbued with supernatural qualities that they had been neither recorded nor probably even heard by outsiders when Cohen investigated them in 1964. No further information is known about them except that they are "played only during the fiesta of Santiago [July 25], which is closely associated with fertility rites and marking of the animals. There are only three melodies

played on the panpipes and these have verses about the alpacas, the cows, and the sheep" (Cohen 1966: 8). The panpipe part is notated in Example 8 (the scale is given afterward) and the transcription reveals an extensive use of microtones. Does this indicate a pre-contact type of tuning system for the *kanchis sipas*, or does it suggest a type of "folk intonation," so prevalent in the Andes?

This example, recorded by Cohen, is followed on the recording by the same song as sung by a woman, and her tuning, transcribed in Example 9, is nearly a pentatonic scale, indicating that the concept in use is "folk intonation," if we consider the vocal version of the song to be the standard (an interesting point when one realizes that the tubes of any panpipe can be easily tuned). Turino (1989: 12) refers to this concept as "dense unison," which he describes as being "the preferred manner of performance [he is referring to aerophones] in which some players within an ensemble will blow slightly sharp or flat of the mean pitch series thereby producing a rich abundance of overtones and combination tones" (1989: 12).

Another point for comparison is the dualistic technique of playing the *kanchis sipas* by overblowing, which causes both the fundamental and the twelfth to sound at the same time. Although the overtones are much louder than the fundamentals, to the extent that the latter do not even register on a stroboscope, the fact that the female singer sings the fundamentals of the *kanchis sipas* and not the much more obvious overtones strongly suggests that the fundamental pitches are more important. Until further research is conducted, we only can speculate about the musical symbolism and the possible dualistic nature of the otherwise monistic *kanchis sipas*.

***Rondador* (Kechua and mestizo: Ecuador).** The *rondador*, a panpipe, is the most important traditional instrument from the Andes of Ecuador, and indeed, it could be considered as the country's national instrument (Fig. 5). The physically monistic *rondador* is distinct because of its visually irregular arrangement of tubes and because it is played by one person who single-handedly can perform two notes at a time, a dualistic technique. Although the origin of the Ecuadorian panpipe is pre-Columbian, the term *rondador* is Spanish, meaning "one who makes rounds." During the colonial period in Quito, Ecuador's capital, a nightwatchman used the panpipe to announce his presence as he made his nightly

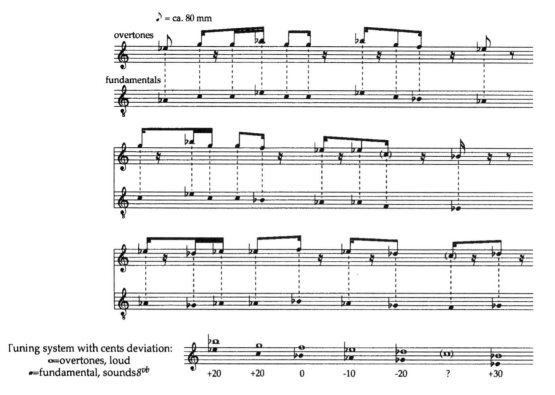

Ex. 8: A song for cows performed on a *kanchis sipas* panpipe of the K'ero, followed by the instrument's tuning system with cents deviation (Cohen 1966: side 2, band 3/A; transcribed by Olsen). "Cent" refers to a pitch measurement system that can accurately quantify microtonal differences by dividing the semitone into 100 equal parts.

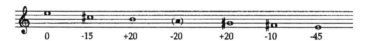

Ex. 9: Tuning system of the same song for cows (See Ex. 8), as sung by a K'ero woman (Cohen 1966: side 2, band 3/A; transcribed by Olsen).

rounds. The name has continued even though the *rondador* currently is played by rural and urban male musicians for rituals, festivals, entertainment, and even begging.

Historically, the four most common types of *rondadores* in Ecuador are the following:

(1) *Rondador* made from condor feather quills of diverse lengths. The feathers at the ends of the quills are maintained, and serve as ornamentation (*Artesanía folclórica en el Ecuador* 1971–1972). Coba Andrade (1981: 99) mentions the feathers of the *buitre* (vulture) as a material, but other sources do not mention feather quill *rondadores*, suggesting a discontinuation of the instrument's use.

(2) *Rondador* made from five small cane tubes (pentatonic), used in religious rituals (*Artesanía folclórica en el Ecuador* 1971–1972). Carvalho-Neto (1964: 367) explains that this small instrument is found only in the Province of Imbabura, and is played but once a year: "It is a ritual instrument . . .

only used in the festivals in homage to the sun, during the equinox of September" (Carvalho-Neto 1964: 367, citing Moreno Andrade).

(3) A 44-tubed (or more) double *rondador* played in a dualistic manner for religious rituals and festivals (*Artesanía folclórica en el Ecuador* 1971–1972). This instrument is not mentioned in other sources.

(4) *Rondador* that has from eight to more than thirty tubes, using a natural minor scale. It is played at festivals, for entertainment, and by beggars.

The fourth type is the most common panpipe in Ecuador today, and the one that is most closely identified with the Ecuadorian patrimony. Hence, use of the term *rondador* hereafter will refer to that popular instrument. The irregular arrangement of the tubes can be seen in Figure 5, and it is important to notice that the playing lengths of some of the tubes coincide with the nodes (natural joints), while the tubes themselves often continue beyond the node. Example 10a, a transcription of the musical scale of a *rondador* (whose notes sound an octave higher than notated), reveals the seemingly irregular and disjunct nature of the instrument's tuning system. This technique serves a very important purpose, however, because two pitches at the interval of a third are sounded together. The brackets in the tuning system indicate those that are blown simultaneously, and a harmonic analysis is provided because the *rondador* often performs with guitars, accordion, or other harmony-producing instruments of European derivation. Example 10b is a transcription of a typical Ecuadorian *sanjuanito* (the most popular dance genre in the Ecuadorian highlands) for *rondador*, in which the parallel thirds are evident. Today's *rondador* is no longer imbued with symbolism, as its pre-Columbian ancestors and their variants surely were.

Edge aerophones: end blown, ductless, simple tube with finger holes (see Table 1, IA, 1b).

Gammu suid **or** ***kammu suid*** **(Kuna: Panama and Colombia).** While very common in the Middle East (where it is known as *nay*), the simple edge aerophone with finger holes is rare in the Americas (Izikowitz 1935 in 1970: 306–11), although it was not always so. Archaeologically found gold effigy figurines from Panama depict musicians playing what are believed to be such instruments, and ancient graves from coastal Peru have yielded similar flutes made from bones (Izikowitz 1935 in 1970: 308). The *gammu suid* is a flute played in pairs (Smith 1984: 129–32), also known as *kammu* (Izikowitz 1935 in 1970: 307; Keeler 1960: 257–61), *kammusui* (Tayler 1972: 82), and *kammu suid* (Velásquez 1987). It is one of the most important sets of instruments of the Kuna because it is performed by the shaman and his assistant during the delivery of the ritual chant dedicated to the ceremonial cutting of hair of the Kuna girl, which is the core of the three-day celebration held when a girl reaches menarche (the *Inna suid* or *Inna wil'la*, which means "long" or "deep" chicha). The composite term *kammu suid* joins the many meanings of *kammu* (see *kammu purwi* above) to *suid* and refers to the performance of these flutes during the "long" chicha.

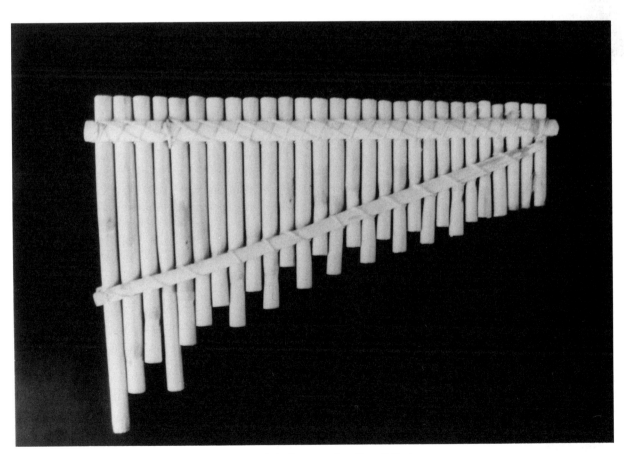

Fig. 5: A *rondador* from Ecuador. Olsen Collection.

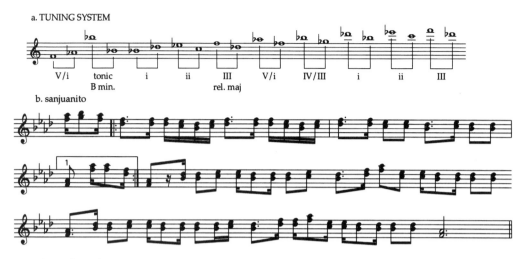

a. TUNING SYSTEM

b. sanjuanito

Ex. 10: A *sanjuanito* performed on *rondador* by Segundo Sandoval (Olsen, Sheehy, and Perrone 1987: 10–11), recorded by Karl Signell and transcribed by Olsen.

The concatenated nature of Kuna thought is manifested in the tradition of performance of the chant, the *kammu ígala*, which consists of 3,584 verses in sixteen sections that mark the various phases of the ritual. Its delivery during the *Inna suid* requires the two *kammu suid* flutes, which are played by the *kantule* and his assistant with their left hands; the maraca (called *násis*) that each of them shakes with the right hand, whether they are playing or singing; and the alternation between the delivery of a verse from the chant by the *kantule*, the reactive response by the assistant confirming the veracity of what the *kantule* has just said, and the resumption of flute playing by either, the *kantule* or the assistant, while the other is chanting, or both. The shaman and his assistant begin by playing a long opening on the two flutes while shaking their maracas; when the *kantule* is about to begin the chant, he separates the flute slightly from his lips and starts his singing. (For an illustration, see Ex. 9 and Recorded Ex. 7 in Velásquez, "The Fundamental Role of Music in Two Central American Ethnic Nations: The Kuna in Panama," in this volume.)

According to Smith (1984), these flutes are considered male and female, the latter being shorter than the former. Measuring between 50 to 80 cm in length, they are constructed from a thin type of cane. The proximal end of the flute consists of a simple horizontal cutting of the cane tube, while its distal end is cut below the node of septum of the cane. In order to keep the flute open-ended, however, a small hole is bored into the node. Two finger holes are made just above the distal end, and each flute "can produce two pitches, which are a neutral third apart. [Each] can be overblown to produce the same interval an octave and a fifth higher. The range of the female flute is a step above that of the male flute" (Smith 1984: 132). The maraca (*násis*) is constructed from a small calabash that is pierced with a bone from a deer's leg as a handle. As two of the most powerful tools of the *kantule* during the female puberty ritual, these instruments have suggested somewhat different symbols of fertility to observers. According to Keeler (1960: 257), the flutes symbolize the erect phallus of Olowaipippilele, the Sungod, while the maraca "represents the Earthmother's [Olokukurtilisop] uterus, and the deer bone handle symbolizes a child in the process of being born to the Earthmother." For Velásquez, and consistent with the meanings of *kammu*, the flutes represent the uterus of the menstruating girl, and their two finger holes allude to penetration of her hymen. This explains why the flutes are bathed in annatto (*Bixa orellana*), a red dye symbolic of blood, as well as in chicha, which represents the fecundity of semen. The maracas also suggest the Earthmother, but in the sense of a world that encloses the seeds and little stones embodying the spirits manipulated by the shaman.

Edge aerophones: end blown, ductless, notched tube with finger holes (see Table 1, IA, 1c).

Muhusemoi **(Warao: Venezuela).** Native American cultures from the tropical forests (Amazon basin,

Orinoco basin, eastern slopes of the Andes, Darién region of Panama, etc.) often take advantage of the natural tubes of animals for making single tubed, end-blown aerophones with finger holes. Even ancient cultures from the Peruvian coast and highlands, such as the Moche, Nazca, Chancay, Inca, and others, used bones from llamas, pelicans, condors, and humans to fabricate flutes. One of the most common tropical forest animals whose leg bones are used for flutes is the deer.

A common aerophone of the Warao from the Venezuelan Orinoco river delta is the *muhusemoi* (*muhu* = bone, *semoi* = wind instrument), a bone flute made from the tibia of a deer (Fig. 6). The Warao, who live in a large swampy jungle area containing hundreds of rivers, hunt deer for food.

The *muhusemoi* belongs to a subcategory of notched edge aerophones having a saddle-shaped cut where the flutist focuses his air stream. An instrument that may be an archaeological prototype of the *muhusemoi* is a bone flute from La Cabrera style in Venezuelan archaeology; however, it has a U-shaped notched mouthpiece (pictured in Cruxent and Rouse 1958: plate 38 A). Both the ancient instrument and the current *muhusemoi* flutes have three finger holes and no thumb hole.

The Warao flutist has a unique way of fingering his *muhusemoi*: he lifts off the bottom finger, returns it; lifts off the middle finger, returns it; and lifts off his upper finger and returns it. Only one finger hole is open at a time. Example 11 presents the tuning systems of three contrasting *muhusemoituma* (plural form). The only standard that exists is an approximate one, and variations of the tuning system are common.

The method of *muhusemoi* construction explains the lack of tuning standardization: the maker's fingers themselves are used as rulers. After he has acquired a fresh deer tibia, he opens both ends of the bone and removes as much marrow as he can with his knife. Then he places the bone out of reach of dogs, but within reach of cockroaches, which will eat out the marrow within several days. Once the bone has dried, the maker forms the saddle-shaped

Fig. 6: *Muhusemoi*, notched aerophone of the Warao, Delta Amacuro Federal Territory, Venezuela. Olsen Collection.

mouthpiece with his knife. Placing the mouthpiece in the crotch between his thumb and first finger, he makes a mark where the tip of his first finger falls. There he will drill the instrument's distal finger hole with the sharpened point of a harpoon, twisting the shaft between his hands like a fire drill. The harpoon point is so sharp that it takes about one minute to drill each finger hole. He then measures the distance for the second finger hole with the back of his thumb (from the tip of the thumb to the first joint). After drilling the second hole he uses the same technique to

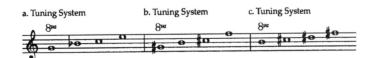

Ex. 11: Tuning systems of three *muhusemoi* flutes. Olsen Collection.

determine the placement of the third finger hole. Because Warao fingers and Orinoco Delta deer tibias all differ in size, there is no standardization in the tuning systems of the final products.

The *muhusemoi* is a man's instrument mostly used for ritual purposes, although it may be played for pleasure while walking in the jungle to cut down trees. Men play several *muhusemoituma* in the jungle while the women collect *yuruma* (*moriche* palm starch) to be offered to the deity Kanobo during the *nahanamu* harvest festival. During the festival itself, several *muhusemoi* flutes are played in ensemble with two *isimoi* sacred clarinets, several *hebu-mataro* rattles, and *sewei* anklet rattles (Recorded Ex. 1). For each of these *muhusemoi* musical contexts a different melody is used, and Example 12 is an excerpt from a melody used while gathering *yuruma*.

Although the *muhusemoi* is played during rituals, it is not an instrument with any particular power of its own. When asked if it contains a spirit, I was told by a powerful Warao shaman, *muhusemoi* maker, and player, "No, this instrument has nothing to do with a spirit. It has very little power . . . . That which has a spirit is the *isimoi*" (a single-reed concussion aerophone). He continued to explain that the instrument and its music come from ancient times, but that there is no particular myth about the flute's creation, nor did the origin of the music appear in a dream. Nevertheless, the *muhusemoi* players are held in great esteem, and they keep their instruments year after year in a basket hung from rafters in their piling houses. Occasionally, a musician will play his bone flute as he relaxes in his hammock.

Kena (Aymara, Kechua: Bolivia, Peru, Chile, Argentina).

The *kena* is a tubular aerophone whose sound is produced by blowing air across a notched mouthpiece (Fig. 7). It is known from pre-Columbian times in ancient Peru, Bolivia, and Chile. In coastal Peru, for example, ancient tombs of the Moche, Chimú, Chancay, Paracas, Ica, Nazca, and other civilizations, have yielded notched flutes made from numerous tubular materials, some vegetable and animal (including human), and some molded from geological substances, such as clay, silver, and gold. Most of the ancient exemplars have four finger holes, although some may have as many as seven. Besides the actual instruments themselves, pre-Columbian pottery from the same areas reveals notched flutes with three or four finger holes performed by priests, shamans, prisoners, death figures, and almost any other type of human except women (pictured in d'Harcourt 1925: vol. 2, plate 25). From these pots religious contexts for the flutes can be surmised, most of them pertaining to some aspect of supernatural communication, especially with regard to sex, fertility, death, and the afterlife (Benson 1975: 121). Many of these magical aspects of the *kena* persisted well into the historical period in certain areas of the Andes, as reported by Spanish and mestizo chroniclers. Especially prevalent is the role of the *kena* as a love charm, as Garcilaso de la Vega wrote in his *Comentarios reales*:

> With this flute [he] accompanied his love songs . . . . The story is told of a Spaniard who, one evening, upon meeting an Indian girl of his acquaintance on a Cuzco street, urged her to come home with him. "Señor," she replied, "kindly let me go my way. The flute you hear is calling me with such tenderness and passion that I can't resist it. Leave me, for your own life's sake; my love is calling me and I must answer him, that he may be my husband and I his wife" (1609 in 1961: 87).

More recent is an account summarized by Jiménez Borja (1951: 36), who writes about the "phallic connotations of the instrument, whose magic voice

Ex. 12: A Warao melody used while gathering *yuruma*, performed on a *muhusemoi* (Olsen Collection, transcribed by Olsen).

defeats death and nurtures life." The source of this account is the 18th-century legend of the *Manchay-Puito* in Ricardo Palma's *Tradiciones peruanas* (1872 in 1968: 790–93). The story involves the Mercedarian Friar Diego de Angulo y Valdivieso, priest of Yanaquihua in the diocese of Cuzco, a virtuous and learned man who was totally devoted to his flock and idolized by his parishioners.

One day, however, perhaps on San Bartolomé, "when the devil breaks loose and raises havoc," the mesmerizing Anita Sielles crossed his path and he succumbed to her charms. From then on, as if bewitched, the shepherd of souls neglected his duties and only dust covered his books. He lavished her with attention, and the Cupid's litany he was singing must have been effective, because one night she left her maternal home to taste the delights awaiting her in the parish residence. After six months of amorous encounters, Don Diego was called to Arequipa to attend to the sale of one of his properties, and the lovers parted with all the tears that accompany such occasions. The business in Arequipa was promptly resolved and, after squandering some money to adorn his beloved with pearls, diamonds, and dresses, he mounted his mule to return to Yanaquihua. Almost at the end of his journey, he met a distraught Indian with a message: "Love of my life, return to me, heaven or hell is separating us, my body fails me and I yearn for the last kiss." That wish was not to be granted: he reached Yanaquihua a few hours after her body had been buried in the church. He fell into silent despair, not shedding even a single tear. That night, however, when the town was asleep, he disinterred her, took her in his arms, and dressed her in the fineries he had brought for her. Then he took his *kena* ("the sublime flute with a voice so strange that it fills the heart with deep sorrow") and started to play it into a clay pot, improvising a *yaraví* that echoed his infinite anguish. This is the *yaraví* that the people of Cuzco know as *Manchay-Puito* (or terrifying hell). Its Kechua verses are filled with despair and raw images that range from the most delicate sensuality to the most explicit expressions of carnal passion. Terrified by the sounds of the *kena* and the lamentations of the poet, people were leaving their homes, dogs were barking, and this went on for three days. Then the *kena* stopped, and the Spaniard who had the courage to venture into the parish residence saw the most horrible sight: Don Gaspar was on the throes of death, embraced to the decomposed body of his beloved.

Such is the story of this popular tradition. Consequently, the Church threatened to excommunicate anyone who

Fig. 7: *Kena*, a notched aerophone from Bolivia. Smith-Olsen Collection.

would sing the *Manchay-Puito* or play the *kena* into a pot. "To this day, this prohibition is respected by the Indians of Cuzco, who would not surrender their souls to the devil for any amount of earthly riches" (Palma 1872 in 1968: 793). In another version of this tale, Don Gaspar arrived many months after the death of his beloved. Thereupon he disinterred her bones, fabricated a *kena* from her tibia, and played it into a clay pot (Jiménez Borja 1951: 36).

In spite of the fact that the Catholic Church banned the practice of playing the *kena* into a pot, Jiménez Borja presents a detailed description of such a mythical jar found in Huamanga, Department of Ayacucho: it has a small opening at the top for inserting the flute, two larger openings in the sides for the player's hands, and two eyelets on the sides so it can be suspended around the *kena* player's neck. If used, the jar must be moistened and contain water only up to a level where it will not touch the flute (1951: 37 and unnumbered photograph). Rigoberto Paredes (1936: 80), writing about Aymara musical instruments, briefly mentions a small animal bone flute called *manchaipuito* that is played into a clay pot, adding that "the people, however, believe this bone to be a tibia taken from the secretly exhumed remains of a beloved woman." Undoubtedly, this flute had taken its name from the *yaraví* in the Cuzco legend documented by Ricardo Palma, and is a part of the same tradition, as Paredes confirms: "No matter how bored or inebriated the Indians might be, they never play this flute for fear of damnation. However, there is always a mestizo who has the audacity to do it."

In spite of the numerous references in Peruvian archaeology and mythology, the term *kena* is not Kechua but Aymara. The Aymara, who inhabit large portions of Bolivia and smaller areas in northern Chile and southern Peru, originally referred to the instrument as *kena-kena*, emphasizing linguistic dualism. Today the singular form of the word is more common. Paredes (1936: 78) describes four notched instruments in Bolivia whose names reflect their differing sizes and number of finger holes: *kena* (50 cm in length, six finger holes and a thumb hole); *kenacho* (44 cm long, four finger holes and a thumb hole); *kenali* (thinner than the rest, with six finger holes and one thumb hole); and *pusi-p'iya* (meaning four holes, i.e., three finger holes and one thumb hole). This latter instrument is the largest of the Aymara *kena* types, measuring up to nearly 70 cm in length (pictured in Buchner 1972: Fig. 117). The Bolivian Chipaya also have a very large notched flute, called *lichiwayu*, which they use mostly during the months of May through July (Baumann 1981: 182). Additionally, *kenas* come in three sizes within many of the groups (González Bravo 1937: 27–28), called *taika* or *jajcha* (mother), *mala* or *malta* (middle, two-thirds the size of the mother, a fifth higher in pitch), and the *kallu* or *chchiti* (son or small, half the size of the mother, an octave higher in pitch).

Kenas presently are made from a variety of tubular materials, notably types of cane known as *chuqui* (González Bravo 1937: 26), *churqui* or *chhojlla* (Díaz Gainza 1962: 180), *chocella* (Vargas 1928: 9), or *mamac*, which grows to over a meter in length between nodes (Jiménez Borja 1951: 35). Other materials currently used are calabash, wood, plastic tubing, and copper pipes. This author observed *kenas* made of copper pipes at a festival in Ayquina in northern Chile, where the *kena* players were workers in the Chuquicamata copper mines.

In pre-Hispanic Peru the notched mouthpieces on cane flutes were carved from the inside of the tubes,

or from the outside in the shape of a V for bone flutes and as a U for silver or gold instruments. Today, however, they are cut on the outside either as a V or a U, conforming to the shapes of either a rat-tail or a square-shaped file.

The tuning systems of the *kenas* vary according to the number of finger holes they have, their quality of craftsmanship, or the region they are from. Most commonly a *kena* will sound the natural minor scale (Aeolian), from which the musician can perform tritonic, pentatonic, hexatonic, diatonic, or even chromatic scales. Modern *kenas* from Lima, La Paz, Paris, Mexico City, and other urban centers are tuned with nonequidistant finger holes, some larger than others, enabling the musician to play modern, equal tempered scales, without using cross-fingerings. Many traditional Andean players finger their *kenas* with two fingers on the top and three on the bottom, leaving the bottom finger hole open, or occasionally covering it with the little finger. Urbanized players, however, as well as many rural flutists, finger their *kenas* like a European aerophone, using three fingers of each hand. Some players place their right hand on the upper finger holes, and others their left hand, the latter seeming to be the most common. Modern instruments may have the bottom hole offset, requiring the musician to finger them much like a European recorder.

Performance styles vary, but the most traditional style consists of many ornaments and a fast vibrato. Modern players, some from European countries who now live in Lima and La Paz, and others who are members of such renowned pan-Andean groups as the Chilean Inti-Illimani and Quilapayún, the Bolivian Savia Andina and Grupo Aymara, and the Peruvian Urubamba, add extensive glissandi that have enamored world audiences with *kena* playing since the 1970s. Many of these "soulful" playing techniques have been copied by the Andean highlanders themselves in a type of cultural backlash. Because of the influence of recordings, ensembles with *kenas* can be found in places where the instrument has not figured into the traditional context, such as in northern Peru, Ecuador, Colombia, and central Chile. The Chilean *nueva canción* groups, such as Inti-Illimani and Quilapayún, chose the *kena* and other central Andean instruments, such as the *siku* and the *charango* (a small chordophone) as expressions of a renewed Native American identity. Additionally, the 1960s recording of "El cóndor pasa" by the North American popular group Simon and Garfunkel, backed up by the Peruvian ensemble known then as Los Incas and today as Urubamba, helped transform the *kena* into the most popular South American aerophone throughout the Western world. In this commercial and popular context, the *kena's* Native American symbolism as a male instrument of magical power has disappeared.

***Pina pinkulucha* (K'ero: Peru).** Possibly the purest forms of the notched flute, its playing techniques, and its music in the Andes, are found among the isolated Kechua-speaking K'eros of the eastern Andean cordillera in southern Peru, who call their instrument the *pina pinkulucha*. The only written information of significance on this instrument is by Cohen (1966: 7–8), who also gives the shortened form *pinkulu* and the Spanish *cana* [*sic*] as names for the flute. While we will see that the most common form of *pinkulu* (many spelling variants will be given) is a duct flute, among the K'ero it is a notched instrument, testifying to both the Aymara and the Kechua meaning for that term which, simply translated, means "flute" (Stevenson 1968: 259). Cohen explains that the *pina pinkulucha* is made from cane, has a rectangular notch, comes in a variety of sizes from 6 to 24 inches in length, has only four finger holes that are rectangular or square in shape, and the finger holes are equidistant in the bottom half of the tube. He further describes a unique manner of fingering the flute, which is to lift off only two fingers at a time, resulting in a total of four combinations: all covered, all off, upper two off, lower two off. As with the Warao system of fingering the *muhusemoi*, the K'ero method also produces music that is totally different from any other musics, whether European or Peruvian. Example 13 is a transcription of a *pina pinkulucha* flute melody of the tritonic type, based on the E–C#–A triad (Holzmann 1986: 240).

The playing technique and music performed on the *pina pinkulucha* is further elaborated by overblowing, producing octaves and other overtones, and rapid dual finger movements. Additionally, several instruments frequently play together in heterophony, each at its own pitch level as dictated by the flute's individual physical characteristics, such as size. The *pina pinkulucha* has a solitary secular function as an instrument of herders, and also a ritual one as a single or small group expression during planting, harvesting, and carnival (Cohen 1966: 7–8). Like the *kanchis sipas*, or *antaras* of the K'eros, and like the Aymara *kenas*, the *pina pinkulucha* is probably very symbolic. Unfortunately, a detailed study of the instrument and its cultural significance among its users has not yet been done.

***Tura* (descendants of the Ayomán and the Hirahara: Venezuela).** In the State of Falcón, near Caracas, and in bordering areas between the states of Falcón and Lara, live the descendants of the Hirahara (Jirajara) and Ayomán (also Ayamán), the latter a subgroup of the former. Aretz documented several pairs of edge aerophones used by them in 1947, each with a notched mouthpiece uniquely in the form of a W (1967: 210–14). The instruments, generically known as *tura*, are grouped into pairs that come in two sizes, the *turas grandes* (large) and *turas chicas* or *turos* (small). Additionally, each member of a pair is conceptualized by the musicians as female (*tura hembra*) and male (*tura macho*), with the latter differentiated from the former by a slightly longer and thinner size and, occasionally, one more finger hole (Aretz 1967: 210). The most common number of finger holes is three, although some have two and others have four.

The *tura* flutes are used for the performance of ancient corn rituals. The most important celebration is the fiesta of the *tura grande*, the harvest or dry corn ceremony, for which the large pair of *tura* flutes is

Ex. 13: *Pina pinkulucha* part from a song entitled "Wallata" (wild web-footed birds that fly in pairs), followed by the instrument's tuning system (Cohen 1966: side 2, band 1/A, transcribed by Holzmann [1986: 238–39]).

used. This is preceded by a smaller celebration, held when the corn is green, which requires the pair of small *tura* flutes. During the rituals the appropriate two flutes perform in an ensemble with a deer skull ocarina *(cacho de venado)* and maracas. The unusual bitonal manner of playing the two *tura* flutes has been notated by Aretz and appears as Example 14. Aretz adds that "... the upper flute is always slightly ahead by a fourth of a beat with respect to the lower, making their music very difficult to write down" (1967: 213).

Within the family of notched flutes, the *tura* is very unusual because of its bipartite notch in the shape of a W. Two other *tura* flutes collected by Aretz, however, have the usual U-shaped *kena* notch, perhaps showing influence from the central Andes, although we must not forget the ancient Venezuelan La Cabrera notched flute pictured in Cruxent and Rouse 1958: plate 38A, which also has a U-shaped notch and three finger holes. The W-shaped notch in most *turas,* and the instrument's paired use regarding both size and gender, suggest a dualistic symbolism. This hypothesis is further strengthened by the dualistic nature of the harvest festival music.

Edge aerophones: side blown, ductless, globular (see Table 1, IA, 2a).

***Cacho de venado* (descendants of the Ayomán and the Hirahara: Venezuela; Guahibo: Colombia).** The *cacho de venado (cacho venao)* is a globular flute made from the skull of a deer, with antlers intact. Between the antlers is a round hole which functions as an embouchure that is blown across, as a side-blown flute. The large opening formed by the neck of the animal is plugged with wax, and the instrument has no finger holes. The musician holds his deer skull flute by grasping an antler with each hand, raising the instrument to his lips to play. Among the descendants of the Ayomán and the Hirahara, in the states of Falcón and Lara, the *cachos de venado* are played in pairs or separately, depending upon the performance requirements (Aretz 1967: 200–202). When played in pairs, a *cacho grande* (large horn) and a *cacho pequeño* or *cacho chico* (small horn) sound their single notes together at the approximate interval of a fourth (Aretz 1967: 201). When they accompany the *baile de las turas,* a dance in celebration of the corn harvest, the *cachos de venado* have a secondary role to the *tura* flutes. During the dance in imitation of the hunt, however, which features the hunters and the hunted (with the latter represented by the *cacho de venado* performers), these deer skull flute players dance and play a leading role.

Closer to the Amazon, the Guahibo of present-day Colombia employed in the past the *cacho de venado* for a dance of the same name (Bermúdez 1985: 40). Among groups affiliated linguistically with the Guahibo who inhabit the plains of eastern Colombia and western Venezuela, however, the *cacho venao* is explicitly excluded from a dance (the *yarake*) performed during sowing festivals, and restricted to

Ex. 14: Corn harvest ceremony music performed by a pair of large *tura* flutes (Aretz 1967: 213).

ritual use and funeral rites in particular. For instance, the instrument is a requisite for the performance of the *Itomo*, the fourth and final phase of funeral rites comprising four ceremonies, each of which is characterized by its specific requirements. The use of the *cacho venao* characterizes the fourth and last phase, or *Itomo*. The instruments are played at the beginning of the ceremony, then thrown into lower ground to dispel evil spirits that still might harm the deceased, and retrieved an hour later to accompany a ritual dance, after which the dead person ceases to exist in the memory of the people (Yépez Chamorro 1999: 855) (Fig. 8).

Naseré **(Pilagá and other Native Americans of the Gran Chaco: Argentina).** While the term *naseré* is used by the Pilagá for their small wooden globular flute (Vega 1946: 185), other Native Americans of the vast Gran Chaco area employ similar instruments whose names do not appear in the literature. In Pilagá, *naseré* refers to an "object that produces sound when blown" (Irma Ruiz, personal communication to Kuss). Izikowitz (1935 in 1970: 292–94) refers to this instrument generally as the wooden whistle of the Chaco Indians. Both Vega

and Izikowitz trace the uncertain origin of the Gran Chaco globular flute to ancient Peru, where pre-contact examples from clay may have served as prototypes. The *naseré* globular flute is characterized by its disk-like flat shape, with a side-blown embouchure hole on one edge (the top or "north" edge), one finger hole on each side ("east" and "west" edges), and two suspension holes opposite the embouchure hole (near the "south" edge). Because of its shape the *naseré* may be an imitation of seashells from the Pacific coast (Izikowitz 1935 in 1970: 293), although its disk form and geometric exterior designs could just as well be in imitation of the sun. There seems to be no evidence of what the Gran Chaco Indians say about the symbolism of the *naseré*. Nevertheless, the small instruments are suspended around the musicians' necks, much like clay effigy figurine globular flutes were carried by musicians in many ancient civilizations (Olsen 1987). Indeed, Nordenskiöld (1919: 179) writes that "nearly every young [Gran Chaco Indian] man carries a small round wooden whistle," and Vega explains that it is used for personal amusement, or as a signaling device during hunting or warfare (1946: 187–88). According to

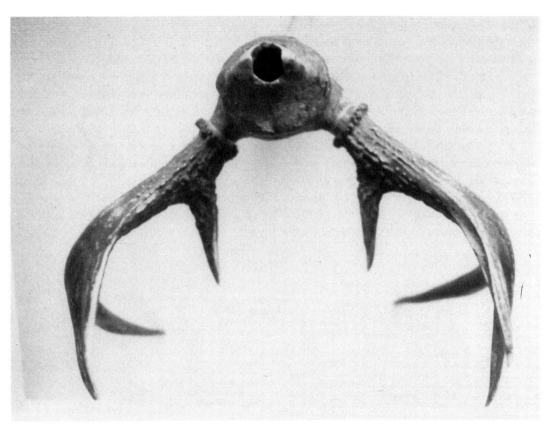

Fig. 8: *Cacho de venado* of the Guahibo, Colombia. Olsen Collection.

Irma Ruiz, who has studied the Pilagá, these instruments also were imbued with the power to seduce women.

***Tsin-hali* (Nambikwára and Paresí: Brazil).** Related to the *naseré* ocarina is a flat disk-shaped globular flute of the Nambikwára and Paresí from the Mato Grosso in Brazil, known as *tsin-hali* among the Paresí (Vale 1978: 33). Made from two similarly shaped pieces of gourd that are joined together with wax (Lévi-Strauss 1955 in 1974: 289), the *tsin-hali* has two finger holes and a side-blown embouchure hole that is blown with the musician's nose rather than his mouth. A Mato Grosso nose-blown ocarina in my possession measures about 9 cm in diameter. Lévi-Strauss (1955 in 1974: 289) explains that the Nambikwára produce "shrill calls" on their nose ocarinas, while Izikowitz (1935 in 1970: 328) mentions Curt Sachs's theory that nose flutes have symbolic significance, cautioning—however—that there is no direct evidence from either the Nambikwára or any other Native Americans to support Sachs's theory in this region.

Edge aerophones: side blown, ductless, single tube with finger holes (see Table 1, IA, 2b).

***Pitu, pfala*, and other transverse flutes from Peru and Bolivia.** *Pitu* is the Kechua and Aymara pronunciation of the Spanish term *pito*, which means simply "whistle." In the Peruvian highlands the instrument is a side-blown edge aerophone, also known in English as a transverse or cross flute, an instrument with many names throughout the Andes. Its most common distribution is in southern Peru, where often it is performed alone (Cohen 1966: 8); in ensemble with many other *pitus*, and Western snare and bass drums (Turino 1989: 8, 11); or with harp, violin, and drum (Arguedas 1977: 16). Although the origin of the instrument may be European, the traditions associated

with it are indigenous. As Arguedas has stated, the ensembles "accompany a great number of dances whose music is pre-Hispanic" (1977: 16).

In Conima, Peru, the transverse flute also is known by its Aymara name, *falawatu* (Turino 1989: 6), a term similar to its counterpart in Bolivia, which is *pfalawita* or simply *pfala* (González Bravo 1938: 171). The Conima *pitu* is made from cane, has six finger holes, and is played throughout the year in three-part ensembles that perform in parallel fashion. Similar to the *sikuri*, the three levels are known as *suli* (smallest), *ankuta* or *malta* (middle), and *sanja* or *tayka* (largest). The *ankuta* or *malta* group performs the main melodic level, which can be a fourth or a fifth above the *tayka*, depending on the particular cultural context (Turino 1989: 8–11).

Among the Kechua-speaking K'ero the *pitu* is played alone by herders, or with drums during the Catholic celebration of Corpus Christi. According to Allard (see Discography, *Musiques du Pérou*, side B), who calls it both *pito* and *pinquillo* (Kechua and Aymara for "flute," usually a duct flute), the instrument has seven finger holes, although Cohen (1966: 9) maintains it has only six. In its festival context the *pitu* performs the representational dance of the Chunchos (or Chunchus), a generic name for neighboring rain forest peoples to whom the K'eros are linked in legends. Example 15 is a transcription of "Chuncho" music played by a K'ero on his *pitu*.

Perhaps because of its association with the Catholic feast, and with its use as a solo instrument performed by herders to pass away the time, the K'ero *pitu* does not seem to carry strong symbolic meaning, as do other K'ero aerophones already discussed. Its music, however, reveals no elements that can be identified as "European," or suggests similarities with any other Andean musics, except for a more virtuosic technique in comparison with that of the *pina pinkulucha*.

Ex. 15: A K'ero melody on the *pitu*, performed during the celebration of Corpus Christi (Cohen 1966: side 2, band 2/C, transcribed by Olsen).

***Tunda* and other transverse flutes from Ecuador.** Several types of transverse flutes are found in Ecuador, of which the *tunda* flutes are the largest. The smaller instruments often are referred to simply as *flauta*. All the transverse flutes are made from several varieties of cane, and are held nearly vertically for the *tunda,* and horizontally either to the left or right for the common *flautas* (Fig. 9). The *tunda* is a ritual instrument played by the Quichua (= Kichua, Kechua) of Imbabura and Pichincha during the Catholic religious celebrations of St. John and St. Peter (Coba Andrade 1981: 95). The musicians play their flutes while large bells attached to their backs resound to their dancing movements. The *tunda* flutes come in three long sizes, from over one meter to about 3/4 of a meter in length, and have three, four, and two finger holes respectively, from longest to shortest. Carvalho-Neto (1964: 410) describes the *tunda* as having a wooden mouthpiece that fits into the proximal end of the flute, while a large cow horn is attached to the distal end. He continues to explain how, at one point in a religious festival, *tundas* are used as weapons during a battle

reenactment, and consequently are broken at the height of the fighting.

The more common six-finger-holed *flauta* has a secular role as well as a ritual one among the Quichua peoples of highland Ecuador. It is played by children as well as adults, for festivals, work, around the house, and for general entertainment (Coba Andrade 1981: 96). For that reason the men and boys carry them by a string around their waists (Carvalho-Neto 1964: 208). When *flautas* are used during festivals and religious rituals, two of them are performed together and are referred to as male and female (Coba Andrade 1981: 96).

***Pinkulwe* (Mapuche: Chile).** The only aerophone with finger holes among the Mapuche of south-central Chile and Argentina is the *pinkulwe,* a transverse flute with four finger holes, measuring about 40 cm in length. Made from bamboo known as *quila,* the nodes are burned out with a red hot poker of iron or bamboo. The mouthpiece and finger holes are likewise burned in. Chilean scholars (Isamitt 1937: 63–64) suggest a

Fig. 9: Transverse edge aerophones from Ecuador. Sigmund-Olsen Collection.

northern influence for the *pinkulwe* because of the linguistic similarity between it and the Kechua-Aymara *pinkullo*, a possible connection already mentioned for the *pifïlka (pifülka)* of the Mapuche. Nevertheless, unlike the northern instruments and the *pifülka*, the *pinkulwe* has only an entertainment function and a solo role, as Isamitt explains:

> It is in the middle of the countryside, and within the intimate setting of the *ruka*, or when the Indian feels the impulse to create something delicate, candid, and sweetly consoling, that one expects to hear the pastoral voice of the *pinkulwe*. The Araucanian boys are accustomed to spontaneously using *pinkulwes* made from tubes of hemlock, making them in a few minutes, with great ease. With them they amuse themselves while they venture into the countryside, or when they herd their animals (1937: 65).

Pífano (folk instrument: northeastern Brazil). The *pífano* (also known as *pífaro, pife, taboca, gaita,* and *búzio* or *buzo*) is commonly a transverse, or side-blown, flute (Rocha and Oliveira Pinto 1986: 92). Usually with a bass drum (*zabumba*), one or two smaller side drums (*tarol*), and a pair of cymbals (*pratos*), two *pífanos* are played together and carry the leading role in the *banda-de-pífano*. This small ensemble is found throughout the Northeast, from Piauí to the south of Bahia, and is known also as *zabumba, banda-cabaçal, esquenta-mulher,* and *banda-de-música-de-couro*, the latter referring to the leather of the bass drum (1986: 90) (see also Elizabeth Travassos, "Oral Traditions of Northeastern Brazil," in these volumes). The *banda-de-pífano* tradition is associated particularly with places such as Caruaru (Pernambuco) (Crook 1991), and with the Cariri, a region in the State of Ceará that is located in the somewhat isolated *sertão* or backland of Brazil's dry northeast, where archaic European characteristics are preserved. *Bandas-de-pífanos* also are found in the states of Minas Gerais and Goiás.

The *pífano* is an instrument of Portuguese provenance. Although in a majority of cases the two instruments of each ensemble are of the same size and tuning, sizes and tunings change from region to region. In Pernambuco, the largest *pífanos* range from 40 to 50 cm in length (*regra inteira* or full length), and others from 30 to 35 cm (*três-quartos* or three-fourths) (Rocha and Oliveira Pinto 1986: 93). These transverse flutes are made of a type of bamboo (*taquara* or *taboca*) reinforced by metal rings, and also of metal or plastic tubing, and are called *pife*, the popular form of *pífano* or *pífaro*. They have seven finger holes, one of which is used as the embouchure, which are bored with a red-hot iron. Metal reinforcement rings around particular regions of the tube are used to keep it from splitting and for ornamentation.

Although the *pífano* is a diatonic instrument, the concept of diatonic steps and modes (major or minor) is applicable only with "deviations" in comparison to the Pythagorean and/or just intonation tuning systems, and equal tempered tuning. The intervallic structure of the following G scale (from g′ to g′′), given in cents, represents the average between corresponding pitches of a pair of *pífanos* from Cabo (Pernambuco), which were carefully tuned in relation to each other. These are shown at the top, with the corresponding intervals in equal tempered tuning at the bottom (Rocha and Oliveira Pinto 1986: 104):

	180		170		140		220		190		120		180	
g′		a′		b′		c′′		d′′		e′′		f′		g′′
	200		200		100		200		200		100		200	

The following table shows intervallic measurements in relation to the tonic in these two *pífanos*, as compared with equal temperament, Pythagorean, and just intonation systems, all measured in cents:

	Two *pífanos*	Equal temperament	Pythagorean	Just intonation
Second	180 = 10/9	200	204	204 = 9/8
Major third	350	400	408	386
Fourth	490	500	498	498
Fifth	710	700	702	702 = 3/2
Major sixth	900	900	906	884
Minor seventh	1020	1000	996	996
Octave	1200	1200	1200	1200 = 2/1

This comparison reveals a very special "neutral third" (or average between 316 and 386, respectively the minor and major thirds in the acoustically "pure" just intonation); a small whole tone of 180 cents (i.e., the 10/9 ratio instead of the 9/8 ratio equal to 204 cents in the Pythagorean and just intonation systems); a "soft" or contracted fourth; and a slightly higher fifth. Rocha and Oliveira Pinto point out that the unique timbral color of these instruments surfaces in the harmonic intervals produced when both *pífanos* play together, stressing the value placed precisely on the two "neutral" thirds (g′–b′ and b′–d′′), which are emphasized by longer time-values and at cadences. The musicians could "correct" the thirds in performance, but this is seldom the case, and therefore "the meaning of this tuning as an expression of aesthetic values should not be underestimated" (1986: 104–105). César Guerra-Peixe (1970) has studied the scales produced by *pífanos* in Caruaro (Pernambuco), which are distinguished by their pitch content, range, and intervallic structure.

Musical contexts for the *banda-de-pífano* are varied and numerous. These ensembles parade the streets soliciting alms for a Catholic festival, accompany processions, and play at weddings, baptisms, dances, and civic celebrations. In Crato (Ceará), the *bandas-cabaçais* perform acrobatic choreography when they play in public places (Figueiredo Filho 1962: 82–83). Pieces may be composed by members of the group or adapted to their instrumentation. The repertoire of *bandas-de-pífanos* includes marches (usually named after the occasion), *dobrados*, *polcas*, *choros*, *tangos*, *baiãos*, and *quadrilhas*, as well as *benditos* and popular Catholic hymns, with the flute duo carrying the traditional melodies (see Elizabeth Travassos, "Oral Traditions of Northeastern Brazil," in these volumes). *Bandas-de-pífanos* attained national prominence shortly after the noted singer and composer Gilberto Gil "discovered" them in the early 1970s (Rocha and Oliveira Pinto 1986: 92).

Edge aerophones: end blown, detachable duct (see Table 1, IB, 1).

Atuñsa (Yuko / Yupa: Colombia, Venezuela) and *kuizi* (Kogi: Colombia): "hatchet" flutes. The colloquial term "hatchet flute" has been given to these duct edge-aerophones because their mouthpiece mechanism has been likened visually to an axe blade, and the tube to an axe handle. Made of a large black clump of flattened beeswax mixed with charcoal, the "hatchet blade" duct mass functions to hold the thin turkey or eagle quill duct tube in place. *Atuñsa (atuja, atunja, atuunsa, atunse)* is the name given to the instrument among the Carib-speaking Yuko (in Colombia) or Yupa (in Venezuela), who live in the northern section of the Sierra de Perijá range, bordering Venezuela and Colombia (Wilbert 1974: 3–5). With the cane tubular flute body measuring over a meter in length, the feather quill pierces the mass of beeswax at an angle, enabling the musician to hold his instrument in a transverse manner while blowing into the quill like a soda straw.

The distal end of the quill nearly touches the edge of the cane tube's proximal end, making the instrument an end-blown edge aerophone. The *atuñsa* has four finger holes and is played alone or in a pair. In Recorded Example 2, a Yuko man (Maraka subtribe) is playing his *atuñsa* with a bird imitating him (or is he imitating the bird?).

When two *atunse* are played together, they are referred to as male and female, as the following folk tale suggests:

Oséema [the Yupa culture hero] ran into the mountains and there he met his companion Kīrīkī (Squirrel), who accompanied Oséema on all his journeyings, since he was invisible to mankind for the most part. Oséema related to Kīrīkī all that had befallen him, and together they decided to forsake mankind and earth. Thereupon they made two *atunse* and set out upon their way, making music as they went. Along their way they happened upon a Yupa village. Three adult women and three girls came running out to meet them, so curious were they about the delightful music. They asked them why they had made these rare instruments and why they made music on them. Oséema explained to them that these were *atunse*: a large one (male) and a little one (female), which he and his companion played as they proceeded on their journey. The women were much taken by the beautiful music and bade the wanderers to tarry a few days (Wilbert 1974: 128).

The *atunse* is a powerful musical instrument associated with fertility because the culture hero Oséema, its creator and first performer, is presumably responsible for introducing corn to the Yupa, as the tale continues:

[Oséema and Kīrīkī] played upon their musical instruments [*atunse*] until midnight. Then suddenly Oséema broke off the music and ordered the women and girls to prepare little fields round about their houses. The women, not knowing how to conduct themselves at first, obediently followed the example of Oséema. He showed them everything, and after this work was done he distributed among them kernels of corn which he carried on his head. He asked them to throw these kernels upon the prepared fields. After all kernels had been sown, the women went back to their houses to rest for the remainder of the night after the strenuous work. During the night the maize sprouted, grew high, and ripened. In the fields, batata, *auyama*, and bananas were also growing (Wilbert 1974: 129).

The legend concludes by telling how the Yupa, to this day, continue to play the *atunse* so that Oséema will give them an abundant harvest. Scholars, however, seldom mention that, today, the *atunse* is played in a pair (Aretz 1967: 224; Bermúdez 1985: 63).

Northwest from the Sierra de Perijá, across the Cesar River Valley and on the slopes of the Sierra Nevada de Santa Marta in northern Colombia, live the Chibchan-speaking Kogi, Ika, and Sanká. The "hatchet" flute, which they call *kuizi,* is also an important means of musical expression for them, although it is much smaller in body length and duct mass, and is held vertically. It is well documented among these possible descendants of the ancient Tairona that *kuizi* flutes are played in pairs. Known as *kuizi hembra* and *kuizi macho* (female and male), the former has five finger holes and the latter has one (Tayler 1972: 14). Other indigenous groups in this area also call the instrument *charu* or *púnkiri.* Both flutes are played by men: the elder plays the five-holed female flute with the fingers of both hands, and the younger man shakes a maraca in one hand while playing the single-holed male flute with the other. In 1965, George List (1983: 65–71) recorded two Spanish-speaking men of "Indian descent" playing two "*carrizos*" and a maraca in the mestizo Kogi village of Atánquez near Valledupar, noting the similarities—in size, respective number of finger holes in the female and male flutes, and tradition of performance (the player of the male flute shakes the rattle)—between these "*carrizos*" and the *kuizis* played by the Kogi. However, List did not identify the "Indian descent" of these men as Kogi. In Atánquez, four decades ago, this ensemble of two flutes and maraca was called *conjunto de carrizos* (a generic term for cane flutes) and accompanied the *chicote,* a round dance (1967: 119–20; 1983: 68–71). List adds that his informants in Atánquez considered both, the flute they called "*carrizo*" and the *chicote,* to be indigenous. Furthermore, he mentions that a British expedition in 1961 recorded two similar flutes and a maraca played by two Kogi men in San Miguel in the Sierra Nevada, where the instruments were called *gaitas* (1967: 120).

Gaita (mestizo: Colombia). As the indigenous "hatchet" flutes made their way from the Kogi settlements into the more mestizo villages and cities of northern Colombia, the axe blade duct mass became smaller, the instruments held vertically, the tubes made from cactus (*Selenicereus grandiflorus*), the music more secular, and their name taken from the Spanish word *gaita.* In Spain and Hispanic America, *gaita* (a generic term for "pipes") is the name given not only to several morphologically different types of aerophones, including bagpipes, but also to a number of musical expressions and danced genres (Pérez Lorenzo *et al.* 1999: 304–13). The instrument called *gaita* in Colombia is the indigenous "hatchet" flute with the changes noted above. It measures from 60 to 70 cm in length, retains the five finger holes for the *gaita hembra,* the player of the *gaita macho* also shakes a maraca, and is an interdependent instrument played mostly in pairs. According to Flórez Forero and Yépez Chamorro, however, the *gaita macho* has two finger holes. The female flute carries the melody, and the male flute has a more rhythmic role, marking the beat and accentuating the last pitches of each measure (1999: 310).

In addition to the changes noted above, List (1967: 120–21) recorded a *gaita* ensemble in San Jacinto (Department of Bolívar) consisting of indigenous female and male flutes, maraca, African-derived membranophones (*tambor mayor* and *llamador,* known on the Coast also as *tambor hembra* and *macho*), and singing in Spanish. In reference to the flutes, which measured 90 cm in length, he remarks that the male flute "utilized in San Jacinto was exceptional in having two finger holes" because most of the *gaitas macho* he had observed had one finger hole. "However, in almost all performances [of the San Jacinto ensemble], one of the two finger holes was closed with wax" (1983: 68). The same applied to the five-holed female flute, whose upper or lower finger hole also was closed with wax. Most importantly, this ensemble belongs to the unique "tri-cultural heritage" that List documented in his classic study of musical traditions in the village of Evitar (1983), as one of the syncretic blends that matches the demographic composition of this tri-ethnic region.

Edge aerophones: end blown, built-in duct (see Table 1, IB, 2).

Uru'a (Kamayurá: Brazil). Although each flute in the two-tubed *uru'a* of the Kamayurá has a built-in duct, a portion of the apparatus responsible for the instrument's sound production is detachable. This portion is a deflector of the airstream that, together with its beeswax mount, can be removed and replaced. Without it, however, the instrument cannot be made to sound. As such, the *uru'a* is very similar to the Indian courting flute of the North American Great Plains, which also has a detachable deflector. The sounding principle of detachable deflector is always the same: the musician's air enters the duct, is forced out through a small hole on the proximal side of a plug (the natural node of the bamboo with the *uru'a*), hits the deflector, which forces the airstream down, against the edge of another hole on the distal side of the plug, thus creating the sound. The *uru'a* consists of two duct flutes without finger holes, constructed from bamboo tubes measuring up to 2.2 meters (Menezes Bastos 1978: 117). The two tubes of each *uru'a* are rafted together and the instrument is played in pairs. Two musicians (each playing two notes, plus one produced by overblowing) interlock and overlap their five notes to create the music.

Uru'a flutes are performed during *kwarìp*, an intertribal ritual complex of the Upper Xingu region of Brazil that commemorates deceased men of great prestige and celebrates the symbolic union of young people in marriage in the presence of their ancestors, thus ensuring the perpetuation and increase of tribal members (Oberg 1963 cited in Hill 1979: 423). Similar flutes also are used by other indigenous groups for this intertribal ritual in the Upper Xingu, although these are given other names. The first part of *kwarìp* is solemn and the second festive, with the latter featuring song and dance, food, wrestling, and *uru'a* flute playing. During the first phase of transition between the solemn and festive parts of the ritual, the *uru'a* are played in the flute house by two young men throughout the first night until daybreak while men gather at the grave site of the deceased being honored. At sunrise, pairs of *uru'a* players appear on the plaza, and they dance from the flute house to the grave site, then to the house of the director of ceremonies, and finally—having multiplied by the addition of new pairs of *uru'a* players and dancers emerging from different houses, including women and small children—they go from house to house around the village, moving in counterclockwise direction. After feasting and several wrestling bouts, beginning in the next early evening, "pairs of *uruá* dancers go around the village and are joined by young women who have recently left puberty seclusion. The women dance behind the men with one hand on the shoulder of the dancer in front" (Hill 1979: 425).

In the context of other rituals—namely the *yaku'i*, which at one level polarizes relations between village men and women on the one hand; and the bamboo (*takwara*) dance, which at the same level polarizes relations between the Kamayurá and outsiders on the other hand—*kwarìp* is a ritual of integration that, at a higher hierarchical level of communication, creates bonds between men and women, as well as between hosts and guests. Moreover, in Jonathan Hill's interpretation, *kwarìp* integrates the ecological time of *yaku'i*, which is celebrated at the beginning of each year's dry season, and the social time of the bamboo dance, which is held whenever the community is struck by misfortune, because *kwarìp* takes place at the beginning of the rainy season (ecological time), but only in years when a prestigious man has died (social time) (1979: 429). All three ceremonies require aerophones: however, the three instruments for *yaku'i* and the *uru'a* for *kwarìp* are technically flutes, and the long *takwara* most likely used for the dance of the same name is an idioglottal single-reed concussion aerophone (see *Tarawi* and *takwara* [Kamayurá: Brazil] below). Furthermore, from analyses of their respective music, Hill proposes a correlation between musical process and ritual function. While the music of the trio of *yaku'i* sacred flutes for *yaku'i*, which is held to bring helpful spirits into the community, expands through lengthening of phrases and addition of pitches in the course of a performance, the music of the *takwara* for the bamboo dance, whose function is to cast away harmful spirits brought into the community by contact with outsiders, contracts by shortening of phrases and deletion of pitches. In this context, the *uru'a* flute music for *kwarìp*, whose function is to integrate opposites at a meta-level of communication, mediates by exclusion of "apparent syntactical changes," remaining constant throughout a performance and emphasizing repetition (Hill 1979: 429).

The *uru'a* is one of the few indigenous flutes that women are allowed to play, but only during one phase of the ritual and never during the symbolic portions of *kwarìp*. Nor do the men need special religious status to play the *uru'a*; rather, their inducement to perform—beyond the traditional role of the *uru'a* in the celebration of *kwarìp*—is aesthetic, as Pedro Agostinho, who studied this ritual, explains: "The *uru'a* players are spontaneous and motivated by the desire to earn [fish] . . . . But the real motivation is to exhibit themselves with great pomp and to gain prestige as good dancers and flute players" (1974: 112 cited in Hill 1979: 427).

***Pito* (Cora: Mexico).** Although *pito* simply means "whistle," this instrument of the Cora in the State of Nayarit, Mexico, has a complex mouthpiece construction, giving it a place in the evolution of duct edge aerophones, between detachable deflector duct flutes (such as the *uru'a* and North American Indian courting flutes), and duct flutes without detachable parts (as in the *yaku'i*, the *pinkullo*, and the recorder). Constructed from cane *(carrizo)* or metal, with five to seven finger holes evenly distributed along its top, the instrument strongly resembles ancient Mexican ceramic beak flutes *(flautas de pico)* because of its protruding mouthpiece construction, which looks like a bird's beak (see photographs in Martí 1968: 342, and Téllez Girón 1964: 99-100). A Cora *pito* measures about 25 cm in length, with about 4 cm of that being the mouthpiece beak (Téllez Girón 1964: 100-101). Initially the proximal end of the cane (or metal) tube is cut about 3/4 of its diameter, leaving the remaining 1/4 to protrude about 4 cm as the mouthpiece beak. This open tube is filled with a plug extending only several centimeters into the tube, to the point where a rectangular hole is cut in line with the beak. Precisely over the beak and covering all but several millimeters of the rectangular hole is placed a perfectly cut piece of cane whose curvature is slightly more acute than that of the tube. When this piece is lashed around the tube a small duct is formed between it and the original protuberance. This detachable portion of the duct functions as part of the duct proper as well as a deflector, causing the musician's airstream to strike the sharp edge of the rectangular hole to produce the sound.

The *pito* is played exclusively by Cora Indian men during Holy Week, between Ash Wednesday and Good Friday (Téllez Girón 1964: 97). For several days and nights the only music heard in a Cora village are the *tonos de Cuaresma*, as each man plays his version of the same "tune," sitting in front of the door of his house. The *pito* melody is performed unaccompanied, and is described as being profoundly pastoral, melancholic, and almost mystical (1964: 97).

***Yaku'i* (Kamayurá: Brazil).** The *yaku'i* is an edge aerophone with a built-in non-detachable duct. Inside the proximal end is a beeswax plug into which the duct is formed, used for directing the musician's air against the edge of a small square window on the upper dorsal part of the flute. Its tubular body is fabricated from a piece of wood, which is split in half, hollowed out, and joined together again with beeswax and bound with fibers. At the extreme distal end of the meter-long flute are four finger holes. Three Kamayurá men—a "master of music" and his assistants—perform upon three *yaku'i* for the ritual of the same name (Menezes Bastos 1978: 118–19). Seated on low benches in front of the sacred flute house in the center of the village square, the master of music in the middle, the assistants begin and continue to blow into their flutes with barely audible, rapid rhythmical reiterations on selected pitches. These are followed by the master's louder, sustained melody, emphasizing a minor third interval, changing to a major third as the music progresses.

The *yaku'i* ritual complex is associated with spirit-mothers of fish, and is held at the beginning of the dry season, in April, to bring about bountiful fishing to the Kamayurá during a time when fish becomes the most important part of their diet. The music of the three *yaku'i* sacred flutes is integral to a dance that summons spirits from the forests and streams to the village, because these "are believed to bring good health and strength to the men." As male-dominated music played for the *yaku'i* ritual, which Hill defined as "a re-enactment of the mythical triumph of male fishermen over female horticulturalists in the struggle for control over the sacred flutes," women are forbidden to even see the sacred instruments; were they to do so, they would risk "being gang-raped by all the men of the village" (Hill 1979: 418). As the *yaku'i* flutists play their music, other men in the village dance next to them in the square; the women and children stay hidden in their houses, out of hearing range and sight from the music and dance.

***Pinkullo* and its linguistic variants (Aymara and Kechua: Peru, Bolivia, Chile).** Along with the central Andean *kena*, the *pinkullo* has a wide distribution from northern Chile to northern Ecuador. The term is used by both the Aymara and the Kechua, and a great variety of spellings are given to accommodate its many pronunciations, including *pinkullo (pincullo)*, *pingollo*, *pingullo*, *pinkillo (pinquilo, pincollo, pinkillu, pincuyllo)*, and so on. Likewise, since the term simply means "flute," it is often qualified as to the material used, such as *cchacca pincollo* (bone flute), *quina quina pincollo* (cane flute), and *tupa pincollo* (made from thick *tocoro* cane) (González Bravo 1937: 29, citing Bertonio 1612). In other instances the flutes take on the names of the materials, such as *tocoro*, the name of the cane it is made from (Jiménez Borja 1951: 45), and *rollano*, because of the different wrappings of leather that bind the entire length of the tube (Bustillos, Oporto, and Fernández 1981: 6). Within other cultures the duct flute has other names, such as *ch'utus* among the Bolivian Chipaya, who also have adapted the Aymara term to become *pinkayllo* (Baumann 1981: 179).

The *pinkullo* is an edge aerophone with a built-in duct that cannot be detached. As such it is related to the European recorder, *flauto dolce, Blockflöte* and other fipple flutes. Jiménez Borja describes the *pinkullo* and its construction in the Kechua provinces of the Department of Cuzco in southern Peru:

> It measures in length up to 1 meter 20 cm . . . [and it] is made from *huarango* wood *(Acacia macrantha)* and also *chachamamo*. Before it is used, the wood soaks for several days, and later it is cut into two halves which are routed out. These halves are joined with llama nerves or *janccu*. When the two parts are joined the tube is ready. There are six finger holes, made with red hot awls. A tongue [plug] is made called *kallo* and it is placed in the proximal end of the flute, where the player's lips are placed . . . . To complete it is a small window whose filed edge breaks the thin strip of breath (1951: 45).

In other regions of southern Peru, as in the Aymara village of Conima in the Department of Puno, the five- and six-holed *pinkillus* are made from cane (Turino 1989: 6), while the Bolivian Chipaya make their *ch'utus* from willow *(sauce)* or tola *(Baccharis tola)* according to Baumann (1981: 179): "The branches, most of which are rather crooked, are cut in half, hollowed out, and tied together again with llama or sheep nerves." In most regions of the Andes the *pinkullo* is seasonal, and it is played only during particular calendrical periods, such as the rainy season from late October or November 1 *(Todos los Santos)* through carnival in late February or March, as Jiménez Borja writes:

> This flute is played during the season when the great rains begin. During this period they celebrate the *señalacuy* or *tincay* in honor of the cattle. At that time they perform the labors of *aporque* [covering the vegetables with earth to make them tender]. These labors are true festivals, which are happily animated by the music of the *pincuyllos*, as they are called in the south of Peru. Before playing the

instrument, it is moistened in *chicha*, alcohol, or water. The coincidence of these festivals with the arrival of the rains, the moistening of the wood before making the flutes, and the moistening of the instruments before playing them, is very significant (1951: 45).

The *pinkullo* is thus associated with fertility, as the symbolism suggested above indicates. Similarly symbolic is the playing of *pinkullos* in pairs among the Kechua (Jiménez Borja 1951: 45), and dualistically among the Chipaya, who perform parallel melodies at the approximate interval of a tritone (Baumann 1981: 179). Among Aymara-speakers in Conima (Puno, southern Peru), *pinkillu* ensembles perform during the rainy season (November 1 through carnival), and for roof-raising fiestas any time of year. Only occasionally are the registers of the instruments in a six-hole *pinkillu* ensemble organized according to the principle of "binary symmetry around a marked center"; most of the time, five- and six-hole *pinkillu* ensembles play in "dense unison" (Turino 1989: 12).

Contrasting with the timbric homogeneity of aerophones in the ensembles documented by Turino in Conima (southern Peru), "where each ensemble is made up of a single type of melodic instrument (*sikus* with *sikus*, *tarkas* with *tarkas*, etc.)" (1989: 8), the *pinkillu* ensembles in northern Potosí (Bolivia), which generally consist of four sizes of melodic instruments of the same type, mix two timbric qualities in the same ensemble (Stobart 1996: 67–69). These are the "hoarse" (*ronco*), buzzing, and dense timbre, rich in harmonics, associated with *tarkas* (see below) of the *machu tara* and *tara pinkillus*, and the "thin" or clear timbric quality, with few harmonics, of the *q'iwa* (also *k'ewa*) and *q'iwita pinkillus*. The four sizes of instruments in the type of *pinkillu* ensembles studied by Henry Stobart in the Kechua-speaking *ayllu* Macha in northern Potosí are called, from largest to smallest, *machu tara* (111 cm), *q'iwa* (72 cm), *tara* (54 cm), and *q'iwita* (37 cm) *pinkillus*. *Taras* are tuned an octave apart, as are the *q'iwas*, and each *q'iwa* is pitched a fifth apart from its lower *tara* pair. In performance, especially the pair of lower instruments (the *machu tara* and *q'iwa*) play their pitches in interlocking fashion. These *pinkillus* are made from wood, have six finger holes, and, except for their sizes, their construction is identical. The differences in timbre are obtained by the manner of performance: *tara pinkillus* produce their buzzing sound when they are played with two fingers, leaving four distal finger holes open; and *q'iwa pinkillus* create their thin sound when played with five fingers, leaving only the proximal finger hole open. Moreover, the mixed timbre occurs only on the final note of *wayñus*, when all the instruments play together (1996: 68). According to Stobart, *pinkillus* are played exclusively during the rainy season. Probing the semantic fields of *tara* and *q'iwa*, "two reciprocal and opposing [concepts applied to] categories of sound or timbre" (1996: 67) in the context of the *pinkillu* ensemble, Stobart transcends the level of binary oppositions to propose an interpretation based on complementary flows of energy. He summarizes the semantic fields of *tara* and *q'iwa* as follows (1996: 77):

TARA	Q'IWA
vibrant / energized	loose / low energy
positive aesthetic	negative aesthetic
broad sound	thin sound
(rich in harmonics)	(few harmonics)
hoarse sound	weeping / crying
in tune (balanced)	out of tune (out of balance)
discontinuous	continuous
stretched / taut	slack / lax
broad / productive	mean / non-productive
equilibrium / even	disequilibrium / uneven
dual (joined / paired)	single (separate / without partner)
highly gendered	mediated gender
arrogant / harsh / obstinate	cowardly / non-aggressive

Of particular interest is Stobart's interpretation of gender in the context of the *pinkillu* ensemble, whose paired *tara* and *q'iwa* instruments are conceptualized as a couple or *qhariwarmi* (Kechua for man and woman). When Stobart asked which instrument was male and which female, "the ambivalent responses quickly made [him] realize that the question was inappropriate. Certain friends considered *tara* female whilst others opted for male or avoided the issue" (1996: 76, 79). Repositioning boundaries in Tristan Platt's concept that each member of a pair, although predominantly male or female, contains an element of the other member (1976: 21), Stobart suggests that *tara*, a dual, dynamic concept, implies heightened sexuality, whether male or female, as well as the balance and strength of paired elements. By contrast, *q'iwa* is single, and its aural and linguistic connotations imply a mediation between polarized dualities—such as silence and dynamic sound, or

"conjunction of male and female"—that disrupts the binary order and creates an imbalance "while permitting contact and the exchange of energies to occur between them," thus linking the concept of *q'iwa* with regeneration (1996: 77–78). In daily tasks, however, "society is viewed to be at its most productive and harmonious when men and women both accomplish their respective, but differentiated, roles equally and individually" (1996: 76), and the concept of *tara* represents control over and balance between these forces.

The flow of substances between the worlds of the dead and the living is crucial for regeneration. In this context, *pinkillus* appear to be associated with the dead, "who, as a 'collective' presence, are said to help the crops to grow through the rainy season" (Harris 1982: 58 in Stobart 1996: 68). According to traditional beliefs, the souls of the dead live in a world that is permanently green and only dance the *wayñus* of the rainy season, never the genres of the dry season (1996: 78). Because the world of the dead is conceptualized as an inversion of that of the living, it can be assumed that the latter would remain dry if paths of communication between them could not be established, "in order to bring liquidity . . . and generate new life" (1996: 78). Stobart explains that, in the Department of La Paz (Bolivia), the cane *pinkillus* that are played to attract rain are described as *q'iwa*, and that the hoarse, wooden *tarkas* are performed to summon dry spells (1996: 79), thus controlling the forces of nature. Moreover, and consistent with the restriction to a single type of aerophones in the configuration of ensembles noted by Turino in Conima (1989: 8), Stobart clarifies that, in the Department of La Paz, *tarkas* and *pinkillus* never are played together in the same ensemble. However, he speculates that the two contrasting categories of sound embodied in the concepts of *tara* and *q'iwa pinkillus*, as brought together in northern Potosí ensembles, might be perceived as fulfilling a function similar to that of mixing *tarkas* and *pinkillus*, and that each of these timbric categories can be interpreted as different yet complementary types of energy:

Weak, thin, and continuous sounds would appear to be associated with generating the flow of substances, instability, and transformation, while strong, dense, and vibrant sounds seem to be linked with controlling the flow of substances and the maintenance of binary equilibrium and stability (1996: 79).

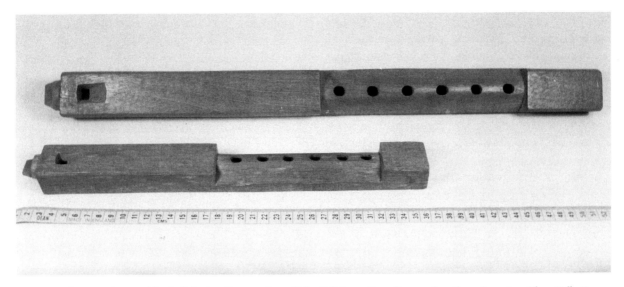

Fig. 10: *Tarkas*, aerophones with a built-in duct from northern Chile, Bolivia, southern Peru, and northern Argentina. Olsen Collection.

Another variant of the *pinkullo* is the *pinkillo mohoceño*, a very large instrument that consists of a detachable extension of the air duct, attached in parallel with the instrument's main body (pictured in d'Harcourt 1959: 12), much like a European bass recorder, and nearly identical to the Slovak *fujara* (pictured in Buchner 1972: Fig. 237). Bustillos (1981: 4) explains that the term *mohoceño* comes from the locale of Mohoza, in the Bolivian Province of Inquisivi. Other names for the instrument are *aykhori* (whining or complaining) and *marimacho* (Paredes 1936: 78).

The Aymara *pinkillos mohoceños* are made from *chuqui* cane, and may be as long as one meter and 60 cm (d'Harcourt 1959: 13). They are normally constructed and performed in five sizes called (from largest to smallest) *bordón, salliva, eraso, requinto,* and *chili* or *cheje,* forming ensembles that can include 24 *pinkillos mohoceños* and four or more drums (Bustillos 1981: 4). The terms *salliva* (large), *liku* (medium), and *contra* (small) also are used, and the respective measurements of the medium and small sizes are 2/3 and 1/2 of the large, producing pitch levels that create parallel fourths and fifths between all three (González Bravo 1937: 30). Some of the members of the family may have detachable duct extensions made from curved metal tubes rather than parallel cane ones, and the smaller members of the *mohoceño* family do not use detachable duct extensions. In principle, the construction of the *pinkillo mohoceño* is nearly identical to the smaller *pinkillo* duct flutes, except for the addition of the detachable extension of the built-in duct on the larger members of the group. Because of the

lengths of the largest flutes, the *mohoceño* player often holds his instrument in a tilted horizontal fashion, although it also may be held vertically. *Pinkillos mohoceños* have five or six finger holes, and several other nonfingered holes at the distal end, which function as the acoustical end of the vibrating tube.

Tarka (Aymara: Bolivia, Chile, southern Peru, and northern Argentina). The Aymara *tarka* is in reality a variant of the *pinkullo* because it is an edge aerophone with a built-in duct (Fig. 10). Its construction and use among the Aymara and the Chipaya (who also call it *tar pinkayllu*), however, is distinct. Currently, it is made from a solid piece of approximately 4 × 4 cm squared orange, pomegranate, or mahogany wood, about 52 cm long for the largest instrument. This piece is drilled out its entire length and partially planed down on its upper two edges, where the six finger holes are placed. Its built-in air duct, while similar to that of the *pinkullo,* is more elaborate and tooled in such a way that it may be the apparatus responsible for the instrument's tone quality. However, the musician also blows the *tarka* in such a forced manner that two tones are produced simultaneously, the fundamental and its octave. In this way, it is said, the *tarka* has a hoarse voice, deriving its name from the Aymara expression for "raspy" or "hoarse," *tarcaca cunca* (González Bravo 1937: 31, citing Bertonio 1612). Montaño, however, claims that its name comes from *tarko,* the tree from which it is made (1988: 17). The *tarka* is played in the usual groups of three registers, called *taika (tayka),* *malta* (*mala* and also *ankuta*), and *chuli* (*suli*, and also *tecle* or *requinto*), producing parallel melodies at intervals of fifths and fourths. They are instruments played in ensembles of nine or more musicians during the Andean spring and fall (from November to April), for dances associated with Christian and calendric festivals (González Bravo 1937: 31), and carnival. The music for *tarkas*, as well as the ensemble itself, is called a *tarkeada*.

In regions of Bolivia the *tarka* is known by other names. For example, in the Bolivian south and in northern Chile it is called *anata*, which means "carnival" (Yévenez Sanhueza 1980: 54). In several areas of the Department of La Paz, the hoarse sound of the *tarkas* is used to "attract dry spells, when the rain becomes too heavy, and at carnival to halt the rains in preparation for harvest" (Stobart 1996: 79). A related instrument that is perhaps an older version of the *tarka* is known as *charkha* (*charka, ch'aje, charge*), another type of *pinkullo* made from curved cane and wrapped with strips of leather or cat gut (Paredes 1936: 79). Marguerite and Raoul d'Harcourt (1959: 13), however, called it the "*pinkullu* of Potosí," explaining that the *charka* is made from a curved piece of hard wood that is cut, hollowed out, placed back together again, and wrapped with animal nerves or gut.

Pingullo (Quichua: Ecuador), cajero, and roncadora (mestizo: Peru) flute-and-drum combinations. The Ecuadorian *pingullo*, while retaining a name linking it to the central Andean Aymara and Kechua traditions, possesses two finger holes and one thumb hole, and it is performed with a *tamboril* membranophone by the same musician. It is most frequently a one-hand edge aerophone with built-in duct, fabricated from bamboo known as *tunda* or *duda*. Although exemplars of *pingullo* with six finger holes and played with both hands also are used, these more commonly are called *pífanos* (a Spanish word) by the Quichua (= Kechua) in Imbabura, Ecuador. The *pingullo* flute and drum combination is played during Christian and calendric festivals (Moreno Andrade 1972: 31–32). Supporting its fertility symbolism as an instrument used during planting festivals is an etymological interpretation of its Quichuan name— from *pinga* and *ullu*, both meaning "penis" (Carvalho-Neto 1964: 342).

Moving southward, the most common term for the one-person ensemble in Cajamarca (Peru) is *cajero*, or one who plays the *flauta y caja*. The flute, played with

Fig. 11: *Cajero* playing *flauta* and *caja*, a duct aerophone (made from plastic tubing) and drum, during the Virgen del Carmen patronal festival, Alto Otuzco, Cajamarca, Peru. Olsen Collection.

the left hand (if the musician is right handed) has two finger holes and one thumb hole. As with the *pingullo*, the *cajero* must overblow and play the upper partials of the overtone series in order to perform melodies. The pitches are, therefore, extremely high, similar to the upper range of a European piccolo. The drum, played with the opposite hand from that holding the flute, provides a constant rhythm by strokes on the drum head and the rim in alternation. The flute is normally made from a hollowed-out tree branch such as willow, although plastic tubing was used by a *cajero* during a 1979 patronal festival in Alto Otuzco, Peru, a small village near Cajamarca (Fig. 11).

The *roncadora* is an end-blown duct flute common in the Callejón de Huaylas, in the Peruvian Department of Ancash. (See also *Mapa de los instrumentos musicales de uso popular en el Perú* 1978: 230). It is played as a one-man combination also called *roncadora*. The flute itself is similar to that of the *cajero* from the Cajamarca area, except that its tubular body is slightly larger and thicker, and the drum is much bigger (Fig. 12). Thus, the Ancash combination is louder than the Cajamarca combo. The term *roncadora* translates from the Spanish as "flute that snores" (from *roncar*, "to snore"), an appropriate appellation because its sound is loud and harsh, consisting of two partials (the fundamental and the octave) sounding simultaneously, as the Ancash flutist forcibly overblows his instrument to obtain the high overtones necessary to produce a melody. A *roncadora* is commonly made from a drilled-out piece of hardwood known as *huaroma* (Otter 1985: 93), *rayán* or *saúco (Sambucus peruviana) (Mapa de los instrumentos musicales de uso popular en el Perú* 1978: 229), although thick bamboo and plastic also may be used. Instruments measure from 50 cm to one meter in length, and have two finger holes and one thumb hole in the extreme distal end. The plug (called *shullun*), which forms a portion of the duct, is constructed in a step-like shape, causing the instrument's tone to be harsh (Otter 1985: 93). With a drumstick in his free hand the *roncadora* player strikes the snare head of his large membranophone, and, like the *cajero* farther north, he hits the drum rim on the offbeats and the skin on the downbeats. In Recorded Example 3, Pablo Milla Balbero from Yungay, Peru, is playing a *wayno* and *fuga* on his *roncadora* (Ex. 16).

The melodies played on the *roncadoras* from Huaylas are distinctly pentatonic, as seen in Example 16, and the rhythm can be recognized as that of the *wayno* (= *huayno*), one of the most characteristic Andean dances. Besides its use in Catholic patron saint festivals, the *roncadora* also participates in the *minga*, or communal work effort. In both instances it can be played as a solo instrument or jointly with other

Fig. 12: Pablo Milla Balbero from Yungay, Ancash, Peru, playing the *roncadora* duct aerophone and drum. Olsen Collection.

roncadoras, performing familiar *waynos*. Roncadoras also are used to perform slower types of music for processionals during patronal feasts.

Lip concussion aerophones: end blown, coiled (see Table 1, IIA, 1).

***Pututu, kepa* (Kechua: Peru), and *heresemoi* (Warao: Venezuela).** Conch shell trumpets have been used as

Ex. 16: A *wayno* performed by a *roncadora* from Yungay (Ancash, Peru). Olsen Collection, transcribed by Olsen. The musician's right-hand rim shots are notated as ×.

sound makers in the Caribbean, circum-Caribbean, Mesoamerican, and Andean regions since pre-contact times. When it was not possible to obtain conch shells, or when they were deemed necessary for ritualistic purposes, ancient cultures in Mexico and Peru fabricated them from clay, complete with the inner spiral, the crucial, symbolic part (pictured in d'Harcourt 1925: vol. 2, plate 9). Whether these ceramic reproductions, such as those found in Moche tombs, were used sonically is not known. They were perhaps only amulets, powerful because of their inner spiral as a symbol of eternity. Or perhaps, when played as lip concussion aerophones, they were revered for their awesome sound as powerful instruments of war. The latter reason was why the *kepa* (also *kheppa* and *qhueppa*), as they called them, were esteemed by the Inca who traveled great distances by raft, from Peru to the warmer waters near Panama, to trade gold, silver, and other valuables for *Strombus galeatus* conch shells (Stevenson 1968: 256, 261). Today Kechua descendants of the Incas in Pisac, near Cuzco, still use conch shell trumpets, called *pututos* or *pututus*, in their Catholic services, sounding them in ensemble during certain portions of the Mass. Other uses today for the *pututo* are to call together village members for communal assembly, to work the fields, clean irrigation ditches, and for similar activities that involve the community (Jiménez Borja 1951: 42). As a sound maker, the *pututo* is a symbol of great authority.

Among the Warao of Venezuela, a conch shell trumpet called *heresemoi* is occasionally found. Since pre-Columbian times the Warao, like the Inca, acquired conch shells (species *Strombus gigas*, Furst 1965: 5) from distant waters, traveling northwest, by canoe, to the Island of Margarita. Today they may purchase them in Tucupita, the capital of the Delta Amacuro Federal Territory. For the Warao the conch shell trumpet is a signaling instrument, used for giving nighttime directions to canoers, announcing the departure and arrival of the crabbing canoes, signaling the completion of a newly made dugout (1965: 27), announcing the death of a tribal member, and calling the annual walking excursion to the *moriche* palm groves in preparation for the *nahanamu* harvest festival (Wilbert 1956: 5–6).

The *heresemoi*, like other conch shell trumpets in the Americas, is end blown. Its cupped mouthpiece is made by cutting off the end of the shell with many short chops of a machete. Since this is the hardest part of the shell, occasional errors are made and the maker may have to repair the embouchure hole with pitch or beeswax. The instrument can be played by anyone, and the music transcribed in Example 17 was played by a *wisiratu* shaman from the Winikina subtribe. His playing technique included gliding gestures, or "portamenti," caused by the intentional increase and decrease of his air pressure (represented by slurs in the notation).

Another Warao playing style consists of three long blasts for signaling grief at the time of a death (Wilbert 1956: 5). The traditional use of the *heresemoi* is becoming increasingly rare, and I never heard one played in an actual context during the months in residence at a Warao village.

Wak'rapuku (Kechua: Peru). The *wak'rapuku* coiled trumpet (also called *waqra pututu* in Bolivia), usually is made from sections of cow horn joined together. This instrument is associated with the indigenous population and used exclusively for cattle-marking rituals. In the central sierra, rituals of increase and animal marking take place twice a year, during carnival and on July 25, the feast of St. James the Apostle (Santiago Apóstol), the animals' saint. On these occasions, the *wak'rapukus*, which always are played in pairs, are joined by a violin and a singer, who also plays the *tinya* (a small membranophone). According to Raúl Romero (1985: 236–37), the most salient characteristic of cattle-marking music is the use of melodies based on tritonic scales. The *wak'rapuku* is found throughout the Department of Apurímac, and in specific localities in the departments of Junín, Huancavelica, Arequipa, Ayacucho, Cuzco, Huánuco, and Pasco (*Mapa de los instrumentos musicales de uso popular en el Perú* 1978: 265). (For a drawing of a *wak'rapuku / waqra pututu*, see the Appendix to Baumann's "Music and

Ex. 17: *Heresemoi* conch shell trumpet as played by a Warao. Olsen Collection, transcribed by Olsen.

Worldview of Indian Societies in the Bolivian Andes," in this volume.)

As a creation of the Kechua during the colonial period (because cows were unknown before the Spanish Conquest in this region), this type of animal horn coiled trumpet—also known in the Mantaro Valley as *cacho* (Romero 1985: 236)—may be a replacement for similarly shaped trumpets made of ceramic in pre-contact times, or for some of the long trumpets perhaps on the way to extinction, such as the maguey *pampa corneta* found in parts of Apurímac, Ayacucho, Huancavelica, and Junín, which—like the *wak'rapuku*—is associated with cattle-marking rituals (*Mapa de los instrumentos musicales de uso popular en el Perú* 1978: 261). *Wak'rapukus* can be made from sections of sheet metal (Cohen 1966: 10), although the bovine model remains the most popular. While instruments of a few decades ago were made from approximately twenty sections of the cow horn, joined together with pegs and covered with pitch at their seams (Jiménez Borja 1951: 43), today they are made from half as many, and their seams are covered with bands made from bicycle inner tubes. The *wak'rapuku*'s small cupped mouthpiece also is made from cow horn.

***Trompeta* (mestizo).** Also an instrument of traditional use in many parts of South and Central America and Mexico, the European trumpet is very common and important in the national patrimony of many countries. The valve trumpet was introduced as part of the expansion of military and civilian bands in the nineteenth century. Although the names of bands and, occasionally, their repertoire, surface in numerous sources, these seldom list the instrumental configuration of each band. In Argentina, for instance, the presence of trumpets by 1882 can be inferred from iconographical sources (Plesch *et al.* 1999: 140). Trumpets today are manufactured in several Latin American countries and are readily available. Throughout many regions of the Andes indigenous wind ensembles, such as the *sikuri*, have been replaced by brass bands. Even muted trumpets occasionally are used in the small mandolin, guitar, and harp ensembles in the Callejón de Huaylas in Ancash, Peru, as a replacement for a *kena* type of flute. Although the trumpet does not carry cosmological associations, it is nevertheless held in high esteem as a loud outdoor instrument in the Andes, perhaps emulating the authoritative role of the indigenous *pututo* or *kepa* from former times.

Lip concussion aerophones: end blown, straight (see Table 1, IIB, 1).

***Trutruka* (Mapuche: Chile).** The *trutruka* is an extremely long, straight, end-blown lip concussion aerophone of the Mapuche in south-central Chile and southwestern Argentina. Measuring between three to four meters or more in length and approximately 5 cm in width, it is made usually from one piece of bamboo that has been slit in half, hollowed out, joined together again, and covered lengthwise with horse gut (Dannemann 1977: 109). The proximal end is open with a slight oblique angle to it, and the distal end has a cow horn attached that serves as an amplifier. Although horse gut and cow horn indicate acculturation, both could have replaced other materials native to the region.

Although a precise standard does not seem to exist for the fundamental pitch of the *trutruka*, it appears that a general range or focal point is sought out since all the *trutrukas* studied by Orrego-Salas are pitched within a minor third of each other (1966: 49). The *trutruka* occasionally is played in the village squares or the countryside for secular entertainment (Dannemann 1977: 109), but in its traditional context it is used as a rhythmic instrument for dancing during the Mapuche *nguillatún* fertility ritual (see María Ester Grebe, "Amerindian Music of Chile," in this volume). Generally, two *trutrukatufes* (trained *trutruka* players) play a series of overtones by overblowing, in a form of heterophonic duet (Grebe 1974a: 75). Titiev (1949: 138) observes that during the *nguillatún* ritual two *trutrukas* occasionally are sounded by players standing north and south of the ceremonial center, while Grebe adds that they face the East while playing (1974a: 75).

Although the horse was introduced by Europeans, it appears as a central, symbolic theme in Mapuche cosmology. The most notable symbolism regarding the *trutruka* is its musical imitation of a galloping horse, including that of the feared ghostrider *wirafün kawellu* (Lavín 1961: 207), as the transcription in Example 18 suggests.

***Pututu* (Aymara: Bolivia).** In Bolivia, the term *pututu* refers to the bull or cow horn used for signaling purposes that replaced the pre-Columbian *kepa* (the conch shell trumpet also called *pututo*), and also to a straight lip-concussion trumpet of traditional use in northern Potosí called *pututu* or *tira tira*. The latter is made of bamboo or cane, measures between three and

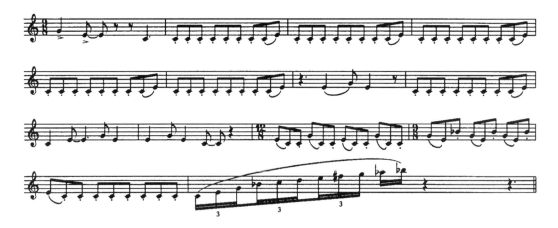

Ex. 18: A *trutruka* melody imitating a galloping horse (Lavín 1961: 208).

four meters in length, and has an animal horn attached to the distal end that functions as an amplifier (see illustrations of both types of *pututus* in the Appendix to Baumann's "Music and Worldview of Indian Societies in the Bolivian Andes," in this volume).

Pututu or *pututo* simply means "horn" (*bocina* in Spanish). The cow horn (Baumann) or bull horn (González Bravo 1938: 170; Sánchez Canedo 1989: 22–24) is known as *pututu* in Bolivia; in Peru, the same instrument is called *pututo* or *pitón* (in Puno), and *cacho* (in Huarochirí, Department of Lima). Also in Peru, the conch shell trumpet with an occasionally added embouchure of metal or cane found in the departments of Cuzco and Puno, is called *pututu* (*Mapa de los instrumentos musicales de uso popular en el Perú* 1978: 259, 263). Surveying traditions in northern Potosí (Bolivia), Wálter Sánchez Canedo (1989: 21–22) explains that the function of the animal horn or *pututu* transcends its specific musical association with the *pinkillo* as a seasonal instrument, as well as its prominent role during the celebration of carnival, because it is utilized throughout the year as a signaling device for such purposes as assembling the members of a community or announcing the arrival of visitors, namely the function of its Inca predecessor (see *Pututo, kepa* [Kechua: Peru] above). (See also Baumann, "Music and Worldview of Indian Societies in the Bolivian Andes," in this volume: Ex. 3 is a transcription of the *liku* pair in a *sikuri* ensemble playing a *wayño*, accompanied by four *cajas* and by a repeated pitch on the *pututu*; Fig. 11 illustrates ceramic trumpets [*pututus*]; and Fig. 13 and the Appendix show illustrations of the animal horn or *pututu*.) In the words of González Bravo (1938: 170), the instrument also was used

to animate the great festivals, and especially at night, during the vespers of these festivals, when [musicians] would display a great ability to create harmony, forming chords with various *pututus*. And it is very colorful to see the Indians riding horseback, making music with this rustic trumpet, and, moreover, it is not so rare to find that the owner of a *pututu* would beautifully tool and cover the bell of his instrument with silver.

Such "chording" as González Bravo mentions is replaced today by brass bands in much of Bolivia.

In northern Potosí the straight lip-concussion *tira tira* or *pututu* consists of two parts: a long tube wrapped with leather strips, and an animal horn which, attached to the tube at the distal end by a very resistant resin, functions as a resonance chamber. The *tira tira* produces a hoarse, low sound, and is played mostly during the celebration of carnival (Sánchez Canedo 1989: 21–23). In Peru, a long straight aerophone made from *saúco* wood, maguey, or cane, with an animal horn attached to its distal end, and with a metal or cane embouchure, is called *kañari* or *cañari* (*Mapa de los instrumentos musicales de uso popular en el Perú* 1978: 262).

Lip concussion aerophones: side blown, straight (see Table 1, IIB, 2).

Clarín (mestizo: Peru). The *clarín* is a northern Peruvian side-blown bamboo trumpet that can measure over three meters in length (Fig. 13). The concept for this instrument antedates contact, and its Kechua name given to this author was *kepa*, another name for the *clarín* in Peru, and the same as that for the ancient conch shell trumpet. However, the side-blown

Fig. 13: Two *clarines* (side-blown lip concussion aerophones) and a *cajero* performing at the Virgen del Carmen patronal festival, Alto Otuzco, Cajamarca, Peru. Olsen Collection.

feature of the *clarín* makes that aspect of its origin moot (Izikowitz 1935 in 1970: 237). Similar side-blown lip concussion instruments are found today in northern Chile, where it is interchangeably called *clarín* (Dannemann 1977), *erke,* and *corneta* (Yévenez Sanhueza 1980: 55); in northwestern Argentina it is known as *erke* (Vega 1946: 239–45); and in Ecuador as *clarín* (Carvalho-Neto 1964: 130).

The *clarín* from the Department of Cajamarca in northern Peru is perhaps an archaic indigenous instrument that may be related, by virtue of its length, to several end-blown trumpets from the pre-contact Moche culture. This ancient civilization, which inhabited the rich coastal portion of the Moche River valley, southwest of Cajamarca (in the vicinity of present Trujillo), fabricated rectangularly coiled trumpets of clay whose uncoiled length would approximate that of the present *clarín*. The body of the Cajamarca *clarín* is constructed from a long piece of bamboo, reinforced with vegetable fibers, ox gut, or nerves to avoid cracking (Jiménez Borja 1951: 42).

A separate adjustable bamboo mouthpiece tube measuring approximately 15 cm in length, and characterized by being closed at one end, open at the other, and by having a rectangular mouth hole near its closed end, is inserted into the proximal end of the instrument's body. The distal end of the *clarín* has a bell made from calabash or metal. A man's instrument, the *clarín* is performed outdoors during Catholic patronal festivals and *mingas,* the traditional communal work effort. In the former context the instrument is played in duet, with the two *clarineros* alternating their melodies (one rests while the other plays). Accompanying their individual sounds are the omnipresent high-pitched melody and rhythm of the *cajero.* During the 1979 Festival of the Virgen del Carmen in Alto Otuzco, the procession carrying the Virgen with her faithful retinue was preceded by two *clarineros* who performed two distinct melodies on their instruments (Recorded Ex. 4), one during the first half of the procession (Ex. 19a) and the other during the second half (Ex. 19b).

All sounds on a *clarín* are produced by overblowing (overtone series) since there are no finger holes. Although the pitches are basically the same for each melody, analysis reveals that the principal tones are different in the two melodies of the example (indicated by the ciphers 1 in the musical scales). During the musical performance for a *minga*, the *clarinero* directs the several aspects of the labor and sets the work rhythms. Gisela Cánepa Koch (cited in Romero 1987) delineates four sections in the *minga*, all determined by the *clarinero*'s music: the *alabado* or announcement; the *llamada,* which tells the workers to begin laboring; the *trabajo* or working period; and the *despedida* or farewell after the workers have returned home. During the *trabajo* the musician plays several distinct melodies, which announce and set the pace for the various

tasks to be accomplished, playing also throughout the resting periods.

Single-reed concussion aerophones: idioglottal and heteroglottal, without finger holes (see Table 1, IIIA, 1).

Erke (Aymara: Bolivia, Argentina, Chile). Although in some regions of the central Andes the name *erke (erkhe)* may refer to a lip concussion aerophone such as the *erke, caña,* or *corneta* (trumpet) of northern Chile and northwestern Argentina (see *clarín* above), *erke* (or *erkencho*) is also the term used for an idioglottal, single-reed concussion instrument. This latter instrument consists of a small cane tube with a bull or cow horn attached to its distal end. Internally, the present-day *erke* (*erkencho* for the largest and *erkenchito* for the smallest) has a small tongue cut into the tube, which vibrates

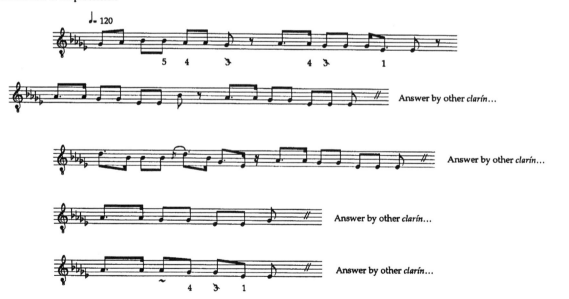

Ex. 19: Two *clarín* melodies performed during the Catholic Festival of the Virgen del Carmen in Alto Otuzco, Department of Cajamarca, Peru, in July 1979. Part a, beginning patterns; part b, ending patterns. Olsen Collection, transcribed by Olsen.

when activated by the player's forced air. Additionally, it is accompanied by a small drum, which the same musician holds and plays, employing the opposite hand from the one used to hold the *erke* to his mouth (Bustillos 1981: 9). According to Vargas (1928: 5), however, an *erke* player produces melodies by covering the end of his horn while playing, thereby raising and lowering his pitches. This technique either represents diversity in the playing tradition of the *erke*, or corresponds to an obsolete style, since it would be impossible for the musician to cover the end of his horn while playing a drum at the same time.

Tekeya (Yekuana: Venezuela). The *tekeya* (*tekeyá*, *tekeyë*, *wanna*) is a single-reed concussion aerophone of the Cariban-speaking Yekuana (Iruaná, Makiritare) of southern Venezuela. The ethnologist Theodor Koch-Grünberg described the instrument during one of his three research trips to South America (1898–1913), and its construction and use continues today in the remote Amazon region of Venezuela. The *tekeya* is made from a large tube of bamboo or *waca* measuring approximately 1.5 meters in length (Aretz 1967: 264). A smaller tube into which a tongue has been cut is inserted into a perforated node near the proximal end of the hollowed bamboo. This single idioglottal reed mouthpiece, capped by the larger tube, vibrates with the forced air of the musician and is amplified by the bamboo tube. This type of instrument, found in numerous regions of the northern Amazon basin, is referred to as a *toré* clarinet by Izikowitz (1935 in 1970: 259; see also Beaudet 1989 and 1997: 58–65). *Tekeyas* always are played in pairs, one instrument considered male and the other female, and their music is symbolic of the "movements and songs of a mythological animal pair (Coppens and Rodríguez V. 1975: 1).

Tarawi and *takwara* (Kamayurá: Brazil). The *tarawi* and *takwara* are idioglottal single-reed concussion aerophones of the Kamayurá, each with a free reed apparatus inserted into a bamboo tube. Menezes Bastos (1999: 158) describes the *tarawi* as consisting of two short tubes measuring 21 and 20 cm in length and played by a pair of musicians in interlocking fashion. He also notes that the *tarawi*, an instrument played while dancing ("instrumento de dançar"), is associated with the *yaku'i* ritual complex whose core instruments are the three *yaku'i* duct flutes (see *Yaku'i* [Kamayurá: Brazil] above).

The *takwara* consists of five tubes that can measure up to two meters in length and requires "as many musicians" playing their pitches in an interlocking fashion (Menezes Bastos 1999: 158, 290 [photo 32]). It is also an "instrumento de dançar," and the Kamayurá say that they do not play the *takwara* properly or correctly ("não saber tocar direito") because this instrument is a specialty of other groups. Regarding its function, the same author indicates *kwarìp*—an intertribal ritual held at the beginning of the rainy season and only when men of great prestige have died, whose core instruments are the pair of double-barreled *uru'a* duct flutes—with a question mark (1999: 158). (See *Uru'a* [Kamayurá: Brazil] above.)

Conflicting information regarding the type of aerophones used by the Kamayurá for the *takwara* (bamboo) dance raised the question of whether *tarawi* or *takwara* were employed, but confirmed the use of single-reed concussion aerophones. This ritual is performed to rid the community of harmful spirits resulting from contact with outsiders, or to appease the Tarawi spirit, the guardian of households who might be angered if "people fail to pray to the garden spirits when planting or to the fish spirits when fishing" (Hill 1979: 421). As such, it "can be held during any season of the year," according to need. In the context of other rituals, such as *yaku'i*, which is performed at the beginning of the dry season, the frequency with which a *takwara* dance might be held is determined by "social," rather than "ecological," time. Also, at one level, this ritual polarizes relationships between the Kamayurá and outsiders, expressing "the cultural ideal of village endogamy, a basic principle of Kamayurá social organization" (1979: 419, 423, 429).

In answer to our question, on the one hand, Rafael José de Menezes Bastos—author of a definitive study (*A musicológica Kamayurá*, first published in 1978 and reprinted with a new preface in 1999) and the recognized authority on this indigenous group, who describes the *takwara* as five, separate, long tubes, not rafted in pairs, as are, for instance, the long *uru'a* duct flutes for *kwarìp*—kindly confirmed that the *takwara* dance requires the long-tubed *takwara* (personal communication to Malena Kuss, May 28, 2003), adding that the same instrument is called *tankwara* by the Waurá and is used also by other Xinguano groups. On the other hand, as cited in Hill (1979: 419), Orlando and Cláudio Villas Bôas (1972) described the instruments as follows:

These flutes, measuring two meters in length, are made of *taquara* (a kind of bamboo). The Indians believe that the chant of these flutes can exorcise the spirits. The players go from house to house in the village, trying to send the spirits away.

Jonathan Hill (1979), working from the literature available at the time (such as the work of the Villas Bôas brothers [1970 and 1972]) and from materials at the Indiana University Archives of Traditional Music, added then that "a pair of male dancers play double-barrelled *tarawi* flutes while proceeding through each household in the village" (1979: 419). It is clear that the instruments used cannot be technically "flutes" and were erroneously identified as such by the Villas Bôas brothers, as Hill kindly confirmed from the sound of "vibrating reeds inside the bamboo tube" in the recording of *takwara* dance music transcribed by him (Villas Bôas 1972: track 1, item 8; Hill 1979: 422; and personal communication to Kuss, May 16, 2003). If the measurements given by Menezes Bastos for the length of the tubes of the *tarawi* (21 and 20 cm) represent the standard for this and similar instruments used by other groups, it would be an acoustical impossibility for these tubes to produce the low sounds we find in Hill's transcription. By the same token, single-reed activated tubes measuring up to two meters, such as those of the *takwara*, might produce sounds lower than those in the same transcription.

There were, on the one hand, compelling reasons for associating the *tarawi* with this ritual: the instrument is named after the guardian spirit of households, known as Tarawi, according to Oberg (1963) and Villas Bôas (1972); and the *takwara* dance "forms a mediating link" between the two objectives of the ritual by employing an instrument believed to embody the benevolent force of this spirit, who has the power "to drive away evil, alien spirits" (Hill 1979: 421). *Takwara*, on the other hand, refers to the ritual as well as to the five-tubed instrument, which is played by five musicians in an interlocking manner, and this applies to the Kamayurá as well as to other groups. If we accept Menezes Bastos's authority on this matter, the description of these instruments—in Hill (1979) after Villas Bôas (1972)—as consisting of two sets of two long tubes each, and played by two musicians / dancers interlocking their four pitches in a manner that musically and visually resembles the pair of *uru'a* duct flutes for *kwarip*, also would be

inaccurate. At this time, an explanation for this discrepancy remains elusive.

Isimoi (Warao: Venezuela). The *isimoi* is a Warao aerophone that has been called everything, from a trumpet (Heinen and Ruddle 1974: 130) and a large flute (Turrado Moreno 1945: 226), to an oboe (Schomburgk, cited in Roth 1924: 461). It is in fact a heteroglottal single-reed concussion aerophone (Fig. 14). The *isimoi* is used during the sacred festivals associated with *nahanamu* (a harvest ritual). Among the Warao aerophones, it is the most culturally significant. It is the sole property of the "owner of the *isimoi*," who is both the maker and the player of the instrument.

Because of the complex nature of the instrument, several days are needed to gather materials and several more to construct it. The first part of the *isimoi* to be made is the single-reed mouthpiece, fabricated from a small tube of *moriche* stalk measuring 8 cm in length, cut and hollowed out to resemble a small trough or canoe. Placed over the open part of this cut tube is a slender stem of a leaf called *sehoro* in Waraoan. Although the stem measures approximately 20 cm in length, only 8 cm of one end covers the small trough. This is firmly attached to the tube, creating a tongue 8 cm long, leaving the remainder to protrude. Next, the "owner of the *isimoi*" uses a small calabash *(amataro)* for an amplifier and mouthpiece holder. One end of the calabash is cut off leaving a hole about 8 cm in diameter, while the other end is drilled just enough so the mouthpiece will fit snugly inside the hole, protruding 8 cm out of the calabash. The nonvibrating portion of the leaf stem protrudes out of the bell end, as decoration. At this point the maker blows through the mouthpiece by inserting it into his mouth, making adjustments on the reed until the sound is to his satisfaction. The main tube of the *isimoi* is made from a burned-out hollowed stalk of *moriche* palm, measuring approximately 35 cm in length and 8 cm in diameter. This functions as an air duct or reed cap, and is placed over the mouthpiece, attached to the calabash with pitch from the *sangrito* tree. The proximal end is partially covered with pitch, leaving a small hole into which the musician blows. More pitch is added to the distal end of the calabash, forming it into a flared bell. Finally, several sticks with tufts of pith (*la barba*, or the beard) are stuck into the flared bell as ornaments.

The owner of the *isimoi* is capable of producing two distinct notes and limited microtonal gliding (glissandi) by increasing and decreasing his air pressure. These two main pitches, like the first interval produced by the majority of the *muhusemoi* flutes, and like the Warao shamanistic healing music, are at the approximate interval of a minor third. Two *isimoi* always are played together in free parallel motion. Example 20 is an excerpt of the music for *nahanamu* (Recorded Ex. 1), featuring two *isimoi*, one *muhusemoi*, several *hebu-mataro* rattles, and *sewei* anklet rattles.

The Warao believe that the *isimoi* has a spirit, which is one and the same as the Kanobo or Supreme Deity. Because of its sacred nature, each *isimoi* is reconstructed each year, prior to use, to provide music during the gathering of the sacred *moriche* starch *(yuruma)* for the Kanobo. When the owner of the *isimoi* returns to his house from the *moriche* grove, deep in the jungle, he must hang his sacred instrument above his hammock in a basket until he needs it again for the main portion of the *nahanamu* festival. When *nahanamu* is over he dismantles his *isimoi* by removing the wax and detaching the mouthpiece. He cleans the small calabash carefully, and saves the unbroken parts because they belong to the Kanobo.

Single-reed concussion aerophones: idioglottal and heteroglottal, with finger holes (see Table 1, IIIA, 2).

Totoy and *massi* (Wayúu: Colombia and Venezuela). The arid Península Guajira in northwestern Venezuela and northeastern Colombia is the habitat of Arawakan-speaking peoples whose self-denomination is Wayúu. Missionaries called them Guajiros, which means "peasants" in Spanish. The Wayúu have two types of idioglottal single-reed aerophones with finger holes: the *totoy* and the *massi* (*maasi*). The sound producing mechanisms in both are nearly identical, consisting of a tongue cut from the tube itself. The uncut end of the tongue may face either the proximal or distal end (Ramón y Rivera 1967), and the entire mouthpiece is placed freely inside the musician's mouth, without lip contact. The physical characteristics of the instruments' bodies, however, are slightly different. For example, the *totoy*, also known as *uótoroyo* among *criollos*, measures

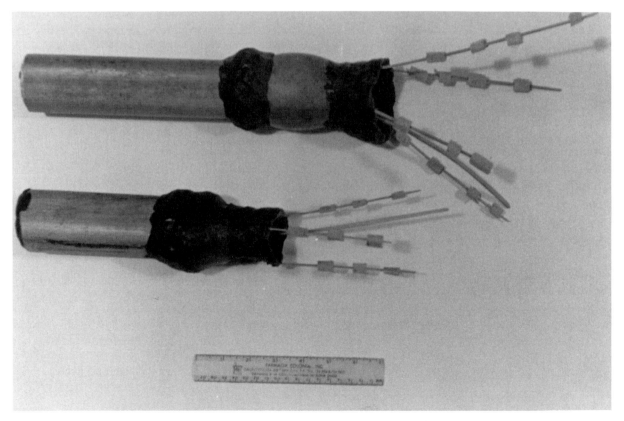

Fig. 14: Two *isimoi*, single-reed concussion aerophones of the Warao, Delta Amacuro Federal Territory, Venezuela. Olsen Collection.

at least 38 cm in length and has a calabash resonator attached to its distal end, while the *massi* measures about 22 cm in length and does not have a resonator (Aretz 1967: 268, 271). In addition, the former instrument is made with a separate cane mouthpiece tube inserted into the larger cane tube of the body, while the latter instrument is made solely from one piece of cane. Another point of contrast are the shapes of the finger holes for each instrument. The four finger holes of the *totoy* are made with a red hot poker and are perfectly round, but the four or five finger holes of the *massi* are cut with a knife and are rectangular. The music performed on the two instruments reveals the greatest difference between them, according to transcriptions by Aretz. Examples 21a and 21b illustrate two melodies played on the *totoy* and the *massi*.

Although two melodies hardly constitute a repertoire from which to draw conclusions, an analysis of these transcriptions reveals the following traits: (1) the *totoy* is approximately one octave lower in pitch than the *massi*; (2) the music of the *totoy* features a lowered third in contrast to the raised third of the *massi* melody; and (3) in performance, the *massi* is characterized by many grace notes, in the manner of the Spanish *gaita* (bagpipe with a single-reed chanter) or *caramillo* (single-reed pipe), while the *totoy* style is much less ornamental. Furthermore, there are "slow" and "fast" melodies or *toques* played on the *massi* (Aretz 1967: 269). About these Wayúu "clarinets," Aretz concludes that they are possibly the result of European influence (1967: 275). Although her hypothesis cannot be proved without more cross-cultural comparison with European as well as Amerindian instruments of similar construction (see Beaudet 1997), traits (2) and (3) reveal distinct differences between the types of melodies played on the two instruments, suggesting perhaps two possibilities for provenance (indigenous and European, respectively), and/or the presence of yet unresearched Wayúu cultural factors that have led to their diverse styles.

Caña de millo (mestizo: Colombia). The *caña de millo* (*flauta de millo, caña de lata, pito*) is an aerophone from Colombia's Caribbean coast. It is nearly identical with the Wayúu *massi*, except for the fact that it is played transversally rather than vertically. It can be constructed from three types of hollowed and open-ended cane: *millo* (millet, *Sorghum vulgare*), *lata*, a thin and spiny palm (Abadía Morales 1973: 125–26), or *carrizo* (List 1983: 54), and can measure from 20 to 40 cm in length. Its single reed is cut at the tube's

proximal end, and four rectangular or circular finger holes are made near the distal end. A thin adjustment string is tied around the tube and under the reed to facilitate and control its vibration, while another is wound around the secure end of the tongue to prevent splitting of the tube. The musician completely encloses the tongue of the *caña de millo* with his mouth, holding the proximal end with his hand, which he also uses to plug the open proximal end. He fingers the usual four finger holes with his other hand. Abadía Morales discusses a unique manner of playing the *caña de millo*, using exhalation for the upper register and inhalation for the lower, as he writes:

> The musicians call the low notes "ripiar," when during the inhalation they make a movement of the jaw, of the reed, and the lips, as if they were going to pronounce a full vowel. There is then a relation between the behavior of the mouth-pharynx shape and the required lowness of the note. During the exhalation, the mouth-pharynx shape is stretched, therefore reducing the air current (1973: 126).

Because the *caña de millo* usually is held horizontally, it often has been mistakenly identified as a flute. In an older context the transversely held instrument performs during Christmas festivities, while in more recent contexts it is played vertically, performing *cumbias* (one of the most representative cluster of genres of the predominantly African-American population of Colombia's Caribbean coast) in ensemble with various African-derived membranophones (drums), and indigenous idiophones (rattles, shakers, scrapers). In this popular musical context, the *caña de millo* usually is called *flauta de cumbia*. On the one hand, George List (1983: 60–65) superbly and convincingly traces the *caña de millo* to African prototypes, and its ensemble role with African-derived membranophones strengthens his conclusions. On the other hand, Adolfo González Henríquez describes the *caña de millo* as an indigenous aerophone used in mestizo musical contexts (1999: 109).

Clarinete, saxofón (mestizo: Peru). The European clarinet and saxophone are two heteroglottal single-reed concussion aerophones that reached Latin America with the expansion of military and civilian bands. Although they are found in bands throughout the region, in the Mantaro Valley of central Peru they are incorporated into the *orquesta típica* as modern replacements for duct and notched edge-aerophones.

Ex. 20: A Warao ensemble of two *isimoi,* one *muhusemoi,* several *hebu-mataro* rattles, and *sewei* anklet rattles (not transcribed), performing music for the ritualistic *nahanamu* harvest dance. Olsen Collection, transcribed by Olsen.

In June 1979, this author studied an *orquesta típica* known professionally as Selección del Centro, which was hired for the patronal festival of St. John the Baptist in the village of Acolla, Department of Junín. The orchestra consisted of three clarinets, three tenor saxophones, five alto saxophones, one harp, and three violins (Fig. 15; Recorded Ex. 5). This is a typical size for an *orquesta típica del centro,* although some ensembles may add a baritone saxophone.

While trumpets are manufactured in Peru, clarinets and saxophones are not, making them difficult to purchase and extremely expensive. The most popular saxophone brands are the silver-plated French Selmer (often purchased from Germany), the

Italian Rampone and Cazzani, and the French Dolnet. To obtain the desired sound, Selmer G-facing or Brilhart number 5 or 6 mouthpieces are used with a number 2, 2-1/2, or 3 reed. The woodwind sound is thus very brilliant, piercing, and reedy. The clarinets, which are predominantly Albert systems, also use the open facing, soft reed combination. Added to the sound is a rather wide vibrato produced on the saxophone by the musician shaking his upper or left hand while playing. On the clarinet the most common vibrato method is to wiggle the instrument back and forth in the mouth. In both instances, the pressure on the reed is constantly being decreased and increased by the movement of the instrument, rather than with a

Ex. 21: Two Wayúu melodies performed by (a) a *totoy* and (b) a *massi;* each melody is preceded by the tuning of each instrument (Aretz 1967: 274, 270–71).

movement of the jaw. Musically, the compositions are in the minor mode, alternating with the relative major. Thirds are emphasized by being doubled in all the voices. Example 22 displays these important, central Andean characteristics.

Multiple single-reed concussion aerophones (Table 1, IIIA, 3).

Acordeón (mestizo: Argentina, Colombia, Peru). The *acordeón* (accordion) is an aerophone whose sound is produced by air passing through multiple single reeds. Aretz (1952: 65) refers to the accordion as a free aerophone because the air is not activated by the player's blowing but set in motion by a bellows producing in (draw) and out (blow or press) flows, comparable to inhalation and exhalation. Unlike other free aerophones, such as the bullroarer—whose sounds are activated by passing a sharp edge rapidly through the air—the accordion is a multiple free-single-heteroglottal-reed, bellows aerophone. The bellows is a mechanical attachment that replaces the human air flow. Several types of accordions are found in the Americas: the *acordeón a botones* (button accordion); the *acordeón a piano* (piano accordion); and the *bandoneón* (the "heart" of Argentina's tango orchestras). The accordion was introduced into many areas of the Americas by Europeans, probably during the early 1900s, not "more than 300 years ago," as Abadía Morales writes (1973: 127). Indeed, the accordion did not become popular in Europe until approximately 1910, although the *bandoneón* was invented in Germany, by Heinrich Band of Krefeld, ca. 1840. Accordions are basically of two types, double action and single action (the former can produce the same note or chords on the draw and blow modes, while the latter produces different notes or chords each time). Some models of *bandoneones* have double action, others single action (Howarth 1969: 325). Many of today's accordions are German instruments made by Hohner, although numerous other companies also manufacture them. While the most common type in rural areas is the button accordion, both varieties are found in urban ensembles that perform folk music throughout the Americas, and on the island of Chiloé in southern Chile (Yévenez Sanhueza 1980: 57), where settlements of Germans have influenced their use.

The factory-made *acordeón* often has replaced either the guitar, or some locally fabricated aerophones found in popular ensembles, such as the *gaita* and *caña de millo*, believed to have been originally used in the Colombian *vallenato*, a tradition specifically associated with accordion performances and virtuosos of that instrument during one phase of its development, ca. 1950 (see Susana Friedmann, "From Tradition to Modernity: *Vallenato* Music [Colombia]," in these volumes). Present-day *vallenato* groups consist of the *acordeón a botones*, *caja* and several other membranophones, a *guacharaca* scraper, and an electric bass (Bermúdez 1985: 74). In urban areas of Colombia, Peru, and elsewhere, the accordion is a common instrument in *tunas* or *estudiantinas* (originally, groups of student musicians who played Hispanic-derived and other folk musics with guitars, mandolins, violins, and other string instruments of European provenance).

Rondín (mestizo: Peru, Ecuador, Colombia). Another multiple single-reed concussion aerophone is the *rondín* or harmonica. In Colombia the instrument is also known as *armónica*, *dulzaina*, and *sinfonía*, and its use has been documented since that country's civil wars (Davidson 1970, vol. 2: 194–95):

> In Cundinamarca . . . *la dulzaina* intervened in our civil wars, as Mora wrote (1936): One morning we took the road to the north, and in the sadness of the farewells and allurement of the adventure, we crossed rugged roads and steep mountains while playing *bandurrias, dulzainas,* and rustic flutes . . . .

In the city of Cajamarca in northern Peru, the *rondín* occasionally has fused with the style of the *cajero*, or single player of the flute and drum. There, the harmonica is played in an unusual manner by one musician who accompanies himself with a drum; since the same hand that holds the drum also must hold the *rondín* (because the other hand holds the drum stick), the musician must move his head back and forth to obtain the different pitches, rather than move the harmonica.

Double-reed concussion aerophones (see Table 1, IIIB).

Chirimía (mestizo: Mexico, Guatemala, Colombia, Ecuador) and *chirisuya* (mestizo: Peru). The *chirimía* (*chirisuya, chirimoya*), a double-reed concussion aerophone (shawm or early oboe), is one of the best documented aerophones brought to the New World by

Fig. 15: Saxophone section of the *orquesta típica* Selección del Centro, playing for a private party during the patronal festival of San Juan Bautista in Acolla, Department of Junín, Peru. Olsen Collection.

Ex. 22: A composition written for an *orquesta típica* of the Mantaro River valley, performed during the San Juan Bautista festival in Acolla, Department of Junín, Peru. Olsen Collection, transcribed by Olsen. The score is for B-flat clarinets, and therefore it is written in B minor for the instruments to sound in A minor.

the Spanish colonists. Perhaps because of its function as a religious instrument for outdoor use in processions, festivals, funerals, and other settings sanctioned by the Catholic Church, and as a secular one for social and political events of the aristocracy, records were kept of its use in Peru from as early as 1551 (Jiménez Borja 1951: 46), and in Mexico from 1569 (Chamorro 1982: 169). It was not long before many native peoples in the viceroyalties of New Spain, New Granada, and Peru learned how to play the *chirimía,* and it became appropriated as an instrument of their own, as noted by José María Arguedas (1977: 16), who wrote about the perception that the harp, violin, transverse flute, and *chirimía* were "Indian instruments in the Peruvian mountains" (complete quote in the opening pages of this essay). Today the *chirimía* is found most often in parts of Mexico, Guatemala, and Peru, where it adopted changes particular to the regions. In Peru, for example, the double reed often is made from the quill of a falcon, seagull, or condor feather, although cane also can be used (García 1978: 7). The use of condor feathers, a sacred bird among Peruvians, strengthens their adoption of the *chirimía* as a "native" instrument. In Mexico, on the other hand, the double reed is often made from the flattened stem of the *chuzpata* palm, while in Guatemala it is made from the royal palm (Chamorro 1982: 172–73). Likewise, the slightly conical or cylindrical *chirimía* body (measuring from 20 to 45 cm in length), with a flared distal end, can be made from a variety of regional woods that are shaped, bored out, and drilled with six or more finger holes and one thumb hole. At one time, however, Peruvian *chirisuyas* from the Department of Lima were made from deer or condor bones (Romero 1987: 11).

Present performance contexts for *chirimías* and *chirisuyas* vary, but most often they are played as a solo instrument, to the accompaniment of a membranophone or idiophone (such as the Aztec *teponaztli* slit-drum in Mexico, or bells in Peru). Occasionally two *chirimías* play together as a duet (García 1978: 7), and a single *chirisuya* may accompany singing (Romero 1987: 11).

In Colombia, the term *chirimía* refers to an aerophone with six finger holes made of ceramic, metal, or from types of bamboo (Yépez Chamorro 1999: 663), as well as to musical ensembles that no longer include the double-reed instrument but several transverse flutes, accompanied by drums, scrapers, and other idiophones (Piñeros Corpas n.d.: 16). In the Chocó region of Colombia, people of African descent have

chirimía ensembles in which a metal or cane keyless transverse flute or a modern clarinet is the melodic instrument, accompanied by membranophones and idiophones (Bermúdez 1985: 77). In other regions of Colombia a *chirimía* ensemble includes a saxophone or accordion as the principal melodic instrument (Ocampo López 1970: 98).

Free aerophones (see Table 1, IV)

A free aerophone is an instrument whose sound is produced by the moving instrument itself passing through still air, rather than moving air passing through a still instrument, as is the case with all the aerophones described above. Several types of free aerophones have been documented in the Americas (Izikowitz 1935 in 1970: 208–13). Of these, the bullroarer is the most common. Known as *zumbador* (buzzer) in Spanish, it can best be described as a piece of wood similar in shape to one-half of a propeller blade, with a hole in one end, through which a string is attached. The performer swings the blade through the air by the string, causing it to spin and create shockwaves in the air, which produce a buzzing or roaring sound. The pitch of the instrument increases or decreases as it is swung respectively faster and slower.

Izikowitz explains that bullroarers are found primarily in the Amazon basin, although they occasionally appear in other areas, such as in the Gran Chaco, the Colombian Chocó, and in Central America (1935 in 1970: 209–10). He suggests that their distribution in the South American rain forest is perhaps related to that of the manioc press complex. Traditionally, bullroarers are sacred instruments, often embodying spirits and carrying their voices. In present-day use, however, they often have been demoted to the role of children's toys.

Aiğe **(Bororo: Brazil).** Among the Bororo of central Brazil, the *aiğe* bullroarer is a sound maker of great significance within traditional culture. Measuring from 30 cm to 150 cm in length, wooden *aiğe* bullroarers are elaborately painted with a red pigment and decorated with a black resin (Lévi-Strauss 1955 in 1974: 230). Such decorations are symbolic of particular totems of Bororo clans. The term *aiğe* also is given to a mythical animal which resembles a type of hippopotamus, represented at burial rituals by a decorated Bororo man who imitates the animal by walking on his hands and feet (Izikowitz 1935 in 1970: 208, 210). The sound of the *aiğe* bullroarer is said to be the voice of the spirit (the animal) and women are excluded from the ceremonies where it is sounded. Women, in fact, are not allowed to view the *aiğe* and, if one looks upon it, she risks being clubbed to death (Lévi-Strauss 1955 in 1974: 230).

Nurá-mëe (**Desana: Colombia**). Among the Tukano-speaking Desana of the Vaupés territory in the Colombian Amazon rain forest, a wooden bullroarer is traditionally used for sacred purposes. It is called *nurá-mëe*, meaning "horsefly," a name chosen by the Desana because of the instrument's buzz, and by its circling path above the musician's head (as horseflies circle around a person's head) (Reichel-Dolmatoff 1971: 59). The *nurá-mëe* represents, however, the voice of the power of the Sun, "through which the Creator exhorts society to observe the rules of exogamy" (Reichel-Dolmatoff 1971: 59). This warning, through symbolic transfer, is related to the Desana creation myth, which speaks of stinging creatures as indiscriminate, stinging horseflies (the masculine principle, symbolic of the man who indiscriminately impregnates any woman). Thus, the sound and power of the *nurá-mëe* bullroarer protects the Desana from endogamy and incest.

CONCLUSIONS

We have seen that wind instruments in many traditional cultures of South America, Central America, and Mexico are used for courting, ritual, battle, entertainment, and other activities where personal and communal music making are important. Although this essay has been organized around sound production and construction as bases for classification, it just as well could have been organized according to musical instrument function. Much of the material presented here has clarified the cultural context within which the instruments are used traditionally, while in other instances the traditional context has not been presented because Westernization has either replaced it, or because it is not known. In order to emphasize the variety and fascination held by organology in the Americas, we conclude with several short examples from the mythological and historical record that suggest an alternative, contextual taxonomy, rather than a descriptive one.

The association of aerophones with courting (i.e., enticing the opposite sex, usually a male seducing a female) is widespread throughout the Americas. The conclusion of the Maya folktale from Guatemala, "The First Flute" (or "the first *chirimía*"), makes this quite clear (Carter 1973: 55–56). In the narrative a Maya princess holds a contest to find a mate, and after rejecting many suitors, the hero (a musician) sings for her, and the princess speaks:

"I like him, Papa. We can sing together, I will marry him. Only first, he must learn the song of each bird of the forest. Then he can teach me."

The minstrel was happy to oblige. He had meant it when he sang of love. At once he disappeared into the jungle. Day after day he practiced, imitating this bird, then that one. But Guatemala is home to hundreds, thousands of birds. Some whistle a complicated tune. The minstrel began to despair of his task.

The god of the forest, after listening for days to the young minstrel's efforts, took pity on him, and also on the birds and other wild inhabitants of the woods—not to mention himself. He appeared before the minstrel, wearing a kindly smile.

"Perhaps I can help you," he offered. "It is a difficult exercise you are engaged in."

Severing a small limb from a tree, the god removed the pith and cut a series of holes in the tube. "Now attend carefully," he said. And he instructed the young man exactly how to blow into one end while moving his fingers over the holes. The notes of the birds tumbled out, clear and sweet.

With a torrent of thanks, the minstrel flew on his way, carrying the *chirimía* . . . . And today the Indians of Guatemala will point to the *chirimía*, the most typical of native instruments, and tell you this is the way it came about.

From this folktale we do not receive clear information about the precise nature of the musical instrument, because the *chirimía* is translated as "flute." Nevertheless, we learn that the instrument originated as an implement for imitating birds, and that the aerophone in question (whether a flute or oboe) seems to have a role in winning the heart of a woman by a man. Another interpretation of this legend would be to associate the instrument with fertility, and throughout this essay we have seen how flutes pertain to that function, as they generally are associated with harvest festivities. Thus, the category of courting merges into ritual.

Aerophones as ritual tools are so categorized because they assist with supernatural communication. They are instruments with special powers. Dualistic panpipes and other wind instruments played in pairs, as male and female, can be classified under this category. Among the Huanca of Peru, so writes Garcilaso de la Vega (1609 in 1961: 200), trumpets made from dogs' heads, and later deer's heads, were used in their rituals:

> These Huancas were especially well known for their strange cult of a dog, which was represented in all their temples .... After he had subjugated them..., General Capac Yupanqui forbade this cult of their idol by the Huancas, but authorized them to make horns out of deer or doe heads, to play at their festivals, as they had been accustomed to doing with the heads of dogs.

Musical instruments made from animal parts take on the power of those animals, and mediate, through performance, in communication with the supernatural.

Battle, as a category for aerophone classification, is most common among those cultures proficient in military pursuits, such as the Aztec and Inca, and the various warring tribes with which they fought. Again Garcilaso de la Vega (1609 in 1961: 167) describes the Inca, this time in confrontation with another enemy, the Chanca, as he writes:

> All night long, the two armies remained facing each other, on the alert. When day broke, the conch horns, timpani, and trumpets began to sound, and they marched toward each other, with loud shouting. Leading his troops, the Inca Viracocha struck the first blow and, in no time, there was a terrible struggle.

Such noise in battle was probably not to summon the supernatural to assist them, but to intimidate the enemy, as suggested by Garcilaso's continued description of the battle: "They gave such shouts and bestirred themselves in such a manner that one would have thought they were ten times more numerous than they actually were, and it was this trick that made the Chancas weaken..." (1609 in 1961: 167–68).

Entertainment as a category for classification is less clear among Native Americans because of the overlapping of functions. For example, Warao men may lay in their hammocks playing harvest festival melodies on their bone flutes as a leisure activity. Traditional love songs or even mourning songs are played by *kenas, sikus,* and string ensembles in the Andes for entertainment, especially by pan-Andean or

folklore revival groups in urban areas. Writing about Andean festivals, José María Arguedas (1957: 33) captures the essence of flutes and other instruments in the context of entertainment: "Later the town's people, too, arrive at the plaza, with *tinya* [drum] and flute. The *tinya* and flute make a concert from afar with the guitars in the plaza. All the town's people are singing. The plaza is the heart of the town; now it is full of happiness."

In any of these contexts, the sounds of instruments produced by concentrated or compressed air are the sounds closest to human singing voices (reed concussion aerophones), human whistles and bird sounds (edge aerophones), human and animal cries, wails, and yells (lip concussion aerophones), and insect buzzes (free aerophones). This affinity with nature, which could yield yet another set of criteria for classification, also accounts for the widespread use of aerophones in American traditional cultures and, indeed, the world.

REFERENCES

Abadía Morales, Guillermo 1973. *La música folklórica colombiana.* Bogotá: Universidad Nacional de Colombia.

Agostinho, Pedro 1974. *Kwarìp: Mito e ritual no Alto Xingú.* São Paulo: Editora Pedagógica e Universitária—Editora da Universidade de São Paulo.

Alemán, Gladys 1998. "Carrizo, baile de" in *Enciclopedia de la música en Venezuela,* 2 vols., ed. by José Peñín and Walter Guido. Caracas: Fundación Bigott, vol. 1, 330–31.

Aretz, Isabel 1952. *El folklore musical argentino.* Buenos Aires: Ricordi Americana.
  1967. *Instrumentos musicales de Venezuela.* Caracas: Universidad de Oriente.

Arguedas, José María 1957. *The singing mountaineers: Songs and tales of the Quechua people,* ed. by Ruth Stephan. Austin: University of Texas Press.
  1977. *Nuestra música popular y sus intérpretes.* Lima: Mosca Azul y Horizonte.

Artesanía folclórica en el Ecuador 1971–1972. Guayaquil: Cromos y Cía.

Auza León, Atiliano 1985. *Historia de la música boliviana,* 2nd edition. La Paz and Cochabamba: Editorial Los Amigos del Libro.

Aytai, Desidério 1981. "A música instrumental Xavante," *Latin American music review* 2/1: 103–29.

Baines, Anthony, ed. 1969. *Musical instruments through the ages.* Middlesex, England: Penguin Books.

Baumann, Max Peter 1981. "Music, dance, and song of the Chipayas (Bolivia)," *Latin American music review* 2/2: 171–222.
  1985. "The Kantu ensemble of the Kallawaya at Charazani (Bolivia)," *Yearbook for traditional music* 17: 146–66.

Beaudet, Jean-Michel 1989. "Les turè, des clarinettes amazoniennes," *Latin American music review* 10/1: 92–115.
  1997. *Souffles d'Amazonie: Les orchestres tule des Wayãpi.* Nanterre: Société d'Ethnologie (Société Française d'Ethnomusicologie, Hommes et musiques, 3).

Bellenger, Xavier 1981. Liner notes to *Bolivia: Panpipes*. See Discography.

Benson, Elizabeth P. 1975. "Death-associated figures on Mochica pottery" in *Death and the afterlife in Pre-Columbian America*, ed. by Elizabeth P. Benson. Washington, D.C.: Dumbarton Oaks Research Library and Collections, 105–44.

Bergman, Billy 1985. *Hot sauces, Latin and Caribbean pop*. New York: Quarto Marketing Ltd.

Bermúdez, Egberto 1985. *Los instrumentos musicales en Colombia*. Bogotá: Universidad Nacional de Colombia.

Bermúdez Silva, Jesús, and Guillermo Abadía Morales 1970. *Aires musicales de los indios guambianos del Cauca (Colombia)*. Bogotá: Universidad Nacional de Colombia.

Bertonio, P. Ludovico 1612 in 1984. *Vocabulario de la lengua aymara*. Cochabamba (Bolivia): CERES.

Boilès, Charles Lafayette 1966. "The pipe and tabor in Mesoamérica," *Yearbook for Inter-American musical research* II: 43–74.

Bolaños, César 1981. *Música y danza en el antiguo Perú*. Lima: Instituto Nacional de Cultura.
1988. *Las antaras Nasca: Historia y análisis*. Lima: Instituto Andino de Estudios Arqueológicos.

Buchner, Alexander 1972. *Folk music instruments*. New York: Crown Publishers.

Bustillos, Freddy, Luis Oporto, and Roberto Fernández 1981. *Música tradicional boliviana*. La Paz: Instituto Boliviano de Cultura.

Carter, Dorothy Sharp 1973. *The enchanted orchard and other folktales of Central America*. New York: Harcourt/Brace/Jovanovich.

Carvalho-Neto, Paulo de 1964. *Diccionario del folklore ecuatoriano*. Quito: Editorial Casa de la Cultura Ecuatoriana.

Chamorro, Arturo 1982. "Chirimías: Sondeo histórico de un modelo islámico en América Hispana," *Latin American music review* 3/2: 165–87.

Chaumeil, J., and J. P. Chaumeil 1977. "El rol de los instrumentos de música sagrados en la producción alimenticia de los Yagua del noreste peruano," *Amazonia peruana* (Lima) 1/2 (July): 101–20.

Claro, Samuel, with Jorge Urrutia Blondel 1971. *Historia de la música en Chile*. Santiago: Editorial ORBE.

Coba Andrade, Carlos Alberto G. 1981. *Instrumentos musicales populares registrados en el Ecuador*. Otavalo, Ecuador: Instituto Otavaleño de Antropología, vol. I.
1992. *Instrumentos musicales populares registrados en el Ecuador*. Quito: Banco Central del Ecuador—Instituto Otavaleño de Antropología, vol. II.

Cohen, John 1966. Liner notes to *Mountain music of Peru*. See Discography.

Coppens, Walter, and Isaías Rodríguez V. 1975. Liner notes to *Music of the Venezuelan Yekuana Indians*. See Discography.

Courlander, Harold 1960. *The drum and the hoe*. Berkeley and Los Angeles: University of California Press.

Crook, Larry Norman 1991. *Zabumba music from Caruaru, Pernambuco: Musical style, gender, and the interpenetration of rural and urban worlds* (PhD diss., Ethnomusicology: University of Texas at Austin).

Cruxent, José María, and Irving Rouse 1958. *An archeological chronology of Venezuela*. Washington, D.C.: Unión Panamericana—Organization of American States.

Dannemann, Manuel 1977. "The musical traditions of the indigenous peoples of Chile," *The world of music* 19/3–4: 104–13.

Davidson, Harry C. 1970. *Diccionario folklórico de Colombia*. Bogotá: Banco de la República.

Densmore, Frances 1925. "A study of Tule Indian music" in *Exploration and fieldwork of the Smithsonian Institution*. Washington, D.C.: Smithsonian Institution Press, 115–27.

Díaz Gainza, José 1962. *Historia musical de Bolivia: Época pre-colonial*. Potosí: Universidad Tomás Frías.

Eli Rodríguez, Victoria 1997. "Aerophones" in *Instrumentos de la música folclórico-popular de Cuba*, 2 vols. and *Atlas*, by Victoria Eli Rodríguez, Ana Victoria Casanova Oliva, Jesús Guanche Pérez, Zobeyda Ramos Venéreo, Carmen María Sáenz Coopat, Laura Delia Vilar Álvarez, and María Elena Vinueza, coordinated by the Centro de Investigación y Desarrollo de la Música Cubana, Olavo Alén Rodríguez, Director. La Habana: Editorial de Ciencias Sociales—Empresa GeoCuba, Ediciones Geo, vol. 2, 495–526.

Figueiredo Filho, José Alves de 1962. *O folclore no Cariri*. Fortaleza, Brazil: Imprensa Universitária do Ceará.

Flores Dorantes, Felipe, and Lorenza Flores García 1981. *Silbatos mayas: Organología aplicada a instrumentos musicales prehispánicos*. Mexico City: Instituto Nacional de Antropología e Historia (INAH)—Museo Nacional de Antropología (Colección científica, Arqueología, Instrumentos musicales prehispánicos, 102).

Flórez Forero, Nubia, and Benjamín Yépez Chamorro 1999. "Gaita (I), Colombia" in *Diccionario de la música española e hispanoamericana*, 10 vols., ed. by Emilio Casares Rodicio, with Victoria Eli Rodríguez and Benjamín Yépez Chamorro. Madrid: Sociedad General de Autores y Editores, vol. 5, 310.

Furst, Peter T. 1965. "West Mexico, the Caribbean, and northern South America: Some problems in New World inter-relationships," *Antropológica* (Caracas) 14 (June): 1–37.

Garces, Marcel 1968. "Limache: Los chinos bailan desde siempre," *El Siglo* (Santiago, Chile, 17 October).

García, Carlos 1998. "Carrizo" in *Enciclopedia de la música en Venezuela*, 2 vols., ed. by José Peñín and Walter Guido. Caracas: Fundación Bigott, vol. 1, 330.
1998. "Maremare" in *Enciclopedia de la música en Venezuela*, 2 vols., ed. by José Peñín and Walter Guido. Caracas: Fundación Bigott, vol. 2, 175–76.

García, Fernando 1978. "Algunas noticias de la chirimía o chirisuya," *Boletín de música y danza* (Lima) 3/4 (July–August): 5–10.
1979. "Algunas notas sobre la zampoña de uso colectivo en Puno," *Folklore* (Lima) 2 (January): 12–13.

Garcilaso de la Vega 1609 in 1961. *The royal commentaries of the Inca*, ed. by Alain Gheerbrant. New York: Orion Press.

Girard, Sharon 1980. *Funeral music and customs in Venezuela*. Tempe: Center for Latin American Studies, Arizona State University.

González Bravo, Antonio 1937. "Kenas, pincollos y tarkas," *Boletín latinoamericano de música* (Montevideo), vol. III: 25–32.
1938. "Trompeta, flauta traversera, tambor y charango," *Boletín latinoamericano de música* (Montevideo), vol. IV: 167–75.

González Henríquez, Adolfo 1999. "Caña de millo" in *Diccionario de la música española e hispanoamericana*, 10 vols., ed. by Emilio Casares Rodicio, with Victoria Eli Rodríguez and Benjamín Yépez Chamorro. Madrid: Sociedad General de Autores y Editores, vol. 3, 109.

Grame, Theodore C. 1962. "Bamboo and music: A new approach to organology," *Ethnomusicology* 6/1: 8–14.

Grebe, María Ester 1973. "El kultrún mapuche: Un microcosmo simbólico," *Revista musical chilena* 27/123–124 (July–December): 3–42.
1974a. "Presencia del dualismo en la cultura y música mapuche," *Revista musical chilena* 28/126–127 (April–September): 47–79.
1974b. "Instrumentos musicales precolombinos de Chile," *Revista musical chilena* 28/128: 5–55.

Guamán Poma de Ayala, Felipe 1615 in 1980. *El primer nueva corónica y buen gobierno*, ed. by John Murra and Rolena Adorno, with translations from Kechua by Jorge L. Urioste. México: Siglo XXI Editores.

Guerra-Peixe, César 1970. "Zabumba, orquestra nordestina," *Revista brasileira do folclore* (Rio de Janeiro) 10/26: 15–38.

d'Harcourt, Marguerite, and Raoul d'Harcourt 1959. *La Musique des Aymaras sur les hauts plateaux boliviens*. Paris: Société des Américanistes, Musée de l'Homme.

d'Harcourt, Raoul, and Marguerite d'Harcourt 1925. *La Musique des Incas et ses survivances*. Paris: Librairie Orientaliste Paul Geuthner.

Harris, Olivia 1978. "Complementarity and conflict: An Andean view of women and men" in *Sex and age as principles of social differentiation*, ed. by Jean Sybil La Fontaine. London: Academic Press, 21–40.

Heinen, Heinz Dieter, and Kenneth Ruddle 1974. "Ecology, ritual, and economic organization in the distribution of palm starch among the Warao of the Orinoco Delta," *Journal of anthropological research* (Albuquerque) 30/2: 116–38.

Henríquez, Alejandro 1973. *Organología del folklore chileno*. Valparaíso: Ediciones Universitarias de Valparaíso.

Hill, Johathan D. 1979. "Kamayurá flute music: A study of music as meta-communication," *Ethnomusicology* 23/3: 417–32.

Hinojosa, Cecilia 1978. "Los ayarachis," *Boletín de música y danza* (Lima) 7/8 (November–December): 1–5.

Holzmann, Rodolfo, ed. 1986. *Q'ero, pueblo y música*. Lima: Patronato Popular y Porvenir Pro Música Clásica.

Hornbostel, Erich M. von, and Curt Sachs 1914 in 1961. "Systematik der Musikinstrumente," *Zeitschrift für Ethnologie* 46: 553–90, translated by Anthony Baines and Klaus P. Wachsmann as "Classification of musical instruments," *The Galpin Society Journal* 14: 3–29.

Howarth, James 1969. "Free-reed instruments" in *Musical instruments through the ages*, ed. by Anthony Baines. Middlesex, England: Penguin Books, 318–26.

Igualada, Fray Francisco de 1938. "Musicología indígena de la Amazonia colombiana," *Boletín latinoamericano de música* (Montevideo), vol. IV: 675–708.

Im Thurn, Everard F. 1883. *Among the Indians of Guiana*. London: Kegan Paul, Trench and Co.

Isamitt, Carlos 1937. "Cuatro instrumentos musicales araucanos," *Boletín latinoamericano de música* (Montevideo), vol. III: 55–66.
1938. "Los instrumentos araucanos," *Boletín latinoamericano de música* (Montevideo), vol. IV : 305–12.

Izikowitz, Karl Gustav 1935 in 1970. *Musical and other sound instruments of the South American Indians: A comparative ethnographical study*. (Göteborg, Elanders), reprint edition. [East Ardsley], England: S.R. Publishers.

Jiménez Borja, Arturo 1951. *Instrumentos musicales del Perú*. Lima: Museo de la Cultura.

Keeler, Clyde E. 1960. *Secrets of the Cuna earthmother*. New York: Exposition Press.

Koch-Grünberg, Theodor 1923. *Vom Roroima zum Orinoco*, vol. III. Stuttgart: Strecker und Schröder Verlag.

Latcham, Ricardo E. 1909. "Ethnology of the Araucanos," *Journal of the Royal Anthropological Institute of Great Britain and Ireland* 34.

Lavín, Carlos 1961. "La música de los araucanos," *Anuario musical*, pp. 201–15, reprinted 1967, *Revista musical chilena* 21/99 (January–March), 57–60.

Lévi-Strauss, Claude 1955 in 1974. *Tristes tropiques*, translated by John and Doreen Weightman. New York: Atheneum.

Lima, Emirto de 1937. "Las flautas indígenas colombianas," *Boletín latinoamericano de música* (Montevideo), vol. III: 67–71.

List, George 1967. "The folk music of the Atlantic littoral of Colombia: An introduction" in *Music in the Americas*, ed. by George List and Juan Orrego-Salas. Bloomington: Indiana University Research Center in Anthropology, Folklore, and Linguistics; The Hague: Mouton, 115–22.
1983. *Music and poetry in a Colombian village: A tri-cultural heritage*. Bloomington: Indiana University Press.

List, George, n.d. "Two flutes and a rattle: The evolution of an ensemble," unpublished manuscript.

Locatelli de Pérgamo, Ana María 1975. "Los Cainguá de Misiones y un curioso instrumento, el mimbú-eta," *Revista INIDEF* (Caracas) I: 21–32.

Loukotka, Cestmír 1968. *Classification of South American Indian languages*, edited and with a preface by Johannes Wilbert. Los Angeles: Latin American Center, University of California, Los Angeles (Reference Series, edited by Johannes Wilbert, vol. 7).

Mapa de los instrumentos musicales de uso popular en el Perú: Clasificación y ubicación geográfica 1978. Lima: Oficina de Música y Danza—Instituto Nacional de Cultura.

Marcuse, Sibyl 1975. *Musical instruments: A comprehensive dictionary*, corrected edition. New York: W. W. Norton.

Martí, Samuel 1968. *Instrumentos musicales precortesianos*. México: Instituto Nacional de Antropología e Historia.

May, Elizabeth, ed. 1980. *Musics of many cultures: An introduction*. Berkeley and Los Angeles: University of California Press.

Mello, Maria Ignez Cruz 1999. "Música e mito entre os Wauja do Alto Xingu" (Master's thesis, Social Anthropology: Universidade Federal de Santa Catarina).

Menezes Bastos, Rafael José de 1978. *A musicológica Kamayurá: Para uma antropologia da comunicação no Alto-Xingu*. Brasília: Fundação Nacional do Indio (FUNAI). Second edition (Florianópolis: Universidade Federal de Santa Catarina, 1999).
1986. "Zur Musikkonzeption der Kamayurá" in *Brasilien*, ed. by Tiago de Oliveira Pinto. Mainz: Schott, 48–57.

Merino, Luis 1974. "Instrumentos musicales, cultura mapuche y el Cautiverio feliz del Maestre de Campo Francisco Núñez y Bascuñán," *Revista musical chilena* 28/128: 56–95.

Millones, Luis, and Mary Pratt 1989. *Amor brujo: Imagen y cultura del amor en los Andes*. Lima: Instituto de Estudios Peruanos.

Montaño, José 1988. "Time, space, culture," Pachamama project, unpublished manuscript.

Moreno Andrade, Segundo Luis 1972. *Historia de la música en el Ecuador*. Quito: Editorial Casa de la Cultura Ecuatoriana, 3 vols.

Nettl, Bruno 1985. *The western impact on world music*. New York: Schirmer Books.

Nordenskiöld, Erland 1919. *An ethno-geographical analysis of the material culture of two Indian tribes in the Gran Chaco*. Göteborg: Elanders.

Oberg, Kalervo 1953. *Indian tribes of northern Mato Grosso, Brazil*. Washington, D.C.: United States Government Printing Office—Smithsonian Institution (Publication No. 13).

Ocampo López, Javier 1970. *El folclor y su manifestación en las supervivencias musicales en Colombia*. Tunja: Universidad Pedagógica y Tecnológica de Colombia.

Olsen, Dale A. 1978–1979. "Musical instruments of the native peoples of the Orinoco Delta, the Caribbean, and beyond," *Revista/Review interamericana* (San Juan, Puerto Rico) 8/4: 577–613.
1980a. "Folk music of South America: A musical mosaic" in *Musics of many cultures: An introduction*, ed. by Elizabeth May. Berkeley and Los Angeles: University of California Press, 386–425.
1980b. "Symbol and function in South American Indian music" in *Musics of many cultures: An introduction*, ed. by Elizabeth May. Berkeley and Los Angeles: University of California Press, 363–85.
1986. "The flutes of El Dorado: An archaeomusicological investigation of the Tairona civilization of Colombia," *Journal of the American Musical Instrument Society* 12: 107–36.
1987. "The flutes of El Dorado: Musical effigy figurines of the Tairona," *Imago musicae* 3 (1986): 79–102.

1990. "The ethnomusicology of archaeology: A model for the musical/cultural study of ancient material culture," *Selected reports in ethnomusicology* 8: 175–97 (Ethnomusicology publications, Department of Ethnomusicology and Systematic Musicology, University of California, Los Angeles).

1992. "Implications of music technologies in the pre-Columbian Andes" in *Musical repercussions of 1492: Encounters in text and performance*, ed. by Carol E. Robertson. Washington, D.C.: Smithsonian Institution Press, 65–88.

1996. *Music of the Warao of Venezuela: Song people of the rain forest*. Gainesville: University Press of Florida.

2002. *Music of El Dorado: The ethnomusicology of ancient South American cultures*. Gainesville: University Press of Florida.

Olsen, Dale A., and Selwyn Ahyoung 1989. "Latin America and the Caribbean" in *Multicultural perspectives in music education*, ed. by William M. Anderson and Patricia Shehan Campbell. Reston, Virginia: Music Educators National Conference, 79–117.

Olsen, Dale A., Daniel E. Sheehy, and Charles A. Perrone 1987. "Music of Latin America," a study guide, in *Sounds of the world*. Reston, Virginia: Music Educators National Conference.

Olsen, Diane 1978. *Precolumbian exhibition: The John and Mary Carter collection of Peruvian precolumbian artifacts and textiles*. Tallahassee: Florida State University Fine Arts Festival.

Orrego-Salas, Juan A. 1966. "Araucanian Indian instruments," *Ethnomusicology* 10/1: 48–57.

Otter, Elisabeth den 1985. *Music and dance of indians and mestizos in an Andean valley of Peru*. Delft, The Netherlands: Eburon.

Palma, Ricardo 1872 in 1968. *Tradiciones peruanas completas*, 6th edition, ed. and with a prologue by Edith Palma. Madrid: Aguilar.

Pardo Tovar, Andrés 1960. *Los cantares tradicionales del Baudó*. Bogotá: Universidad Nacional de Colombia.

Paredes, Rigoberto 1936. "Instrumentos musicales de los Kollas," *Boletín latinoamericano de música* (Montevideo), vol. II: 77–82.

1977. *El arte folklórico de Bolivia*. La Paz: Ediciones Puerta del Sol.

Perdomo Escobar, José Ignacio 1986. *Colección de instrumentos musicales*, ed. by Egberto Bermúdez. Bogotá: Banco de la República.

Pérez Lorenzo, Miguel, Nubia Flórez Forero, Benjamín Yépez Chamorro, Gisela Cánepa Koch, Gladys Alemán Felibert, and Carlos García Carbó 1999. "Gaita (I) and (II)" in *Diccionario de la música española e hispanoamericana*, 10 vols., ed. by Emilio Casares Rodicio, with Victoria Eli Rodríguez and Benjamín Yépez Chamorro. Madrid: Sociedad General de Autores y Editores, vol. 5, 304–13.

Piñeros Corpas, Joaquín, n.d. Liner notes to *Introducción al cancionero noble de Colombia*. See Discography.

Platt, Tristan 1976. *Espejos y maíz: Temas de la estructura simbólica andina*. La Paz: Cuadernos de Investigación CIPCA 10.

Plesch, Melanie, Walter Sánchez, Manuel Dannemann, Raquel Bustos Valderrama, Carolina Iriarte, Jorge Luis Acevedo, Victoria Eli Rodríguez, Mario Godoy Aguirre, Juan Mullo Sandoval, Víctor Manuel López Guzmán, Salvador Marroquín, Dieter Lehnhoff, Alfred E. Lemmon, Irene Vásquez Valle, Fernando Nava, Leslie E. George, Isis de Bárcena, and Fredy Moncada 1999. "Bandas" in *Diccionario de la música española e hispanoamericana*, 10 vols., ed. by Emilio Casares Rodicio, with Victoria Eli Rodríguez and Benjamín Yépez Chamorro. Madrid: Sociedad General de Autores y Editores, vol. 2, 137–60.

Pumarino V., Ramón, and Arturo Sangüeza 1968. *Los bailes chinos en Aconcagua y Valparaíso*. Santiago de Chile: Consejería Nacional de Promoción Popular.

Ramón y Rivera, Luis Felipe 1966. "Music of the Motilone Indians," *Ethnomusicology* 10/1: 18–27.

1967. "A riddle of cultural diffusion: The existence of inverted reed clarinets among the Indians of the Guajira Peninsula," *Journal of the International Folk Music Council* 19: 37–41.

Rawcliffe, Susan 1992. "Complex acoustics in pre-Columbian flute systems" in *Musical repercussions of 1492: Encounters in text and performance*, ed. by Carol E. Robertson. Washington, D.C.: Smithsonian Institution Press, 35–63.

Reichel-Dolmatoff, Gerardo 1971. *Amazonian cosmos: The sexual and religious symbolism of the Tukano Indians*. Chicago: University of Chicago Press.

Rocha, José Maria Tenório, and Tiago de Oliveira Pinto 1986. "Bandas de pífanos, die Instrumental-Ensembles des Nordostens" in *Brasilien*, ed. by Tiago de Oliveira Pinto. Mainz: Schott, 89–107.

Romero, Raúl 1985. "La música tradicional y popular" in *La música en el Perú* by César Bolaños, Enrique Iturriaga, Enrique Pinilla, José Quezada, and Raúl Romero. Lima: Patronato Popular y Porvenir Pro Música Clásica, 215–74.

1987. Liner notes to *Música andina del Perú*. See Discography.

2001. *Debating the past: Music, memory, and identity in the Andes*. New York: Oxford University Press.

Roth, Walter E. 1924. "An introductory study of the arts, crafts, and customs of the Guiana Indians," *38th annual report of the Bureau of American Ethnology 1916–1917* (Washington, D.C.), 25–745.

Ruiz, Irma 2000. "Mimby retá" in *Diccionario de la música española e hispanoamericana*, 10 vols., ed. by Emilio Casares Rodicio, with Victoria Eli Rodríguez and Benjamín Yépez Chamorro. Madrid: Sociedad General de Autores y Editores, vol. 7, 585–86.

Ruiz, Irma, and Rubén Pérez Bugallo 1980. *Instrumentos musicales etnográficos y folkóricos de la Argentina*. Buenos Aires: Instituto Nacional de Musicología "Carlos Vega."

Salas Salazar, Marcos Angelo 1998. *Banda Departamental de Músicos de Nariño*. Nariño, Colombia: Fondo Mixto de Cultura.

Sánchez Canedo, Wálter 1989. "Música autóctona del norte de Potosí," *Boletín* (Cochabamba, Bolivia, Centro Pedagógico y Cultural de Portales—Centro de Documentación de Música Boliviana), No. 12 (April-May).

Seeger, Anthony 1987. *Why Suyá sing*. Cambridge: Cambridge University Press.

Smith, Sandra 1984. *Panpipes for power, panpipes for play: The social management of cultural expression in Kuna society* (PhD diss., Anthropology: University of California at Berkeley).

Smith McCosker, Sandra 1974. *The lullabies of the San Blas Cuna Indians of Panama*. Göteborg: Göteborgs Etnografiska Museum (Etnologiska Studier, 33).

1980. "Ethno-theories of music: An example from the Kuna in Panama," unpublished manuscript.

Stevenson, Robert 1968. *Music in Aztec and Inca territory*. Berkeley and Los Angeles: University of California Press.

Stobart, Henry 1996. "*Tara and q'iwa*: Worlds of sound and meaning" in *Cosmología y música en los Andes*, ed. by Max Peter Baumann. Frankfurt am Main: Vervuert; Madrid: Iberoamericana, 67–81.

Sullivan, Lawrence E. 1988. *Icanchu's drum: An orientation to meaning in South American religions*. New York: Macmillan.

Tayler, Donald 1972. Liner notes to *The music of some Indian tribes of Colombia*. See Discography.

Téllez Girón, Roberto 1964. *Investigación folklórica en México*. México: Secretaría de Educación Pública—Instituto Nacional de Bellas Artes, Departamento de Música, Sección de Investigaciones Musicales.

Thorrez López, Marcelo 1977. *El huayño en Bolivia*. La Paz: Instituto Boliviano de Cultura.

Titiev, Mischa 1949. *Social singing among the Mapuche*. Ann Arbor: University of Michigan Press (Anthropological papers, Museum of Anthropology, 2).

Turino, Thomas 1988. "The music of Andean migrants in Lima, Peru: Demographics, social power, and style," *Latin American music review* 9/2: 127–49.

———. 1989. "The coherence of social style and musical creation among the Aymara in southern Peru," *Ethnomusicology* 33/1: 1–30.

———. 1993. *Moving away from silence: Music of the Peruvian Altiplano and the experience of urban migration.* Chicago: University of Chicago Press.

Turrado Moreno, Ángel 1945. *Etnografía de los indios guaraúnos.* Caracas: Litografía y Tipografía Vargas.

Urrutia Blondel, Jorge 1968. "Danzas rituales en la provincia de Santiago," *Revista musical chilena* 22/103 (January–March): 43–76.

Vale, Flausino Rodrigues 1978. *Elementos de folclore musical brasileiro,* 2nd ed., revised and enlarged. São Paulo: Companhia Editora Nacional.

Valencia Chacón, Américo 1983. *El siku bipolar altiplánico.* Vol. I: *Los sikuris y pusamorenos.* Lima: Editorial Artex.

———. 1989. *El siku o zampoña.* Lima: Centro de Investigación y Desarrollo de la Música Peruana.

———. 1990. *El siku altiplánico: Estudio de los conjuntos orquestales de sikus bipolares del altiplano peruano.* La Habana: Casa de las Américas.

Vargas, Teófilo 1928. *Aires nacionales de Bolivia.* Santiago: Casa Amarilla.

Vega, Carlos 1946. *Los instrumentos musicales aborígenes y criollos de la Argentina.* Buenos Aires: Ediciones Centurión.

Velásquez, Ronny 1987. *Chamanismo, mito y religión en cuatro naciones étnicas de América aborigen.* Caracas: Academia Nacional de la Historia (Colección Estudios, Monografías y Ensayos 97).

———. 1992. "Kammu purwi (flautas de pan de los Kunas de Panamá)," *Anuario FUNDEF* (Caracas, Fundación de Etnomusicología y Folklore) 3: 7–22.

Villas Bôas, Orlando, and Cláudio Villas Bôas 1970. *Xingu: Os índios, seus mitos.* Rio de Janeiro: Zahar Editores. English translation by Susana Hertelendy Rudge, as *Xingu: The Indians, their myths,* ed. by Kenneth S. Brecher (New York: Farrar, Straus and Giroux, 1973).

———. 1972. Liner notes to *Xingu: Cantos e ritmos.* See Discography.

Wara Céspedes, Gilka 1984. "New currents in 'música folklórica' in La Paz, Bolivia," *Latin American music review* 5/2: 217–42.

Wilbert, Johannes 1956. "Los instrumentos musicales de los indios Warrau (Guarao, Guaraúno)," *Antropológica* (Caracas) I: 2–22.

———. 1972. *Survivors of Eldorado.* New York: Praeger.

———. 1974. *Yupa folktales.* Los Angeles: Latin American Center, University of California (Latin American Studies, 24).

Yábar Palacio, Luis 1922 in 1986. "El ayllu de Qqeros—Paucartambo" in *Q'ero, pueblo y música,* ed. by Rodolfo Holzmann. Lima: Patronato Popular y Porvenir Pro Música Clásica, 173–96.

Yépez Chamorro, Benjamín 1984. *La música de los Guahibo: Sikuani—Cuiba.* Bogotá: Fundación de Investigaciones Arqueológicas Nacionales—Banco de la República.

———. 1999. "Cachovenao" and "Chirimía" (Colombia) in *Diccionario de la música española e hispanoamericana,* 10 vols., ed. by Emilio Casares Rodicio, with Victoria Eli Rodríguez and Benjamín Yépez Chamorro. Madrid: Sociedad General de Autores y Editores, vol. 2, 855; vol. 3, 663.

Yévenez Sanhueza, Enrique 1980. *Chile: Proyección folklórica.* Santiago: Edward W. Leonard.

DISCOGRAPHY

Amerindian ceremonial music from Chile. Liner notes by Manuel Dannemann. LP, Philips 6586 026 (UNESCO Collection, "Musical sources").

Amerindian music of Chile (Aymara, Qaqashqar, Mapuche). Liner notes by Christos Clair-Vasiliadis *et al.* LP, Folkways FE 4054.

Anthology of Brazilian Indian music. Liner notes by Harold Schultz. LP, Folkways 4311.

Bandinha de pífano: Cultural de Caruaru. LP, Companhia Industrial de Discos CID 8040.

Bolivia: Panpipes. Recordings by Louis Girault (1950–73). Edited by The International Institute for Comparative Music Studies. Commentary by Xavier Bellenger. 1 LP stereo, EMI Italiana 3C/06418528 (1981) (UNESCO Collection, Musics and musicians of the world); reissued on CD, AUVIDIS D8009 (1987).

Bolivien: Musik im Andenhochland. Liner notes by Max Peter Baumann. LP, Museum für Völkerkunde Berlin, MC 14.

Brazil: The Bororo world of sound. Liner notes by Ricardo Canzio. CD, AUVIDIS D 8201 (1989) (International Music Council/ UNESCO, Musics and musicians of the world).

Brésil Central: Chants et danses des Indiens Kaiapó. Liner notes by Gustaaf Verswijver. CD, AIMP XIV–XV, disques VDE-GALLO, VDE, CD 554/555 (1989) (Archives internationales de musique populaire).

Brésil: Musiques du Haut Xingú. Liner notes by Patrick Menget. LP, Musidisc-Europe MU 218 Y 558 517.

Chile: Hispano-Chilean mestizo traditional music. Liner notes by Manuel Dannemann. CD, AUVIDIS D 8001 (UNESCO Collection).

The Indians of Colombia. Liner notes, no author given. LP, Lyrichord LLST 7365.

Instruments and music of Bolivia. Recorded in Bolivia by Bernard Keiler. Liner notes by Bernard Keiler. 1 LP, Ethnic Folkways Library, FM 4012.

Introducción al cancionero noble de Colombia. Liner notes by Joaquín Piñeros Corpas. LP, Industrias Fonoton/Antares Ltda. Edición especial de la Universidad de los Andes, Bogotá.

Lowland tribes of Ecuador. Liner notes by David Blair Stiffler. LP, Folkways FE 4375.

Mountain music of Peru. Recorded and with liner notes by John Cohen. 2 LPs, Folkways FE 4539 (1966).

Music from Mato Grosso, Brazil. Liner notes by Edward M. Weyer, Jr. LP, Folkways FE 4446.

The music of some Indian tribes of Colombia. Liner notes by Donald Tayler. 3 LPs, British Institute of Recorded Sound (1972).

Music of the Jívaro of Ecuador. Liner notes by Michael J. Harner. LP, Folkways FE 4386.

Music of the Venezuelan Yekuana Indians. Collected and edited by Walter Coppens. Liner notes by Walter Coppens and Isaías Rodríguez V. LP, Folkways FE 4104 (1975).

Música andina del Perú. Liner notes by Raúl Romero. LP, Pontificia Universidad Católica del Perú (1987).

Música indígena y folklórica de Colombia. Liner notes by Manuel Benavides. LP, Importaciones Daro. Bogotá: Instituto Colombiano de Antropología.

Música indígena Guajibo. Liner notes by Igor Colima Castillo *et al.* LP, Fundación La Salle and Instituto Interamericano de Etnomusicología y Folklore.

Música tradicional del Valle del Mantaro. Liner notes by Raúl Romero. LP, Pontificia Universidad Católica del Perú.

Musique indienne du Brésil. Liner notes by Simone Dreyfus. LP, Collection Musée de L'Homme, VG 403 LDM 30112 B.

Musique des Indiens Bora et Witoto d'Amazonie colombienne. Liner notes by Mireille Guyot. Office de la Recherche Scientifique et Technique Outre-Mer (1976).

Musiques du Pérou: Paucartambo, Indiens Q'eros. Recorded and with liner notes by Pierre Allard. LP, OCORA OCR 30 (1967).

Pérou: Taquile, île du ciel. Liner notes by Xavier Bellenger. LP, OCORA, Festival de Lille 558651.

Peru: Ayarachi and Chiriguano. DC, MTC 1 (UNESCO Collection, Digital Archives of Traditional Music).

Soul vine shaman. Recording ed. by Neelon Crawford. Liner notes by Norman E. Whitten, Jr. *et al.* LP, NC-S-7601, Sacha Runa Research Foundation.

Wayãpi, Guyane. Liner notes by Jean-Michel Beaudet. Office de la Recherche Scientifique et Technique Outre-Mer (1980).

Xingu: Cantos e ritmos. Liner notes by Orlando and Claudio Villas Boas. LP, Phillips Records 6349-022 (1972).

RECORDED EXAMPLES

1. *Nahanamu* harvest festival of the Warao, Delta Amacuro Federal Territory, Venezuela. *Muhusemoi* (flute), two *isimoi* clarinets, *hebu-mataro* rattles, and *sewei* anklet rattles (see also Figs. 6 and 14, and Ex. 20). Recorded by Dale A. Olsen (1972). Ethnomusicology Archive, Florida State University, Tallahassee.

2. *Atuñsa* flute and bird. *Atuñsa* played by a Yuko man, imitating a bird. The Yuko are a subgroup of the Maraka who live in the Sierra de Perijá, Colombia. Recorded by Kenneth Ruddle (ca. 1970). Ethnomusicology Archive, Florida State University, Tallahassee.

3. Pablo Milla Balbero from Yungay, Ancash, Peru, playing a *wayno* and *fuga* on his *roncadora* (flute and drum, see also Fig. 12 and Ex. 16). Recorded by Dale A. Olsen (1979). Ethnomusicology Archive, Florida State University, Tallahassee.

4. Procession during the patronal festival of the Virgen del Carmen in Alto Otuzco, Cajamarca, Peru. Two alternating *clarines* (trumpets), *cajero* (flute and drum), female singers, fireworks, and church bells (see also Fig. 13 and Exs. 19a and 19b). Recorded by Dale A. Olsen (16 July 1979). Ethnomusicology Archive, Florida State University, Tallahassee.

5. *Orquesta típica* Selección del Centro of the Valle del Mantaro directed by Julio Rosales Huatuco, performing the *huayno* "No le cuentes a nadie" (Don't tell anybody) at a private party during the patronal festival of San Juan Bautista in Acolla, Department of Junín, Peru (see Fig. 15). Harp, three violins, clarinets, and alto and tenor saxophones. Recorded by Dale A. Olsen (24 June 1979). Ethnomusicology Archive, Florida State University, Tallahassee.

EPILOGUE

CAROL E. ROBERTSON

DURING THE LAST five hundred years of cultural contact, the peoples of America, Africa, and Europe have used images of each other to renegotiate new identities. Cast in the womb of what—to some—was a "New World" and to others a "Fourth World," these identities have taken tacit form in performance. At the beginning of the twenty-first century, and within the arena of representation and enactment, the monumental forces of time, nature, and cultural encroachment are brought into the flux of a modern world that substitutes boom boxes for shamans and hardhats for feather headdresses. As men and women build roads across the Andes, fight for a political toehold in southern Mexico, organize weaving cooperatives in Ecuador, and manifest their resistance to five hundred years of occupation by raising their voices in *nueva canción* (an ancient American tradition), their musical practices seldom have been represented as integral to the fabric of nationhood in music histories that, written mostly by Latin Americans, span well over a century (Kuss 1984: 52–65; 1987: 615–63).

In the European discourse on the Indigenous Other we tend to "totalize" populations, painting cultural images with broad strokes that obscure the intricate dynamics between individuals and communities. Thus, while the Andean *ayllu* remains a nexus of community, traditional rituals, and ancient modes of social actions, it also becomes the cornerstone for agricultural revolution. It seems difficult for us to simultaneously hold images of traditions being reconstituted over time by changing communities, and of radical change wrought by individuals whose identities are lost to the leveling power of ethnographic writing. Our tendencies to standardize and depersonalize data forfeit the passion of individuals like Nobel laureate Rigoberta Menchú, who, in 1992, focused worldwide attention on the plight of the Quiché Maya of Guatemala. We also tend to lose sight of dedicated men like Don Herminio Ricaldi Chávez, a copper-mine worker in the highland Peruvian town of Carhuamayo, who brought the drama of Atahualpa's life and death to his community in an effort to revise the complex relationship between conquered and conqueror, and to integrate a local version of oral Inca history into the national discourse.

The individuals subsumed under our ethnomusicological rhetoric are crucial players in these cultural dramas, for—like their pre-Columbian ancestors—they are the key to experimentation and change. While indigenous healers use musical and medical formulas handed down for generations, they also continue to run biochemical experiments on themselves, testing new herbs and novel techniques of sonic and spiritual manipulation. Like their predecessors, who explored timbre and experienced periods of intense change followed by periods of quiet assimilation of technologies, today's indigenous composers, performers, and ritual practitioners live at a crossroads in which old and new forms of knowledge are becoming intertwined.

The historical presence of the European often is articulated through ritual enactment. These representations, for all their stereotyping, offer complex perceptions of five centuries of occupation. In "The Death of the Coya" dance described by Luis

Millones (1992: 242–48), the women of the town of Carhuamayo perform the stately gestures and foot movement of Inca royalty, aware that they are being approached by Pizarro, who weasels among them sowing his deceit. Suddenly, in a burst of traitorous energy, Pizarro unsheaths his hidden dagger and slits the throat of the leading Coya, whose *wira*, or life force, spills onto the ground in the form of corn liquor. This dramatic act encapsulates a betrayal that, for all our efforts to document and honor indigenous cultures, cannot be undone. It also demonstrates how the trauma of Conquest becomes incorporated into ritual enactments of cultural identity.

Many of the images central to indigenous ritual life are composites drawn from Iberian and mestizo culture, infused with local meanings. Victoria Reifler Bricker (1973), writing on the Passion of Christ among Chamula Indians in Chiapas, Mexico, interprets the representation of Christ as one of these composites:

The passion cult is the only cult in Chamula for which the object of devotion is not a saint figure in the church. The emphasis is on impersonation rather than idolatry. The theme of the fiesta is war, and one of the wars being commemorated is the Caste War of 1867-1870, which originated in Chamula. The leaders of this rebellion exhorted the Indians to reject the Catholic saints and, on Good Friday in 1868, crucified a ten- or eleven-year-old boy, Domingo Gómez Checheb, to be worshipped as the Indian Christ (Pineda 1888: 76-77). There is abundant evidence that the Christ whom the Passion impersonates is this Indian Christ rather than the Ladino Savior (1973: 88–89).

In the examples documented by Millones and Reifler Bricker, symbolic impersonation and representation take on staggering depth. What is at play here is the uncanny ability of human populations under siege to redress imbalances perceived in the cosmos. As shown in the articles in this volume, performance plays a central role in the mediation of meaning and in "restoring order" to a world that is constantly in danger of running amok.

The complexity of indigenous musical thought was best illustrated in Charles Boilès's classic exploration of Tepehua "thought-song" (1967), in which musical "conjugation" parallels the semantic structures of language. The intricacies of Tepehua sound structures point us toward a theoretical/conceptual current in

indigenous musical creativity that also surfaces in the essays included in this volume. The diversity of performance contexts and symbolic meanings documented by Hill, Travassos, Menezes Bastos, Baumann, Turino, Grebe, Ruiz, Robertson, Velásquez, and Nava López, adduces modes of ethnomusicological analysis that honor the musical maturity of the peoples of the Americas. Alonso Bolaños's survey of indigenous groups in Mexico provides one concrete example of the breadth of this diversity.

Our millennial challenge is to open new forms of dialogue between cultures, incorporating these voices into our discourse: yet, few indigenous sages seek our form of wisdom, our way with words, our interpretations. The discourse we create, however, must imbibe the *wira*, the life force of the traditions we seek to understand. Scientific inquiry, or knowledge "about" the musical traditions of indigenous groups must not be kept at arm's length: instead, knowledge "of" their rituals and worldviews must be burned into our psyche and become integral to our own experience of the Americas.

The Conquest may have submerged and extinguished many indigenous voices, but it did not silence them. Increasingly, indigenous peoples are raising their own voices. They will not settle for being ignored, and have taken their case to the world's tribunals, to the polls, and into continued wars of resistance. In this volume we have given voice to only a sample of musical experiences of Native Americans. There is a long road ahead in our quest to map the wealth of their musical legacy.

REFERENCES

Boilès, Charles L. 1967. "Tepehua thought-song: A case of semantic signaling," *Ethnomusicology* 11/3: 267–92.

Kuss, Malena 1984. *Latin American music: An annotated bibliography of reference sources and research materials.* Paris: International Music Council—UNESCO.
1987. "Toward a comprehensive approach to Latin American music bibliography: Theoretical foundations for reference sources and research materials" in *Latin American masses and minorities: Their images and realities*, 2 vols., ed. by Dan C. Hazen. Madison: SALAM Secretariat—Memorial Library, University of Wisconsin, vol. II, 615–63.

Millones, Luis 1992. "The Death of Atahualpa" in *Musical repercussions of 1492: Encounters in text and performance*, ed. by Carol E. Robertson. Washington, D.C.: Smithsonian Institution Press, 237–56.

Pineda, Vicente 1888. *Historia de las sublevaciones indígenas habidas en el estado de Chiapas.* Chiapas: Tipografía del Gobierno.

Reifler Bricker, Victoria 1973. *Ritual humor in Highland Chiapas.* Austin and London: University of Texas Press.

INDEX

MALENA KUSS

This index highlights peoples, instruments, concepts, and countries. In hierarchical terms, the main entries on peoples (e.g., Atacameño, Aymara, Mapuche, P'urhépecha, Wakuénai, etc.) are analyzed in greatest detail. Subheadings under peoples generate main subject headings (e.g., demographics, cosmology, dance, rituals and ceremonies, song, etc.) which themselves collect more synthetically analyzed references. Consistent with the obvious lack of coincidence between cultural areas and geopolitical boundaries, main headings on countries collect references at the most synthetic level (e.g., peoples in the respective nations).

The structure of this index also reflects the value placed on localizing traditions. Consequently, countries' names and specific regions qualify ethnic groups in the following cases:

(1), when the territory and/or area of cultural influence associated with a single, linguistically differentiated group extends over two or more countries, and/or when a number of factors—including different sociopolitical histories—defines an interplay between a metalevel of commonalities and a microlevel of local differences in traditional practices (e.g., the Aymara in Argentina, Bolivia, Chile, and Peru; the Mapuche in Argentina and Chile); and

(2), when linguistically differentiated groups in the same country share traditions (e.g., the Aymara and Kechua in Bolivia), or, conversely, when their respective traditional practices differ significantly at the local level (e.g., Aymara-speakers in Conima District and Kechua-speakers in Canas Province, both in southern Peru).

Indexing of instruments—and especially the extensive coverage of aerophones in this volume—prioritizes two contrasting types of terminological concordances: homonymic, namely the use of the same term for different instruments; and synonymic, namely the use of different terms for the same instrument. Concordances also reflect changing approaches to orthography and transliteration (for instance, *kena* and *mimby retá* supersede *quena* and *mimbü-eta*, respectively). For areas still untouched by the age of plastic substitution, an entry on "aerophones, materials for" underscores the importance of material culture as anthropological trait and suggests the possibility of area differentiation according to basic material used, such as bamboo vis-à-vis cane.

Page numbers in italics refer to iconographical and musical illustrations.

A

Abadía Morales, Guillermo, 314, 316
abajeño (P'urhépecha musical genre; sung and danced types), 248–49, *249*, 251–52, 255–56, 259
abisúa (Kuna ritual specialist), 213, 222–23
absogued (*absoguedi*; Kuna chant; chant owner; great shaman), 213–15, 217, 224–25
absogued ígala (Kuna shamanic chant-type), path of, 213–14, 224–25
accordion (*acordeón*; multiple single-reed aerophone)
    button accordion (*acordeón a botones*), 316
    in Chile, 316

    in Colombia, 316, 318
    description of, 263, 267, 316
    Mbyá people, 177
    in Peruvian *orquesta cuzqueña*, 133
    piano accordion (*acordeón a piano*), 316
acculturation. *See also* cultural change; *mestizaje*; transculturation
    in the Argentinian Northwest, 163
    in Brazil, 52–53, 59–60
    as concept, 4–5
    identity retention in, and *mestizaje*, 2–5, 238

acculturation (*continued*)
  by peoples
    Atacameño, 153
    Aymara and Kechua, in Bolivia, 116
    indigenous population, in Chile, 145
    Kawéskar, 158–60
    Mapuche, in Chile, 156
    Mískito, in creole music, 207–10
    P'urhépecha, 258–59
    Xavante, in *louvores* (praise songs for Catholic
      saints), 59–60
Achach K'umu (Aymara dance-drama tradition), in Conima
    District, Peru, 126, 132, *133*
achachilas (*apus*; Aymara for Andean mountain divinities,
    male centers of power), 103, 126, 130, 132
achachis (*achichis*; ancestral spirits; male spirits of the
    mountain), in Bolivia, 109, 113, 116
achichis (*achachis*; ancestral spirits, Aymara people), in
    Chile, 150
acordeón. See accordion
acoustics
  classification of sound categories, basis for, Kamayurá
    people, 64
  interlocking performance technique, evidence of, in
    Mochica and Nazca panpipes, 275
  in *pífano* tunings, northeastern Brazil, 296–97
  in timbral aesthetics of
    clarín (long side-blown trumpet), 310
    kanchis sipas (double-row panpipes), 283
    pinkillus (duct flutes), 127
    pitus (*falawatus*; side-blown flutes), 127
    sikus (double-row panpipes), 127, 276
    tarkas (duct flutes), 127, 303
Adzanéni people, 18n, 25
aerophones. *See also* aerophones, by instruments
  aesthetics, in general, 267–69. *See also under*
    aesthetics
  classification of, 261–63, 284–85, 319–20
  construction techniques, 266–67
  defined, 261–63
  functions of, in general, 319–20
  gender attribution. *See under* gender attribution
  materials for. *See* aerophones, materials for
  mouthpiece types, technological scale of, 266–67
  performance practice, in general, 267–69. *See also*
    under performance practice
  sources, primary and secondary, 263–64
  survey of, 261–320, *265* (map)
  symbolism of, in general, 56, 102–103, 267–69,
    319–20. *See also under specific aerophones*
  tunings, in general, 267. *See also under* tuning
aerophones, by instruments. *See also* ensembles, by type
  accordion (*acordeón*)
    button accordion (*acordeón a botones*), 316
    in Chile, 316
    in Colombia, 316, 318
    description of, 263, 267, 316
    Mbyá people, 177
    in Peruvian *orquesta cuzqueña*, 133
    piano accordion (*acordeón a piano*), 316
    aige (bullroarer), 318–19

anata (name for *tarka* in southern Bolivia and northern
    Chile; duct flute). See *tarka* below
antara
  as Kechua term for dualistic panpipes, 103–104, 118
  as Kechua term for monistic panpipes, 266, 275,
    277n, 282–83
are're (panpipes), 280
armónica. See *rondín* below
atuñsa (*atunse*, plural for the pair; "hatchet" duct flute),
    267, 297–98
auloi (double pipes of ancient Greeks), 263
ayarachi (*ayarichi*; as panpipes), 276–78
ayarichi (*ayarachi*; as panpipes), 104, 118, *118*
aykhori. See *pinkillo mohoceño* below
aymara. See *pinkillo mohoceño* below
bandoneón, 316
bullroarers, 316, 318–19
burdón (*contrabajo*; duct aerophone), 119
búzio. See *pífano* below
buzo. See *pífano* below
cacho, in Peru
  as name for the animal horn coiled trumpet
    (*wak'rapuku*), in Mantaro Valley, 307
  as name for the bull or cow horn (*pututo* or *pututu*),
    in Huarochirí, 308
cacho de venado (*cacho venao*; deer-skull ocarina),
    292–93, *293*
caña
  in Argentina, as long side-blown trumpet (*corneta*,
    erke), 163, 309
  in Bolivia, as end-blown bamboo tube with
    resonator, 120, *120*
  in Peru
    as long side-blown trumpet (*erke*), 163. See also
      clarín
    as name for K'ero notched flute (*pina pinkulucha*,
      pinkulu), 291
caña de lata. See *caña de millo* below
caña de millo (*caña de lata, flauta de millo, pito*; side-
    blown single-reed aerophone), 267, 314,
    316
cañari (*kañari*), 308
capador (panpipe), 266, 269
caracoles (conch-shell trumpets), 247
caramillo (panpipe), 280
carrizo (panpipes)
  in Colombia, 298
  description of, 266
  in Venezuela, 278, 280–82, *281*
ch'aje. See *charka* below
charazani (side-blown flute), 120
charge. See *charka* below
charka (*ch'aje; charge; charkha*; curved duct flute), 102,
    119, 304
charu. See *kuizi* below
chino flute (*flauta de chino, flautón, pito*)
  description of, 266, 271–73, *272,*
  interlocking technique in performance, 268,
    272–74
  performance styles, 278
chirimía (*chirimoya, chirisuya*; double-reed aerophone)

in Colombia
    as ensemble, 318
    as single-reed aerophone, 316, 318
description of, 316, 318
in Mexico
    in general, 316, 318
    P'urhépecha people, 248, 251
origin of, 263
in Peru, 262, 316, 318
chirimoya (name for *chirimía* in Lucanas, Department of
    Ayacucho, Peru), 316
chirisuya (name for *chirimía* in areas of southern Peru),
    263, 316, 318
chiriwanos
in Bolivia
    as panpipe ensembles, 104
    as panpipes of Aymara and Kechua peoples, 104,
      118, *118*
    as panpipes of Chipaya people (*maizus*), 104, 118,
      118
in Peru
    as Aymara name for *siku* panpipes, 274
    as Aymara tradition of *siku* panpipes
      performance, 276–78
chokela (notched flute)
in Bolivia, 103, 118, 120
in Peru, 127
ch'unchu (as side-blown flute), 120
ch'utu (*pinkayllo*; duct flute), 102, 119, 301
clarín (long straight side-blown trumpet)
in Argentina (*caña, corneta, erke*), 163, 309
in Chile
    Atacameño people, 153–54
    under other names (*corneta, erke*), 309
in Ecuador, 309
in Peru, 308–10, *309*, *310*
clarinet (*clarinete*)
in army and civilian bands, 269
description of, 267
in Peru, 314–16, *317*
contrabajo (*burdón*), 119
corneta (Spanish for "trumpet"; lip concussion
    aerophones)
in Argentina, as long side-blown trumpet (*caña,
      erke*), 163
in Chile
    as long side-blown trumpet (*clarín, erke*), 309
    as short end-blown trumpet, Mapuche peoples,
      271
dápa (trumpets), 31–32, 46
déetu (as flute), 35, 37–38, 40–41, 42, *42*, 44–46
doti (Chipaya name for *pututu* as bull or cow horn), in
    Bolivia, 120
dulzaina. See *rondín* below
dzáate (as flute), 31, 33, 46
dzáwinápa (large "Jaguar-bone" trumpets), 25, 29–32,
    46
erke
as long side-blown trumpet (*caña, clarín, corneta,
    erkhe*)
    in Argentina, 309–310

in Chile, 309–310
in Peru, 163
as single-reed animal horn (*erkencho*)
    in Argentina, 310–11
    in Bolivia (*erkencho*), 120, *120*, 310–11
    in Chile, 310–11
    description of, 267
erkencho (*erke*; single-reed animal horn), 120, *120*, 267,
    310–11
falawatu (*pitu*; side-blown flute), in Peru, 126–28, 132,
    133, 294
flauta (as smaller types of transverse flutes in Ecuador),
    295, *295*
flauta de chino. See *chino* flute *above*
flauta de millo. See *caña de millo* above
flautas de pico (generic term for beak flutes), 300
flautón. See *chino* flute *above*
flawata. See *pflawata*
flutes. *See also specific types*
    Kayabi people, 72
    Makuxí, Taulipáng, and Yekuâna peoples, 54
    Wakuénai peoples, 26
gaita
as "hatchet" duct flute, in Colombia
    gaita hembra (female flute), 298
    gaita macho (male flute), 268, 298
as name for side-blown ductless flute (*pífano*), in
    Brazil, 296–97
as single open pipe with finger holes and detachable
    duct, 267
gammu-burui. See *kammu purwi* below
gammu suid. See *kammu suid* below
guli (*kuli*; set of separate but complementary end-blown
    ductless tubes), 273, *273*
harehare (single closed pipe with finger holes), 267
harmonica, in Peruvian string band music, 134
he (flutes), 18
heresemoi (conch-shell trumpet), 305–306, *306*
hito (*wichu*; duct aerophone), 267
horn, baritone, in army and civilian bands, 269
isimoi (single-reed aerophone), 267, 288, 312–13, *313*, *315*
jiwa (panpipes), 280
julajulas (single-row panpipes)
    description of, 105, 107–108, *105–107*, 118
    dry season, association with, 103
    with *pulus* (vessel flutes), in ensembles, 120
    symbolic dualism in interlocking performance
      technique, 103–105, *105–106*, 107–108
julu-julus (panpipes), 104, 118
kagutu (large flutes), 21
kallamachu (single-row panpipes), 127–28
kammu (as aerophone). See *kammu suid* below
kammu purwi (*gammu-burui, kammupurui, kamu-purrui*;
    panpipes), 226–27, *227–28*, 278–80, *279*
kammu suid (*gammu suid*; *kammu*; *kammusui*; flutes
    played in pairs), 266, 285–86
kammupurui. See *kammu purwi* above
kammusui. See *kammu suid* above
kamu-purrui. See *kammu purwi* above
kañari (*cañari*; long straight aerophone with attached
    animal horn), 308

aerophones, by instruments (*continued*)
  kanchis sipas (double-row panpipes), 267, 282–83, *284*
  kanojí (bone whistle), 169
  kena (*qena, quena*; notched flute)
    in Bolivia, 103–104, 116, 118, *118*, 120
    in Chile, 150–51, 153
    description of, 288–91, *289*
    diffusion of, 290–91
    distribution of, 266
    history of, 288–91
    performance styles, 290–91
    Peru
      in Kechua traditions, Canas Province, 134
      in *orquesta cuzqueña*, 133
      in string-band tradition, 134
    symbolism of, 116, 288–91, 320
    tunings, 290
  kena-kena (notched flute), 103, 118, 290
  kenacho (a type of *kena*; notched flute), 290
  kenali (a type of *kena*; notched flute), 290
  kepa (*kheppa, qhueppa*)
    conch shells, symbolism of, 269
    in Peru
      as conch-shell trumpet (*kheppa, pututo, pututu, qhueppa*), 305–306
      as name for long straight side-blown trumpet (*clarín*), 308
      as pre-Columbian conch-shell trumpet, 305–307
  kheppa. See *kepa* above
  kuai (as flute), 18
  kuizi (*charu, púnkiri*; "hatchet" duct flute), 267, 297–98
  kuli. See *guli* above
  kúlirrína (large Wakuénai trumpets), 35–36, *36*, 38–39, 40–42, 44, *44*, 46
  laka (*pusa*; panpipes), 274
  lakitas (double-row panpipes)
    in Bolivia
      description of, 108–109, *108–109*, 118
      dry season, association with, 103, 109
      ensembles, 104
      function of, 109
      with membranophones, in ensembles, 104, 120
      symbolic dualism in interlocking performance technique, 103–105, 108
    in Chile, 148, 150–51
  lichiguayo (*lichiwayu*; as large type of *kena*; notched flute), 148, 150–51
  lichiwayu (*lichiguayo*; as large type of notched flute), 103, 118, 290
  locopallapalla (single-row panpipes), 127
  lolkiñ (vertical natural trumpet), 271
  máariawa (flutes), 31–34, 42, 46
  maasi. See *massi* below
  maizus (*chiriwanos*; panpipes), 104, 118, *118*
  manchaipuito (bone flute), 290
  mare-mare (as panpipes), in Venezuela
    as name for *carrizo* panpipes, 280–82
    as pluralistic panpipes, 280–82, *281–82*
  marimacho. See *pinkillo mohoceño* below
  massi (*maasi*; single-reed aerophone), 267, 313–14, *315*
  máwi (flutes), 35, *36*, 38–39, 41, *43*, 46

  mimbü-eta. See *mimby retá* below
  mimby (flutes), 174, 176
  mimby retá (*mimbü-eta*; panpipes), 174, 176, 178, 273–74
  mohoceño. See *pinkillo mohoceño* below
  molítu (as flutes), 30, 31–33, 42–43, 44–46
  much'a (a type of *pinkillo*; duct flute), 119, *119*
  muhusemoi (notched flute)
    centric melodic interval, 313
    description of, 266, 286–88, *287*
    fingering of, 287, 291
    function of, 288, 320
    music for, 288, *315*
    tuning of, 267, 287, *287*
  naseré (globular flute), 293–94
  nolkiñ (short vertical trumpets), 158
  nose ocarina (*tsin-hali*), 54, 294
  nurá-mĕe (bullroarer), 319
  ocarina, 120, 264
  paceño (a type of notched flute), 118
  pampa corneta (long maguey trumpet), 307
  pfala (*pfalawita*; side-blown ductless flute), 120, 266, 294
  pfalawita. See *pfala* above
  pflawata (*flawata*; duct flute), 119
  phalawita (side-blown ductless flute), 120, *120*
  phuko (*siku* panpipes performance tradition), 275
  phukunas (panpipes), 104, 118
  phulu-pututu (end-blown trumpet), 120
  phululu (end-blown trumpet), 120
  pífano
    as Quichua end-blown duct flute with six finger holes (*pingullo*), in Ecuador, 304
    as side-blown ductless flute (*búzio, buzo, gaita, pífaro, pife, taboca*), in Brazil, 296–97
    as side-blown flute, in Bolivia, 120
  pífaro. See *pífano* above
  pife. See *pífano* above
  pifilka. See *pifülka* below
  pifülka (*pifilka*; end-blown flute without finger holes)
    in Argentina (as *pifilka*), 170–71, 184, *185*
    in Chile (as *pifülka*), 158
    description of, 266, 269–71, *271*
    function of, 270
    performance techniques, 270–71, 274, 278
  pina pinkulucha (*caña, pinkulu*; notched flute), 291, *291*, 294
  pincollo (*pinkollo*). See *pinkillo* below
  pincullo. See *pinkullo* below
  pincuyllo (duct flute), 300
  pingollo (duct flute), 300
  pingúio. See *pinkullo* below
  pingullo (duct flute)
    as Quichua duct flute with six finger holes (*pífano*), in Ecuador, 304
    as Quichua one-hand duct flute with two finger holes and a thumb hole, in Ecuador, 304
    as variant spelling of *pinkullo*, 300
  pinkayllo (*ch'utu*; duct flute), 119, 301
  pinkillo (*pinquillo, pinquilo*; duct flute)
    in Bolivia, 102, 104, 116, 119–20, *119*
    in Chile, 149

compared with *pinkillo mohoceño*, 303
as seasonal instrument, 308
symbolism of, 116
as variant spelling of *pinkullo*, 300
pinkillo mohoceño (*aykhori, aymara, marimacho, mohoceño*; large duct aerophone), 102, 119, 119, 303
pinkillu (duct flute)
  in Peru, 126–27, 130, 131, 141, 301
  timbric symbolism, in northern Potosí ensembles, Bolivia, 301–302
  as variant spelling of *pinkullo*, 300
pinkollo (*pincollo*). See *pinkillo* above
pinkullo (*pincullo*; duct flute)
  Chiriguano-Chané peoples (*pingüio*), 171
  description of, 266–67, 300–303
  function of, 301–303
  variants of, 303
pinkullu
  as end-blown duct flute, in Peru, 134–35, 137–40, 140, 141
  as "*pinkullu* of Potosí" (name for *charka*; curved duct flute), in Bolivia, 304
pinkulu. See *pina pinkulucha* above
pinkulwe (side-blown flute), 295–96
pinquillo (*pinquilo*). See *pinkillo* above
pinquilo (*pinquillo*). See *pinkillo* above
píti (whistles), 35
pito
  as "beak" flute of the Cora people, in Mexico, 300
  as name for *caña de millo* (*caña de lata, flauta de millo*; side-blown single-reed aerophone), in Colombia, 314
  as name for *chino* flute (*flauta de chino, flautón*), in Chile, 271
  as transverse flute, in Bolivia, 120
pitón (as name for *pututo*; bull or cow horn), in Peru, 308
pitu (as transverse flute)
  in Bolivia (*pfala, pfalawita*), 120, 294
  description of, 266, 294
  in Peru
    Aymara people, in Conima District (*falawatu*), 126–28, 132, 133, 294
    K'ero people, 294, 294
pulu (vessel flute), 120
púnkiri. See *kuizi* above
pusa (*laka*; panpipes), 274
pusamoreno (*sikumoreno*; panpipes; *siku* panpipes performance tradition), 276–78
pusi-p'iya (*pusi-ppia*; as largest type of *kena*; notched flute), 290
pusi-ppia (*pusi-p'iya*; as type of notched flute),103
putu (natural horn), 153–54
pututo. See also *pututu* below
  as bull or cow horn
    in Bolivia (*pututu*), 307–308
    in Chile, 153
    in Peru (*cacho, pitón*), 308
  as conch-shell trumpet (*kepa, pututu*)
    in Bolivia, 307–308

in Peru, 305–308
pututu. See also *pututo* above
  as bull or cow horn
    in Bolivia, 102, 109, 111–12, 115, 120, 120, 307–308
    in Peru (*cacho, pitón, pututu*), 308
  as ceramic trumpet, 114
  as conch-shell trumpet (*kepa, pututo*)
    in Bolivia, 307–308
    in Peru, 305–308
  as straight, long lip-concussion trumpet (*tira tira*), in Bolivia, 307–308
qena. See *kena* above
qhueppa. See *kepa* above
quena. See *kena* above
rollano (curved duct flute), 119, 119, 301
roncadora (end-blown duct flute; flute-and-drum combination)
  description of, 267, 304–305
  music for, 305
rondador (panpipe), 266, 283–85, 285–86
rondín (*armónica, dulzaina, sinfonía*; harmonica), 263, 267, 316
saxophone (*saxofón*)
  as calabash lip concussion instrument, in Colombia, 269
  European
    in army and civilian bands, 269
    in *chirimía* ensembles, Colombia, 318
    description of, 267
    as imported instrument, 263
    in Peru, 314–16, 317
    in P'urhépecha *bandas*, 251
siku (double-row dualistic panpipes)
  in Argentina's Northwest, 163
  in Aymara healing practices, 189
  in Bolivian Andes, 103–104, 114–17, 115, 118, 118
  description of, 266, 274–78, 274
  interlocking technique in peformance, 126–27, 268, 274–76, 275
  in *nueva canción* groups, Chile, 290
  in Peru, 126–32, 128, 141
  sikuris (ensembles of *sikus*)
    performance traditions, 267, 275–78
    replaced by brass bands, 307
    symbolism of, 114–17, 115, 278, 320
    tunings, 275, 275
sikumoreno (*pusamoreno*; panpipes; *siku* panpipes performance tradition), 276–78
sikuras (*sikuris*; large type of double-row panpipes)
  in Bolivia
    description of, 109–13, 110, 115, 118, 118
    dry season, association with, 103
    function of, 109, 113
    music for, 111–12
    symbolic dualism in interlocking performance technique, 103–105, 109, 114–16
    tuning, 110
  in Chile, 148, 150–51
sikuris
  as another name for *sikuras*. See *sikuras* above
  as ensemble of *sikus*. See under *siku* above

aerophones, by instruments (*continued*)
  silbatillo (small whistle), 247
  sinfonía. See *rondín* above
  single-reed aerophones. *See also specific types*
    indigenous types, contested European origin of, 263
    Makuxí, Taulipáng, and Yekuâna peoples, 54
  suduchu (panpipes), 280
  taboca. See *pífano* above
  takwara (as single-reed aerophone), 65, 299, 311–12
  tankwara (Waurá term for *takwara* as single-reed
      aerophone), 311
  tar pinkayllu (Chipaya name for *tarka*; duct aerophone),
      303
  tarawi (single-reed concussion aerophone), 311–12
  tarka (duct flute)
    in Bolivia (*anata, tar pinkayllu*), 102, 104, 116,
        119–20, *119*, 303–304
    in Chile (*anata*), 149–50, 304
    description of, 267, 303–304, *303*
    in Peru, 126–28, 130–31, 141, 301
    symbolism of, 116, 127
    traditional performance practice, in ensembles
        (*tarkeadas*), 303–304
  ted-nono (flute), 225
  tekeya (*tekeyá, tekeyë, wanna*; single-reed concussion
      aerophone), 267, 311
  tekeyá. See *tekeya* above
  tekeyë. See *tekeya* above
  tira tira (*pututu*; straight long trumpet with attached
      animal horn), in Bolivia, 120, 307–308
  tocoro (duct flute), 301
  tokuru (long duct aerophone), 102, 119, *119*
  toré (as single-reed aerophone), 311
  totoy (*uótoroyo*; single-reed concussion aerophone), 267,
      313–14, *315*
  trombone
    as calabash lip-concussion instrument, 269
    European
      in army and civilian bands, 269
      in ensembles of P'urhépecha people, 251–52
  trompetas. See trumpets *below*
  trumpets (*trompetas*). *See also specific types*
    as calabash lip-concussion instrument, 269
    as European valve aerophone
      in Argentina, 307
      in army and civilian bands, 269
      Aymara people, in Chile, 151
      in Peru, 307
      P'urhépecha people, 248, 251
      in South America, 307
    Huanca culture, dog- and deer-head, 320
    Makuxí, Nambikwára, Paresí, Taulipáng, and
        Yekuâna peoples, 54
    Wakuénai peoples, 26
  trutruka (long straight end-blown trumpet), 158, 170–71,
      271, 307, 308
  tsidupo (two-tubed flute), 60
  tsikóta (small flutes), 35, 38–39, 41, 46
  tsin-hali (nose-blown, flat disk-shaped ocarina), 54, 294
  tuba
    as calabash lip-concussion instrument, 269

    European
      in army and civilian bands, 269
      bass tuba, Aymara people in Chile, 151
  tule (single-reed concussion aerophone), 268
  tunda (large type of side-blown flute), 266, 295, *295*
  tura (notched flute), 267, 291–92, *292*
  umreñiduruture (flute-rattle), 60
  uótoroyo (*totoy*; single-reed concussion aerophone),
      313–14
  upawã (side-blown flute), 60
  uru'á (two-tubed duct flutes), 65, 298–300, 311–12
  verékushi (panpipes), 280, 282
  waka-pinkillo (duct flute), 119
  wak'rapuku (animal horn coiled trumpet)
    in Bolivia (*waqra pututu*), 120, *120*
    in Peru (*cacho*), 306–307
  wáliáduwa (flutes), 31–34, 41–42, 46
  wanna. See *tekeya* above
  waqra pututu (animal horn coiled trumpet)
    in Bolivia, 120, *120*
    in Peru (*cacho, wak'rapuku*), 306–307
  wara (long notched flute), 266–67
  wauqu (vessel flute), 118, 120, *120*
  whistles: Makuxí, Taulipáng, and Yekuâna peoples, 54.
      See also specific types
  wichu (*hito*; duct aerophone), 267
  yaku'i (as duct flutes), 65, 79, 299–300, 311
  zampoña (panpipe), 118, 266, 274
  zumbador (bullroarer), 318
aerophones, materials for
  about, 263–64, 266
  animal horns
    about, 263
    as amplifiers or resonators, 120, 295, 307–308, 310
    doti (Chipaya name for *pututu*), in Bolivia, 120
    erke (*erkencho*; as single-reed bovine horn), 120, *120*,
        267, 310–11
    pututo (as bovine horn)
      in Bolivia, 307–308
      in Chile, 153
      in Peru (*cacho, pitón, pututu*), 308
    pututu (as bovine horn)
      in Bolivia, 102, 109, 111–12, 115, 120, *120*, 307–308
      in Peru (*cacho, pitón, pututu*), 308
    wak'rapuku (*cacho*; coiled trumpet), in Peru,
        306–307
    waqra pututu (coiled trumpet), in Bolivia, 120, *120*
  bamboo
    about, 114, 264, 266
    association with wind and dry season, Aymara and
        Kechua, in Bolivia, 108
    caña (as long end-blown aerophone with resonator),
        in Bolivia, 120
    chino flutes (*flautón*), 272
    chirimía (as single-reed aerophone), in Colombia,
        318
    clarín (long straight side-blown trumpet),
        308–309
    flautón (*chino* flutes), 272–73
    kena (notched flute), 116
    mimby retá (*mimbü-eta*; panpipes, Mbyá), 273

notched flutes, in the Bolivian Andes, 102–103
phulu-pututu (trumpet), 120
phululu (trumpet), 120
pífanos (*pífaros, pife*; side-blown flutes), in
    northeastern Brazil, 296
pifïlka (*pifülka*; flute, Mapuche), 184
pingullo (duct flute), in Ecuador, 304
pinkulwe (flute, Mapuche), 295
roncadora (flute in flute-and-drum combination), 305
sikus (double-row panpipes), 116, 276
single-reed aerophones: Makuxí, Taulipáng, and
    Yekuâna peoples, 54. *See also specific types*
takwara ("bamboo"; single-reed aerophone), 65, 299,
    311–12
tarawi (two-tubed single-reed aerophone,
    Kamayurá), 311
tekeya (single-reed aerophone, Yekuana), 311
tira tira (trumpet), 120, 307
trutruka (trumpet, Mapuche), 307
tsidupo (two-tubed flutes, Xavante), 60
upawã (flute, Xavante), 60
uru'a (two-tubed duct flutes, Kamayurá), 299
bone
    about, 263–64, 266, 286–87
    antaras (panpipes), 282
    cacho de venado (*cacho venao*, deer-skull ocarina),
        292, *293*
    cchacca pincollos (duct flutes), 300
    chirisuyas (double-reed aerophones), in Peru, 318
    dzáwinápa (Wakuénai "Jaguar-bone" trumpets), 29
    flutes. *See also specific types*
        Kawéskar people, 159
        Kayabi people, 72
        Makuxí, Taulipáng, and Yekuâna peoples, 54
        notched, 288
        simple edge aerophones, coastal Peru, 285
        kena (notched flute), 289–90
        manchaipuito (flute, Peru), 289–90
        muhusemoi (notched flute, Warao), 267, 287, 320
        pifülkas (flute, Mapuche), 270
        ted-nono (armadillo skull and tubular bone flute,
            Kuna), 225
        trumpets, deer- or dog-skull (Huanca culture, Peru),
            320
cactus, *gaita* ("hatchet" duct flute), in Colombia, 298
calabashes
    as amplifiers or resonators, 120, 309, 312–14
    gourd aerophones, in ensembles, Colombia and
        Ecuador, 269
    kenas (notched flutes), 290
    tsin-hali (nose ocarina, Paresí and Nambikwára), 54,
        294
    umreñiduruture (flute-rattle, Xavante), 60
cane
    about, 264, 266
    antara (panpipe), 282–83
    atuñsa (*atunse*; pair of "hatchet" duct flutes,
        Yuko/Yupa), 297
    caña de millo (side-blown single-reed aerophone),
        314
    cañari (*kañari*), 308

caramillo (name of the cane; panpipes), 280
carrizo (name of the cane; panpipes), 280
charka (curved duct flute), 304
erke (as single-reed aerophone), 310
erkencho (single-reed aerophone), 310
falawatu. See pitu
flautas (small side-blown flutes), in Ecuador, 295
flutes, side-blown, in *chirimía* ensembles, Colombia,
    318. *See also specific types*
gammu suid. See kammu suid
kammu purwi (panpipes, Kuna), 278, 280
kammu suid (*gammu suid*; flutes, Kuna), 285–86
kañari (*cañari*; long straight aerophone with attached
    animal horn), 308
kanchis sipas (panpipes, K'ero), 283
kenas (notched flutes), 134, 290
mare-mare (*mare*, name of the cane; panpipes), 280
massi (single-reed aerophone, Wayúu), 313–14
panpipes, pre-Hispanic, 275
pina pinkulucha (notched flute, K'ero), 291
pinkillo mohoceño (duct flute, Aymara), 303
pinkillus (duct flutes)
    Aymara, in Conima District, Peru, 134, 301
    in Department of La Paz, Bolivia, 302
pinkullu of Potosí (*charka*; duct flute), 304
pinkullus (as short duct flutes), Aymara, in Conima
    District, Peru, 134
pito (as "beak" flute, Cora), 300
pitu (*falawatu*; side-blown flute), in Conima District,
    Peru, 294
quina quina pincollo (duct flute), 300
rondador (monistic panpipe), 284, *285*
sikus (double-row panpipes), 275–76
tira tira (long straight aerophone with attached
    animal horn), 307
tocoro (name of the cane; duct flute), 300
totoy (*uótoroyo*; single-reed aerophone with calabash
    resonator, Wayúu), 313–14
tunda (name of the cane; large side-blown flute), in
    Ecuador, 295
tupa pincollo (*tocoro* cane duct flute), 300–301
uótoroyo. See totoy
ceramic
    about, 114, 263–64, 266
    "beak" flutes, in Mexico, 300
    chirimías (as single-reed aerophones), in Colombia,
        318
    coiled trumpets, pre-Hispanic, 307, 309
    globular flutes, 293
    notched flutes, pre-Hispanic, 288
    panpipes, pre-Hispanic, 114, *114*, 275
    pifülkas (flutes, Mapuche), 270
    trumpets, pre-Hispanic, 114, *114*, 306
    wauqu (vessel flute, Chipaya), 120, *120*
copper, *kenas* (notched flutes), in Chile, 290
gold
    about, 264
    figurines, depicting flutes, in Panama, 285
    notched flutes, in pre-Hispanic Peru, 288, 290
    panpipes, pre-Hispanic, 275
metal (unspecified)

aerophones, materials for (*continued*)
    bells, as resonators, 309
    chirimías (as single-reed aerophones), in Colombia,
        318
    kenas (notched flutes), 134
    pífanos (as side-blown flutes), in northeastern Brazil,
        296
    pito (as "beak" flute, Cora), 300
    wak'rapukus (coiled trumpets), 307
  plastic
    cajero (flute, in flute-and-drum combination), *304*
    kenas (notched flutes), 134, 290
    lakitas (panpipes, Aymara), in Chile, 150
    pífanos (as side-blown flutes), in northeastern Brazil,
        296
    roncadora (flute, in flute-and-drum combination),
        305
    sikus (double-row panpipes), 276
  quill, *rondador* (monistic panpipe), in Ecuador, 284
  shell
    conch-shell trumpets, symbology of, 269,
        305–306
    heresemoi (conch-shell trumpet, Warao), 305–306
    horns, 320
    kepa (*pututo, pututu*; conch-shell trumpet), 269,
        305–308
    trumpets: Makuxí, Taulipáng, and Yekuâna peoples,
        54. *See also specific types*
  silver
    in general, 264
    notched flutes, pre-Hispanic, 288, 290
    panpipes, pre-Hispanic, 275
  stone
    in general, 264
    panpipes, pre-Hispanic, 275
    pifülkas (flutes, Mapuche), 270
  wood
    about, 263–64
    bullroarers (*aige* [Bororo] and *nurá-mĕe* [Desana]),
        318–19
    cajero (flute, in flute-and-drum combination), 304
    charkas (duct flutes), 304
    chino flutes, 272–73
    chirimías (double-reed aerophones), in Peru, 318
    ch'utus (duct flutes, Chipaya), 301
    duct flutes, in the Bolivian Andes, 102. *See also*
        specific types
    flutes (*déetu, máwi, tsikóta, wáliáduwa*, Wakuénai),
        31, 33, 41
    isimoi (single-reed aerophone, Warao), 312, *313*
    kañari (*cañari*; long straight aerophone with attached
        animal horn), 308
    kenas (notched flutes), 290
    molítu (palmwood flute, Wakuénai), 32
    naseré (globular flute, Pilagá and other Chaco area
        peoples), 293
    pifülkas (*pifilkas*; flutes, Mapuche), 184, 269, 270
    pinkillo (duct flute), in the Bolivian Andes, 116
    pinkillus (duct flutes), in northern Potosí, Bolivia,
        301
    pinkullos (duct flutes), 301

    pinkullus (as large duct flutes), in Canas Province,
        Peru, 134
    pinkulwe (side-blown flute, Mapuche), 296
    roncadora (duct flute, in flute-and-drum
        combination), *305, 305*
    tarkas (duct flutes), 116, 127, 148, 302–303, *303*
    trumpets
      Hohódeni-Wakuénai people, 18
      Makuxí, Taulipáng, and Yekuâna peoples, 54
      Wakuénai peoples, 31, 33
    yaku'i (duct flutes, Kamayurá), 300
aesthetics, by peoples. *See also* composition; dynamics;
    formal structure; meter; performance
    practice; pitch organization; register;
    rhythm; tempo; texture; timbre; tuning
  Aymara, in Chile, high tessitura, 149
  Aymara, in Conima District, Peru
    collectivity as ideal, vis-à-vis individuality, in
        aerophone ensembles, 128, 141, 278
    contrast, subtlety in concept of, 124
    cosmology, in three-part registral texture: *pitu, sikuri*,
        and *tarka* ensembles, 126
    dense sound, concept of, 124, 127–28, 141, 267
    dense unison, concept of, 267, 283, 301
    high tessitura, 124, 127, 141
    repetition, 124, 128, 141
    style differentiation, in aerophone ensembles,
        129–30
    texture, binary symmetry framing central part, in
        aerophone ensembles, 124, 126–28, 301
    timbric homogeneity, in traditional aerophone
        ensembles, 126–27, 141, 301
  Aymara, in general, 104, 267–69, 278
  Aymara and Kechua, in Bolivia, timbric homogeneity in
    traditional panpipe ensembles, 104
  Gê-speaking groups, in Brazil, 70
  Kamayurá, songs, pitch organization of, as critical
    language, in *yawari* ritual, 89–90, *89*, *94*,
    96, *98*
  Kechua, in Canas Province, Peru
    change and contrast, concepts of, 124, 137
    dense sound, 124, 135, 141
    high tessitura, 134–35, 269
    individuality vis-à-vis collectivity, in aerophone
        ensembles, 141
    repetition, 124, 137–38, 141
    timbric homogeneity, in indigenous ensemble
        traditions, 141
    timbric mixture, in mestizo ensembles, 133
  nordestinos, Brazil, in *pífano* tunings, 296–97
  P'urhépecha, 248–49
  Suyá, 67, 69–70, 73
  Tarahumara (Rarámuri), 5
  Tupi-speaking groups, in Brazil, 70–72, *71–72*
  Wakuénai (in *kwépani* and *pudáli* ceremonial cycles)
    music acting upon myth, 38–39, 42–46
    myth acting upon music, 33–34, 43–46
  Xavante, 57, 59
African descendants
  in Colombia
    chirimía ensembles, 318

use of *caña de millo*, 314
in Ecuador, use of calabashes in ensembles, 269
in Mexico, 238, 241
in Viceroyalty of New Spain, 237
Agerkop, Terry, 202
Agostinho, Pedro, 65, 80, 299–300
agriculture. *See also* agricultural cycles *under* rituals and ceremonies, by function
    Argentina
        Mapuche peoples, 169
        Mbyá people, 173
    Bolivia: Aymara, Callawaya, Chipaya, and Kechua peoples, 101–103
    Chile
        Atacameño people, 152
        Aymara people, 145
    Inca culture, 2
    Mexico, indigenous population, by region
        central, 240
        central valleys and northern Oaxaca, 242
        eastern, 239
        northwestern, 238
        southern, 241
        western, 239
    Peru
        agrarian reform movement, 123–24
        Canas Province, Department of Cuzco, 132
        Conima District, Department of Puno, 126
    politics and, 327
Ahuitzotl, Lord of Tenochtitlan, 14
Ahyoung, Selwyn, 276
aiğe (free aerophone; bullroarer, Bororo people), 318–19
aikulki inanka (a type of Mískito lament), 200–201
aimasihbi inanka (a type of Mískito lament), 200–201
AIRA (Asociación Indígena de la República Argentina), 163
akia (Suyá song genre), 22, 67–70, *68–69*, 73, 191
akwa nusa ígala (Kuna shamanic healing chant-type), 221–22, *223*
alabados (*alabanzas*; songs of praise and invocations of religious character)
    Catholicism, as symbols of conversion to, 17
    as invocations, in communal labor (*minga*), 310
    P'urhépecha people, as mestizo genre, 252
alabanzas. See alabados
Alakaluf people. *See* Kawéskar people
algarroba (rite of passage ceremony, Mataco and Guaycurú peoples), 168
All Saints' Day (Todos los Santos, November 1), 102, 127, 130, 301
Allard, Pierre, 294
Alonso Bolaños, Marina, 328
altered states. *See* hallucinogens
alüaluntu (Mapuche sacred time-space), 182, 184
Alvarado, Pedro de, 8
Alwani (Mískito mythical thunder-figure), 199
Amáru (primordial mother in Wakuénai creation myth

cycles), 26, 28–34, 40, 42, 45–46
Amerindian peoples. *See* Native Americans; *specific groups*
amupurrún (Mapuche gender-specific dance), in Argentina, 170–71
Amuzgo (Tzjon Non) people, 235, 241
anata (Aymara for "carnival"; name for *tarka* in southern Bolivia and northern Chile; duct flute), 102, 304. *See also tarka*
ancestors, by peoples
    Atacameño, 152
    Chiriguano-Chané, 172
    Kamayurá, in *kwarỹ'p* ritual, 65
    Karajá, 189
    Kuna, 279–80. *See also* Kuna *under* cosmology
    Mapuche, 9, 155, 170, 182, 184–85
    Mískito, in *inankas* (laments), 199–203, *200*, *202–203*
    Wakuénai, 25–26, 34
angúa aretepe (*anguaguásu*; double-headed drum, Chiriguano-Chané peoples), 172
anguaguásu (*angúa aretepe*; double-headed drum, Chiriguano-Chané peoples), 172
anguapú (*mbaepú*; double-headed drum, Mbyá people), 174, 176
anguarái (double-headed drum, Chiriguano-Chané peoples), 172
animal increase rituals. *See* cattle-marking and animal increase *under* rituals and ceremonies, by function
animal sacrifice
    in Aymara Carnival of Isluga, Chile, 149
    Aymara and Kechua peoples, in Bolivia (*wilancha*), 102–103
    in Kechua ritual battle of Chiaraje, Canas Province, Peru, 138
animals. *See also* animal sacrifice; birds; bull; cattle-marking and animal increase *under* rituals and ceremonies, by function; condor; horse; jaguar; llama; ocelot; rhea; *tero*
    in Bororo mythology, 318–19
    in instrument construction, use of, 29, 167, 225, 320
    in Mataco and Guaycurú cosmology, 167
    powers of, in myth/cosmology, 17–20, *19*, 25, 29–30, 167, 320
    as sources of song, Suyá people, 69–70
    symbolic role of
        in Kamayurá intertribal ritual, 82–95
        in Kuna *toques* and dances, 227
        Mapuche peoples
            in dances, 156, 184, 271
            in *trutruka* music, *307*, *308*
        in Mbyá *mimby retá* panpipes music, 274
        in songs
            Aymara people, in Chile, 147–48
            Kawéskar people, 159–60
            K'ero people, 283
         in Wakuénai ceremonial cycles, 31, 33, 35, 37–39, 41, 44–46. *See also under* jaguar
        in Yekuana (Venezuela) *tekeya* music, 311

Annals of Cuauhtitlan, 13–14

antara (Kechua for "panpipes")
    as Kechua term for dualistic panpipes, in Bolivia,
        103–104, 118
    as Kechua term for monistic panpipes, in Peru, 266,
        275, 277n, 282–83
    symbolism of, 282

"Antarctic France" (French colony), 49

anthropophagy, 79, 97, 195

Anumania people (as ancestors of the Awetí), 97

Anunciación, Fiesta de la (Annunciation, March 25),
        Chiriguano-Chané peoples, 171

Aöniken people (Tehuelche subgroup), 169

Apapocuvá people, funerary rite of passage, 191

Apayaya (Canelos Quichua mythical black jaguar;
        grandfather figure), 18

Apolinar, Victoriano Sebastián, 250

apus (*achachilas*; Kechua for Andean mountain divinities,
        male centers of power), 103, 126, 130, 132

Apỳap people, 79

ára pyau (Mbyá annual ceremony for new seasonal cycle),
        174

aras napat (idiophone; Mískito horse-jaw scraper), 207

"La Araucana" (Ercilla y Zúñiga), 181

Araucanian empire, 270, 182 (map)

Araucanian peoples. *See* Mapuche peoples

Arawak (Arawakan)
    affiliated languages, 18n, 25, 61, 65, 77, 164, 171
    linguistic stock, 51

Arawété people, 71–72

archaeo-organology, of aerophones, 263–64, 267–68, 270,
        275, 287

archaeology
    Andean sites, 1–2
    La Cabrera (notched flute), in Venezuela, 292
    gold artifacts, in Panama, 285
    healing ritual artifacts, 187
    Moche culture. *See* Moche culture
    naseré (Pilagá small globular flute), prototypes of, in
        Peru, 293
    Nazca culture. *See* Nazca culture

Archibold, Sam, 193–94

areíto (*areyto*; ceremony of Arawakan Taínos in the Greater
        Antilles, extinct), 10

are're (panpipes, Panare people), in Venezuela, 280

aréte avati (corn festival, Chiriguano-Chané peoples),
        171–72

Aretz, Isabel, 163, 280–82, 291, 314, 316

areyto. See *areíto*

Argentina
    dance
        bailecito, 172
        chacarera, 172
        chamamé, 171
        takirari, 172
    demographics, 2, 163–64, 166, 178–79
    institutions
        Asociación Indígena de la República Argentina
            (AIRA), 163
        Servicio Nacional de Asuntos Indígenas (Argentina),
            163

instruments
    aerophones
        accordion, 316
        bandoneón, 316
        corneta (*caña*; *clarín*; *erke*; long straight side-blown
            trumpet), 163, 309
        kanojí (Mataco shaman's bone whistle), 169
        mimby (Mbyá flute), 174, 176
        mimby retá (Mbyá dualistic panpipes), 174, 176,
            178, 273–74
        naseré (Pilagá term; wooden globular flute),
            293–94
        pifilka (*pifülka*; Mapuche flute), 170–71, 184, *185*
        pinkulwe (Mapuche flute with finger holes),
            295–96
        sikus (Aymara double-row dualistic panpipes), 163
        trutruka (Mapuche long straight end-blown
            trumpet), 170–71, 271, 307, *308*
    chordophones
        guitar, six-string, 174, 176–77
        mbaraká (Mbyá five-string guitar), 173–76, 177
        ravé (Mbyá rebec), 173–76, 177
        turumi (*miorí*; Chiriguano-Chané violin), 171–72
    idiophones
        kaskawilla (Mapuche pellet-bell rattles), 170–71,
            271
        maracas (gourd rattle), 166–69
        palo sonajero de uñas (Mataco and Guaycurú
            stamping tube rattle), 167–69
        takuapú (Mbyá stamping tube), 174–75, 178
    membranophones
        anguaguásu (*angúa aretepe*; Chiriguano-Chané
            largest drum), 172
        anguapú (*mbaepú*; Mbyá double-headed drum),
            174, 176
        anguarái (Chiriguano-Chané medium-sized
            drum), 172
        kataki (Mataco and Guaycurú water drum),
            167–69
        kultrún (Mapuche drum), 170, 182, *183*, 189
        michirái (Chiriguano-Chané smallest drum), 172

missionaries and missionization, 164, 166, 171–73, 181

peoples
    Aymara, 147, 268, 310–11
    Chiriguano-Chané, 163–64, 165 (map), 171–72, 179
    Mapuche. *See* Mapuche peoples, in general;
        Mapuche peoples, in Argentina
    Mataco and Guaycurú, 163–69, 165 (map), 178–79,
        189, 293–94
        Mataco subgroups
            Chorote, 163–64, 168, 189
            Chulupí (Nivaklé), 163–64, 167
            Mataco proper (Wichí), 163–64, 166, 168–69,
              189
        Guaycurú subgroups
            Mocoví. *See* Mataco and Guaycurú *above*
            Pilagá, 163–64, 166, 168–69, 293–94
            Toba, 163–64, 166–69, 178–79
    Mbyá, 163–64, 165 (map), 172–78, 177–78,
        273–74
    Selk'nam (extinct), 20–21, 161n, 163–64, 179

Tehuelche (Mapuche subgroup), 158, 163–64, 169, 179, 181, 189
regions
Northcentral, Chaco area. *See* Chiriguano-Chané; Mataco and Guaycurú peoples *above*
Northeast. *See* Mbyá people *above*
Northwest (formerly part of the Inca empire or Tawantinsuyu)
corneta (*caña*), religious instrumental music for, 163
early cultural crossbreeding in, 163
pitch organization, pentatonic and tritonic scales in, 163
sikus (Aymara double-row dualistic panpipes) in, 163
song
baguala (tritonic song genre), 163
coplas (song genre associated with the *baguala*), 163
South. *See* Mapuche; Selk'nam; Tehuelche peoples *above*
Patagonia, 163–64, 169, 181–85. *See also* Mapuche peoples, in Argentina
Tierra del Fuego. *See* Selk'nam people *above*
song
baguala (tritonic song genre), 163
coplas (song genre associated with the *baguala*), 163
tourism in, 173
Arguedas, José María, 262, 294, 318, 320
Aridamerica (macrostructural area), 231, 232 (map), 233
Arikêm linguistic family, 51
arka. See *ira/arka* principle
armónica. See rondín
arpa. See harp
aruaña (Karajá healing ceremony), 189
Asociación Indígena de la República Argentina (AIRA), 163
Assumption (Fiesta de la Virgen de la Asunción, August 15)
Mamita Asunta (Mama Asunta; Virgen de la Asunción), in Bolivia, 102, 108
mestizo population, in Conima District, Peru, 130
astrology, Aztec (Mexica) people, 12
astronomy, Maya culture, 9, 233
Asunción, Fiesta de la Virgen de la. *See* Assumption
Atacameño people (Likan-Antai), 145, 151–54
ancestor worship, 152
cosmology, 152–54
dance. *See also* rituals and ceremonies *below*
chururito (dance-songs for cattle-marking ritual), 152
túskalu (tap-dance for sowing ritual), 152
demographics, 145, 151–52
ensembles (in acculturated music), 153
gender attribution, to instruments, 153–54
history of, 151–52
influences, Aymara and Hispanic, 153
instruments
chorromón (pre-Hispanic metal bell-set), 153–54
clarín (long straight side-blown trumpet), 153–54
guitar (in acculturated music), 153
putu (animal horn), 153–54

language (Kunza, extinct), in rituals, 152
missionaries and missionization, 153
music, mythic origin of, 153–54
rituals and ceremonies
carnival, 152–53
cattle-marking (*floramiento del ganado*), 152
cleansing of pre-Hispanic irrigation ducts (*limpia de canales*), 151–54
sowing (*fiesta de la semilla*), 152
style characteristics, music for, 153–54
song
in Kunza and Spanish, 152
talatur (dance-songs for ritual cleansing of irrigation ducts), 153–54
Atahualpa (Inca ruler), reenactments, death of, 4, 10–11, 327
atuñsa (*atunse*, plural for the pair; "hatchet" duct flute)
description of, 267, 297
symbolism of, 297–98
Augusta, Félix José de, 145, 181
Augustine, St. (Tata Agustín), feast of, Aymara and Kechua, in Bolivia, 103
Augustinian order, in Mexico, 248
Auki Auki (mountain divinity; name for *Achach K'umu* dance-drama), 132
auloi (double pipes of ancient Greeks), 263
"authenticity," as concept, 52–53
"*Awbia daktar*" (variant of "Yankee Doodle"), as Mískito children's game-song (*pulanka*), 209, 209
Awetí people, 61, 63, 71–72, 77, 80, 97–98
awicha (female spirit of the arable land), 109, 113, 116
ayahuasca vine (hallucinogen), 188
ayahuasquero (Peruvian Amazon healer), 188–89
Ayamán people. *See* Ayomán
ayarachi (*ayarichi*; panpipes; tradition associated with burial ceremonies)
as ceremonial music, 275
as Kechua tradition of panpipe performance, in Peru, 276–78
ayarichi (*ayarachi*; Kechua double-row panpipes), in Bolivia, 104, 118, 118
aykhori. See pinkillo mohoceño
ayllu (smallest unit of Andean socioeconomic organization; community), by peoples
Atacameño, 152
Aymara, in Conima District, Peru, 126–28, 130
Aymara and Kechua, in Bolivia, 107, 116
Kechua, in Canas Province, Peru, 138
Kechua, in northern Potosí, Bolivia, 301
social function of, in present-day Andean life, 327
Aylwin, José, 158
aymara. See pinkillo mohoceño
Aymara people, in general
aesthetics, 104, 124, 127–30, 141, 267, 278, 283, 301
cosmology, 101–17, 123–24, 126–27, 132, 147–48, 150–51, 301
demographics, 2, 101, 125 (map), 126, 145, 147
ensembles
bandas (brass bands), 148, 150–51
julajulas (panpipes), 103–105, 105–107, 107–108
julu-julus (panpipes), 104

Aymara people, in general (*continued*)
  lakitas (panpipes), 103–105, 108–109, *108–109*, 118, 120, 148, 150–51
  lichiguayos (large *kenas*), 148, 150–51
  orquesta, 148–50
  pinkillus (five- and six-hole duct flutes), 126–27, 130–31, 301
  pitus (*falawatus*; side-blown flutes), 126–28, 132, *133*, 294
  sikuras (large panpipes), 103–105, 109, *110–13*, 113, *115*, 148, 150–51
  sikus (*sikuris*; panpipes)
    in Bolivia, 103–105, 114–17, *115*, 118, *118*
    in Bolivia and Peru, 274–78
    in Peru, 126–32, *128–29*, 141
  tarkas (duct flutes), 126–28, 130–31, 141, 148–49, 301, 303–304
  instruments. *See also* ensembles *above*
    erke. See *erke* (as single-reed animal horn)
    kena. See *kena*
    pututu. See *pututu*; *pututo* (as bull or cow horn)
  language, 101, 126
Aymara people, in Argentina, 147, 268, 310–11
Aymara people, in Bolivia. *See* Aymara and Kechua peoples, in Bolivia
Aymara people, in Chile
  cosmology, 147–48, 150–51
  dance
    carnival *rueda* (round dance), 151
    cueca, 150
    cumbia andina, 150
    huayño, 146, 150
    takirari, 150, 151
    vals, 150
  demographics, 145, 147
  gender attribution, to songs, 148
  genres (religious music), *benditos*, *dianas*, marches, processions, 150
  healing, 189
  language, 147
  music, concept of, 147
  rituals and ceremonies
    carnival, as fertility ritual
      orquesta, 148–50
      ruedas (round dances), 148–49, 151
      tarkeadas (*tarka* ensembles), 148–49
      takiraris (dances), 150
      tonos (vocal tunes), 148–49
    cattle-marking, songs, classification of, addressed to animals, 147–48
    patron-saint fiestas (as syncretic ritual)
      bandas (brass bands), 148, 150–51
      lakitas (ensembles of small panpipes), 148, 150–51
      lichiguayos (ensembles of large *kenas*), 148, 150–51
      sikuras (ensembles of large panpipes), 148, 150–51
    potato-sowing (*Pachallampe*)
      ruedas (round dances), 148
      tonos (accompanied songs), 148, 151
Aymara people, in Peru (Conima District, Department of Puno)

aesthetics
  collectivity, in principle of "group blend," 128, 141, 278
  contrast, concept of, 124
  dense sound, concept of, 124, 127–28, 141, 267
  dense unison, concept of, 267, 283, 301
  high tessitura, 124, 127, 141
  repetition, 124, 128, 141
  style differentiation, in aerophone ensembles, 129–30
  timbric homogeneity, in traditional aerophone ensembles, 127, 141, 301
celebrations. *See also* rituals and ceremonies *below*
  Assumption (Virgen de la Asunción), mestizo-controlled, 130
  Candlemas (Virgen de la Candelaria), as harvest ritual, 130, 132
  Holy Cross Day (Fiesta de Santa Cruz), *Achach K'umu* dance-drama for, 132
  San Isidro (May 15), *satiri* dance-drama for, 131–32
  San Miguel (patron-saint fiesta), mestizo-controlled, 126, 130
composition, 128–29
cosmology, 123–24, 126–27, 132, 301
cultural change, 127
dance
  Achach K'umu (dance-drama), for Holy Cross Day, 124, 126, 132, *133*
  pastores (children's Christmas dance), 127
  Satiri (dance-drama), for San Isidro, 131–32
  wifala (courting dance), for Candlemas, 130, *131*
demographics, 125 (map), 126
ensembles, aerophones with membranophone accompaniment
  pinkillus (five- and six-hole), 126–27, 130–31, 301
  pitus (*falawatus*), 126–28, 132, *133*, 294
  sikus, 126–32, *128–29*, 141
  tarkas, 126–28, 130–31, 141, 301, 303–304
gender roles, in instrumental performance, 127, 320
language, 126
migration, 141–42
rituals and ceremonies (syncretic). *See also* celebrations *above*
  Achach K'umu (dance-drama), 132, *133*
  Candlemas (Candelaria), as harvest ritual, 130, 132
  carnival, 127, 130–32, 301
  satiri (dance-drama; reenactment of agricultural rituals), 131–32
traditions, Aymara and Kechua, in Conima and Canas, compared, 140–42
Aymara and Kechua peoples, in Bolivia
  aesthetics, timbric homogeneity, in aerophone ensembles, 104
  carnival, 102, 120, 308
  cosmology
    anthropomorphic, representations of, 114–17, *115*
    in gender attribution, 102–104, 116, 301–302
    panpipe ensembles, symbolic dualism in
      julajulas, 105, *105–107*, *107–108*
      lakitas, 103–105, 108–109, *108–109*, 118, 120
      sikuras, 105, 109, *110–13*, 113, *115*
    in panpipe representations, pre-Columbian, 113–14, *114*

as syncretic belief system, 102–104, 114–17
dance
    in general, 101–103
    of *julajula* panpipe players, in *tinku*, 103, *106–107*,
        107–108
    of *sikura* panpipe players, representational circle
        dance, 109, 113, *113*
    in *sikuri* ensemble traditions, 274–78
    wayño (huayno), 111–12
demographics, 101
ensembles, of aerophones
    julajulas (single-row panpipes), 103–105,
        105–107, *107–108*
    lakitas (double-row panpipes), 103–105, 108–109,
        108–109, 118, 120
    pinkillus (duct flutes; Kechua, in northern Potosí),
        301–302
    sikuras (large double-row panpipes), 103–105,
        109, *110–13*, *113*, *115*
    sikus (sikuris; double-row panpipes), 103–105,
        114–18, *115*, *118*, 274–78
healers and healing, 189
rituals and ceremonies
    agricultural cycles, 102
    fertility, 103
    in general, 101
    tinku (ritual battle and encounter), 103, *106–107*,
        107–108, 116
song
    in general, 101–102
    tonadas (wirsus; functional song repertoire),
        102
Ayomán (Ayamán) descendants, in Venezuela
    cacho de venado (globular flutes), 292–93, *293*
    turas (notched flutes), 291–92, *292*
Ayquina (Chilean village; site of ceremonial events,
    Atacameño people), 153
Aytai, Desidério
    O mundo sonoro Xavante, 57, 59–60
    research on scales, indigenous peoples, Brazil, 73
Azevedo, Luiz Heitor Corrêa de, 53, 55–56, 73
Aztec (Mexica) culture
    Annals of Cuauhtitlan (codex), 13–14
    astrology, 12
    calendrical systems, 5, 11–14
    composition, 14–16, 17
    cosmology, 11–17, *12–13*, *15*
    jaguar, as Aztec Lord of the Animals, 17–18, *19*
    records, destruction of, 14
    rituals and ceremonies, New Fire, 11–12, *12*
    sacrifice, human, 14, 16
    song
        Cantares mexicanos (extant poetic texts in Nahuatl),
            2, 14, 16
        death and warfare, as themes in, 11–15
        "flower and song," concept of, 14–17, *15*
    time, concept of, 5, 9–10, 11–14, 233–35
    Toltec influence on, 5
    warfare
        aerophone classification, basis for, 320
        in Aztec cosmology, 14

B

baguala (lyric genre within tritonic repertoire of northern
    Argentina), 163
Bahana (Warao eastern Supreme Spirit), 190
bahanarotu (Warao healer), 190
baiano. *See baião*
baião (baiano; Brazilian dance genre), 297
baile chúkaro (chúcaro; "fierce dance," Aymara and Kechua
    peoples), in Bolivia, *106–107*, *107–108*
baile de las turas (corn rituals, Ayomán and Hirahara
    descendants), in Venezuela, 291–92, *292*
bailecito (colonial dance; folk dance of Argentina's
    Northwest), Chiriguano-Chané peoples,
    172
bailes chinos (confraternities of musician/dancers or
    chinos), dances of, 271–73
bajeo (syncopated, improvised contrapuntal bass line),
    in P'urhépecha *sones* and *abajeños*,
    249, 252, 255
Balfour, Henry, 262
Band, Heinrich, 316
"La Banda de los Borrachos" (Colombian ensemble),
    269
bandas-de-pífanos (ensemble), in northeastern Brazil,
    296–97
bandola (plucked chordophone), Aymara people, in Chile,
    148–49
bandoneón (multiple single-reed concussion aerophone),
    316
bands (*bandas*). *See* brass bands *under* ensembles, by type
bandurria (plucked chordophone)
    in Chile, Aymara people, 148–49
    in Colombia, 316
    in Peru, 134–35, 141
Baniwa peoples, 18n
bans. *See also* censorship
    indigenous traditions, by Catholic missionaries, 233
    indigenous traditions and shamanism, by Protestant
        missionaries, 166
    on playing *kena* into a pot, after Kechua legend, 289
Barasana people, in Colombia, male initiation ritual, 18
baritone horn, in army and civilian bands, 269
Barreto, Oscar, 181
bass, electric, in *vallenato* ensembles, Colombia, 316
bass drum
    in army and civilian bands, 269
    in brass bands, Aymara people, in Chile, 151
    in Brazil (zabumba), 296
    in Peruvian *orquesta cuzqueña*, 133
    in *pitu*, *siku*, and *tarka* ensembles, Aymara people, in
        Peru, 126–27
Basso, Ellen, 21
Bastide, Roger, 196
Bastien, Joseph W., 115
Bastos, Rafael José de Menezes, 62–64, 66, 70,
    311, 328
battles, ritual. *See* ritual battles *under* rituals and
    ceremonies
Baumann, Max Peter, 301, 328
Beaudet, Jean-Michel, 49–50, 73

Belize
    formerly territory of ancient Mexico, 231
    Garífuna ethnic nation (Black Caribs) in, 196–97
bells. *See under* idiophones
Beltrán de Guzmán, Nuño, 237
Beltrán y Rózpide, Ricardo, 197
benditos (religious folk songs; collective prayers sung in
            praise of saints)
    in Brazil, 297
    in Chile, 150
Benson, Elizabeth, 10
Bering Sea, 187
Bering Strait, 1, 5
Bermúdez, Egberto, 269
Bernal Jiménez, Miguel, 251. See also *Tata Vasco*
beverages
    chicha
        Aymara and Kechua, in Bolivia and Peru, 103, 301
        Chiriguano-Chané peoples, 172
        Kechua people, in Conquest dance-drama, 4, 327–28
        Kuna people
            in secular contexts, 279–80
            in shamanic rituals, 212, 217, 219–22, 224, 286
        Mapuche peoples, in Chile, 157
        Mískito people, in shamanic rituals, 204–206
        in ritual offerings (*tinka*), Atacameño people (*chicha
            de aloja*), 152
    kÿe (regurgitation-inducing tea for purification
            ceremonies), Kamayurá, 95
    manioc beer, Wakuénai peoples, 32, 36–37
    mohet, in *yawari* myth, Kamayurá people, 97
birds
    Kamayurá people, sound domain, in conceptualization
            of, 64
    symbolic representations of
        in *atunse* music, 297–98
        in Aymara dances, Chile, 148
        in Kamayurá *yawari* (intertribal ritual), 90, 93–94,
            98
        in Kechua panpipe music, 278
        in Kuna *Mete sikwi uurma kali* dance, 227, 227–28
        in legends and myths, 4, 10, 80, 82, 88–89
        in Mapuche cosmology, 156
        in Mapuche dances
            ostrich, in Chile, 156
            rhea and *tero* (South American bird), in
                Argentina, 184
        in Maya legend of "first *chirimía*" (first flute), 319
        in Mbyá *mimby retá* panpipes music, 274
Black Caribs. *See* Garífuna ethnic nation
body ornamentation, by peoples .
    Chibcha, 233
    Kamayurá, 80
    Kuna, 222, *222*
    Suyá, 67–68
    Xavante, 57
Boehm, Theobald, "Boehm flute," 266
Boilès, Charles, L., 328
Bolaños, César, 275
Bolivia
    aesthetics: Aymara, Chipaya, and Kechua peoples, 104

carnival, 102, 120, 308
celebrations, Catholic feasts (syncretic), cyclic calendar
            of, 102–103
cosmology (syncretic)
    gender attribution, in anthropomorphic, 102–104,
            116
    and social organization, 115–16
    symbolic dualism, in panpipe ensembles, 104–17,
            105–15
dance
    in general, 101–102
    of *julajula* panpipe players, 103, *106–107*, 107–108
    sikura panpipe players
        representational circle dance of, 109, 113, *113*
        wayño (*huayno*), *111–12*
    in *sikuri* ensemble traditions, 275, 277–78
demographics, 2, 101
ensembles. *See also* groups *below*
    Aymara people, *julu-julus* (panpipes), 104
    Aymara and Kechua peoples
        julajulas (panpipes), 103–105, *105–107*, 107–108
        lakitas (panpipes), 103–105, 108–109, *108–109*,
            118, 120
        sikuras (large panpipes), 103–105, 109, *110–13*, *113*,
            115
        sikus (*sikuris*; panpipes), 103–105, 114–17, *115*, 118,
            118, 274–78
    Callawaya people, *phukunas* (panpipes), 104, 118
    Chipaya people, *maizus* (panpipes), 104, 118, *118*
    Kechua people
        ayarichis (panpipes), 104, 118, *118*
        pinkillus (duct flutes), in northern Potosí,
            301–302
    panpipe ensembles, types and distribution of, 104
    survey of, 117–21
groups. *See also* ensembles *above*
    Grupo Aymara, 290
    Savia Andina, 290
instruments, 117–21, *118–21*
    aerophones. *See also* ensembles *above*
        erke. *See* erke (as single-reed animal horn)
        kena. *See* kena
        lichiwayu, 103, 118, 290
        pfala, 120, 266, 294
        pinkayllo (ch'utu), 102, 119, 301
        pinkillo. *See* pinkillo
        pinkillo mohoceño. *See* pinkillo mohoceño
        pinkillu. *See* pinkillu
        pinkullo. *See* pinkullo
        pinkullu. *See* pinkullu
        pitu (pfala, pfalawita), 120, 294
        pututu. *See* pututu
        tar pinkayllu (tarka), 303
        tarka. *See* tarka
        tira tira, 120, 307–308
languages, 101
peoples
    Aymara. *See* Aymara people, in general; Aymara and
            Kechua peoples, in Bolivia
    Callawaya, 101, 104, 118, 120
    Chipaya. *See* Chipaya people

Kechua. *See* Kechua people, in general; Aymara and
  Kechua peoples, in Bolivia
  Toba, in Bolivian Chaco, *nahôre* dances (female
    initiation ritual), 18, 20
bombo (large double-headed drum)
  in Bolivia, 118, 120
  in Chile, 149–51, 272
  in Ecuador, 269
  in Peru, 126
Bororo linguistic family, 51
Bororo people, aerophones of, 318–19
Botocudo linguistic family, 51
Botocudo people, early research on, 53–54
Boudin, Max, 56
brass bands. *See under* ensembles, by type
Brazil
  "Antarctic France" (16th-century French colony) in,
    49
  demographics, 50, 51, 63 (map), 77–79
  ensembles, *bandas-de-pífanos*, in the Northeast,
    296–97
  ethnomusicological research, history of, 49–56,
    50, 52
  iconography, music, 53
  Indians, enslavement of, by the Portuguese, 164
  indigenous cultural areas, early classification of,
    51, 52 (map)
  indigenous groups
    comparative studies, musics of, 49–51, 56,
      70–74
    land conflicts, 79
    in State of Mato Grosso
      Capoto Indian area, 58, 63 (maps)
      cultural interaction among, 5, 77–79, 98
      Jarina Indian Area, 58, 63 (maps)
      Jarina Indian Reserve, 63 (map)
      Xingu Indian Park, 58 (map), 60–67, 63 (map),
        77–79
  institutions
    Ecumenical Center for Documentation and
      Information (CEDI), 51
    Flute House, Kamayurá people, 82–83, 82, 90–91,
      90–91
    Fundação Nacional do Índio (FUNAI), 77
    Indigenous Missionary Council (CIMI),
      50
    National Library, Music Division, 53
  linguistic stocks and families, list of, 51
  missionaries and missionization, 49, 51–53, 57,
    59–60
  music iconography, survey of, National Library, Music
    Division, 53
  peoples
    Apapocuvá, 191
    Apỳap, 79
    Araweté, 71
    Awetí, 61, 63, 71–72, 77, 80, 97–98
    Bororo, 318–19
    Botocudo, 53–54
    Guaraní, 56, 189
    Juruna, 61–62, 71–72, 77, 79, 80

Kadiwéu, 56, 73
Kaingang, 67
Kalapálo, 21, 61, 65, 77, 188, 299, 311–12
Kamayurá. *See* Kamayurá people
Karajá, 189
Kayabi, 61–62, 70–72, 71, 77
Kayapó, 26
Kayowá, 70, 72
Kiriri, 5
Krahó, 70
Kuikúro, 61, 65–66, 77, 299, 311–12
  list of, in Xingu River region, 63 (map)
Makiritare. *See* Makiritare people
Makuxí, 54–55
Matipúhy, 80, 95–96
Maxakali, 56
Mbayá (Mbyá), 56, 73, 172
Mehináku, 61, 65, 77, 80
Metuktire, 61–62, 77
Nahukwá-Matipú, 61, 77
Nahukwá-Matipúhy. *See* Nahukwá-Matipú *above*
Nambikwára, 53–54, 294
Ofayé, 56
Panará , 61–62, 77
Paresí, 53–55, 294
Suyá. *See* Suyá people
Tapayuna, 77
Taulipáng, 54–55
Tremembé, 51
Trumai, 61, 77, 79–80, 96–98
Tupinambá (extinct), 49, 50, 53–55
Txikão, 61–62, 77
Urubu, 56
Urubu-Kaapor, 56, 73
Wapixána, 54
Waurá, 61, 77, 79, 311
Wayãpí, 268
Xavante, 56–60, 58–62, 67, 70, 73–74
Xokleng, 67
Yanomami (Yanomamö), 51, 188, 190, 262
Yawalapiti, 61, 65, 77, 80, 299, 311–12
Yekuâna, 54–55
  song. *See under* Kamayurá people; Suyá people;
    Xavante people
  transcription, of indigenous music, 49, 53–55, 57
bride service, 28, 35–36
Brinton, Daniel, 3
"Brit ayang-kra ba kaikisma ki" ("The Muffin Man"), as
  Mískito children's game-song (*pulanka*),
  209, 209
British colonizers, 194–96, 208–209, 209
buccaneers, 195–96
bull. See *kiríngwa* and *toritos* under P'urhépecha people
bullroarers (free aerophones), 316, 318–19
burdón (*contrabajo*; duct aerophone), in Bolivia, 119
burials. *See* funerary *under* rituals and ceremonies, by
  function
Bustillos, Freddy, 303
button accordion (*acordeón a botones*), 316
búzio. See *pífano*
buzo. See *pífano*

C

caboclo (Portuguese term for person of mixed Indian and European heritage), in Brazil, 4
cacho (aerophone), in Peru
as name for the animal horn coiled trumpet (*wak'rapuku*) in the Mantaro Valley, 307
as name for the bull or cow horn (*pututo* or *pututu*) in Huarochirí, 308
cacho de venado (*cacho venao*; globular deer-skull aerophone), 292–93, *293*
caja (double-headed drum)
in Bolivia, Aymara and Kechua peoples, 109, *111–12*, 120
in Chile
Atacameño people, 153
Aymara people, 149–50
in Colombia, 316
in Peru
Aymara people, 126–27, 130
in flute-and-drum combination (*cajero*), Peru, 304, *304*, 309, *309*, 316
Cajamarquilla cultural area, wooden aerophones of, 264
cajero (performer on *flauta* and *caja*; flute-and-drum combination), 304, *304*, 309, *309*, 314, 316
cajita (diminutive of *caja*; small double-headed drum), in Bolivia, 120
calendrical systems. *See also* time, concepts of
agricultural cycles, syncretized with Gregorian and Inca calendars, in Bolivia, 102
in Maya culture, 11–14
in Mesoamerica, 233–35
and myth/cosmology, 9–17
Nahuatl-speaking peoples, in Mexico, 5
Callawaya people
demographics, 101
flutes (*ch'unchus*), 120
language (Machchj-juyai), 101
panpipe ensembles (*phukunas*), 104, 118
Calvin, John, 49
camaruco. See *nguillipún*
Camêu, Helza, 52–56, 70, 73
campana (Spanish for "bell"). See *campanilla*
campanilla (*campana* ; idiophone; bronze llama bell), in Bolivia, 109, 121, *121*
Campbell, Joseph, 7–8
campesino (Spanish for "peasant"), 123
caña (Spanish for "tube"; aerophone)
in Argentina, as long side-blown trumpet (*corneta*, *erke*), 163, 309
in Bolivia, as end-blown bamboo tube with resonator, 120, *120*
in Peru
as long side-blown trumpet (*erke*), 163. See also *clarín*
as name for the K'ero notched flute (*pina pinkulucha*, *pinkulu*), 291
caña de lata. See *caña de millo*
caña de millo (*caña de lata*, *flauta de millo*, *pito*; side-blown single-reed aerophone), in Colombia, 267, 314, 316
canajqua (*kanákwa*; pre-contact P'urhépecha song), 247

cañari (*kañari*; long straight aerophone with attached animal horn), in Peru, 308
Candelaria, Fiesta de la Virgen de la. *See* Candlemas
Candlemas (Fiesta de la Virgen de la Candelaria, February 2)
Aymara people, in Conima District, Peru, as harvest ritual, 130, 132
Aymara and Kechua peoples, in Bolivia, 102
P'urhépecha people, 254
Canelo Quichua peoples, myths of, 18
Cánepa Koch, Gisela, 310
"*Canidé ioune*" (apocryphal Tupinambá melody), 49, 50, 53–55
cannibalism. *See* anthropophagy
cantal (Atacameño ritual leader), 152–53
cantares históricos (Inca epic song genre), 10
Cantares mexicanos (extant poetic texts in Nahuatl), 2, 14, 16
cantos de pastores (as P'urhépecha shepherds' songs), 253
capador (panpipe), in Colombia, 266, 269
Capriccio italien (Tchaikovsky), 255
caracoles (conch-shell trumpets, P'urhépecha people), 247
caramillo (term for panpipes, Carib descendants), in Venezuela, 280
Cárdenas del Río, Lázaro, 251
Carib descendants, in Venezuela, panpipe traditions of, 280
Carib linguistic stock, 51, 61, 77
Carles, Rubén Darío, 196
carnival (*carnaval*, *carnavales*)
anata (Aymara term for "carnival"; another name for *tarka*, in Bolivia and Chile), 304
cattle-marking rituals, association with, in Peru, 306
duct flutes, association with
pinkillos
Aymara people, in Chile, 149–50
Aymara and Kechua peoples, in Bolivia, 102
pinkillus, Aymara people, in Conima District, Peru, 130–31
pinkullos, in Andean region, 301
pinkullus, Kechua people, in Canas Province, Peru, 139–40
tarkas (*tarkeada* music)
Aymara people, in general, 303–304
Aymara people
in Chile, 149–50
in Conima District, Peru, 127, 130–31
Aymara and Kechua peoples, in Bolivia, 102
horns and trumpets, association with
bamboo trumpets, in Bolivia, 120
pututu (*pututo*; as animal horn), in Bolivia, 308
tira tira (trumpet), in Bolivia, 308
wak'rapuku (coiled animal-horn trumpet), in Peru, 306
by peoples
Atacameño, 152–53
Aymara
in Chile, as fertility ritual, 147–50
in Peru, Conima District, 127, 130–32, 301
Aymara and Kechua, in Bolivia, 102, 120–21, 308

Chiriguano-Chané (merged with *aréte awati* festival), 171–72
Kechua, in Canas Province, Peru, 134, 139–40, 141
K'ero, 291
P'urhépecha
carnival *torito* (culture-specific musical genre), 249, *249*, 251, 254
as ritual, 254, *254*, 255–56
carrizo (panpipes)
in Colombia, 298
description of, 266
in Venezuela, 278, 280–82, *281*
Carvalho-Neto, Paulo de, 269, 284, 295
Casamiquela, Rodolfo, 159, 170, 181
Caste War (Mexico), 328
Catherine II, Empress of Russia, 3
Catholic Church
feasts of. *See* celebrations, Catholic feasts (syncretic), cyclic calendar of
missionaries and missionization
Augustinian and Franciscan orders, in Mexico, 248
Jesuits
in Argentina, 164, 172–73, 181
in Brazil, 49
Salesian order, 4, 57
rituals of, Mass, in P'urhépecha language, 257
cattle-marking and animal increase rituals. *See under* rituals and ceremonies, by function
CEDI (Ecumenical Center for Documentation and Information), Brazil, 51
celebrations, Catholic feasts (syncretic), cyclic calendar of. *See also* carnival; civic holidays; life-cycle (rites of passage); New Year's; rituals and ceremonies
Christmas
Atacameño people, 152
Aymara people, in Conima District, Peru, *pastores* (children's dance), 127
Aymara and Kechua peoples, in Bolivia, 102
in Colombia, *caña de millo* performances, association with, 314
Mískito people, *Krismes* (as children's dance-songs), 208
P'urhépecha people, 252–54
Epiphany, P'urhépecha people, 253–54
Lent (Cuaresma), Cora people, *tonos de Cuaresma* (tunes for), 300
Holy Week
Chamula people, Passion of Christ, interpretation of, 328
Cora people, *tonos de Cuaresma* (Lent tunes), performed on *pitos*, 300
Mayo people, *pascola* dances, performed during, 239, *239*
Easter
Aymara people, in Conima District, Peru, 126, 132
Chiriguano-Chané peoples, 171
dry season and *sikus*, association with, 127
Holy Cross Day (Fiesta de la Santa Cruz, Fiesta de la Cruz, May 3)

Aymara people, in Conima District, Peru, *Achach K'umu* dance-drama on, 132
Aymara and Kechua peoples, in Bolivia, 102, 107
Corpus Christi
Aymara and Kechua peoples, in Bolivia, 102–103
K'ero people, 294, *294*
P'urhépecha people, *249*, 251, 254, 257
Cristo de los Milagros, feast of, P'urhépecha people, 253
patron-saint fiestas and saints. *See also* Virgin Mary *below*
aerophones, association with
cajero (flute and drum), in Peru, 304–305, *304*, *309*, *309*
chino flutes, in Chile, 271–73, *272*
clarín, in Peru, 309–10, *309–10*
roncadora and drum, in Peru, 304–305, *305*
sikuri ensemble traditions, 277–78
tundas, Quichua people, in Ecuador, 295
by peoples
Atacameño, 153
Aymara, in Chile, 147–48, 150–51
indigenous population, in Mexico, 234
Kechua, in Canas Province, Peru, 132–33
mestizo population, in Conima District, Peru, 126, 130
P'urhépecha, 255, 257, 259
by saints
All Saints' Day (Todos los Santos, November 1), 102, 127, 130, 301
Augustine, St. (Tata Agustín), Aymara and Kechua, in Bolivia, 103
Isidro, Fiesta de San (May 15), Aymara people, in Conima District, Peru, *satiri* dance-drama on, 131–32
James, St. (Fiesta de Santiago)
Aymara and Kechua peoples (Tata Santiago), in Bolivia, 103
K'ero people (July 25; as fertility ritual), *kanchis sipas* played only on, 283
John the Baptist, St. (Fiesta de San Juan Bautista, June 24)
in Acolla, Department of Junín, Peru, 315, *317*
Atacameño people, 152
Aymara and Kechua peoples, in Bolivia, 103
Chiriguano-Chané peoples, 171
Quichua people, in Ecuador, 295
Michael, St. (San Miguel, September 29), mestizo population, in Conima District, Peru, 126, 130
Peter and Paul, Saints (San Pedro y San Pablo, June 29), Quichua people, in Ecuador, 295
Roque, Fiesta de San, in Tarija, Bolivia, 120
Virgin Mary (Proper of the Saints)
in Andean cosmology, syncretic, 102, 116
Annunciation (Fiesta de la Anunciación, March 25), Chiriguano-Chané peoples, 171
Assumption (Fiesta de la Virgen de la Asunción, August 15)
Mamita Asunta (Mama Asunta; Virgen de la Asunción), in Bolivia, 102, 108
mestizo population, in Conima District, Peru, 130

celebrations (*continued*)
    Candlemas (Fiesta de la Virgen de la Candelaria,
        February 2)
        Aymara people, in Conima District, Peru, as
          harvest ritual, 130, 132
        Aymara and Kechua peoples, in Bolivia, 102
        P'urhépecha people, 254
    Immaculate Conception (Fiesta de la Concepción,
        December 8), Aymara and Kechua peoples,
        in Bolivia, 102
    Virgen del Carmen
        in Bolivia, 102
        in Peru, Alto Otuzco, Cajamarca, 304, *304*,
          309–10, *309–10*
    Virgen de Copacabana, in Bolivia, 102
    Virgen de Guadalupe, patron of Mexico, 257
    Virgen del Rosario, Fiesta de la, in Andacollo,
        Chile, 271–73, *272*
Cencio, Luis, 181
censorship, and Aztec composition, 14. *See also* bans
cent (pitch measurement system based on division of
    semitone into 100 equal parts), 54, 284
Centeotl (Mesoamerican god/goddess of maize), 11, 189
Centro de Investigación de la Cultura P'urhépecha, 257
ceremonial dress. *See* costumes and ceremonial dress
ceremonies. *See* rituals and ceremonies
chacarera (traditional folk dance of northwestern
    Argentina), Chiriguano-Chané peoples, 172
Chaco War, 171
ch'ajch'as (idiophone; rattles), in Bolivia, 121, *121*
ch'aje. See charka
ch'alla (ritual offerings)
    Aymara people, in Conima District, Peru, 130
    Aymara and Kechua peoples, in Bolivia, 103
chamamé (dance genre from rural tradition of Corrientes
    in northeastern Argentina), 171
Chamula people, Passion cult of, 328
Chanca people, 320
Chancay culture, materials for flutes in, 286–88
Chané (Arawakan-affiliated people). *See* Chiriguano-Chané
    peoples
change, cultural. *See* cultural change
chant, by peoples. *See also* song
    Botocudo, 53–54
    Huichol, shamanic, 190
    Kamayurá, shamanic, 66
    Kayabi, 71
    Kayowá, 72
    Keres, 8–9
    Kuna, shamanic
        ígala, paths of, 212–26, *216*, 228, 278, 285–86
        ritual specialists, 214
        transcriptions of, *218*, *221*, *223*, *226*
    Mapuche, in Argentina, 9, *189*. *See also under* song
    Tremembé, 51
    Tupinambá (extinct group), 49, *50*, 53–55
    Wakuénai (*málikái*; ritual speech, chant, and song), 26,
        34, 46. *See also under* song
    Warao, shamanic, 190
Chapman, Anne, 20–21, 159
charango (plucked and strummed chordophone)

    in Bolivia, 104, 118
    in Canas Province, Peru
        description of, 135–37, *136*
        function of, 134–37
        genres, 137
        indigenous vis-à-vis mestizo traditions, 135–37, *137*,
          141
        stringing of, 137
        tunings of, 135, 137, *137*
    in Chile, in *nueva canción* groups, 290
charazani (side-blown flute), in Bolivia, 120
charge. See charka
charka (*ch'aje*, charge, *charkha*; curved cane wrapped duct
    flute), 102, 119, 304
charkha. See charka
charu. See kuizi
Chatino (Kitse cha'tnio) people, 235, 241
Cherokee people, Eastern, in the United States, 3
Chibcha linguistic family, 194, 212
Chibcha people, 233
chicha, as beverage, by peoples
    Atacameño, *chicha de aloja* in ritual offerings (*tinka*),
        152
    Aymara and Kechua, in traditional practices of, 103, 301
    Chiriguano-Chané, 172
    Kechua, in Conquest dance-drama, 4, 327–28
    Kuna
        in secular contexts, 279–80
        in shamanic rituals, 212, 217, 219–22, 224, 286
    Mapuche, in Chile, 157
    Mískito, in shamanic rituals, 204–206
Chichen Itza (major Maya site in Yucatán), 12
Chichicastenango (Quiché-Maya town in Guatemala where
    Popol Vuh manuscript was found), 8
Chichimec (Úza) people
    demographics, 235, 240
    ritualized warfare drama of, 248
chicote (round dance), in Colombia, 298
chilames (*Chilam Balam*, sacred books of Yucatec-Maya
    people), 12
children's songs
    Kawéskar people, 159
    Mískito people (*pulanka*; game-songs), 208–10, *209*
Chile
    dance
        bailes chinos, in Limache, 271–73, *272*
        cueca, 150
        cumbia andina, 150
        huayño (*huayno*), 146, 150
        takirari, 150–51
        vals (waltz), 150
    ensembles. *See also* groups *below*
        bandas (brass bands), 148, 150–51
        lakitas (ensembles of small panpipes), 148, 150–51
        lichiguayos (ensembles of large *kenas*), 148, 150–51
        of Mapuche peoples, 158, 271
        orquesta, 148–50
        sikuras (ensembles of large panpipes), 148, 150–51
        tarkeadas (*tarka* ensembles), 148–49
    groups. *See also* ensembles *above*
        Inti-Illimani, 290

Quilapayún, 290
instruments. *See also* ensembles *above*; Mapuche
    peoples, in general
  bandola, 148–49
  bandurria, 149
  chino flutes, 266, 268, 271–74, *272*, 278
  chorromón (pre-Hispanic metal bell-set), 153–54
  clarín (*erke*; *corneta*; long straight side-blown
    trumpet), 153–54, 309
  erke. See *erke*
  guitar, 149–50, 152–53
  kena. See *kena*
  pinkillo, 149
  pinkullo, 301–303
  putu (animal horn), 153–54
  sikus. See *siku*
  tarka. See *tarka*
peoples
  Atacameño, 145, 151–54
  Aymara, 145, 147–51
  German descendants, in Chiloé Island, 316
  indigenous groups, in general
    cosmology and ritual, 146
    demographics, 145
    languages, 145
    research on musics of, 145
    style characteristics, in music of, 146–47
    traditional vis-à-vis acculturated practices, 145
  Kawéskar, 145, 158–60, 161n
  Mapuche, 145, 154–58, 169, 188, 190–91, 271, 307,
    308
  Selk'nam, 20–21, 145, 158–60, 161n
  Yámana, 145, 158–59, 161n
song
  benditos (religious folk songs), 150
  nueva canción, use of traditional instruments in,
    290–91
  tonos (tunes, accompanied songs), 148–49
Chimú culture
  aerophones, materials for, 288
  epics, recorded in chronicles, 10
  panpipe representations, in ceramics of, 113–14
Chinantec (Tsa ju jmí) people, 235, 242
chino (member of confraternities of musicians/dancers), in
    Chile, 271–73
chino flute (*flauta de chino*, *flautón*, *pito*; end-blown
    aerophone played by *chinos*)
  description of, 266, 271–73, *272*
  interlocking technique in performance, 268, 272–73,
    274
  traditional performance style, 278
Chipaya people
  aerophones
    ch'utus (duct flutes), 102, 119, 301
    doti (horn), 120
    functionality of, 266
    lichiwayu (large notched flute), 103, 118, 290
    maizus (panpipes), 104, 118, *118*
    pinkayllo (duct flute), 119, 301
    tar pinkayllu (*tarka*; wooden duct flute), 303
    wauqu (vessel flute), 118, 120, *120*

cosmology, 103–104
demographics, 101
ensembles, panpipes
  maizus, 104, 118, *118*
  sikus (*sikuris*), 277
texture, parallel polyphony, at tritone, in *pinkullo*
    performance, 301
Chiriguano (Guaraní-affiliated people). *See* Chiriguano-
    Chané peoples
Chiriguano-Chané peoples, 163–64, *165* (map), 171–72, 179
  ancestor worship, 172
  celebrations, Roman Catholic feasts, adoption of,
    171–72
  cultural change, 172, 178–79
  dance
    creole, *bailecitos*, *chacareras*, *takiraris*, 172
    traditional
      carnival, circular dances, and ritualized dance-
        drama, 171–72
      with *zapateo* (footwork), to *turumi* music, 171
  demographics, 163–64, *165* (map), 171
  gender roles, 172
  genres, *tonadas* (instrumental), 171
  instruments
    chordophones, *turumi* (*miorí*; violin), 171–72
    membranophones, family of
      anguaguásu (*angúa aretepe*; largest-sized), 172
      anguarái (medium-sized), 172
      michirái (smallest), 172
  languages, 171
  missionaries and missionization, 171
  national society, interaction with, 179
  rituals and ceremonies
    aréte awati (corn festival), 171–72
    carnival (merged with *aréte awati*), 171–72
    funerary, 171
chirimía (*chirimoya*, *chirisuya*; term for "shawm" in Spain;
    double-reed aerophone)
  in Colombia
    as ensemble, 318
    as single-reed aerophone, 316, 318
  description of, 316, 318
  in Mexico, 316, 318
  origin of, 263
  in Peru, 262, 316, 318
  P'urhépecha people, 248, 251
chirimoya (double-reed aerophone; name for the *chirimía*
    in Lucanas, Peru), 316
Chiripá people, 164
chirisuya (double-reed aerophone; name for the *chirimía* in
    areas of southern Peru), 263, 316, 318
chiriwanos (panpipes)
  in Bolivia
    as panpipe ensembles, 104
    as panpipes of Aymara and Kechua peoples, 104,
      118, *118*
    as panpipes of Chipaya people (*maizus*), 104, 118, *118*
  in Peru
    as Aymara name for *siku* panpipes, 274
    as Aymara tradition of *siku* panpipes performance,
      276–78

Chocho (Chocholtecas, Runixa ngiigua) people, 235, 242
choike-purrún (Mapuche ostrich dance), 156, 271
chokela (notched flute)
   in Bolivia, 103, 118, 120
   in Peru, 127
Ch'oles (Winik) people, 235, 243
Chomsky, Noam, 83
Chontal of Oaxaca people, 235, 241
chordophones
   adoption of
      Chiriguano-Chané peoples, violin (*turumi; miorí*),
         171–72
      Mbyá people
         five-string guitar and rebec (*ravê*), 173–76, 177
         harp, 177
      Mískito people, six-string guitar, 207
      Púrhépecha people, 248–49
   arpa. See harp *below*
   bandola, Aymara people, in Chile, 148–49
   bandurria
      in Chile, Aymara people, 149
      in Colombia, 316
      in Peru, 134, 135, 141, 148
   bass, electric, in *vallenato* ensembles, Colombia, 316
   charango
      in Bolivia, 104, 118
      in Canas Province, Peru, 134–37, 136–37, 141
      in Chile, in *nueva canción* groups, 290
   cuatro ("four-course" instrument), in *mare-mare*
         performance traditions, Venezuela, 280,
         282
   double bass, in P'urhépecha ensembles, 251
   ensembles, by type
      of *charangos*, in Peru, 136–37
      estudiantinas (*tunas*; ensembles of mostly plucked
         chordophones), 316
      of flute, guitar, harp, and *caja*, Atacameño people,
         153
      string bands, in Peru, 133–34, 141–42
      of violin, guitar, Mexican *vihuela*, and string bass,
         P'urhépecha people, 251
   guitar (*guitarra*; six-string)
      Bolivia, 104
      Chile
         Atacameño people, 152–53
         in Aymara Carnival of Socoroma, 149
         in Aymara *orquesta*, 150
      Ecuador, in ensembles with *rondador* panpipe, 285
      in *estudiantina* ensembles, 316
      Mbyá people
         five-string (*mbaraká*), 173–76, 177
         six-string, 174, 176–77
      Mískito people, 207
      in Nahuatl song-texts, 16
      Peru
         in Canas Province, 135–37
         in chordophone ensembles with muted trumpets,
           Ancash, 307
         in string-band music, 134
      P'urhépecha people
         construction and marketing of, 258

      in dance accompaniment, 252
      in ensembles, 251–52
      as instrument played by women, 256
      sétima (replaced guitar of three single and four
         double courses), 251
      in song accompaniment, 249, 250, 251–52, 257
   guitarra. See guitar *above*
   harp (*arpa*; diatonic)
      Mbyá people, 177
      Peru
         in chordophone ensembles with muted trumpets,
           Ancash, 307
         in *orquesta cuzqueña*, 133
         in *orquesta típica del centro*, 315
   lungku (*lunku*; Mískito musical bow), 204
   mandolin
      Chile, in Aymara *orquesta*, 150
      in *estudiantina* ensembles, 316
      Peru
         in chordophone ensembles with muted trumpets,
           Department of Ancash, 307
         in *orquesta cuzqueña*, 133
         in string-band music, 134
   mbaraká (as five-string guitar of the Mbyá people),
         173–76, 177
   miorí. See turumi
   ravé (rebec), 173–76, 177
   rebec. See *ravé above*
   tina (Mískito monochord), 207
   turumi (*miorí*; violin of the Chiriguano-Chané peoples),
         171–72
   vihuela (as Mexican five-string strummed instrument),
         in P'urhépecha ensembles, 251
   violin
      Chile, in Aymara *orquesta*, 150
      in *estudiantina* ensembles, 316
      Peru
         in orquesta *cuzqueña*, 133
         in *orquesta típica del centro*, 315
      in P'urhépecha ensembles, 251
      turumi (*miorí*; Chiriguano-Chané peoples), 171–72
choreography. *See also* dance; *specific dances*
   by country, northeastern Brazil, *bandas-cabaçais*, in
         performances of, 297
   by peoples
      Aymara
         in Chile
           carnival dances, 149–50
           Pachallampe (potato-sowing ritual) dances, 151
         in Peru, Conima District, *wifala* dance, 130
      Aymara and Kechua, in Bolivia
         julajula panpipe players, in dances of, 103,
           106–107, 107–108
         sikura panpipe players, in dances of, 109, 113, 113
      Chiriguano-Chané, 171
      Kamayurá, in *yawari* intertribal ritual, symbolism of,
         82–83, 90–94, 91
      Kechua, in Canas Province, Peru, of *kashuas*, 137
      Mapuche
         in Argentina, 170–71, 184
         in Chile, 155

Mbyá, of ritual dances, 174
P'urhépecha, of *abajeño, son,* and "Dance of the Moors," 252–53
Wakuénai, of *dzúdzuápani,* 38
choros (from the Portuguese "chorar," to weep), as Xavante laments (*dawawa*), 57, 59–60, *59,* 70
choros femininos, as Suyá women's laments, 69
Chorote people. *See also* Mataco and Guaycurú peoples
    demographics, 163–64
    gender roles, in dance and song, 168
    healing, shamanic, 168, 189
chorromón (idiophone; pre-Hispanic metal bell-set), 153–54
Christianity. *See also* missionaries and missionization
    Protestant denominations
        Moravian Church, 196–97, 199, 207
        Native Americans, cultural borrowings from, 5
        Pentecostal Church, in Chaco region, Argentina, 166, 169, 178–79
    Roman Catholicism
        feasts of. *See* celebrations, Catholic feasts (syncretic), cyclic calendar of
        Mass, 257, 306
        religious celebrations, adoption of, Chiriguano-Chané peoples, 171–72
        in syncretic belief systems
            Aymara and Kechua peoples, in Bolivia, 101–103
            Chiriguano-Chané peoples, 171–72
            in Mesoamerica, 16–17, 231, 233–35
Christmas
    Atacameño people, 152
    Aymara people, in Conima District, Peru, *pastores* (children's dance), 127
    Aymara and Kechua peoples, in Bolivia, 102
    in Colombia, *caña de millo* performances, association with, 314
    Mískito people, *Krismes* (as children's dance-songs), 208
    P'urhépecha people, 252–54
chronicles. *See also* chroniclers
    aerophones, descriptions of, 113, 264, 276
    Brazil, 49–53, *50*
    Comentarios reales de los Incas. See Garcilaso de la Vega
    Crónicas de Indias, 10
    hallucinogen usage, described in, 190
    healing rituals, described in, 187
    kashuas (circle dances), described in, 137
    musical competence of Indians, references to, 248
    nguillipún tradition, described in, 181
    shamans' identification with jaguar, described in, 20
chroniclers. *See also* chronicles
    Cuauhtlehuanitzin, Chimalpain, 13
    Díaz del Castillo, Bernal, 264
    Durán, Diego, 14
    Garcilaso de la Vega. *See* Garcilaso de la Vega
    Guamán Poma de Ayala, Felipe, 264
    Havestadt, Bernhard, 181
    Léry, Jean de, *50,* 53–55
    Oviedo y Valdés, Gonzalo Fernández de, 264
    Sahagún, Bernardino de, 11, 13–14, 187
ch'ullu-ch'ullus (idiophone; rattles), in Bolivia, 121

Chulupí (Nivaklé) people. *See also* Mataco and Guaycurú peoples
    demographics, 163–64
    status and rank, non-shamanic, 167
ch'unchu (as side-blown flute), Callawaya people, in Bolivia, 120
chururito (Atacameño circular dance-songs for cattle-marking and increase rituals), 152
ch'utu (*pinkayllo;* duct flute, Chipaya people), 102, 119, 301
Cihuacoatl (Mesoamerican earth goddess), 14
CIMI (Indigenous Missionary Council), Brazil, 50
civic holidays, celebrations of, P'urhépecha people, 256
clarín (long straight side-blown bamboo trumpet)
    in Argentina (*caña, corneta, erke*), 163, 309
    in Chile
        Atacameño people, 153–54
        under other names (*corneta, erke*), 309
    in Ecuador, 309
    in Peru, 308–10, *309–10*
clarinet (*clarinete;* single-reed aerophone)
    in army and civilian bands, 269
    description of, 267
    in Peru, 314–16, *317*
Claro Valdés, Samuel, 270, 279
classification
    of aerophones, 261–63, 266–67, 284–85, 319–20
    of indigenous instruments, in Brazil, 52–56, 70, 73
    of indigenous languages
        in Brazil, 51
        in Mexico, 231, 235, *236* (map), 237
        in South America, 3, 262
    of music, by peoples
        Aymara, in Chile, of musical traditions, within cosmological orders, 147–48
        Kamayurá
            of musical domain, 64, *64,* 73
            of sound domain, acoustical and semiological basis for, 64, 73
        Mapuche, in Chile
            rituals and ceremonies, of danced and sung music in, 155–57
            of *ülkantún* (generic term for mostly vocal music), 156
    of musical genres, P'urhépecha people, 248–49, *249,* 252
    of rituals, within cosmological orders, Aymara people, in Chile, 147–48
    of songs, by peoples
        Aymara, in Chile, for cattle-marking rituals, 148
        Suyá, 67–70
        Xavante, 59–60
Clastres, Pierre, 80
cleansing, ritual. *See* ritual cleansing *under* rituals and ceremonies, by function
Coatlicue (Mesoamerican goddess), 11
Coba Andrade, Carlos Alberto G., 284
Codex Madrid. See *Códice Matritense*
Códice Borbónico, 12
Códice Fejérvary-Mayer, 13, 187
Códice Florentino, 11, 13–14, 17
Códice Matritense (Codex Madrid), 11, 14, 187

Códice Telleriano-Remensis, 19

Cohen, John, 283, 291, 294

Colombia. *See also* New Granada, Viceroyalty of
    dance
        cacho de venado (deer hunt), 292
        chicote (round dance), 298
        cumbia, traditional, 314
    ensembles. *See also* groups *below*
        brass bands, 269
        carrizos (panpipes), *conjunto de*, 298
        chirimía (as ensemble), accordion in, 318
        gaita ensembles, in San Jacinto, Department of
            Bolívar, tri-ethnic, 298
        rondín-and-drum combination, 316
        vallenato, accordion in, 316
    epics, pre-contact, 10
    groups, "La Banda de los Borrachos," 269. *See also*
        ensembles *above*
    institutions, Gold Museum, Bogotá, 264
    instruments. *See also* ensembles *above*
        accordion, in *vallenato* and *chirimía* ensembles, 316,
            318
        atuñsa (*atunse*; Yuko pair of "hatchet" duct flutes) ,
            267, 297–98
        bullroarer, in Chocó region, 318
        cacho de venado (deer-skull globular flute), 292–93,
            293
        caña de millo (*gaita*, *flauta de cumbia*; side-blown
            single-reed aerophone), 267, 314, 316
        chirimía (as single-reed aerophone), 316, 318
        collections of, 263
        gaita, 268, 298. See also *kuizi below*
        kuizi (Kogi "hatchet" duct flute), 267, 297–98.
            See also *gaita* above
        massi (Wayúu single-reed aerophone), 267, 313–14,
            315
        nurá-mëe (Desana wooden bullroarer), 319
        rondín (harmonica), 263, 267, 316
        totoy (Wayúu single-reed aerophone), 267, 313–14,
            315
    peoples
        Barasana, 18
        Curripaco (term for Wakuénai groups in Colombia),
            18n, 25
        Desana (Tukano-affiliated), 20, 189–90, 319
        Guahibo-affiliated, 292–93, *293*
        Ika, 298
        Kogi, 297–98
        Sanká, 198
        Wayúu, 313–14, *315*
        Yuko, 297–98
    rituals and ceremonies, *Ítomo* (funerary), Guahibo-
        affiliated people, 292–93, *293*
    syncretism, in tri-ethnic ensemble, San Jacinto
        (Department of Bolívar), 298

Colombia (as name of Kuna ritual specialist [*kandur*]),
    214

colonization
    of Brazil, 49–50, 52
    of Chile, 152
    of Mexico, 233, 237, 248

Columbus, Christopher (Cristóbal Colón), 2, 195

Columbus, Ferdinand (Fernando Colón), 195

Comentarios reales de los Incas (Garcilaso de la Vega), 21, 22,
    113, 187, 276, 288, 320

communal labor
    as ancient Andean tradition, 278
    as core value, in Mesoamerica, 234
    in Peru
        exchange of, in Canas Province, 132, 137
        minga (traditional collective work effort)
            clarín, function of, in, 309–10
            roncadora and drum, association with, 305

communication media. *See* radio

competition
    "Concurso Artístico de la Raza P'urhépecha," 257
    inter-communal
        Aymara, in Conima District, Peru, ensembles in,
            126, 128–30, 131–32, 141, 278
        P'urhépecha people, brass bands in, 255, 259

The Complete Muu-ígala in Picture Writing (Holmer and
    Wassen), 218

composition. *See also* improvisation
    by country, Peru
        in Canas Province, 137–40
        in Conima District, 128–31, 137, 141
        for *orquesta típica del centro*, 314–15, *317*
        for panpipe ensembles, 128–30
    by peoples
        Aymara
            in Chile, *kena*, ornamentation in, 150
            in Conima District, Peru
                innovation, concept of, 128–29, 141
                motivic juxtaposition in, 128
        Aztec (Mexica), censorship on, 14
        Kechua, in Canas Province, Peru,
            formulaic approach to, 141
            in general, 137
        K'ero, *pina pinkulucha* music, ornamentation in,
            291, 294
        Mapuche, in Chile, ritual and secular "human"
            music, traits of, 157–58
        P'urhépecha
            concept of, 251
            Day of the P'urhépecha Composer (May 24),
                257
            repertoire renewal, 253, 259

Concepción, Fiesta de la (Immaculate Conception,
        December 8), Aymara and Kechua, in
        Bolivia, 102

condor
    Andean cult of, in Kechua *ayarachi* tradition, 278
    bones, for *chirisuyas*, in Peru, 318
    as male manifestation, in Andean symbolic dualism,
        Bolivia, 116
    as spirit of the mountains (*mallku*, Mallku), in Andean
        cosmology, 103, 113, 116

conjuntos. *See* ensembles, by type

Conquest (of America)
    genocide and, 2, 5, 164
    of Mexico, 2, 8, 11, 231, 248
    of Peru, 2, 10–11

prefigured, in Aztec and Yucatec-Maya cosmology, 9–10, 12–14
representations of, in dance-dramas, plays, and myths
 "The Death of Atahualpa," 4, 10–11, 327
 "The Death of the Coya," in Carhuamayo, Peru, 4, 327–28
 in Makiritare creation myth (Watunna), 4, 17
 Moors and Christians
  P'urhépecha people
   "Danza de los moros," 249, 249, 251, 253, 255, 257, 259. See also "Danza de los soldados"
   "Danza de moros y cristianos," 248–49, 259
   "Danza de los soldados," 255, 259. See also "Danza de los moros"
  symbolism of, 4
 responses to, 4, 327–28
 of southwestern Inca Empire, 163
"Conquest of the Desert" campaign, in Argentina, 164
contests. See competition
contrabajo (burdón; duct aerophone), in Bolivia, 119
Conzemius, Edward, 196
Coons, Carleton S., 159–60
coplas (as tritonic song genre), in Argentina, 163
Cora (Nayeri) people, 235, 239–40, 300
corneta (Spanish for "trumpet"; lip-concussion aerophones)
 in Argentina, as long straight side-blown trumpet (caña, erke), 163
 in Chile
  as long straight side-blown trumpet (clarín, erke), 309
  as short end-blown trumpet, Mapuche peoples, 271
"La corona" (The Crown; canajqua [kanákwa]; pre-contact P'urhépecha song), 247
Corpus Christi
 Aymara and Kechua peoples, in Bolivia, 102–103
 K'ero people, 294, 294
 P'urhépecha people, 249, 251, 254, 257
Corrêa de Azevedo, Luiz Heitor. See Azevedo, Luiz Heitor Corrêa de
corrido (narrative vocal genre), as mestizo repertoire, P'urhépecha people, 252, 255
Cortés, Hernán, 13–14
cosmology. See also Christianity; myth; rituals and ceremonies; shamans and shamanism
 as explanation, system of, 22–23, 146
 healing and, 187–89
 in Mesoamerica, 233–34
 by peoples
  Atacameño, 152–54
  Aymara, in Chile, 147–48, 150–51
  Aymara, in Conima District, Peru, 123–24, 126–27, 132, 301
  Aymara and Kechua, in Bolivia, 101–105, 107–109, 113–17, 114–15
  Aztec (Mexica), 11–17, 12–13, 15
  Guaraní, 189
  indigenous groups, in general
   Chile, 146–47
   Mexico, 234
  Kamayurá, 80–82, 88–89, 93–94, 97–98
  Kawéskar, 158

Kechua, in Canas Province, Peru, 123–24, 137
Kuna, 212–14, 216–26, 278, 285–86
Makiritare, 4
Mapuche, 9, 154–58, 179, 182, 184–85, 307, 308
Mataco and Guaycurú, 166–68
Maya, 11–17, 13
Mazatec, 190
Mbyá, 172–73, 174–75
Mískito, 197–207
P'urhépecha, 248, 253, 256
Suyá, 67–70
Toltec, 11–17, 13
Wakuénai, 18n, 25–35, 39–40, 45–46
Warao, 268, 313
Xavante, 57, 59
Costa Rica, formerly territory of ancient Mexico, 231
costume and ceremonial dress, by peoples
 Aymara
  in Conima District, Peru, 130, 133
  in sikuri traditions, 278
 Aymara and Kechua, in Bolivia, 113
 Aztec (Mexica), 14
 indigenous groups, in Mexico, identity, as marker of, 234
 Kechua, in Canas Province, Peru, 139
 Mapuche, in Argentina, for nguillipún fertility ritual, 170, 184
 P'urhépecha, 252–53, 258
 Selk'nam, for Hain initiation ceremony, 20
 Wakuénai, for kwépani ceremony, 31, 33
counterpoint, European, taught to P'urhépecha people, 248
courtship, by peoples
 Aymara, in Chile, 149
 Kechua, in Peru, association with
  charango music, in Canas Province, 137, 141
  kena, 288–90
 Mataco and Guaycurú, in algarroba festival, 168
 Maya, in Guatemala, "first flute," in legend of, 319
 P'urhépecha, 253
creation myths. See under myth
criollo (as born in the Americas of Spanish descent), 123–24
Cristo de los Milagros, feast of, P'urhépecha people, 253
criticism, music, Kamayurá people, in yawari ritual, pitch organization as critical language, 89–90, 89, 94, 96, 98
Crónicas de Indias (chronicles), 10
Cruxent, José María, 292
Cruz, Fiesta de la (Holy Cross Day, May 3)
 Aymara people, in Conima District, Peru, Achach K'umu dance-drama on, 132
 Aymara and Kechua peoples, in Bolivia, 102, 107
cuatro ("four-course" plucked chordophone), in Venezuelan mare-mare traditions, 280, 282
Cuauhtlehuanitzin, Chimalpain, 13
Cubeo people, 34n, 27–28
cueca (widespread national folk dance of Chile), Aymara people, 150
Cuicuilco (archaeological site in Valley of Mexico, major center ca. 300–100 B.C.E.), 1

cultural change. *See also* acculturation; *mestizaje*;
    transculturation
  in Atacameño traditions, 152–53
  Aymara people, in Chile, *lakitas*, in construction of, 150
  Aymara people, in Conima District, Peru, 127
  in Chiriguano-Chané traditions, 172, 178–79
  Conquest and, 2
  identity construction, in processes of, 4–5
  indigenous peoples, in Chile, 145
  in Kawéskar traditions, 159–60
  in *kena* performance styles, 290–91
  in Mapuche traditions, Argentina, 171, 179
  in Mataco and Guaycurú traditions, 166, 178–79
  Native Americans, in general, 327–28
  Peru
    in Conima and Canas traditions, comparatively,
      141–42
    in string-band tradition, 133–34
  P'urhépecha people, 252, 257–59
  social resistance to, 5, 328
cultural extinction
  Fuegian peoples, 158–60
  Pikunches (Mapuche peoples of the North), in Chile,
    154
  Selk'nam people, 163–64
  Tehuelche people, in Patagonia, 163–64
cultural policies. *See* state policies
cumbia (cluster of traditional choreographic genres, in
    Colombia; urban-popular style)
  caña de millo (*gaita, flauta de cumbia*) in, Colombia, 314
  P'urhépecha people, in repertoire categorized as
    mestizo, 252, 255
cumbia andina (melodic-rhythmic hybrid of Andean
    huayno and Colombian *cumbia*)
  in Chile, Aymara people, 150
  in Peru, 124
curandera (as Mazatec female healer), 189
Curassow Head (archetypal character in *yawari* mythic
    narrative), 89, 96–98
Curripaco (name for Wakuénai peoples in Colombia and
    Venezuela), 18n
Cusi-Coyllur (Inca princess), 10
cymbals (idiophones; *pratos*), in Brazil, 296

D

Dada saila tummadi (Great Father-creator in Kuna
    cosmology), 216, 222, 224
dadzarono (Xavante noon songs), 57, 59–60, *61*
dahipopo (Xavante evening songs), 57, 59
Dama Prapit (Mískito for "Elder Wise Prophet"; honorific
    title given to ritual specialists), *208*
dance. *See also* choreography; rituals and ceremonies;
    specific dances and types
  Conquest dance-dramas
    "The Death of the Coya," in Carhuamayo, Peru, 4,
      327–28
    Moors and Christians
      P'urhépecha people
        "Danza de los moros," 249, *249*, 251, 253, 255,

        257, 259. *See also* "Danza de los soldados"
        "Danza de moros y cristianos," 248–49, 259
        "Danza de los soldados," 255, 259. *See also*
          "Danza de los moros"
  symbolism of, 4
  by country
    Argentina
      bailecito, 172
      chacarera, 172
      chamamé, 171
      takirari, 172
    Bolivia
      in general, 101–102
      julajula panpipe players, dance of, 103, *106–107*,
        107–108
      sikura panpipe players
        representational dance of, 109, 113, *113*
        wayño (*huayno*), *111–12*
      in *sikuri* ensemble traditions, 275, 277–78
    Chile
      bailes chinos, in Limache, 273
      cueca, 150
      cumbia andina, 150
      huayño (*huayno*), 146, 150
      takirari, 150–51
      vals (waltz), 150
    Colombia
      cacho de venado (deer hunt), 292
      chicote (round dance), 298
      cumbia, traditional, 314
    Peru
      Achach K'umu (dance-drama), for Holy Cross
        Day, 124, 126, 132, *133*
      cumbia andina, 124
      "The Death of the Coya" (dance-drama), in
        Carhuamayo, 4, 327–28
      kashuas (circle dances), 137–38, *138*, 141
      marinera, 133
      pastores (children's Christmas dance), 127
      satiri (dance-drama), for San Isidro, 131–32
      wayno (*huayno*), 133–34
      wifala (courting dance), for Candlemas, 130, *131*
  by peoples
    Atacameño, 152–54
    Aymara
      in Chile, 146, 150–51
      in Conima District, Peru, 124, 126–27, 130–32,
        131, 133
      in general, accompanied by *tarkeadas*, 304
    Aymara and Kechua
      in Bolivia, 101–103, *106–107*, *107–109*, 113,
        111–13
      in Bolivia and Peru, 274–78
    Ayomán descendants (*baile de las turas*), in
      Venezuela, 292
    Botocudo, 54
    Chiriguano-Chané, 171–72
    Guahibo, *cacho de venado* dance (deer hunt), in
      Colombia, 292
    Hirahara descendants (*baile de las turas*), in
      Venezuela, 292

Kamayurá, 65, 81–82, 90–91, 94, 299–300, 312
Kawéskar, 160
Kechua, in Canas Province, Cuzco, Peru, 133–34, 137–41, *138*
Kogi, 298
Kuna, 227, *227–28*
Mapuche
   in Argentina, 170–71, 182, 184
   in Chile, 156–57, 271
Mataco and Guaycurú, 166–69
Mayo, 239, *239*
Mbyá, 174–77, *177*
Mískito, 208–210, *209*
Nahua, *242*
Pur'hépecha, 247–49, *249*, 251–54, 256–59
Wakuénai, 25–26, 29, 31–34, 38–40, 42, 44, 46
Xavante, 57
Zoque, *243*
"Dance of *tlacololeros*" (ocelots), Nahua peoples, *242*
daño're (Xavante term for "collective dance and song"), 57, 59, 60, *61–62*
"Danza de los cúrpites" (representational dance genre), P'urhépecha people, 253–54
"Danza de la flor" (P'urhépecha pre-contact dance tradition), 247, 256
"Danza de los moros" (Dance of the Moors; P'urhépecha dance-drama), 249, *249*, 251, 253, 255, 257, 259. *See also* "Danza de los soldados"
"Danza de moros y cristianos" (Moors and Christians cycle of conquest dance-dramas), 4, 248–49, 259
"Danza de los negritos" (representational dance genre), P'urhépecha people, 253, 256–57
"Danza de San Lorenzo," Zoque people, in State of Chiapas, *243*
"Danza de los soldados" (Dance of the Soldiers; P'urhépecha dance-drama), 255, 259. *See also* "Danza de los moros"
"Danza de las uananchas" (representational dance genre), P'urhépecha people, 253
"Danza de las uarecitas" (representational dance genre), P'urhépecha people, 258
"Danza de los viejitos" (representational dance genre), P'urhépecha people, 253, 258
danzón (Cuban dance-genre), in repertoire categorized as mestizo, P'urhépecha people, 252
dápa (Wakuénai sacred trumpet), 31–32, 46
dapraba (Xavante morning songs), 57, *59*–60, 62
datun (Mapuche shamanic healing ritual for chronic or severe diseases), 156–57
dawawa (Xavante type of *choro* or lament), 57, 59–60, *59*, 70
Day of the Dead (Todos los Muertos, November 2), P'urhépecha people, 256
death. *See also* funerary *under* rituals and ceremonies, by function; sacrifice
  in cosmology of
    Aztec (Mexica) people, 11–14
    Kamayurá people, 80, 81–82, 88–89, 93–94, 96–98
    Kuna people, 218–21, 225–26
    Mískito people, 199–202, 205–207

    Toltec people, 11–14
    Wakuénai peoples, 38, 40
Day of the Dead (Todos los Muertos, November 2), P'urhépecha people, 256
instruments, role of, in afterlife, 10
Peruvian Conquest history, in dramatizations of
    "The Death of Atahualpa," 4, 10–11, 327
    "The Death of the Coya," 4, 327–28
pinkillus, association with, in Andean cosmology, 302
  in pre-Hispanic ceramic vessels, Andean peoples, 10, 114, *114*
  in representational *sikuri* dances, Bolivia, 109, 113, *113*
  in song-themes of
    Aztec and Yucatec-Maya peoples, 11–17
    Xavante people, 59
deer
  bones, for *chirisuyas*, in Peru, 318
  cacho de venado dance (deer hunt), in Colombia, 292
  in myths, 8
  skull
    as globular aerophone (*cacho de venado, cacho venao*), 292–93, *293*
    as trumpet, 320
  tibia, as flute, 286–88
déetu
  as symbolic coconut palm weevils, 37, 41, 44–46
  as Wakuénai flute named after the palm weevil
    definition of, 46
    function, in *pudáli* ceremonial cycle, 35, 37–38, 42
    symbolism of, 40–42, 44–46
demographics
  the Americas, pre-Columbian population of, 2
  the Antilles, Greater and Lesser, 2
  by country
    Argentina, 2, 163–64, *165* (map), 169, 171–72, 181
    Bolivia, 2, 101
    Brazil, 2, 50–51, *58* (map), 60–62, *63* (map), 67, 77–79
    Chile, 145, 147, 151–52, 154, 158
    Guatemala, 2
    Mexico, 237–44, 248
    Peru, 2, *125* (map), 126, 132
    Uruguay, 2
  by peoples
    Atacameño, 145, 151–52
    Aymara
      in Bolivia, 101
      in Chile, 145, 147
      in Conima District, Peru, *125* (map), 126, 132
    Callawaya, 101
    Chipaya, 101
    Chiriguano-Chané, 163–64, *165* (map), 171
    Kamayurá, 60–64, *63* (map), 77, 79
    Kechua, in Bolivia, 101
    Kechua, in Canas Province, Peru, *125* (map), 132
    Kuna (in Panama), 210, *210* (map), *211*, 212
    Mapuche
      in Argentina, 163–64, *165* (map), 169, 181
      in Chile, 145, 154
    Mataco and Guaycurú, 163–64, *165* (map)
    Mbyá, 163–64, *165* (map), 172–73, 273

demographics (*continued*)
    Mískito (in Honduras and Nicaragua), 194–97, *195*
        (map), *198–99*
    Suyá, 61–62, *63* (map), 77, 79
    Wakuénai (in Venezuela), 18n, 25
    Xavante, 57, *58* (map), 67
  social categories and, 123–24
Densmore, Frances, 279
Desana (Tukano-affiliated) people
  aerophones of, 319
  healers and healing, 189–90
  shaman's identification with jaguar, 20
Diaguita-Calchaquí peoples, 153
Diaguita culture
  aerophones of, 270–71, *270*
  shamanic knowledge, in rock drawings of, 187
dianas (signals or calls in Aymara repertoire of religious
      instrumental music), in Chile, 150
Díaz del Castillo, Bernal, 264
Dictionnaire de musique (Rousseau), 53
dobrado (march-like genre, in repertoire of *bandas-de-
      pífanos*), northeastern Brazil, 297
Dobyns, Henry F., 2
dog, Huanca cult of, 320
Dorialina (Mískito shaman or *sukia*), 207
doti (Chipaya name for *pututu* as bull or cow horn), in
      Bolivia, 120
double bass, in P'urhépecha ensembles, 251
dreams
    Aymara people, oracular, 189
    Kamayurá songs, received in, 65
    Mataco and Guaycurú peoples, shamanic vocation,
        revealed through, 167
    Mískito people
      links to Kuna people, established in, 193
      shamanic vocation, revealed through, 198
      songs and shamanic knowledge, received in, 193,
        203
    Nahua children, oracular, 189
    Xavante songs, received in, 57, 60
dress. *See* costume and ceremonial dress
drinking, ritual. *See* ritual drinking *under* rituals and
      ceremonies
drinks. *See* beverages
drugs. *See* hallucinogens
drums. *See under* membranophones; idiophones
dulzaina. See *rondín*
Durán, Diego, *Historia de las Indias de Nueva España*,
      14
Durand (Spaniard credited with description of
      Moctezuma's coronation), 190
dynamics
    in Atacameño music, 153
    in Aymara aerophone ensembles, Conima District,
      Peru, 128, 130–31
    in Kawéskar song, 159
    in P'urhépecha music, 252, 255
dzáate (toucan; Wakuénai sacred flutes), 31, 33, 46
Dzáwinai people, 18n, 25
dzáwinápa (Wakuénai large "Jaguar-bone" trumpets), 25,
      29–32, 46

dzúdzuápani (Wakuénai "wheel" dance-songs), 25, 38–40,
      44, 46
Dzúli (Wakuénai mythical figure, first owner of sacred
      chants or *málikái*), 26, 28–29, 45–46

E

Easter
  Aymara people, in Conima District, Peru, 126, 132
  Chiriguano-Chané peoples, 171
  dry season and *tarkas*, association with, 127
ecology, as theme, in P'urhépecha songs, 251
economy
  by country
    Argentina, 164, 166
    Brazil, land conflicts, 79
    Mexico
      central region, 240, 252
      central valleys and northern Oaxaca, 242
      in colonial regional reconfiguration, 237
      eastern region, 239
      northwestern region, mining centers, 238
      southeastern region, 243
      southern Pacific region, 241
      western region, 239–40
    Peru, in *ayllus* of Conima, Department of Puno, 126
  by peoples
    Kamayurá, in sponsorship of *yawari* ritual, 81
    Kawéskar, Selk'nam, and Yámana, 158
    Kechua, in Canas Province, Peru, 132
    Kuna, in chant transmission, 213–14
    Mapuche
      in Argentina, 181
      in Chile, 154
    Mataco and Guaycurú, 166
    Mbyá, 173
    pre-Hispanic
      Inca, 1–2
      Teotihuacan, 1
Ecuador
  aerophones
    chirimía (double-reed aerophone) in, 316, 318
    clarín (long straight side-blown trumpet) in, 309
    flautas, 295, *295*
    pingullo
      as Quichua duct flute with six finger holes
        (*pífano*), 304
      as Quichua one-hand duct flute with two finger
        holes and a thumb hole, 304
    rondador (monistic panpipe), 266, 283–85, *285–86*
    rondín (harmonica), 263, 267, 316
    tunda (side-blown flutes), 295
  dance, *sanjuanito*, 285, *286*
  ensembles, *pingullo*-and-*tamboril* combination, 304
  Inca culture in, 2
  peoples
    Quichua, 295, *295*, 304
    Shuar (formerly Jíbaro or Jívaro), 153
  regions
    Chota Valley, calabashes, in ensembles, 269

Imbabura Province, 284, 295, 304
Pichincha Province, 295
Quito, 283
Ecumenical Center for Documentation and Information
    (CEDI), Brazil, 51
education
    healers, traditional training of, 188–89
    missionaries, as music instructors, 49, 52, 248
    state-sponsored, impact of
        on Kawéskar traditions, 160
        on Mískito children's traditions, 210
    traditional culture, oral transmission of, by peoples
        Atacameño, 153
        Kamayurá, 65, 71
        Kuna, 193, 212–15, 214, 216–17
        Mataco and Guaycurú, 167
        Mbyá, 175
        P'urhépecha, 248–50, 256–57
        Suyá, 71, 73–74
        Xavante, 73–74
Elchén F'Chau (Mapuche Venerable Old Father), 182
Elchén Kushé (Mapuche Venerable Old Mother), 182
eluwün. See machi-elwün
Emperaire, Joseph, 159
enculturation, Kawéskar people, 160
enfloramiento or floreo del ganado (Aymara cattle-marking
    and increase ritual), in Chile, 148
ensembles (bandas, conjuntos, orquestas, tropas), by type. See
    also groups
    of aerophones, performance techniques, in general,
        267–68
    aerophonic/membranophonic combinations
        aerophone-and-drum single-player combinations
            chirimía and drum, P'urhépecha people, 251
            erke (as single-reed aerophone) and drum, 311
            fife and drum, P'urhépecha people, 251
            flauta and caja (cajero), in Peru, 304, 304, 309,
                309, 314, 316
            flute and drum, Chiriguano-Chané peoples,
                171–72
            panpipe and drum, as pre-contact tradition, 268
            pingullo and tamboril, in Ecuador, 304
            pipe and tabor, 268
            roncadora and drum, in Peru, 304–305, 305
            rondín (harmonica) and drum, in Peru, 316
        in Bolivia, 117–21
        as symbolic timbral dualism, 268
    of antaras (panpipes), in Nazca culture, 275
    of ayarichis (panpipes), Kechua people, in Bolivia, 104,
        118
    bandas-de-pífanos, in northeastern Brazil, 296–97
    bands (bandas; brass bands) and "orchestras"
        (orquestas), 269
    brass bands (bandas)
        Aymara people
            in Chile, 148, 150–51
            in Peru, 126, 130
        in Colombia, 269
        in mestizo traditions, Peru, 133
        military and civilian, 269
        P'urhépecha people, 251–57, 259

replacing
    pututu groups (bovine horns), in Bolivia, 308
    traditional aerophone ensembles, 307
    traditional performance techniques in, retention of,
        267
    valve trumpets in, 307
calabashes (as aerophones)
    with aerophones and chordophones, in Colombia,
        269
    with tin cans and banana leaves, in Ecuador, 269
carrizos (panpipes), conjunto de
    in Colombia, 298
    in Venezuela, 280–81, 281
of charangos, in Peru, 136–37
chirimía (as ensemble with transverse flutes), in
    Colombia, 318
of chiriwanos (panpipes)
    Aymara and Kechua peoples, in Bolivia, 104, 118
    maizus (chiriwanos; panpipes), Chipaya people, in
        Bolivia, 104, 118
of chordophones (violin, guitar, Mexican vihuela, string
    bass), P'urhépecha people, 251
for cumbia, traditional, in Colombia, 314
estudiantinas (tunas; ensembles of mostly plucked
    chordophones), 316
of flute, guitar, harp, and caja, Atacameño people, 153
gaita (as ensemble), in Colombia, 298
of julajulas (panpipes), Aymara and Kechua peoples, in
    Bolivia, 104–108, 105–106
of julu-julus (panpipes), Aymara people, in Bolivia, 104
kenas (notched flutes)
    in Aymara orquesta, Chile, 150
    in Bolivia, 118
    instruments' sizes (registers), in ensembles, 290
    in non-traditional contexts, 290
    in nueva canción groups, Chile, 290–91
kepas and wankaras, in Inca culture, 269
of lakitas (panpipes)
    Aymara people, in Chile, 148, 150–51
    Aymara and Kechua peoples, in Bolivia, 104–105,
        108–109, 108–109, 118, 120
lichiguayos (as ensembles of large type of kenas),
    Aymara people, in Chile, 148, 150–51
of maizus (chiriwanos; panpipes), Chipaya people, in
    Bolivia, 104, 118
of Mapuche peoples, in Chile
    for healing rituals, 158
    for ritual dances, 271
of mare-mare panpipes, in Venezuela, 281–82, 282
orquesta
    Aymara people, in Chile, 148–50
    of chordophones and aerophones, P'urhépecha
        people, 251–52, 255, 257
    in Peru
        orquesta cuzqueña, 133
        orquesta típica del centro, 269, 314–15, 317
        saxophone, in orquesta típica del centro, 314–15,
            317
of panpipes. See also specific types above and below
    in Bolivia, 104–13, 105–13
    pre-Columbian, 113–14, 114

ensembles (*continued*)
    of *phukunas* (panpipes), Callawaya people, 104
    of *pinkillos*, in Bolivia, 120
    of *pinkillos mohoceños* and drums, 303
    of *pinkillus*
        Aymara people, in Conima District, Peru, 126–27,
            130–31, 301
        Kechua people
            in Canas Province, Peru, 134–35
            in northern Potosí, Bolivia, timbric mixture in,
                301–302
    of *pitus* (*falawatus, pitos*; side-blown flutes)
        Aymara people, in Conima District, Peru, 126–28,
            132, *133*, 294
        with harp, violin, and drum, in Peru, 294
    of *sikuras* (*sikuris*; as ensemble of large type of double-
            row panpipes)
        Aymara people, in Chile, 148, 150–51
        Aymara and Kechua peoples, in Bolivia, 104–105,
            109, 110–13, 113, 115, 118
    sikuris (as ensembles of *sikus*; double-row panpipes)
        aesthetics, 128, 267
        in Argentina's Northwest, 163
        Aymara people, in Conima District, Peru, 126–32,
            128–29, 141
        Aymara and Kechua peoples, in Bolivia, 103–104,
            114–17, 115, 118, 118
        distribution of, 275
        performance traditions, in Bolivia and Peru,
            274–78
        registers in, 276
        symbolism of, 104–105, 114–17, 115, 278
    string bands, in Peru, 133–34, 141–42
    tango orchestras, *bandoneón* in, 316
    of *tarkas* (duct flutes; *tarkeadas* as *tarka* ensembles),
            Aymara people
        in Argentina, 303–304
        in Bolivia (*anata*), 303–304
        in Chile (*anata*), 148–51, 303–304
        in Conima District, Peru, 126–28, 130–31, 141, 301,
            303–304
    tropas, as rural panpipe ensembles, in Bolivia, 104
    tunas. See *estudiantinas*
    for *vallenato* music, accordion in, 316
    of Warao people, for *nahanamu* harvest festival, 288,
            312–13, *315*
epics
    areíto (*areyto*; ceremonies of Arawakan-affiliated
            Taínos), 10
    Aztec people (*teocuicatl*), 10–11, 14
    Ercilla y Zúñiga's "La Araucana," 181
    Inca people, *cantares históricos* and dramas,
            10–11
    P'urhépecha people, history, in sung narratives,
            250–51
    time, concept of, in, 10–11
Epiphany, P'urhépecha people, 253–54
epurba (secret shamanic knowledge embedded in Kuna
            chant), 214–15
Ercilla y Zúñiga, Alonso de, "La Araucana," 181
erke (aerophone)

as long side-blown trumpet (*caña, clarín, corneta, erkhe*)
        in Argentina, 309–310
        in Chile, 309–310
        in Peru, 163
    as single-reed animal horn (*erkencho*)
        in Argentina, 310–11
        in Bolivia (*erkencho*), 120, *120*, 310–11
        in Chile, 310–11
        description of, 267
erkencho (*erke*; single-reed animal horn), 120, *120*, 267,
            310–11
eschatology
    Kuna people, 216, 225–26, *226*
    Mískito people, 205–207, *208*
espuelas (idiophone; spur-rattles), in Bolivia,
            121, *121*
esthetics. *See* aesthetics
estudiantina (*tuna*; ensemble of mostly plucked
            chordophones), 316
ethnicity. *See* identity
ethnographic research, critique of, 3–5
ethnomusicology
    classification issues in, 3–5
    comparative studies in, 49–50, 70–74
    history of, in Brazil, 49–56, *50*, *52*
    methodological issues in, 2–5, 70–74, 328
    organological issues in, 264, 266–67
extinction, cultural. *See* cultural extinction

F

falawatu (*pitu*; side-blown flute), in Peru, 126–28, 132,
            133, 294
falsetto. *See under* performance practice
fañuru (Fañuru's manifestations, in Makiritare creation
            myth), 4, 17
Fañuru (Spanish invader figure, in Makiritare creation
            myth), 4, 17
Faron, Louis C., 181
Fernández de Oviedo y Valdés, Gonzalo. *See* Oviedo y
            Valdés, Gonzalo Fernández de
fertility rituals. *See under* rituals and ceremonies, by
            function
festivals. *See* carnival; celebrations; civic holidays; life-cycle
            (rites of passage); New Year's; patron-saint
            fiestas; rituals and ceremonies
fiddle. *See* violin
Fiesta de la Cruz. *See* Holy Cross Day
Fiesta de la Santa Cruz. *See* Holy Cross Day
Fiesta de la semilla (Atacameño sowing ritual), 152
fiestas. *See* carnival; celebrations; civic holidays; life-cycle
            (rites of passage); New Year's; patron-saint
            fiestas; rituals and ceremonies
fire
    emergence of, 20
    Kuna people, origin of, 220
    Mískito people, shamanic control of, 199
    P'urhépecha people, pre-contact offerings of, 247
    Wakuénai peoples, in *kwépani* and *pudáli* ceremonies,
            29, 37–38

fish
  Kamayurá people, in *yaku'i* ritual, symbolism of, 300
  Wakuénai peoples
    kúlirrína trumpets, function and symbolism of, 35–36, *36*, 38–39, 40–42, 44, 46
    spawning behavior of, in *pudáli* ceremonies, 37
flauta (as smaller types of transverse flutes in Ecuador), 295, *295*
flauta de chino. See *chino* flute
flauta de millo. See *caña de millo*
flautas de pico (beak flutes), 300
flautón. See *chino* flute
flawata. See *pflawata*
"Flor de canela" (*pirékwa*; P'urhépecha song), 258
"Flor de clavel" (carnation; *pirékwa*, P'urhépecha song), 250
floramiento or *floreo del ganado* (cattle-marking and increase ritual, Acatameño people), 152
Flórez Forero, Nubia, 298
"flower and song" (metaphor for the creative process in Nahuatl semiotic discourse), 16
Flute House, as institution
  Barasana people, *He* (flute) House, 18
  Kamayurá people, 79, 82–83, *82*, 90–91, *90–91*, 299–300
flutes. *See also specific types*
  Kayabi people, 72
  Makuxí, Taulipáng, and Yekuâna peoples, 54
  Wakuénai peoples, 26
food, ritual uses of. *See* ritual uses of food *under* rituals and ceremonies
formal structure (musical)
  Aymara and Kechua peoples, in Bolivia, symbolic dualism in *julajula* dances, 108
  comparatively
    in Canas (Kechua) and Conima (Aymara) traditions, Peru, 141
    in Caneño (Kechua) and mestizo *charango* traditions, Peru, 136
  Kechua people, in Canas Province, Peru
    in carnival melodies,139–40
    in *kashuas* (Kechua), 137, *138*
    in *papa tarpuy* song-dances, 137, *138*
    in ritual battle of Chiaraje melodies, 138
  Mapuche peoples, in Chile, symbolic dualism in, 157
  in mestizo music
    of Atacameño people, 153
    for *charango*, in Peru, 136
  in music of
    Aymara people, in Conima District, Peru, 128
    indigenous peoples, in Chile, 146
    Yekuâna people, in Brazil, 55
    P'urhépecha people, in *abajeño* and *son* genres, 249, 259
  in songs
    of Aymara people, in Chile
      for carnival, 149
      for cattle-marking rituals, 148
    of Kawéskar people, 159
    of P'urhépecha people, 251
    of Suyá people, 68–69, *68–69*

Franciscan order, in Mexico, 248
French Guiana, Wayãpí people, 268
F'ta Chau (Mapuche Great Father), 182
Fuegian cultures
  Kawéskar people (formerly Alakaluf)
    cosmology, 158
    cultural change, 159–60
    demographics, 145, 158–59
    history of, 145, 158
    name of, 161n
    near-extinction of, 159–60
    repertoires, types of, 159
    songs, types and style characteristics of, 159–60
    traditional music, preservation of, in field recordings, 159
  Selk'nam people (formerly Ona; in Argentina and Chile)
    annihilation of, 163–64
    Hain initiation ceremony, 20–21
    history of, 145, 158–59
    Kiepja, Lola (as last representative of her people), 20–21
    name of, 161n
    song, preservation of, in field recordings, 159, 164, 179
  Yámana people (formerly Yahgan)
    history of, 145, 158
    name of, 161n
    preservation of traditions, in field recordings, 159
fuga (closing section with contrasting theme in faster tempo)
  in *huayno*, 305
  in sectional mestizo *charango* music, 136
fujara (Slovak duct aerophone), 303
FUNAI (Fundação Nacional do Índio), 77
Fundação Nacional do Índio (FUNAI), 77
funerary rituals. *See* funerary *under* rituals and ceremonies, by function
fur-mantles, shaken (idiophones), Kawéskar people, 159
Furlong, C. Wellington, 145, 159

G

gaita (Spanish term for "pipes")
  as ensemble, in Colombia, 298
  as "hatchet" duct flute, in Colombia. See also *kuizi*
    gaita hembra (female flute), 298
    gaita macho (male flute), 268, 298
  as name for side-blown ductless flute (*pífano*), in Brazil, 296–97
  as single open pipe with finger holes and detachable duct, 267
Gallet, Luciano, 55, 73
Galvão, Eduardo, 51, 80
games
  ball (*juego de pelota*), in pre-contact Mesoamerica, 233
  pulanka (Mískito children's game-songs), 208–10, *209*
gammu-burui. See *kammu purwi*
gammu suid. See *kammu suid*
García, Carlos, 281

Garcilaso de la Vega (Inca), *Comentarios reales de los Incas*
  aerophonic performance, contexts for, 264
  healing practices, descriptions of, 187
  Huanca dog cult, description of, 320
  Inca song on gender reciprocity, 21–22
  Inca warfare, instruments in, description of, 320
  kena, association with courting, 288
  panpipes, interlocking technique in performance, 113,
    276
Garífuna ethnic nation (Black Caribs), 3, 196–97
Gê linguistic family, 51, 67, 70, 74, 77
gender attribution
  to aerophones
    atunse (pair of "hatchet" duct flutes), Yupa people,
      in Venezuela, 297–98
    carrizos (panpipes), in Venezuela, 278, 280–82, *281*
    clarín (*tatai clarín-clarín*; trumpet), Atacameño
      people, 154
    flautas, in Ecuador, 295
    gaita (as "hatchet" duct flute), in Colombia, 298
    guli (*kuli*; Kuna set of complementary pipes), 273,
      273
    julajulas (single-row panpipes), Aymara and Kechua,
      in Bolivia, 104–105, 118
    kammu purwi (Kuna dualistic panpipes), 226–27,
      227–28, 278–80, *279*
    kammu suid (Kuna flutes played in pairs), 266,
      285–86
    kuizi (Ika, Kogi, and Sanká "hatchet" duct flutes), in
      Colombia, 297–98
    lakitas (double-row panpipes), Aymara and Kechua,
      in Bolivia, 104–105, 118
    mimby (Mbyá flute), 174, 176
    mimby retá (Mbyá dualistic panpipes), 174, 176, *178*,
      273–74
    panpipes, Guahibo people, 280
    pifülka (*pifïlka*; Mapuche flutes), 158, 170, 184, *185*,
      266, 269–71, 271, 274, 278
    pinkillu ensemble registers, Kechua, in northern
      Potosí, Bolivia, 301–302
    putu (*mamai putu-putu*; horn), Atacameño people,
      154
    sikuras (large double-row panpipes)
      Aymara people, in Chile, 150
      Aymara and Kechua peoples, in Bolivia, 104–105,
        118
    tekeya (single-reed aerophone), Yekuana people, in
      Venezuela, 311
    trutruka (Mapuche trumpets), 158, 170–71, 271, 307,
      308
    tura (notched flutes), Ayomán and Hirahara, in
      Venezuela, 267, 291–92, *292*
    verékushi (Kariña panpipes), 280
    Wakuénai peoples, in *kwépani* and *pudáli*,
      contrasting criteria for, 42–46, *43*
    yaku'i (duct flutes), Kamayurá people, 65, 79,
      299–300, 311
  to Andean topography, 103
  in identity construction, 70
  to idiophones, *chorromón* (bells), Atacameño people,
    153–54

to membranophones
  llamador (*tambor macho*; African-derived single-
    headed drum), in Colombia, 298
  tambor mayor (*tambor hembra*; African-derived
    single-headed drum), in Colombia, 298
to seasons, Aymara and Kechua peoples, in Bolivia,
  102–103
to songs, in Aymara cattle-marking rituals, Chile, 148
gender roles
  by country
    Mexico, fiestas, in organization of, 234
    Peru, female-owned *tinya* drum performance
      tradition, 127, 306, 320
  in invocations to sacred beings of myth, 8
  by peoples
    Aymara, in Chile, in ritual music, 151
    Aymara, in Conima District, Peru, in instrumental
      performance, 127
    Aymara and Kechua
      in aerophonic performance, 268–69
      in anthropomorphic cosmology, 101–105, 108,
        116
    Bororo, gender-based power, in rituals, 318–19
    Chiriguano-Chané, in instrumental performance,
      172
    Guayakí, gender-based power, in rituals, 21
    Kalapálo, in *kagutu* and *yamarikumalu* ceremonies,
      21
    Kamayurá
      in sacred *yaku'i* flutes performance tradition,
        65, 300
      in *uru'a* flutes performance tradition, 299–300
    Kawéskar, labor, in division of, 158
    Kechua, in Bolivia, in *pinkillu* ensembles,
      301–302
    Kuna, in *kammu purwi* performances, 280
    Macoa, female-owned tradition of panpipe
      performance, 280
    Mapuche, in Argentina and Chile
      in *kultrún* (drum) performance tradition, 155, 158,
        170, 182, *183*, 189, 271
      in rituals, 170, 182, 184, 188
    Mataco and Guaycurú, in dances, instruments, and
      songs, 168
    Mbyá
      female-owned performance traditions
        mimby retá (panpipes), 174, 176, *178*, 273–74
        takuapú (stamping tubes), 174–75, *178*
      male-owned performance traditions
        anguapú (*mbaepú*; Mbyá double-headed
          drum), 174, 176
        mbaraká (Mbyá five-string guitar), 173–76,
          177
        ravé (Mbyá rebec), 173–76, *177*
    Mískito, in shamanic practices and songs, 198–99,
      202
    P'urhépecha, in performance traditions, 252–53,
      256–57, 259
    Selk'nam, Hain ceremony, gender-based power in,
      20–21
    Suyá, in oratory and song, 67, 69

Wakuénai
  in *kwépani* and *pudáli* ceremonies, 31, 38, 40–42,
      45–46
  pákamarántakan songs, in *kwépani* vis-à vis
      pudáli, 32, 34, 37, 40, 46
Warao, male-owned *muhusemoi*, 288
Xavante, in song performance, 57
German descendants, in Chile, accordion, use of, 316
Gil, Gilberto, 297
Gold Museum (Bogotá), 264
Goldman, Irving, 34n
Gómez, Milceades (Kuna ritual specialist), 217
Gómez Checheb, Domingo, 328
González, Raúl, 145
González Bravo, Antonio, 308
González Henríquez, Adolfo, 314
González Sánchez, Filemón, 250
Good, Catharine, 234
Graham, Laura, 57
Grame, Theodore, 264
Grebe, María Ester, 159–60, 270, 307, 328
Groeber, Pablo, 181
groups. *See also* ensembles, by type
  "La Banda de los Borrachos," 269
  Grupo Aymara, 290
  Los Incas (later Urubamba), 290–91
  Inti-Illimani, 290
  Quilapayún, 290
  Savia Andina, 290
  Selección del Centro (*orquesta típica del centro*), 315, 317
  Simon and Garfunkel, 290–91
  Trio Los Chapás, 250
  Urubamba (formerly Los Incas), 290–91
Grupo Aymara (Bolivian ensemble), 290
guacharaca (idiophone; scraper), in Colombia, 316
Guahibo and Guahibo-affiliated peoples, in Colombia and
      Venezuela
  cacho de venado (globular flute), 292–93, *293*
  jiwa (panpipes), 280
Guaikurú (Guaycurú, Guaykurú) linguistic family, 51
Guamán Poma de Ayala, Felipe, 264
Guaraní linguistic family, 164, 171–72
Guaraní peoples (in Brazil and Paraguay). *See also* Mbyá
      people
  mbaraká (gourd rattle), symbolism of, 189
  Mbayá music, field recordings of, in Brazil, 56
  migration, 164, 172–73
  missionaries and missionization, Jesuits, in
      northeastern Argentina, 172
Guarijío (Macurawe) people, 235, 238
Guatemala. *See also* Maya culture
  in Chiapas (Mexico), political refugees from, 244
  demographics, 1–2
  formerly territory of ancient Mexico, 231
  instruments
    chirimía (double-reed aerophone) in, 316, 318
    legend, of first flute or "*chirimía*," Maya people, 319
  peoples
    Garífuna ethnic nation (Black Caribs) in, 196–97
    Mame, 244
    Maya, in general, 319

Quiché-Maya, 1–2, 8, 244, 327
Guayakí people, gender-based power, in rituals, 21
Guaycurú subgroups. *See also* Mataco and Guaycurú
      peoples
  Mocoví. *See* Mataco and Guaycurú peoples
  Pilagá, 163–64, 166, 168–69, 293–94
  Toba, 163–64, 166–69, 178–79
Guaymí people, 193, 196
Gucumatz (Quiché-Maya mythical figure), 8, 11. *See also*
      Kukulcán; Quetzalcoatl
Guerra-Peixe, César, 297
guitar (*guitarra*; six-string plucked and strummed
      chordophone)
  in Bolivia, 104
  in Chile
    Atacameño people, 152–53
    in Aymara Carnival of Socoroma, 149
    in Aymara *orquesta*, 150
  in Ecuador, in ensembles with *rondador* panpipe, 285
  in *estudiantina* ensembles, 316
  Mbyá people
    five-string (*mbaraká*), 173–76, 177
    six-string, 174, 176–77
  Mískito people, in secular repertoire, 207
  in Nahuatl song-texts, 16
  in Peru
    Canas Province, 135–37
    in chordophone ensembles with muted trumpets,
        307
    in string-band music, 134
  P'urhépecha people
    commodification and construction of, 258
    in dance accompaniment, 252
    in ensembles, 251–52
    sétima (replaced guitar of three single and four
        double courses), 251
    in song accompaniment, 249, 250, 251–52, 257
    women, as instrument played by, 256
guitarra. *See* guitar
guli (*kuli* ; Kuna ductless set of complementary tubes
      without finger holes), 273, *273*
Gumilla, Joseph, 264
Günuna Kena people (Guénaken; northern Tehuelche),
      169, 181, 188
Gusinde, Martin, 145, 159–60
Guzmán, Nuño de, 248

H

Hain (male initiation ceremony, Selk'nam people), 20–21
hallucinogens
  alkaloids, 190
  ayahuasca vines, 188–90
  coca leaves, in *t'inka* ritual offerings
    Atacameño people, 152
    Aymara people, in Peru, 126
  ebene, 190
  healing rituals and, 188–90
  mushrooms, 8, 189–90
  as pathways to mystical flight, 8, 10

hallucinogens (*continued*)
 peyote (*hikuri*; cactus), 190
 psychoactive plants, ritual use of, in pre-contact Mexico, 234
 yagé (psychotropic drink), 18
d'Harcourt, Marguerite, 276, 304
d'Harcourt, Raoul, 276, 304
harehare (Warao aerophone; flat edge, single closed pipe with finger holes), 267
harmonica, in Peruvian string-band music, 134
harmony (functional)
 in Aymara cattle-marking songs, Chile, 148
 in mestizo *charango* traditions, Peru, 137
 in music of indigenous groups, Chile, 146
 in music for mestizo fiestas, Cuzco, Peru, 133–34
 in *tiuns* ("tunes") with guitar, Mískito people, 207
harp (*arpa*; diatonic)
 Mbyá people, 177
 Peru
  in chordophone ensembles with muted trumpets, Ancash, 307
  in *orquesta cuzqueña*, 133
  in *orquesta típica del centro*, 315
Hausch people, 158
Havestadt, Bernhard, 181
he (sacred flutes, Barasana people), in Colombia, 18
healers and healing. *See also* hallucinogens; illness; shamans and shamanism
 as ancient tradition in the Americas, 10, 187, 191
 botanical and musical skills of, 187–90, 327
 drums, song, and rattles as central components in, 188–91
 by peoples
  Aymara, in Chile, 189
  Chorote, 168, 189
  Desana (Tukano-affiliated), 189
  Günuna Kena, 188
  Huarpe, 188
  Huichol (Wirr'arika, Wixárika), 190
  Kalapálo, 188
  Kamayurá, 64–66, 66, 72
  Karajá, 189
  Kechua, 188
  Kuna, 213–14, 217–18, 218, 221–25, 223
  Mapuche
   in Argentina, 188, 190–91
   in Chile, 156–57, 189, 191
  Mataco (Wichí), 168, 189
  Mataco and Guaycurú, 167–68, 189
  Mazatec, 188–90
  Mískito, 197–99, 203–205, 204–206
  Nahua, 16, 189
  Otomí, 189
  Puelche, Ranquel, northern Tehuelche, 188–89
  Tepehua, 188
  Toba, 168
  Tukano, 190
  Tupi-affiliated groups, in Brazil, 71–72
  Wakuénai, 34, 37–38, 40
  Warao, 190, 267, 313

Xavante, 59
Yanomami (Yanomamö), 188, 190
plants, knowledge of, 189–90
rituals, as forms of communal regeneration, 190–91
sound, role of, within multidimensional time-concept, 10, 188–91
tasks and training of, 187–90
wellness, concepts of, 187–88, 191
hebu-mataro (idiophone; Warao rattles), 288, 313, 315
hekura (Yanomami [Yanomamö] demons), 190
Henríquez, Alejandro, 272
heresemoi (Warao conch-shell trumpet), 305–306, 306
Hermo, Elena, 193n
Herrera, Filemón, 193n
Hérri (Wakuénai mythical figure), 28–29, 46
heterophony. *See under* texture
Hill, Jonathan D., 18n, 65, 74, 299–300, 311–12, 328
Hípana (Wakuénai mythic center of the world), 18n, 25, 28–30, 40, 46
Hirahara descendants, in Venezuela
 cacho de venado (globular flutes), 292–93, 293
 turas (notched flutes), 291–92, 292
Hispaniola (island in the Greater Antilles), *areíto* ceremony in, 10
Histoire d'un voyage faict en la Terre du Brésil ... (de Léry), 50, 53–55
Historia de las Indias de Nueva España (Durán), 14
An Historical and Ethnological Survey of the Cuna Indians (Nordenskiöld), 214
historiography, music, Amerindians' lack of representation in, 327
history
 myth and, 9–11, 14
 social construction of, and musical practices, 74
hito (*wichu*; Yekuana duct aerophone; single closed pipe with finger holes), 267
Hohódeni-Wakuénai people, 18n, 25
Holmer, Nils M.
 The Complete Muu-ígala in Picture Writing (with Wassen), 218
 Muu-ígala or the Way of Muu, A Medicine Song from the Cuna Indians of Panama (with Wassen), 217
Holy Cross Day (Fiesta de la Santa Cruz, Fiesta de la Cruz, May 3)
 Aymara people, in Conima District, Peru, *Achach K'umu* dance-drama on, 132
 Aymara and Kechua peoples, in Bolivia, 102, 107
Holy Week
 Chamula people, Passion of Christ, interpretation of, 328
 Cora people, *tonos de Cuaresma* (Lent tunes), played on *pitos*, 300
 Mayo people, *pascola* dances, 239, 239
Holzmann, Rodolfo, 283
Honduras
 demographics, 1
 epics, pre-contact, 10
 formerly territory of ancient Mexico, 231
 peoples
  British colonizers, 194–96

Garífuna ethnic nation (Black Caribs), 196–97
Mískito. *See* Mískito people
Paya, 196–97
Spanish colonizers, 194–95
Sumo, 196
Horcasitas, Fernando, 16
horn, baritone, in army and civilian bands, 269
Hornbostel, Erich M. von
Fuegian songs, studies of, 145, 159, 160
indigenous groups in Brazil, studies of, 54–55, 73
instrument classification system, 262
horse, use of, by peoples
Chorote, in shamanic rituals, 168
Kechua, in Canas Province, Peru, 132, 138–39
Mapuche, in Argentina and Chile, 164, 169, 171, 182, 184, *307*, *308*
Pilagá and Toba, 166
Huamán Poma de Ayala, Felipe. *See* Guamán Poma de Ayala, Felipe
Huanca culture, dog cult, dog- and deer-head trumpets, 320
Huarpe people, 181, 188
Huave (Mareños) people, 235, 241
huayno (*huayño*, *huayñu*, *waiñu*, *wayno*, *wayño*; widespread traditional Andean dance-complex)
Aymara people (*huayño*), in Chile, 146, 150
Aymara and Kechua peoples (*wayño*), in Bolivia, *111–12*
and *cumbia*, hybrid of (*cumbia andina*), 124
Kechua people (*wayno*), in Canas Province, Peru, 133–34
on *roncadora* (duct flute) and drum, in Peru, *305, 305*
sikuri ensembles, in repertoire of, 275–78
huayño. See huayno
huayñu. See huayno
Huichol (Wirr'arika, Wixárika) people
demographics, 235, 239, 240
peyote (*hikuri*), use of, in shamanic healing, 190
Huitzilopochtli (Aztec deity; form of Toltec Tezcatlipoca and primeval Ometeotl), 13–14, 16
human sacrifice
Aztec (Mexica) people, 14, 16
in pre-contact Mesoamerica, 233, 247
P'urhépecha people, in pre-contact Tzintzuntzan, 248
Huracán ("Divine Mind" in the *Popol Vuh*), 8

I

Iaranavi (Spanish invader figure in Makiritare creation myth), 4
Ibe (Kuna for "Sun"), 220
Ibelele ("Sun"; "House of the Sun" in Kuna cosmology; deity), 215–17, 219, 225, 278
Ibeorgun (Ibelele's son; Sun; Kuna mythical great chief), 216–17
Ibeorgun Nega ("House of Grandfather Sun"; Kuna Congress; house of daily teachings), 193, 212, 215
Ica (pre-contact) culture, notched flutes, materials for, 288
Icco inna (Kuna girls' body ornamentation ceremony), 222, *222*
iconography, music

in Brazil, survey of, National Library, Music Division, 53
in ceramics of pre-contact cultures
aerophone-and-drum combinations, 268
notched flutes, 288
panpipes, 113–14, *114*, 275, 278
identity
constructions of
collective vis-à-vis individual, in Aymara *ayllus*, 126
ensembles, as emblems in, Aymara people, in Conima District, Peru, 126, 129–30
ethnicity and language correlations, critique of, 2–5, 51
political language, importance of, 79
rituals and ceremonies, role of, 70
social categories and, Aymara and Kechua peoples, 123–24, 141–42
dress, indigenous groups, in Mexico, as marker of, 234
renegotiation of, in performance, 4–5, 327
retention of, in acculturation, *mestizaje*, 2–5, 51, 141, 238
idiophones
aras napat (Mískito horse-jaw scraper), 207
bells
campana (Spanish for "bell"). See *campanilla* below
campanilla (*campana*; bronze llama bell), in Bolivia, 109, 121, *121*
with *chirimías*, in Peru, 318
chorromón (pre-Hispanic metal bell-set), 153–54
P'urhépecha people, 247
espuelas (spur-rattles), in Bolivia, 121, *121*
fur-mantles, shaken, Kawéskar people, 159
guacharaca (scraper), in Colombia, 316
kaskawilla (Mapuche pellet-bell rattles), 158, 170–71, 271
kiríngwa (zoomorphic hollowed-out log, P'urhépecha people), 247, 251–52, 254, *254*
maracas (gourd rattles)
Kogi people, 298
Kuna people
with flutes, in initiation rituals, 219, 221
násisi (*násis*; Kuna gourd rattle with deer-bone handle), 227, 279, 286
Mataco and Guaycurú peoples, 166–69
mbaraká (sacred gourd rattles, Guaraní peoples), 189
Mískito people, 204, 207
Venezuela
in creole and mestizo *mare-mare* traditions, 282
with *tura* flutes, 292
wada (Mapuche gourd rattles), 158, 271
matraca (cog rattle), in Bolivia, 121, *121*
palo sonajero de uñas de ciervo (stamping deer-hoof rattle, Mataco and Guaycurú peoples), 167–69
percussion sticks, Kawéskar people, 159
pratos (Portuguese for "cymbals"), in *bandas-de-pífanos*, northeastern Brazil, 296
raspador (Spanish for "scraper"; striated stick), P'urhépecha people, 247
rattles
ch'ajch'as, in Bolivia, 121, *121*
chu'ullu-ch'ullus, in Bolivia, 121
espuelas (spur-rattles), in Bolivia, 121, *121*
gourd. *See* maracas *above*

idiophones (*continued*)
    hebu-mataro (Warao rattles), 288, 313, *315*
    Kamayurá people, 66
    kaskawilla (Mapuche pellet-bell rattles), 158, 170–71, 271
    Kuna people, 273
    Makuxí, Taulipáng, and Yekuâna peoples, 54
    sewei (Warao anklet rattles), 288, 313, *315*
    shell-rattles, Kawéskar people, 159
    snake-rattles, P'urhépecha people, 247
    suila jut'as, in Bolivia, 121
    turtle-shell rattles, P'urhépecha people, 247
    Xavante people, 60
    stamping tubes
        takuapú, Mbyá people, 174–75, 178
        wáana, Wakuénai peoples, 36, 38–39, 46
        Xavante people, 60
    teponaztli (Aztec slit drum), 247, 251–52, 318
    triangle (*triángulo*), in Bolivia, 121, *121*
    triángulo. See triangle *above*
    umreñiduruture (Xavante flute-rattle), 60
ígala (journey of Kuna chant during ritual performance), 212–14, 217–26, 228–29, 278, 286
ihbaia láwana (Mískito song of self-edification), 200, 202
Ika people (Chibchan-speaking Arhuacos; Ijca), in Colombia, 298
Ilche Dzomó (Mapuche Young Woman), 182
Ilche Wentrú (Mapuche Young Man), 182
Illampu (mountain), in Bolivia, 103
illness. *See also* healers and healing; shamans and shamanism
    Mapuche peoples, in Chile, healing songs, category-specific
        datun (shamanic, for severe, chronic diseases), 156–57
        pewutún (shamanic, diagnostic), 156–57
        ülutún (mild or acute diseases), 156–57, 189
    Mískito people, hierarchical classification of
        isingni ulan ("mounted or ridden soul"), 203–205
        iumu (minor ailments), 203–204, 204–205
        paun (severe, unknown cause), 203, 205
    seizure, concept of, in Andean healing, 189
Im Thurn, Everard F., 264
Immaculate Conception (Fiesta de la Concepción, December 8), Aymara and Kechua, in Bolivia, 102
improvisation. *See also* composition
    indigenous groups, in Chile, 146–47
    Kechua people, in Canas Province, Peru, in texts, 140
    Mapuche peoples
        in Argentina, *kantún* (vocal and instrumental), 170
        in Chile, in ritual and secular "human" music, 157
    P'urhépecha people, in *bajeo* (bass line), 249, 252, 255
    Wakuénai peoples, in *máwi* and *tsikóta* flute duets for *pudáli*, 38–39, 42
inanka (Mískito laments, communication with ancestors), 199–203, *200*, 202–203, 207
inanka nani (Mískito type of lament), 199–200, 202
inanka upla pruan bara (Mískito type of lament), 200–202, *202*

Iñápirríkuli (Yaperikuli; trickster-creator in Wakuénai creation myth), 18, 28–32, 34–35, 39, 45, 46
inatuledi (Kuna ritual specialist; "owner of medicines"), 217, 221
Inca culture
    calendar, 102
    cantares históricos (epic song genre), 10
    chronicles, Garcilaso de la Vega, *Comentarios reales de los Incas*
        aerophonic performance, contexts for, 264
        healing practices, 187
        Kechua song on gender reciprocity, 21–22
        kena, association with courting, 288
        panpipes, interlocking technique in performance, 113, 276
        warfare, instruments in, description of, 320
    Conquest, foretold in myths of, 9
    ensembles, of *kepas* and *wankaras*, 269, 306
    epics, 10–11
    instruments
        aerophones, materials for, 264, 286–87
        antara (as monistic panpipe), 266, 275, 277n, 282–83
        drums, from human skin, 282
        kepa (conch-shell tumpets), 305–306
    language (Runa Simi [Kechua]), in Bolivia, 101
    Tawantinsuyu (Inca Empire)
        Argentinian Northwest as part of, 163
        epics and dramas, as representations of resistance to, 10–11
        history of, 1–2
        number symbolism, in sociopolitical organization of, 116
        uprisings against, 10
        warfare in, 269, 306, 320
Inca Empire. *See* Tawantinsuyu *under* Inca culture
Los Incas (Peruvian ensemble, *later* Urubamba), 290–91
incense
    cacao, pepper, and tobacco, in shamanic rituals, Kuna people, 215, 222–23, 225, 227
    q'oa, in ritual offerings, Aymara and Kechua peoples, in Bolivia, 103
    sahumerio, in ritual offerings, Atacameño people, 152
Indiana University Archives of Traditional Music, 312
Indigenous Missionary Council (CIMI), Brazil, 50
inebriation, ritual. *See* ritual inebriation *under* rituals and ceremonies
initiation rituals. *See* initiation *under* rituals and ceremonies, by function
Inna mutikit (Kuna, three year-old girls' hair-cutting ceremony), 218–19
Inna tutsikaledi (Kuna, six year-old girls' hair-cutting ceremony), 218–19
Inna wil'la (*Inna suid*; Kuna women's puberty ceremony, three-night chicha), 218–21, 222, 278, 285–86
institutions
    Asociación Indígena de la República Argentina (AIRA), 163
    Centro de Investigación de la Cultura P'urhépecha, 257

Ecumenical Center for Documentation and Information (CEDI), Brazil, 51
Flute House, as traditional institution, 18, 79, 82–83, 82, 90–91, 90–91, 299–300
Fundação Nacional do Índio (FUNAI), 77
Gold Museum, Bogotá, 264
Indiana University Archives of Traditional Music, 312
Indigenous Missionary Council (CIMI), Brazil, 50
Instituto Nacional Indigenista (Mexico City), 237, 238, 257
Kuna Congress (*Ibeorgun Nega*; house of daily teachings), 193, 212, 215
Museum of Anthropology and Ethnography, Russian Academy of Sciences, 53
National Library, Music Division, Brazil, 53
Servicio Nacional de Asuntos Indígenas (Argentina), 163
Universidad Michoacana de San Nicolás de Hidalgo, 257
Instituto Nacional Indigenista (Mexico City), 237–38, 257
instruments, traditional. *See also* aerophones; aerophones, by instruments; chordophones; ensembles, by type; idiophones; membranophones
    adoption of
        accordion and harp, Mbyá people, 177
        chirimía, 318
        chordophones, in general, P'urhépecha people, 248, 255
        five-string guitar (*mbaraká*), Mbyá people, 173–76, 177
        rebec (*ravé*), Mbyá people, 173–76, 177
        violin (*turumi* or *miorí*), Chiriguano-Chané peoples, 172
    of Aymara, Callawaya, Chipaya, and Kechua peoples, in Bolivia, 117–21
    classification of, in Brazil, 56. *See also* Camêu, Helza
    conceptualization of, according to roles, Kamayurá people, 64
    Kawéskar people, 159
    in pre-contact Tzintzuntzan (P'urhépecha territory), 247–48
interlocking technique in aerophonic performance. *See under* performance practice
intervals. *See under* pitch organization
Inti-Illimani (Chilean ensemble), 290
Inti Raymi (Bolivian winter solstice, June 21; dry season, festival of The Inca), 102–103
ira/arka principle (Aymara and Kechua symbolic dualism; leader/follower roles in panpipe performance)
    evidence of, in pre-contact artifacts and chronicles, 113–17, 114
    in general, 104–105
    julajulas, 104–108, 105–106
    lakitas, 105, 108–109, 108–109
    sikuras, 105, 109, 110–12, 113, 115
    sikus (*sikuris*), 126–27, 268, 274–76, 275, 274–75
Iruaná people, *tekeya* (single-reed aerophone) of, 311
Isamitt, Carlos, 145, 181, 270, 296
isimoi (Warao single-reed aerophone), 267, 288, 312–13, 313, 315
isingni ulan ("mounted or ridden soul"; Mískito illness category), 203–205

Ítomo (funerary ritual phase, Guahibo-affiliated people), in Colombia, 292–93
itseke (Kalapálo spiritual forms of energy), 188
iumu (Mískito illness category), 203–204, 204–205
Izikowitz, Karl Gustav, *Musical and Other Sound Instruments of the South American Indians*
    aerophones
        definition of, 262–63
        descriptions of, 276, 279, 293–94
    bullroarers, distribution of, 318
    description of, 262
    toré, as term for single-reed aerophones, 311

J

jaguar
    as Aztec Lord of the Animals, 19
    as core symbol, in myths, 8, 17–20, 19, 25
    fire, links to mythical emergence of, 20
    in initiation rituals, by peoples
        Barasana, in Colombia, 18
        Toba, in Bolivian Chaco, *nahôre* dances, 18, 20
    masks of, in Olmec sites, 18
    in myth-cosmology, by peoples
        Canelos Quichua, 18
        Desana, 20
        Hohódeni-Wakuénai, 18, 18n
        Kamayurá, 65, 83, 88–89, 93
        Makiritare, 4, 17
        Wakuénai, 25, 29–31, 33–34, 38, 40, 46
Jakairá (Mbyá god of mist [tobacco] and wisdom), 173
James, St. (Fiesta de Santiago)
    Aymara and Kechua (Tata Santiago), in Bolivia, 103
    K'ero people (July 25; as fertility ritual), *kanchis sipas* played only on, 283
jaripeo (rodeo), in patron-saint fiestas, P'urhépecha people, 255
Jeldes, Fidel, 145
Jesuits
    in Argentina, 164, 172–73, 181
    in Brazil, 49, 52
Jiménez Borja, Arturo, 282–83, 288–89, 301
jiwa (Guahibo panpipes), in Venezuela, 280
John the Baptist, St. (Fiesta de San Juan Bautista, June 24)
    in Acolla, Department of Junín, Peru, patronal, 315, 317
    Atacameño people, 152
    Aymara and Kechua peoples, in Bolivia, 103
    Chiriguano-Chané peoples, 171
    Quichua people, in Ecuador, *tundas* (flutes), for feast of, 295
juego de pelota (as Mesoamerican ball game), 233
julajulas (single-row panpipes; Aymara and Kechua peoples), in Bolivia
    description of, 105, 105–107, 107–108, 118
    dry season, association with, 103
    with *pulus* (vessel flutes), in ensembles, 120
    symbolic dualism, in interlocking performance technique, 103–108, 105–106

julu-julus (single-row panpipes; Aymara people), in Bolivia, 104, 118
Juruna linguistic family, 51
Juruna people, 61–62, *63* (map), 71–72, 77, 79–80

K

Káali (plant species creator in Wakuénai myth cycles), 35, 39–40, 45–46
kabur (hot pepper), in Kuna healing ceremonies, 222
Kadiwéu people, 56, 73
kagutu (Kalapálo large flutes), 21
Kagutu (Kalapálo male-owned ceremony), 21
Kalapálo people
  demographics, 61, *63* (map), 77
  gender-based power, in *Yamarikumalu* and *Kagutu* ceremonies, 21
  healing, shamanic, 188
  instruments, *takwara* (single-reed aerophone), 65, 299, 311–12
kalfumalén (Mapuche girls embodying ancestors in *nguillipún*), 182, *183*, 184
kallamachu (single-row panpipes, Aymara people), in Conima District, Peru, 127–28
kamarikún (*kamarrikún*). See *nguillipún*
Kamayurá people, 60–66, 79–98, *84–91*
  classification
    of musical domain (*maraka*), 64, *64*, 73
    of sound domain, acoustical and semiological basis for, 64, 73
  cosmology, 80–82, 88–89, 93–94, 97–98
  dance, in rituals and ceremonies, 65, 81–82, 90–91, 94, 299–300, 312
  demographics, 60–64, *63* (map), 77, 79
  education, music masters, rank and status of, 65, 71
  gender roles, in instrumental performance, 65
  healing
    kewere (non-shamanic ritual), 64, 72
    payemeramaraka (shamanic ritual), 65–66, *66*, 72. See also shamans and shamanism *below*
  history of, 79–80
  instruments
    aerophones
      takwara ("bamboo"; five-tubed single-reed aerophone): of Kalapálo, Kuikúro, and Yawalapiti peoples
        tarawi (two-tubed single-reed aerophone), 311–12
        uru'a (two-tubed duct flutes), 65, 298–300, 311–12
        yaku'i (sacred duct flutes), 65, 79, 299–300, 311
      conceptualization of, according to roles, 64
      function of, 64–65
      gender-based power, in *yaku'i* flutes performance, 65
      instrumental music, practice of, 72
  language, 61, 65, 77, 93
  music, conceptualization of, 64–66, 81
  myth
    flutes, creation of, 65
    music, creation of, jaguar's role in, 65
    of *yawari*'s origin, 80, 82, 96–98

performance practice, interlocking technique in aerophonic performance, 65, 298–300, 311–12
rituals and ceremonies. *See also* shamans and shamanism *below*
  classification of musical domain, correlation with, 64
  intertribal, in context of cultural exchange and factional politics, 65, 77–79
  kwarỳ'p (commemoration of deceased chiefs), 65, 80, 89, 299–300, 311–12
  syntax, musical, symbolic correlations with, 65
  takwara (bamboo dance; held to rid community of evil spirits), 65, 299, 311–12
  yaku'i (held to attract benefic spirits), 65, 299–300, 311
  yawari ("ocelot"; intertribal ritual; death as cosmic trade), case study of, 80–98
    dance and choreographic formations in, 82–83, 90–94, *91*
    interpretation of, 88–89, 96–98
    macrostructure of, 81–88, 94–95
    martial arts in, 89–91, 93, 95–96
    music, critical role of, analysis of referential scales, 89–90, *89*, 94, 96, 98
    mythical origin of, 80, 96–97
    nucleus/periphery, in spatial and musical organization of, 81–82, *82*, 90, *90*
    songs in, 81–83, 88, *84–88*, 91–94
    sponsorship of, 81
  shamans and shamanism
    in general, 64, 71–72
    payemeramaraka (shamanic healing ritual), 65–66, *66*, 72
  song, in rituals and ceremonies
    in general, 65
    in *yawari*, 81–83, 88, *84–88*, 91–94
  texture, multi-part, in instrumental performance, 65, 70, 72
Kamibe (heaven's ruler in Kuna cosmology; Sun), 216, 219–20, 225, 278
Kaminaljuyú (major Maya site on outskirts of present-day Guatemala City), 1
kammu
  as aerophone. See *kammu purwi* and *kammu suid*
  as prefix (Kuna for "reed, sonorous reed, throat, flute"), 220, 278, 280, 285–86
kammu ígala (Kuna shamanic chant-type, for women's puberty ceremony), *214*, 218–21, *221*, 278, 285–86
kammu purwi (*gammu-burui*, *kammupurui*, *kamu-purrui*; Kuna dualistic panpipes)
  description of, 226–27, *227–28*, 278, *279*
  symbolism of, 227, 278–80
kammu suid (*gammu suid*, *kammu*, *kammusui*; Kuna flute played in pairs), 266, 285–86
kamsuedi (Kuna specialist in reed-panpipe construction), 227, 278
kamu-purrui. See *kammu purwi*
kanákwa (*canajqua*; pre-contact P'urhépecha song, "La corona" [The Crown]), 247

kanalekwa (Kuna Muu *ígala* ritual specialist; childbirth), 217

kañari (*cañari*, long straight aerophone with attached animal horn), in Peru, 308

kanchis sipas (double-row panpipes, K'ero people)
description of, 267, 282–83, *284*
symbolism and tuning of, 283

kandur (Kuna ritual specialist), 217–20. See also *kantule*

Kanobo (Supreme Deity of Warao people), 288, 313

kanojí (Mataco shaman's bone whistle), 169

kantule (Kuna ritual specialist), 217, 278–79, 286. See also *kandur*

Kantule, Nele (architect of Kuna ethnic nation's independence), 210, 212, 214

kantún (Mapuche, in Argentina; vocal and instrumental improvisations), 170

kápetiápani (Wakuénai collective dance-songs marked by ritual whips), 26, 29, 31–34, 46

Karaí (Mbyá god of fire, protector of agricultural crops), 173

Karajá linguistic family, 51

Karajá people, healing ceremonies of, 189

Kariña people, in Venezuela, *verékushi* panpipes of, 280–82

kashua (*kashwa*; Kechua pre-contact collective dance-genre), in Canas Province, Peru, 137–38, *138*, 141

kaskawilla (from the Spanish "cascabel"; idiophone; Mapuche pellet-bell rattles), 158, 170–71, 271

katakí (membranophone; Toba and Pilagá single-headed water drum), 167–69

Katukina linguistic family, 51

Kawéskar people (*formerly* Alakaluf; Fuegian people)
cosmology, 158
cultural change, 159–60
demographics, 145, 158–59
history of, 145, 158
name of, 161n
near-extinction of, 159–60
repertoires, types of, 159
songs, types and style characteristics of, 159–60
traditional music, preservation of, in field recordings, 159

Kayabi people
demographics, 61–62, *63* (map), 77
shamans and shamanism, 71–72
yawaci ritual, 70, *71*

Kayowá people, 70, 72

Kechua (Runa Simi) language, in Bolivia, 101

Kechua people, in general. *See also* Aymara and Kechua peoples, in Bolivia; Quichua people, in Ecuador
ensembles
ayarachi (panpipes; tradition associated with burial ceremonies)
as ceremonial music, 275
as tradition of panpipe performance, 276–78
pinkillus (duct flutes; Kechua, in northern Potosí), 301–302
sikuri performance traditions, 274–78
instruments

antara. See *antara*

charango, in Caneño and mestizo traditions, 134–37, *136–37*, 141

kena. See *kena*

pinkullu, 134–35, 137–39, *140*

pututo, kepa (conch-shell trumpets), 305–308

wak'rapuku (*cacho*, animal horn coiled trumpet, 306–307

Kechua people, in Bolivia. *See also* Aymara and Kechua peoples, in Bolivia
demographics, 101
ensembles (of aerophones)
ayarichis (panpipes), 104, 118, *118*
pinkillus (duct flutes), in northern Potosí, timbric symbolism in, 301–302
sikuri performance traditions, 274–78
languages, Kechua (Runa Simi), 101

Kechua people, in Peru (Canas Province, Department of Cuzco)
aesthetics
change and contrast, subtlety in concepts of, 124, 137
dense sound quality, 124, 135, 141
high tessitura, 134–35, 269
individuality, in performer's relationship to ensemble, 141
repetition, 124, 137–38, 141
timbric homogeneity, in traditional aerophone ensembles, 141
timbric mixture, in mestizo ensembles, 133
composition
formulaic approach to, 141
in general, 137
cosmology, symbolic dualism, within tri-layered worldview, 123–24, 137
dance
carnival, 134, 139–40
kashuas (circle dance-songs), 137–38, *138*, 141
marineras, 133
in mestizo fiestas, 133
in *papa tarpuy* (potato planting song-dances), 137
waynos, 133–34
demographics, *125* (map), 132
ensembles, in mestizo traditions
brass bands, 133
orquestas cuzqueñas, 133
string-band tradition, 133–34, 141
instruments
charango, in Caneño and mestizo traditions, 134–37, *136–37*, 141
kena, 134. See also *kena*
pinkullu, 134–35, 137–39, *140*
language, 132
migration, 132, 141
rituals and ceremonies
carnival, 139–40
fertility
association with rainy season, 135
tinku (ritual battle of Chiaraje), 137–39, *140*, 141
papa tarpuy (potato planting), 134–37
song
for carnival, 139–40

Kechua people, in Peru (*continued*)
  in general, 134, 140
  in ritual battle of Chiaraje, 137–39
  traditions, Aymara and Kechua, in Conima and Canas,
      compared, 140–42
Keeler, Clyde E., 279, 286
kena (*qena, quena*; Aymara term; notched flute, Aymara
      and Kechua peoples)
  Bolivia, 103–104, 116, 118, *118*, 120
  Chile
    in Aymara-influenced Atacameño ceremonies, 153
    in Aymara *orquesta*, 150
    as *lichiguayos* (ensembles of large notched flutes),
        151
    in *nueva canción* groups, 290–91
  description of, 288–91, *289*
  distribution of, 266
  history of, 288–91
  instruments' sizes (registers), in ensembles, 290
  in non-traditional contexts, 290–91
  performance styles, 290–91
  Peru
    in Kechua traditions, Canas Province, 134
    in *orquesta cuzqueña*, 133
    in string-band tradition, 134
  symbolism of, 116, 288–91, 320
  tunings, 290
kena-kena (Aymara dualistic term for *kena*, notched flute),
      103, 118, 290
kenacho (a type of *kena*; notched flute), 290
kenali (a type of *kena*; notched flute), 290
kepa (*kheppa, qhueppa*; aerophone)
  conch-shells, symbolism of, 269, 306
  in Peru
    as conch-shell trumpet (*kheppa, pututo, pututu,
        qhueppa*), 305–306
    as name for long straight side-blown trumpet
        (*clarín*), 308
  as pre-Columbian conch-shell trumpet, 305–307
Keres people, creation myth of, 8–9
K'ero people
  aerophones
    kanchis sipas (monistic panpipes), 267, 282–83, *284*
    pina pinkulucha (notched flute), 291, *291*, 294
    pitu (side-blown flute), 294, *294*
  celebrations, Catholic feasts (syncretic), cyclic calendar
      of
    Corpus Christi, *pitus* played on, 294
    Santiago, Fiesta de (July 25; as fertility ritual),
        kanchis sipas played only on, 283
  dance, of the Chunchos (representational), 294
  songs, animals, in themes of, 283
  tunings, instrumental and vocal correlations in, 267,
      283, *284*
kewere ("prayer," as category in Kamayurá classification of
      musical domain; healing ritual), 64, 72
Key, Mary Ritchie, 3
kheppa. See *kepa*
Kiepja, Lola (as last representative of now-extinct Selk'nam
      people), 20–21
Kikapú (Kikaapoa) people, 235, 238

kimpeñ (shared patrilineage soul, Mapuche peoples), 170,
      179. See also *tayil*
Kirchhoff, Paul, 231, 233
kiríngwa (idiophone; zoomorphic hollowed-out log,
      P'urhépecha people), 247, 251–52, 254, *254*
Kiriri people, *toré* ritual, adoption of, 5
Koch-Grünberg, Theodor
  indigenous cultures, studies of, 264
  tekeya, description of, 311
  Vom Roroima zum Orinoco, 54
Kogi people, 297–98
Koppers, Wilhelm, 159
Koya (Coya, Kolla)
  "Death of the Coya," dance-drama, in Carhuamayo,
      Peru, 4, 327–28
  Koya Raymi (Inca festival of the Kolla, wife of The
      Inca), 102
Kra (Selk'nam Moon Woman), 20
Krahó people, 70
Kran (Selk'nam Sun Man), 20
krismes (Mískito children's Christmas round-dances, a type
      of *pulanka*), 208
kuai (sacred flute, Hohódeni-Wakuénai people), 18
Kuai (Kuwái; jaguar-engendered primordial hero in
      Hohódeni-Wakuénai myths), 18, 18n
Kuikúro people
  demographics, 61, *63* (map), 77
  instruments, *takwara* (single-reed aerophone), 65,
      299, 311–12
  payemeramaraka (shamanic healing ritual), 66
kuizi (*charu, púnkiri*; "hatchet" duct flute), 267, 297–98.
      See also *gaita*
Kukulcán (Yucatec-Maya mythical figure), 8, 11–12.
      See also Gucumatz; Quetzalcoatl
kuli. See *guli*
kúlirrína (Wakuénai large trumpets)
  construction of, *44*
  definition of, 46
  function of, in *pudáli* ceremonial cycle, 35–36, *36*,
      38–39
  symbolism of, 40–42, 44
kultrún (Mapuche single-headed membranophone; larger
      male drum; smaller drum of female ritual
      specialist), 155, 158, 170, 182, *183*, 189, 271
Kulturkreislehre (early 20th-century theory of
      theomonogenetic cultural diffusionism),
      54
Kumadámnainai people, 18n, 25
Kuna Congress (*Ibeorgun Nega*; house of daily teachings),
      193, 212, 215
Kuna people, in Panama, 193–229
  ancestors, 279–80. *See also* cosmology *below*
  chants, shamanic (*ígala*; journey through song in ritual
      performance), 212–26. *See also* rituals and
      ceremonies, shamanic *below*
  cultural knowledge, as sources of, 213–26
  defined, 212
  notation (ideographic) of, 215–16, *216*
  oral transmission of, 213–17, *214*
  structure of, 215, 219–20
  system of

absogued ígala (paths of knowledge; healing), 213–14, 224–25

akwa nusa ígala (paths of healing), 221–22, *223*

kammu ígala (for women's puberty ceremony [*Inna wil'la, Inna suid*]), 214, 218–21, 221, 278, 285–86

massar ígala (for journey of the dead), 225–26, *226*

Muu *ígala* (to assist in childbirth), 217–18, *218*, 222

Sia·ba kabur unaedi (healing; soul retrieval), 222–23

Ukku naibe ígala (mythical serpent's origin; healing), 223–24

Congress (*Ibeorgun Nega*; house of teachings, daily meetings), 193, 212, 215

cosmology, 212–13, 216–17, 219, 223–26, 278. *See also* chant, system of *above*

dance, secular, on *kammu purwi* panpipes (*Mete sikwi uurma kali*), 227, *227–28*

demographics, 210, *210* (map), 211, 212

education, 212–16, *214*

fire, origin of, 220

history of, 210, 212, 229

instrumental performances (*toques*), 212, 226–27, *227–28, 273, 273,* 280

instruments

flute-and-rattle tradition, 268

functionality of, 266

guli (*kuli* ; ductless set of complementary flutes), 273, *273*

kammu purwi (dualistic panpipes), 226–27, *227–28,* 278–80, *279*

kammu suid (flute played in pairs), 266, 285–86

násisi (maracas), 227, 286

ted-nono (bone flute), 225

language, 194, 212

Mískito people, links to, 193–94, 228–29

music, concept of, 212

myth, creation, 216–17, 220, 226

naming, tradition of, 220

paraphernalia, ritual, 214–15, 217, 219, 222

plants, in shamanic rituals (cacao [*sia*] and hot pepper [*kabur*]), 215, 222–23

rituals and ceremonies, shamanic. *See also* chants, shamanic *above*

Icco inna (girls' body ornamentation, at birth), 222, *222*

Inna mutikit (three year-old girls' hair-cutting, one-night chicha), 218–19

Inna tutsikaledi (six year-old girls' hair-cutting, two-night chicha), 218–19

Inna wil'la (*Inna suid*; women's puberty; three-night long / deep chicha), 218–21, 222, 278, 285–86

shamans and shamanism, 193, 212–26, 228–29, 278, 285–86

songs, socioeconomic function of, 212. *See also* chants, shamanic *above*

Kunza (extinct language), Atacameño people, in ritual music of, 145, 152–53

Kuwái (Kuai; primordial human in Wakuénai creation myth cycles), 18, 26, 28–34, 40, 42, 45–46

Kwal taya (Mískito funerary ritual, journey of the dead), 205–207, *208*

kwarìp (*kwarỳp*; Kamayurá ritual; to honor deceased chiefs), 65, 80, 89, 299–300, 311–12

kwépani (Wakuénai ceremonies; male-controlled construction of mythical/human vertical relations), 26–34, 41–46

L

labor, communal. *See* communal labor

Lacandón (Hach winik) people, 237, 243

Lafkenches (Mapuche peoples of the West), in Chile, 154

lahtubi inanka (Mískito type of lament), 200–201

laka (*pusa*; Aymara term for *siku* panpipes), in Chile, 274

Lakatuhún Hatupasdíqal (Tepehua marijuana goddess; Santa Rosa), in healing ritual, 188

lakitas (double-row panpipes)

in Bolivia

description of, 108–109, *108–109,* 118

dry season, association with, 103, 109

ensembles, 104

function of, 109

membranophones, in ensembles, 104, 120

symbolic dualism in interlocking performance technique, 103–105, 108

in Chile, 148, 150–51

laments

Mískito *inankas*, 199–203, *200, 202–203,* 207

Suyá *choros femininos* (women's laments), 69

Xavante *dawawa*, 57, 59–60, *59,* 70

language

classification, indigenous linguistic stocks, families, and languages

in Brazil, 51

in Mexico, 231, 235, *236* (map), 237

in South America, 3, 262

classifications of, and ethnic identity correlations, 3–5

linguistic kinship, early approaches to, 3

pidgin, Portuguese as, in Xingu Indian Park, 79

Lastres, Juan, 190

láwana (Mískito shamanic song), 193, 197, 199, 203–205, *204,* 207

legends

of first *atunse* (pair of *atuñsa* "hatchet" duct flutes), Yupa people, in Venezuela, 297–98

of first flute or "*chirimía*," Maya people, in Guatemala, 319

of *Manchay-Puito yaraví* played on *kena*, Kechua people, in Peru, 288–90

songs, as illustrations of, Xavante people, 59

Lehmann-Nitsche, Robert, 181

Lent, Cora people, *tonos de Cuaresma* (tunes for), 300

León-Portilla, Miguel, 14, 237–38

Léry, Jean de

expedition, mid-16th-century, to Brazil, 49

Histoire d'un voyage faict en la Terre du Brésil..., 50, 53–55

Lévi-Strauss, Claude
  on Nambikwára nose ocarinas (*tsin-hali*), 294
  The Raw and the Cooked, 20, 22
  Structural Anthropology, Muu ígala Kuna chant, analysis
    of, 217–18
lichiguayos (*lichiwayu*; as ensembles of large type of *kenas*,
    Aymara people), in Chile, 148, 150–51
lichiwayu (*lichiguayo*; as large type of notched flute,
    Chipaya people), in Bolivia, 103, 118, 290
life cycle (rites of passage)
  death, commemorations of, P'urhépecha people, 256
  first hair-cutting, Aymara people, in Conima District,
    Peru, 130
  roof-raising
    Aymara people in Conima District, Peru, 130, 141
    P'urhépecha people, 256
  weddings
    Aymara people, in Conima District, Peru, 127, 130
    P'urhépecha people, 256
Limpia de canales (Atacameño ritual cleansing of irrigation
    ducts), 151–54
Liscano, Juan, 281–82
List, George, 298, 314
llama
  Atacameño people, 152
  Aymara people, in Chile, 149
llamador (Spanish for "caller"; *tambor macho* or male;
    African-derived single-headed drum), in
    Colombia, 298
locopallapalla (single-row panpipes, Aymara people), in
    Conima District, Peru, 127
lolkiñ (Mapuche vertical natural trumpets), 271
lonkomeo (Mapuche gender-specific dance), 170–71, 184
López Austin, Alfredo, 233–34
Loukotka, Cestmír, 3, 262
louvores (Portuguese for "praise songs"; homages to
    Catholic saints), Xavante people, 59–60
lukutún (Mapuche ritual discourse), 9, 182, 184
lullabies, by peoples
  Kawéskar, 159
  Mapuche, in Chile, 157
  Mataco and Guaycurú, 167
  Mbyá, 174
  Toba, 167
  Xavante, 59
Lumholtz, Carl, 253
lungku (*lunku*; Mískito musical bow), 204

M

máariawa (Wakuénai sacred flutes), 31–34, 42, 46
maasi. See *massi*
Machchj-juyai language (Callawaya people), in Bolivia, 101
machi (Mapuche ritual specialist), 154–55, 188–90, 271
machi-elwün (Mapuche shaman's funerary song-dance
    categorized as ritual "human" music),
    156–57, 271
Macoa people, in Venezuela, female-owned tradition of
    panpipe performance, 280
Macro-Chibcha linguistic stock, 194

Macro-Gê linguistic stock, 51
Macuilxochitl ("Five Flower")
  as Aztec woman composer, 14–15, 17
  as one name of Xochipilli (deity of song, dance, and
    poetry), 11, 14, 15
Madrid Codex (*Códice Matritense*), 14, 187
mádzeru (Wakuénai genre, for *pudáli* ceremonies), 34
Mahaiwadi (Makiritare mythical shaman whose spirit
    double is the jaguar [*demodede*]), 17
maizus (*chiriwanos*; panpipes, Chipaya people), in Bolivia,
    104, 118, *118*
Makiritare people (in Brazil and Venezuela)
  creation myth (Watunna) of
    Fañuru (negative figure of Spanish conqueror) in, 4,
      17
    Iaranavi (positive figure of White Man) in, 4, 17
    jaguar, as spirit double (*demodede*) of the shaman in,
      17
  tekeya, as single-reed aerophone of, 311
Makú linguistic family, 51
Makuxí people, 54–55
málikái (Wakuénai ritual speech, chant, and song), 26, 34,
    46
málirríkairi (Wakuénai shaman's songs), 40
Mallku (condor; Andean master of the mountains). *See also*
    condor
  as Chipaya protective spirits (Mallkus), 103
  as male manifestation, in Andean symbolic dualism,
    Bolivia, 116
  as spirit of the mountains, 103
Mama Asunta. *See* Assumption
Mama Killa (Mother Moon; Andean pre-contact deity,
    later Mama Santísima), 103, 116
Mame people, 237, 244
Mamita Asunta. *See* Assumption
mamitas (Spanish for "mothers"; Andean local virgins),
    102
mañanitas (Mexican serenades), as mestizo genre,
    P'urhépecha people, 252
manchaipuito (bone flute played into a pot), 290. See also
    Manchay-Puito
Manchay-Puito ("terrifying hell"; Kechua legend), 288–90
mandolin (plucked chordophone)
  Chile, in Aymara *orquesta*, 150
  in *estudiantina* ensembles, 316
  Peru
    in chordophone ensembles with muted trumpets,
      Department of Ancash, 307
    in *orquesta cuzqueña*, 133
    in string-band music, 134
manioc beer, 32, 36, 37
Manizer, H. H., 53–54
Mapuche peoples, in general
  horse, significance of (in Argentina and Chile), 164,
    169, 171, 182, 184, 307, *308*
  instruments (in Argentina and Chile)
    aerophones
      corneta (as short end-blown trumpet), 271
      lolkiñ (vertical natural trumpet), 271
      nolkiñ (short vertical trumpets), 158
      pifilka (*pifülka*; flutes). See *pifülka*

pinkulwe (flute with finger holes), 295–96
trutruka (long straight end-blown trumpet), 158, 170–71, 271, 307, *308*
idiophones
kaskawilla (pellet-bell rattles), 158, 170–71, 271
wada (gourd rattles), 158, 271
membranophones, *kultrún*, 155, 158, 170, 182, *183*, 189, 271
language (Mapu-dungu), 154, 156, 169
Mapuche peoples, in Argentina
ancestors, 9, 155, 170, 182, 184–85
cosmology, 9, 182, 184–85
dance (*"purrún,"* holistic term for choreography and dance-music)
creole, adoption of *chamamé*, 171
traditional
amupurrún, 170–71
lonkomeo, 170–71, 184
in *nguillipún* fertility ritual, 170–71, 182, 184
puelpurrún, 170, 182, 184
rinkürrinküpurrún, 170
shafshafpurrún, 170
demographics, 163–64, *165* (map), 169, 181
gender attribution, to instruments, 170
gender roles, 170, 182, 184, 188
healers and healing, shamanic, 188, 190–91
history of, 164, 169, *182* (map)
identity, construction of, ethnicity and language correlations in, 4
improvisation (*kantún*; vocal and instrumental), 170
missionaries and missionization, 4
national society, interaction with, 171
ritual speech (*lukutún*), 9, 182, 184
rituals and ceremonies, *nguillipún* (annual fertility cycle), 181–85
distribution of, 181–82, *182* (map)
functions of, 181–82, 191
Jesuits, documentation on, 181
leadership structure of, 182, *183–84*
lineage traditions, 181–82
retention of, 171, 179
ritual dance and song in, 170–71, 182, 184
structure of, 182, 184–85
shamans and shamanism, 182, 184–85, 188, 190–91
song
non-ritual (as *ülkantún*), 170. See also *ülkantún* under Mapuche peoples, in Chile
ritual (*öl, nöl, ül*; term for song and poetry), 9, 170, 184. See also *ül* under Mapuche peoples, in Chile
subgroups (subsumed under Mapuche), 169, 181
tayil, definition and function of, 9, 170–71, 179, 181–82, 184, 190
Mapuche peoples, in Chile, 154–58
cosmology, 154–58, 307, *308*
dance, ritual
choike-purrún (ostrich), 156, 271
(*See also* rituals and ceremonies; song *below*)
demographics, 145, 154
ensembles
for healing rituals, 158

for ritual dances, 271
healing, shamanic
datun (for severe or chronic diseases), 156–57
pewutún (diagnostic songs), 156–57
ülutun (for mild or acute diseases), 156–57, 189
history of, 154
languages, 145
improvisation, in ritual and secular "human" music, 157
rituals and ceremonies (as "human" *ülkantún* ritual music)
auxiliary spirits, communication with, 156–57
classification of, song-music and dance in, 156–57
communal (*ngillatun, nguillatún*; fertility), 156–57, 271, 307
healing, shamanic, 156–57, 189, 191
initiation, 156–57
(*See also* shamans and shamanism *below*)
shamans and shamanism, 154–57, 188–91
song
ül (song and poetry; term for music), 156
ülkantún (as term for all sacred and "human" [vocal] music)
"human" *ülkantún* (ritual and secular), styles of, 156–58
sacred *ülkantún* (*tayil*, as communication between *wenu-mapu* cosmic strata), 156. See also *ülkantún* under Mapuche peoples, in Argentina
mara'akáme (Huichol healer), 190
maracas (idiophones; gourd rattles)
Kogi people, 298
Kuna people
with flutes, in initiation rituals, 219, 221
násisi (*násis*), 227, 279, 286
Mataco and Guaycurú peoples, 166–69
mbaraká (sacred gourd rattle of Guaraní peoples), 189
Mískito people, 204, 207
Venezuela
in creole and mestizo *mare-mare* traditions, 282
with *tura* flutes, 292
wada (Mapuche gourd rattles), 158, 271
maraka (Kamayurá term for "domain of music"), 64, *64*
maraká (properly musical shamanic ritual, Kayabi people), 72
marakatap (Kamayurá term for instruments, conceptualized according to roles), 64
mara'wawa (Xavante midnight songs), 57
marches (*marchas*)
in *bandas-de-pífanos* repertoire, northeastern Brazil, 297
as mestizo genre, in *bandas* repertoire, P'urhépecha people, 252, 255
as religious music, Aymara people, in Chile, 150
in *sikuri* ensembles repertoire, 275
mare-mare (in Venezuela)
as dance-genre linked to panpipe music, 280–82, *282*
as name for *carrizo* panpipes, 280–82
as pluralistic panpipes, 280–82, *281–82*
mariachi music, and P'urhépecha *abajeño*, 249
marimacho. See *pinkillo mohoceño*
marinera (song-dance genre from creole traditions in coastal Peru)

marinera (*continued*)
  in *orquestas cuzqueñas*, 133
  in repertoire of brass bands, 133
Martí, Samuel, 263
martial arts, in *yawari* intertribal ritual, Kamayurá people, 89–91, 93, 95–96
Martín, Gustavo, 282
masks, Olmec, 18. *See also* jaguar
Mass (Roman Catholic ritual)
  in P'urhépecha language, 257
  pututos or *pututus* (as Kechua conch-shell trumpets), used in, 306
massar ígala (Kuna shamanic chant-type for journey of the dead), 225–26, *226*
massar tuledi (Kuna ritual specialist in *massar ígala* funerary chant), 216–17, 225–26
massi (*maasi*; single-reed aerophone, Wayúu people), in Colombia and Venezuela, 267, 313–14, *315*
Mataco (Wichí) people. *See also* Mataco and Guaycurú peoples
  demographics, 163–64, 166
  healing, shamanic, 168, 189
  instruments, *kanojí* (shaman's bone whistle), 169
  missionaries and missionization, response to, 166
Mataco and Guaycurú peoples, 163–69. *See also subgroups:* Chorote, Chulupí (Nivaklé), Mataco (Wichí); Pilagá, Toba
  cosmology, 166–68
  dance, in rituals and ceremonies, 166–69
  demographics, 163–64, *165* (map)
  economy, 166
  gender roles, 168
  healers and healing, shamanic, 167–68, 189
  instruments
    aerophones
      kanojí (Mataco shaman's bone whistle), 169
      naseré (Pilagá term; wooden globular flute), 293–94
    idiophones
      maracas (gourd rattle), 166–69
      palo sonajero de uñas de ciervo (stamping tube rattle), 167–69
    membranophones, *katakí* (water drum), 167–69
  missionaries and missionization
    impact of, 166
    Pentecostal Church, 166, 169, 178–79
    United Evangelical Church, Toba people, founded by, 169
  oral transmission, traditional music, 167
  rituals and ceremonies
    as initiation into musical practices, 167
    non-shamanic, *algarroba* (adolescents' rite of passage), 168
    shamanic, 167–69
  secular traditions
    lullabies, 167
    mating dances, 167–68
  shamans and shamanism, 167–69
  song
    heterophony, in multiplicity of individual performances, 167

individual ownership of, 168–69
    subgroups, 164
    syncretism, 169
Matipúhy people, 80, 95–96
Matlatzinca people, 235, 240
matraca (idiophone; cog rattle), in Bolivia, 121, *121*
máwi (longest type of Wakuénai flute), 35, *36*, 38–39, 41, *43*, 46
Mawucini (demiurge in Kamayurá cosmology), 89, 93
Maxakali linguistic family, 51
Maxakali people, 56
Maya culture
  astronomy, 9, 233
  calendrical systems, 11–14, 233–34
  chilames (*Chilam Balam*, sacred books of Yucatec-Maya people), 12
  cosmology, 11–17, *13*
  Popol Vuh (Quiché-Maya "Counsel Book"), 1, 8
  shamanic knowledge, recorded in codices of, 187
  time, concepts of, 9–14, 233–34
Maya people, Peninsular, in Mexico, 235, *236* (map), 237, 243
Mayo (Yoreme) people, 235, 239, *239*
  demographics, 235, 239
  pascola dance, Holy Week performances of, 239, *239*
Mazahua people, 235, 241
Mazatec (Ha Shuta Enima) people
  demographics, 235, 242
  dreams, oracular, 189
  healing, 188–90
  psilocybine mushroom, symbolism of, 190
mazurka, in Mískito creole repertoire, 207
mbaepú. See anguapú
mbaraká (as chordophone; as idiophone)
  as five-string guitar of the Mbyá (Guaraní-affiliated) people, 173–76, 177
  as sacred gourd rattle, Guaraní peoples, 189
Mbayá (Mbyá) people, in Brazil, 56, 73, 172. *See also* Mbyá people
Mbyá people (Guaraní-affiliated, in Argentina), 172–78
  cosmology, 172–75
  dance
    ceremonial
      choreographic types, 174–75
      yeroky sondaro (ritual dance of the soldiers), 174–77, *177*
    secular, 176–77
  demographics, 163–64, *165* (map), 172–73, 273
  economy, 173
  gender roles, in instrumental performance and rituals, 174–76, 178, 273–74
  instruments
    aerophones
      mimby (male-owned bamboo flute), 174, 176
      mimby retá (female-owned bamboo dualistic panpipes), 174, 176, 178, 273–74
    chordophones
      guitar, six-string, 174, 176–77
      mbaraká (male-owned five-string guitar)
        adoption and function of, 173–76, 177
        tuning, 176, 177

ravé (male-owned rebec)
    adoption and function of, 173–76, *177*
    melodic structure, 176
    tuning, 176, *177*
    idiophones, *takuapú* (female-owned bamboo
        stamping tube), 174–75, *178*
    membranophones, *anguapú* (*mbaepú*; male-owned
        double-headed drum), 174, 176
  migration, 164, 172–73
  missionaries and missionization, resistance to, 172, 178
  rituals and ceremonies, shamanic
    ára pyau (new seasonal cycle), annual celebration of,
        174
    central evening ceremony (daily), 174–75, 177
    Ñemongaraí (annual consecration of first harvest;
        child-naming), 174–76
  shamans and shamanism
    Pa'i (religious leader)
      functions and skills, 175, 177
      status and rank, 173–74
    (*See also* rituals and ceremonies *above*)
  song
    non-ritual
      creole, with six-string guitar, parallel thirds in,
        176–77
      lullabies, 174
    ritual
      deity-specific melodies in, 175
      melodic structure of, 176
  tourism, crafts, commodification of, 173
  traditions, retention strategies, 177–78
McCosker, Sandra Smith. *See* Smith McCosker, Sandra
Means, Philip Ainsworth, 2
Medina, Alberto, 159–60
Mehináku people
  demographics, 61, 63 (map), 77
  participation of, in Kamayurá shamanic healing ritual
    (*payemeramaraka*), 65
  yawari intertribal ritual, adoption of, 80
Melfi, María Teresa, 193n
melody, by peoples
  Atacameño, 153
  Aymara, in Chile
    kena, ornamentation in, 150
    in songs
      for carnival, 149
      for cattle-marking rituals, 148
      for potato-sowing ritual (*Pachallampe*), 151
  Aymara, in Conima District, Peru, ornamentation as
    stylistic difference, 129
  Botocudo, 54
  Kamayurá
    instruments' roles, in conceptualization of, 64
    phrase-theme syntax and ritual function
      correlations, 65
  K'ero, *pina pinkulucha* music, ornamentation in, 291,
    294
  Mapuche, in Chile, symbolic dualism in construction
    of, 157
  Mbyá, structure of, in *ravé* (rebec) music and ritual
    song, 176

Mískito, of secular *tiuns* ("tunes"), 207–208
P'urhépecha, in conceptualization of music, 248, 252
Wayúu, *massi* (single-reed aerophone), ornamentation
    in, 314
Xavante
  in laments (*dawawa*), 59
  in praise songs (*louvores*) for Catholic saints, 59–60
membranophones
  angúa aretepe (*anguaguásu*; double-headed drum,
    Chiriguano-Chané peoples), 172
  anguaguásu (*angúa aretepe*; double-headed drum,
    Chiriguano-Chané peoples), 172
  anguapú (*mbaepú*; double-headed drum, Mbyá people),
    174, 176
  anguarái (double-headed drum, Chiriguano-Chané
    peoples), 172
  bass drum
    in army and civilian bands, 269
    in brass bands of Aymara people, in Chile, 151
    in Brazil (*zabumba*), 296
    in Peruvian *orquesta cuzqueña*, 133
    in *pitu, siku,* and *tarka* ensembles, Aymara people,
      in Peru, 126–27
  bombo (large double-headed drum)
    in Bolivia, 118, 120
    in Chile, 149–51, 272
    in Ecuador, 269
    in Peru, 126
  caja (double-headed drum)
    in Bolivia, Aymara and Kechua peoples, 109, *111–12*,
      120
    in Chile
      Atacameño people, 153
      Aymara people, 149–50
    in Colombia, 316
    in Peru
      Aymara people, 126–27, 130
      in flute-and-drum combination (*cajero*), Peru,
        304, 304, 309, 316
  cajita (small double-headed drum), in Bolivia, 120
  Inca culture, human skin drum, 282
  kataki (single-headed water drum, Pilagá and Toba
    peoples), 167–69
  kultrún (Mapuche; larger male drum; smaller drum of
    female ritual specialist), 155, 158, 170, 182,
    183, 189, 271
  llamador ("caller"; *tambor macho* or male; African-
    derived single-headed drum), in Colombia,
    298
  mbaepú. See anguapú
  michirái (double-headed drum, Chiriguano-Chané
    peoples), 172
  military drum, in brass bands of Aymara people, in
    Chile, 151
  pfutu wankara (large double-headed drum), in Bolivia,
    120, *120*
  P'urhépecha people, in *chirimía*-and-drum
    combination, 251
  retuela (small double-headed drum), in Bolivia, 120
  snare drum
    in army and civilian bands, 269

membranophones (continued)
    in *pitu* and *tarka* ensembles, Aymara people, in
        Peru, 127
    in *roncadora* flute-and-drum combination, Peru,
        304–305, *305*
    tambor (Spanish for "drum")
        in Bolivia, as small drum, 118
        in Chile, 272
    tambor hembra. See *tambor mayor*
    tambor macho. See *llamador*
    tambor mayor ("largest, principal drum"; *tambor hembra*
        or female; African-derived single-headed
        drum), in Colombia, 298
    tambora (small double-headed drum), in Bolivia, 120
    tamborcito (small double-headed drum), in Bolivia, 120
    tamboril (small double-headed drum)
        in Bolivia, 120
        in Ecuador, 304
    tarol (small side-drum), in *bandas-de-pífanos*,
        northeastern Brazil, 296
    tinya (small drum), in Peru, 127, 306, 320
    wankara (large double-headed drum), in Bolivia and
        Peru, 108, *115*, 120, *120*, 269
    wankarita (small double-headed drum), in Bolivia, 120,
        120
    water drum (*katakí*; single-headed membranophone),
        Mataco and Guaycurú peoples, 167–69
    zabumba (bass drum), in *bandas-de-pífanos*,
        northeastern Brazil, 296
men. See gender roles
Menchú, Rigoberta, 327
Menezes Bastos, Rafael José de. See Bastos, Rafael José de
    Menezes
Mersenne, Marin, 53
Mesoamerica (macrocultural area)
    concept of, 231, *232* (map), 233–34
    core system of thought in, 233–35, 253
    flute-and-rattle tradition, in gold effigy figurines of, 268
    flutes, with built-in ducts, in ancient Mexico, 267
mestizaje. See also acculturation; cultural change;
    transculturation
    as concept, 4–5
    identity retention in, and acculturation, 2–5, 238
Mete sikwi uurma kali (Kuna secular dance), on *kammu
    purwi* panpipes, 227, *227–28*
meter, by peoples. See also rhythm
    Atacameño, in ritual music, 153
    Aymara, in Chile
        in carnival songs, 149
        in cattle-marking songs, 148
    Aymara, in Conima District, Peru, 128
    Kamayurá, 66
    Kawéskar, 159–60
    Mapuche, in Chile, 157
    Xavante, in songs, 60, *60*
metonymy, Aymara people, in Chile, 149–51
Metuktire people, 61–62, *63* (map), 77
Mexica. See Aztec people
Mexicaneros people, 235, 240
Mexico. See also New Spain, Viceroyalty of
    cultural areas, regions, and peoples, 237–44

cultural policies, traditions, preservation of, 257–58
dance, by peoples
    Mayo, *pascola*, 239, *239*
    Nahua, "Dance of *tlacololeros*," 242
    P'urhépecha. See dance *under* P'urhépecha people
groups, Trio Los Chapás, 250
institutions
    Centro de Investigación de la Cultura P'urhépecha,
        257
    Instituto Nacional Indigenista (Mexico City), 237–38
        257
    Universidad Michoacana de San Nicolás de Hidalgo,
        257
instruments. See also ensembles, by type *under*
    P'urhépecha people
    chirimía (double-reed aerophone)
        in general, 316, 318
        P'urhépecha people, 248, 251
    guitar (six-string), 249, 251–52, 256–58
    kiríngwa (bull-shaped hollowed-out log; idiophone),
        247, 251–52, 254, *254*
    vihuela (Mexican type), 251
linguistic families, list and distribution of, 231, 235, *236*
    (map), 237
mariachi music, and P'urhépecha *abajeño*, 249
missionaries and missionization, 237–38, 248
Passion cult, Chamula people, 328
peoples
    Amuzgo (Tzjon Non), 235, 241
    Chamula, 328
    Chatino (Kitse cha'tnio), 235, 241
    Chichimec, 235, 240, 248
    Chinantec (Tsa ju jmí), 235, 242
    Chocho (Chocholtecas, Runixa ngiigua), 235, 242
    Ch'oles (Winik), 235, 243
    Chontal of Oaxaca, 235, 241
    Cora (Nayeri), 235, 239–40, 300
    Guarijío (Macurawe), 235, 238
    Huave (Mareños), 235, 241
    Huichol (Wirr'arika, Wixárika), 190, 235, 239, 240
    Kikapú (Kikaapoa), 235, 238
    Lacandón (Hach winik), 237, 243
    Mame, 237, 244
    Matlatzinca, 235, 240
    Maya, Peninsular, 235, *236* (map), 237, 243
    Mayo (Yoreme), 235, 239, *239*
    Mazahua, 235, 241
    Mazatec (Ha Shuta Enima). See Mazatec people
    Mexicaneros, 235, 240
    Mixe (Ayukk), 235, 241
    Mixtec, 235, 241
    Mochó (Motozintlec), 237, 244
    Nahua. See Nahua people
    Otomí (Hña hñu), 189, 235, 240
    Pame, 235, 239
    Pápago (O'tham), 235, 238
    Pima (O'ob), 235, 238
    Popoluca, 235, 242
    P'urhépecha. See P'urhépecha people
    Seri (Konkaak), 235, 238
    Tarahumara (Rarámuri), 5, 235, 238

Tepehua (Ódami; northern and southern), 188, 235, 238–39, 328
Tlapanec (Mbo me'phaa), 235, 241
Tojolabales (Tojolwinik'otik), 237, 244
Totonac, 235, 239
Trique, 235, 241
Tzotzil (Batsil winik'otik), 237, 244
Yaqui (Yoreme), 235, 238–39
Zapotec, 235, 243
Zoque (O'de püt), 235, 242, *243*
reception, of popular music, in Mískito secular *tiuns* ("tunes"), 207
Michael, St. (San Miguel, September 29), patronal, mestizo population, in Conima District, Peru, 126, 130
michirái (double-headed drum, Chiriguano-Chané peoples), 172
migration
Chiriguano-Chané peoples, 171
Guaraní–affiliated peoples, in general, 164
Kawéskar people, in Chile, 158–59
Mbyá (Guaraní-affiliated) people, 172–73
Mexico
in general, 237
peoples in central valleys and northern Oaxaca, 242
P'urhépecha people, 237, 250, 258
Peru, rural-urban shifts, 123–24, 127, 134, 141–42, 275
military drum, in brass bands, Aymara people, in Chile, 151
Milla Balbero, Pablo, *305*
Miller, Elmer, 166–67, 169
Milliapi, Carolina (Mapuche ritual specialist), *183*
Millones, Luis, 327–28
mimbü-eta. See mimby retá
mimby (male-owned flute, Mbyá people), 174, 176
mimby retá (*mimbü-eta*; female-owned panpipes, Mbyá people), 174, 176, 178, 273–74
minga (traditional collective work effort). *See also* communal labor
alabados (*alabanzas*), as invocations in, 310
clarín, function of, in, 309–10
roncadora and drum, association with, 305
miorí (*turumi*; violin of the Chiriguano-Chané peoples), 171–72
Mískito people (in Honduras and Nicaragua), 193–210
acculturation, in creole music of, 207–10
ancestors, in *inankas* (laments), 199–203, *200, 202–203*
British folk songs, retention of, in *pulankas*, 208–209, *209*
cosmology, 197–207
demographics, 194–97, *195* (map), *198–99*
healers and healing, shamanic, 197–99, 203–205, *204–206*
history of, 194–97, 229
illness, hierarchical classification of
isingni ulan ("mounted or ridden soul"), 203–205
iumu (minor ailments), 203–204, *204–205*
paun (extremely serious, unknown cause), 203, 205
instruments
aras napat (idiophone; horse-jaw scraper), 207

guitar, adoption of, 207
lungku (*lunku*; musical bow), 204
tina (monochord), 207
Kuna people, links to, 193–94, 228–29
language, 194, 196, 209
Mexican music, influence of, on *tiuns* ("tunes"), 207
missionaries and missionization, Moravian Church, 196–97, 199, 207, 229
name, history of, 194
rituals and ceremonies, *Kwal taya* (funerary), 200, 205–207, *207–208*. *See also* shamans and shamanism; *sukia láwana* (shamanic) *under* song *below*
Sandinistas, autonomy of, implemented by, 197
shamans and shamanism, 193, 197–99, 203–207, *204–208*, 228–29
song, 197–210
inankas (laments; communication with ancestors), 199–203
aikulki inanka (of fatherless sons), 200–201
aimasihbi inanka (of childless adults), 200–201
ihbaia láwana (of self-edification), 200, 202
inanka nani (of communication with ancestors), 199–200, 202
inanka upla pruan bara (funerary), 200–202, *202*
lahtubi inanka (curses), 200–201
sary inanka (recollections of past grief), 200–202, *200*
pulankas (children's round-dances and game-songs), 208–210, *209*
sukia láwana (shamanic), 193, 197, 199, 203–205, *204, 207*
defined, 197, 199
isingni ulan (to heal a "mounted soul"), 203–205
iumu (to heal minor illnesses), 203–204, *204–205*
received in dreams, 193
tiuns ("tunes"; secular songs with guitar), 207–208
United States, links to the, 197
missionaries and missionization
Catholic Church
Augustinian and Franciscan orders, in Mexico, 248
Jesuits
in Argentina, 164, 172–73, 181
in Brazil, 49
Salesian order, 4, 57
by country
in Brazil, 49, 51–53, 56–57, 59–60
in Mexico, 238, 248
pacification
in Brazil, 56–57
in Mexico, 237–38
by peoples
Atacameño, 153
Chiriguano-Chané, 171
Mapuche, in Argentina, 4
Mataco and Guaycurú, 166, 169, 178–79

missionaries and missionization (*continued*)
  Mbyá, in Argentina, resistance to, 172, 178
  Mískito, 196–97, 199, 207, 229
  P'urhépecha, 248
  Xavante, 57, 59–60
  Protestant denominations
    Moravian Church, and Mískito people, 196–97,
      199, 207
    Native Americans, cultural borrowings from, 5
    Pentecostal Church, in Chaco region, Argentina,
      166, 169, 178–79
    shamanism, eradication of, 166
    United Evangelical Church (founded by Toba people),
      169
Mixe (Ayukk) people, 235, 241
Mixtec people, 235, 241
Moche culture
  coiled clay trumpets, 309
  conch-shell trumpets, in ceramics of, 306
  flutes, materials for, 286–88
  history of, 10n, 265 (map)
  panpipe representations, in ceramics of, 113–14, 114, 275
  shamanic knowledge, in rock drawings of, 187
  sound-induced trance, depicted in ceramics of, 10
  stone panpipes, 264
Mochica. *See* Moche culture
Mochó (Motozintlec) people, 237, 244
Mocoví people. *See* Mataco and Guaycurú peoples
Moctezuma (Montezuma, Motecuhzoma II; ninth
    Aztec ruler, d. 1520), 14
mohoceño. See *pinkillo mohoceño*
molítu
  as symbolic frog, in Wakuénai myth cycle, 30, 33, 44–46
  as Wakuénai flute named after frog's species, 30, 31–33,
    42–43, 44–46
  Wakuénai *molítu* flute players, oracular role of, 32–33
Mondé linguistic family, 51
Montaño, José, 303
Monte Albán (ancient Zapotec capital, major center ca.
    600–800 C.E.), 1
Montezuma. *See* Moctezuma
Montoya, Edwin, 132
Montoya, Luis, 132
Montoya, Rodrigo, 132
Moors and Christians (Conquest dance-dramas)
  conqueror in, representation of, 4
  P'urhépecha people
    "Danza de los moros," 249, 249, 251, 253, 255, 257,
      259. *See also* "Danza de los soldados"
    "Danza de moros y cristianos," 248–49, 259
    "Danza de los soldados," 255, 259. *See also* "Danza
      de los moros"
Moravian Church, missionaries and missionization,
    Mískito people, 196–97, 199, 207
La Mosquitia (colonial name for territory inhabited by
    Mískito people), 194–96, 199, 207, 209
Mosquitos. *See* Mískito people
Mostny, Grete, 145
Motecuhzoma II. *See* Moctezuma
mourning rituals. *See* funerary *under* rituals and
    ceremonies, by function

Mouse Ceremony (initiation, Suyá people), 22, 67–69,
    74, 191
Mozart, Wolfgang Amadeus, P'urhépecha *bandas*,
    overtures in repertoire of, 255
much'a (a type of *pinkillo*; duct flute), in Bolivia, 119, *119*
"La muerte de Atahualpa" ("Death of Atahualpa"),
    dramatic representation of, in Peru, 4,
    10–11, 327
"The Muffin Man" ("Brit ayang-kra ba kaikisma ki"), as
    Mískito children's game-song (*pulanka*),
    209, *209*
muhusemoi (Warao bone notched flute)
  centric melodic interval, 313
  description of, 266, 286–88, *287*
  fingering of, 287, 291
  function of, 288, 320
  music for, *288*, *315*
  tuning of, 267, 287, *287*
O mundo sonoro Xavante (Aytai), 57, 59–60
Munduruku linguistic family, 51
Mura linguistic family, 51
Museum of Anthropology and Ethnography, Russian
    Academy of Sciences, 53
mushrooms. *See* hallucinogens
music. *See also* composition; dynamics; formal structure;
    improvisation; melody; meter;
    performance practice; pitch organization;
    register; rhythm; tempo; texture; timbre;
    tuning
  classification of, by peoples
    Kamayurá, 64, *64*, 73
    P'urhépecha, 248–49, *249*, 252
  concepts of, by peoples
    Aymara, 147
    Kamayurá, 64–66, 81
    Kuna, 212
    P'urhépecha, 248, 252
    Suyá, 67
  origins of, by peoples
    Atacameño (mythic), 153–54
    Aymara (mythic), 147, 154
    Kamayurá, 65
    Mapuche (mythic), 154–55
    Suyá, 69–70
música norteña (of northern Mexico and U.S. border
    region), in P'urhépecha *bandas* repertoire,
    255
*Musical and Other Sound Instruments of the South American
    Indians* (Izikowitz)
  aerophones
    definition of, 262–63
    description of, 276, 279, 293–94
  bullroarers, distribution of, 318
  description of, 262
  toré, as term for single-reed aerophones, 311
Musiguí (Guaymí name for Mískito people), 196
mútsi (palm grubs), Wakuénai peoples, 29, 41, 44–46
Muu (Kuna life-force; deity of creation), 216, 217–19,
    222
Muu *ígala* (Kuna shamanic healing chant-type), 217–18,
    218, 222

*Muu-ígala or the Way of Muu, A Medicine Song from the
        Cuna Indians of Panama* (Holmer and
        Wassen), 217
myth. *See also* cosmology; rituals and ceremonies
    as concept, 7–10, 17, 20, 22–23, 146
    creation myths
        animal powers in, 17–20, *19*. *See also* jaguar
        by peoples
            Canelos Quichua, in Ecuador, 18
            Desana (Tukano-affiliated), 319
            Hohódeni-Wakuénai, 18, 18n
            Keres, in Laguna Pueblo, 8–9
            Kuna, 216–17, 220, 226
            Makiritare (*Watunna*), 4, 17
            Mbyá, 172–73
            Olmec, 17–18, *19*
            Quiché-Maya (*Popol Vuh*), 1, 8
            Wakuénai, 18n, 25–35, 39–40, 45–46
    gender antagonisms and reciprocity in, 8, 20–23
    instruments, in contextual study of, 264
    mythic center
        Hípana (Wakuénai peoples), 18n, 25, 28–30, 40, 46
        Takarkuna (Kuna people), 216, 225
    by peoples
        Atacameño, of Tata-Purajni (water and water-music
            spirit), 153–54
        Aymara, in Chile
            of *carnavalón* (carnival spirit), 149
            of Sereno (water and water-music spirit), 150, 154
        Desana (Tukano-affiliated), healer's knowledge of,
            189
        Inca, in song texts, 21–22
        Kamayurá
            flutes and music, creation of, 65
            of *yawari*'s origin, 80, 82, 96–98
        Kuna, in chant texts, 222–26
        Mapuche, in Chile, in ritual songs and recitations,
            154–56
        Mataco and Guaycurú, songs' origin, as explanation
            of, 167
        Selk'nam, gender-based power in, 20–21
        Yupa, of first *atunse* (pair of "hatchet" duct flutes),
            297–98
    ritual performance, song, and speech, as agency and
        embodiment of, 8–11, 20–23, 80, 94
    time, concepts of, in, 9–11, 22–23

N

nahanamu (Warao harvest festival), 288, 306, 312–13, *315*
nahôre (ritual dances; female initiation into jaguar powers),
        Toba people, in Bolivia, 18, 20
Nahua people
    "Dance of *tlacololeros*" (ocelots), in State of Guerrero,
        242
    demographics, 235, 239, 240, 241
    healers and healing, 16, 189
    language, 235, 240–41
    migration, 237
    time, concept of, 5, 233–34

traditions, retention of, 234
Nahuatl language, 235, 240–41. *See also* Aztec culture
Nahukwá-Matipú (Nahukwá-Matipúhy) people, 61, *63*
        (map), 77
namake (Kuna term for the action of singing), 212
Ñamandú (Mbyá primal creator, Sun god and source of
        light), 173
Nambikwára linguistic family, 51
Nambikwára people, 53–54, 294
Naotsete ("She Who Remembers"; sacred twin in Keres
        creation myth), 8–9
naseré (Pilagá term for small wooden globular flutes),
        293–94
násisi (*násis*; idiophone; Kuna gourd rattle with deer-bone
        handle), 227, 279, 286
National Library, Music Division (Brazil), music
        iconography, survey of, 53
Native Americans, in general
    contact with Europeans, responses to, 4
    demography, 2
    early history of, 1–2, 231–34
    identity, construction of, ethnicity and language
        correlations in, 2–5
    traditional healing practices, history of, 187–88
Nava López, E. Fernando, 328
Navas, Odis (Kuna ritual specialist and community leader
        or *saila*), 215
Nazca culture
    antara (panpipes) ensembles, 275
    ceramic trumpets, 263
    flutes, materials for, 286–88
    history of, 1, 1n, *265* (map)
    panpipe representations, in ceramics of, 113–14, 275,
        278
    sound-induced mystical flight, depicted in ceramics of,
        10
ñe ẽngaraí (Apapocuvá shamanic song for journey of the
        dead), 191
nele (Kuna sage; diviner/shaman by birth; auxiliary spirits),
        213, 216–17, 221, 225, 229
nellipún. See nguillipún
Ñemongaraí (Mbyá ceremony, annual consecration of first
        harvest), 174–76
New Fire ceremony, in Aztec cosmology, 11–12, *12*
New Granada, Viceroyalty of, 318
New Spain, Viceroyalty of, *chirimía* in, 318
New Year's
    Atacameño people, 152
    Aymara and Kechua peoples, in Bolivia, 102
    P'urhépecha people, 257
Nezahualcoyotl (Aztec poet/composer, *tlanatinime* or sage,
        Lord of Texcoco), 15–16, 23
ngeikurrewén (Mapuche post-initiation song-dance
        categorized as "human" ritual music), 157,
        271
Ngeñechén ("She/He Who Creates"; chief deity in
        Mapuche cosmology), 182
ngére (Suyá [Gê] term for "music" and "ceremony";
        collective song genre), 67–69, *68*, 73
ngillatún (*nguillatún*; Mapuche fertility ritual), in Chile,
        156–57, 271, 307. *See also nguillipún*

nguillipún (*camaruco, kamarikún, kamarrikún, nellipún, nguillatún*; Mapuche fertility ritual), in Argentina, 181–85. See also *nguillatún*
    distribution of, 181–82, *182* (map)
    functions of, 181–82, 191
    Jesuits, documentation on, 181
    leadership structure of, 182, *183–84*
    lineage traditions, 181–82
    retention of, 171, 179
    ritual dance and song in, 170–71, 182, 184
    structure of, 182, 184–85
Nicaragua
    epics, pre-contact, 10
    formerly territory of ancient Mexico, 231
    missionaries and missionization, Moravian Church in, 196–97, 199, 207
    peoples
        British colonizers, 194–96
        Garífuna ethnic nation (Black Caribs), 3, 196–97
        Mískito. See Mískito people
        Rama, 196–97
        Spanish colonizers, 194–95
        Sumo, 196
    state policies, Sandinistas, Mískito autonomy, implemented by, 197
niga (life force of Muu, Kuna deity of creation), 216. See also *purba*
Nivaklé (Chulupí) people, 164, 167
nolkiñ (Mapuche short vertical trumpets), 158
Nordenskïold, Erland
    An Historical and Ethnological Survey of the Cuna Indians, 214
    on wooden whistles of Chaco area peoples, 293
nose ocarina (*tsin-hali*), 54, 294
notation, ideographic, of Kuna chant, 215–16, *216*
nuchus (Kuna wooden anthropomorphic figures; ritual auxiliary spirits), 214, 217, *219*, 222
nueva canción (Latin American sociopolitical movement expressed through folk and urban popular song)
    as ancient American tradition, 327
    use of *kena, siku,* and *charango,* in Chilean tradition of, 290–91
Ñuke Mapu (Mapuche Earth Mother), 182
Nunghuí (female spirit of garden soil and pottery clay, in Canelos Quichua cosmology), 18
nurá-mëe (wooden bullroarer, Tukano-affiliated Desana people), in Colombia, 319
ñusta (Inca woman or maiden of royal lineage), 21

O

Oasisamerica (macrocultural area), 231, *232* (map), 233
Oberg, Kalervo, 312
Oberhauser, Fernando, 145
ocarina, 120, 264
ocelot
    jaguatirica, yawari (mediating core symbol in intertribal ritual), Kamayurá people, 80–98

tlacololeros ("ocelots"; dance tradition of Nahua people), in Mexico, 242
Ofayé people, 56
offerings, ritual. *See* ritual offerings *under* rituals and ceremonies
oká (ceremonial dance space, Mbyá people), 174–75
öl (*nöl, ül*; Mapuche ritual song and poetry), 9, 156, 170, 184
Oliveira Filho, João Pacheco de, 53
Oliveira Pinto, Tiago de, 296–97
Ollantay (Inca drama of contested pre-Hispanic origin), 10
Olmec people, jaguar as deity, in creation myth cycles of, 17–18
Olsen, Dale A., 263, 276
Ometeotl (Mesoamerican dual deity; primeval God of creation), 11, 14
Ona people. *See* Selk'nam people
opy (Mbyá place of worship; house of religious leader), 174–75, 178
oral transmission. *See* education
oratory
    Suyá people, 67
    Xavante people, 57, 59
ornamentation, melodic. *See* melody
orquestas. See under ensembles, by type
Orrego-Salas, Juan, 270, 307
Oséema (Yupa culture hero, creator of first *atunse* flute pair), 297–98
Otomí (Hña hñu) people
    demographics, 235, 240
    fertility ritual, healer's song in, 189
overture, as mestizo genre, P'urhépecha people, 252
Oviedo y Valdés, Gonzalo Fernández de, 264
oyné (funerary ceremony, Cubeo people), 34n

P

paceño (a type of notched flute), in Bolivia, 118
Pachacamac (Early Lima) cultural area, in Peru, 264
Pachacutec, Inca, 10
Pachallampe (potato-sowing ritual), Aymara people, in Chile, 147–48, 151
Pachamama (Andean Earth Mother syncretized with attributes of the Virgin Mary)
    in Bolivia, 102–103, 108–109, 113, 116
    in Chile, 151–52
    in Peru, 126, 130, 132, 135, 138, 139
Pachatata (Tatapacha, Andean Earth Father), in Bolivia, 102–103, 108, 113, 116
pacification, in Brazil, 56–57
Pa'i (Mbyá religious leader), 173–75, 177
pákamarántakan (Wakuénai songs; in *kwépani* and *pudáli*), 32, 34, 37, 40, 46
Palavecino, Eduardo, 181
Pallas, Peter, 3
Palma, Ricardo, *Tradiciones peruanas*, 289–90
palo sonajero de uñas de ciervo (idiophone; Mataco and Guaycurú stamping deer-hoof rattle), 167–69
Pame people, 235, 239

pampa corneta (long maguey trumpet), in Peru, 307
Pampa people (group subsumed under Mapuche), in
        Argentina, 169
Panama
    gold artifacts, flutes with finger holes in, 285
    peoples
        Guaymí, 193, 196
        Kuna. *See* Kuna people
    tourism in, 229
Panará people, 61–62, *63* (map), 77
Panare people, in Venezuela, *are're* (panpipes), 280
Pano linguistic family, 51
panpipes, 266. *See also under* aerophones, by instruments;
        specific types
papa tarpuy (potato harvest), Kechua people, in Canas
        Province, Peru, 134–37
Pápago (O'tham) people, 235, 238
Paracas culture, notched flutes, materials for, 288
Paraguay
    epics, pre-contact, 10
    peoples
        Guaraní-affiliated, in general, 164, 172–73, 189
        Guayakí, 21
    migration, 164, 172–73
Paresí people, 53–55, 294
pascola (Mayo dance performed during Holy Week), 239, *239*
pasodoble (Spanish dance-genre), as mestizo genre,
        P'urhépecha people, 252, 255
Passion cult, Chamula people, interpretation of, 328
pastores (children's Christmas dance), Aymara people, in
        Conima District, Peru, 127
patron-saint fiestas. *See also* All Saints' Day; saints,
        Catholic
    aerophones, association with
        cajero (flute and drum), in Peru, 304–305, *304*, 309,
            309
        chino flutes, in Chile, 271–73, *272*
        clarín, in Peru, 309–10, *309–10*
        kanchis sipas, in Peru, 283
        roncadora and drum, in Peru, 304–305, *305*
        sikuri ensemble traditions, 277–78
        tundas, in Ecuador, 295
    by peoples
        Atacameño, 153
        Aymara, in Chile, 147–48, 150–51
        indigenous peoples, in Mexico, 234
        Kechua, in Canas Province, Peru, 132–33
        K'ero, in Peru, 283
        mestizo population, in Conima District, Peru, 126,
            130
        P'urhépecha, 255, 257, 259
        Quichua, in Ecuador, 295
    by saints
        Augustine, St. (Tata Agustín), Aymara and Kechua,
            in Bolivia, 103
        Isidro, Fiesta de San (May 15), Aymara, in Conima
            District, Peru, *satiri* dance-drama on,
            131–32
        James, St. (Fiesta de Santiago)
            Aymara and Kechua (Tata Santiago), in Bolivia,
                103

        K'ero people (July 25; as fertility ritual), *kanchis
            sipas* played only on, 283
        John the Baptist, St. (Fiesta de San Juan Bautista,
            June 24)
            in Acolla, Department of Junín, Peru, patronal,
                315, *317*
            Atacameño people, 152
            Aymara and Kechua peoples, in Bolivia, 103
            Chiriguano-Chané peoples, 171
            Quichua people, in Ecuador, *tundas* (flutes), for
                feast of, 295
        Michael, St. (San Miguel, September 29), mestizo
            population, in Conima District, Peru, 126,
            130
        Peter and Paul, Saints (San Pedro y San Pablo, June
            29), Quichua, in Ecuador, *tundas* (flutes)
            for, 295
        Roque, Fiesta de San, in Tarija, Bolivia, 120
        Virgin Mary (Proper of the Saints)
            in Andean syncretic cosmology, 102, 116
            Annunciation (Fiesta de la Anunciación, March
                25), Chiriguano-Chané peoples, 171
            Assumption (Fiesta de la Virgen de la Asunción,
                August 15)
                Mamita Asunta (Mama Asunta; Virgen de la
                    Asunción), in Bolivia, 102, 108
                mestizo population, in Conima District, Peru,
                    130
            Candlemas (Fiesta de la Virgen de la Candelaria,
                February 2)
                Aymara people, in Conima District, Peru, as
                    harvest ritual, 130, 132
                Aymara and Kechua peoples, in Bolivia, 102
                P'urhépecha people, 254
            Immaculate Conception (Fiesta de la Concepción,
                December 8), Aymara and Kechua peoples,
                in Bolivia, 102
            Virgen del Carmen
                in Bolivia, 102
                in Peru, Alto Otuzco, Cajamarca, 304, *304*,
                    309–10, *309–10*
            Virgen de Copacabana, in Bolivia, 102
            Virgen de Guadalupe, patron of Mexico, 257
            Virgen del Rosario, Fiesta de la, in Andacollo,
                Chile, 271–73, *272*
paun (Mískito illness category), 203, 205
Paya people, 196–97
payé (Desana [Tukano-affiliated] and Tukano healer),
        189–90
payemeramaraka (Kamayurá shamanic healing ritual),
        65–66, *66*, 72
Payeta people (as Trumai ancestors), 97
Pederek, Elerio (Mískito ritual specialist), *205–206*. See also
        iumu
Pehuenche (Pewenche; Mapuche peoples of the East;
        group subsumed under Mapuche)
    in Argentina, 169, 181
    in Chile, 154
penitentes (self-flagellating Christian sects), 16–17
Pentecostal Church, missionaries and missionization, in
        Chaco region, 166, 169, 178–79

Perdomo Escobar, José Ignacio, 263
performance practice. *See also* texture
  aerophones, in general, 267–69
  alternating technique in aerophonic performance
    carrizos (panpipes), in Venezuela, 278, 280–82, *281*
    sikuras (panpipes), Aymara and Kechua, in Bolivia,
        105, 109, *110–12*, 113, *115*
  falsetto
    in Kechua songs, Canas Province, Peru, 134
    in P'urhépecha songs, 251
    in rainy season music for Pachamama, Aymara and
        Kechua, in Bolivia, 102
    as trait shared by indigenous groups, in Chile, 146
  high tessitura (vocal and instrumental)
    Aymara people, in Conima District, Peru, 124, 127,
        141
    Kechua people, in Canas Province, Peru, 134–35,
        141
  interlocking technique in aerophonic performance
    about, 268
    carrizos (panpipes), in Venezuela, 278, 280–82, *281*
    chino flutes, in Chile, 268, 272–73, *272*, *274*
    guli (*kuli*; Kuna set of complementary pipes), 273,
        273
    in Inca culture, panpipes, descriptions of, 113, 276
    julajulas (Aymara and Kechua single-row panpipes),
        104–108, *105–106*
    kammu purwi (Kuna panpipes), 226–27, *227–28*,
        278–80, *279*
    lakitas (Aymara panpipes), 105, 108–109, *108–109*,
        150
    mare-mare (pluralistic panpipes), in Venezuela,
        280–82, *282*
    in *máwi* flute duets, Wakuénai peoples, 39
    mimby retá (Mbyá panpipes), 174, 176, *178*,
        273–74
    in Moche and Nazca cultures, ceramics of, 113–14,
        114
    panpipes (dualistic), Guahibo people, 280
    pifülkas (*pifilkas*; Mapuche flutes), 184, 270–71,
        271, 274, 278
    sikuras (Aymara large double-row panpipes), in
        Chile, 150
    sikus (Aymara double-row panpipes), 126–27, 268,
        274–76, *274–75*
    takwara ("bamboo"; five-tubed single-reed
        aerophone), 65, 299, 311–12
    tarawi (two-tubed single-reed aerophone), Kamayurá
        people, 311–12
    tule (Wayãpí single reed aerophone), 268
    uru'a (Kamayurá two-tubed duct flutes), 65,
        298–300, 311–12
  ornamentation, melodic, in aerophonic performance
    kena (notched flute), Aymara people, in Chile, 150
    massi (single-reed aerophone), Wayúu people,
        314
    pina pinkulucha (notched flute), K'ero people,
        291, 294
  paired flutes, excluding interlocking techniques
    atunse (pair of Yuko and Yupa *atuñsa* "hatchet"
        duct flutes), 297–98

gaita ("hatchet" duct flute), in Colombia, 298
kammu suid (*gammu suid*; Kuna flutes
        interdependent in performance), 266,
        285–86
kuizi (Ika, Kogi, and Sanká "hatchet" duct flutes), in
        Colombia, 297–98
pinkullos (duct flutes), Kechua people, in Peru, 301
tekeya (single-reed aerophone), Yekuana people, in
        Venezuela, 267, 311
techniques, instrument-specific
  caña de millo (single-reed aerophone), in Colombia,
        314
  charango, 134, 135–37, *136–37*, 141
  vibrato
    clarinet and saxophone, in traditional contexts,
        314–16
    kena (notched flute)
      in general, 290
      in mestizo style, Peru, 134
Peru
  carnival
    Aymara people, in Conima District, 127,
        130–32, 301
    Kechua people, in Canas Province, 139–40
  celebrations, Catholic feasts (syncretic), cyclic calendar
        of
    All Saints' Day (Todos los Santos, November 1), 127,
        130, 301
    Assumption (Virgen de la Asunción), 130
    Candlemas (Virgen de la Candelaria), 130, 132
    Corpus Christi, 294, *294*
    Holy Cross Day (Fiesta de la Santa Cruz), 132
    Isidro, Fiesta de San (May 15), 131–32
    James, St. (Fiesta de Santiago, July 25; as fertility
        ritual), 283
    John the Baptist, St. (Fiesta de San Juan Bautista,
        June 24), 315, *317*
    Michael, St. (San Miguel, September 29), patron-
        saint fiesta, 126, 130
    Virgen del Carmen, 304, *304*, 309–10, *309–10*
  dance
    Achach K'umu (dance-drama), for Holy Cross Day,
        124, 126, 132, *133*
    cumbia andina, 124
    "The Death of the Coya" (dance-drama), in
        Carhuamayo, 4, 327–28
    kashuas (circle dances), 137–38, *138*, 141
    marinera, 133
    pastores (children's Christmas dance), 127
    satiri (dance-drama), for San Isidro, 131–32
    wayno (huayno), 133–34
    wifala (courting dance), for Candlemas, 130, *131*
  demographics, 2, 125 (map), 126, 132
  ensembles. *See also* groups *below*
    aerophone and drum, single-player combinations
      cajero (*flauta* and *caja*), 304, *304*, 309, *309*, 314,
        316
      roncadora (duct flute) and drum, 304–305, *305*
      rondín (harmonica) and drum, 316
    aerophones, with membranophone accompaniment
        (Aymara and Kechua)

ayarachi (panpipes; tradition associated with burial ceremonies), 275–78
pinkillus (five- and six-hole duct flutes), 126–27, 130–31, 301
pitus (*falawatus*; side-blown flutes), 126–28, 132, *133*, 294
sikus (*sikuris*; panpipes), 126–32, *128–29*, 141, 274–78
tarkas (duct flutes), 126–28, 130–31, 141, 301, 303–304
brass bands, 133
orquestas cuzqueñas, 133
string-band tradition, 133–34, 141
groups. *See also* ensembles *above*
Los Incas (later Urubamba), 290–91
Selección del Centro (*orquesta típica del centro*), 315, *317*
Urubamba (formerly Los Incas), 290–91
identity, Aymara and Kechua peoples, social construction of, 123–24, 141–42
instruments. *See also* ensembles *above*
antara. *See* antara
charango, in Caneño and mestizo traditions, 134–37, *136–37*, 141
chirimía (double-reed aerophone), 262, 316, 318
chirimoya (name for the *chirimía* in Lucanas, Department of Ayacucho), 316
chirisuya (name for the *chirimía* in areas of southern Peru), 263, 316, 318
clarín (long straight side-blown trumpet), 308–10, *309–310*
kanchis sipas. *See* kanchis sipas
kena. *See* kena
pina pinkulucha. *See* pina pinkulucha
pinkullo. *See* pinkullo
pinkullu, 134–35, 137–39, *140*
pitu. *See* pitu
pututu, kepa (conch-shell trumpets), 305–308
wak'rapuku (*cacho*; animal horn coiled trumpet), 306–307
language, 126, 132
migration, rural-urban shifts, 123–24, 127, 134, 141–42, 275
peoples
Aymara. *See* Aymara people, in general; Aymara people, in Peru (Conima District, Department of Puno)
Kechua. *See* Kechua people, in general; Kechua people, in Peru (Canas Province, Department of Cuzco)
K'ero. *See* K'ero people
rituals and ceremonies (syncretic). *See also* celebrations *above*
Aymara people, in Conima District
Achach K'umu (dance-drama), 132, *133*
Candlemas (Candelaria), as harvest ritual, 130, 132
satiri (dance-drama; reenactment of agricultural rituals), 131–32
Kechua people, in Canas Province

papa tarpuy (potato planting), 134–37
tinku (ritual battle of Chiaraje), 137–39, *140*, 141
song
Kechua people, in Canas Province
for carnival, 139–40
in general, 134, 140
in ritual battle of Chiaraje, 137–39
K'ero people, 283
state policies, 123–24, 132
syncretism, 123–24, 130, 132
traditions, Aymara and Kechua, in Conima and Canas, compared, 140–42
Peru, Viceroyalty of, 318
Peter and Paul, Saints (San Pedro y San Pablo, June 29), Quichua, in Ecuador, *tundas* (flutes) for, 295
Pewenche. *See* Pehuenche
pewutún (Mapuche shamanic diagnostic ritual), in Chile, 156–57
peyote (*hikuri*; hallucinogenic cactus), in shamanic healing, Huichol people, 190
pfala (*pfalawita*; side-blown ductless flute with finger holes), in Bolivia, 120, 266, 294
pfalawita. *See* pfala
pflawata (*flawata*; duct flute), in Bolivia, 119
pfutu wankara (large double-headed drum), in Bolivia, 120, *120*
phalawita (side-blown ductless flute with finger holes), in Bolivia, 120, *120*
phuko (Kechua of Paratía, *siku* panpipes performance tradition), in Peru, 275
phukunas (Callawaya panpipes), in Bolivia, 104, 118
phulu-pututu (end-blown bamboo trumpet), in Bolivia, 120
phululu (end-blown bamboo trumpet), in Bolivia, 120
piano accordion (*acordeón a piano*), 316
pichi-pillantún (Mapuche shaman's ritual songs), in Chile, 157
pífano (aerophone)
as Quichua end-blown duct flute with six finger holes (*pingullo*), in Ecuador, 304
as side-blown ductless flute (*búzio, buzo, gaita, pífaro, pife, taboca*), in Brazil, 296–97
as side-blown flute, in Bolivia, 120
pífaro. *See* pífano
pife. *See* pífano
pifilka. *See* pifülka
pifülka (*pifilka*; Mapuche end-blown flute without finger holes)
in Argentina (as *pifilka*), 170–71, 184, *185*
in Chile (as *pifülka*), 158
description of, 266, 269–71, *271*
function of, 270
performance techniques, 270–71, 274, 278
Pikunche (Mapuche peoples of the North; extinct group), in Chile, 154, 270
Pilagá people. *See also* Mataco and Guaycurú peoples
demographics, 163–64, 166
horse, adoption of, 166
kataki (Pilagá and Toba name for the water drum; membranophone), 168–69
naseré (Pilagá term; wooden globular flute), 293–94

pillantún (Mapuche shaman's ritual songs), in Chile, 157

Pima (O'ob) people, 235, 238

pina pinkulucha (*caña*, *pinkulu*; K'ero notched flute), 291, 291, 294

pincollo (*pinkollo*). See *pinkillo*

pincullo. See *pinkullo*

pincuyllo (duct flute), as variant spelling of *pinkullo*, 300

pingollo (duct flute), as variant spelling of *pinkullo*, 300

pingúio (*pinkullo*; duct flute, Chiriguano-Chané peoples), 171

pingullo (end-blown duct flute)
    as Quichua duct flute with six finger holes (*pífano*), in Ecuador, 304
    as Quichua one-hand duct flute with two finger holes and a thumb hole, in Ecuador , 304
    as variant spelling of *pinkullo*, 300

pinkayllo (*ch'utu*; duct flute of the Chipaya people), in Bolivia, 119, 301

pinkillo (*pinquillo*, *pinquilo*; end-blown duct flute)
    in Bolivia, 102, 104, 116, 119–20, 119
    in Chile, 149
    compared with *pinkillo mohoceño*, 303
    as seasonal instrument, 308
    symbolism of, 116
    as variant spelling of *pinkullo*, 300

pinkillo mohoceño (*aykhori*, *aymara*, *marimacho*, *mohoceño*; large duct aerophone with detachable extension of air duct), in Bolivia, 102, 119, 119, 303

pinkillu (end-blown duct flute)
    in Peru, 126–27, 130, 131, 141, 301
    timbric symbolism, in northern Potosí ensembles, Bolivia, 301–302
    as variant spelling of *pinkullo*, 300

pinkollo (*pincollo*). See *pinkillo*

pinkullo (*pincullo*; Aymara and Kechua term for "flute"; duct aerophone)
    Chiriguano-Chané peoples (*pingúio*), 171
    description of, 266–67, 300–303
    function of, 301–303
    variants of, 303

pinkullu (duct aerophone)
    as end-blown duct flute, in Peru, 134–35, 137–41, 140
    as "*pinkullu* of Potosí" (name for *charka*; wrapped curved duct flute), in Bolivia, 304

pinkulu. See *pina pinkulucha*

pinkulwe (Mapuche side-blown ductless flute with finger holes), 295–96

pinquillo (*pinquilo*). See *pinkillo*

pinquilo (*pinquillo*). See *pinkillo*

Pinto, Tiago de Oliveira. See Oliveira Pinto, Tiago de

pirates. See buccaneers

pirékwa (generic term for songs in P'urhépecha language), 249–50, 252–53, 257–58

pitch organization. See also tuning
    intervals
        in Kawéskar songs, 159
        in Miskito laments (*inanka*), range of, 202
        in Warao *muhusemoi* melodies, centricity of, 313
    scales
        as critical language, in Kamayurá intertribal ritual, interpretation of, 89–90, 89, 94, 96, 98
        in general, by peoples
            Aymara and Kechua, in Peru, in *sikuri* traditions, 277
            Botocudo, 54
            indigenous groups, in Brazil, 55, 72–73
            Kamayurá, referential, from songs, in *yawari* ritual, 89–90, 89, 94, 96, 98
            Kawéskar, 159
            Kechua, in Canas Province, Peru, 137–38, 141
            K'ero, referential, for *kanchis sipas* panpipes and song, 283, 284
            Makuxí, Taulipáng, and Yekuâna, 54–55
            Mapuche, in Chile, 157
            Paresí, 54
            Xavante, 60, 73
        heptatonic
            Aymara people
                in Chile, 149–50
                in Peru, 128, 141, 277
            Kechua people, in Taquile Island, Lake Titicaca, 277
        hexatonic, Aymara people
            in Chile, 149–51
            in Peru, 128, 141, 277
        major modes, Aymara people, in Chile, 148, 151
        minor modes, Aymara people, in Chile, 151
        pentatonic
            in Aymara-influenced Atacameño music, 153
            Aymara people
                in Bolivia, 105, 109
                in Chile, 148–51, 153
                in Peru, 128, 277
            Chiriguano-Chané peoples, 171
            indigenous groups, in Chile, 146
            Kechua people
                in Bolivia, 105, 109
                in Peru, 277, 283, 284
            Mapuche peoples, in Chile, 157
            in music of *sikus*, Argentinian Northwest, 163
            in *roncadora* melodies (duct flutes), Peru, 305
        tetratonic
            Atacameño people, in ritual music of, 153–54
            indigenous groups, in Chile, 146
            Kechua people, in Canas Province, Peru, 137–38, 141
        tritonic
            Atacameño people, 153–54
            in *bagualas* and *coplas*, Argentinian Northwest, 163
            indigenous groups, in Chile, 146
            Kechua people, in Canas Province, Peru, 137–38, 141
            Mapuche peoples, in Chile, 157
            in melodies for cattle-marking rituals, central sierra, Peru, 306–307
            in religious *corneta* (*caña*) music, Argentinian Northwest, 163

píti (Wakuénai whistles), 35

pito (Spanish for "whistle"; aerophone)

as "beak" duct flute of the Cora people, in Mexico, 300
as name for *caña de millo* (*caña de lata, flauta de millo*);
    side-blown single-reed aerophone, in
    Colombia, 314
as name for *chino* flute (*flauta de chino, flautón*);
    aerophone without finger holes, in Chile,
    271
as side-blown flute with finger holes, in Bolivia, 120
pitón (as name for *pututo*; bull or cow horn), in Peru, 308
pitu (Aymara and Kechua pronunciation of *pito*, Spanish
    for "whistle"; side-blown flute)
    in Bolivia (*pfala, pfalawita*), 120, 294
    description of, 266, 294
    in Peru
        Aymara people, in Conima District (*falawatu*),
            126–28, 132, *133*, 294
        K'ero people, 294, *294*
piwichén (Mapuche boys embodying original ancestors in
    nguillipún), 182, 184, *184–85*
Pizarro, Francisco, 4, 328
plants
    hallucinogenic. *See* hallucinogens
    pharmacological knowledge of, healers and healing,
        189–90
    role of, in healing practices
        in general, 189–90, 327
        Kuna people, in shamanic healing rituals, 215,
            221–23, 226
Platt, Tristan, 302
plegaria (Spanish for "prayer"), in Aymara and Kechua
    tinku, Bolivia, 108
polka, in P'urhépecha repertoire, categorized as mestizo,
    252
polyphony, European, taught to P'urhépecha people,
    248
Popol Vuh (Quiché-Maya for "Counsel Book"; foundational
    cosmological narrative), 1, 8
Popoluca people, 235, 242
potatoes
    Pachallampe (Aymara sowing ritual), in Chile, 147–48,
        151
    papa tarpuy (Kechua harvest festival), in Canas
        Province, Peru, 137, *138*
praise songs
    alabados (*alabanzas*)
        Catholicism, as symbols of conversion to, 17
        as invocations, in communal labor (*minga*), 310
        P'urhépecha people, as mestizo genre, 252
    benditos (religious folk songs; collective prayers sung in
        praise of saints)
        in Brazil, 297
        in Chile, 150
    louvores (for Catholic saints), Xavante people, 59–60
pratos (Portuguese for "cymbals"; idiophone), in *bandas-de-
    pífanos*, northeastern Brazil, 296
Pravia Lacayo, Nathan, 193n
pregoneros (street criers), in pre-contact Tzintzuntzan,
    247
Protestant denominations
    Moravian Church, missionaries and missionization,
        Mískito people, 196–97, 199, 207

Native Americans, cultural borrowings from, 5
Pentecostal Church, in Chaco region, Argentina, 166,
    169, 178–79
pudáli (Wakuénai ceremonial cycle; male- and female-
    controlled expansion of horizontal social
    relations), 26–27, 34–46. *See also under*
    Wakuénai peoples
puelpurrún (Mapuche gender-specific "dances to the East,"
    in *nguillipún* fertility ritual), 170, 182, 184
pulanka (Mískito children's round-dances and game-
    songs), 208–10, *209*
pulu (Aymara vessel flute without finger holes), in Bolivia,
    120
Pumarino V., Ramón, 272
púnkiri. See kuizi
purba (Kuna for "breath of life"; soul, body's guardian),
    216–17, 219–20, 225–26
P'urhépecha people (*formerly* Tarascos), 247–59
    acculturation, 248, 258–59
    aesthetics, 248–49
    Aztecs and, 247
    carnival, as regional ritual, 254–56, *254*. *See also* carnival
        torito under genres *below*
    celebrations, Catholic feasts (syncretic), cyclic calendar
        of
        Candlemas, regional, 254
        Christmas, regional, 252–54
        Corpus Christi, regional, 249, 251, 254, 257
        danced prayers, religious tradition of, 253
        Epiphany, regional, 253–54
    civic holidays, 256
    composition
        concept of, 251
        repertoire renewal, 253, 259
    Conquest prophecies, in myths of, 9
    cultural change, 252
    cultural policies, traditional music, preservation and
        dissemination of, 257–58
    dance
        choreography, 252–53
        danced prayers, religious tradition of, 253
        gender roles in, 252–53, 257
        genres
            abajeño de danza (danced type), 249, *249*, 252–53,
                259
            "Danza de los cúrpites" (representational),
                253–54
            "Danza de la flor" (representational), 247, 256
            "Danza de los moros" (Dance of the Moors;
                dance-drama), 249, *249*, 251, 253, 255, 257,
                259. *See also* "Danza de los soldados"
            "Danza de moros y cristianos" (Moors and
                Christians cycle of conquest dance-
                dramas), 248–49, 259
            "Danza de los negritos" (representational), 253,
                256–57
            "Danza de los soldados" (Dance of the Soldiers;
                dance-drama), 255, 259. *See also* "Danza de
                los moros"
            "Danza de las uananchas" (representational), 253
            "Danza de las uarecitas" (representational), 258

P'urhépecha people (*continued*)
    "Danza de los viejitos" (representational), 253,
        258
    ritualized warfare, with Chichimecas, 248
    son de danza (danced type), 249, *249*, 252–53, 259
  Day of the Dead (November 2), commemorations on,
    256
  demographics, 235, 240–41
  ensembles, by type. *See also* groups *below*
    bandas (brass bands)
      in intra-community competitions, 255, 259
      performance contexts, 254, 256
      repertoire of, 251, 253, 255
      replacing *orquestas*, 255
      in song accompaniment, 252
    chirimía-and-drum, fife-and-drum combinations, 251
    of chordophones (violin, guitar, Mexican *vihuela*,
        string bass), 251
    orquesta, of chordophones and aerophones, 251–52,
        255, 257
  gender roles, in traditions of, 252–53, 256, 259
  genres
    classification of, native, 248–49, *249*, 252
    culture-specific
      abajeño (danced [*abajeño de danza*]; not danced
        [sung] types)
        choreography, 252
        cultural density of, 259
        description of, 248–49, *249*
        formal structure and tempo, 249, 259
        gender roles in danced type, 252
        performance contexts, 255–56
        style characteristics (*bajeo*) of, 249, 252
      carnival *torito* ("little bull"), 249, *249*, 251, 254
      son (danced [*son de danza*]; not danced [sung]
        types)
        choreography, 252
        cultural density of, 259
        description of, 248–49, *249*
        formal structure and tempo, 249, 259
        gender roles in danced type, 252
        performance contexts, 255
        style characteristics (*bajeo*) of, 249, 252, 255
      son del Corpus (Corpus Christi's *son*), 249, 251,
        254
    mestizo
      toritos (defined by function)
        function and structure of, 249
        toritos de cambio de autoridades (for change of
          authorities), 256
        toritos de jaripeo (a type of rodeo), 255
        toritos de levantamiento (for Candlemas), 254
        toritos de quema de castillo (castle-burning), for
          patron-saint fiestas, 255
        for weddings, 252, 256
        repertoire categorized as, 252, 255
  groups, Trio Los Chapás, 250. *See also* ensembles, by
    type *above*
  history of, 247–48
  human sacrifice, in pre-contact Tzintzuntzan, 248
  identity retention, 258–59

instruments
  chordophones, adoption of, 248–49
  guitar (six-string)
    commodification and construction of, 258
    in dance accompaniment, 252
    in ensembles, 251–52
    as instrument played by women, 256
    sétima (superseded guitar of three single and
        four double courses), 251
    in song accompaniment, 249, 250, 251–52, 257
  kiríngwa (bull-shaped hollowed-out log; idiophone),
    247, 251–52, 254, *254*
language (P'urhépecha, an isolate), 235, *236* (map),
    241, 252
life-cycle
  roofraising, 256
  weddings, 252, 256
migration, 237, 250, 258
missionaries and missionization, 248
music, concept of, 248, 252
national society, interaction with, 257–58
New Year's, "The P'urhépecha New Year" (festival),
    257
patron-saint fiestas, communal
  jaripeo (a type of rodeo) in, 255
  ritualized rivalries in, "Moros" and "Soldados"
    dance-dramas as, 255
  social organization of, 257
  sociomusical competition, bands in, 255, 259
regional and communal events, social organization of,
    253, 255–56, 257
rituals and ceremonies, funerary, in pre-contact
    Tzintzuntzan, 248
songs
  culture-specific
    abajeño (not danced), as vocal genre, 248–49,
      249, 252
    canajqua (*kanákwa*; pre-contact P'urhépecha
      song), 247
    formal structure of, 251
    pirékwa (generic term for songs in P'urhépecha),
      249–50, 252–53, 257–58
    repertoire renewal, 251, 259
    son (not danced), as vocal genre, 248–49, *249*,
      252
    song-text substitution, 251
    song-text themes
      ecology, 251
      flowers as love metaphors, 250, 257
      historical narratives, 250–51
      personal narratives, 250
      weeping, 250
  mestizo
    alabanzas, 252
    for Christmas, 252
    corrido (Mexican), 252
    mañanitas (Mexican serenades), 252
    shepherds' songs, 252–53
Western traditions, adoption of, 248
purification, ritual. *See* cleansing *under* rituals and
    ceremonies, by function

purrún (Mapuche holistic term for choreography and dance-music), 156, 170–71, 184, 271
purumpacha (uninhabited or empty time; beginning of time in Inca thought), 10
pusa (*laka*; Aymara term for *siku* panpipes), in Chile, 274
pusamoreno (*sikumoreno*; panpipes; mestizo tradition of *siku* panpipes performance), in Peru, 276–78
pusi-p'iya (*pusi-ppia*; as largest type of *kena* or notched flute), 290
pusi-ppia (*pusi-p'iya*; as type of notched flute), 103
putu (natural horn related to the Aymara *pututo*, Atacameño people), 153–54
pututo (aerophone). See also *pututu*
    as bull or cow horn, Aymara people
        in Bolivia (*pututu*), 307–308
        in Chile, 153
        in Peru (*cacho*, *pitón*), 308
    as conch-shell trumpet (*kepa*, *pututu*)
        in Bolivia, 307–308
        in Peru, 305–308
pututu (aerophone). See also *pututo*
    as bull or cow horn
        in Bolivia, 102, 109, *111–12*, 115, 120, *120*, 307–308
        in Peru (*cacho*, *pitón*, *pututo*), 308
    as ceramic trumpet, *114*
    as conch-shell trumpet (*kepa*, *pututo*)
        in Bolivia, 307–308
        in Peru, 305–308
    as straight, long lip-concussion trumpet (*tira tira*), in Bolivia, 307–308

Q

qena. See *kena*
qhueppa. See *kepa*
Quechua. *See* Kechua
quena. See *kena*
Quetzalcoatl (Toltec historical figure; Mesoamerican deity), 8, 11–12, 14, 16, 190. *See also* Gucumatz; Kukulcán
Quiché-Maya people. *See also* Maya culture
    demographics, 2
    as Guatemala's civil war victims, 327
    language, 8, 235, *236* (map), 237
    Popol Vuh (creation narrative) of, 1, 8
    as refugees in Chiapas, 244
Quichua people, in Ecuador, 295, *295*, 304
Quilapayún (Chilean ensemble), 290
Quiroga, Vasco de ("Tata Vasco"), Bishop of Michoacán, 250–51

R

radio
    creole traditions, influence of, on Mbyá secular music, 177
    "Mañanitas P'urhépecha," traditional music, broadcasts of, 257

Mexican music, influence of, on Mískito *tiuns* ("tunes"), 207
string-band music, Peru, dissemination of, 133–34
University of Michoacán station, 257
XEPUR, "The Voice of the P'urhépecha" station, 257
Rama people, 196–97
Ramarâma linguistic family, 51
Ramón y Rivera, Luis Felipe, 193n, 203
Ranquel people (group subsumed under Mapuche), 169, 181, 188
Rarámuri people. *See* Tarahumara people
raspador (Spanish for "scraper"; idiophone; striated stick), P'urhépecha people, 247
rattles. *See under* idiophones
ravé (rebec; bowed chordophone, Mbyá people), 173–76, 177
The Raw and the Cooked (Lévi-Strauss), 20, 22
rebec. See *ravé*
reception, of Mexican popular music, in Mískito secular *tiuns* ("tunes"), 207
Reclus, Elisée, 196–97
recordings. *See* sound recordings
Reeland, Adrianus, 3
register. *See also* high tessitura *under* aesthetics, by peoples; texture
    Aymara people, in general
        kenas, 290
        pinkillos mohoceños, 303
        in *sikuri* (*siku* ensembles) performance traditions, 276–78
        tarkas, 303–304
    Aymara people, in Chile, in aerophone ensembles
        lakitas, 150
        lichiguayos, 151
        sikuras, 150
        tarkas, 149
    Aymara people, in Conima District, Peru, in aerophone ensembles
        pitus, 126–28, 294
        sikus (*sikuris*), 126–28, *128–29*
        tarkas, 126–28, 303–304
    Aymara and Kechua peoples, Bolivia, in panpipe ensembles
        julajulas, 104–108, *105–106*
        lakitas, 108–109, *108–109*
        sikuras, 109, *110–12*, 113, *115*
    cosmology, in three-part structure of Aymara *pitu*, *sikuri*, and *tarka* ensembles, 126
    Kechua people, in northern Potosí, Bolivia, in *pinkillu* ensembles, 301–302
Reifler Bricker, Victoria, 328
religions. *See* Christianity; cosmology
retreta (outdoor concert), 269
retuela (small double-headed drum), in Bolivia, 120
rewe (Mapuche ceremonial center; shaman's sacred space, symbol of cosmos), 155, 170–71, 182
reza (prayer; "properly musical" shamanic ritual, Kayabi people), 72
rhea, Mapuche *nguillipún* dances, zoomorphic mimetism in, 184

rhythm, by peoples. *See also* meter
  Atacameño, in ritual and mestizo music, 153
  Aymara, in Conima District, Peru, in general, 128
  indigenous groups, in Chile, in general, 146
  Kamayurá and Kuikúro, in *payemeramaraka* shamanic
      healing chants, 65–66, *66*
  Kawéskar, in songs, 159
  Kechua, in Canas Province, Peru, in *kashuas*, 137
  Makuxí, Taulipáng, and Yekuâna, in songs, 55
  Mapuche
      in Argentina, in *lonkomeo* dance-patterns, 170
      in Chile, in general, 157
  Mbyá, in rebec (*ravê*) and five-string guitar (*mbaraká*)
      music, 176, 177
  P'urhépecha, music, in conceptualization of, 248
  Xavante, in songs, 60
Ribeiro, Darcy, 50–51, 56
Ricaldi Chávez, Herminio, 327
rinkürrinküpurrún (Mapuche dance), in Argentina, 170
"Ritual of the Bacabs" (Yucatec-Maya manuscript), 187
rituals and ceremonies. *See also* carnival; cosmology;
              healers and healing; myth; sacrifice;
              shamans and shamanism
  classification of, Aymara people, in Chile, 147–48
  commemoration in, 21–22, 248, 327–28
  cosmology and, Andean peoples, in Bolivia, 102–104
  by function
      agricultural cycles
          Aymara people, in Conima District, Peru, *satiri*,
              131–32
          Aymara and Kechua peoples, in Bolivia, 102
          harvest
              Aymara people, in Conima District, Peru,
                  Candlemas as, 130
              Ayomán and Hirahara peoples, in Venezuela,
                  291–92, *292*
              Chiriguano-Chané peoples, 171–72
              Mbyá people, 174–76
              Warao people, 288, 306, 312–13, *315*
          Mbyá people, 174
          planting
              Atacameño people (*fiesta de la semilla*), 152
              Aymara people, in Chile (*Pachallampe*),
                  147–48, 151
              Kechua people, in Canas Province, Peru (*papa
                  tarpuy*), 134–37
          seasons, defining Andean ritual calendar and
              instrument use, 102–103
      carnival, as ritual. *See also* carnival
          Atacameño people, 152–53
          Aymara people, in Chile, 147–50
          Aymara people, in Conima District,
              Peru, 130–31
          Chiriguano-Chané peoples (merged with *aréte
              awati*), 171–72
          Kechua people, in Canas Province, Peru,
              139–40
          P'urhépecha people, 254–56, *254*
      cattle-marking and animal increase
          Atacameño people, 152
          Aymara people, in Chile, 147–48

Kechua people, in Peru
    in Canas Province, 139, 141
    wak'rapuku, association with, 306–307
  cleansing, Atacameño people, of irrigation ducts,
      151–54
  fertility. *See also* agricultural cycles; cattle-marking
          and animal increase *above*
      Aymara and Kechua peoples, in Bolivia, 103
      Kechua people, in Peru
          in Canas Province, 135, 137–39, *140*, 141
          wak'rapuku, association with, 306–307
      Mapuche peoples
          in Argentina (*nguillipún*), 4, 170–71, 179,
              181–85, *182* (map), *183–84*, 191
          in Chile (*ngillatún, nguillatún*), 156–57, 271,
              307, *308*
  funerary
      Apapocuvá people, 191
      Chiriguano-Chané peoples, 171
      Guahibo-affiliated peoples (*Ítomo*), 292–93, *293*
      Mískito people (*Kwal taya*), 200, 205–207,
          207–208
  initiation
      Barasana people, in Colombia, 18
      Kuna people, 218–21, 222, 278, 285–86
      Mapuche peoples, in Chile, 156–57
      Selk'nam people, 20–21
      Suyá people, 22, 67–69, 74, 191
      Toba people, in Bolivian Chaco, 18, 20
      Wakuénai peoples, 25
  patron-saint fiesta, as ritual. *See also* patron-saint
          fiestas
      Atacameño people, 153
      Aymara people
          in Chile, 147–48, 150–51
          in Conima District, Peru (Candlemas as
              harvest), 130
myth, embodied in performance of, 7–10, 20–23, 146
by peoples
  Apapocuvá, *ñe ēngaraí* (funerary, for journey of the
      dead), 191
  Atacameño
      carnival, as ritual, 152–53
      cattle-marking and increase (*floramiento del
          ganado*), 152
      cleansing of irrigation ducts (*limpia de canales*),
          151–54
      sowing (*fiesta de la semilla*), 152
  Aymara, in Chile
      carnival, as ritual, 147–50
      cattle-marking and increase, 147–48
      classification of, 147–48
      patron-saint fiesta, as ritual, 147–48, 150–51
      potato sowing (*Pachallampe*), 147–48, 151
  Aymara, in Conima District, Peru
      Achach K'umu (dance-drama), 132, *133*
      Candlemas (Candelaria), as harvest ritual, 130,
          132
      carnival, as ritual, 130–31
      satiri (dance-drama; reenactment of agricultural
          rituals), 131–32

Aymara and Kechua, in Bolivia
agricultural cycles, 102
fertility, 103
in general, 101
tinku (ritual battle and encounter), 103, *106–107*, 107–108, 116
Ayomán and Hirahara, in Venezuela, *baile de las turas* (corn harvest), 291–92, *292*
Aztec (Mexica), New Fire ceremony (creation renewal), 11–12, *12*
Barasana, in Colombia (initiation), 18
Bororo, bullroarer in, 318–19
Chiriguano-Chané
aréte awati (corn festival), 171–72
carnival (merged with *aréte awati*), 171–72
funerary, 171
Guahibo-affiliated, *Ítomo* (funerary), in Colombia, 292–93, *293*
Kalapálo, *Yamarikumalu* and *Kagutu*, gender-based power in, 21
Kamayurá
classification of musical domain, correlation with, 64
intertribal, cultural exchange and factional politics in, 65, 78–79
kwarÿ'p (commemoration of deceased chiefs), 65, 80–89, 299–300, 311–12
syntax, musical, symbolic correlations with functions of, 65, 299
takwara (bamboo dance; held to rid community of evil spirits), 65, 299, 311–12
yaku'i (held to attract benefic spirits), 65, 299–300, 311
yawari ("ocelot"; intertribal ritual; "death" as cosmic trade), 80–98, *82, 84–91, 96*
Kayabi, *yawaci*, 70, *71*
Kechua, in Canas Province, Peru
carnival, as ritual, 139–40
fertility
association with rainy season, 135
tinku (ritual battle of Chiaraje), 137–39, *140*, 141
papa tarpuy (potato planting), 134–37
Kiriri, *toré*, adoption of, 5
Kuna, shamanic. *See also* chants, system of *under* Kuna people
Icco inna (girls' body ornamentation), 222, *222*
Inna mutikit (girls' hair-cutting, one-night chicha), 218–19
Inna tutsikaledi (girls' hair-cutting, two-night chicha), 218–19
Inna wil'la (*Inna suid*; women's initiation; long/deep chicha), 218–21, *222*, 278, 285, 286
Mapuche, in Argentina, *nguillipún* (fertility), 4, 170–71, 179, 181–85, *182* (map), *183–84*, 191
Mapuche, in Chile
healing, 156–57, 189, 191
initiation, 156–57
ngillatún (*nguillatún*; fertility), 156–57, 271, 307, *308*
Mataco and Guaycurú

non-shamanic (*algarroba* festival, adolescents' rite of passage), 168
shamanic, 167–69
Mbyá, shamanic
ára pyau (annual celebration of new seasonal cycle), 174
central evening ceremony (daily), 174–75, *177*
Ñemongaraí (annual consecration of first harvest; child-naming), 174–76
Mískito, 193, 197–200, 203–207, *204–208*, 228–29
Selk'nam, Hain ceremony (initiation), 20–21
Suyá, Mouse Ceremony (initiation), 22, 67–69, 74, 191
Toba, in Bolivian Chaco, *nahôre* (initiation dances), 18, 20
Tremembé, *torém*, 51
Wakuénai
initiation, sacred "Jaguar-bone" trumpets in, 25
kwépani (male-controlled construction of mythic/human vertical relations), 26–34, 41–46
pudáli (male- and female-controlled expansion of horizontal social relations), 26–27, 34–46
Warao, *nahanamu* (harvest festival), 288, 306, 312–13, *315*
Xavante, songs for, 59
ritual battles
Moors and Christians, 248. *See also* Conquest dance-dramas *under* dance
tinku (pre-contact Andean tradition of ritual battle and encounter)
Aymara and Kechua peoples, in Bolivia, 103, *106–107*, 107–108, 116
Kechua people, in Canas Province, Peru, 137–39, *140*, 141
ritual drinking
Kamayurá people
kÿe in *yawari* intertribal ritual, 95
mohet, in *yawari* myth, 97
Wakuénai, manioc beer, in *kwépani* and *pudáli* ceremonies, 32, 36, 37
ritual inebriation
Mapuche peoples, in Argentina, 170
Mataco and Guaycurú peoples, in *algarroba* festival, 168
P'urhépecha people, 247, 254
Wakuénai peoples, 32
ritual offerings
of alcohol, coca, and food, in Kechua ritual battle of Chiaraje, Canas Province, Peru, 139
ch'alla
Aymara people, in Conima District, Peru, 130
Aymara and Kechua peoples, in Bolivia, 103
kajcher, Atacameño people, in ritual cleansing of irrigation ducts, 152–53
t'inka (*tinka*)
Atacameño people (*convido*), in sowing ritual, 152
Aymara people, in Conima District, Peru, 126, 130, 132
ritual uses of food
Kamayurá, in *yawari* intertribal ritual, 95

rituals and ceremonies (*continued*)
>> Wakuénai peoples, in *kwépani* and *pudáli*
>>> ceremonies, 25–26, 29, 31, 33–41, 45–46
> ritual whipping
>> *penitentes*, in Mesoamerica, 16–17
>> Toba people, in Bolivian Chaco, in *nahôre* initiation
>>> dances, 18, 20
>> Wakuénai peoples, 26–27, 31–34, 46
> sacred and ordinary time, fusion of, as function of
>> ritual, 182
Rivet, Paul, 2
Robertson, Carol E. (Carolina), 170, 181, 233, 328
Robles Rodríguez, Eulogio, 181
Rocha, José Maria Tenório, 296–97
rollano (wrapped curved duct flute), in Bolivia, 119, *119*, 301
Roman Catholicism. *See under* Christianity
roncadora (end-blown duct flute; one-man flute and snare-
> drum combination), in Peru
>> description of, 267, 304–305
>> music for, *305*
rondador (monistic panpipe), in Ecuador
> description of, 266, 283–85, *285*
> music for, *286*
> types of, 284
rondín (*armónica, dulzaina, sinfonía*; harmonica), in
> Ecuador, 263, 267, 316
Rondon, Cândido Mariano da Silva, 54–55
Rondônia (Roquette-Pinto), 54
roof-raising
> Aymara people, in Conima District, Peru, 130, 141
> P'urhépecha people, 256
Roquette-Pinto, Edgardo
> indigenous music, first recordings of, in Brazil, 53–55
> *Rondônia*, 54
Rosales, Diego de, 181
Rossini, Gioacchino, P'urhépecha *bandas*, overtures in
> repertoire of, 255
Roth, Walter E., 264
Rouse, Irving, 292
Rousseau, Jean-Jacques, *Dictionnaire de musique*, 53
rueda (Aymara round-dance), in Chile, 148–49, 151
Rueda, Ismael Bautista, 250
Ruiz, Irma, 294, 328
Runa Simi (Kechua for "language of the people"), 101

S

Sachs, Curt
> instrument classification system, 262
> nose flutes (*tsin-hali*), symbolism of, 54, 294
sacrifice
> animal
>> in Aymara Carnival of Isluga, Chile, 149
>> Aymara and Kechua peoples, in Bolivia (*wilancha*),
>>> 102–103
>> in Kechua ritual battle of Chiaraje, Canas Province,
>>> Peru, 138
> human
>> Aztec (Mexica) people, 14, 16
>> in pre-contact Mesoamerica, 233, 247

P'urhépecha people, in pre-contact Tzintzuntzan,
> 248
Sahagún, Bernardino de, 11, 13–14, 187
sailas (Kuna community leaders; healing-chants
> specialists), 212, 215, 217, 229
saints, Catholic. *See also* patron-saint fiestas
> All Saints' Day (Todos los Santos, November 1), 102,
>> 127, 130, 301
> in Aymara and Kechua cosmology, 102–103, 126
> Xavante praise songs (*louvores*) for, 59–60
Sajama (holy mountain), in Bolivia, 103
Salas Salazar, Marcos A., 269
Salesian order, 4, 57
El Salvador, *formerly* territory of ancient Mexico, 231
Samiris (Chipaya protective spirits), 103
San Isidro, Fiesta de (May 15), Aymara, in Conima District,
> Peru, *satiri* agricultural ritual on, 131–32
San Juan Bautista, Fiesta de (St. John the Baptist, June 24)
> in Acolla, Department of Junín, Peru, patronal, 315, *317*
> Atacameño people, 152
> Aymara and Kechua peoples, in Bolivia, 103
> Chiriguano-Chané peoples, 171
> Quichua, in Ecuador, *tundas* (flutes), for feast of, 295
San Miguel, Fiesta de (St. Michael, September 29),
> patronal, mestizo population, in Conima
> District, Peru, 126, 130
San Pedro y San Pablo, Fiesta de (St. Peter and St. Paul,
> June 29), Quichua, in Ecuador, 295
San Roque, Fiesta de, in Tarija, Bolivia, 120
Sánchez Canedo, Wálter, 308
Sandinistas, Mískito autonomy, implemented by, 197
Sandoval, Segundo, *286*
Sangüeza, Arturo, 272
sanjuanito ("St. John"; popular dance-song in the
> Ecuadorian Andes), mestizo type of, 285, *286*
Sanká people, 298
Santa Cruz, Fiesta de la (Holy Cross Day, May 3)
> Aymara people, in Conima District, Peru, *Achach
>> K'umu* dance-drama on, 132
> Aymara and Kechua peoples, in Bolivia, 102, 107
Santiago, Fiesta de (St. James)
> Aymara and Kechua peoples (Tata Santiago), in Bolivia,
>> 103
> K'ero people (July 25; as fertility ritual), *kanchis sipas*
>> played only on, 283
Sapper, Karl, 2
sary inanka (Mískito type of lament), 200–202, *200*
satiri (Aymara dance-drama), in Conima District, Peru,
> 131–32
Saussure, Ferdinand de, 83
Savia Andina (Bolivian ensemble), 290
saxophone (*saxofón*)
> as calabash lip-concussion instrument, in Colombia,
>> 269
> European
>> in army and civilian bands, 269
>> in *chirimía* ensembles, Colombia, 318
>> description of, 267
>> as imported instrument, 263
>> in Peru, 314–16, *317*
>> in P'urhépecha *bandas*, 251

scales. *See under* pitch organization
Schaden, Egon, 56
Schmidt, M., 80
seasons. *See* agricultural cycles *under* rituals and
        ceremonies, by function
Seeger, Anthony
    indigenous peoples in Brazil, interaction with
        Europeans, 52–53
    on Kiriri reconstruction of identity, 5
    musical phenomena, contextualization of, 56
    Suyá vocal genres, studies of, 22, 67–70, 68–69, 73–74
    Why Suyá Sing, 68
    yawari intertribal ritual, Suyá subtradition of, 81
Selección del Centro (Peruvian *orquesta típica del centro*),
        315, 317
Selk'nam people (*formerly* Ona; Fuegian people, in
        Argentina and Chile)
    annihilation of, 163–64
    Hain male initiation ceremony, 20–21
    history of, 145, 158–59
    Kiepja, Lola (as last representative of her people), 20–21
    name of, 161n
    songs, preservation of, in field recordings, 159, 164, 179
Seren'-mallku. *See* Sereno
Sereno (Seren'-mallku; Aymara water and water-music
        spirit), 147, 150, 154. *See also* Tata-Putarajni
Seri (Konkaak) people, 235, 238
Servicio Nacional de Asuntos Indígenas (Argentina), 163
"La Severianita" (*pirékwa*, P'urhépecha song), 258
sewei (idiophone; Warao anklet rattles), 288, 313, 315
shabori (Yanomami [Yanomamö] shaman), 190
shafshafpurrún (Mapuche dance), in Argentina, 170
shamans and shamanism. *See also* dreams; hallucinogens;
        healers and healing; rituals and
        ceremonies
    Diaguita and Moche cultures, shamanic knowledge,
        evidence of, 187
    in healing rituals
        performance, function of, 187–91
        pharmacology, 189–90
    jaguar, shamanic healers' identification with, 20
    in Mesoamerica, 234
    missionaries and missionization, eradication of, 166
    by peoples
        Apapocuvá, 191
        Apỹap, 79
        Arawété, 71–72
        Awetí (Tupi-speakers), 71–72
        Barasana, in Colombia, 18
        Chorote, 168, 189
        Desana (Tukano-affiliated), in Colombia, 20
        Kamayurá, 64–66, 66, 71–72
        Kayabi, 71–72
        Kuikúro, 65–66
        Kuna, 212–26
            ceremonies and chants (*ígala*), 212–26, 214, 216,
            228–29, 278, 285–86
            chants, transcriptions of, 218, 221, 223, 226
        Mapuche
            in Argentina, 182, 184–85, 188, 190–91
            in Chile, 154–57, 188–91

Mataco and Guaycurú, 167–69
Mbyá, 173–77
Mískito, 193, 197–99, 203–207, 204–208, 228–29
Wakuénai, 34, 37–38, 40–41
Warao, 267, 306, 313
shell-rattles (idiophones), Kawéskar people, 159
Shuar people (*formerly* Jíbaro or Jívaro), 153
sia (cacao), in Kuna healing ceremonies, 222–23
sia ba kabur unaedi (Kuna shamanic healing chant-type),
        222–23
siku (Aymara term for double-row dualistic panpipes)
    in Argentina's Northwest, 163
    in Aymara healing practices, 189
    in Bolivian Andes, 103–104, 114–17, 115, 118, 118
    description of, 266, 274–78, 274
    interlocking technique in peformance, 126–27, 268,
        274–76, 275
    in *nueva canción* groups, Chile, 290
    in Peru, 126–30, 128, 131–32, 141
sikuris (ensembles of *sikus*)
    performance traditions, 275–78
    symbolism of, 114–17, 115, 278, 320
    tunings, 275, 275
sikumoreno (*pusamoreno*; panpipes; *siku* panpipes
        performance tradition), in Peru, 276–78
sikuras (*sikuris*; type of large double-row panpipes)
    in Bolivia
        description of, 109–13, 110, 115, 118, 118
        dry season, association with, 103
        function of, 109, 113
        music for, 111–12
        symbolic dualism, in interlocking performance
        technique, 103–105, 109, 114–16
        tuning, 110
    in Chile, 148, 150–51
sikuris (as ensembles of *sikus*; double-row panpipes)
    aesthetics, 128, 267
    in Argentina's Northwest, 163
    Aymara people, in Conima District, Peru, 126–32,
        128–29, 141
    Aymara and Kechua peoples, in Bolivia, 103–104,
        114–17, 115, 118, 118
    brass bands, as replacements for, 307
    distribution of, 275
    performance traditions, in Bolivia and Peru, 274–78
    registers in, 276
    symbolism of, 104–105, 114–17, 115, 278
silbatillo (pre-Hispanic small whistle), 247
Simmons, Merle L., 10
Simon and Garfunkel, recording of "El cóndor pasa,"
        290–91
sinfonía. See rondín
single-reed aerophones. *See also specific types*
    indigenous, contested European origin of, 263
    Makuxí, Taulipáng, and Yekuâna peoples, 54
sïrángwa (P'urhépecha for "root" or "core"; ceremony
        honoring community leaders), 256, 258
sitan láwana (Mískito "sinful" secular songs with guitar),
        207
slavery, of Guaraní peoples, 164, 172
Smith Kantule, Jesús, 193n

Smith McCosker, Sandra, 278, 280, 286
snake-rattles (idiophones), P'urhépecha people, 247
snare drum
    in army and civilian bands, 269
    in *pitu* and *tarka* ensembles, Aymara people, Peru, 127
    in *roncadora* flute-and-drum combination, Peru,
        304–305, *305*
son (as P'urhépecha genre; applies to the sung and danced
        types), 248–49, *249*, 251–52, 255, 259
son del Corpus (Corpus Christi's *son*; culture-specific
        P'urhépecha genre), *249*, 251, 254
song. *See also* chant; rituals and ceremonies; shamans and
        shamanism; *specific types*
    as agency of creation, in myths, 8–11, 21–23
    classification of, for cattle-marking rituals, Aymara
        people, in Chile, 148
    epics
        areíto (*areyto*; ceremonies of Arawakan-affiliated
            Taínos), 10
        cantares históricos (Inca epics) and dramas, 10–11
        history, commemorated in sung narratives,
            P'urhépecha people, 250–51
        teocuicatl (Aztec epics), 10–11, 14
        time, intersections of myth and history in, 10–11
    by function
        children's game-songs
            Kawéskar people, 159
            Mískito people (*pulankas*), 208–10, *209*
        Christmas
            Atacameño people, 152
            Mískito people, *Krismes* (as children's dance-
                songs), 208
            P'urhépecha people, 252–54
        healing. *See also* chant *under* Kuna people; song
            under Mískito people
            in general, 188–91
            Tepehua "thought songs," 188
        laments
            Mískito *inankas*, 199–203, *200*, *202–203*, 207
            Suyá *choros femininos* (women's laments), 69
            Xavante *dawawa*, 57, 59–60, *59*, 70
        lullabies, by peoples
            Kawéskar, 159
            Mapuche, in Chile, 157
            Mataco and Guaycurú, 167
            Mbyá, 174
            Toba, 167
            Xavante, 59
        narrative
            corrido (Mexican), P'urhépecha people, 252, 255
            Mapuche peoples, in Chile, 157
        praise
            alabados (*alabanzas*)
                Catholicism, as symbols of conversion to, 17
                as invocations, in communal labor (*minga*),
                     310
                P'urhépecha people, as mestizo genre, 252
            benditos (religious folk songs; collective prayers in
               praise of saints)
               in Brazil, 297
               in Chile, 150

louvores (for Catholic saints), Xavante people,
    59–60
warfare
    Kayabi people, in *yawaci* ritual, 70, 71
    Xavante people, 59–60, *60*
work
    alabados (*alabanzas*), as invocations, in
        communal labor (*minga*), 310
    Mapuche peoples, in Chile, 157
by peoples
    Atacameño
        in Kunza and Spanish, 152
        mestizo types of, 153
        talatur, 153–54
    Aymara, in Chile
        for carnival, 148–49
        for cattle-marking rituals, classification of,
            147–48
        for potato-sowing ritual, 148, 151
    Aymara and Kechua, in Bolivia
        in general, 101–102
        tonadas (*wirsus*; functional song repertoire), 102
    Aztec (Mexica)
        Cantares mexicanos (extant poetic texts in
            Nahuatl), 2, 14, 16
        death and warfare, as themes in, 11–15
        "flower and song," concept of, 14–17, *15*
    Botocudo, 53–54
    British, folk songs, retention of, Mískito people,
        208–209, *209*
    Inca, myth in, 21–22
    Kalapálo, in female-owned *Yamarikumalu* rituals,
        21
    Kamayurá, in rituals and ceremonies
        in general, 65
        in *yawari* , 81–83, 88, *84–88*, 91–94
    Kawéskar, 159–60
    Kayabi, in *yawaci* ritual, 70, 71
    Kayowá, 72
    Kechua, in Canas Province, Peru
        for carnival, 139–40
        in general, 134, 140
        in ritual battle of Chiaraje, 137–39
    Kuna, 212. *See also* Kuna *under* chant
    Makuxí, Taulipáng, and Yekuâna, 54–55
    Mapuche, in Argentina. *See also* rituals and
        ceremonies *under* Mapuche peoples, in
        Argentina
        non-ritual (as *ülkantún*), 170. See also *ülkantún*
            under Mapuche peoples, in Chile
        ritual (*öl, nöl, ül*; term for song and poetry), 9,
            170, 184
    Mapuche, in Chile. *See also* rituals and ceremonies
        under Mapuche peoples, in Chile
        ül (song and poetry; term for music), 156
        ülkantún (as term for all sacred and "human"
            [vocal] music)
            "human" *ülkantún* (ritual and secular), styles
                of, 156–58
            sacred *ülkantún* (*tayil*), 156. See also *ülkantún*
                under Mapuche peoples, in Argentina

song (*continued*)
    Mataco (Wichí), 168
    Mataco and Guaycurú, 167–69
    Mbyá
        non-ritual
            creole, with six-string guitar, 176–77
            lullabies, 174
        ritual
            deity-specific melodies in, 175
            melodic structure of, 176
    Mískito
        inankas (laments, communication with
            ancestors), 199–203, *200, 202–203*, 207
        pulankas (children's game-songs), 208–10, *209*
        sukia láwana (shamanic), 193, 197, 199, 203–205,
            204, 207
        tiuns ("tunes"; secular, with guitar), 207–208
    Paresí, 54
    P'urhépecha
        categorized as culture-specific
            abajeño (not danced), as vocal genre, 248–49,
                249, 252
            canajqua (*kanákwa*; pre-contact P'urhépecha
                song), 247
            formal structure of, 251
            pirékwa (generic term for songs in
                P'urhépecha), 249–50, 252–53, 257–58
            repertoire renewal, 251, 259
            son (not danced), as vocal genre, 248–49, *249*,
              252
            song-text substitution, 251
            song-text themes, 250–51, 257
        categorized as mestizo, 252–53
    Selk'nam
        in Hain male initiation ceremony, 20–21
        preservation of, in field recordings, 159, 164, 179
    Suyá
        conceptualization of
            origins, 69–70
            structure, 68–69, *68*, 73
        genres, ceremonial
            akia (individual song in "shouted" style), 22,
                67–70, *68–69*, 191
            ngére (collective song), 67–69, *68*, 73
            intonation levels, in *agachi ngére* (collective songs
                for rainy season), 73
            laments (*choros femininos*), 69
    Tepehua, "thought-songs," 188, 328
    Toba, 167, 169
    Tupinambá (extinct group), 49, *50*, 53–55
    Wakuénai
        málikái (ritual speech, chant, and song), 26, 34, 46
        málirríkairi (shaman's songs), 40
        pákamarántakan (in *kwépani* and *pudáli*), 32, 34,
            37, 40, 46
        wáanapáni (stamping-tube song-dances), in
            pudáli ceremonies, 36, 38, 46
    Xavante
        classification of, by function, 59
        laments (*choros* or *dawawa*), 57, 59–60, *59*, 70
        life-cycle, daily, 57, 59–60, *61–62*

    louvores (praise songs for Catholic saints), 59–60
    lullabies, 59
    warfare, 59–60, *60*
sorcery, by peoples
    Apỹap, 79
    Kamayurá, 81
    Mískito, 195–96, 202
    Suyá, 22, 67, 69–70
sound archives
    Indiana University Archives of Traditional Music, 312
    of P'urhépecha traditional music, 257
sound recordings, field, research based on, 49–50, 54–56,
    145, 159–60, 312
Sousa, Antônio Pirineus de, 54
speech. *See* oratory
Squier, George, *Waikna: Adventures on the Mosquito Shore,*
    195, 199
stamping tubes (idiophones)
    takuapú, Mbyá people, 174–75, 178
    wáana, Wakuénai peoples, 36, 38–39, 46
    Xavante people, 60
Stannard, David E., 2
state policies
    Argentina, 163–64, 178–79
    Brazil
        pacification, 56–57
        Xingu Indian Park, creation of, 50–51, 77–78
    Mexico, P'urhépecha people, 257–58
    Nicaragua, Mískito autonomy, Sandinista
        establishment of, 197
    Peru, agrarian and sociocultural reforms, 123–24, 132
Steinen, Karl von den, 79–80
Stevenson, Robert, 263
Stobart, Henry, 301–302
Strauss, Johann, Jr., waltzes, P'urhépecha *bandas*, in
    repertoire of, 255
Structural Anthropology (Lévi-Strauss), 217–18
structure. *See* formal structure
Suárez, Jorge, 3
suduchu (Yekuana term for "panpipes"), in Venezuela, 280
suila jut'as (idiophones; rattles), in Bolivia, 121
sukia (Mískito shaman), 193, 197–99, 203–207, *205–208*,
    229
sukia láwana (Mískito shamanic song tradition), 193, 197,
    199, 203–205, *204*, 207
Sullivan, Lawrence E., 21
Sumo people, 196
Supay (Zupay; mythical ruler of evil's domain in Andean
    cosmology), 109, *113*
Suppé, Franz von, overtures, P'urhépecha *bandas*, in
    repertoire of, 255
Suyá people
    aesthetics, 67, 69–70, 73
    cosmology, in social organization and musical
        structures, 67–70
    demographics, 61–62, *63* (map), 77, 79
    education
        ceremonial leaders, rank and status of, 71
        oral transmission, 73–74
    gender roles, in continuum of oral expressions, 67, 69
    instruments, 262

Suyá people (*continued*)
language, 51, 67
music (*ngére*), as concept, 67
oratory, 67
performance practice, 70, 73
rituals and ceremonies (*ngére*)
as institutions, cultural knowledge, oral
transmission of, 74
Mouse Ceremony (initiation), 22, 67–69, 74, 191
song
conceptualization of
origins, 69–70
structure, 68–69, *68*, 73
genres, ceremonial
akia (individual song in "shouted" style), 22,
67–70, *68–69*, 191
ngére (collective song), 67–69, *68*, 73
intonation levels, in *agachi ngére* (collective songs
for rainy season), 73
laments (*choros femininos*), 69
sorcery, 22, 67, 69–70
texture, heterophony, in simultaneous multiplicity of
individual performances (*akia*), 59,
69–70
Why Suyá Sing (Seeger), 68
yawari intertribal ritual, subtradition of, 80–81. See also
yawari under Kamayurá people
Swadesh, Morris, 3
syncretism
by area, in Mesoamerica, 16–17, 231, 233–35
by country
Chile, in *bailes chinos* (dances of *chino* flute players),
273
Colombia, in tri-ethnic ensemble, San Jacinto
(Department of Bolívar), 298
Peru
Conima District, in celebrations, 130
in *cumbia andina*, 124
by peoples
Aymara, in Chile, in patron-saint fiestas, 150
Aymara, in Conima District, Peru, in cosmology of,
126
Aymara and Kechua, in Bolivia, in cosmology of,
101–103
Chamula, in interpretation of Passion, 328
Kechua, in Canas Province, Peru, 123–24, 130, 132
Mataco and Guaycurú, in rituals and ceremonies,
169
Mazatec, in carriers of healing power, 190

T

taboca. See *pífano*
Tahuantinsuyu. *See* Tawantinsuyu
Taíno people
areíto (*areyto*) ceremony, 10
Conquest prophecies, in myths of, 9
Tairona culture, 298
Takarkuna (mountain; Kuna mythic origin of the world),
216, 225

taki (*taqui*; Kechua term for sung language, rhythmicized
melody, and dance), 101–102
takirari (Andean dance genre of probable Bolivian origin)
Aymara people, in Chile, 150–51
Chiriguano-Chané peoples, in Argentina, 172
takiy (in Kechua, "to sing"), 101–102
takuapú (idiophone; female-owned stamping tube of the
Mbyá people), 174–75, 178
takwara ("bamboo")
as ritual dance, Kamayurá people, 65, 299, 311–12
as single-reed aerophone: Kalapálo, Kuikúro, and
Yawalapiti peoples, 65, 299, 311–12
talatur (Atacameño dance-songs for ritual cleansing of
irrigation ducts), 153–54
tambor (Spanish for "drum")
in Bolivia, as small drum, 118
in Chile, 272
tambor hembra. See *tambor mayor*
tambor macho. See *llamador*
tambor mayor (Spanish for "largest, principal drum";
tambor hembra or female; African-derived
single-headed drum), in Colombia, 298
tambora (small double-headed drum), in Bolivia, 120
"Tambora sinaloense," as factor of cultural change in
P'urhépecha song, 252
tamborcito (small double-headed drum), in Bolivia,
120
tamboril (small double-headed drum)
in Bolivia, 120
in Ecuador, 304
tango, *bandoneón* in, 316
tankwara (Waurá name for *takwara*; single-reed concussion
aerophone), 311
Tapayuna people, *63* (map), 77
tar pinkayllu (Chipaya name for *tarka*; duct aerophone),
in Bolivia, 303
Tarahumara (Rarámuri) people, 5, 235, 238
Tarascos. *See* P'urhépecha people
tarawi (Kamayurá single-reed concussion aerophones),
311–12
Tarawi (Kamayurá spirit, guardian of households),
311–12
tarka (duct flute)
in Bolivia (*anata*, *tar pinkayllu*), 102, 104, 116, 119–20,
119, 303–304
in Chile (*anata*), 149–50, 304
description of, 267, 303–304, *303*
in Peru, 126–28, 130–31, 141, 301
symbolism of, 116
traditional performance practice, in ensembles
(*tarkeadas*), 303–304
tarkeadas (*tarka* ensembles; repertoire of *tarka* ensembles),
Aymara people
in Argentina, 303–304
in Bolivia (*anata*), 303–304
in Chile (*anata*), 148–51, 303–304
in Conima District, Peru, 126–28, 130–31, 141, 301,
303–304
tarol (small side-drum), in *bandas-de-pífanos*, northeastern
Brazil, 296
tasba láwana (Mískito secular songs), 207

Tata Agustín (St. Augustine), Fiesta de, Aymara and
    Kechua peoples, in Bolivia, 103
Tata Inti (Father Sun; Andean pre-contact deity, *later* Tata
    Santísimo), 103, 116
Tata-Putarajni (Atacameño water and water-music spirit),
    153–54. *See also* Sereno
Tata Vasco (opera by Miguel Bernal Jiménez), 251.
    See also Quiroga, Vasco de
Taulipáng people, 54–55
Tavares, Astolfo, 54
Tawantinsuyu (Inca Empire). *See also* Inca culture
    Argentinian Northwest, as part of, 163
    epics and dramas, as representations of resistance to,
        10–11
    history of, 1–2
    number symbolism, in sociopolitical organization of,
        116
    Runa Simi (Kechua), as language spoken in Bolivia, 101
    uprisings against, 10
    warfare in, 320
taxonomy. *See* classification
tayil (Mapuche vocalization of the shared lineage soul or
        kimpeñ)
    as communication with sacred domain, 9, 156
    in healing rituals, 190
    in *nguillipún* fertility rituals, 181–82, 184
    research on, 170
    retention of, 171, 179
Tchaikovsky, Pyotr Il'yich, *Capriccio italien*, P'urhépecha
        bandas, in repertoire of, 255
ted-nono (Kuna bone flute), 225
Tehuelche people (group subsumed under Mapuche)
    as ancient inhabitants of the Americas, 158
    annihilation of, 163–64
    cultural traditions, retentions of, 179
    demographics, 169
    nguillipún (fertility ritual), variants of, 181
    shamans and shamanism, 189
tekeya (*tekeyá, tekeyĕ, wanna*; Yekuana single-reed
        concussion aerophone), in Venezuela, 267,
        311
tekeyá. See tekeya
tekeyĕ. See tekeya
tempo
    in anthropology, as insufficiently studied trait, 55
    by peoples
        Atacameño, in ritual music, 153
        Aymara, in Chile
            in carnival songs, 149
            in cattle-marking songs, 148
        Aymara, in Conima District, Peru, 129
        indigenous groups, in Chile, 146
        Kamayurá and Kuikúro, in *payemeramaraka*
            shamanic healing chant, 66
        Kawéskar, in songs, as evidence of cultural change,
            159–60
        Makuxí, Taulipáng, and Yekuâna, comparison of, in
            songs, 55
        Mapuche, in Chile, 157
        P'urhépecha, *abajeño* and *son*, as stylistic contrast
            between, 249, 259

Xavante, in songs, 60
Tenochtitlan (capital city of Aztec Empire), 1, 14
teocuicatl (Nahuatl for "divine songs"; Aztec epics), 10–11,
    14
Teotihuacan (Mesoamerican center of power, ca. 100
    B.C.E.–750 C.E.), 1
teotlatolli (Nahuatl for "speakers of divine words"), 11
Tepehua (Ódami) people, northern and southern
    demographics, 235, 238–39
    "thought-songs," 188, 328
Tepeu (creator and sovereign figure in the *Popol Vuh*), 8
teponaztli (idiophone; Aztec slit drum), 247, 251–52,
    318
tero (South American bird), Mapuche *nguillipún* dances,
    zoomorphic mimetism in, 184
texture. *See also* performance practice; register
    heterophony
        Atacameño people, 153
        Guahibo people, in monistic panpipe performances,
            280
        indigenous groups, in Chile, 146
        as simultaneous multiplicity of individual
            performances
            K'ero people, *pina pinkulucha* (notched flute),
                291, *291*, 294
            Krahó songs, 70
            in laments for the dead
                Mískito people, 201
                Xavante people, 59, 70
            Mataco and Guaycurú peoples, 167
            Suyá *akia*, 59, 69, 70
            Wakuénai peoples, in *pudáli* ceremonial cycle,
                35, 40–41
    multi-part relationships
        indigenous groups, in Brazil, in general, 56, 65,
            70, 72
        Kamayurá people, 65, 70, 72
        Kayabi people, 70, 71
        Kayowá people, 70, 72
    parallel polyphony
        absence of, in Kechua traditions, Canas Province,
            Peru, 134
        Aymara people, in Chile, in aerophone ensembles
            lichiguayos (large *kenas*), 151
            sikuras (large double-row panpipes), 150
            tarkas (*tarkeadas*; duct flutes), 149
        Aymara people, in Conima District, Peru, in
            aerophone ensembles
            cosmology, in three-part structure of *pitu, sikuri,*
                and *tarka* ensembles, 126
            pinkillus (duct flutes), 301
            pitus (*falawatus*; side-blown flutes), 126–28,
                294
            sikus (*sikuris*; double-row panpipes), 126–28,
                128, 276
            tarkas (duct flutes), 126–28, 303–304
        Aymara and Kechua peoples, in general, in
            aerophone ensembles
            pinkillos mohoceños (duct aerophone), 303
            sikus (double-row panpipes), 276
            tarkas (duct flutes), 303–304

texture (*continued*)
    Aymara and Kechua peoples, in Bolivia, in panpipe
        ensembles
            julajulas (single-row panpipes), 104–108, *105–106*
            lakitas (double-row panpipes), 108–109, *108–109*
            sikuras (large double-row panpipes), 109, *109–12*,
                113, *115*
        Chipaya people, in *pinkullo* performance, at tritone,
            301
        in general, 267–68
        Kechua people, in northern Potosí, Bolivia, in
            pinkillu ensembles, 301–302
        Kuna people, in *kammu purwi* panpipes
            performance, 227, *227–228*
        in pre-contact panpipe ensembles, 113–14, *114*
        Warao people, in *isimoi* (single-reed aerophone)
            performance, 288, 313, *315*
    polyphony (as European counterpoint), P'urhépecha
        people, 248
Tezcatlipoca (Toltec deity; double and fourfold
            manifestation of primeval Dual God
            Ometeotl), 11, 14
Tezcatlipocas (Mesoamerican deities; four sons or
            manifestations of Ometeotl, each a symbol
            and ruler of a quadrant of the universe), 11
Tiahuanaco. *See* Tiwanaku
Tikal (Maya site), 1
timbre
    homogeneity (lack of timbric mixture in aerophone
            ensembles)
        flutes, with drum accompaniment
            pinkillus (five- and six-hole), Aymara in Conima
                District, Peru, 126–27
            pitus (*falawatus*), Aymara in Conima District,
                Peru, 126–27
            tarkas, Aymara in Conima District, Peru, 126–27
        panpipes, double-row, with drum accompaniment
            lakitas, Aymara and Kechua peoples, in Bolivia,
                104
            sikuras, Aymara and Kechua peoples, in Bolivia,
                104
            sikus, Aymara in Conima District, Peru, 126–27
        panpipes, single-row, without drum accompaniment
            julajulas, Aymara and Kechua peoples, in Bolivia,
                104
        in *pífano* pairs, northeastern Brazil, 196–97. *See* also
            pífano under tuning
    as sound frequency, in shamanic healing, 188–89, 327
    timbric mixture
        homogeneity, subversion of, in Kechua *pinkillu*
            ensembles, Bolivia, 301–302
        in mestizo ensembles, Kechua in Canas Province,
            Peru, 133
time, concepts of. *See also* calendrical systems
    Aymara and Kechua peoples, in Bolivia, calendrical
        systems, syncretism in, 102
    in Inca cosmology, *purumpacha* (uninhabited beginning
        of time), 10–11
    Kamayurá daily cycle, 82–83
    in Maya cosmology, 9–14, 233–34
    in Mesoamerica, 5, 9–17, 233–35

    in myth, 9–11
    in pre-contact epics, 10–11
    sacred and ordinary time, fusion of, as function of
        ritual, 182
    in shamanic healing, 188
tina (Mískito monochord used as "string bass"), 207
t'inka (ritual offerings)
    Atacameño people, 152
    Aymara people, in Conima District, Peru, 126, 130, 132
tinku (Andean pre-contact tradition of ritual battle and
        encounter)
    Aymara and Kechua peoples, in Bolivia, 103, 107–108,
        107, 116
    Kechua people, in Canas Province, Peru, 137–39, *140*,
        141
tinya (small drum; female-owned instrumental tradition),
        in Peru, 127, 306, 320
tira tira (*pututu*; long straight trumpet with attached
        animal horn), in Bolivia, 120, 307–308
Titicaca, Lake, 103, 126, 275, 276
Titiev, Mischa, 270, 307
tiun ("tune"; Mískito secular song, with guitar), 207–208
Tiwanaku culture (Andean empire, ca. 100–ca. 1200 C.E.),
        1, 103, 152, 263–64
tlacololeros ("ocelots"; ancient dance tradition of Nahua
        people), in Mexico, *242*
Tlaloc (Nahuatl for the Mesoamerican Rain God), 18
tlamatinime (Aztec composer, poet, sage), 16
Tlapanec (Mbo me'phaa) people, 235, 241
Tlatelolco (late pre-Hispanic center of Mexica subgroup), 1
Tloque Nahuaque (Aztec "Lord of Near and Close"), 16, 23
Toba people. *See also* Mataco and Guaycurú peoples
    in Argentina
        cosmology, 166–67
        demographics, 163–64
        horse, adoption of, 166
        missionaries and missionization
            Pentecostal Church, 169
            response to, 166, 178–79
        power and status, shamanic and non-shamanic,
            166–67
        rituals and ceremonies, *algarroba* festival, 168
        song, lullabies, 167
        United Evangelical Church (hybrid), founded by,
            169, 178–79
    in Bolivia, *nahôre* dances (women's initiation into
        jaguar powers), 18, 20
tobacco
    in Barasana male initiation rituals, 18
    in Kamayurá *payemeramaraka* (shamanic healing
        ritual), 65–66
    in Kuna shamanic rituals, 215, 220, 225, 227
    in Makiritare creation myth, 17
    Mbyá people
        in healing and food purification rituals, 173
        Jakairá (god of mist [tobacco] and wisdom),
            173
    in Wakuénai creation myth cycle, 30
    in Warao shamanic healing, 190
tocoro (end-blown duct flute), 301
Todorov, Tzvetan, 9

Todos los Santos (All Saints' Day, November 1), 102, 127, 130, 301
Tojolabales (Tojolwinik'otik) people, 237, 244
tokuru (long duct aerophone), in Bolivia, 102, 119, *119*
Toltec culture
    cosmology, 11–17, *13*
    influence on Aztec (Mexica) people, 5, 14
tonada (Spanish for "melody," vocal or instrumental)
    Aymara and Kechua peoples, in Bolivia, 102
    Chiriguano-Chané peoples, 171
    P'urhépecha people, 253
tonal organization. *See* pitch organization
Tonalamatl (Aztec sacred astrological books), 12
tonos (Spanish for "tunes," vocal or instrumental)
    instrumental, for Lent (*tonos de Cuaresma*), Cora people, 300
    vocal, Aymara people, in Chile, 148–49, 151
toques (from the Spanish "tocar," to play; instrumental performance)
    Kuna people
        on *guli* (*kuli*) set of complementary flutes, 213, 273, *273*
        on *kammu purwi* panpipes, 213, 226–27, *227–28*, 280
    Wayúu people, on *massi* (single-reed aerophones), 314
toré ("clarinets," Izikowitz's term for single-reed aerophones in northern Amazon basin), 311
toré (*torém*; ritual adopted by the Kiriri in Brazil), 5
torém (*toré*; ritual practiced by the Tremembé in Brazil), 51
toritos (Spanish for "little bulls"; musical genre, defined by function)
    as culture-specific P'urhépecha genre, carnival *torito*, 249, *249*, 251, 254
    description of, 249
    as mestizo genre, in repertoire of P'urhépecha people
        toritos de cambio de autoridades (for change of authorities), 256
        toritos de jaripeo (for a type of rodeo), 255
        toritos de levantamiento (for Candlemas), 254
        toritos de quema de castillo (castle-burning), for patron-saint fiestas, 255
        for weddings, 252, 256
Totonac people, 235, 239
totoy (*uótoroyo*; single-reed aerophone, Wayúu people), in Colombia and Venezuela, 267, 313–14, *315*
tourism
    commodification of
        Andean globular ocarinas, 264, 266
        Mbyá crafts, 173
        P'urhépecha folk arts and guitars, 258
    Kuna people, exploited by, 229
Tradiciones peruanas (Palma), 289–90
"traditional," as concept, 262
trance. *See* shamans and shamanism
transcription, of indigenous music, in Brazil, 49, 53–55, 57
transculturation. *See also* acculturation; cultural change; *mestizaje*
    in the Argentinian Northwest, 163
    Mataco (Wichí) and Toba peoples, 166, 178–79

Travassos, Elizabeth, 328
travelers' accounts, 53, 198–99. *See also* chroniclers; chronicles
Tremembé people, 51
triangle (*triángulo*; idiophone), in Bolivia, 121, *121*
triángulo. *See* triangle
Trio Los Chapás (Michoacán ensemble), *250*
Trique people, 235, 241
trombone
    as calabash lip concussion aerophone, in Colombia, 269
    European
        in army and civilian bands, 269
        in ensembles of P'urhépecha people, 251, 252
trompetas. *See* trumpets
tropas. *See* ensembles, by type
Trumai people
    demographics, 61, 63 (map), 77
    yawari intertribal ritual, role in mythical history of, 79–80, 96–98
trumpets (*trompetas*). *See also specific types*
    as calabash lip-concussion instrument, 269
    as European valve aerophone
        in Argentina, 307
        in army and civilian bands, 269
        Aymara people, in Chile, 151
        in Peru, 307
        P'urhépecha people, 248, 251
        in South America, 307
    Huanca culture, dog- and deer-head, 320
    Makuxí, Nambikwára, Paresí, Taulipáng, and Yekuâna peoples, 54
    Wakuénai peoples, 26
trutruka (Mapuche long straight end-blown trumpet), 158, 170–71, 271, 307, *308*
Tse che nako (Thought Woman in Keres creation myth), 8–9
tsépani (final dances of Kuwái, in Wakuénai *kwépani* ceremonies), 32–34, 42, 46
tsidupo (Xavante two-tubed flute), 60
tsikóta (Wakuénai small *máwi*-palm flutes), 35, 38–39, 41, 46
tsin-hali (Paresí term; nose-blown ocarina), 54, 294
tuba
    as calabash lip-concussion aerophone, in Colombia, 269
    European
        in army and civilian bands, 269
        bass tuba, Aymara people, in Chile, 151
Tukano linguistic family, 51
Tukano peoples
    aerophones, made of bone, 266
    healing rituals, 189–90
    sexual symbolism, to instrumental sounds, attribution of, 268
tuktan-pulanka (Mískito children's game-songs), 208–10
tukuy (in Kechua, corruption of the Spanish *tocar*, "to play"), 101–102
Tula (Toltec city), 11
tule (single-reed concussion aerophone, Wayãpí people), 268

tuna. See *estudiantina*

tunda (side-blown flute), in Ecuador, 266, 295

tuning

    of aerophones

        carrizos (panpipes), in Venezuela, 278, 280–82, *281*

        chino flutes, 272

        julajulas (panpipes), 105, *105*

        kammu purwi (panpipes), 226–27, 227–28, 278–80, *279*

        kammu suid (flutes played in pairs), 286

        kanchis sipas (panpipes), 267, 282–83, *284*

        kenas (notched flutes), 290

        lakitas (panpipes), 108–109, *108*

        mare-mare (as pluralistic panpipes), 280–82, *281–82*

        mimby-retá (panpipes), 176, *178*

        muhusemoi (notched flute), 267, 286–88, *287*

        pífanos (side-blown flutes), in northeastern Brazil, 296–97

        pina pinkulucha (notched flute), 291, *291*

        pinkullus (duct flutes), 138

        rondador (monistic panpipe), 266, 283–85, *285–86*

        siku (double-row panpipes)

            in ensembles, "dense unison," 127, 267

            in pair of panpipes, 274–75, *275*

        in *sikura* ensembles (large double-row panpipes), 109, *110*

        trutrukas (long straight trumpets), 307

    of chordophones

        charango, 135, *136*, 137, *137*, 141

        mbaraká (Mbyá five-string guitar), 176, *177*

        ravé (Mbyá rebec), 176, *177*

    concepts of

        dense sound

            in aerophonic performance, Aymara, in Conima District, Peru, 127, 267

            in *charango* performance, Kechua, in Canas Province, Peru, 135

            dense unison, 127, 267

            instrumental and vocal correlations in, 267

        intonation levels, in songs

            indigenous groups, in Brazil, in general, 72–73

            Suyá people, 73

Tupã (Mbyá god of waters, creator of rains and thunder), 173

Tupari linguistic family, 51

Tupi-Guarani linguistic family, 51. *See also* Kamayurá people

Tupi linguistic stock, 51, 61

Tupi peoples, in general, 70–72

Tupinambá people (extinct), 49, *50*, 53–55

tura (notched flute, Ayomán and Hirahara descendants), in Venezuela, 267, 291–92, *292*

Turino, Thomas, 267, 278, 283, 301–302, 328

Turner, Terence, 26n

turtle-shell rattles (idiophones), P'urhépecha people, 247

turumi (*miorí*; violin, Chiriguano-Chané peoples), 171–72

túskalu (Atacameño tap-dance for planting ritual), 152

tusuy (in Kechua, "to dance"), 101–102

Txapakúra linguistic family, 51

Txikão people, 61–62, *63* (map), 77

Tzintzuntzan (pre-contact P'urhépecha territory, in present-day Michoacán), 247–48

Tzotzil (Batsil winik'otik) people, 237, 244

U

Ukku naibe (Kuna ritual specialist; snake-bites healer), 223–24

Ukku naibe ígala (Kuna shamanic healing chant-type), 223–24

ukur war (*neles*, auxiliary spirits; Kuna anthropomorphic figures of *balso* wood), 225

ül (*öl*, *nöl*; Mapuche song and poetry), 9, 156, 170, 184

ülkantún (Mapuche song)

    in Argentina, as non-ritual song, 170

    in Chile, as term for all sacred (*tayil*) and "human" (ritual and secular) vocal music, 156–58

ulpiada (ritual offerings), Atacameño people, 152

ülutún (Mapuche healing songs for mild or acute illnesses), 156–57, 189

umreñiduruture (Xavante flute-rattle), 60

United Evangelical Church (founded by the Toba people), 169

United States

    courting flute (Great Plains), 299

    Keres people, in Laguna Pueblo, 8–9

    Mískito people, links to, 197

    Native Americans, tribal affiliation, criteria for determination of, 2–3

    Pápago people, in Mexico and, 235, 238

    stamping-tube rattles, indigenous groups, in California, 169

    territory, formerly part of ancient Mexico, 231

Universidad Michoacana de San Nicolás de Hidalgo, 257

uótoroyo (creole name for the Wayúu *totoy*; single-reed concussion aerophone), in Colombia and Venezuela, 313–14

upawã (Xavante side-blown flute), 60

urbanization. *See* migration

Uretsete ("She Who Matters"; sacred twin in Keres creation myth), 8–9

uru'a (Kamayurá two-tubed duct flute), 65, 298–300, 311–12

Urubamba (*formerly* Los Incas; Peruvian ensemble), 290–91

Urubu-Kaapor people, 56, 73

Urubu people, 56

Uruguay, Native American population of, 2

Utatlán, destruction of, 8

V

Valdivia, Luis de, 181

Valdivia, Pedro de, 181, 270

Valencia Chacón, Américo, 275–77, 277n

Valiñas, Leopoldo, 235

vallenato (regional style), in Colombia, use of accordion in, 316

vals (Spanish for "waltz"), 150, 248, 255. *See also* waltz

Vargas, Teófilo, 311
Vega, Carlos, 163, 269–70, 293
Velasco Alvarado, Juan, 123–24
Velásquez, Ronny, 278, 286, 328
Venezuela
    dance
        baile de las turas, 291–92
        mare-mare, 280–82, 282
    instruments. See also under Wakuénai peoples; Warao
        people
        atuñsa (atunse; pair of "hatchet" duct flutes), 267,
            297–98
        cacho de venado (globular flute), 292–93, 293
        cuatro (chordophone), 280, 282
        massi (Wayúu single-reed aerophone), 267, 313–14,
            315
        tekeya (Yekuana single-reed aerophone), 267, 311
        totoy (Wayúu single-reed aerophone), 267, 313–14,
            315
        turas (notched flutes, Ayomán and Hirahara
            descendants), 291–92, 292
    panpipe performance traditions
        are're, Panare people, 280
        carrizos, 278, 280–82, 281
        jiwa, Guahibo people, 280
        mare-mare
            as dance-genre linked to panpipe music, 280–82,
                282
            as name for carrizo panpipes, 280–82
            as pluralistic panpipes, 280–82, 281
        suduchu, Yekuana people, 280, 311
        verékushi, Kariña people, 280–82
    peoples
        Ayomán, 291–93, 292–93
        Curripaco (in Venezuela, name for Wakuénai
            peoples), 18n
        Guahibo, 280
        Hirahara, 291–93, 292–93
        Kariña, 280, 282
        Makiritare, 4, 17, 311
        Panare, 280
        Wakuénai. See Wakuénai peoples
        Warao. See Warao people
        Wayúu, 313–14, 315
        Yanomami (Yanomamö), 188, 190, 262
        Yekuana, 266–67, 280, 311
        Yupa, 297–98
    rituals and ceremonies, corn harvest festivals (baile de
        las turas), 291–92, 292
verékushi (Kariña term for "panpipes"), in Venezuela,
    280, 282
vibrato. See under performance practice
vihuela (Mexican type; five-string strummed chordophone),
    in P'urhépecha ensembles,
    251
Villas Bôas, Cláudio, 78, 311–12
Villas Bôas, Leonardo, 77–78
Villas Bôas, Orlando, 78, 311–12
violin
    Chile, in Aymara orquesta, 150
    in estudiantina ensembles, 316

Peru
    in orquesta cuzqueña, 133
    in orquesta típica del centro, 315
    in P'urhépecha ensembles, 251
    turumi (miorí; Chiriguano-Chané peoples),
        171–72
Virgen de la Asunción, Fiesta de la (Assumption,
        August 15)
    Mamita Asunta (Mama Asunta; Virgen de la Asunción),
        in Bolivia, 102, 108
    mestizo population, in Conima District, Peru, 130
Virgen de la Candelaria, Fiesta de la (Candlemas,
        February 2)
    Aymara people, in Conima District, Peru, as harvest
        ritual, 130, 132
    Aymara and Kechua peoples, in Bolivia, 102
    P'urhépecha people, 254
Virgen del Carmen
    in Bolivia, 102
    in Peru, Alto Otuzco, Cajamarca, patron-saint fiesta of,
        304, 304, 309–10, 309–10
Virgen de Copacabana, in Bolivia, 102
Virgen de Guadalupe, patron of Mexico, 257
Virgin Mary (Proper of the Saints), veneration of
    in Andean cosmology, syncretic, 102, 116
    Annunciation (Fiesta de la Anunciación, March 25),
        Chiriguano-Chané peoples, 171
    Assumption (Fiesta de la Virgen de la Asunción,
        August 15)
        Mamita Asunta (Mama Asunta; Virgen de la
            Asunción), in Bolivia, 102, 108
        mestizo population, in Conima District, Peru, 130
    Candlemas (Fiesta de la Virgen de la Candelaria,
        February 2)
        Aymara people, in Conima District, Peru, as harvest
            ritual, 130, 132
        Aymara and Kechua peoples, in Bolivia, 102
        P'urhépecha people, 254
    Immaculate Conception (Fiesta de la Concepción,
        December 8), Aymara and Kechua peoples,
        in Bolivia, 102
    Virgen del Carmen
        in Bolivia, 102
        in Peru, Alto Otuzco, Cajamarca, patron-saint fiesta
            of, 304, 304, 309–10, 309–10
    Virgen de Copacabana, in Bolivia, 102
    Virgen de Guadalupe, patron of Mexico, 257
    Virgen del Rosario, Fiesta de la, in Andacollo, Chile,
        271–73, 272
Virgen del Rosario, Fiesta de la, in Andacollo, Chile,
    271–73, 272
Vom Roroima zum Orinoco (Koch-Grünberg), 54

W

wáana (idiophone; Wakuénai stamping tubes), 36,
    38–39, 46
wáanapáni (Wakuénai stamping-tube dance-songs),
    36, 38, 46
wada (idiophone; Mapuche gourd rattles), 158, 271

Waikna: Adventures on the Mosquito Shore (Squier), 195, 199
waiñu. See huayno
waka-pinkillo (duct flute), in Bolivia, 119
wakes. *See* funerary *under* rituals and ceremonies
wak'rapuku (animal horn coiled trumpet)
    in Bolivia (*waqra pututu*), 120, *120*
    in Peru (*cacho*), 306–307
Waku (Arawakan language), 18n, 25, 28
Wakuénai peoples (in Venezuela), 25–46
    chant (*málikái*; ritual speech, chant, and song), 26, 34, 46. *See also* song *below*
    composition
        in *kwépani*, stability as symbol of myth acting upon music, 33–34, 43–46. See also in *pudáli below*
        in *kwépani* and *pudáli*, ritual functions mirrored in, 26–27, 38–39, 42–46
        in *pudáli*, change and improvisation as symbols of music acting upon myth, 38–39, 42–46. See also in *kwépani* above
    dance, in rituals and ceremonies
        dzúdzuápani ("wheel" dance-songs), 25, 38–40, 44, 46
        kápetiápani (dance-songs marked by ritual whips), 26, 29, 31–34, 46
        tsépani (final dances of Kuwái, in *kwépani* ceremonies), 32–34, 42, 46
    demographics, 18n, 25
    healing, shamanic, 34, 37–38, 40
    instruments (aerophones). See also *déetu; kúlirrína; máariawa; máwi; molítu; tsikóta; wáliáduwa*
        gender attribution to, in *kwépani* and *pudáli* ceremonies, 42, *43*, 44
        mythic origin of, 25–26
        symbolism of flutes, in *kwépani*
            máariawa, 42
            molítu, 42–46
            wáliáduwa, 41–42
        symbolism of, in *pudáli*
            déetu flutes, 40–42, 44–46
            kúlirrína trumpets, 40–42, 44
            máwi flutes, 41, *43*
            tsikóta flutes, 41
    jaguar, as mythic ancestor-creator, 25, 29–31, 33–34, 38, 40, 46
    language (Waku), 18n, 25, 28
    myth-cosmology (creation cycles), 18n, 25–35, 39–40, 45–46
    performance practice, interlocking technique in *máwi* flute duets, 39
    rituals and ceremonies
        initiation, sacred "Jaguar-bone" trumpets in, 25
        kwépani (male-controlled construction of mythic/human vertical relations), 26–34, 41–46. See also *pudáli below*
        kwépani and *pudáli*
            gender roles in, 31, 38, 40–42, 45–46
            symbolic opposition and mediation in, 41–46
            symbolism of
                déetu weevil, 42, 44–46

máwi palm tree, 41
molítu frog, 42, 44–46
palm grub (*mútsi*), 41, 44–46
whipping, ritual, 26–27, 31, 33–34, 46
pudáli (male- and female-controlled expansion of horizontal social relations), 26–27, 34–46. See also *kwépani above*
social organization, 27–28, 27 (map), 36
song. *See also* chant *above*
    málirríkairi (shamanic), 40
    pákamarántakan, in *kwépani* and *pudáli*, 32, 34, 37, 40, 46
    wáanapáni (stamping-tube song-dances), in *pudáli* ceremonies, 36, 38, 46
texture, heterophony, in *pudáli* ceremonial cycle, 35, 40–41
wáliáduwa (Wakuénai sacred flutes), in *kwépani* ceremonies, 31–34, 41–42, 46
waltz, P'urhépecha *bandas*, in repertoire of, 255. See also *vals*
Wanadi (Makiritare creation deity), 17
wankara (large double-headed drum), in Bolivia and Peru, 108, *115*, 120, *120*, 269
wankarita (small double-headed drum), in Bolivia, 120, *120*
wanna. See tekeya
Wapixána people, 54
wapté (Xavante young adept), 57
waqra pututu (animal horn coiled trumpet)
    in Bolivia, 120, *120*
    in Peru (*cacho, wak'rapuku*), 306–307
war. *See* warfare
wara (Warao hollowed plant-stalk flutes), 266–67
Warao people
    cosmology, 268, 313
    healing, shamanic, 190, 267, 313
    instruments
        aerophones
            bone, as material for, 266, 286–87
            functionality of, 266, 320
            harehare (flute), 267
            heresemoi (conch-shell trumpet), 305–306, *306*
            isimoi (single-reed), 267, 288, 312–13, *313, 315*
            muhusemoi (bone flute), 266–67, 286–88, *287–88*, 291, *315*, 320
            wara (hollowed plant-stalk flute), 266–67
        idiophones, *hebu-mataro* and *sewei* anklet rattles, 288, 313, *315*
    rituals and ceremonies, *nahanamu* (harvest festival), 288, 306, 312–13, *315*
    tunings, instrumental and vocal, 267, 286–88, *287*
warfare
    as category, in hypothetical classification of aerophones by function, 320
    Chichimec (Úza) people, ritualized, 248
    "Conquest of the Desert" campaign, in Argentina, 164
    cult of, in pre-contact Tzintzuntzan, 247
    in history of
        Kuna people, 210, 212
        Mapuche peoples, in Argentina, 164, 169
        Mískito people, 193, 196
        Xingu River region peoples, 79

warfare (*continued*)
    Inca culture, *kepas* and *wankaras* in, 269, 306
    in Mesoamerica, 233
    in Mexico
        Caste War, 328
        indigenous uprisings, 237–38, 243
    naseré (Pilagá small globular flute), used in, 293
    songs, by peoples
        Kayabi, in *yawaci* ritual, 70, 71
        Xavante, 59–60, *60*
Waríperídakéna people, 18n, 25
Washington, George, 3
Wassen, Henry
    The Complete Muu-ígala in Picture Writing (with
        Holmer), 218
    *Muu-ígala or the Way of Muu, A Medicine Song from the
        Cuna Indians of Panama* (with Holmer),
        217
water drum (*kataki*; single-headed membranophone,
        Mataco and Guaycurú peoples), 167–69
Watunna (Makiritare creation myth), 4, 17
wauqu (vessel flute or ocarina, Chipaya people), in Bolivia,
        118, 120, *120*
Waurá people, 61, *63* (map), 77, 79, 311
Wayãpí people, in Brazil and French Guiana, interlocking
        technique in aerophonic performance, 268
wayno. See *huayno*
wayño. See *huayno*
Wayúu people, in Colombia and Venezuela, 313–14, *315*
weaving designs, in Cuzco, symmetrical conceptualization
        of, 137
weddings
    Aymara people, in Conima District, Peru, 127, 130
    P'urhépecha people, 252, 256
whipping, ritual. *See* ritual whipping *under* rituals and
        ceremonies
whistles: Makuxí, Taulipáng, and Yekuâna peoples, 54.
        See also specific types
Why Suyá Sing (Anthony Seeger), 68
wichu (*hito*; Yekuana duct aerophone; single closed pipe
        with finger holes), 267
wifala (courting dance), Aymara people, in Conima
        District, Peru, for Candlemas, 130, *131*
wilancha (animal sacrifice), Aymara and Kechua peoples,
        in Bolivia, 102, *103*
Williches (Mapuche peoples of the South), in Chile, 154
wirsus (ritual-specific melodies), Aymara and Kechua
        peoples, in Bolivia, 102
witakultruntufe ("she-who-carries-the-drum"; Mapuche
        ritual specialist), 9, 182, *183*
witchcraft. *See* sorcery
women. *See* gender roles
Won-yu (Won-Aisa; creator figure in Mískito cosmology),
        199–201
work. *See* communal labor
work songs
    alabados (*alabanzas*), as invocations, in communal labor
        (*minga*), 310
    Mapuche peoples, in Chile, 157
worldview. *See* cosmology
Wright, Robin, 18

X

Xavante people, 56–60
    acculturation, in praise songs (*louvores*) for Catholic
        saints, 59–60
    cosmology, in social organization of, 57, 59
    dance (*dañore*; as collective dance), 57
    demographics, 57, *58* (map), 67
    education, oral transmission, 73–74
    gender roles, in musical practices of, 57
    healing songs and instrumental music, 59
    instruments
        rattles (idiophones), 60
        stamping tube (idiophone), 60
        tsidupo (two-tubed bamboo aerophone), 60
        umreñiduruture (flute-rattle), 60
        upawã (side-blown flute without finger holes), 60
    laments (*choros* or *dawawa*; not categorized as "song" by
        the Xavante), 57, 59, *59*, 70
    language, 56
    missionaries and missionization, 56–57, 59–60
    oratory, 57, 59
    pacification, 56–57
    pitch organization, 60, 73
    song. *See also* laments *above*
        classification of, by function, 59–60
        healing, 59
        life-cycle, daily (*dañore*; as collective song)
            dapraba (morning), 57, 59–60, *62*
            dadzarono (noon), 57, 59–60, *61*
            dahipopo (evening), 57, 59
            mara'wawa (midnight), 57
        louvores (praise songs for Catholic saints), 59–60
        lullabies, 59
        received in dreams, 57, 60
        style characteristics of, 60, *60–61*
        warfare, 59–60, *60*
    texture, heterophony, in simultaneous multiplicity of
        laments' performance, 59, 70
    vocal music, primacy of, 67
Ximénez, Francisco, *Popol Vuh*, translation of, 8
Xingu Indian Park, 60–64, 67, 77–79, *78* (map), 81
Xochipili (Mesoamerican deity of song, dance, and poetry),
        11, 14, *15*. *See also* Macuilxochitl

Y

yachaj (Kechua for "wise men"), 103
Yahgan people. *See* Yámana people
yaku'i
    as duct flutes, Xingu River region peoples, 65, 79,
        299–300, 311
    as Kamayurá ritual (held to attract benefic spirits), 65,
        299–300, 311
Yámana people (*formerly* Yahgan; Fuegian people)
    history of, 145, 158
    name of, 161n
    traditional music, preservation of, in field recordings,
        159
Yamarikumalu (Kalapálo female-owned ceremony), 21

"Yankee Doddle" (as "Awbia daktar," Mískito children's
        game-song or *pulanka*), 209, *209*
Yanomami (Yanomamö) linguistic family, 51
Yanomami (Yanomamö) people
    lack of aerophones, 262, 266
    shamanic healing, 188, 190
Yaperikuli (Iñápirríkuli; jaguar-creator of primordial
        human in Hohódeni-Wakuénai creation
        myth), 18
Yaqui (Yoreme) people, 235, 238–39
yarake (dance for sowing festivals of Guahibo-affiliated
        peoples), in Colombia and Venezuela,
        292–93
yaraví (*harawi*; plaintive love song documented in colonial
        Peru in 1791–92, hypothetically linked to
        the pre-contact *harawi*), 288–90
yatiri (Aymara for "wise men"), 103
yawaci (Kayabi ritual), 70, 71
Yawalapiti people
    demographics, 61, *63* (map), 77
    instruments, *takwara* (single-reed aerophone), 65, 299,
        311–12
    in Kamayurá *yawari* (intertribal ritual), as hosts,
        80, 95
    participation of, in Kamayurá shamanic healing ritual
        (*payemeramaraka*), 65
yawari (*Jaguatirica*, ocelot; Kamayurá intertribal ritual),
        80–98
    dance and choreographic formations in, 82–83,
        90–94, *91*
    interpretation of, 88–89, 96–98
    macrostructure of, 81–88, 94–95
    martial arts in, 89–91, 95–96
    music in, critical role of, analysis of referential scales,
        89–90, *89*, 94, 96, 98
    mythical origin of, 80, 96–97

nucleus/periphery, in spatial and musical organization
        of, 81–82, *82*, 90, *90*
    songs in, 81–83, 88, *84–88*, 91–94
    sponsorship of, 81
Yekuâna (Yekuana) people
    in Brazil, 54–55
    in Venezuela, 266–67, 280, 311
Yépez Chamorro, Benjamín, 298
yeroky sondaro (Mbyá ceremonial "dance of the soldiers"),
        174–77, *177*
Yuko people, in Colombia, *atuñsa* (*atunse*; pair of "hatchet"
        duct flutes), 267, 297–98
Yupa people, in Venezuela, legend of first *atunse*,
        symbolism of, 297–98
Yvy marã eÿ (mythical "Land purged of Evil" in cosmology
        of Guaraní peoples), 172–73, 175

Z

zabumba (bass drum), in *bandas-de-pífanos*, northeastern
        Brazil, 296
zambo (as derogatory mixed-race classification), 196–97
Zamorano, Mariano, 181
zampoña (Spanish term for "panpipe"), 118, 266, 274
zapateo (choreographic rhythmic footwork)
    Aymara people, in Chile, 149
    Chiriguano-Chané peoples, 171
    P'urhépecha people, 252
Zapatista Army of National Liberation, uprisings of, 243
Zapotec people, 235, 243
Zoque (O'de püt) people
    "Danza de San Lorenzo," in State of Chiapas, *243*
    demographics, 235, 242
zumbador (Spanish term for "buzzer"; bullroarer, free
        aerophone), 318

Music in Latin America and the Caribbean
An Encyclopedic History

Malena Kuss, Editor

A project of The Universe of Music: A History,
initiated by and developed in cooperation with the International Music Council

CONTRIBUTORS TO VOLUME I

CAROL E. ROBERTSON is former President of the Society for Ethnomusicology and editor of *Musical Repercussions of 1492: Encounters in Text and Performance,* a book that received the National Publishers' Award for outstanding scholarly edition of 1992. She holds a Ph.D. in Folklore from Indiana University and is Professor of Music / Ethnomusicology at the University of Maryland, College Park.

JONATHAN D. HILL is the author of *Keepers of the Sacred Chants: The poetics of ritual power in an Amazonian society;* editor of two books, *Rethinking History and Myth: Indigenous South American perspectives on the past* and *History, Power, and Identity: Ethnogenesis in the Americas, 1492–1992;* and co-editor of *Comparative Arawakan Histories: Rethinking language family and culture area in Amazonia.* He is also the current editor of *Identities: Global Studies in Culture and Power.* He holds a Ph.D. in Anthropology from Indiana University and is Professor and Chair of the Department of Anthropology at Southern Illinois University at Carbondale.

ELIZABETH TRAVASSOS is the author of *Xamanismo e música entre os Kayabi do Parque do Xingu, Modernismo e música brasileira,* and *Os mandarins milagrosos: Arte e etnografia em Mário de Andrade e Béla Bartók.* She holds a Ph.D. in Social Anthropology from the Universidade Federal do Rio de Janeiro and is Professor of Music at the Instituto Villa-Lobos and at the Universidade do Rio de Janeiro (UNIRIO).

RAFAEL JOSÉ DE MENEZES BASTOS is Coordinator of the Núcleo de Estudos sobre Arte, Cultura e Sociedade na América Latina e Caribe at the Universidade Federal de Santa Catarina and the author of *A musicológica Kamayurá: Para uma antropologia da comunicação no Alto Xingu.* He holds a Ph.D. in Social Anthropology from the Universidade de São Paulo and is Professor of Anthropology at the Universidade Federal de Santa Catarina.

MAX PETER BAUMANN is former Director of the Internationales Institut für Traditionelle Musik in Berlin and the editor of several books, among them *World Music, Musics of the World: Aspects of documentation, mass media, and acculturation; Music in the Dialogue of Cultures: Traditional music and cultural policy;* and *Kosmos der Anden: Weltbild und Symbolik indianischer Tradition in Südamerika.* He holds a Ph.D. in Musicology from Universität Bern and is Professor of Ethnomusicology at the Otto-Friedrich-Universität Bamberg.

THOMAS TURINO is the author of two books, *Moving Away from Silence: Music of the Peruvian Altiplano and the experience of urban migration* and *Nationalists, Cosmopolitans, and Popular Music in Zimbabwe*. He holds a Ph.D. in Ethnomusicology from the University of Texas at Austin and is Professor of Musicology and Anthropology at the University of Illinois at Urbana-Champaign.

MARÍA ESTER GREBE has written several books, among them *Generative Models, Symbolic Structures, and Acculturation in the Panpipe Music of the Aymara of Tarapacá, Chile*; *The Chilean Verso: A study in musical archaism*; and *Culturas indígenas de Chile: Un estudio preliminar*. She holds a Ph.D. in Social Anthropology from The Queen's University of Belfast and is Professor of Anthropology at the Universidad de Chile.

IRMA RUIZ is co-author of *Instrumentos musicales etnográficos y folklóricos de la Argentina: Síntesis de datos obtenidos en investigaciones de campo (1931–1992)*; *Antología del tango rioplatense: Desde sus comienzos hasta 1920*; and *Mekamunnaa: Estudio etnomusicológico sobre los Bora de la Amazonia peruana*. She also served as Director for the coverage of Argentina in the 10-volume *Diccionario de la música española e hispanoamericana*, of which she was one of the principal contributors. She holds a Licenciatura in Anthropological Sciences from the Universidad de Buenos Aires and is Principal Researcher at CONICET (Consejo Nacional de Investigaciones Científicas) and Professor of Anthropology of Music at the Universidad de Buenos Aires.

RONNY VELÁSQUEZ is the author of *Mitos de creación de la cuenca del Orinoco*; *Chamanismo, mito y religión en cuatro naciones étnicas de América aborigen* and a principal contributor to the *Enciclopedia histórica de Honduras*. He holds a Ph.D. in Social Sciences from the Universidad Central de Venezuela in Caracas and is President of the Fundación Internacional de Etnomusicología y Folklore (FINIDEF). He also heads the Department of Cultural Promotion at the Escuela de Artes of the Universidad Central de Venezuela.

MARINA ALONSO BOLAÑOS holds a Licenciatura in Ethnology from the Escuela Nacional de Antropología e Historia in Mexico City and occupies the position of Researcher at the Instituto Nacional de Antropología e Historia (INAH).

E. FERNANDO NAVA LÓPEZ is one of the principal contributors to publications of the Instituto Nacional Indigenista in Mexico City and the author of *El campo semántico del sonido musical P'urhépecha*. He holds a Ph.D. in Anthropology from the Universidad Nacional Autónoma de México (UNAM) and works as Researcher at the Instituto de Investigaciones Antropológicas of UNAM in Mexico City. He is also Visiting Researcher at the Instituto de Investigaciones en Ecosistemas of UNAM in Morelia, and Visiting Professor at the Escuela de Lengua y Literaturas Hispánicas of the Universidad Michoacana de San Nicolás de Hidalgo.

DALE A. OLSEN is President of the College Music Society; author of *Music of the Warao in Venezuela: Song people of the rain forest* and *Music of El Dorado: The ethnomusicology of ancient South American cultures*; and co-editor of *South America, Mexico, Central America, and the Caribbean* in *The Garland Encyclopedia of World Music*. He holds a Ph.D. in Ethnomusicology from the University of California at Los Angeles and is Distinguished Research Professor of Music at The Florida State University in Tallahassee.

RECORDED EXAMPLES

Compact disc I

I, 1. Duet of sacred *wáliáduwa* flutes played at the beginning of *kwépani* (Wakuénai: Venezuela). *Kwépani*, or the dance of Kuwái (the primordial human being whose musical voice and instruments powerfully opened up the world), is a ceremonial exchange of wild fruits during which the sacred flutes and trumpets of Kuwái are played by adult, initiated males, while lashing each other with ritual whips (*kapéti*). In this excerpt, two *wáliáduwa* flutes are played in a circle around a display of wild fruits in the hosts' village. While the male hosts watch, the male guests, dancing behind the *wáliáduwa* flute players, strike them on their backs with *kapéti* whips, punctuating the mournful melody of the flutes. Recorded by Jonathan D. Hill (1985). Used by permission, courtesy of Jonathan D. Hill (2:18).

I, 2. *Kápetiápani* song-dance performed by men between midnight and dawn (Wakuénai: Venezuela). This performance takes place during the social and musical high point of *kwépani*, marked by the men's entrance into the women's house to dance with them. The women superimpose their own singing of *pákamarántakan* songs (the most generalized and unrestricted vocal genre in Wakuénai culture), laughing and drinking manioc liquor, while the sound of a *molítu* flute (named after a species of small frog) and sacred *dápa* trumpets (named after a large rodent) can be heard in the background. Recorded by Jonathan D. Hill (1985). Used by permission, courtesy of Jonathan D. Hill (3:56).

I, 3. *Máariawa* flute duet played shortly before dawn (Wakuénai: Venezuela). It announces the beginning of *tsépani* and is performed after the celebration of the previous night comes to a halt. *Tsépani*, the final dances of Kuwái, commemorates the mythic episode in which Kuwái ate the three nephews of Iñapirríkuli (the trickster-creator of myth and father of Kuwái) who had broken their fast by eating *guaco* fruits. Recorded by Jonathan D. Hill (1985). Used by permission, courtesy of Jonathan D. Hill (1:19).

I, 4. Two *máariawa* and three *wáliáduwa* flute players join in a simultaneous performance of their respective music during *tsépani* (Wakuénai: Venezuela). The *wáliáduwa* flutes are repeating the same music played at the beginning of *kwépani*. The superimposition of two *máariawa* and three *wáliáduwa* flutes symbolizes the integration of the five fingers of Kuwái's mythic hand and connects the five segments of his complete body, thereby closing the circuit between jaguar-ancestors and human descendants. Recorded by Jonathan D. Hill (1985). Used by permission, courtesy of Jonathan D. Hill (2:01).

I, 5. *Wáliáduwa* flute duet played in a canoe while leaving the village (Wakuénai: Venezuela). After the men send Kuwái back to the forests and rivers and away from the village by playing the *wáliáduwa* and *molítu* flutes as they embark in a canoe, the sound of Kuwái's flutes, fading into the distance, marks the end of *kwépani*. Recorded by Jonathan D. Hill (1985). Used by permission, courtesy of Jonathan D. Hill (1:48).

I, 6. *Máwi* flute duet, playing the highly standardized and most commonly heard music during the first phase of male-owned *pudáli* ceremonies (Wakuénai: Venezuela). This music accompanies the opening dances, named after various species of *Leporinus* fish. *Máwi*, a species of palm used to make flutes and trumpets, is also the name given to the longest flutes. The low and rumbling sound of the ceremonial *kulírrina* trumpets, named after a species of large, striped catfish, imitates the sound of a river teeming with fish. If *kwépani* enacts a socioreligious process of constructing the vertical, generational dimension of social and cosmic relations, *pudáli*, the ceremonial exchange of meat and manioc products between affines, represents the horizontal opening up of the family by creating and renewing relations of exchange between groups outside the blood-related patrilineal family. At a symbolic metalevel, however, *pudáli* transcends and overrides initial social oppositions between hosts and guests, and kin and affines, and its music, although secular, outlines a process of collectively constructing the space-time of mythic beginnings. Recorded by Jonathan D. Hill (1981). Used by permission, courtesy of Jonathan D. Hill (1:49).

I, 7. Two *máwi* flutes and *déetu* flutes (named after a species of coconut palm weevil) performing simultaneously during the opening dances of *pudáli* (Wakuénai: Venezuela). In addition to the duet of *máwi* flutes, musicians playing other instruments (such as *déetu* flutes) often join in the *leporinus* dances to enlarge the procession, creating a heterophonic collage framed by the low-sounding *máwi* and the ear-piercing *déetu* flutes. Recorded by Jonathan D. Hill (1981). Used by permission, courtesy of Jonathan D. Hill (1:49).

I, 8. *Déetu* flute performance during the late-night period of *pudáli* (Wakuénai: Venezuela). The performance of *déetu* flutes to the exclusion of other instruments marks an important transitional phase in the meaning of *pudáli*. By playing their flutes into the space between the roof and the wall of the hosts' house, the guests imitate the natural behavior of *déetu* insects, metaphorically "sucking" fermented drinks out of their hosts. When the hosts bring out manioc beer, which the guests drink and regurgitate, they also are evoking the transformational power of shamanic curing (sucking and spitting out a disease). The reversal of basic physiological processes (sucking and vomiting) evokes the reversible space-time of shamanistic transformation, signaling the transition from a secular process of food exchange to a mythical process of dismantling symbolic boundaries between humans and animals, and between men and women. Recorded by Jonathan D. Hill (1981). Used by permission, courtesy of Jonathan D. Hill (0:44).

I, 9. *Dzúdzuápani*, or "wheel-dance," one of the sub-genres of *wáanapáni* song-dance performed around a bonfire just before dawn, at the end of the transitional late-night period in female-owned *pudáli* ceremonies (Wakuénai: Venezuela). *Wáanapáni* is a generic term for dance-songs performed with *wáana* stomping tubes. In female-owned *pudáli* ceremonies, *wáanapáni* dance-songs replace the function of *kulírrina* trumpet-dances in male-owned *pudáli* ceremonies. During the performance of *dzúdzuápani* ("wheel-dance"), a fish-net is suspended between two poles carried by the lead singers of the hosts and guests and their female dance-partners, who whirl around the fire in rapid motions to prevent the net from dipping into the flames. Two line formations of singers and female dancers respond to the verse "We open the jaguar's mouth" by moving away from each other, reversing this motion in response to the lead singers' "I want to close the jaguar's mouth." Recorded by Jonathan D. Hill (1981). Used by permission, courtesy of Jonathan D. Hill (4:59).

I, 10. *Dzawírra* (fish), *máwi* flute duet that exemplifies the individualized and improvisatory approach to the music performed during the final stage of feasting in *pudáli*, expressing in musical terms the dissolution of boundaries between hosts and guests, and kin and affines. Whether male- or female-owned, the three stages of *pudáli* outline a process of establishing, transforming, and dissolving the social boundaries between hosts and guests, or kin and affines. Thus, the unchanging character of the standardized flute duets performed during the opening stage of *pudáli* contrasts with the improvisatory character of the flute duets played during the third stage. These are based on variations that, taking on different shapes with each performance, elaborate on a six-pitch theme played in an interlocking manner on longer male and shorter female *máwi* flutes. The duets are named after animal species, the *dzawírra* (a fish) in this case (Wakuénai: Venezuela). Recorded by Jonathan D. Hill (1981). Used by permission, courtesy of Jonathan D. Hill (1:57).

I, 11. *Dapraba* (morning song), sung by Tsipre (Xavante: Brazil). The Xavante, a Gê-speaking group, totaled approximately 5,000 persons ca. 1987. The music of the Xavante was studied by Desidério Aytai, who contributed one of the most extensive repertoires of transcriptions on any indigenous group in Brazil. Xavante songs are received in dreams, when the spirit wanders through distant places. The extensive repertoire of the Xavante includes songs for rituals; songs related to subsistence, such as hunting and home construction; and songs articulating the cycle of daily life, such as morning, noon, evening, and midnight. The generic term that designates song and dance is *daño're*. The *dapraba*, one of several types of *daño're*, are differentiated from other daily songs by dance gestures and the appropriate time at which they are performed. Although received in dreams by individuals, the process of transmission makes these songs collective. *Daño're* are male-owned songs associated with public life. In addition to the predominantly collective and vocal nature of Xavante music, other characteristics include a firmly regular rhythmic pulse, as illustrated in this *dapraba* sung by Tsipre. Recorded by Desidério Aytai in the Sangradouro area in 1969 or 1974. Used by permission, courtesy of Elizabeth Travassos (1:40).

I, 12.   *Akia* ("Akia de adultos," or song of adult males in "shouted" style) (Suyá: Brazil). The Suyá are a Gê-speaking group of approximately 150 persons who live on the Suyá-Miçu River, a tributary of the Xingu. Practically all Suyá music is vocal. Singing is part of a larger system that assigns high value to oral expression, and to masculine oratory in particular. The music of the Suyá has been studied by Anthony Seeger, the author of a paradigmatic musical anthropology (*Why Suyá Sing*) published in 1987. He approached Suyá vocal genres from the comparative perspective of a continuum ranging from speech to song, rather than as a roster of discrete or contrasting forms. According to Seeger, songs are restricted to certain sex-, age-, and named-based groups. The singing of songs in "shouted" style (*akia*), for instance, is both a form of expression and a way of achieving culturally sanctioned ideals for adult men. The Suyá conceptualize the structure of their songs by separating, in each strophe, the parts sung with text (*sinti iarén*, or "telling the name") and parts in which only song-syllables are sung (such as the *kuré*, or coda, sung to the syllables te-te-te-te in this example). As a whole, songs consist of two parts (*kradi* and *sindaw*), each of which is structured according to the same four corresponding sections ("song syllables," "approaching the name," "telling the name," and "coda"). These individual, masculine songs, are a source of pride for the Suyá. In this performance, the individual singing of an *akia* is followed by several men singing their *akia* independently and simultaneously, as is the custom in Suyá ceremonies. *Akia* are, in a certain sense, identified with individuals, unlike the collective songs called *ngére*, which are identified with ceremonial groups and sung in unison. According to the Suyá, men sing *akia* for their sisters. (In other contexts, *akia* means "to shout.") In Anthony Seeger's interpretation, the shouted style of these songs overcomes the spatial, social, and psychological separation between a Suyá man and his sisters, given that, after a man leaves his birthhome, he must follow rules of residence restricting relations with female blood relatives. Included in *A arte vocal dos Suyá*, one LP and notes, side B, band 4, compiled by Judith Seeger, Anthony Seeger, and the Suyá community. São João del Rei, Brazil: Tacape 007, 1982 (Série etnomusicológica). Used by permission, courtesy of Anthony Seeger (3:16).

I, 13.   Dusk "instance" of the Yawari studied and recorded by Brazilian anthropologist Rafael José de Menezes between June 7 and June 18, 1981, with the Kamayurá as hosts and the Matipúhy as guests; the Yawalapiti were associated with the Kamayurá at that time and also described themselves as hosts (Brazil). The Kamayurá are a Tupi-Guarani-speaking group of approximately 200 persons living in a single village in the southern part of the Xingu Indian Park, in the State of Mato Grosso. The ethnically different indigenous groups living in the southern part of the Upper Xingu River region that Menezes Bastos calls "Xinguano" make up an intertribal, polyethnic society in which intertribal rituals play an extremely important role. According to Menezes Bastos, these intertribal rituals only can be considered in the context of cultural exchange and factional politics. He also notes that the Kamayurá system of social articulation in relation to other Xinguano groups should be defined as a process of organization of differences, rather than viewed from the perspective of sociocultural uniformity. The musical practices of the Kamayurá have been studied by Menezes Bastos, the author of a major study (*A musicológica Kamayurá*) published in 1978 and reissued in 1999. Within the eminently relational world of Xinguano groups, the Yawari ("Jaguatirica," or ocelot) is an intertribal ritual whose wide dissemination in the region led Menezes Bastos to call it "Xinguano" without detracting from its origin in a historical juncture that joins the Trumai with the Tupi Kamayurá and Awetí. Even the Juruna and Suyá, who live in the northern part of the Xingu Indian Park and are among those groups Menezes Bastos calls "Xinguese," have marginal access to this ritual. In this author's interpretation, Yawari is a discourse on cosmic trade, using the world of humans as a metaphor. The Dusk "instance" documented in this example marked the formal opening of the Yawari at the beginning of the Kamayurá day on June 7, 1981. The Yawari repertoire is classified by the Kamayurá according to emblematic animals. This recorded example constitutes an "instance" of the Dusk sequence from the repertoire of the Forest Cat. The "instance"—a term Menezes Bastos uses to define a concrete manifestation in performance of conceptual rules not operating at a conscious level in the minds of the practitioners—consists of *cantos* (a sequentially arranged group of songs) and vignettes (characteristically, onomatopoeias of the voices of various animals performed by the periphery, within an overall distribution of roles and space into nucleus and periphery). The four vignettes (1, 8, 9, and 10) and the six songs (2, 3, 4, 5, 6, and 7) comprising the Dusk "instance" are performed without interruption in the following order: 1, M; 2, Motekey; 3, He nu yawari; 4, Horowỳ; 5, Kamiwaye; 6, Nuterihiyu; 7, Yahaha; 8, M; 9, T; 10, T'. In Menezes Bastos' interpretation, the texts of songs 2 through 5 stress disjunction (to burn, to desire, as in jealousy and envy), while the texts of songs 6 and 7 highlight conjunction (to share) within the ritual's overall symbolic system. Used by permission, courtesy of Rafael José de Menezes Bastos (7:19).

I, 14. *Julajula* panpipe players performing a *baile chúkaro* (Kechua and Aymara: Bolivia). *Julajulas* are single-row panpipes that play in pairs of *ira* (leader) and *arka* (follower) instruments, performing the pitches of a melody in interlocking fashion. *Julajula* ensembles (*tropas*) perform without drum accompaniment. This group of campesinos from Lagua Lagua (Cantón Santiago, General Bilbao Province, Department of Potosí) comprised eight pairs of different-sized *julajulas* (sixteen panpipes) tuned in five octave registers distributed as follows, from low to high: one pair of *machus*, one pair of *malis*, two pairs of *likus*, three pairs of *tijlis*, and one pair of *ch'ilis*. The *baile chúkaro* of the *julajulas* is performed during the dry season, particularly during the Fiesta de la Cruz (Holy Cross Day, May 3). The oldest and most experienced musicians play the largest and lowest panpipes. Recorded by Max Peter Baumann (June 1980, Q 706). Used by permission, courtesy of Max Peter Baumann (2:16).

I, 15. *Lakita* panpipe players performing a *wayñu* (huayno) (Aymara and Kechua: Bolivia). These are double-row panpipes that perform in ensembles with drum accompaniment. *Lakitas* ("the chosen ones") are played during the dry season, as is usually the case with panpipes. The *lakita* dancers express the ritual purification and preparation of the land before sowing begins, entreating Pachamama (the Earth Mother) to grant a good harvest. The group Mallkus de Aransaya y sus Lakitas was recorded in the community of Lauro Llokolloko (Cantón Caquiaviri, Pacajes Province, Department of La Paz). Accompanied by four *wankaras* (drums), twelve *lakitas* (namely six pairs of *ira* and *arka* instruments) are playing in three octave registers distributed as follows, from low to high: two pairs of *sanjas* or *jachas*, three pairs of *likus*, and one pair of *ch'ilis*. Recorded by Max Peter Baumann (October 1978, Q 567). Used by permission, courtesy of Max Peter Baumann (2:35).

I, 16. *Sikura* panpipe players performing a *wayño* (Aymara and Kechua: Bolivia). *Sikuras* are a large type of double-row panpipes and play in ensembles with drum accompaniment. Unlike the *julajulas* and *lakitas*, whose ensembles include different-sized instruments, an ensemble of *sikuras* consists of same-sized panpipes playing their melody within the range of an octave, with the *liku* and *ch'ili* pairs sounding an octave apart and the *tarke* pair playing a fifth above the *liku*. Instead of performing the pitches of a melody in an interlocking manner, as do the pairs of *ira* and *arka* *julajulas* and *lakitas*, *sikuras* play melodies in an alternating technique whereby the *arka* instrument always echoes the pitch played by the *ira* panpipe. In this performance by campesinos from Chilca Grande (Tapacarí Province, Department of Cochabamba), the panpipe players, accompanying themselves with four *cajas* (drums), dance in a circle around three dancers representing an old man (*achachi* or *abuelo*), his small child (*kulyaqa*, or child of the ancestors), and the *umajala* ("naked head," perhaps symbolizing death) who rings a llama bell (*campanilla*). Outside the circle there is an old woman, the *awicha* or *abuela*, who is the child's mother. The *achachi* adopts the symbolic role of the old man who plows the field and represents the male spirit of the mountain; the *awicha* is the woman who sows and represents the spirit of the arable land; both of them are constantly surrounded by danger. The circle dances of all these panpipe ensembles are associated with the dry season of the agricultural cycle and represent the giving of thanks for the past harvest, as well as the prayers for the next season. These are addressed to Pachamama and Pachatata, who are manifestations of the Andean concept of the earth as a dualistic principle of energy, and respectively the female and male spirits of the ancestors (*awicha* and *achachi*). The *wayño* (*wayñu* or *huayno*) documented in this example was performed on nine *sikuras* (five *likus*, one pair of *tarkes*, and one pair of *ch'ilis*) accompanied by four *cajas* (drums), one *pututu* (cow horn), and a *campanilla* (small llama bell). Recorded by Max Peter Baumann (June 1980, Q 689a). Used by permission, courtesy of Max Peter Baumann (3:24).

I, 17. Untitled piece in the *lento* genre typical of *sikuris*, or ensembles of *siku* panpipes, performed by the group Centro Social Conima, which illustrates one of the wind ensemble traditions practiced in the Aymara-speaking rural district of Conima on the northern shore of Lake Titicaca (Province of Huancané, Department of Puno, Peru). *Sikus* are double-row panpipes played in pairs of 'ira (leader) and *arka* (follower) instruments that perform the pitches of a melody in interlocking fashion. Consistent with tradition, ensembles of *sikus* or *sikuris* in Conima are accompanied by large double-headed drums *(bombos)*. Conimeño musical culture revolves mostly around five Andean wind ensemble traditions, each with its own specific genres and association with particular occasions and times of year. *Sikus* are played at public fiestas during the dry season (Easter through October) and at weddings throughout the year. With one exception, only men play musical instruments in Conima, and, as is generally true in the Andes, melodic types of instruments are not mixed in indigenous ensemble traditions, which adhere to the aesthetic principle of timbric homogeneity. The high value placed on unity and identity of the community overrides individual identity. Communal solidarity is reflected in the aesthetic ideal of "playing as one," or "sounding as one instrument" in *sikuri* ensemble performances. The resulting sound is that of a "collective single instrument" within which individuality, rather than being obliterated, is subsumed into the dense texture of the whole. On unisons and octaves, for instance, pitch variations of up to forty cents (twenty cents above and below) are common in the tuning of a given pair of *sikus* and between instruments of a tuned ensemble, thus creating a dense sonic fabric that Thomas Turino calls "dense unison." The related concept of "dense sound," also according to Turino, refers to a consistent overlapping and blending of discrete fundamentals and overtones to produce a thick unified texture. Individual variations and improvisatory techniques are present, oftentimes moving performances from parallel polyphony to blended heterophony without causing an individual player to stand out. *Sikuris* may be organized into three groups covering a range of three parallel octaves, within which the middle or *malta* register is the main melody-carrying voice and therefore is played by the largest number of pairs of instruments, with the high and low groups balanced around the *maltas* at the center in a symmetrical distribution of roles that Turino relates to Aymara cosmology. The strong identity of individual groups, for which music serves as a primary emblem, also fuels a tendency toward intercommunity musical competition. Twenty panpipe players (ten pairs) and two *bombos* (drums) are heard in this example. This performance, which took place at the home of one of the musicians, was recorded by Thomas Turino (August 1986). Used by permission, courtesy of Thomas Turino (3:11).

I, 18. Solo *charango*-vocal rendition of a *tuta kashua* performed by Raúl Quispe, a boy in his late teens who was recorded at the weekly market in Descanso (Province of Canas, Department of Cuzco, Peru). This example illustrates one of several musical traditions practiced by Kechua speakers who live at high altitudes in districts around Descanso, especially Langui, Layo, and Checca, in the Province of Canas. According to Thomas Turino, whose observations were confirmed by local stereotypes, Caneños are more individualistic in spirit than the Kechua valley people or the Aymara in Conima. The older musical traditions practiced by Kechua-speaking people in Canas include Kechua songs and such instruments as the *pinkullu*, *kena*, and *charango* (a chordophone). In contrast to Conima in the Department of Puno, music in Canas in the Department of Cuzco sometimes is performed solo in formal and informal contexts; vocal music is extremely important; and the *charango* has been incorporated into local festivals and agricultural rituals, including the *papa tarpuy* (potato planting). The Andean *charango*, which by its very nature is a mestizo instrument, was developed during the colonial period, around the turn of the seventeenth century. Although the instrument is a hybrid innovation based on the model of the guitar or vihuela but smaller in size, both the Kechua-speaking people as well as mestizos in the Province of Canas associate it with the former group. In this area, and excepting the *papa tarpuy* fiesta, the *charango* is played primarily during courtship by young Kechua-speaking musicians who perform a limited repertoire of *kashuas* or circle dances. Mestizos play the *charango* elsewhere in southern Peru, but in a manner that differs fundamentally from the indigenous approach to performance. For instance, several different tunings are used by Kechua speakers in Canas, depending on the player, and they can be a step or more above the standard A minor tuning used by mestizos. The higher-pitched tunings, the flat-backed sound box, and the numerous thin metal strings that characterize the instruments played by Kechua speakers create a sound that is consistent with the Andean preference for a high, strident, and dense sound. Techniques of performance also differentiate Kechua speakers from mestizo players: the former use only strumming, while the latter alternate between plucking and strumming within a single performance. Also characteristic of the indigenous style is a melodic approach to performance whereby the melody is played on a single course and strummed along with the remaining open strings, creating a dense sound. During courtship, young men use a limited repertoire of *kashuas*. Two main types of *kashuas* are used for courting in Canas, namely the "day" (*punchay*) and "night" (*tuta*) *kashuas*, whose melodies rely on three and four pitches, respectively. The performance of a *tuta kashua* (or "night" circle dance) by Raúl Quispe illustrates the indigenous style. The instrument used by Quispe had twelve metal strings. Recorded by Thomas Turino (March 1981). Used by permission, courtesy of Thomas Turino (2:43).

I, 19. Carnival dance recorded in Layo (Province of Canas, Department of Cuzco, Peru). An unidentified, informal group of people from the districts of Langui and Layo are performing during the celebration of carnival, which is an important context for *pinkullu* performance. *Pinkullus* are duct flutes associated with the rainy season. During carnival, the capital of each district holds a major fiesta. The carnival dance is performed by couples or by groups of men and women. Men play *pinkullus*, and both men and women sing to accompany the dance, which combines a wealth of meaning. Carnival is a time of heightened sexual activity and earth and animal fertility rituals. The male dancer's role as a male llama combines the images of animal fertility and human sexuality. Men play the carnival melody solo, in pairs, or in groups in unison. They also may alternate performing the melody on *pinkullus* and singing verses. Often one or two women sing basically in unison with their partner's flute melody. Toward the end of the performance, men and women also alternate sung verses in a kind of duel between the sexes. The performance includes occasional *pinkullu* interludes. As the performance warms up, men and women begin their singing simultaneously, without reference or concern for where the other may be, melodically or in the text. These are gleefully aggressive shouting/singing competitions during which people enter into the singing, play *pinkullus*, and dance at will. Recorded by Thomas Turino (February 1982). Used by permission, courtesy of Thomas Turino (3:37).

I, 20. "Arakú," *mimby retá* (panpipe) tune recorded in Cuña Pirú, Province of Misiones, performed by Agustina Cáceres and Luisa Ramírez (Mbyá: Argentina). The Mbyá are a Guaraní-affiliated group of mostly subsistence farmers who, less than a century ago, migrated to the northeastern Province of Misiones in Argentina from bordering Paraguay, by all accounts their original habitat. The present Mbyá population in Argentina should not be considered a remnant of the Guaraní from Jesuit settlements in what is today the Province of Misiones, in part because they were the most fierce in resisting that force. Almost all musical expression currently in practice is sacred or associated with ritual. Vocal music is the domain of men and women, but the function they fulfill varies according to the role assigned to each in ritual. Instrumental performance is gender-specific. While the rebec (*ravé*) and guitar are played only by men, the *mimby-retá* panpipes are played only by women. The case of the *mimby-retá* or female flute is unusual. It is a type of bamboo panpipe consisting of loose tubes (from 5 to 8, usually 7) on which two women play a single melody in interlocking fashion. They distribute among them the tubes of one panpipe according to the specifications of each melody (for instance, 4 and 3; 4 and 2; 5 and 2; or 3 and 3). The second flute player is always responsible for a short repeated pattern of two, three, or four pitches, creating with the first flute a composed, single melody in predominantly conjunct motion, or a diaphony. Although a *mimby retá* performance can be addressed to a deity, most women play it for entertainment. Recorded by Irma Ruiz (1980). Used by permission, courtesy of Irma Ruiz (0:30).

I, 21. Ritual dance of the Mbyá (*toque para danza*) for rebec and five-string guitar recorded in Fracran, Province of Misiones, performed by Mario Silva on the rebec and Gervasio Martínez on the guitar (Mbyá: Argentina). Traditional practice among the Guaraní-affiliated Mbyá includes the appropriation of a three-string rebec (*ravé*) and a five-string guitar (the *mbaraká*), two chordophones that the Mbyá have assimilated fully into worship. Brought from Europe during the colonial period, these instruments have been appropriated to the extent that they no longer are considered exogenous. Although the Mbyá are fully aware of the tuning and performance techniques of the widespread six-string guitar, playing with skill some of the "exogenous" creole dances they hear on the radio, they retain the five-string *mbaraká* and its tuning for their own repertoire. These distinctive features allow them to clearly separate one guitar from the other and to claim the five-string guitar as their own, along with the rebec. The vitality of traditional practices varies from village to village. In communities that can claim the presence of a ritual specialist, one or two daily ceremonies may take place. The daily ceremony at dusk is preceded by a dance performed in the *oká*, or dance-space in front of the house of the religious leader, which is also the place of worship, or *opy*. The presence of the religious leader, his wife, and the political chief lends an institutional character to the dance as preamble to the ritual. All participants meet in the *oká*—men, women, and children—and dance to rebec and guitar music for an hour or more until dark. The counterclockwise circle dance is suggestive of aggression and resistance, expressed by the subtle movements of the dancers. The Mbyá experience all ritual acts as earthly replicas of events in the heavenly domain or "city of the gods." In the *oká*, the dancers represent the soldiers (*sondaro*) of deities; just as soldiers guard the deities, dancers protect the sacred space of worship (the *opy*) by dancing outside, in front of the house. Their action signifies the daily renewal of a sense of respect for the gods and those who represent divine power on earth. The generic term for this dance is *yeroky sondaro* (dance of the soldiers). The rebec carries the melodic line, and the guitar's strumming on open strings underscores the rhythmic pulse. While the rebec melody proceeds in duple simple meter, the guitar accompaniment maintains a rhythmic subdivision of the beat into triplets. From village to village, the tunings of both chordophones preserve the same intervallic distance between the pitches of each string, but the concept of pitch is relative, not absolute. This example documents one of several *toques de danza* performed during the *yeroky sondaro*, or dance of the soldiers, which lasts until nightfall. Recorded by Irma Ruiz (1977). Used by permission, courtesy of Irma Ruiz (2:03).

I, 22. *Kawel tayil* ("horse" lineage song), as delivered by ritual specialist Carolina Milliapi in Huilquimenuco, Province of Neuquén (Mapuche: Argentina). The *nguillipún* is a fertility ritual currently celebrated by Native American peoples of southern Chile and Argentina. It used to be held to increase animal and crop fertility, mark a successful harvest, or entreat deities when a community was in crisis. At the present time, however, the celebration of *nguillipún* is limited to an annual cycle based on the completion of summer grazing and the marking of lineage flocks. The objective of *nguillipún* is to reach the inhabitants of sacred time through the performance of chants and dances that, by breaking down and fusing the temporal boundaries between sacred and ordinary time, can move supernatural beings to compassionate action. The *nguillipún* is led by two adolescent girls (*kalfumalén*) and two adolescent boys (*piwichén*) who embody the part-human, part-supernatural nature of the original ancestors. At daybreak, men stand behind the altar and invoke the inhabitants of sacred space-time through a form of ritual discourse (*lukutún*), while women of their lineage stand behind them and sing *tayil*, thereby "pulling" the lineage soul out of the bodies of the male supplicants, into the sacred ritual space, and into the time of sacred beings. *Tayil* can be defined as a vocalization of the lineage soul. It is a vocal genre that gives tangible, active form to the cumulative soul shared by all members (living, deceased, and unborn) of a lineage. The lineage soul, or *kimpeñ*, can be actualized by being "birthed" (*entún*) through performance. Inheritance patterns and associations of *tayil* with the birthing process make this repertoire the exclusive domain of women. Recorded by Carol E. Robertson (1995). Used by permission, courtesy of Carol E. Robertson (1:46).

I, 23. Women during a *nguillipún* held in Malleo, Province of Neuquén, performing for the saddling of ritual horses of the *piwichén*. In addition, the ritual specialist Carolina Milliapi is performing on the *kultrún* (Mapuche: Argentina). The female ritual specialist is called *witakultrunfe* (she-who-carries-the-drum). The *kultrún* played by the female ritual specialist is an icon depicting the Mapuche's multi-layered conception of cosmic space. As a symbolic microcosmos, the *kultrún* represents not only a dynamic synthesis of the universe, which embodies both immaterial and material components, but also her owner, the ritual specialist. Recorded by Carol E. Robertson (1995). Used by permission, courtesy of Carol E. Robertson (2:56).

Compact disc II

II, 1. *Sary inanka*, one of several types of laments (Mískito: Honduras and Nicaragua). The Mískito are a thriving ethnic nation inhabiting the part of the Caribbean coastal area of Honduras and Nicaragua that conquistadores called "La Mosquitia." *Inanka*, a generic term for laments, refers to one of two general categories of songs of the Mískito. The laments, sorrowful songs, or wailful singing, are intimately related to the sound of thunder during the tropical storms that beseech La Mosquitia for eight months of the year. *Inankas* express deep emotions, such as sorrow, hope, resignation, supplication, gratitude, indignation, hatred, curses, joy, and personal exaltation. Normally, *inanka* texts address the spirits of ancestors, reaffirming and establishing earthly as well as spiritual communication between them and a world that is familiar to the spirits of the dead because it was a part of their experience when they were alive and shared it with their living relatives. The composite term *sary inanka*, or mournful weeping, alludes to all types of recollections of past grief. In general, all *sary inanka* addressed to ancestors or to dead children avoid exteriorizing grief, except for sobbing at the end of each melodic phrase. Recorded by Ronny Velásquez (1975–1986). Used by permission, courtesy of Ronny Velásquez (1:39).

II, 2. *Inanka upla pruan bara*, or collective laments for the dead (Mískito: Honduras and Nicaragua). For the Mískito, death is the start of a journey to the unknown; the road is dark, yet conceived as an intangible representation of the world on earth. Through this road, the spirits of the dead will travel the same path they followed during their lifetime. The singing of *inanka upla pruan bara* is the vehicle through which the entire community weeps at wakes in the presence of the body of the deceased. According to the Mískito, the most important *inanka upla pruan bara* are about remembrance, rather than about the actual farewell. Through a heterophonous intersection of multiple messages, the dead receive instructions for the long journey, are entrusted with special requests, and are asked not to forget the relatives on earth, all of which prepares and guides the spirit to its proper place in the afterlife. Death among the Mískito is a social event, grieved by the whole community and those who live in neighboring villages. Recorded by Ronny Velásquez (1975–1986). Used by permission, courtesy of Ronny Velásquez (1:17).

II, 3. *Iumu*, or preparation of the water to heal minor illnesses (Mískito: Honduras and Nicaragua). The *sukia* or shaman is the owner and keeper of traditional knowledge and, as such, he has an obligation to transmit it in order to perpetuate the tradition. It is also the *sukia*'s responsibility to watch over the health of the community and apply the therapy required for each illness. *Láwana* is a general term for song. Shamanic songs, or *sukia láwana*, as differentiated from the laments (*inanka*), constitute the second of two general categories of traditional songs. The shaman's ritual and spiritual songs traverse the roads of the life cycle and the paths of death. Shamanic songs can be learned from another shaman, or taught by spirits through dreams interpreted as voyages into the spirit's domain. As a healer, the shaman classifies illnesses into three categories, among which *iumu* refers to minor ailments. In the practice of healing, the shaman extracts various objects through suction, explaining that the spirit in the form of that object intended to take possession of the soul of the patient. The element that determines the cure is not the object, but the shaman's identification of the spirit ailing the patient. In communities where no shaman is available, exhalation experts can apply curative blowing to water (*iumu*) with verbal formulas addressed to the spirits considered to be causing the illness. Treatment consists of taking medicinal waters that have been prepared by the power of the healer's word. These formulas penetrate the water through a small cannula introduced by the shaman or by an exhalation expert, through which he speaks to the water, whispering phrases of indefinite semantic content, but of symbolic and practical effectiveness for the users. *Iumu*, or preparation of the water to heal minor illnesses, is characterized by the intermittent sound of blowing on the water through a hollow reed serving as a mirliton, through which the healer intones a shamanic melody whose semantic content he develops mentally. Recorded by Ronny Velásquez (1975–1986). Used by permission, courtesy of Ronny Velásquez (1:45).

II, 4. Song to capture the soul of the dead (Mískito: Honduras and Nicaragua). As the spiritual leader of the community, the *sukia* is responsible for rituals to guide the souls of the dead to their dwelling in the afterlife. The final abode is described as an ancestral mother (*Yapti-misri*) who shelters all the souls of the Mískito, therein the use of the expression *Kwal taya*, or "that which encloses," to allude to the ritual itself. One of the most important phases of the ritual is the capture of the soul because, consistent with its nature, it struggles to remain on earth and the *sukia* must take control of its arbitrary will. The shaman has special soul-capturing songs, many of which are based on improvisations. The capture, which involves the entire community, only can take place between the hours of the afternoon and evening. Only after the soul has been captured and interred next to the body of the deceased can the soul initiate the great voyage to the afterlife. Recorded by Ronny Velásquez (1975–1986). Used by permission, courtesy of Ronny Velásquez (2:38).

II, 5. *Tiun* ("tune"), creole music accompanied by guitar illustrating Hispanic influence (Mískito: Honduras and Nicaragua). Although the *inanka* and *sukia láwana* song traditions are firmly established, the younger Mískito have adopted the guitar to accompany songs they call *tiuns* (from the English word "tune"), a polysemic term meaning sound, tuning, tune, concordance, and harmony. *Tiuns* are constructed according to the melodic principles of *inankas*, with weeping and communication with the spirits, but they can be danced. In recent years, the same *tiuns* have acquired characteristics of Mexican music heard on the radio in La Mosquitia. These are called *sitan láwana* (songs of the demons) by the Moravian priests who settled among the Mískito, or *kitar láwana* (songs with guitar), and they rely on the simple harmonic principles of rhythmic strumming on dominant and tonic chords. Another designation for this repertoire is *tasba láwana*, meaning secular or "earthly" songs that young Mískito sing during moonlit nights. The Mískito texts are sung to periodic phrases, in binary or ternary meter, and the melodies are always in major keys, reflecting Hispanic influence. Recorded by Ronny Velásquez (1975–1986). Used by permission, courtesy of Ronny Velásquez (2:23).

II, 6. Muu *ígala*, or, through the paths of the divinity of creation, a chant that the great shaman performs to aid in the birth of a child during difficult labor (Kuna: Panama). The Kuna population of approximately 30,000 persons lives on some forty-five islands and on stretches along the Panamanian coast on the Caribbean Sea. Kuna Yala is the indigenous name for this thriving ethnic nation, which was created by an ordinance called Ley Segunda in 1938 and emerged after a successful revolt against Panama's central government in February of 1925. The Kuna have established one of the strongest ethnic nations on the American continent, fighting not only the Spanish colonists but also the Panamanian creoles to preserve their culture, dignity, and freedom. The Kuna's traditional structure has remained resilient to changes proposed by governmental programs, and their culture is respected to such a degree that, in present-day Panama, one principal Kuna chief and three regional chiefs represent the Kuna ethnic nation in the political structure of the country. The leading figure of this successful political movement was the great sage Nele Kantule (1868–1944), whose wisdom continues to guide the destiny of the Kuna nation. The Kuna have a complex system of chants that, embedded in a broad symbolic structure and defined by them as a secret language, subsumes their entire system of beliefs. For Kuna chant, the most important term is *ígala*, which means path, road, "the way" to the known and unknown through song. Each chant represents a totality within the specific phase of the ritual of which it is a part, while referring the performer to other chants of the same type. Thus, each chant is a part of an enormous mental structure within a symbolic network known only to the specialist. An isolated chant cannot account for the entire system and, conversely, an understanding of the system results only from analyses of each specific chant. Moreover, each chant must follow a strict internal order because that is the path followed by the primordial ancestors. Two simultaneous actions coalesce in the shaman's performance: the sung-speech delivery of the chant, and the mental reiteration and elaboration of the *epurba*, the secret that ensures the chant's effectiveness. The simultaneous performance of this dual role only can be achieved through exalted communication with the divine. The Kuna distinguish two principal elements in human beings: *niga*, or the life force emanating from Muu, the deity of creation who engenders movement; and *purba*, or the breath of life and guardian of *abargana*, the body. The Muu *ígala* is a chant that the shaman performs when a woman experiences difficulties during labor. Muu—the force that breathes life into a fetus and inhabits the depths of the maternal uterus with her twelve daughters who preside over the development of the new being—is causing a disturbance, and has captured the mother-to-be's *purba*, sapping all her strength. Muu probably is reacting to some offense to her honor during one of the rituals that Kuna women must undergo from early childhood onward. The objective of the shaman performing the Muu *ígala* is to confront Muu, engage in a struggle, and defeat her and the Muugan (her daughters), after which point the child can descend through the paths of Muu. The research on this chant by Nils M. Holmer and Henry Wassen (1947) served Claude Lévi-Strauss as a basis for "The Effectiveness of Symbols" in *Structural Anthropology* (1958 in 1967: 181–201). Recorded by Ronny Velásquez (1982–1992). Used by permission, courtesy of Ronny Velásquez (2:30).

II, 7. *Kammu ígala*, or, through the paths of the sonorous reeds. Excerpt from the ritual chant of the great shaman (*kandur*) that marks the path of the ceremonial cutting of hair of the Kuna girl, with two flutes alternating with each verse of the chant, accompanied by maracas (Kuna:

Panama). In Kuna mythology, the hair of a woman is an enormous tree whose entanglement symbolizes an impenetrable jungle. Moreover, each woman's hair represents the enormous, entangled tree that the soul or *purba* of her husband must climb when he dies. If her hair is not cut according to all the corresponding rituals, the tangles, branches, trees, lianas, and great rivers in that symbolic jungle will not let the husband's soul get through and climb to the heaven of Kamibe, but will die asphyxiated by the tree that is his own wife's hair. Hair-cutting ceremonies take place at three fundamental stages in a girl's life, the third of which is celebrated when she reaches menarche. According to Ronny Velásquez, the chant for the ceremony of initiation of Kuna women that takes place at the onset of menses reflects perhaps the most traditional religious structure of the Kuna because it represents the life-giving power of women in an eminently matrilineal society. There are three types of hair-cutting ceremonies, each varying in length. The *Inna suid* (long chicha) or *Inna wil'la* (deep chicha), the ceremony lasting three days and three nights, is one of the longest and most splendid ceremonies of the Kuna. The entire *kammu ígala*, which describes in detail every step of the ritual, consists of 3,584 verses, each of which is sung twice, first by the *kandur* or ritual specialist and then by him with his principal assistant, who repeats each verse, with two flutes alternating with the verses of the chant, accompanied by maracas. Recorded by Ronny Velásquez (1982–1992). Used by permission, courtesy of Ronny Velásquez (2:03).

II, 8. *Akwa nusa ígala*, or, through the paths of the stones that hold the power to heal (Kuna: Panama). Healers use various stones in their medical practices. According to traditional beliefs, these stones are of divine origin because they are the *neles* or great sages who were transformed into stone and sent to live on the various layers of the earth. The stones are found on the banks of prestigious rivers, some of which may no longer exist. The stones only can be in the possession of the shaman and become auxiliaries in the practice of his profession. The manner in which the power of these stones is used varies according to the type of illness the shaman diagnoses. Consistent with all other shamanic practices of the Kuna, the various stones, or *akwa nusa*, will be effective only if the secret of their origin is known, and if the corresponding chants that empower them are performed, leading the *akwa nusa* and the patient through the paths of their incantation. In this excerpt from an *akwa nusa ígala*, a male voice delivers the text syllabically, over two recitation tones occasionally reinforced by appoggiaturas. Recorded by Ronny Velásquez (1982–1992). Used by permission, courtesy of Ronny Velásquez (1:51).

II, 9. *Sia ba kabur unaedi*, healing chant instructing the cacao and hot pepper to search for the soul of a patient (Kuna: Panama). This chant searches for the soul of a patient that has been captured by an evil spirit. *Sia* (cacao) and *kabur* (hot pepper) play an extremely important role in healing practices of the Kuna because they never fail to assist in every medical treatment. The smoke of cacao nourishes the benefic spirits, and the smoke of hot pepper drives evil spirits away. For specific cases, the joining of *sia* and *kabur* creates an indestructible formula, with *sia* as the diplomat who enters into a dialogue with the spirits and *kabur* as the warrior who attacks. If both travel to the world of the spirits where the soul of the patient is trapped, it is believed that soon the afflicted person's soul will return to his or her body. The cure does not depend on the intrinsic properties of the medicinal plants, but on the transformative mediation of the appropriate chant that sends *sia* and *kabur* through the path holding the mystery of their efficacy. In this excerpt from a shamanic *Sia ba kabur unaedi*, cacao and hot pepper are instructed to search for the soul of a patient, which he lost in the mountain where he was working. The sick person is lying in his hammock, burning with fever in the community of Coetupo (Koetupo), while the ritual specialist is performing the chant in the neighboring village of Tubualá. Recorded by Ronny Velásquez (1982–1992). Used by permission, courtesy of Ronny Velásquez (1:44).

II, 10. *Ukku naibe ígala*, or, through the paths of the serpent. Excerpt from the chant describing the origin of the rattlesnake (Kuna: Panama). In general, the Kuna believe that animals were prestigious humans in primeval times. Among them, Ukku Naibe was the great healer who specialized in the cure of snakebites. The *Ukku naibe* chant describes not only the origin of the rattlesnake, extolling its characteristics and the powers given to it by the divine ancestors, but also the origin of other poisonous snakes; it also gives minute detail about where the snakes live, depicting the stones and caves where they are curled up, sleeping or lying in ambush. The chant also narrates how a poisonous serpent (Kirpali), an enemy of humankind, bit one of Ukku Naibe's patients, causing acute pain and blood sputum. As the chant travels the path of the plants, bushes, and reeds displaying the same designs and colors of the rattlesnakes, it awakens the sleeping spirits of these plants, which then join Ukku Naibe in his path to defeat the malignant spirits of the snakes that bit the patient. When the battle is won, a mythical bird

(Wekku) who devours poisonous snakes appears in the chant's narrative. Thus, the earth joins the forces of heaven in a struggle to defeat Kirpali and return the soul to the affected patient. Recorded by Ronny Velásquez (1982–1992). Used by permission, courtesy of Ronny Velásquez (2:17).

II, 11. *Absogued ígala*, the chant of the great shaman through the paths of knowledge and the power of *balso* spirits (Kuna: Panama). This chant is performed to defeat harmful spirits (*poni*) causing illnesses and epidemics in Kuna communities. The narrative delivered by the great shaman is the longest of the Kuna chants, exceeding 5,000 verses. It describes, step by step, the creation of the world, its plants, animals, minerals, and marine flora and fauna. It also explains the origin of *ukur war*, or *balso* wood, the main powerful spirit who will multiply into legions of supernatural beings to assist the great shaman in his struggle to defeat harmful ones who, called *kilu gana* in shamanic language, bring epidemics and attract poisonous snakes that bite workers in the fields. The *ukur war* takes on anthropomorphic shapes of *balso* wood, of the same size or larger than a human shape, carved by the shaman and placed by him in strategic places, which then multiply into thousands of benefic spirits that assist him in his struggle to defeat harm. In his spiritual flight, the great shaman or *absoguedi* traverses the cosmos and descends through the layers of the earth toward the fifth layer, where the great shaman of evil dwells in the company of a legion of harmful spirits. Here is where the *absoguedi* will apply his power, seizing all the evil spirits and transporting them to the eighth layer, under the earth, where they will remain captive, tied with reeds. Recorded by Ronny Velásquez (1982–1992). Used by permission, courtesy of Ronny Velásquez (1:46).

II, 12. *Massar ígala*, or, through the paths of the solid reeds. Chant of the great shaman to lead the soul of the dead to the afterlife (Kuna: Panama). *Massar ígala* is an expression interpreted as "journey of the dead," or as "paths of the sacred reeds." Although *massar* means "bristly reed" in everyday language, shamanic interpretation links reeds intimately to the world of the dead. The chant guides eight solid reeds accompanying the *purba* and instructs them about their behavior and care they must exercise along the difficult roads of penance they must traverse. The eight solid reeds cut from the top of the *massar*, which the ritual specialist has prepared himself, are entrusted with guiding and defending the *purba*, the soul of the deceased. Four of them will accompany the soul up to the Takarkuna, the sacred mountain of the Kuna, and the other four will guide it until it reaches the house of the *Paba saila tummadi*, or heaven of Kamibe, the Sun and great mythical god of origins. The spirit of the great shaman travels with the *purba*, which must climb up the *palu wala*, the mythical tree of death, and cross over wells of boiling water, swamps of hungry alligators, oceans filled with sharks, mountains infested with snakes, and precipices crossed by turbulent waters, while also overcoming dangers in places where other souls have been trapped and will try to stop it. When the soul has passed through all the possible ordeals, it will disappear into an immense abyss for a long time until it finally emerges cleansed and prepared to dwell in the eternal world of the dead, wherefrom it will assist in ruling the destiny of beings left behind in the material world. Recorded by Ronny Velásquez (1982–1992). Used by permission, courtesy of Ronny Velásquez (1:32).

II, 13. *Mete sikwi uurma kali*, a secular instrumental melody played on panpipes (*kammu purwi*) accompanying a festive dance (Kuna: Panama). Panpipes are linked to a tradition of daily performances in each Kuna community. The *kammu purwi* panpipes always are played accompanied by maracas (*násisi*). In ritual contexts, the panpipes are played by males and the maracas by females, while in secular contexts both men and women play these panpipes. The *kammu purwi* is a composite instrument consisting of four male tubes and three female tubes, each tied with plant fiber and also joined by a rope that the player hangs around the neck for the instrument to reach breast level. Thus, the performer can join the two smallest tubes of each group to form a composite instrument in the shape of a V. Moreover, the performance of melodies requires two interdependent sets of instruments, also conceptualized as male and female, which are played by a pair of musicians who alternate and combine the pitches of a complete melody. In performance, the female and male sets produce most of the time a melodic texture in parallel fifths between the leader or female set of panpipes, and the follower or male set of panpipes. A *toque* or performance usually involves several pairs of players, with maracas marking the pulse of the melody. These performances always are danced, and the tradition of playing while dancing also is observed when a youngster is being taught how to play the panpipes. The *Mete sikwi uurma kali* is a secular melody for a festive dance that imitates the song and movements of a bird. Recorded by Ronny Velásquez (1982–1992). Used by permission, courtesy of Ronny Velásquez (1:42).

II, 14. "Klabéli tsïtsïki–Flor de clavel," *pirékwa* in *abajeño* style performed by the Trio Los Chapás from Comachuén, Michoacán (P'urhépecha: Mexico). For this indigenous group whose self-denomination is P'urhépecha, music is the exclusive domain of human beings. The P'urhépecha concept of music centers on melody and, consequently, all musical expressions require a melodic component. Elements such as rhythmic patterns or percussive practices are viewed as subordinate to the melody and relegated to the role of accompaniment. In the worldview of the P'urhépecha, there are only two types of music: their own, which they situate mythically in the pre-Hispanic era, and that of the mestizos, or people of mixed race. Music they consider their own is associated with weddings and with specific rituals within the cycle of religious celebrations; it is sung in the P'urhépecha language, which is an isolate; and it is organized rhythmically in ternary subdivisions of time. The native taxonomy of genres centers on the *son* and *abajeño*, two genres whose essential difference is the tempo, with the *son* being particularly slow and the *abajeño* decidedly quick. Consistent with the high value placed on melody, singing holds the place of privilege in the musical life of the P'urhépecha. *Pirékwa* is the generic term for songs sung in their language. Among the recurring themes of the song texts are love and the beauty of women, represented in a metaphorical language that summons images of flowers, birds, stars, the moon, the mist, and the rain. This imagery surfaces in the titles of songs, such as "Klabéli tsïtsïki" or "Flor de clavel" (carnation). Included in *Música P'urhépecha. Antología, Vol. 3: Trío "Los Chapás" de Comachuén / Banda Juvenil "Ecor,"* compiled by the Centro de Investigación de la Cultura P'urhépecha. Discos Pentagrama, PCD 220, one CD and notes. Morelia: Universidad Michoacana de San Nicolás de Hidalgo. Used by permission, courtesy of E. Fernando Nava López (2:49).

II, 15. "Flor de chicalote," a *son* by Francisco Salmerón Equihua, performed by La Orquesta de Quinceo conducted by the composer (P'urhépecha: Mexico). All forms of P'urhépecha music include some type of instrumental performance. The most important post-Conquest ensemble of the P'urhépecha is the *orquesta*, which is made up of approximately eight musicians. This is an ensemble of chordophones and aerophones whose leader is one of the musicians, usually a violinist or saxophone player. In this example, which illustrates a typical *orquesta* of the P'urhépecha and features a clarinet solo, the composer of the piece and leader of the group, Francisco Salmerón Equihua, plays the saxophone, and Juan Crisóstomo Valdés, the founding conductor of La Orquesta de Quinceo, plays the violin. The instruments performing this *son* are clarinet, saxophone, trombone, three violins, violoncello, and double bass. The *orquesta's* repertoire is basically the same as that of smaller ensembles, playing mostly *sones* and *abajeños*. Included in *Música P'urhépecha. Antología, Vol. 2: Orquesta de Quinceo / Los Hermanos Dimas*, compiled by the Centro de Investigación de la Cultura P'urhépecha. Discos Pentagrama PCD 219, one CD and notes. Morelia: Universidad Michoacana de San Nicolás de Hidalgo. Used by permission, courtesy of E. Fernando Nava López (2:55).

II, 16. "Torito 'para castillo'," or castle-burning *torito*, performed by the *banda* La Michoacana of Ichán conducted by Argemiro Ascencio, as recorded in Tzintzuntzan during the feast of the Señor del Rescate in 1981 (P'urhépecha: Mexico). The largest ensemble of the P'urhépecha is the *banda* of wind and percussion instruments with an average of twenty musicians. This is the only ensemble that plays all the types of music included in the native taxonomy of P'urhépecha genres (namely *sones* and *abajeños*, the carnival *torito*, and the "Dance of the Moors"), as well as marches, overtures, and arrangements of popular symphonic works. The leader of a *banda* sometimes plays the trumpet or trombone, or stands apart from the band, conducting with a baton. Unlike vocal music, whose poetry and music remain in the domain of oral tradition, compositions for *orquesta* and *banda* require musical notation. The *torito* (little "bulls") is a genre with several specific functions, but only the *torito* related to carnival is considered P'urhépecha; all other types of *toritos* are mestizo. An air of rivalry surrounds the celebration of large festivals, because they are organized by people who belong to different sectors of the population. This competitiveness is played out at different levels, including proficiency in musical performance, dance, and pyrotechnical displays. Musical competition usually involves two opposing *bandas* that compete from the afternoon until dawn, although the encounter may last one, two, or three nights. During the late evening the *bandas* may play *sones*, but the end of the confrontation at dawn always is marked by the performance of *abajeños*. The competition reaches its climax around midnight, during the series of "castle burnings" from each part of the community. Each respective *banda* then must play "Toritos de quema de castillo," which tend to be compositions of recent vintage. Included in *Abajeños y sones de la fiesta purépecha*, compiled by Arturo Chamorro and María del Carmen Díaz de Chamorro. One LP and notes. México: Instituto Nacional de Antropología e Historia—El Colegio de Michoacán, 1983 (Series INAH, 24). Used by permission, courtesy of E. Fernando Nava López (3:08).

II, 17. *Nahanamu* harvest festival, one of the contexts of *muhusemoi* performance. Several *muhusemoi* flutes are played in ensemble with two *isimoi* (a heteroglottal single-reed concussion aerophone), *hebu-mataro* rattles, and *sewei* anklet rattles (Warao: Venezuela). Native American cultures from the tropical forests often take advantage of the natural tubes of animals for making single tubed, end-blown aerophones with finger holes. One of the most common tropical forest animals whose leg bones are used for flutes is the deer. The *muhusemoi* (*muhu* = bone, *semoi* = wind instrument), a bone flute made from the tibia of a deer, is a common aerophone of the Warao in the Venezuelan Orinoco river delta. The Warao, who live in a large swampy jungle area containing hundreds of rivers, hunt deer for food. The *muhusemoi* is a man's instrument mostly used for ritual purposes, although it may be played for pleasure while walking in the jungle to cut down trees. Men play several *muhusemoituma* in the jungle while the women collect *yuruma* (*moriche* palm starch) to be offered to the deity Kanobo during the *nahanamu* harvest festival. During the festival itself, several *muhusemoi* flutes are played in ensemble with two *isimoi* sacred "clarinets," several *hebu-mataro* rattles, and *sewei* anklet rattles. A different melody is used for each of these *muhusemoi* musical contexts. This example is an excerpt from a melody performed while gathering *yuruma*. Recorded by Dale A. Olsen (1972). Ethnomusicology Archive, The Florida State University, Tallahassee. Used by permission, courtesy of Dale A. Olsen (1:58).

II, 18. *Atuñsa* flute and bird. The *atuñsa* is played by a Yuko man, imitating a bird (Yuko: Colombia = Yupa: Venezuela). *Atuñsa* is the name given to the "hatchet" flute among the Carib-speaking Yuko (in Colombia) or Yupa (in Venezuela), a subgroup of the Maraka who live in the northern Sierra de Perijá range bordering Venezuela and Colombia. These duct edge-aerophones are known colloquially as "hatchet" flutes because their mouthpiece mechanism has been likened visually to an axe blade, and the tube to an axe handle. The *atuñsa* has four finger holes and is played alone or in a pair. In this example, a Yuko man (Maraka subtribe) is playing his *atuñsa* with a bird imitating him, or, perhaps, he is imitating the bird. Recorded by Kenneth Ruddle (ca. 1970). Ethnomusicology Archive, The Florida State University, Tallahassee. Used by permission, courtesy of Dale A. Olsen (2:31).

II, 19. Pablo Milla Balbero from Yungay, Department of Ancash (Peru), playing a *wayno* and *fuga* on his *roncadora* (flute-and-drum combination). The *roncadora* is an end-blown duct flute common in the Callejón de Huaylas, in the Peruvian Department of Ancash. It is played as a one-man flute-and-drum combination also called *roncadora*. These flutes measure from 50 cm to one meter in length, and have two finger holes and one thumb hole in the extreme distal end. With a drumstick in his free hand, the *roncadora* player strikes the snare head of his large membranophone, hitting the drum rim on the offbeats and the skin on the downbeats. The melodies played on the *roncadoras* from Huaylas are distinctly pentatonic, and the rhythm can be recognized as that of the *wayno* (or *huayno*), one of the most characteristic Andean dances. Recorded by Dale A. Olsen (1979). Ethnomusicology Archive, The Florida State University, Tallahassee. Used by permission, courtesy of Dale A. Olsen (1:58).

II, 20. Procession during the patronal festival of the Virgen del Carmen in Alto Otuzco, Department of Cajamarca (Peru), preceded by two alternating *clarines* (trumpets) accompanied by *cajero* (flute-and-drum combination) and female singers, with fireworks and church bells. The *clarín* is a northern Peruvian side-blown bamboo trumpet that can measure over three meters in length. A man's instrument, the *clarín* is performed outdoors during Catholic patronal festivals and also for *mingas*, the communal work effort. During a *minga*, the *clarinero* directs the several aspects of the labor and sets the work rhythms. *Cajero*, or the person who plays both *flauta y caja* (a small drum), is the most common term for the flute-and-drum combination in the Department of Cajamarca. The flute has two finger holes and a thumb hole, and the drum provides a constant rhythm by strokes on the drumhead and rim in alternation. In the context of Catholic patronal festivals, two *clarineros* alternate their melodies (one rests while the other plays). Accompanying their individual sounds are the high-pitched melody and rhythm of the *cajero*. During the 1979 Festival of the Virgen del Carmen in Alto Otuzco, the procession carrying the Virgin and her faithful retinue was preceded by two *clarineros* performing two distinct melodies on the instruments, one during the first half of the procession, and the other during the second half. Recorded by Dale A. Olsen (16 July 1979). Ethnomusicology Archive, The Florida State University, Tallahassee. Used by permission, courtesy of Dale A. Olsen (1:30).

II, 21. *Orquesta típica* Selección del Centro of the Valle del Mantaro conducted by Julio Rosales Huatuco, performing the *huayno* "No le cuentes a nadie" (Don't tell anybody) at a private party during the patronal festival of San Juan Bautista (June 24) in Acolla, Department of Junín

(Peru). The European clarinet and saxophone are two heteroglottal single-reed concussion aerophones that reached Latin America with the expansion of military and civilian bands. Although they are found in bands throughout the region, in the Mantaro Valley of central Peru they are incorporated into the *orquesta típica* as modern replacements for duct and notched edge-aerophones. In June of 1979, Dale A. Olsen studied an *orquesta típica* known professionally as Selección del Centro, which was hired for the patronal festival of St. John the Baptist in the village of Acolla, Department of Junín. The orchestra consisted of three clarinets, three tenor saxophones, five alto saxophones, one harp, and three violins. This is a typical size for an *orquesta típica del centro*, although some ensembles might add a baritone saxophone. Usually, the compositions are in the minor mode, sometimes alternating with the relative major, and intervals of a third are emphasized by doublings in all the voices. Recorded by Dale A. Olsen (24 June 1979). Ethnomusicology Archive, The Florida State University, Tallahassee. Used by permission, courtesy of Dale A. Olsen (2:44).